FORD PICK-UPS
2004-12 REPAIR MANUAL

Deleted

CHILTON'S

**Covers U.S. and Canadian models of Ford F-150 Pick-ups
2004 through 2012**

*Does not include F-250, Super Duty or diesel models.
Does not include information specifc to F-150 Heritage, Lightning or
Raptor models*

by Mike Stubblefield

CHILTON *Automotive Books*

PUBLISHED BY **HAYNES NORTH AMERICA, inc.**

Manufactured in USA
©2009, 2012 Haynes North America, Inc.
ISBN-13: 978-1-62092-009-1
Library of Congress Control Number 2012947884

Haynes Publishing Group
Sparkford Nr Yeovil
Somerset BA22 7JJ England

Haynes North America, Inc
861 Lawrence Drive
Newbury Park
California 91320 USA

ABCDE
FGHIJ
KLMN

9Q7-2

Contents

INTRODUCTORY PAGES

About this manual – 0-5
Introduction – 0-5
Vehicle identification numbers – 0-6
Recall information - 0-7
Buying parts – 0-10
Maintenance techniques, tools and working facilities – 0-11
Jacking and towing – 0-19

Booster battery (jump) starting – 0-20
Automotive chemicals and lubricants – 0-21
Conversion factors – 0-22
Fraction/decimal/millimeter equivalents – 0-23
Safety first! – 0-24
Troubleshooting – 0-25

1

TUNE-UP AND ROUTINE MAINTENANCE – 1-1

2

4.2L V6 ENGINE – 2A-1
3.5L AND 3.7L V6 ENGINES – 2B-1
V8 ENGINES – 2C-1
GENERAL ENGINE OVERHAUL PROCEDURES – 2D-1

3

COOLING, HEATING AND AIR CONDITIONING SYSTEMS – 3-1

4

FUEL AND EXHAUST SYSTEMS – 4-1

5

ENGINE ELECTRICAL SYSTEMS – 5-1

6

EMISSIONS AND ENGINE CONTROL SYSTEMS – 6-1

MANUAL TRANSMISSION – 7A-1
AUTOMATIC TRANSMISSION – 7B-1
TRANSFER CASE – 7C-1

7

CLUTCH AND DRIVELINE – 8-1

8

BRAKES – 9-1

9

SUSPENSION AND STEERING SYSTEMS – 10-1

10

BODY – 11-1

11

CHASSIS ELECTRICAL SYSTEM – 12-1
WIRING DIAGRAMS – 12-28

12

GLOSSARY – GL-1

GLOSSARY

MASTER INDEX – IND-1

MASTER INDEX

Mechanic and photographer with a 2004 F-150

ACKNOWLEDGEMENTS

We are grateful to Solution Builders for providing wiring diagrams. Technical writers who contributed to this project include Joe L. Hamilton, Robert Maddox and John Wegmann

While every attempt is made to ensure that the information in this manual is correct, no liability can be accepted by the authors or publishers for loss, damage or injury caused by any errors in, or omissions from, the information given.

About this manual

ITS PURPOSE

The purpose of this manual is to help you get the best value from your vehicle. It can do so in several ways. It can help you decide what work must be done, even if you choose to have it done by a dealer service department or a repair shop; it provides information and procedures for routine maintenance and servicing; and it offers diagnostic and repair procedures to follow when trouble occurs.

We hope you use the manual to tackle the work yourself. For many simpler jobs, doing it yourself may be quicker than arranging an appointment to get the vehicle into a shop and making the trips to leave it and pick it up. More importantly, a lot of money can be saved by avoiding the expense the shop must pass on to you to cover its labor and overhead costs. An added benefit is the sense of satisfaction and accomplishment that you feel after doing the job yourself.

USING THE MANUAL

The manual is divided into Chapters. Each Chapter is divided into numbered Sections. Each Section consists of consecutively numbered paragraphs.

At the beginning of each numbered Section you will be referred to any illustrations which apply to the procedures in that Section. The reference numbers used in illustration captions pinpoint the pertinent Section and the Step within that Section. That is, illustration 3.2 means the illustration refers to Section 3 and Step (or paragraph) 2 within that Section.

Procedures, once described in the text, are not normally repeated. When it's necessary to refer to another Chapter, the reference will be given as Chapter and Section number. Cross references given without use of the word "Chapter" apply to Sections and/or paragraphs in the same Chapter. For example, "see Section 8" means in the same Chapter.

References to the left or right side of the vehicle assume you are sitting in the driver's seat, facing forward.

Even though we have prepared this manual with extreme care, neither the publisher nor the author can accept responsibility for any errors in, or omissions from, the information given.

➡ **NOTE**

A *Note* provides information necessary to properly complete a procedure or information which will make the procedure easier to understand.

�֎ CAUTION

A *Caution* provides a special procedure or special steps which must be taken while completing the procedure where the Caution is found. Not heeding a Caution can result in damage to the assembly being worked on.

✖ WARNING

A *Warning* provides a special procedure or special steps which must be taken while completing the procedure where the Warning is found. Not heeding a Warning can result in personal injury.

Introduction

These pick-ups are available in standard and quad-cab body styles. All cabs are single welded unit construction and bolted to the frame. Short-bed and long-bed models are available. All models are available in two-wheel drive (2WD) and four-wheel drive (4WD) versions.

Powertrain options include a 4.2L V6, as well as two V8 engines: a 4.6L and 5.4L. In 2011 and later models, four new engines were introduced; two OHC V6 engines - a turbocharged "Eco-Boost" 3.5L and a 3.7L; and 5.0L and 6.2L V8 engines. Transmissions used are either a four-speed automatic, a six-speed automatic or five-speed manual.

Chassis layout is conventional, with the engine mounted at the front and the power being transmitted through either the manual or automatic transmission to a driveshaft and solid rear axle. On 4WD models, in addition to power being delivered to the rear axle and wheels, a transfer case transmits power via a driveshaft, front differential, then to the wheels through independent drtiveaxles.

All models feature an independent coil spring, upper and lower A-arm type front suspension, and have a solid axle and leaf springs at the rear.

All models are equipped with power-assisted front and rear disc brakes with a four-wheel Anti-lock Braking System (ABS).

Vehicle identification numbers

Modifications are a continuing and unpublicized process in vehicle manufacturing. Since spare parts lists and manuals are compiled on a numerical basis, the individual vehicle numbers are necessary to correctly identify the component required.

VEHICLE IDENTIFICATION NUMBER (VIN)

This very important identification number is stamped on a plate attached to the dashboard inside the windshield on the driver's side of the vehicle (see illustration). The VIN also appears on the Vehicle Certificate of Title and Registration. It contains information such as where and when the vehicle was manufactured, the model year and the body style.

VIN ENGINE AND MODEL YEAR CODES

Two particularly important pieces of information found in the VIN are the engine code and the model year code. Counting from the left, the engine code letter designation is the 8th digit and the model year code letter designation is the 10th digit.

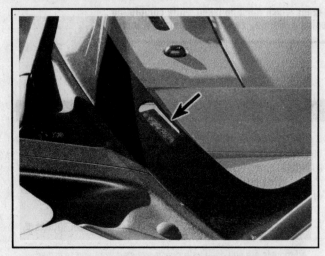

The VIN is visible through the windshield on the driver's side

On the models covered by this manual the engine codes are:

2	4.2L V6
W	4.6L 2-valve V8
8	4.6L 3-valve V8
5	5.4L 3-valve V8
V	5.4L 3-valve V8
M	3.7L V6
T	3.5L V6
F	5.0L V8
6	6.2L V8

On the models covered by this manual the model year codes are:

4	2004
5	2005
6	2006
7	2007
8	2008
9	2009
A	2010
B	2011
C	2012

VEHICLE CERTIFICATION LABEL

The Vehicle Certification Label is attached to the driver's side door pillar (see illustration). Information on this label includes the name of the manufacturer, the month and year of production, as well as information on the options with which it is equipped. This label is especially useful for matching the color and type of paint for repair work.

ENGINE IDENTIFICATION NUMBER

Labels containing the engine code, engine number and build date can be found on the valve cover (see illustration). The engine number is also stamped onto a machined pad on the external surface of the engine block.

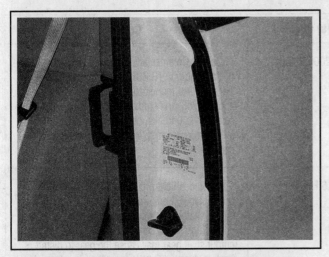

The vehicle certification label is affixed to the driver's side door pillar (or on the front of the driver's side rear door on quad-cab models)

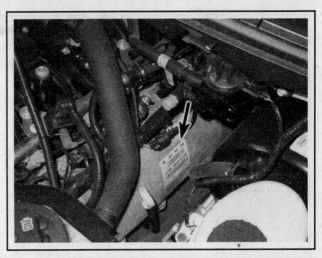

The engine identification label is affixed to the valve cover

Recall information

Vehicle recalls are carried out by the manufacturer in the rare event of a possible safety-related defect. The vehicle's registered owner is contacted at the address on file at the Department of Motor Vehicles and given the details of the recall. Remedial work is carried out free of charge at a dealer service department.

If you are the new owner of a used vehicle which was subject to a recall and you want to be sure that the work has been carried out, it's best to contact a dealer service department and ask about your individual vehicle - you'll need to furnish them your Vehicle Identification Number (VIN).

The table below is based on information provided by the National Highway Traffic Safety Administration (NHTSA), the body which oversees vehicle recalls in the United States. The recall database is updated constantly.

For the latest information on vehicle recalls, check the NHTSA website at www.nhtsa.gov, www.safercar.gov, or call the NHTSA hotline at 1-888-327-4236.

Recall date	Recall campaign number	Model(s) affected	Concern
4/16/2004	04V20000	2004 F-150	On certain trucks equipped with 4.2L, 4.6L and 5.4L gasoline engines, the fuel tank may have a depression at the seam between the top and the bottom halves of the tank. If the depression is large enough, fuel may permeate the fuel tank wall resulting in a fuel odor, a fuel leak, or illumination of the "Service Engine Soon" light
9/9/2004	04V443000	2004 F-150	On certain trucks equipped with 4.2L, 4.6L and 5.4L gasoline engines, the fuel tank may have a depression at the seam between the top and the bottom halves of the tank. If the depression is large enough, fuel may permeate the fuel tank wall resulting in a fuel odor, a fuel leak, or illumination of the "Service Engine Soon" light.

Recall date	Recall campaign number	Model(s) affected	Concern
11/21/05	05T022000	2005/2006 F-150	Certain Continental Contitrac TR Owl, Contitrac BSW, Contritrac TR BSW and General Grabber TR BSW tires manufactured between 5/29/05 and 6/11/05, and sold as original equipment on certain F-150 trucks, can wear prematurely, which fails to to conform to federal motor vehicle safety standard No. 119.
11/7/2005	05V520000	2006 F-150	The windshield wiper motor may have been assembled without grease being applied to the output shaft gear. After a period of continuous use on the high speed setting, lack of grease on the output shaft gear may cause the gear to distort or fracture during operation, resulting in a loss of wiper function.
2/6/2006	06V033000	2005/2006 F-150	Certain pickup trucks fail to comply with either the requirements of Federal Motor Vehicle Safety Standard (FMVSS) No. 105, "Hydraulic and Electric Brake Systems" or FMVSS No. 135, "passenger car brake systems." These vehicles were built with a software error in the instrument cluster.
6/20/2007	07V278000	2007 F-150	On certain trucks built with 26 gallon fuel tanks, the fuel tank may have a depression at the seam between the top and bottom halves of the tank (not visible from outside the fuel tank). If a depression is large enough, fuel may permeate the fuel tank wall resulting in a fuel odor, or a "Service Engine Soon" indicator light.
8/2/2007	07V336000	2004 F-150	On certain vehicles, the speed control deactivation switch may, under certain conditions, leak internally and then overheat, smoke, or burn.
5/5/2008	08V208000	2005/2006 F-150	On some models equipped with 5.4L 3-valve engines, the brake booster vacuum supply hose attached to the intake manifold fitting may swell over time and lose retention force. This condition could allow the hose to become detached from the fitting during an intake manifold backfire. Should the hose detach from the intake manifold, several brake applications with power assist will be available before the vacuum reserve is depleted.
4/29/2009	09V150000	2009 F-150	Certain vehicles fail to comply with the requirements of Federal Motor Vehicle Safety Standard no. 108, "lamps, reflective devices, and associated equipment." The brake stop lamp switch may be improperly adjusted. This may result in a delay in brake stop lamp illumination when the brake pedal is depressed. In situations of very mild brake application, the brake stop lamps may not illuminate.

Recall date	Recall campaign number	Model(s) affected	Concern
12/29/2010	10V659000	2011 F-150	The manufacturer is recalling certain model year 2011 F-150 vehicles. During a six-day production period, the supplier of the Body Control Module manufactured modules that may have the potential for an internal short.
1/28/2011	11V049000	2009/2010 F-150	On some models, the interior door handle housing embossment retaining the interior door handle spring may fracture during normal usage resulting in insufficient spring force to return the handle to the fully stowed position.
2/21/2011	11V107000	2004/2005/2006 F-150	On some models, if the clockspring jumper wire comes in contact with the driver side frontal airbag lower horn plate, the wire insulation may become chafed, creating a potential for a short circuit. If this occurs the airbag warning lamp may illuminate indicating that service is required.
2/21/2011	11V128000	2011 F-150	Some vehicles were inspected using Integrated Diagnostic System (IDS) that had a custom software routine to read the suspect Body Control Module (BCM) serial number. Based on the serial number the BCM was either not affected or replaced. The custom software routine was not reading the correct set of characters, and was not able to identify a BCM that required replacement; affected BCMs may have the potential for an internal short.
7/29/2011	11V385000	2004 F-150	On certain models, prolonged exposure to road deicing chemicals may cause severe corrosion of the fuel tank straps which secure the tank to the vehicle.
12/5/2011	11V582000	2011 F-150	Some vehicles fail to comply with the requirements of Federal Motor Vehicle Safety Standard number 114, "theft protection." The transmission can be shifted out of the park position without pressing the brake pedal due to a brake shift interlock switch problem.

Buying parts

Replacement parts are available from many sources, which generally fall into one of two categories - authorized dealer parts departments and independent retail auto parts stores. Our advice concerning these parts is as follows:

Retail auto parts stores: Good auto parts stores will stock frequently needed components which wear out relatively fast, such as clutch components, exhaust systems, brake parts, tune-up parts, etc. These stores often supply new or reconditioned parts on an exchange basis, which can save a considerable amount of money. Discount auto parts stores are often very good places to buy materials and parts needed for general vehicle maintenance such as oil, grease, filters, spark plugs, belts, touch-up paint, bulbs, etc. They also usually sell tools and general accessories, have convenient hours, charge lower prices and can often be found not far from home.

Authorized dealer parts department: This is the best source for parts which are unique to the vehicle and not generally available elsewhere (such as major engine parts, transmission parts, trim pieces, etc.).

Warranty information: If the vehicle is still covered under warranty, be sure that any replacement parts purchased - regardless of the source - do not invalidate the warranty!

To be sure of obtaining the correct parts, have engine and chassis numbers available and, if possible, take the old parts along for positive identification.

Maintenance techniques, tools and working facilities

MAINTENANCE TECHNIQUES

There are a number of techniques involved in maintenance and repair that will be referred to throughout this manual. Application of these techniques will enable the home mechanic to be more efficient, better organized and capable of performing the various tasks properly, which will ensure that the repair job is thorough and complete.

Fasteners

Fasteners are nuts, bolts, studs and screws used to hold two or more parts together. There are a few things to keep in mind when working with fasteners. Almost all of them use a locking device of some type, either a lockwasher, locknut, locking tab or thread adhesive. All threaded fasteners should be clean and straight, with undamaged threads and undamaged corners on the hex head where the wrench fits. Develop the habit of replacing all damaged nuts and bolts with new ones. Special locknuts with nylon or fiber inserts can only be used once. If they are removed, they lose their locking ability and must be replaced with new ones.

Rusted nuts and bolts should be treated with a penetrating fluid to ease removal and prevent breakage. Some mechanics use turpentine in a spout-type oil can, which works quite well. After applying the rust penetrant, let it work for a few minutes before trying to loosen the nut or bolt. Badly rusted fasteners may have to be chiseled or sawed off or removed with a special nut breaker, available at tool stores.

If a bolt or stud breaks off in an assembly, it can be drilled and removed with a special tool commonly available for this purpose. Most automotive machine shops can perform this task, as well as other repair procedures, such as the repair of threaded holes that have been stripped out.

Flat washers and lockwashers, when removed from an assembly, should always be replaced exactly as removed. Replace any damaged washers with new ones. Never use a lockwasher on any soft metal surface (such as aluminum), thin sheet metal or plastic.

Fastener sizes

For a number of reasons, automobile manufacturers are making wider and wider use of metric fasteners. Therefore, it is important to be able to tell the difference between standard (sometimes called U.S. or SAE) and metric hardware, since they cannot be interchanged.

All bolts, whether standard or metric, are sized according to diameter, thread pitch and length. For example, a standard 1/2 - 13 x 1 bolt is 1/2 inch in diameter, has 13 threads per inch and is 1 inch long. An M12 - 1.75 x 25 metric bolt is 12 mm in diameter, has a thread pitch of 1.75 mm (the distance between threads) and is 25 mm long. The two bolts are nearly identical, and easily confused, but they are not interchangeable.

In addition to the differences in diameter, thread pitch and length, metric and standard bolts can also be distinguished by examining the bolt heads. To begin with, the distance across the flats on a standard bolt head is measured in inches, while the same dimension on a metric bolt is sized in millimeters (the same is true for nuts). As a result, a standard wrench should not be used on a metric bolt and a metric wrench should not be used on a standard bolt. Also, most standard bolts have slashes radiating out from the center of the head to denote the grade or strength of the bolt, which is an indication of the amount of torque that can be applied to it. The greater the number of slashes, the greater the strength of the bolt. Grades 0 through 5 are commonly used on automobiles. Metric bolts have a property class (grade) number, rather than a slash, molded into their heads to indicate bolt strength. In this case, the higher the number, the stronger the bolt. Property class numbers 8.8, 9.8 and 10.9 are commonly used on automobiles.

Strength markings can also be used to distinguish standard hex nuts from metric hex nuts. Many standard nuts have dots stamped into one side, while metric nuts are marked with a number. The greater the number of dots, or the higher the number, the greater the strength of the nut.

Metric studs are also marked on their ends according to property class (grade). Larger studs are numbered (the same as metric bolts), while smaller studs carry a geometric code to denote grade.

It should be noted that many fasteners, especially Grades 0 through 2, have no distinguishing marks on them. When such is the case, the only way to determine whether it is standard or metric is to measure the thread pitch or compare it to a known fastener of the same size.

Standard fasteners are often referred to as SAE, as opposed to metric. However, it should be noted that SAE technically refers to a non-metric fine thread fastener only. Coarse thread non-metric fasteners are referred to as USS sizes.

Since fasteners of the same size (both standard and metric) may have different strength ratings, be sure to reinstall any bolts, studs or nuts removed from your vehicle in their original locations. Also, when replacing a fastener with a new one, make sure that the new one has a strength rating equal to or greater than the original.

Tightening sequences and procedures

Most threaded fasteners should be tightened to a specific torque value (torque is the twisting force applied to a threaded component such as a nut or bolt). Overtightening the fastener can weaken it and cause it to break, while undertightening can cause it to eventually come loose. Bolts, screws and studs, depending on the material they are made of and their thread diameters, have specific torque values, many of which are noted in the Specifications at the end of each Chapter. Be sure to follow the torque recommendations closely. For fasteners not assigned a specific torque, a general torque value chart is presented here as a guide. These torque values are for dry (unlubricated) fasteners threaded into steel or cast iron (not aluminum). As was previously mentioned, the size and grade of a fastener determine the amount of torque that can safely be applied to it. The figures listed here are approximate for Grade 2 and Grade 3 fasteners. Higher grades can tolerate higher torque values.

Fasteners laid out in a pattern, such as cylinder head bolts, oil pan bolts, differential cover bolts, etc., must be loosened or tightened in sequence to avoid warping the component. This sequence will normally be shown in the appropriate Chapter. If a specific pattern is not given, the following procedures can be used to prevent warping.

Initially, the bolts or nuts should be assembled finger-tight only. Next, they should be tightened one full turn each, in a criss-cross or diagonal pattern. After each one has been tightened one full turn, return to the first one and tighten them all one-half turn, following the same

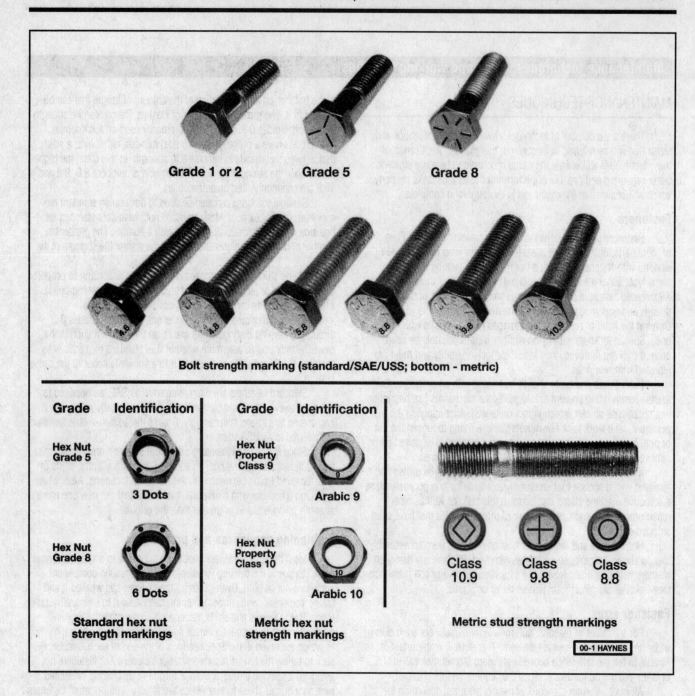

Grade 1 or 2   Grade 5   Grade 8

Bolt strength marking (standard/SAE/USS; bottom - metric)

Grade	Identification
Hex Nut Grade 5	3 Dots
Hex Nut Grade 8	6 Dots

Standard hex nut strength markings

Grade	Identification
Hex Nut Property Class 9	Arabic 9
Hex Nut Property Class 10	Arabic 10

Metric hex nut strength markings

Class 10.9   Class 9.8   Class 8.8

Metric stud strength markings

00-1 HAYNES

pattern. Finally, tighten each of them one-quarter turn at a time until each fastener has been tightened to the proper torque. To loosen and remove the fasteners, the procedure would be reversed.

Component disassembly

Component disassembly should be done with care and purpose to help ensure that the parts go back together properly. Always keep track of the sequence in which parts are removed. Make note of special characteristics or marks on parts that can be installed more than one way, such as a grooved thrust washer on a shaft. It is a good idea to lay the disassembled parts out on a clean surface in the order that they were removed. It may also be helpful to make sketches or take instant photos of components before removal.

When removing fasteners from a component, keep track of their locations. Sometimes threading a bolt back in a part, or putting the washers and nut back on a stud, can prevent mix-ups later. If nuts and bolts cannot be returned to their original locations, they should be kept in a compartmented box or a series of small boxes. A cupcake or muffin tin is ideal for this purpose, since each cavity can hold the bolts and nuts from a particular area (i.e. oil pan bolts, valve cover bolts, engine

Metric thread sizes

	Ft-lbs	Nm
M-6	6 to 9	9 to 12
M-8	14 to 21	19 to 28
M-10	28 to 40	38 to 54
M-12	50 to 71	68 to 96
M-14	80 to 140	109 to 154

Pipe thread sizes

	Ft-lbs	Nm
1/8	5 to 8	7 to 10
1/4	12 to 18	17 to 24
3/8	22 to 33	30 to 44
1/2	25 to 35	34 to 47

U.S. thread sizes

	Ft-lbs	Nm
1/4 - 20	6 to 9	9 to 12
5/16 - 18	12 to 18	17 to 24
5/16 - 24	14 to 20	19 to 27
3/8 - 16	22 to 32	30 to 43
3/8 - 24	27 to 38	37 to 51
7/16 - 14	40 to 55	55 to 74
7/16 - 20	40 to 60	55 to 81
1/2 - 13	55 to 80	75 to 108

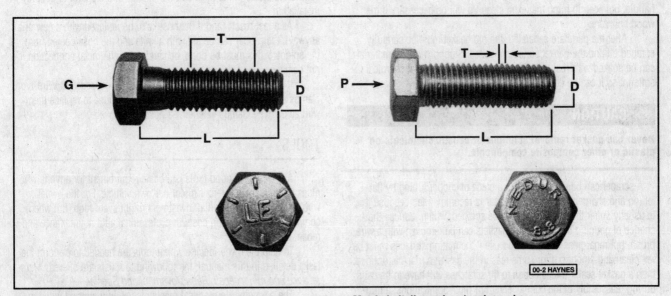

Standard (SAE and USS) bolt dimensions/grade marks

G   Grade marks (bolt strength)
L   Length (in inches)
T   Thread pitch (number of threads per inch)
D   Nominal diameter (in inches)

Metric bolt dimensions/grade marks

P   Property class (bolt strength)
L   Length (in millimeters)
T   Thread pitch (distance between threads in millimeters)
D   Diameter

mount bolts, etc.). A pan of this type is especially helpful when working on assemblies with very small parts, such as the carburetor, alternator, valve train or interior dash and trim pieces. The cavities can be marked with paint or tape to identify the contents.

Whenever wiring looms, harnesses or connectors are separated, it is a good idea to identify the two halves with numbered pieces of masking tape so they can be easily reconnected.

Gasket sealing surfaces

Throughout any vehicle, gaskets are used to seal the mating surfaces between two parts and keep lubricants, fluids, vacuum or pressure contained in an assembly.

Many times these gaskets are coated with a liquid or paste-type gasket sealing compound before assembly. Age, heat and pressure can sometimes cause the two parts to stick together so tightly that they are very difficult to separate. Often, the assembly can be loosened by striking it with a soft-face hammer near the mating surfaces. A regular hammer can be used if a block of wood is placed between the hammer and the part. Do not hammer on cast parts or parts that could be easily damaged. With any particularly stubborn part, always recheck to make sure that every fastener has been removed.

Avoid using a screwdriver or bar to pry apart an assembly, as

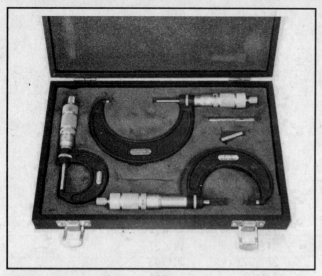

Micrometer set

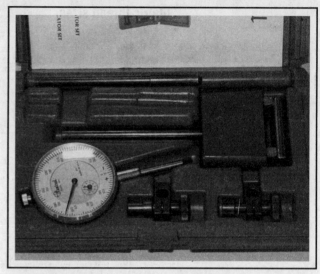

Dial indicator set

they can easily mar the gasket sealing surfaces of the parts, which must remain smooth. If prying is absolutely necessary, use an old broom handle, but keep in mind that extra clean up will be necessary if the wood splinters.

After the parts are separated, the old gasket must be carefully scraped off and the gasket surfaces cleaned. Stubborn gasket material can be soaked with rust penetrant or treated with a special chemical to soften it so it can be easily scraped off.

✳ CAUTION:

Never use gasket removal solutions or caustic chemicals on plastic or other composite components.

A scraper can be fashioned from a piece of copper tubing by flattening and sharpening one end. Copper is recommended because it is usually softer than the surfaces to be scraped, which reduces the chance of gouging the part. Some gaskets can be removed with a wire brush, but regardless of the method used, the mating surfaces must be left clean and smooth. If for some reason the gasket surface is gouged, then a gasket sealer thick enough to fill scratches will have to be used during reassembly of the components. For most applications, a non-drying (or semi-drying) gasket sealer should be used.

Hose removal tips

✳ WARNING:

If the vehicle is equipped with air conditioning, do not disconnect any of the A/C hoses without first having the system depressurized by a dealer service department or a service station.

Hose removal precautions closely parallel gasket removal precautions. Avoid scratching or gouging the surface that the hose mates against or the connection may leak. This is especially true for radiator hoses. Because of various chemical reactions, the rubber in hoses can bond itself to the metal spigot that the hose fits over. To remove a hose, first loosen the hose clamps that secure it to the spigot. Then, with slip-joint pliers, grab the hose at the clamp and rotate it around the spigot. Work it back and forth until it is completely free, then pull it off. Silicone or other lubricants will ease removal if they can be applied

between the hose and the outside of the spigot. Apply the same lubricant to the inside of the hose and the outside of the spigot to simplify installation.

As a last resort (and if the hose is to be replaced with a new one anyway), the rubber can be slit with a knife and the hose peeled from the spigot. If this must be done, be careful that the metal connection is not damaged.

If a hose clamp is broken or damaged, do not reuse it. Wire-type clamps usually weaken with age, so it is a good idea to replace them with screw-type clamps whenever a hose is removed.

TOOLS

A selection of good tools is a basic requirement for anyone who plans to maintain and repair his or her own vehicle. For the owner who has few tools, the initial investment might seem high, but when compared to the spiraling costs of professional auto maintenance and repair, it is a wise one.

To help the owner decide which tools are needed to perform the tasks detailed in this manual, the following tool lists are offered: *Maintenance and minor repair, Repair/overhaul and Special.*

The newcomer to practical mechanics should start off with the *maintenance and minor repair* tool kit, which is adequate for the simpler jobs performed on a vehicle. Then, as confidence and experience grow, the owner can tackle more difficult tasks, buying additional tools as they are needed. Eventually the basic kit will be expanded into the *repair and overhaul* tool set. Over a period of time, the experienced do-it-yourselfer will assemble a tool set complete enough for most repair and overhaul procedures and will add tools from the special category when it is felt that the expense is justified by the frequency of use.

Maintenance and minor repair tool kit

The tools in this list should be considered the minimum required for performance of routine maintenance, servicing and minor repair work. We recommend the purchase of combination wrenches (box-end and open-end combined in one wrench). While more expensive than open end wrenches, they offer the advantages of both types of wrench.

Combination wrench set (1/4-inch to 1 inch or 6 mm to 19 mm)
Adjustable wrench, 8 inch
Spark plug wrench with rubber insert

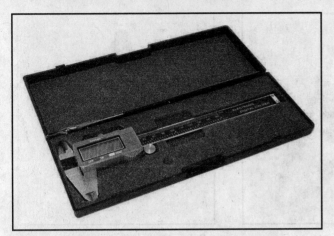

Dial caliper

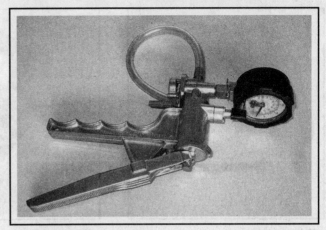

Hand-operated vacuum pump

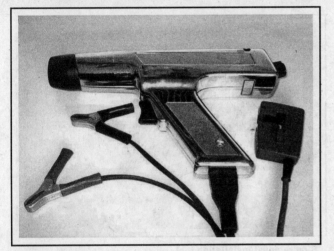

Timing light

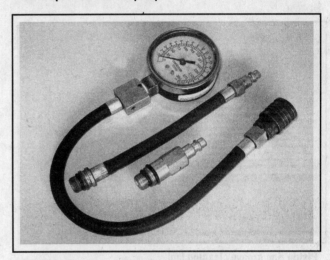

Compression gauge with spark plug hole adapter

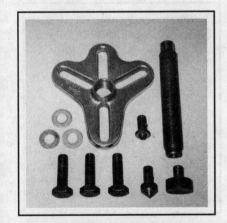

Damper/steering wheel puller

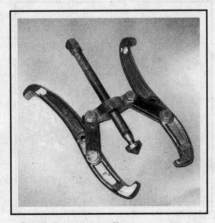

General purpose puller

Hydraulic lifter removal tool

Spark plug gap adjusting tool
Feeler gauge set
Brake bleeder wrench
Standard screwdriver (5/16-inch x 6 inch)
Phillips screwdriver (No. 2 x 6 inch)
Combination pliers - 6 inch
Hacksaw and assortment of blades
Tire pressure gauge
Grease gun

Oil can
Fine emery cloth
Wire brush
Battery post and cable cleaning tool
Oil filter wrench
Funnel (medium size)
Safety goggles
Jackstands (2)
Drain pan

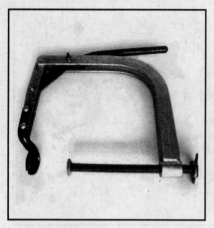

Valve spring compressor

Valve spring compressor

Ridge reamer

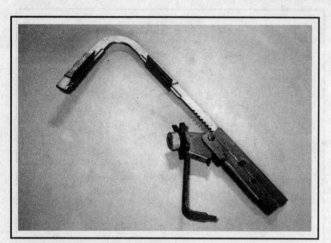

Piston ring groove cleaning tool

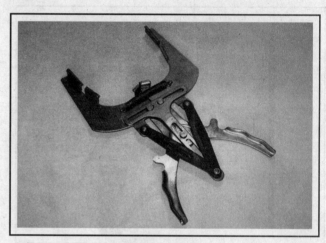

Ring removal/installation tool

Ring compressor

Cylinder hone

Brake hold-down spring tool

➡ **Note: If basic tune-ups are going to be part of routine maintenance, it will be necessary to purchase a good quality stroboscopic timing light and combination tachometer/dwell meter. Although they are included in the list of special tools, it is mentioned here because they are absolutely necessary for tuning most vehicles properly.**

Repair and overhaul tool set

These tools are essential for anyone who plans to perform major repairs and are in addition to those in the maintenance and minor repair tool kit. Included is a comprehensive set of sockets which, though expensive, are invaluable because of their versatility, especially when various extensions and drives are available. We recommend the 1/2-inch drive over the 3/8-inch drive. Although the larger drive is bulky and more expensive, it has the capacity of accepting a very wide range of large sockets. Ideally, however, the mechanic should have a 3/8-inch drive set and a 1/2-inch drive set.

Torque angle gauge

Clutch plate alignment tool

Socket set(s)
Reversible ratchet
Extension - 10 inch
Universal joint
Torque wrench (same size drive as sockets)
Ball peen hammer - 8 ounce
Soft-face hammer (plastic/rubber)
Standard screwdriver (1/4-inch x 6 inch)
Standard screwdriver (stubby - 5/16-inch)
Phillips screwdriver (No. 3 x 8 inch)
Phillips screwdriver (stubby - No. 2)
Pliers - vise grip
Pliers - lineman's
Pliers - needle nose
Pliers - snap-ring (internal and external)
Cold chisel - 1/2-inch
Scribe
Scraper (made from flattened copper tubing)
Centerpunch
Pin punches (1/16, 1/8, 3/16-inch)
Steel rule/straightedge - 12 inch
Allen wrench set (1/8 to 3/8-inch or 4 mm to 10 mm)
A selection of files
Wire brush (large)
Jackstands (second set)
Jack (scissor or hydraulic type)

➡ **Note: Another tool which is often useful is an electric drill with a chuck capacity of 3/8-inch and a set of good quality drill bits.**

Special tools

The tools in this list include those which are not used regularly, are expensive to buy, or which need to be used in accordance with their manufacturer's instructions. Unless these tools will be used frequently, it is not very economical to purchase many of them. A consideration would be to split the cost and use between yourself and a friend or friends. In addition, most of these tools can be obtained from a tool rental shop on a temporary basis.

This list primarily contains only those tools and instruments widely available to the public, and not those special tools produced by the vehicle manufacturer for distribution to dealer service departments. Occasionally, references to the manufacturer's special tools are included in the text of this manual. Generally, an alternative method of doing the job without the special tool is offered. However, sometimes there is no alternative to their use. Where this is the case, and the tool cannot be purchased or borrowed, the work should be turned over to the dealer service department or an automotive repair shop.

Valve spring compressor
Piston ring groove cleaning tool
Piston ring compressor
Piston ring installation tool
Cylinder compression gauge
Cylinder ridge reamer
Cylinder surfacing hone
Cylinder bore gauge
Micrometers and/or dial calipers
Hydraulic lifter removal tool
Balljoint separator
Universal-type puller
Impact screwdriver
Dial indicator set
Stroboscopic timing light (inductive pick-up)
Hand operated vacuum/pressure pump
Tachometer/dwell meter
Universal electrical multimeter
Cable hoist
Brake spring removal and installation tools
Floor jack

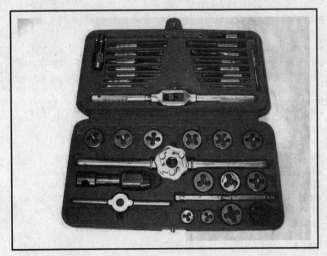

Tap and die set

Buying tools

For the do-it-yourselfer who is just starting to get involved in vehicle maintenance and repair, there are a number of options available when purchasing tools. If maintenance and minor repair is the extent of the work to be done, the purchase of individual tools is satisfactory. If, on the other hand, extensive work is planned, it would be a good idea to purchase a modest tool set from one of the large retail chain stores. A set can usually be bought at a substantial savings over the individual tool prices, and they often come with a tool box. As additional tools are needed, add-on sets, individual tools and a larger tool box can be purchased to expand the tool selection. Building a tool set gradually allows the cost of the tools to be spread over a longer period of time and gives the mechanic the freedom to choose only those tools that will actually be used.

Tool stores will often be the only source of some of the special tools that are needed, but regardless of where tools are bought, try to avoid cheap ones, especially when buying screwdrivers and sockets, because they won't last very long. The expense involved in replacing cheap tools will eventually be greater than the initial cost of quality tools.

Care and maintenance of tools

Good tools are expensive, so it makes sense to treat them with respect. Keep them clean and in usable condition and store them properly when not in use. Always wipe off any dirt, grease or metal chips before putting them away. Never leave tools lying around in the work area. Upon completion of a job, always check closely under the hood for tools that may have been left there so they won't get lost during a test drive.

Some tools, such as screwdrivers, pliers, wrenches and sockets, can be hung on a panel mounted on the garage or workshop wall, while others should be kept in a tool box or tray. Measuring instruments, gauges, meters, etc. must be carefully stored where they cannot be damaged by weather or impact from other tools.

When tools are used with care and stored properly, they will last a very long time. Even with the best of care, though, tools will wear out if used frequently. When a tool is damaged or worn out, replace it. Subsequent jobs will be safer and more enjoyable if you do.

HOW TO REPAIR DAMAGED THREADS

Sometimes, the internal threads of a nut or bolt hole can become stripped, usually from overtightening. Stripping threads is an all-too-common occurrence, especially when working with aluminum parts, because aluminum is so soft that it easily strips out.

Usually, external or internal threads are only partially stripped. After they've been cleaned up with a tap or die, they'll still work. Sometimes, however, threads are badly damaged. When this happens, you've got three choices:

1) Drill and tap the hole to the next suitable oversize and install a larger diameter bolt, screw or stud.

2) Drill and tap the hole to accept a threaded plug, then drill and tap the plug to the original screw size. You can also buy a plug already threaded to the original size. Then you simply drill a hole to the specified size, then run the threaded plug into the hole with a bolt and jam nut. Once the plug is fully seated, remove the jam nut and bolt.

3) The third method uses a patented thread repair kit like Heli-Coil or Slimsert. These easy-to-use kits are designed to repair damaged threads in straight-through holes and blind holes. Both are available as kits which can handle a variety of sizes and thread patterns. Drill the hole, then tap it with the special included tap. Install the Heli-Coil and the hole is back to its original diameter and thread pitch.

Regardless of which method you use, be sure to proceed calmly and carefully. A little impatience or carelessness during one of these relatively simple procedures can ruin your whole day's work and cost you a bundle if you wreck an expensive part.

WORKING FACILITIES

Not to be overlooked when discussing tools is the workshop. If anything more than routine maintenance is to be carried out, some sort of suitable work area is essential.

It is understood, and appreciated, that many home mechanics do not have a good workshop or garage available, and end up removing an engine or doing major repairs outside. It is recommended, however, that the overhaul or repair be completed under the cover of a roof.

A clean, flat workbench or table of comfortable working height is an absolute necessity. The workbench should be equipped with a vise that has a jaw opening of at least four inches.

As mentioned previously, some clean, dry storage space is also required for tools, as well as the lubricants, fluids, cleaning solvents, etc. which soon become necessary.

Sometimes waste oil and fluids, drained from the engine or cooling system during normal maintenance or repairs, present a disposal problem. To avoid pouring them on the ground or into a sewage system, pour the used fluids into large containers, seal them with caps and take them to an authorized disposal site or recycling center. Plastic jugs, such as old antifreeze containers, are ideal for this purpose.

Always keep a supply of old newspapers and clean rags available. Old towels are excellent for mopping up spills. Many mechanics use rolls of paper towels for most work because they are readily available and disposable. To help keep the area under the vehicle clean, a large cardboard box can be cut open and flattened to protect the garage or shop floor.

Whenever working over a painted surface, such as when leaning over a fender to service something under the hood, always cover it with an old blanket or bedspread to protect the finish. Vinyl covered pads, made especially for this purpose, are available at auto parts stores.

Jacking and towing

JACKING

The jack supplied with the vehicle should only be used for raising the vehicle when changing a tire or placing jackstands under the frame. NEVER work under the vehicle or start the engine when the vehicle supported only by a jack.

The vehicle should be parked on level ground with the wheels blocked, the parking brake applied and the transmission in Park (automatic) or Reverse (manual). If the vehicle is parked alongside the roadway, or in any other hazardous situation, turn on the emergency hazard flashers. If a tire is to be changed, loosen the lug nuts one-half turn before raising off the ground.

Place the jack under the vehicle in the indicated positions (see illustrations). Operate the jack with a slow, smooth motion until the wheel is raised off the ground. Remove the lug nuts, pull off the wheel, install the spare and thread the lug nuts back on with the beveled side facing in. Tighten the lug nuts snugly, lower the vehicle until some weight is on the wheel, tighten them completely in a criss-cross pattern and

remove the jack. Note that some spare tires are designed for temporary use only - don't exceed the recommended speed, mileage or other restriction instructions accompanying the spare.

TOWING

Two-wheel drive models can be towed from the rear with the front wheels on the ground, using a wheel lift type tow truck. Four-wheel drive models must be towed with all four wheels off the ground. The best way to tow the vehicle is with a flat-bed car carrier. A sling-type tow truck cannot be used, as body damage will result.

If any vehicle is to be towed with the front wheels on the ground and the rear wheels raised, the ignition key must be turned to the OFF position to unlock the steering column and a steering wheel clamping device designed for towing must be used or damage to the steering column lock may occur.

Front jacking point

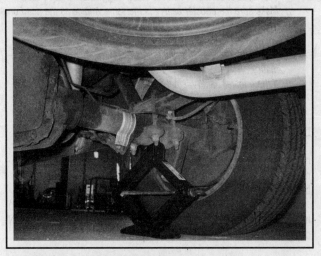

Rear jacking point (all models)

Booster battery (jump) starting

Observe these precautions when using a booster battery to start a vehicle:

a) *Before connecting the booster battery, make sure the ignition switch is in the Off position.*
b) *Turn off the lights, heater and other electrical loads.*
c) *Your eyes should be shielded. Safety goggles are a good idea.*
d) *Make sure the booster battery is the same voltage as the dead one in the vehicle.*
e) *The two vehicles MUST NOT TOUCH each other!*
f) *Make sure the transmission is in Neutral (manual) or Park (automatic).*
g) *If the booster battery is not a maintenance-free type, remove the vent caps and lay a cloth over the vent holes.*

Connect the red jumper cable to the positive (+) terminals of each battery (see illustration).

Connect one end of the black jumper cable to the negative (-) terminal of the booster battery. The other end of this cable should be connected to a good ground on the vehicle to be started, such as a bolt or bracket on the body.

Start the engine using the booster battery, then, with the engine running at idle speed, disconnect the jumper cables in the reverse order of connection.

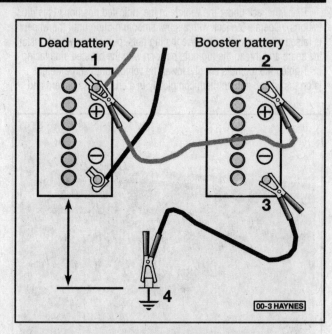

Make the booster battery cable connections in the numerical order shown (note that the negative cable of the booster battery is NOT attached to the negative terminal of the dead battery)

Automotive chemicals and lubricants

A number of automotive chemicals and lubricants are available for use during vehicle maintenance and repair. They include a wide variety of products ranging from cleaning solvents and degreasers to lubricants and protective sprays for rubber, plastic and vinyl.

CLEANERS

Carburetor cleaner and choke cleaner is a strong solvent for gum, varnish and carbon. Most carburetor cleaners leave a dry-type lubricant film which will not harden or gum up. Because of this film it is not recommended for use on electrical components.

Brake system cleaner is used to remove brake dust, grease and brake fluid from the brake system, where clean surfaces are absolutely necessary. It leaves no residue and often eliminates brake squeal caused by contaminants.

Electrical cleaner removes oxidation, corrosion and carbon deposits from electrical contacts, restoring full current flow. It can also be used to clean spark plugs, carburetor jets, voltage regulators and other parts where an oil-free surface is desired.

Demoisturants remove water and moisture from electrical components such as alternators, voltage regulators, electrical connectors and fuse blocks. They are non-conductive and non-corrosive.

Degreasers are heavy-duty solvents used to remove grease from the outside of the engine and from chassis components. They can be sprayed or brushed on and, depending on the type, are rinsed off either with water or solvent.

LUBRICANTS

Motor oil is the lubricant formulated for use in engines. It normally contains a wide variety of additives to prevent corrosion and reduce foaming and wear. Motor oil comes in various weights (viscosity ratings) from 0 to 50. The recommended weight of the oil depends on the season, temperature and the demands on the engine. Light oil is used in cold climates and under light load conditions. Heavy oil is used in hot climates and where high loads are encountered. Multi-viscosity oils are designed to have characteristics of both light and heavy oils and are available in a number of weights from 0W-20 to 20W-50.

Gear oil is designed to be used in differentials, manual transmissions and other areas where high-temperature lubrication is required.

Chassis and wheel bearing grease is a heavy grease used where increased loads and friction are encountered, such as for wheel bearings, ball-joints, tie-rod ends and universal joints.

High-temperature wheel bearing grease is designed to withstand the extreme temperatures encountered by wheel bearings in disc brake equipped vehicles. It usually contains molybdenum disulfide (moly), which is a dry-type lubricant.

White grease is a heavy grease for metal-to-metal applications where water is a problem. White grease stays soft under both low and high temperatures (usually from -100 to +190-degrees F), and will not wash off or dilute in the presence of water.

Assembly lube is a special extreme pressure lubricant, usually containing moly, used to lubricate high-load parts (such as main and rod bearings and cam lobes) for initial start-up of a new engine. The assembly lube lubricates the parts without being squeezed out or washed away until the engine oiling system begins to function.

Silicone lubricants are used to protect rubber, plastic, vinyl and nylon parts.

Graphite lubricants are used where oils cannot be used due to contamination problems, such as in locks. The dry graphite will lubricate metal parts while remaining uncontaminated by dirt, water, oil or acids. It is electrically conductive and will not foul electrical contacts in locks such as the ignition switch.

Moly penetrants loosen and lubricate frozen, rusted and corroded fasteners and prevent future rusting or freezing.

Heat-sink grease is a special electrically non-conductive grease that is used for mounting electronic ignition modules where it is essential that heat is transferred away from the module.

SEALANTS

RTV sealant is one of the most widely used gasket compounds. Made from silicone, RTV is air curing, it seals, bonds, waterproofs, fills surface irregularities, remains flexible, doesn't shrink, is relatively easy to remove, and is used as a supplementary sealer with almost all low and medium temperature gaskets.

Anaerobic sealant is much like RTV in that it can be used either to seal gaskets or to form gaskets by itself. It remains flexible, is solvent resistant and fills surface imperfections. The difference between an anaerobic sealant and an RTV-type sealant is in the curing. RTV cures when exposed to air, while an anaerobic sealant cures only in the absence of air. This means that an anaerobic sealant cures only after the assembly of parts, sealing them together.

Thread and pipe sealant is used for sealing hydraulic and pneumatic fittings and vacuum lines. It is usually made from a Teflon compound, and comes in a spray, a paint-on liquid and as a wrap-around tape.

CHEMICALS

Anti-seize compound prevents seizing, galling, cold welding, rust and corrosion in fasteners. High-temperature anti-seize, usually made with copper and graphite lubricants, is used for exhaust system and exhaust manifold bolts.

Anaerobic locking compounds are used to keep fasteners from vibrating or working loose and cure only after installation, in the absence of air. Medium strength locking compound is used for small nuts, bolts and screws that may be removed later. High-strength locking compound is for large nuts, bolts and studs which aren't removed on a regular basis.

Oil additives range from viscosity index improvers to chemical treatments that claim to reduce internal engine friction. It should be noted that most oil manufacturers caution against using additives with their oils.

Gas additives perform several functions, depending on their chemical makeup. They usually contain solvents that help dissolve gum and varnish that build up on carburetor, fuel injection and intake parts. They also serve to break down carbon deposits that form on the inside surfaces of the combustion chambers. Some additives contain upper cylinder lubricants for valves and piston rings, and others contain chemicals to remove condensation from the gas tank.

MISCELLANEOUS

Brake fluid is specially formulated hydraulic fluid that can withstand the heat and pressure encountered in brake systems. Care must be taken so this fluid does not come in contact with painted surfaces or plastics. An opened container should always be resealed to prevent contamination by water or dirt.

Weatherstrip adhesive is used to bond weatherstripping around doors, windows and trunk lids. It is sometimes used to attach trim pieces.

Undercoating is a petroleum-based, tar-like substance that is designed to protect metal surfaces on the underside of the vehicle from corrosion. It also acts as a sound-deadening agent by insulating the bottom of the vehicle.

Waxes and polishes are used to help protect painted and plated surfaces from the weather. Different types of paint may require the use of different types of wax and polish. Some polishes utilize a chemical or abrasive cleaner to help remove the top layer of oxidized (dull) paint on older vehicles. In recent years many non-wax polishes that contain a wide variety of chemicals such as polymers and silicones have been introduced. These non-wax polishes are usually easier to apply and last longer than conventional waxes and polishes.

CONVERSION FACTORS

LENGTH (distance)
Inches (in)	X 25.4	= Millimeters (mm)	X 0.0394	= Inches (in)
Feet (ft)	X 0.305	= Meters (m)	X 3.281	= Feet (ft)
Miles	X 1.609	= Kilometers (km)	X 0.621	= Miles

VOLUME (capacity)
Cubic inches (cu in; in³)	X 16.387	= Cubic centimeters (cc; cm³)	X 0.061	= Cubic inches (cu in; in³)
Imperial pints (Imp pt)	X 0.568	= Liters (l)	X 1.76	= Imperial pints (Imp pt)
Imperial quarts (Imp qt)	X 1.137	= Liters (l)	X 0.88	= Imperial quarts (Imp qt)
Imperial quarts (Imp qt)	X 1.201	= US quarts (US qt)	X 0.833	= Imperial quarts (Imp qt)
US quarts (US qt)	X 0.946	= Liters (l)	X 1.057	= US quarts (US qt)
Imperial gallons (Imp gal)	X 4.546	= Liters (l)	X 0.22	= Imperial gallons (Imp gal)
Imperial gallons (Imp gal)	X 1.201	= US gallons (US gal)	X 0.833	= Imperial gallons (Imp gal)
US gallons (US gal)	X 3.785	= Liters (l)	X 0.264	= US gallons (US gal)

MASS (weight)
Ounces (oz)	X 28.35	= Grams (g)	X 0.035	= Ounces (oz)
Pounds (lb)	X 0.454	= Kilograms (kg)	X 2.205	= Pounds (lb)

FORCE
Ounces-force (ozf; oz)	X 0.278	= Newtons (N)	X 3.6	= Ounces-force (ozf; oz)
Pounds-force (lbf; lb)	X 4.448	= Newtons (N)	X 0.225	= Pounds-force (lbf; lb)
Newtons (N)	X 0.1	= Kilograms-force (kgf; kg)	X 9.81	= Newtons (N)

PRESSURE
Pounds-force per square inch (psi; lbf/in²; lb/in²)	X 0.070	= Kilograms-force per square centimeter (kgf/cm²; kg/cm²)	X 14.223	= Pounds-force per square inch (psi; lbf/in²; lb/in²)
Pounds-force per square inch (psi; lbf/in²; lb/in²)	X 0.068	= Atmospheres (atm)	X 14.696	= Pounds-force per square inch (psi; lbf/in²; lb/in²)
Pounds-force per square inch (psi; lbf/in²; lb/in²)	X 0.069	= Bars	X 14.5	= Pounds-force per square inch (psi; lbf/in²; lb/in²)
Pounds-force per square inch (psi; lbf/in²; lb/in²)	X 6.895	= Kilopascals (kPa)	X 0.145	= Pounds-force per square inch (psi; lbf/in²; lb/in²)
Kilopascals (kPa)	X 0.01	= Kilograms-force per square centimeter (kgf/cm²; kg/cm²)	X 98.1	= Kilopascals (kPa)

TORQUE (moment of force)
Pounds-force inches (lbf in; lb in)	X 1.152	= Kilograms-force centimeter (kgf cm; kg cm)	X 0.868	= Pounds-force inches (lbf in; lb in)
Pounds-force inches (lbf in; lb in)	X 0.113	= Newton meters (Nm)	X 8.85	= Pounds-force inches (lbf in; lb in)
Pounds-force inches (lbf in; lb in)	X 0.083	= Pounds-force feet (lbf ft; lb ft)	X 12	= Pounds-force inches (lbf in; lb in)
Pounds-force feet (lbf ft; lb ft)	X 0.138	= Kilograms-force meters (kgf m; kg m)	X 7.233	= Pounds-force feet (lbf ft; lb ft)
Pounds-force feet (lbf ft; lb ft)	X 1.356	= Newton meters (Nm)	X 0.738	= Pounds-force feet (lbf ft; lb ft)
Newton meters (Nm)	X 0.102	= Kilograms-force meters (kgf m; kg m)	X 9.804	= Newton meters (Nm)

VACUUM
Inches mercury (in. Hg)	X 3.377	= Kilopascals (kPa)	X 0.2961	= Inches mercury
Inches mercury (in. Hg)	X 25.4	= Millimeters mercury (mm Hg)	X 0.0394	= Inches mercury

POWER
Horsepower (hp)	X 745.7	= Watts (W)	X 0.0013	= Horsepower (hp)

VELOCITY (speed)
Miles per hour (miles/hr; mph)	X 1.609	= Kilometers per hour (km/hr; kph)	X 0.621	= Miles per hour (miles/hr; mph)

FUEL CONSUMPTION *
Miles per gallon, Imperial (mpg)	X 0.354	= Kilometers per liter (km/l)	X 2.825	= Miles per gallon, Imperial (mpg)
Miles per gallon, US (mpg)	X 0.425	= Kilometers per liter (km/l)	X 2.352	= Miles per gallon, US (mpg)

TEMPERATURE
Degrees Fahrenheit = (°C x 1.8) + 32   Degrees Celsius (Degrees Centigrade; °C) = (°F - 32) x 0.56

It is common practice to convert from miles per gallon (mpg) to liters/100 kilometers (l/100km), where mpg (Imperial) x l/100 km = 282 and mpg (US) x l/100 km = 235

FRACTION/DECIMAL/MILLIMETER EQUIVALENTS

DECIMALS TO MILLIMETERS

Decimal	mm	Decimal	mm
0.001	0.0254	0.500	12.7000
0.002	0.0508	0.510	12.9540
0.003	0.0762	0.520	13.2080
0.004	0.1016	0.530	13.4620
0.005	0.1270	0.540	13.7160
0.006	0.1524	0.550	13.9700
0.007	0.1778	0.560	14.2240
0.008	0.2032	0.570	14.4780
0.009	0.2286	0.580	14.7320
		0.590	14.9860
0.010	0.2540		
0.020	0.5080		
0.030	0.7620		
0.040	1.0160	0.600	15.2400
0.050	1.2700	0.610	15.4940
0.060	1.5240	0.620	15.7480
0.070	1.7780	0.630	16.0020
0.080	2.0320	0.640	16.2560
0.090	2.2860	0.650	16.5100
		0.660	16.7640
0.100	2.5400	0.670	17.0180
0.110	2.7940	0.680	17.2720
0.120	3.0480	0.690	17.5260
0.130	3.3020		
0.140	3.5560		
0.150	3.8100		
0.160	4.0640	0.700	17.7800
0.170	4.3180	0.710	18.0340
0.180	4.5720	0.720	18.2880
0.190	4.8260	0.730	18.5420
		0.740	18.7960
0.200	5.0800	0.750	19.0500
0.210	5.3340	0.760	19.3040
0.220	5.5880	0.770	19.5580
0.230	5.8420	0.780	19.8120
0.240	6.0960	0.790	20.0660
0.250	6.3500		
0.260	6.6040		
0.270	6.8580	0.800	20.3200
0.280	7.1120	0.810	20.5740
0.290	7.3660	0.820	20.8280
		0.830	21.0820
0.300	7.6200	0.840	21.3360
0.310	7.8740	0.850	21.5900
0.320	8.1280	0.860	21.8440
0.330	8.3820	0.870	22.0980
0.340	8.6360	0.880	22.3520
0.350	8.8900	0.890	22.6060
0.360	9.1440		
0.370	9.3980		
0.380	9.6520		
0.390	9.9060		
		0.900	22.8600
0.400	10.1600	0.910	23.1140
0.410	10.4140	0.920	23.3680
0.420	10.6680	0.930	23.6220
0.430	10.9220	0.940	23.8760
0.440	11.1760	0.950	24.1300
0.450	11.4300	0.960	24.3840
0.460	11.6840	0.970	24.6380
0.470	11.9380	0.980	24.8920
0.480	12.1920	0.990	25.1460
0.490	12.4460	1.000	25.4000

FRACTIONS TO DECIMALS TO MILLIMETERS

Fraction	Decimal	mm	Fraction	Decimal	mm
1/64	0.0156	0.3969	33/64	0.5156	13.0969
1/32	0.0312	0.7938	17/32	0.5312	13.4938
3/64	0.0469	1.1906	35/64	0.5469	13.8906
1/16	0.0625	1.5875	9/16	0.5625	14.2875
5/64	0.0781	1.9844	37/64	0.5781	14.6844
3/32	0.0938	2.3812	19/32	0.5938	15.0812
7/64	0.1094	2.7781	39/64	0.6094	15.4781
1/8	0.1250	3.1750	5/8	0.6250	15.8750
9/64	0.1406	3.5719	41/64	0.6406	16.2719
5/32	0.1562	3.9688	21/32	0.6562	16.6688
11/64	0.1719	4.3656	43/64	0.6719	17.0656
3/16	0.1875	4.7625	11/16	0.6875	17.4625
13/64	0.2031	5.1594	45/64	0.7031	17.8594
7/32	0.2188	5.5562	23/32	0.7188	18.2562
15/64	0.2344	5.9531	47/64	0.7344	18.6531
1/4	0.2500	6.3500	3/4	0.7500	19.0500
17/64	0.2656	6.7469	49/64	0.7656	19.4469
9/32	0.2812	7.1438	25/32	0.7812	19.8438
19/64	0.2969	7.5406	51/64	0.7969	20.2406
5/16	0.3125	7.9375	13/16	0.8125	20.6375
21/64	0.3281	8.3344	53/64	0.8281	21.0344
11/32	0.3438	8.7312	27/32	0.8438	21.4312
23/64	0.3594	9.1281	55/64	0.8594	21.8281
3/8	0.3750	9.5250	7/8	0.8750	22.2250
25/64	0.3906	9.9219	57/64	0.8906	22.6219
13/32	0.4062	10.3188	29/32	0.9062	23.0188
27/64	0.4219	10.7156	59/64	0.9219	23.4156
7/16	0.4375	11.1125	15/16	0.9375	23.8125
29/64	0.4531	11.5094	61/64	0.9531	24.2094
15/32	0.4688	11.9062	31/32	0.9688	24.6062
31/64	0.4844	12.3031	63/64	0.9844	25.0031
1/2	0.5000	12.7000	1	1.0000	25.4000

Safety first!

Regardless of how enthusiastic you may be about getting on with the job at hand, take the time to ensure that your safety is not jeopardized. A moment's lack of attention can result in an accident, as can failure to observe certain simple safety precautions. The possibility of an accident will always exist, and the following points should not be considered a comprehensive list of all dangers. Rather, they are intended to make you aware of the risks and to encourage a safety conscious approach to all work you carry out on your vehicle.

ESSENTIAL DOS AND DON'TS

DON'T rely on a jack when working under the vehicle. Always use approved jackstands to support the weight of the vehicle and place them under the recommended lift or support points.

DON'T attempt to loosen extremely tight fasteners (i.e. wheel lug nuts) while the vehicle is on a jack - it may fall.

DON'T start the engine without first making sure that the transmission is in Neutral (or Park where applicable) and the parking brake is set.

DON'T remove the radiator cap from a hot cooling system - let it cool or cover it with a cloth and release the pressure gradually.

DON'T attempt to drain the engine oil until you are sure it has cooled to the point that it will not burn you.

DON'T touch any part of the engine or exhaust system until it has cooled sufficiently to avoid burns.

DON'T siphon toxic liquids such as gasoline, antifreeze and brake fluid by mouth, or allow them to remain on your skin.

DON'T inhale brake lining dust - it is potentially hazardous (see Asbestos below).

DON'T allow spilled oil or grease to remain on the floor - wipe it up before someone slips on it.

DON'T use loose fitting wrenches or other tools which may slip and cause injury.

DON'T push on wrenches when loosening or tightening nuts or bolts. Always try to pull the wrench toward you. If the situation calls for pushing the wrench away, push with an open hand to avoid scraped knuckles if the wrench should slip.

DON'T attempt to lift a heavy component alone - get someone to help you.

DON'T rush or take unsafe shortcuts to finish a job.

DON'T allow children or animals in or around the vehicle while you are working on it.

DO wear eye protection when using power tools such as a drill, sander, bench grinder, etc. and when working under a vehicle.

DO keep loose clothing and long hair well out of the way of moving parts.

DO make sure that any hoist used has a safe working load rating adequate for the job.

DO get someone to check on you periodically when working alone on a vehicle.

DO carry out work in a logical sequence and make sure that everything is correctly assembled and tightened.

DO keep chemicals and fluids tightly capped and out of the reach of children and pets.

DO remember that your vehicle's safety affects that of yourself and others. If in doubt on any point, get professional advice.

STEERING, SUSPENSION AND BRAKES

These systems are essential to driving safety, so make sure you have a qualified shop or individual check your work. Also, compressed suspension springs can cause injury if released suddenly - be sure to use a spring compressor.

AIRBAGS

Airbags are explosive devices that can CAUSE injury if they deploy while you're working on the vehicle. Follow the manufacturer's instructions to disable the airbag whenever you're working in the vicinity of airbag components.

ASBESTOS

Certain friction, insulating, sealing, and other products - such as brake linings, brake bands, clutch linings, torque converters, gaskets, etc. - may contain asbestos or other hazardous friction material. Extreme care must be taken to avoid inhalation of dust from such products, since it is hazardous to health. If in doubt, assume that they do contain asbestos.

FIRE

Remember at all times that gasoline is highly flammable. Never smoke or have any kind of open flame around when working on a vehicle. But the risk does not end there. A spark caused by an electrical short circuit, by two metal surfaces contacting each other, or even by static electricity built up in your body under certain conditions, can ignite gasoline vapors, which in a confined space are highly explosive. Do not, under any circumstances, use gasoline for cleaning parts. Use an approved safety solvent.

Always disconnect the battery ground (-) cable at the battery before working on any part of the fuel system or electrical system. Never risk spilling fuel on a hot engine or exhaust component. It is strongly recommended that a fire extinguisher suitable for use on fuel and electrical fires be kept handy in the garage or workshop at all times. Never try to extinguish a fuel or electrical fire with water.

FUMES

Certain fumes are highly toxic and can quickly cause unconsciousness and even death if inhaled to any extent. Gasoline vapor falls into this category, as do the vapors from some cleaning solvents. Any draining or pouring of such volatile fluids should be done in a well ventilated area.

When using cleaning fluids and solvents, read the instructions on the container carefully. Never use materials from unmarked containers.

Never run the engine in an enclosed space, such as a garage. Exhaust fumes contain carbon monoxide, which is extremely poisonous. If you need to run the engine, always do so in the open air, or at least have the rear of the vehicle outside the work area.

THE BATTERY

Never create a spark or allow a bare light bulb near a battery. They normally give off a certain amount of hydrogen gas, which is highly explosive.

Always disconnect the battery ground (-) cable at the battery before working on the fuel or electrical systems.

If possible, loosen the filler caps or cover when charging the battery from an external source (this does not apply to sealed or maintenance-free batteries). Do not charge at an excessive rate or the battery may burst.

Take care when adding water to a non maintenance-free battery and when carrying a battery. The electrolyte, even when diluted, is very corrosive and should not be allowed to contact clothing or skin.

Always wear eye protection when cleaning the battery to prevent the caustic deposits from entering your eyes.

HOUSEHOLD CURRENT

When using an electric power tool, inspection light, etc., which operates on household current, always make sure that the tool is correctly connected to its plug and that, where necessary, it is properly grounded. Do not use such items in damp conditions and, again, do not create a spark or apply excessive heat in the vicinity of fuel or fuel vapor.

SECONDARY IGNITION SYSTEM VOLTAGE

A severe electric shock can result from touching certain parts of the ignition system (such as the spark plug wires) when the engine is running or being cranked, particularly if components are damp or the insulation is defective. In the case of an electronic ignition system, the secondary system voltage is much higher and could prove fatal.

HYDROFLUORIC ACID

This extremely corrosive acid is formed when certain types of synthetic rubber, found in some O-rings, oil seals, fuel hoses, etc. are exposed to temperatures above 750-degrees F (400-degrees C). The rubber changes into a charred or sticky substance containing the acid. *Once formed, the acid remains dangerous for years. If it gets onto the skin, it may be necessary to amputate the limb concerned.*

When dealing with a vehicle which has suffered a fire, or with components salvaged from such a vehicle, wear protective gloves and discard them after use.

Troubleshooting

CONTENTS

Section Symptom

Engine

1 Engine will not rotate when attempting to start
2 Engine rotates but will not start
3 Starter motor operates without rotating engine
4 Engine hard to start when cold
5 Engine hard to start when hot
6 Starter motor noisy or excessively rough in engagement
7 Engine starts but stops immediately
8 Engine lopes while idling or idles erratically
9 Engine misses at idle speed
10 Engine misses throughout driving speed range
11 Engine stalls
12 Engine lacks power
13 Engine backfires
14 Pinging or knocking engine sounds during acceleration or uphill
15 Engine continues to run after switching off

Engine electrical system

16 Battery will not hold a charge
17 Ignition light fails to go out.
18 Ignition light fails to come on when key is turned on

Fuel system

19 Excessive fuel consumption
20 Fuel leakage and/or fuel odor

Cooling system

21 Overheating
22 Overcooling
23 External coolant leakage
24 Internal coolant leakage
25 Coolant loss
26 Poor coolant circulation

Clutch

27 Fails to release (pedal pressed to the floor - shift lever does not move freely in and out of Reverse)
28 Clutch slips (engine speed increases with no increase in vehicle speed)
29 Grabbing (chattering) as clutch is engaged
30 Squeal or rumble with clutch fully engaged (pedal released)
31 Squeal or rumble with clutch fully disengaged (pedal depressed)
32 Clutch pedal stays on floor when disengaged

Manual transmission

33 Noisy in Neutral with engine running
34 Noisy in all gears
35 Noisy in one particular gear
36 Slips out of high gear

Section Symptom

37 Difficulty in engaging gears
38 Oil leakage

Automatic transmission

39 General shift mechanism problems
40 Transmission will not downshift with accelerator pedal pressed to the floor
41 Transmission slips, shifts rough, is noisy or has no drive in forward or reverse gears
42 Fluid leakage

Transfer case

43 Transfer case is difficult to shift into the desired range
44 Transfer case noisy in all gears
45 Noisy or jumps out of four-wheel drive Low range
46 Lubricant leaks from the vent or output shaft seals

Driveshaft

47 Oil leak at front of driveshaft
48 Knock or clunk when the transmission is under initial load (just after transmission is put into gear)
49 Metallic grinding sound consistent with vehicle speed
50 Vibration

Axles

51 Noise
52 Vibration
53 Oil leakage

Brakes

54 Vehicle pulls to one side during braking
55 Noise (high-pitched squeal with the brakes applied)
56 Excessive brake pedal travel
57 Brake pedal feels spongy when depressed
58 Excessive effort required to stop vehicle
59 Pedal travels to the floor with little resistance
60 Brake pedal pulsates during brake application

Suspension and steering systems

61 Vehicle pulls to one side
62 Shimmy, shake or vibration
63 Excessive pitching and/or rolling around corners or during braking
64 Excessively stiff steering
65 Excessive play in steering
66 Lack of power assistance
67 Excessive tire wear (not specific to one area)
68 Excessive tire wear on outside edge
69 Excessive tire wear on inside edge
70 Tire tread worn in one place

This section provides an easy reference guide to the more common problems which may occur during the operation of your vehicle. These problems and possible causes are grouped under various components or systems; i.e. Engine, Cooling System, etc., and also refer to the Chapter and/or Section which deals with the problem.

Remember that successful troubleshooting is not a mysterious black art practiced only by professional mechanics. It's simply the result of a bit of knowledge combined with an intelligent, systematic approach to the problem. Always work by a process of elimination, starting with the simplest solution and working through to the most complex - and never overlook the obvious. Anyone can forget to fill the gas tank or leave the lights on overnight, so don't assume that you are above such oversights.

Finally, always get clear in your mind why a problem has occurred and take steps to ensure that it doesn't happen again. If the electrical system fails because of a poor connection, check all other connections in the system to make sure that they don't fail as well. If a particular fuse continues to blow, find out why - don't just go on replacing fuses. Remember, failure of a small component can often be indicative of potential failure or incorrect functioning of a more important component or system.

ENGINE

1   Engine will not rotate when attempting to start

1   Battery terminal connections loose or corroded. Check the cable terminals at the battery. Tighten the cable or remove corrosion as necessary.

2   Battery discharged or faulty. If the cable connections are clean and tight on the battery posts, turn the key to the On position and switch on the headlights and/or windshield wipers. If they fail to function, the battery is discharged.

3   Automatic transmission not completely engaged in Park or Neutral or clutch pedal not completely depressed.

4   Broken, loose or disconnected wiring in the starting circuit. Inspect all wiring and connectors at the battery, starter solenoid and ignition switch.

5   Starter motor pinion jammed in flywheel ring gear. If manual transmission, place transmission in gear and rock the vehicle to manually turn the engine. Remove starter and inspect pinion and flywheel at earliest convenience (Chapter 5).

6   Starter solenoid faulty (Chapter 5).

7   Starter motor faulty (Chapter 5).

8   Ignition switch faulty (Chapter 12).

2   Engine rotates but will not start

1   Fuel tank empty, fuel filter plugged or fuel line restricted.

2   Fault in the fuel injection system (Chapter 4).

3   Battery discharged (engine rotates slowly). Check the operation of electrical components as described in the previous Section.

4   Battery terminal connections loose or corroded (see previous Section).

5   Fuel pump faulty (Chapter 4).

6   Excessive moisture on, or damage to, ignition components (see Chapter 5).

7   Worn, faulty or incorrectly gapped spark plugs (Chapter 1).

8   Broken, loose or disconnected wiring in the starting circuit (see previous Section).

9   Broken, loose or disconnected wires at the ignition coil (Chapter 5).

10 Contaminated fuel.

3   Starter motor operates without rotating engine

1   Starter pinion sticking. Remove the starter (Chapter 5) and inspect.

2   Starter pinion or flywheel teeth worn or broken. Remove the flywheel/driveplate access cover and inspect.

4   Engine hard to start when cold

1   Battery discharged or low. Check as described in Section 1.

2   Fault in the fuel or electrical systems (Chapters 4 and 5).

5   Engine hard to start when hot

1   Air filter clogged (Chapter 1).

2   Fault in the fuel or electrical systems (Chapters 4 and 5).

3   Fuel not reaching the injectors (see Chapter 4).

4   Low cylinder compression (Chapter 2).

6   Starter motor noisy or excessively rough in engagement

1   Pinion or flywheel gear teeth worn or broken. Remove the cover at the rear of the engine (if equipped) and inspect.

2   Starter motor mounting bolts loose or missing.

7   Engine starts but stops immediately

1   Loose or faulty electrical connections at coil or alternator.

2   Fault in the fuel or electrical systems (Chapters 4 and 5).

3   Vacuum leak at the gasket surfaces of the intake manifold or throttle body. Make sure all mounting bolts/nuts are tightened securely and all vacuum hoses connected to the manifold are positioned properly and in good condition.

4   Restricted intake or exhaust systems (Chapter 4)

5   Contaminated fuel.

8   Engine lopes while idling or idles erratically

1   Vacuum leakage. Check the mounting bolts/nuts at the throttle body and intake manifold for tightness. Make sure all vacuum hoses are connected and in good condition. Use a stethoscope or a length of fuel hose held against your ear to listen for vacuum leaks while the engine is running. A hissing sound will be heard. A soapy water solution will also detect leaks.

2   Fault in the fuel or electrical systems (Chapters 4 and 5).

3   Plugged PCV valve or hose (see Chapters 1 and 6).

4   Air filter clogged (Chapter 1).

5   Fuel pump not delivering sufficient fuel to the fuel injectors (see Chapter 4).

6   Leaking head gasket. Perform a compression check (Chapter 2).

7   Camshaft lobes worn (Chapter 2).

9 Engine misses at idle speed

1 Spark plugs worn, fouled or not gapped properly (Chapter 1).
2 Fault in the fuel or electrical systems (Chapters 4 and 5).
3 Faulty spark plug wires (Chapter 1).
4 Vacuum leaks at intake or hose connections. Check as described in Section 8.
5 Uneven or low cylinder compression. Check compression as described in Chapter 2.

10 Engine misses throughout driving speed range

1 Fuel filter clogged and/or impurities in the fuel system (Chapter 1).
2 Faulty or incorrectly gapped spark plugs (Chapter 1).
3 Fault in the fuel or electrical systems (Chapters 4 and 5).
4 Defective spark plug wires (Chapter 1).
5 Faulty emissions system components (Chapter 6).
6 Low or uneven cylinder compression pressures. Remove the spark plugs and test the compression with a gauge (Chapter 2).
7 Weak or faulty ignition system (Chapter 5).
8 Vacuum leaks at the throttle body, intake manifold or vacuum hoses (see Section 8).

11 Engine stalls

1 Idle speed incorrect. Refer to the VECI label.
2 Fuel filter clogged and/or water and impurities in the fuel system (Chapter 1).
3 Fault in the fuel system or sensors (Chapters 4 and 6).
4 Faulty emissions system components (Chapter 6).
5 Faulty or incorrectly gapped spark plugs (Chapter 1). Also check the spark plug wires (Chapter 1).
6 Vacuum leak at the throttle body, intake manifold or vacuum hoses. Check as described in Section 8.

12 Engine lacks power

1 Fault in the fuel or electrical systems (Chapters 4 and 5).
2 Faulty or incorrectly gapped spark plugs (Chapter 1).
3 Faulty coil (Chapter 5).
4 Brakes binding (Chapter 1).
5 Automatic transmission fluid level incorrect (Chapter 1).
6 Clutch slipping (Chapter 8).
7 Fuel filter clogged and/or impurities in the fuel system (Chapter 1).
8 Emissions control system not functioning properly (Chapter 6).
9 Use of substandard fuel. Fill the tank with the proper fuel.
10 Low or uneven cylinder compression pressures. Test with a compression tester, which will detect leaking valves and/or a blown head gasket (Chapter 2).
11 Restriction in the intake or exhaust system (Chapter 4).

13 Engine backfires

1 Emissions system not functioning properly (Chapter 6).
2 Fault in the fuel or electrical systems (Chapters 4 and 5).
3 Faulty secondary ignition system (cracked spark plug insulator or faulty plug wires) (Chapters 1 and 5).

4 Vacuum leak at the throttle body, intake manifold or vacuum hoses. Check as described in Section 8.
5 Valves sticking (Chapter 2).
6 Crossed plug wires (Chapter 1).

14 Pinging or knocking engine sounds during acceleration or uphill

1 Incorrect grade of fuel. Fill the tank with fuel of the proper octane rating.
2 Fault in the fuel or electrical systems (Chapters 4 and 5).
3 Improper spark plugs. Also check the plugs and wires for damage (Chapter 1).
4 Faulty emissions system (Chapter 6).
5 Vacuum leak. Check as described in Section 8.

15 Engine continues to run after switching off

Fault in the fuel or electrical systems (Chapters 4 and 5).

ENGINE ELECTRICAL SYSTEM

16 Battery will not hold a charge

1 Alternator drivebelt defective or not adjusted properly (Chapter 1).
2 Electrolyte level low or battery discharged (Chapter 1).
3 Battery terminals loose or corroded (Chapter 1).
4 Alternator not charging properly (Chapter 5).
5 Loose, broken or faulty wiring in the charging circuit (Chapter 5).
6 Short in the vehicle wiring causing a continuous drain on the battery (refer to Chapter 12 and the Wiring Diagrams).
7 Battery defective internally.

17 Ignition light fails to go out

1 Fault in the alternator or charging circuit (Chapter 5).
2 Alternator drivebelt defective or not properly adjusted (Chapter 1).

18 Ignition light fails to come on when key is turned on

1 Instrument cluster warning light bulb defective (Chapter 12).
2 Alternator faulty (Chapter 5).
3 Fault in the instrument cluster printed circuit, dashboard wiring or bulb holder (Chapter 12).

FUEL SYSTEM

19 Excessive fuel consumption

1 Dirty or clogged air filter element (Chapter 1).
2 Emissions system not functioning properly (Chapter 6).
3 Fault in the fuel or electrical systems (Chapters 4 and 5).
4 Low tire pressure or incorrect tire size (Chapter 1).
5 Restricted exhaust system (Chapter 4).

20 Fuel leakage and/or fuel odor

1 Leak in a fuel feed line (Chapter 4).
2 Tank overfilled.
3 Evaporative emissions system canister clogged (Chapter 6).
4 Vapor leaks from system lines (Chapter 4).

COOLING SYSTEM

21 Overheating

1 Insufficient coolant in the system (Chapter 1).
2 Water pump drivebelt defective or not adjusted properly (Chapter 1).
3 Radiator core blocked or radiator grille dirty and restricted (see Chapter 3).
4 Thermostat faulty (Chapter 3).
5 Fan blades broken or cracked (Chapter 3).
6 Cooling system pressure cap not maintaining proper pressure (Chapter 3).

22 Overcooling

1 Thermostat faulty (Chapter 3).
2 Inaccurate temperature gauge (Chapter 12).

23 External coolant leakage

1 Deteriorated or damaged hoses or loose clamps. Replace hoses and/or tighten the clamps at the hose connections (Chapter 1).
2 Water pump seals defective. If this is the case, water will drip from the weep hole in the water pump body (Chapter 3).
3 Leakage from the radiator core or side tank(s). This will require the radiator to be professionally repaired (see Chapter 3 for removal procedures).
4 Engine drain plug(s) leaking (Chapter 1) or water jacket core plugs leaking (see Chapter 2).

24 Internal coolant leakage

➡ **Note: Internal coolant leaks can usually be detected by examining the oil. Check the dipstick and inside of the valve cover for water deposits and an oil consistency like that of a milkshake.**

1 Leaking cylinder head gasket. Have the cooling system pressure tested.
2 Cracked cylinder bore or cylinder head. Dismantle the engine and inspect (Chapter 2).
3 Leaking intake manifold gasket.

25 Coolant loss

1 Too much coolant in the system (Chapter 1).
2 Coolant boiling away due to overheating (see Section 15).
3 External or internal leakage (see Sections 23 and 24).
4 Faulty pressure cap (Chapter 3).

26 Poor coolant circulation

1 Inoperative water pump. A quick test is to pinch the top radiator hose closed with your hand while the engine is idling, then let it loose. You should feel the surge of coolant if the pump is working properly (see Chapter 1).
2 Restriction in the cooling system. Drain, flush and refill the system (Chapter 1). If necessary, remove the radiator (Chapter 3) and have it reverse flushed.
3 Water pump drivebelt defective or not adjusted properly (Chapter 1).
4 Thermostat sticking (Chapter 3).
5 Drivebelt incorrectly routed, causing the pump to turn backwards (Chapter 1).

CLUTCH

27 Fails to release (pedal pressed to the floor - shift lever does not move freely in and out of Reverse)

1 Leak in the clutch hydraulic system. Check the master cylinder, slave cylinder and lines (Chapters 1 and 8).
2 Clutch plate warped or damaged (Chapter 8).

28 Clutch slips (engine speed increases with no increase in vehicle speed)

1 Clutch plate oil soaked or lining worn. Remove clutch (Chapter 8) and inspect.
2 Clutch plate not seated (Chapter 8).
3 Pressure plate worn (Chapter 8).
4 Weak diaphragm springs (Chapter 8).
5 Clutch plate overheated. Allow to cool.

29 Grabbing (chattering) as clutch is engaged

1 Oil on clutch plate lining. Remove (Chapter 8) and inspect. Correct any leakage source.
2 Worn or loose engine or transmission mounts. These units move slightly when the clutch is released. Inspect the mounts and bolts (Chapter 2).
3 Worn splines on clutch plate hub. Remove the clutch components (Chapter 8) and inspect.
4 Warped pressure plate or flywheel. Remove the clutch components and inspect.

30 Squeal or rumble with clutch fully engaged (pedal released)

Release bearing binding on transmission bearing retainer. Remove clutch components (Chapter 8) and check bearing. Remove any burrs or nicks; clean and relubricate bearing retainer before installing.

31 Squeal or rumble with clutch fully disengaged (pedal depressed)

1   Worn, defective or broken release bearing (Chapter 8).
2   Worn or broken pressure plate springs (or diaphragm fingers) (Chapter 8).

32 Clutch pedal stays on floor when disengaged

1   Linkage or release bearing binding. Inspect the linkage or remove the clutch components as necessary.
2   Make sure proper pedal stop (bumper) is installed.

MANUAL TRANSMISSION

➡ **Note: All the following references are in Chapter 7A, unless noted.**

33 Noisy in Neutral with engine running

1   Input shaft bearing worn.
2   Damaged main drive gear bearing.
3   Worn countershaft bearings.
4   Worn or damaged countershaft endplay shims.

34 Noisy in all gears

1   Any of the above causes, and/or:
2   Insufficient lubricant (see the checking procedures in Chapter 1).

35 Noisy in one particular gear

1   Worn, damaged or chipped gear teeth for that particular gear.
2   Worn or damaged synchronizer for that particular gear.

36 Slips out of high gear

1   Transmission loose on clutch housing.
2   Internal transmission problem (Chapter 7A).

37 Difficulty in engaging gears

1   Clutch disc worn (see Chapter 8).
2   Loose, damaged or out-of-adjustment shift linkage. Make a thorough inspection, replacing parts as necessary (Chapter 7A).

38 Oil leakage

1   Excessive amount of lubricant in the transmission (see Chapter 1 for correct checking procedures). Drain lubricant as required.
2   Transmission oil seal or speedometer oil seal in need of replacement (Chapter 7A).

AUTOMATIC TRANSMISSION

➡ **Note: Due to the complexity of the automatic transmission, it's difficult for the home mechanic to properly diagnose and service this component. For problems other than the following, the vehicle should be taken to a dealer service department or a transmission shop.**

39 General shift mechanism problems

1   Chapter 7B deals with checking and adjusting the shift linkage on automatic transmissions. Common problems which may be attributed to poorly adjusted linkage are:
   a) *Engine starting in gears other than Park or Neutral.*
   b) *Indicator on shifter pointing to a gear other than the one actually being selected.*
   c) *Vehicle moves when in Park.*
2   Refer to Chapter 7B to adjust the linkage.

40 Transmission will not downshift with accelerator pedal pressed to the floor

Since these transmissions are electronically controlled, check for any diagnostic trouble codes stored in the PCM. The actual repair will most likely have to be performed by a qualified repair shop with the proper equipment.

41 Transmission slips, shifts rough, is noisy or has no drive in forward or reverse gears

1   There are many probable causes for the above problems, but the home mechanic should be concerned with only one possibility - fluid level.
2   Before taking the vehicle to a repair shop, check the level and condition of the fluid as described in Chapter 1. Correct fluid level as necessary or change the fluid and filter if needed. If the problem persists, have a professional diagnose the probable cause.

42 Fluid leakage

1   Automatic transmission fluid is a deep red color. Fluid leaks should not be confused with engine oil, which can easily be blown by air flow to the transmission.
2   To pinpoint a leak, first remove all built-up dirt and grime from around the transmission. Degreasing agents and/or steam cleaning will achieve this. With the underside clean, drive the vehicle at low speeds so air flow will not blow the leak far from its source. Raise the vehicle and determine where the leak is coming from. Common areas of leakage are:
   a) *Pan: Tighten the mounting bolts and/or replace the pan gasket as necessary (see Chapter 7).*
   b) *Filler pipe: Replace the rubber seal where the pipe enters the transmission case.*
   c) *Transmission oil lines: Tighten the connectors where the lines enter the transmission case and/or replace the lines.*
   d) *Vent pipe: Transmission overfilled and/or water in fluid (see checking procedures, Chapter 1).*
   e) *Speedometer connector: Replace the O-ring where the speedometer sensor enters the transmission case (Chapter 7).*

TRANSFER CASE

43 Transfer case is difficult to shift into the desired range

1 Speed may be too great to permit engagement. Stop the vehicle and shift into the desired range.
2 Shift linkage loose, bent or binding. Check the linkage for damage or wear and replace or lubricate as necessary (Chapter 7C).
3 If the vehicle has been driven on a paved surface for some time, the driveline torque can make shifting difficult. Stop and shift into two-wheel drive on paved or hard surfaces.
4 Insufficient or incorrect grade of lubricant. Drain and refill the transfer case with the specified lubricant (Chapter 1).
5 Worn or damaged internal components. Disassembly and overhaul of the transfer case may be necessary (Chapter 7C).

44 Transfer case noisy in all gears

Insufficient or incorrect grade of lubricant. Drain and refill (Chapter 1).

45 Noisy or jumps out of four-wheel drive Low range

1 Transfer case not fully engaged. Stop the vehicle, shift into Neutral and then engage 4L.
2 Shift linkage loose, worn or binding. Tighten, repair or lubricate linkage as necessary.
3 Shift fork cracked, inserts worn or fork binding on the rail. Disassemble and repair as necessary (Chapter 7C).

46 Lubricant leaks from the vent or output shaft seals

1 Transfer case is overfilled. Drain to the proper level (Chapter 1).
2 Vent is clogged or jammed closed. Clear or replace the vent.
3 Output shaft seal incorrectly installed or damaged. Replace the seal and check contact surfaces for nicks and scoring.

DRIVESHAFT

47 Oil leak at seal end of driveshaft

Defective transmission or transfer case oil seal. See Chapter 7 for replacement procedures. While this is done, check the splined yoke for burrs or a rough condition which may be damaging the seal. Burrs can be removed with crocus cloth or a fine whetstone.

48 Knock or clunk when the transmission is under initial load (just after transmission is put into gear)

1 Loose or disconnected rear suspension components. Check all mounting bolts, nuts and bushings (see Chapter 10).
2 Loose driveshaft bolts. Inspect all bolts and nuts and tighten them to the specified torque.
3 Worn or damaged universal joint bearings. Check for wear (see Chapter 8).

49 Metallic grinding sound consistent with vehicle speed.

Pronounced wear in the universal joint bearings. Check as described in Chapter 8.

50 Vibration

➡ Note: Before assuming that the driveshaft is at fault, make sure the tires are perfectly balanced and perform the following test.

1 Install a tachometer inside the vehicle to monitor engine speed as the vehicle is driven. Drive the vehicle and note the engine speed at which the vibration (roughness) is most pronounced. Now shift the transmission to a different gear and bring the engine speed to the same point.
2 If the vibration occurs at the same engine speed (rpm) regardless of which gear the transmission is in, the driveshaft is NOT at fault since the driveshaft speed varies.
3 If the vibration decreases or is eliminated when the transmission is in a different gear at the same engine speed, refer to the following probable causes.
4 Bent or dented driveshaft. Inspect and replace as necessary (see Chapter 8).
5 Undercoating or built-up dirt, etc. on the driveshaft. Clean the shaft thoroughly and recheck.
6 Worn universal joint bearings. Remove and inspect (see Chapter 8).
7 Driveshaft and/or companion flange out of balance. Check for missing weights on the shaft. Remove the driveshaft (see Chapter 8) and reinstall 180-degrees from original position, then retest. Have the driveshaft professionally balanced if the problem persists.

AXLES

51 Noise

1 Road noise. No corrective procedures available.
2 Tire noise. Inspect tires and check tire pressures (Chapter 1).
3 Rear wheel bearings loose, worn or damaged (Chapter 8).

52 Vibration

See probable causes under Driveshaft. Proceed under the guidelines listed for the driveshaft. If the problem persists, check the rear wheel bearings by raising the rear of the vehicle and spinning the rear wheels by hand. Listen for evidence of rough (noisy) bearings. Remove and inspect (see Chapter 8).

53 Oil leakage

1 Pinion seal damaged (see Chapter 8).
2 Axleshaft oil seals damaged (see Chapter 8).
3 Differential inspection cover leaking. Tighten the bolts or replace the gasket as required (see Chapters 1 and 8).

BRAKES

➡ **Note: Before assuming that a brake problem exists, make sure that the tires are in good condition and inflated properly (see Chapter 1), that the front end alignment is correct and that the vehicle is not loaded with weight in an unequal manner.**

54 Vehicle pulls to one side during braking

1   Defective, damaged or oil contaminated disc brake pads on one side. Inspect as described in Chapter 9.
2   Excessive wear of pad material or disc on one side. Inspect and correct as necessary.
3   Loose or disconnected front suspension components. Inspect and tighten all bolts to the specified torque (Chapter 10).
4   Defective caliper assembly. Remove the caliper and inspect for a stuck piston or other damage (Chapter 9).
5   Inadequate lubrication of front brake caliper slide rails. Remove caliper and lubricate slide rails (Chapter 9).

55 Noise (high-pitched squeal with the brakes applied)

1   Disc brake pads worn out. The noise comes from the wear sensor rubbing against the disc (does not apply to all vehicles) or the actual pad backing plate itself if the material is completely worn away. Replace the pads with new ones immediately (Chapter 9). If the pad material has worn completely away, the brake discs should be inspected for damage as described in Chapter 9.
2   Missing or damaged brake pad insulators. Replace pad insulators (see Chapter 9).
3   Linings contaminated with dirt or grease. Replace pads.
4   Incorrect linings. Replace with correct linings.

56 Excessive brake pedal travel

1   Partial brake system failure. Inspect the entire system (Chapter 9) and correct as required.
2   Insufficient fluid in the master cylinder. Check (Chapter 1), add fluid and bleed the system if necessary (Chapter 9).

57 Brake pedal feels spongy when depressed

1   Air in the hydraulic lines. Bleed the brake system (Chapter 9).
2   Faulty flexible hoses. Inspect all system hoses and lines. Replace parts as necessary.
3   Master cylinder mounting bolts/nuts loose.
4   Master cylinder defective (Chapter 9).

58 Excessive effort required to stop vehicle

1   Power brake booster not operating properly (Chapter 9).
2   Excessively worn pads. Inspect and replace if necessary (Chapter 9).
3   One or more caliper pistons seized or sticking. Inspect and replace as required (Chapter 9).

4   Brake pads contaminated with oil or grease. Inspect and replace as required (Chapter 9).
5   New pads installed and not yet seated. It will take a while for the new material to seat against the disc.

59 Pedal travels to the floor with little resistance

1   Little or no fluid in the master cylinder reservoir caused by leaking caliper piston(s), loose, damaged or disconnected brake lines. Inspect the entire system and correct as necessary.
2   Worn master cylinder seals (Chapter 9).

60 Brake pedal pulsates during brake application

1   Caliper improperly installed. Remove and inspect (Chapter 9).
2   Disc defective. Remove (Chapter 9) and check for excessive lateral runout and parallelism. Have the disc resurfaced or replace it with a new one.

SUSPENSION AND STEERING SYSTEMS

61 Vehicle pulls to one side

1   Tire pressures uneven (Chapter 1).
2   Defective tire (Chapter 1).
3   Excessive wear in suspension or steering components (Chapter 10).
4   Front end in need of alignment.
5   Front brakes dragging. Inspect the brakes as described in Chapter 9.

62 Shimmy, shake or vibration

1   Tire or wheel out-of-balance or out-of-round. Have professionally balanced.
2   Worn front wheel bearings (Chapter 10).
3   Shock absorbers and/or suspension components worn or damaged (Chapter 10).

63 Excessive pitching and/or rolling around corners or during braking

1   Defective shock absorbers. Replace as a set (Chapter 10).
2   Broken or weak springs and/or suspension components. Inspect as described in Chapter 10.

64 Excessively stiff steering

1   Lack of fluid in power steering fluid reservoir (Chapter 1).
2   Incorrect tire pressures (Chapter 1).
3   Lack of lubrication at steering joints (see Chapter 1).
4   Front end out of alignment.
5   Lack of power assistance (see Section 66).

65 Excessive play in steering

1 Worn front wheel bearings (Chapter10).
2 Excessive wear in suspension or steering components (Chapter 10).
3 Steering gearbox damaged or out of adjustment (Chapter 10).

66 Lack of power assistance

1 Steering pump drivebelt faulty or not adjusted properly (Chapter 1).
2 Fluid level low (Chapter 1).
3 Hoses or lines restricted. Inspect and replace parts as necessary.
4 Air in power steering system. Bleed the system (Chapter 10).

67 Excessive tire wear (not specific to one area)

1 Incorrect tire pressures (Chapter 1).
2 Tires out-of-balance. Have professionally balanced.
3 Wheels damaged. Inspect and replace as necessary.
4 Suspension or steering components excessively worn (Chapter 10).

68 Excessive tire wear on outside edge

1 Inflation pressures incorrect (Chapter 1).
2 Excessive speed in turns.
3 Front end alignment incorrect. Have professionally aligned.
4 Suspension arm bent or twisted (Chapter 10).

69 Excessive tire wear on inside edge

1 Inflation pressures incorrect (Chapter 1).
2 Front end alignment incorrect. Have professionally aligned.
3 Loose or damaged steering components (Chapter 10).

70 Tire tread worn in one place

1 Tires out-of-balance.
2 Damaged or buckled wheel. Inspect and replace if necessary.
3 Defective tire (Chapter 1).

TUNE-UP AND ROUTINE MAINTENANCE

Section

1 Maintenance schedule
2 Introduction
3 Tune-up general information
4 Fluid level checks
5 Tire and tire pressure checks
6 Engine oil and filter change
7 Tire rotation
8 Windshield wiper blade inspection and replacement
9 Battery check, maintenance and charging
10 Cooling system check
11 Seat belt check
12 Underhood hose check and replacement
13 Brake check
14 Steering and suspension check
15 Fuel system check
16 Air filter check and replacement
17 Exhaust system check
18 Fuel filter replacement
19 Brake fluid change
20 Drivebelt check and replacement
21 Manual transmission lubricant change
22 Positive Crankcase Ventilation (PCV) valve replacement
23 Spark plug check and replacement
24 Ignition coil check (3.5L and 3.7L V6, and V8 engines)
25 Spark plug wire check and replacement (OHC V6 and 6.2L V8 engines)
26 Differential lubricant change
27 Cooling system servicing (draining, flushing and refilling)
28 Automatic transmission fluid and filter change
29 Transfer case lubricant change (4WD models)

1 Maintenance schedule

The maintenance intervals in this manual are provided with the assumption that you, not the dealer, will be doing the work. These are the minimum maintenance intervals recommended by the factory for vehicles that are driven daily. If you wish to keep your vehicle in peak condition at all times, you may wish to perform some of these procedures even more often. Because frequent maintenance enhances the efficiency, performance and resale value of your car, we encourage you to do so. If you drive in dusty areas, tow a trailer, idle or drive at low speeds for extended periods or drive for short distances (less than four miles) in below freezing temperatures, shorter intervals are also recommended.

When your vehicle is new, it should be serviced by a factory authorized dealer service department to protect the factory warranty. In many cases, the initial maintenance check is done at no cost to the owner.

EVERY 250 MILES OR WEEKLY, WHICHEVER COMES FIRST

Check the engine oil level (Section 4)
Check the engine coolant level (Section 4)
Check the brake and clutch fluid level (Section 4)
Check the windshield washer fluid level (Section 4)
Check the power steering fluid level (Section 4)
Check the automatic transmission lubricant level (Section 4)
Check the tires and tire pressures (Section 5)

EVERY 3000 MILES OR 3 MONTHS, WHICHEVER COMES FIRST

All items listed above plus:
Change the engine oil and oil filter (Section 6)
Rotate the tires (Section 7)
Check the manual transmission lubricant level (Section 4)
Check the transfer case lubricant level (4WD models) (Section 4)
Check the differential lubricant level (Section 4)

EVERY 7500 MILES OR 6 MONTHS, WHICHEVER COMES FIRST

All items listed above plus:
Inspect and replace, if necessary, the windshield wiper blades
   (Section 8)
Check and service the battery (Section 9)
Check the cooling system (Section 10)
Check the seat belts (Section 11)

EVERY 15,000 MILES OR 12 MONTHS, WHICHEVER COMES FIRST

All items listed above plus:
Inspect and replace, if necessary, all underhood hoses (Section 12)

Inspect the brake system (Section 13)*
Inspect the suspension and steering components (Section 14)
Fuel system check (Section 15)
Inspect and replace, if necessary, the air filter (Section 16)*

EVERY 30,000 MILES OR 24 MONTHS, WHICHEVER COMES FIRST

All items listed above plus:
Check the exhaust system (Section 17)
Replace the fuel filter (Section 18)
Replace the air filter (Section 16)*
Change the brake fluid (Section 19)
Check the engine drivebelt (Section 20)

EVERY 60,000 MILES OR 48 MONTHS, WHICHEVER COMES FIRST

All items listed above plus:
Replace manual transmission lubricant (Section 21)*
Replace the Positive Crankcase Ventilation (PCV) valve (Section 22)
Check and replace, if necessary, the spark plugs (Section 23)
Check the ignition coils (V8 engines) (Section 24)
Inspect and replace, if necessary, the spark plug wires
   (V6 engines) (Section 25)
Replace the differential lubricant (Section 26)*

EVERY 100,000 MILES

Service the cooling system (drain, flush and refill) (Section 27)
Replace the automatic transmission fluid (Section 28)**
Replace the transfer case lubricant (Section 29)
Replace the spark plugs (Section 23)
   *This item is affected by "severe" operating conditions as described
   below. If your vehicle is operated under "severe" conditions, perform all maintenance indicated with an asterisk (*) at 3000 mile/3
   month intervals. Severe conditions are indicated if you mainly
   operate your vehicle under one or more of the following conditions:
Operating in dusty areas
Towing a trailer
Idling for extended periods and/or low speed operation
Operating when outside temperatures remain below freezing and
   when most trips are less than 4 miles
** If operated under one or more of the following conditions, change
   the automatic transmission fluid every 15,000 miles:
In heavy city traffic where the outside temperature regulary reaches
   90-degrees F or higher.
In hilly or mountainous terrain.
Frequent trailer pulling.

Engine compartment layout (5.4L V8 model shown, others similar)

1   Coolant expansion tank
2   Underhood fuse/relay block
3   Brake fluid reservoir
4   Power steering fluid reservoir

5   Air filter housing
6   Engine oil filler cap
7   Upper radiator hose

8   Automatic transmission fluid dipstick
9   Battery
10 Windshield washer fluid reservoir

Engine compartment layout (3.7L model shown)

1	Coolant expansion tank	4	PCV valve hose	7	Upper radiator hose
2	Underhood fuse/relay block	5	Air filter housing	8	Battery
3	Brake fluid reservoir	6	Engine oil dipstick	9	Windshield washer fluid reservoir

Typical underside components (2WD 5.4L V8 model shown, others similar)

1	Exhaust pipe	3	Engine oil drain plug	5	Steering gear boot
2	Automatic transmission pan	4	Lower control arm		

Typical rear underside components

1	Muffler	2	Fuel tank	3	Shock absorber

2 Introduction

This Chapter is designed to help the home mechanic maintain the F-150 with the goals of maximum performance, economy, safety and reliability in mind.

Included is a master maintenance schedule, followed by procedures dealing specifically with each item on the schedule. Visual checks, adjustments, component replacement and other helpful items are included. Refer to the accompanying illustrations of the engine compartment and the underside of the vehicle for the locations of various components.

Servicing the vehicle, in accordance with the mileage/time maintenance schedule and the step-by-step procedures will result in a planned maintenance program that should produce a long and reliable service life. Keep in mind that it is a comprehensive plan, so maintaining some items but not others at the specified intervals will not produce the same results.

As you service the vehicle, you will discover that many of the procedures can - and should - be grouped together because of the nature of the particular procedure you're performing or because of the close proximity of two otherwise unrelated components to one another.

For example, if the vehicle is raised for chassis lubrication, you should inspect the exhaust, suspension, steering and fuel systems while you're under the vehicle. When you're rotating the tires, it makes good sense to check the brakes since the wheels are already removed. Finally, let's suppose you have to borrow or rent a torque wrench. Even if you only need it to tighten the spark plugs, you might as well check the torque of as many critical fasteners as time allows.

The first step in this maintenance program is to prepare yourself before the actual work begins. Read through all the procedures you're planning to do, then gather up all the parts and tools needed. If it looks like you might run into problems during a particular job, seek advice from a mechanic or an experienced do-it-yourselfer.

OWNER'S MANUAL AND VECI LABEL INFORMATION

Your vehicle owner's manual was written for your year and model and contains very specific information on component locations, specifications, fuse ratings, part numbers, etc. The Owner's Manual is an important resource for the do-it-yourselfer to have; if one was not supplied with your vehicle, it can generally be ordered from a dealer parts department.

Among other important information, the Vehicle Emissions Control Information (VECI) label contains specifications and procedures for applicable tune-up adjustments and, in some instances, spark plugs (see Chapter 6 for more information on the VECI label). The information on this label is the exact maintenance data recommended by the manufacturer. This data often varies by intended operating altitude, local emissions regulations, month of manufacture, etc.

This Chapter contains procedural details, safety information and more ambitious maintenance intervals than you might find in manufacturer's literature. However, you may also find procedures or specifications in your Owner's Manual or VECI label that differ with what's printed here. In these cases, the Owner's Manual or VECI label can be considered correct, since it is specific to your particular vehicle.

3 Tune-up general information

The term tune-up is used in this manual to represent a combination of individual operations rather than one specific procedure.

If, from the time the vehicle is new, the routine maintenance schedule is followed closely and frequent checks are made of fluid levels and high wear items, as suggested throughout this manual, the engine will be kept in relatively good running condition and the need for additional work will be minimized.

More likely than not, however, there will be times when the engine is running poorly due to lack of regular maintenance. This is even more likely if a used vehicle, which has not received regular and frequent maintenance checks, is purchased. In such cases, an engine tune-up will be needed outside of the regular routine maintenance intervals.

The first step in any tune-up or diagnostic procedure to help correct a poor running engine is a cylinder compression check. A compression check (see Chapter 2D) will help determine the condition of internal engine components and should be used as a guide for tune-up and repair procedures. If, for instance, a compression check indicates serious internal engine wear, a conventional tune-up will not improve the performance of the engine and would be a waste of time and money. Because of its importance, the compression check should be done by someone with the right equipment and the knowledge to use it properly.

The following procedures are those most often needed to bring a generally poor running engine back into a proper state of tune.

MINOR TUNE-UP

Check all engine related fluids (Section 4)
Clean, inspect and test the battery (Section 9)
Check all underhood hoses (Section 12)
Check the cooling system (Section 10)
Check the fuel system (Section 15)
Check the air filter (Section16)

MAJOR TUNE-UP

All items listed under Minor tune-up, plus . . .
Replace the fuel filter (Section 18)
Replace the air filter (Section 16)
Check the drivebelt (Section 20)
Replace the PCV valve (Section 22)
Replace the spark plugs (Section 23)
Replace the spark plug wires, if equipped (Section 25)
Check the charging system (Chapter 5)

4 Fluid level checks (every 250 miles or weekly)

1 Fluids are an essential part of the lubrication, cooling, brake and windshield washer systems. Because the fluids gradually become depleted and/or contaminated during normal operation of the vehicle, they must be periodically replenished. See *Recommended lubricants and fluids* in this Chapter's Specifications before adding fluid to any of the following components.

→ **Note: The vehicle must be on level ground when fluid levels are checked.**

ENGINE OIL

▶ **Refer to illustrations 4.2, 4.4 and 4.6**

2 The oil level is checked with a dipstick, which is attached to the engine block (see illustration). The dipstick extends through a metal tube down into the oil pan.

3 The oil level should be checked before the vehicle has been driven, or about 5 minutes after the engine has been shut off. If the oil is checked immediately after driving the vehicle, some of the oil will remain in the upper part of the engine, resulting in an inaccurate reading on the dipstick.

4 Pull the dipstick out of the tube and wipe all the oil from the end with a clean rag or paper towel. Insert the clean dipstick all the way back into the tube and pull it out again. Note the oil at the end of the dipstick. At its highest point, the level should be between the MIN and MAX marks on the dipstick (see illustration).

5 It takes one quart of oil to raise the level from the MIN mark to the MAX mark on the dipstick. Do not allow the level to drop below the MIN mark or oil starvation may cause engine damage. Conversely, overfilling the engine (adding oil above the MAX mark) may cause oil fouled spark plugs, oil leaks or oil seal failures. Maintaining the oil level above the upper mark can cause excessive oil consumption.

6 To add oil, remove the filler cap from the valve cover (see illustra-

tion). After adding oil, wait a few minutes to allow the level to stabilize, then pull out the dipstick and check the level again. Add more oil if required. Install the filler cap and tighten it by hand only.

7 Checking the oil level is an important preventive maintenance step. A consistently low oil level indicates oil leakage through damaged seals, defective gaskets or past worn rings or valve guides. If the oil looks milky in color or has water droplets in it, the cylinder head gasket(s) may be blown or the head(s) or block may be cracked. The engine should be checked immediately. The condition of the oil should also be checked. Whenever you check the oil level, slide your thumb and index finger up the dipstick before wiping off the oil. If you see small dirt or metal particles clinging to the dipstick, the oil should be changed (see Section 6).

4.2 Engine oil dipstick location

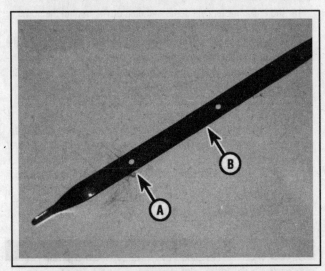

4.4 It takes one quart of oil to raise the level from ADD mark (A) to the FULL mark (B). Don't allow the oil level to exceed the upper hole

4.6 Engine oil filler cap location (5.4L V8 shown, others similar)

4.8 The coolant expansion tank is located at the side of the engine compartment

4.9 Keep the level in the COLD FILL RANGE - DO NOT remove the cap until the engine has cooled completely

4.15a The brake fluid level should be kept between the MIN and MAX marks on the translucent plastic reservoir

ENGINE COOLANT

▶ **Refer to illustrations 4.8 and 4.9**

❋❋ **WARNING:**

Do not allow antifreeze to come in contact with your skin or painted surfaces of the vehicle. Flush contaminated areas immediately with plenty of water. Don't store new coolant or leave old coolant lying around where it's accessible to children or pets - they're attracted by its sweet smell. Ingestion of even a small amount of coolant can be fatal! Wipe up garage floor and drip pan spills immediately. Keep antifreeze containers covered and repair cooling system leaks as soon as they're noticed.

8   All vehicles covered by this manual are equipped with a pressurized coolant recovery system. A plastic expansion tank located at the side of the engine compartment is connected by a hose to the engine (see illustration). As the engine heats up during operation, the expanding coolant fills the tank.

9 The coolant level in the tank should be checked regularly.

❋❋ **WARNING:**

Do not remove the expansion tank cap to check the coolant level when the engine is warm!

The level in the tank varies with the temperature of the engine. When the engine is cold, the coolant level should be in the COLD FILL RANGE on the expansion tank (see illustration). If it isn't, remove the cap from the tank and add a 50/50 mixture of ethylene glycol based antifreeze and water.

10 Drive the vehicle, let the engine cool completely then recheck the coolant level. Don't use rust inhibitors or additives. If only a small amount of coolant is required to bring the system up to the proper level, water can be used. However, repeated additions of water will dilute the antifreeze and water solution. In order to maintain the proper ratio of antifreeze and water, always top up the coolant level with the correct mixture. An empty plastic milk jug or bleach bottle makes an excellent container for mixing coolant.

11 If the coolant level drops consistently, there may be a leak in the system. Inspect the radiator, hoses, filler cap, drain plugs and water pump (see Section 10). If no leaks are noted, have the expansion tank cap pressure tested by a service station.

12 If you have to remove the expansion tank cap wait until the engine has cooled completely, then wrap a thick cloth around the cap and unscrew it slowly, stopping if you hear a hissing noise. If coolant or steam escapes, let the engine cool down longer, then remove the cap.

13 Check the condition of the coolant as well. It should be relatively clear. If it's brown or rust colored, the system should be drained, flushed and refilled. Even if the coolant appears to be normal, the corrosion inhibitors wear out, so it must be replaced at the specified intervals.

BRAKE AND CLUTCH FLUID

▶ **Refer to illustrations 4.15a and 4.15b**

14 The brake master cylinder is mounted on the front of the power booster unit in the engine compartment. The hydraulic clutch master cylinder used on manual transmission vehicles is located inboard of the brake master cylinder, attached to the cowl panel.

15 To check the fluid level of the brake and clutch master cylinders, simply look at the MAX and MIN marks on the reservoir (see illustrations). The level should be within the specified distance from the maximum fill line.

16 If the level is low, wipe the top of the reservoir cover with a clean rag to prevent contamination of the brake system before lifting the cover.

17 Add only the specified brake fluid to the brake and clutch reservoirs (refer to *Recommended lubricants and fluids* in this Chapter's Specifications or to your owner's manual). Mixing different types of brake fluid can damage the system. Fill the brake master cylinder reservoir only to the MAX line.

❋❋ **WARNING:**

Use caution when filling either reservoir - brake fluid can harm your eyes and damage painted surfaces. Do not use brake fluid that has been opened for more than one year or has been left open. Brake fluid absorbs moisture from the air. Excess moisture can cause a dangerous loss of braking.

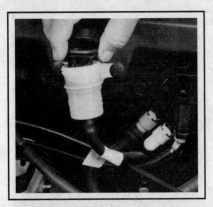

4.15b The clutch fluid reservoir is mounted on the firewall - add fluid until it reaches the FULL line

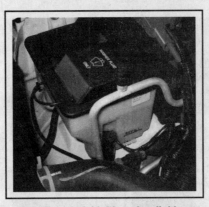

4.22 The windshield washer fluid reservoir is located in the front corner of the engine compartment

4.25 The power steering fluid reservoir is located on the left side of the engine (5.4L V8 engine shown, others similar)

18 While the reservoir cap is removed, inspect the master cylinder reservoir for contamination. If deposits, dirt particles or water droplets are present, the system should be drained and refilled.

19 After filling the reservoir to the proper level, make sure the lid is properly seated to prevent fluid leakage and/or system pressure loss.

20 The fluid in the brake master cylinder will drop slightly as the brake pads at each wheel wear down during normal operation. If either master cylinder requires repeated replenishing to keep it at the proper level, this is an indication of leakage in the brake or clutch system, which should be corrected immediately. If the brake system shows an indication of leakage check all brake lines and connections, along with the calipers, wheel cylinders and booster (see Section 13 for more information). If the hydraulic clutch system shows an indication of leakage check all clutch lines and connections, along with the clutch slave cylinder (see Chapter 8 for more information).

21 If, upon checking the brake or clutch master cylinder fluid level, you discover one or both reservoirs empty or nearly empty, the systems should be bled (see Chapters 8 and 9).

WINDSHIELD WASHER FLUID

▶ **Refer to illustration 4.22**

22 Fluid for the windshield washer system is stored in a plastic reservoir located at the right front corner of the engine compartment (see illustration).

4.28 With the engine cold, the fluid level should be between the MIN and MAX marks on the reservoir

23 In milder climates, plain water can be used in the reservoir, but it should be kept no more than 2/3 full to allow for expansion if the water freezes. In colder climates, use windshield washer system antifreeze, available at any auto parts store, to lower the freezing point of the fluid. Mix the antifreeze with water in accordance with the manufacturer's directions on the container.

> ❋❋ **CAUTION:**
>
> **Do not use cooling system antifreeze - it will damage the vehicle's paint.**

POWER STEERING FLUID

▶ **Refer to illustrations 4.25 and 4.28**

24 Check the power steering fluid level periodically to avoid steering system problems, such as damage to the pump.

> ❋❋ **CAUTION:**
>
> **DO NOT hold the steering wheel against either stop (extreme left or right turn) for more than five seconds. If you do, the power steering pump could be damaged.**

25 The power steering reservoir, located at the right side of the engine compartment (see illustration), has MIN and MAX fluid level marks on the side. The fluid level can be seen without removing the reservoir cap.

26 Park the vehicle on level ground and apply the parking brake.

27 Run the engine until it has reached normal operating temperature. With the engine at idle, turn the steering wheel back and forth about 10 times to get any air out of the steering system. Shut the engine off with the wheels in the straight-ahead position.

28 Note the fluid level on the side of the reservoir. It should be between the two marks (see illustration).

29 Add small amounts of fluid until the level is correct.

> ❋❋ **CAUTION:**
>
> **Do not overfill the reservoir. If too much fluid is added, remove the excess with a clean syringe or suction pump.**

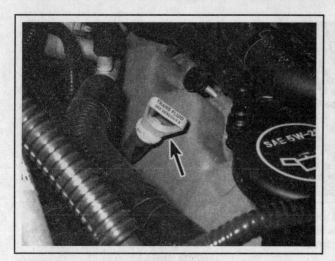

4.33 The automatic transmission dipstick is located at the right side of the engine compartment

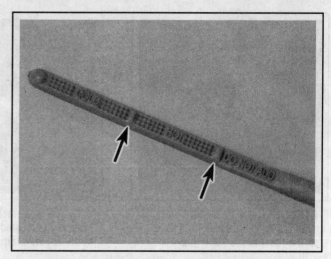

4.36 Check the fluid with the transmission at normal operating temperature - the level should be in the HOT range

30 Check the power steering hoses and connections for leaks and wear.

AUTOMATIC TRANSMISSION FLUID

2010 and earlier models

▶ **Refer to illustrations 4.33 and 4.36**

31 The automatic transmission fluid level should be carefully maintained. Low fluid level can lead to slipping or loss of drive, while overfilling can cause foaming and loss of fluid.

32 With the parking brake set, start the engine, then move the shift lever through all the gear ranges, ending in Neutral. The fluid level must be checked with the vehicle level and the engine running at idle.

➡ **Note: Incorrect fluid level readings will result if the vehicle has just been driven at high speeds for an extended period, in hot weather in city traffic, or if it has been pulling a trailer. If any of these conditions apply, wait until the fluid has cooled (about 30 minutes).**

33 With the transmission at normal operating temperature, remove the dipstick from the filler tube. The dipstick is located near the right-side valve cover (see illustration).

➡ **Note: Normal operating temperature is after a few minutes of engine operation or after 15 miles of driving.**

34 Wipe the fluid from the dipstick with a clean rag and push it back into the filler tube until the cap seats.

35 Pull the dipstick out again and note the fluid level.

36 At normal operating temperature, the fluid level should be between the two upper reference holes (HOT) (see illustration). If it's hot, the level should be in the area marked OK (crosshatched area). If additional fluid is required, add it directly into the tube using a funnel. Add the fluid a little at a time and keep checking the level until it's correct.

➡ **Note: Wait at least two minutes before rechecking the fluid level allowing the fluid to fully drain into the transmission.**

37 The condition of the fluid should also be checked along with the level. If the fluid at the end of the dipstick is a dark reddish-brown color, or if it smells burned, it should be changed. If you are in doubt about

the condition of the fluid, purchase some new fluid and compare the two for color and smell.

2011 and later models

38 There is no conventional dipstick for the automatic transmission on these models. To check or add fluid, the vehicle must be on a lift, with the engine running in Park at normal temperature. Remove the short fill-plug at the left-front corner of the transmission case.

39 Separate the short dipstick from the filler plug, and insert the dipstick into the transmission case at the fill-plug hole.

40 If the fluid level is at the upper mark, reassemble the dipstick to the filler plug and reinstall it in the transmission.

41 If the fluid is low, add only as much fluid as it takes to show fluid at the upper mark.

MANUAL TRANSMISSION FLUID

▶ **Refer to illustration 4.42**

➡ **Note: It isn't necessary to check this lubricant weekly; every 3000 miles (4800 km) or 3 months will be adequate.**

42 The manual transmission does not have a dipstick. To check the fluid level, raise the vehicle and support it securely on jackstands. On the transmission housing, remove the fluid fill plug (see illustration). If the lubricant level is correct, it should be up to the lower edge of the hole.

43 If the transmission needs more lubricant (if the level is not up to the hole), use a syringe or a gear oil pump to add more. Stop filling the transmission when the lubricant begins to run out the hole.

44 Install the plug and tighten it securely. Drive the vehicle a short distance, then check for leaks.

TRANSFER CASE FLUID

➡ **Note: It isn't necessary to check this lubricant weekly; every 3000 miles (4800 km) or 3 months will be adequate.**

45 The lubricant level is checked by removing a plug from the side of the case. If the vehicle is raised to gain access to the plug, be sure to

support it safely on jackstands - DO NOT crawl under the vehicle when it's supported only by a jack!

46 With the engine and transfer case cold, remove the plug. If lubricant immediately starts leaking out, thread the plug back into the case - the level is correct. If it doesn't, completely remove the plug and reach inside the hole with your little finger. The level should be even with the bottom of the plug hole.

47 If more lubricant is needed, use a syringe or small pump to add it through the opening.

48 Thread the plug back into the case and tighten it securely. Drive the vehicle, then check for leaks around the plug.

DIFFERENTIAL FLUID

▶ **Refer to illustration 4.49**

➡ **Note 1: It isn't necessary to check this lubricant weekly; every 3000 miles (4800 km) or 3 months will be adequate.**

➡ **Note 2: 4WD vehicles have two differentials; one in the front as well as one in the rear - be sure to check the lubricant level in both differentials.**

49 To check the fluid level, raise the vehicle and support it securely on jackstands. On the axle housing, remove the check/fill plug (see illustration). If the lubricant level is correct, it should be up to the lower edge of the hole.

50 If the differential needs more lubricant (if the level is not up to the hole), use a syringe or a gear oil pump to add more. Stop filling the differential when the lubricant begins to run out the hole.

51 Install the plug and tighten it securely. Drive the vehicle a short distance, then check for leaks.

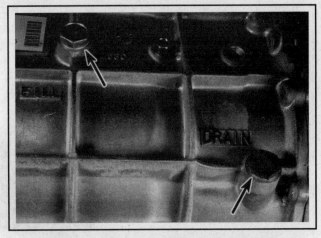

4.42 The manual transmission fill plug and drain plug are located on the side of the transmission case

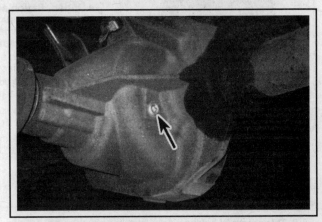

4.49 Differential check/fill plug (rear differential shown)

5   Tire and tire pressure checks (every 250 miles or weekly)

▶ **Refer to illustrations 5.2, 5.3, 5.4a, 5.4b and 5.8**

1 Periodic inspection of the tires may spare you the inconvenience of being stranded with a flat tire. It can also provide you with vital information regarding possible problems in the steering and suspension systems before major damage occurs.

2 The original tires on this vehicle are equipped with 1/2-inch wide bands that will appear when tread depth reaches 1/16-inch, at which point they can be considered worn out. Tread wear can be monitored with a simple, inexpensive device known as a tread depth indicator (see illustration).

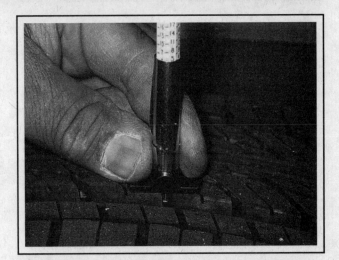

5.2 A tire tread depth indicator should be used to monitor tire wear - they are available at auto parts stores and service stations and cost very little

UNDERINFLATION

CUPPING

Cupping may be caused by:
- Underinflation and/or mechanical irregularities such as out-of-balance condition of wheel and/or tire, and bent or damaged wheel.
- Loose or worn steering tie-rod or steering idler arm.
- Loose, damaged or worn front suspension parts.

OVERINFLATION

INCORRECT TOE-IN OR EXTREME CAMBER

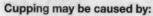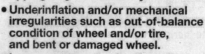

FEATHERING DUE TO MISALIGNMENT

5.3 This chart will help you determine the condition of your tires, the probable cause(s) of abnormal wear and the corrective action necessary

3   Note any abnormal tread wear (see illustration). Tread pattern irregularities such as cupping, flat spots and more wear on one side than the other are indications of front end alignment and or balance problems. If any of these conditions are noted, take the vehicle to a tire shop or service station to correct the problem.

4   Look closely for cuts, punctures and embedded nails or tacks. Sometimes a tire will hold air pressure for a short time or leak down very slowly after a nail has embedded itself in the tread. If a slow leak persists, check the valve stem core to make sure it is tight (see illustration). Examine the tread for an object that may have embedded itself in the tire or for a "plug" that may have begun to leak (radial tire punctures are repaired with a plug that is installed in a puncture). If a puncture is suspected, it can be easily verified by spraying a solution of soapy water onto the puncture area (see illustration). The soapy solution will bubble if there is a leak. Unless the puncture is unusually large, a tire shop or service station can usually repair the tire.

5   Carefully inspect the inner sidewall of each tire for evidence of brake fluid leakage. If you see any, inspect the brakes immediately.

6   Correct air pressure adds miles to the life span of the tires, improves mileage and enhances overall ride quality. Tire pressure cannot be accurately estimated by looking at a tire, especially if it's a radial. A tire pressure gauge is essential. Keep an accurate gauge in the glove compartment. The pressure gauges attached to the nozzles of air hoses at gas stations are often inaccurate.

7   Always check tire pressure when the tires are cold. Cold, in this case, means the vehicle has not been driven over a mile in the three hours preceding a tire pressure check. A pressure rise of four to eight pounds is not uncommon once the tires are warm.

8   Unscrew the valve cap protruding from the wheel or hubcap and

5.4a If a tire loses air on a steady basis, check the valve core first to make sure it's snug (special inexpensive wrenches are commonly available at auto parts stores)

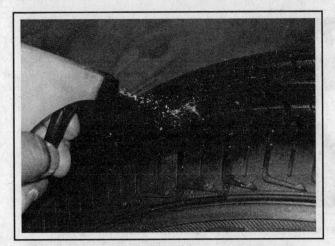

5.4b If the valve core is tight, raise the corner of the vehicle with the low tire and spray a soapy water solution onto the tread as the tire is turned slowly - slow leaks will cause small bubbles to appear

5.8 To extend the life of your tires, check the air pressure at least once a week with an accurate gauge (don't forget the spare!)

push the gauge firmly onto the valve stem (see illustration). Note the reading on the gauge and compare the figure to the recommended tire pressure shown on the tire placard on the driver's side door. Be sure to reinstall the valve cap to keep dirt and moisture out of the valve stem

mechanism. Check all four tires and, if necessary, add enough air to bring them up to the recommended pressure.

9   Don't forget to keep the spare tire inflated to the specified pressure (refer to the pressure molded into the tire sidewall).

6   Engine oil and filter change (every 3000 miles or 3 months)

▶ **Refer to illustrations 6.2, 6.7, 6.12, 6.13 and 6.15**

1   Frequent oil changes are the most important preventive maintenance procedures that can be done by the home mechanic. As engine oil ages, it becomes diluted and contaminated, which leads to premature engine wear.

2   Make sure that you have all the necessary tools before you begin this procedure (see illustration). You should also have plenty of rags or newspapers handy for mopping up oil spills.

3   Access to the oil drain plug and filter will be improved if the vehicle can be lifted on a hoist, driven onto ramps or supported by jackstands.

❋❋ WARNING:

Do not work under a vehicle supported only by a jack - always use jackstands!

4   If you haven't changed the oil on this vehicle before, get under it and locate the oil drain plug and the oil filter. The exhaust components will be warm as you work, so note how they are routed to avoid touching them when you are under the vehicle.

5   Start the engine and allow it to reach normal operating temperature - oil and sludge will flow out more easily when warm. If new oil, a

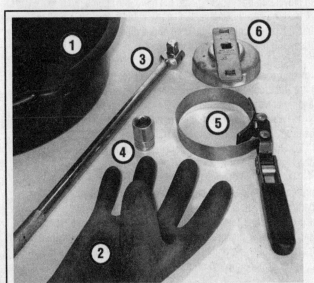

6.2 These tools are required when changing the engine oil and filter

1   *Drain pan* - It should be fairly shallow in depth, but wide in order to prevent spills

2   *Rubber gloves* - When removing the drain plug and filter, it is inevitable that you will get oil on your hands (the gloves will prevent burns)

3   *Breaker bar* - Sometimes the oil drain plug is pretty tight and a long breaker bar is needed to loosen it

4   *Socket* - To be used with the breaker bar or a ratchet (must be the correct size to fit the drain plug)

5   *Filter wrench* - This is a metal band-type wrench, which requires clearance around the filter to be effective

6   *Filter wrench* - This type fits on the bottom of the filter and can be turned with a ratchet or beaker bar (different size wrenches are available for different types of filters)

6.7 Use a proper size box-end wrench or socket to remove the oil drain plug and avoid rounding it off

6.12 Use an oil filter wrench to remove the filter

6.13 On 5.0L V8 engines, there is a plastic channel below the oil filter to catch and direct oil while the filter is draining

6.15 Lubricate the oil filter gasket with clean engine oil before installing the filter on the engine

filter or tools are needed, use the vehicle to go get them and warm up the engine/oil at the same time. Park on a level surface and shut off the engine when it's warmed up. Remove the oil filler cap from the valve cover.

6   Raise the vehicle and support it on jackstands. Make sure it is safely supported!

7   Being careful not to touch the hot exhaust components, position a drain pan under the plug in the bottom of the engine, then remove the plug (see illustration). It's a good idea to wear a rubber glove while unscrewing the plug the final few turns to avoid being scalded by hot oil.

8   It may be necessary to move the drain pan slightly as oil flow slows to a trickle. Inspect the old oil for the presence of metal particles.

9   After all the oil has drained, wipe off the drain plug with a clean rag. Any small metal particles clinging to the plug would immediately contaminate the new oil.

10 Clean the area around the drain plug opening, reinstall the plug and tighten it securely, but don't strip the threads.

11 Move the drain pan into position under the oil filter.

12 Loosen the oil filter by turning it counterclockwise with a filter wrench (see illustration). Any standard filter wrench will work.

13 Once the filter is loose, use your hands to unscrew it from the block. Just as the filter is detached from the block, immediately tilt the open end up to prevent the oil inside the filter from spilling out (see illustration).

14 Using a clean rag, wipe off the mounting surface on the block. Also, make sure that none of the old gasket remains stuck to the mounting surface. It can be removed with a scraper if necessary.

15 Compare the old filter with the new one to make sure they are the same type. Smear some engine oil on the rubber gasket of the new filter and screw it into place (see illustration). Overtightening the filter will damage the gasket, so don't use a filter wrench. Most filter manufacturers recommend tightening the filter by hand only. Normally they should be tightened 3/4-turn after the gasket contacts the block, but be sure to follow the directions on the filter or container.

16 Remove all tools and materials from under the vehicle, being careful not to spill the oil in the drain pan, then lower the vehicle.

17 Add new oil to the engine through the oil filler cap. Use a funnel to prevent oil from spilling onto the top of the engine. Pour four quarts of fresh oil into the engine. Wait a few minutes to allow the oil to drain into the pan, then check the level on the dipstick (see Section 4 if necessary). If the oil level is in the OK range, install the filler cap.

18 Start the engine and run it for about a minute. While the engine is running, look under the vehicle and check for leaks at the oil pan drain plug and around the oil filter. If either one is leaking, stop the engine and tighten the plug or filter slightly.

19 Wait a few minutes, then recheck the level on the dipstick. Add oil as necessary to bring the level into the OK range.

20 During the first few trips after an oil change, make it a point to check frequently for leaks and proper oil level.

21 The old oil drained from the engine cannot be reused in its present state and should be disposed of. Check with your local auto parts store, disposal facility or environmental agency to see if they will accept the oil for recycling. After the oil has cooled it can be drained into a container (capped plastic jugs, topped bottles, milk cartons, etc.) for transport to one of these disposal sites. Don't dispose of the oil by pouring it on the ground or down a drain!

7   Tire rotation (every 3000 miles or 3 months)

▶ **Refer to illustration 7.2**

1   The tires should be rotated at the specified intervals and when-ever uneven wear is noticed. Since the vehicle will be raised and the tires removed anyway, check the brakes also (see Section 13).

2   Radial tires must be rotated in a specific pattern (see illustration). If your vehicle has a compact spare tire, don't include it in the rotation pattern.

3   Refer to the information in *Jacking and towing* at the front of this manual for the proper procedure to follow when raising the vehicle and changing a tire. If the brakes must be checked, don't apply the parking brake as stated.

4   The vehicle must be raised on a hoist or supported on jackstands to get all four wheels off the ground. Make sure the vehicle is safely supported!

5   After the rotation procedure is finished, check and adjust the tire pressures as necessary and be sure to tighten the lug nuts to the torque listed in this Chapter's Specifications.

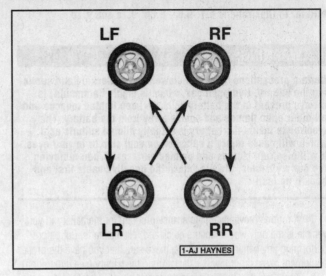

7.2 The recommended tire rotation pattern

8   Windshield wiper blade inspection and replacement (every 7500 miles or 6 months)

▶ **Refer to illustrations 8.4a and 8.4b**

1   The windshield wiper and blade assembly should be inspected periodically for damage, loose components and cracked or worn blade elements.

2   Road film can build up on the wiper blades and affect their effi-ciency, so they should be washed regularly with a mild detergent solu-tion.

3   If the wiper blade elements are cracked, worn or warped, or no longer clean adequately, they should be replaced with new ones.

4   Lift the arm assembly away from the glass for clearance, press on the release lever, then slide the wiper blade assembly out of the hook in the end of the arm (see illustrations).

5   Attach the new wiper to the arm. Connection can be confirmed by an audible click.

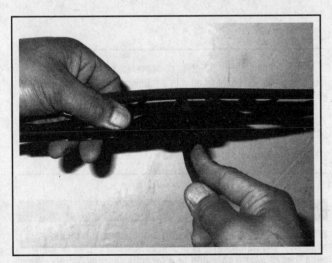

8.4a To release the blade holder, push the release lever . . .

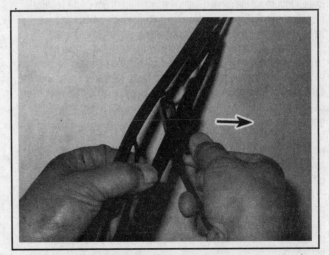

8.4b . . . and pull the wiper blade in the direction of the arrow to separate it from the arm

9   Battery check, maintenance and charging (every 7500 miles or 6 months)

▶ Refer to illustrations 9.1, 9.6a, 9.6b, 9.7a and 9.7b

✵ WARNING:

Certain precautions must be followed when checking and servicing the battery. Hydrogen gas, which is highly flammable, is always present in the battery cells, so keep lighted tobacco and all other open flames and sparks away from the battery. The electrolyte inside the battery is actually diluted sulfuric acid, which will cause injury if splashed on your skin or in your eyes. It will also ruin clothes and painted surfaces. When removing the battery cables, always detach the negative cable first and hook it up last!

1   A routine preventive maintenance program for the battery in your vehicle is the only way to ensure quick and reliable starts. But before performing any battery maintenance, make sure that you have the proper equipment necessary to work safely around the battery (see illustration).

2   There are also several precautions that should be taken whenever battery maintenance is performed. Before servicing the battery, always turn the engine and all accessories off and disconnect the cables from the negative terminal of the battery (see Chapter 5).

3   The battery produces hydrogen gas, which is both flammable and explosive. Never create a spark, smoke or light a match around the battery. Always charge the battery in a ventilated area.

4   Electrolyte contains poisonous and corrosive sulfuric acid. Do not allow it to get in your eyes, on your skin, or on your clothes. Never ingest it. Wear protective safety glasses when working near the battery. Keep children away from the battery.

5   Note the external condition of the battery. If the positive terminal and cable clamp on your vehicle's battery is equipped with a rubber protector, make sure that it's not torn or damaged. It should completely cover the terminal. Look for any corroded or loose connections, cracks in the case or cover or loose hold-down clamps. Also check the entire length of each cable for cracks and frayed conductors.

6   If corrosion, which looks like white, fluffy deposits (see illustration) is evident, particularly around the terminals, the battery should be removed for cleaning. Loosen the cable clamp bolts with a wrench, being careful to remove the ground cable first, and slide them off the terminals (see illustration). Then disconnect the hold-down clamp bolt and nut, remove the clamp and lift the battery from the engine compartment.

7   Clean the cable clamps thoroughly with a battery brush or a terminal cleaner and a solution of warm water and baking soda (see illustration). Wash the terminals and the top of the battery case with the same solution but make sure that the solution doesn't get into the battery. When cleaning the cables, terminals and battery top, wear safety goggles and rubber gloves to prevent any solution from coming in contact with your eyes or hands. Wear old clothes too - even diluted, sulfuric acid splashed onto clothes will burn holes in them. If the terminals have been extensively corroded, clean them up with a terminal cleaner (see illustration). Thoroughly wash all cleaned areas with plain water.

8   Make sure that the battery tray is in good condition and the hold-down clamp fasteners are tight. If the battery is removed from the tray, make sure no parts remain in the bottom of the tray when the battery is reinstalled. When reinstalling the hold-down clamp bolts, do not over-tighten them.

9   Information on removing and installing the battery can be found in Chapter 5. Information on jump starting can be found at the front of this manual.

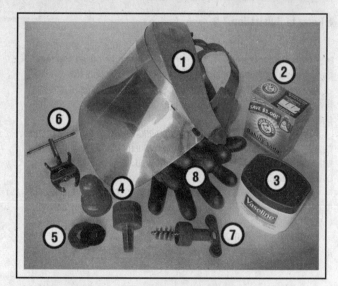

9.1 Tools and materials required for battery maintenance

1   *Face shield/safety goggles* - *When removing corrosion with a brush, the acidic particles can easily fly up into your eyes*

2   *Baking soda* - *A solution of baking soda and water can be used to neutralize corrosion*

3   *Petroleum jelly* - *A layer of this on the battery posts will help prevent corrosion*

4   *Battery post/cable cleaner* - *This wire brush cleaning tool will remove all traces of corrosion from the battery posts and cable clamps*

5   *Treated felt washers* - *Placing one of these on each post, directly under the cable clamps, will help prevent corrosion*

6   *Puller* - *Sometimes the cable clamps are very difficult to pull off the posts, even after the nut/bolt has been completely loosened. This tool pulls the clamp straight up and off the post without damage*

7   *Battery post/cable cleaner* - *Here is another cleaning tool which is a slightly different version of number 4 above, but it does the same thing*

8   *Rubber gloves* - *Another safety item to consider when servicing the battery; remember that's acid inside the battery!*

CLEANING

10 Corrosion on the hold-down components, battery case and surrounding areas can be removed with a solution of water and baking soda. Thoroughly rinse all cleaned areas with plain water.

11 Any metal parts of the vehicle damaged by corrosion should be covered with a zinc-based primer, then painted.

CHARGING

✵ WARNING:

When batteries are being charged, hydrogen gas, which is very explosive and flammable, is produced. Do not smoke or allow open flames near a charging or a recently charged battery. Wear eye protection when near the battery during charging. Also, make sure the charger is unplugged before connecting or disconnecting the battery from the charger.

9.6a Battery terminal corrosion usually appears as light, fluffy powder

9.6b Removing a cable from the battery post with a wrench - sometimes a pair of special battery pliers are required for this procedure if corrosion has caused deterioration of the nut hex (always remove the ground (-) cable first and hook it up last!)

9.7a When cleaning the cable clamps, all corrosion must be removed

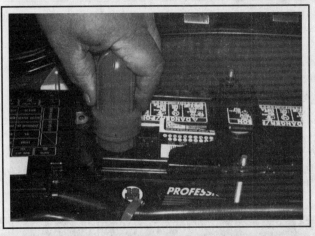

9.7b Regardless of the type of tool used to clean the battery posts, a clean, shiny surface should be the result

12 Slow-rate charging is the best way to restore a battery that's discharged to the point where it will not start the engine. It's also a good way to maintain the battery charge in a vehicle that's only driven a few miles between starts. Maintaining the battery charge is particularly important in the winter when the battery must work harder to start the engine and electrical accessories that drain the battery are in greater use.

13 It's best to use a one or two-amp battery charger (sometimes called a "trickle" charger). They are the safest and put the least strain on the battery. They are also the least expensive. For a faster charge, you can use a higher amperage charger, but don't use one rated more than 1/10th the amp/hour rating of the battery. Rapid boost charges that claim to restore the power of the battery in one to two hours are hardest on the battery and can damage batteries not in good condition. This type of charging should only be used in emergency situations.

14 The average time necessary to charge a battery should be listed in the instructions that come with the charger. As a general rule, a trickle charger will charge a battery in 12 to 16 hours.

10 Cooling system check (every 7,500 miles or 6 months)

▶ **Refer to illustration 10.4**

1 Many major engine failures can be caused by a faulty cooling system.

2 The engine must be cold for the cooling system check, so perform the following procedure before the vehicle is driven for the day or after it has been shut off for at least three hours.

3 Remove the pressure-relief cap from the expansion tank at the left side of the engine compartment. Clean the cap thoroughly, inside and out, with clean water. The presence of rust or corrosion in the expansion tank means the coolant should be changed (see Section 27). The coolant inside the expansion tank should be relatively clean and transparent. If it's rust colored, drain the system and refill it with new coolant.

Check for a chafed area that could fail prematurely.

Overtightening the clamp on a hardened hose will damage the hose and cause a leak.

Check for a soft area indicating the hose has deteriorated inside.

Check each hose for swelling and oil-soaked ends. Cracks and breaks can be located by squeezing the hose.

10.4 Hoses, like drivebelts, have a habit of failing at the worst possible time - to prevent the inconvenience of a blown radiator or heater hose, inspect them carefully as shown here

4 Carefully check the radiator hoses and the smaller diameter heater hoses. Inspect each coolant hose along its entire length, replacing any hose which is cracked, swollen or deteriorated (see illustration). Cracks will show up better if the hose is squeezed. Pay close attention to hose clamps that secure the hoses to cooling system components. Hose clamps can pinch and puncture hoses, resulting in coolant leaks.

5 Make sure that all hose connections are tight. A leak in the cooling system will usually show up as white or rust colored deposits on the area adjoining the leak. If wire-type clamps are used on the hoses, it may be a good idea to replace them with screw-type clamps.

6 Clean the front of the radiator and air conditioning condenser with compressed air, if available, or a soft brush. Remove all bugs, leaves, etc. embedded in the radiator fins. Be extremely careful not to damage the cooling fins or cut your fingers on them.

7 If the coolant level has been dropping consistently and no leaks are detectable, have the expansion tank cap and cooling system pressure checked at a service station.

11 Seat belt check (every 7,500 miles or 6 months)

1 Check seat belts, buckles, latch plates and guide loops for obvious damage and signs of wear.

2 See if the seat belt reminder light comes on when the key is turned to the Run or Start position. A chime should also sound.

3 The seat belts are designed to lock up during a sudden stop or impact, yet allow free movement during normal driving. Make sure the retractors return the belt against your chest while driving and rewind the belt fully when the buckle is unlatched.

4 If any of the above checks reveal problems with the seat belt system, replace parts as necessary.

12 Underhood hose check and replacement (every 15,000 miles or 12 months)

✳✳ WARNING:

Replacement of air conditioning hoses must be left to a dealer service department or air conditioning shop that has the equipment to depressurize the system safely. Never remove air conditioning components or hoses until the system has been depressurized.

tems operation. Periodic inspection should be made for cracks, loose clamps, material hardening and leaks.

2 Information specific to the cooling system hoses can be found in Section 10.

3 Most (but not all) hoses are secured to the fittings with clamps. Where clamps are used, check to be sure they haven't lost their tension, allowing the hose to leak. If clamps aren't used, make sure the hose has not expanded and/or hardened where it slips over the fitting, allowing it to leak.

GENERAL

1 High temperatures under the hood can cause deterioration of the rubber and plastic hoses used for engine, accessory and emission sys-

PCV SYSTEM HOSE

4 To reduce hydrocarbon emissions, crankcase blow-by gas is

vented through the PCV valve in the valve cover to the intake manifold via a rubber hose on most models. The blow-by gases mix with incoming air in the intake manifold before being burned in the combustion chambers.

5   Check the PCV hose for cracks, leaks and other damage. Disconnect it from the valve cover and the intake manifold and check the inside for obstructions. If it's clogged, clean it out with solvent.

VACUUM HOSES

6   It's quite common for vacuum hoses, especially those in the emissions system, to be color coded or identified by colored stripes molded into them. Various systems require hoses with different wall thickness, collapse resistance and temperature resistance. When replacing hoses, be sure the new ones are made of the same material.

7   Often the only effective way to check a hose is to remove it completely from the vehicle. If more than one hose is removed, be sure to label the hoses and fittings to ensure correct installation.

8   When checking vacuum hoses, be sure to include any plastic T-fittings in the check. Inspect the fittings for cracks and the hose where it fits over each fitting for distortion, which could cause leakage.

9   A small piece of vacuum hose (1/4-inch inside diameter) can be used as a stethoscope to detect vacuum leaks. Hold one end of the hose to your ear and probe around vacuum hoses and fittings, listening for the "hissing" sound characteristic of a vacuum leak.

❊❊ WARNING:

When probing with the vacuum hose stethoscope, be careful not to come into contact with moving engine components such as drivebelts, the cooling fan, etc.

FUEL HOSE

❊❊ WARNING:

Gasoline is flammable, so take extra precautions when you work on any part of the fuel system. Don't smoke or allow open flames or bare light bulbs near the work area, and don't work in a garage where a gas-type appliance (such as a water heater or clothes dryer) is present. Since fuel is carcinogenic, wear fuel-resistant gloves when there's a possibility of being exposed to fuel, and, if you spill any fuel on your skin, rinse it off immediately with soap and water. Mop up any spills immediately and do not store fuel-soaked rags where they could ignite. The fuel system is under constant pressure, so, if any fuel lines are to be disconnected, the fuel pressure in the system must be relieved first (see Chapter 4 for more information). When you perform any kind of work on the fuel system, wear safety glasses and have a Class B type fire extinguisher on hand.

10   The fuel lines are usually under pressure, so if any fuel lines are to be disconnected be prepared to catch spilled fuel.

❊❊ WARNING:

Your vehicle is equipped with fuel injection and you must relieve the fuel system pressure before servicing the fuel lines. Refer to Chapter 4 for the fuel system pressure relief procedure.

11   Check all flexible fuel lines for deterioration and chafing. Check especially for cracks in areas where the hose bends and just before fittings, such as where a hose attaches to the fuel pump, fuel filter and fuel injection unit.

12   When replacing a hose, use only hose that is specifically designed for your fuel injection system.

13   Spring-type clamps are sometimes used on fuel return or vapor lines. These clamps often lose their tension over a period of time, and can be "sprung" during removal. Replace all spring-type clamps with screw clamps whenever a hose is replaced. Some fuel lines use spring-lock type couplings, which require a special tool to disconnect. See Chapter 4 for more information on this type of coupling.

METAL LINES

14   Sections of metal line are often used for fuel line between the fuel pump and the fuel injection unit. Check carefully to make sure the line isn't bent, crimped or cracked.

15   If a section of metal fuel line must be replaced, use seamless steel tubing only, since copper and aluminum tubing do not have the strength necessary to withstand vibration caused by the engine.

16   Check the metal brake lines where they enter the master cylinder and brake proportioning unit (if used) for cracks in the lines and loose fittings. Any sign of brake fluid leakage calls for an immediate thorough inspection of the brake system.

13   Brake check (every 15,000 miles or 12 months)

❊❊ WARNING:

The dust created by the brake system is harmful to your health. Never blow it out with compressed air and don't inhale any of it. An approved filtering mask should be worn when working on the brakes. Do not, under any circumstances, use petroleum-based solvents to clean brake parts. Use brake system cleaner only! Try to use non-asbestos replacement parts whenever possible.

➡ **Note: For detailed photographs of the brake system, refer to Chapter 9.**

1   In addition to the specified intervals, the brakes should be inspected every time the wheels are removed or whenever a defect is suspected.

2   Any of the following symptoms could indicate a potential brake system defect: The vehicle pulls to one side when the brake pedal is depressed; the brakes make squealing or dragging noises when applied; brake pedal travel is excessive; the pedal pulsates; or brake fluid leaks, usually onto the inside of the tire or wheel.

3   Loosen the wheel lug nuts.

4   Raise the vehicle and place it securely on jackstands.

5   Remove the wheels (see *Jacking and towing* at the front of this book, or your owner's manual, if necessary).

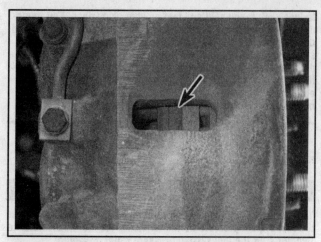

13.7a With the wheel off, check the thickness of the inner pad through the inspection hole (front caliper shown, rear caliper similar)

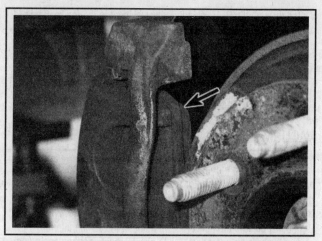

13.7b The outer pad is more easily checked at the edge of the caliper

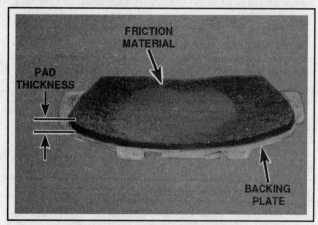

13.9 If a more precise measurement of pad thickness is necessary, remove the pads and measure the remaining friction material

DISC BRAKES

▶ **Refer to illustrations 13.7a, 13.7b and 13.9**

6   There are two pads (an outer and an inner) in each caliper. The pads are visible with the wheels removed. The vehicles covered by this manual have disc brakes front and rear, with a mechanical, drum-type parking brake mechanism inside the rear discs.

7   Check the pad thickness by looking at each end of the caliper and through the inspection window in the caliper body (see illustrations). If the lining material is less than the thickness listed in this Chapter's Specifications, replace the pads.

➡ **Note: Keep in mind that the lining material is riveted or bonded to a metal backing plate and the metal portion is not included in this measurement.**

8   If it is difficult to determine the exact thickness of the remaining pad material by the above method, or if you are at all concerned about the condition of the pads, remove the caliper(s), then remove the pads from the calipers for further inspection (refer to Chapter 9).

9   Once the pads are removed from the calipers, clean them with

brake cleaner and re-measure them with a ruler or a vernier caliper (see illustration).

10   Measure the disc thickness with a micrometer to make sure that it still has service life remaining. If any disc is thinner than the specified minimum thickness, replace it (refer to Chapter 9). Even if the disc has service life remaining, check its condition. Look for scoring, gouging and burned spots. If these conditions exist, remove the disc and have it resurfaced (see Chapter 9).

11   Before installing the wheels, check all brake lines and hoses for damage, wear, deformation, cracks, corrosion, leakage, bends and twists, particularly in the vicinity of the rubber hoses at the calipers. Check the clamps for tightness and the connections for leakage. Make sure that all hoses and lines are clear of sharp edges, moving parts and the exhaust system. If any of the above conditions are noted, repair, reroute or replace the lines and/or fittings as necessary (see Chapter 9).

BRAKE BOOSTER CHECK

12   Sit in the driver's seat and perform the following sequence of tests.

13   With the brake fully depressed, start the engine - the pedal should move down a little when the engine starts.

14   With the engine running, depress the brake pedal several times - the travel distance should not change.

15   Depress the brake, stop the engine and hold the pedal in for about 30 seconds - the pedal should neither sink nor rise.

16   Restart the engine, run it for about a minute and turn it off. Then firmly depress the brake several times - the pedal travel should decrease with each application.

17   If your brakes do not operate as described, the brake booster has failed. Refer to Chapter 9 for the replacement procedure.

PARKING BRAKE

18   One method of checking the parking brake is to park the vehicle on a steep hill with the parking brake set and the transmission in Neutral (be sure to stay in the vehicle for this check). If the parking brake cannot prevent the vehicle from rolling, it's in need of attention (see Chapter 9).

14 Steering and suspension check (every 15,000 miles or 12 months)

➡ **Note: The steering linkage and suspension components should be checked periodically. Worn or damaged suspension and steering linkage components can result in excessive and abnormal tire wear, poor ride quality and vehicle handling and reduced fuel economy. For detailed illustrations of the steering and suspension components, refer to Chapter 10.**

SHOCK ABSORBER CHECK

▶ **Refer to illustration 14.6**

1 Park the vehicle on level ground, turn the engine off and set the parking brake. Check the tire pressures.

2 Push down at one corner of the vehicle, then release it while noting the movement of the body. It should stop moving and come to rest in a level position within one or two bounces.

3 If the vehicle continues to move up-and-down or if it fails to return to its original position, a worn or weak shock absorber is probably the reason.

4 Repeat the above check at each of the three remaining corners of the vehicle.

5 Raise the vehicle and support it securely on jackstands.

6 Check the shock absorbers for evidence of fluid leakage (see illustration). A light film of fluid is no cause for concern. Make sure that any fluid noted is from the shocks and not from some other source. If leakage is noted, replace the shocks as a set.

7 Check the shocks to be sure that they are securely mounted and undamaged. Check the upper mounts for damage and wear. If damage or wear is noted, replace the shocks as a set (front or rear).

8 If the shocks must be replaced, refer to Chapter 10 for the procedure.

STEERING AND SUSPENSION CHECK

▶ **Refer to illustrations 14.9 and 14.11**

9 Visually inspect the steering and suspension components (front and rear) for damage and distortion. Look for damaged seals, boots and bushings and leaks of any kind. Examine the bushings where the control arms meet the chassis (see illustration).

10 Clean the lower end of the steering knuckle. Have an assistant grasp the lower edge of the tire and move the wheel in-and-out while you look for movement at the steering knuckle-to-control arm balljoint. If there is any movement the suspension balljoint(s) must be replaced.

11 Grasp each front tire at the front and rear edges, push in at the front, pull out at the rear and feel for play in the steering system components. If any freeplay is noted, check the idler arm and the tie-rod ends for looseness (see illustration).

12 Additional steering and suspension system information and illustrations can be found in Chapter 10.

14.6 Check for signs of fluid leakage at this point on shock absorbers (rear shock shown)

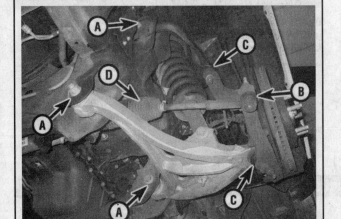

14.9 Examine the mounting points for the upper and lower control arms on the front suspension (A), the tie-rod ends (B), the balljoints (C), and the steering gear boots (D)

14.11 With the steering wheel in the locked position and the vehicle raised, grasp the front tire as shown and try to move it back-and-forth - if any play is noted, check the steering gear mounts and tie-rod ends for looseness

14.14 Inspect the inner and outer driveaxle boots on 4WD models for loose clamps, cracks or signs of leaking lubricant

DRIVEAXLE BOOT CHECK (4WD MODELS)

▶ **Refer to illustration 14.14**

13 The driveaxle boots are very important because they prevent dirt, water and foreign material from entering and damaging the constant velocity (CV) joints. Oil and grease can cause the boot material to deteriorate prematurely, so it's a good idea to wash the boots with soap and water. Because it constantly pivots back and forth following the steering action of the front hub, the outer CV boot wears out sooner and should be inspected regularly.

14 Inspect the boots for tears and cracks as well as loose clamps (see illustration). If there is any evidence of cracks or leaking lubricant, they must be replaced as described in Chapter 8.

15 Fuel system check (every 15,000 miles or 12 months)

✳ WARNING:

Gasoline is flammable, so take extra precautions when you work on any part of the fuel system. Don't smoke or allow open flames or bare light bulbs near the work area, and don't work in a garage where a gas-type appliance (such as a water heater or clothes dryer) is present. Since fuel is carcinogenic, wear fuel-resistant gloves when there's a possibility of being exposed to fuel, and, if you spill any fuel on your skin, rinse it off immediately with soap and water. Mop up any spills immediately and do not store fuel-soaked rags where they could ignite. When you perform any kind of work on the fuel system, wear safety glasses and have a Class B type fire extinguisher on hand. The fuel system is under constant pressure, so, before any lines are disconnected, the fuel system pressure must be relieved (see Chapter 4).

1 If you smell gasoline while driving or after the vehicle has been sitting in the sun, inspect the fuel system immediately.

2 Remove the fuel filler cap and inspect it for damage and corrosion. The gasket should have an unbroken sealing imprint. If the gasket is damaged or corroded, install a new cap.

3 Inspect the fuel feed line for cracks. Make sure that the connections between the fuel lines and the fuel injection system and between the fuel lines and the in-line fuel filter are tight.

✳ WARNING:

Your vehicle is fuel injected, so you must relieve the fuel system pressure before servicing fuel system components. The fuel system pressure relief procedure is outlined in Chapter 4.

4 Since some components of the fuel system - the fuel tank and part of the fuel feed line, for example - are underneath the vehicle, they can be inspected more easily with the vehicle raised on a hoist. If that's not possible, raise the vehicle and support it on jackstands.

5 With the vehicle raised and safely supported, inspect the gas tank and filler neck for punctures, cracks and other damage. The connection between the filler neck and the tank is particularly critical. Sometimes a rubber filler neck will leak because of loose clamps or deteriorated rubber. Inspect all fuel tank mounting brackets and straps to be sure that the tank is securely attached to the vehicle.

✳ WARNING:

Do not, under any circumstances, try to repair a fuel tank (except rubber components). A welding torch or any open flame can easily cause fuel vapors inside the tank to explode.

6 Carefully check all rubber hoses and metal lines leading away from the fuel tank. Check for loose connections, deteriorated hoses, crimped lines and other damage. Repair or replace damaged sections as necessary (see Chapter 4).

16 Air filter check and replacement (every 15,000 miles or 12 months)

2004 THROUGH 2008 MODELS

▶ **Refer to illustrations 16.2a, 16.2b, 16.2c and 16.2d**

1 The air filter is located inside a housing at either the right (passenger's) side of the engine compartment on 4.2 and 4.6L models, or at the center of the engine compartment on 5.4L models.

2 To remove the air filter on a 4.2 or 4.6L engine, loosen the clamp securing the inlet tube to the air filter cover, release the clamps that secure the two halves of the air cleaner housing together, then separate

16.2a On earlier 4.2 and 4.6L engines, release the clamp (A) then separate the housing halves to access the air filter

16.2b On earlier 5.4L engines, release the two clamps . . .

16.2c . . . then pull the filter tray out . . .

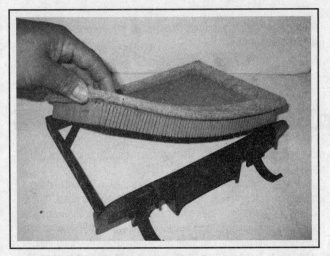

16.2d . . . and remove the air filter element

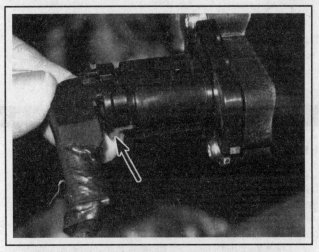

16.8 Pull the red lock out, depress the tab and pull off the connector

the cover halves and remove the air filter element (see illustration). If you are working on a 5.4L engine, release the clamps, then slide the air filter tray assembly outward and remove the air filter element (see illustrations).

2009 AND 2010 MODELS

3   Loosen the clamp securing the air intake duct to the air filter cover, then disconnect the Mass Air Flow (MAF) sensor electrical connector. Release the clamps that secure the two halves of the air cleaner housing together, then separate the cover and remove the air filter element.

4   Inspect the outer surface of the filter element. If it is dirty, replace it. If it is only moderately dusty, it can be reused by blowing it clean from the back to the front surface with compressed air. Because it is a pleated paper type filter, it cannot be washed or oiled. If it cannot be cleaned satisfactorily with compressed air, discard and replace it. While the cover is off, be careful not to drop anything down into the housing.

⁑ CAUTION:

Never drive the vehicle with the air cleaner removed. Excessive engine wear could result and backfiring could even cause a fire under the hood.

5   Wipe out the inside of the air cleaner housing.
6   Place the new filter into the air cleaner housing, making sure it seats properly.
7   The remainder of installation is the reverse of removal.

2011 AND LATER MODELS

▶ **Refer to illustrations 16.8, 16.9 and 16.10**

8   Disconnect the MAF sensor connector.

➡ **Note: You must pull the red locking tab to disconnect the sensor (see illustration).**

16.9 Loosen the hose clamp connected to the air filter box cover and wiggle the hose from the cover

16.10 Release the clips to access the air filter for replacement

9   Loosen the large hose clamp and slide the air intake hose from the cover (see illustration).

10   Release the clips and pull the cover up to remove the air filter (see illustration).

17 Exhaust system check (every 30,000 miles or 24 months)

▶ **Refer to illustration 17.2a and 17.2b**

1   With the engine cold (at least three hours after the vehicle has been driven), check the complete exhaust system from the engine to the end of the tailpipe. Ideally, the inspection should be done with the vehicle on a hoist to permit unrestricted access. If a hoist isn't available, raise the vehicle and support it securely on jackstands.

2   Check the exhaust pipes and connections for evidence of leaks, severe corrosion and damage. Make sure that all brackets and hangers are in good condition and tight (see illustrations).

3   At the same time, inspect the underside of the body for holes, corrosion, open seams, etc. which may allow exhaust gases to enter the passenger compartment. Seal all body openings with silicone or body putty.

4   Rattles and other noises can often be traced to the exhaust system, especially the mounts and hangers. Try to move the pipes, muffler and catalytic converter. If the components can come in contact with the body or suspension parts, secure the exhaust system with new mounts.

5   Check the running condition of the engine by inspecting inside the end of the tailpipe. The exhaust deposits here are an indication of engine state-of-tune. If the pipe is black and sooty or coated with white deposits, the engine may need a tune-up, including a thorough fuel system inspection.

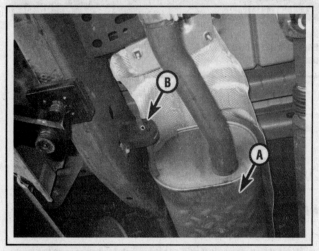

17.2a Inspect the muffler (A) and all hangers (B) for signs of deterioration

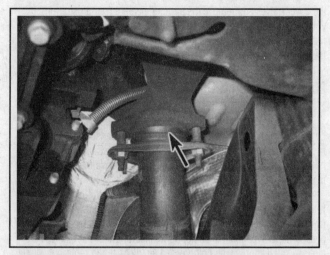

17.2b Inspect all flanged joints (arrow indicates pipe-to-manifold joint) for signs of exhaust gas leakage

18 Fuel filter replacement (every 30,000 miles or 24 months)

▶ Refer to illustration 18.1

➡ Note: 2009 and later models do not have a serviceable fuel filter. A filter is part of the fuel pump module in the fuel tank, but it does not have a service interval.

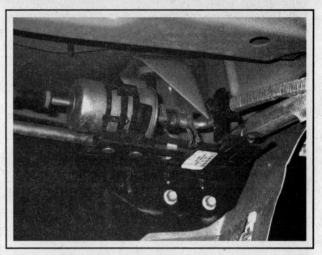

18.1 The fuel filter is located in front of the gas tank

✳ WARNING:

Gasoline is extremely flammable, so take extra precautions when you work on any part of the fuel system. Don't smoke or allow open flames or bare light bulbs near the work area, and don't work in a garage where a gas-type appliance (such as a water heater or clothes dryer) is present. Since fuel is carcinogenic, wear fuel-resistant gloves when there's a possibility of being exposed to fuel, and, if you spill any fuel on your skin, rinse it off immediately with soap and water. Mop up any spills immediately and do not store fuel-soaked rags where they could ignite. When you perform any kind of work on the fuel system, wear safety glasses and have a Class B type fire extinguisher on hand.

1   The fuel filter is mounted under the vehicle on the left side, in front of the gas tank (see illustration).

2   Relieve the fuel system pressure (see Chapter 4), then disconnect the cable from the negative terminal of the battery.

3   If necessary, raise the vehicle and support it securely on jackstands.

4   Inspect the fittings at both ends of the filter to see if they're clean. If more than a light coating of dust is present, clean the fittings before proceeding.

5   Release the clips holding the fuel lines to the filter (see Chapter 4, Section 4).

6   Detach the fuel hoses, one at a time, from the filter. Be prepared for fuel spillage.

7   After the lines are detached, check the fittings for damage and distortion. If they were damaged in any way during removal, new ones must be used when the lines are reattached to the new filter (if new clips are packaged with the filter, be sure to use them in place of the originals).

8   Remove the fuel filter from the mounting bracket, while noting the direction the fuel filter is installed.

9   Install the new filter in the same direction. Carefully push each hose onto the filter until it's seated against the collar on the fitting, then install the clips (see Chapter 4, Section 4). Make sure the clips are securely attached to the hose fittings - if they come off, the hoses could back off the filter and a fire could result!

10 Start the engine and check for fuel leaks.

19 Brake fluid change (every 30,000 miles or 24 months)

✳ WARNING:

Brake fluid can harm your eyes and damage painted surfaces, so use extreme caution when handling or pouring it. Do not use brake fluid that has been standing open or is more than one year old. Brake fluid absorbs moisture from the air. Excess moisture can cause a dangerous loss of braking effectiveness.

1   At the specified intervals, the brake fluid should be drained and replaced. Since the brake fluid may drip or splash when pouring it, place plenty of rags around the master cylinder to protect any surrounding painted surfaces.

2   Before beginning work, purchase the specified brake fluid (see *Recommended lubricants and fluids* in this Chapter's Specifications).

3   Remove the cap from the master cylinder reservoir.

4   Using a hand suction pump or similar device, withdraw the fluid from the master cylinder reservoir.

5   Add new fluid to the master cylinder until it rises to the base of the filler neck.

6   Bleed the brake system as described in Chapter 9 at all four brakes until new and uncontaminated fluid is expelled from the bleeder screw. Be sure to maintain the fluid level in the master cylinder as you perform the bleeding process. If you allow the master cylinder to run dry, air will enter the system.

7   Refill the master cylinder with fluid and check the operation of the brakes. The pedal should feel solid when depressed, with no sponginess.

✳ WARNING:

Do not operate the vehicle if you are in doubt about the effectiveness of the brake system.

20 Drivebelt check and replacement (every 30,000 miles or 24 months)

1   A single serpentine drivebelt is located at the front of the engine and plays an important role in the overall operation of the engine and its components. Due to its function and material make up, the belt is prone to wear and should be periodically inspected. Although the belt should be inspected at the recommended intervals, replacement may not be necessary for more than 100,000 miles.

2   The vehicles covered by this manual are equipped with a single self-adjusting serpentine drivebelt, which is used to drive all of the accessory components such as the alternator, power steering pump, water pump and air conditioning compressor.

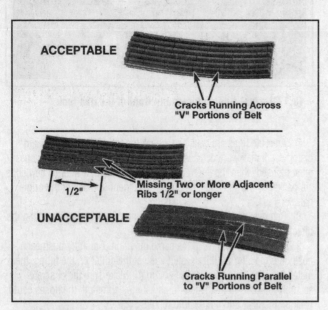

20.4 Small cracks in the underside of a V-ribbed belt are acceptable - lengthwise cracks, or missing pieces that cause the belt to make noise, are cause for replacement

CHECK

▶ **Refer to illustrations 20.4 and 20.5**

3   With the engine off, open the hood and locate the drivebelt at the front of the engine. Using your fingers (and a flashlight, if necessary), move along the belts checking for cracks and separation of the belt plies. Also check for fraying and glazing, which gives the belt a shiny appearance. Both sides of each belt should be inspected, which means you will have to twist the belt to check the underside.

4   Check the ribs on the underside of the belt. They should all be the same depth, with none of the surface uneven (see illustration).

5   The tension of the belt is automatically adjusted by the belt tensioner and does not require any adjustments. Drivebelt wear can be checked visually by inspecting the wear indicator marks located on the side of the tensioner body. Locate the belt tensioner at the front of the engine, adjacent to the lower crankshaft pulley, then find the tensioner operating marks. If the indicator mark is outside the operating range, the belt should be replaced (see illustration).

REPLACEMENT

▶ **Refer to illustrations 20.6 and 20.8**

6   To replace the belt, rotate the tensioner counterclockwise on V6 models, or clockwise on V8 models to relieve the tension on the belt (see illustration).

7   Remove the belt from the auxiliary components.

8   Route the new belt over the various pulleys, again rotating the tensioner to allow the belt to be installed, then release the belt tensioner. Make sure the belt fits properly into the pulley grooves - it must be completely engaged.

➡ **Note: Most models have a drivebelt routing decal on the upper radiator panel to help during drivebelt installation (see illustration).**

20.5 Belt wear indicator marks are located on the side of the tensioner body - when the belt reaches the maximum wear mark it must be replaced (5.4L engine shown)

A   Maximum length (belt worn out when indicator reaches this point)
B   Belt length indicator

20.6 Rotate the tensioner arm to relieve belt tension

A   Tensioner   *B   Wrench*

TENSIONER REPLACEMENT

9   Remove the drivebelt as described previously.

10 On V6 models, remove the bolt in the center of the tensioner, then detach the tensioner from the engine.

11 On V8 models, remove the three bolts securing the tensioner to the engine block.

12 Installation is the reverse of removal. Be sure to tighten the tensioner bolt(s) to the torque listed in this Chapter's Specifications.

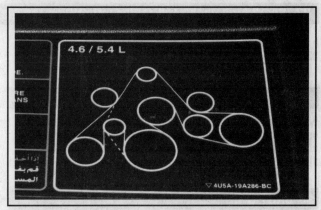

20.8 The routing schematic for the drivebelt is usually found on the fan shroud

21 Manual transmission lubricant change (every 60,000 miles or 48 months)

1   Raise the vehicle and support it securely on jackstands.

2   Move a drain pan, rags, newspapers and wrenches under the transmission.

3   Remove the fill plug from the side of the transmission case, then remove the transmission drain plug at the bottom of the case and allow the lubricant to drain into the pan (see illustration 4.42).

4   After the lubricant has drained completely, reinstall the plug and

tighten it securely.

5   Using a hand pump, syringe or funnel, fill the transmission with the specified lubricant until it is level with the lower edge of the filler hole. Reinstall the fill plug and tighten it securely.

6   Lower the vehicle.

7   Drive the vehicle for a short distance, then check the drain and fill plugs for leakage.

22 Positive Crankcase Ventilation (PCV) valve replacement (every 60,000 miles or 48 months)

▶ **Refer to illustrations 22.3 and 22.4**

➡ **Note: For additional information on the PCV system refer to Chapter 6.**

➡ **Note: The PCV valve on 5.4L engines is built into the valve cover. This is not a maintenance item and needs replacement only when defective.**

1   On V6 and 4.6L, 5.0L and 6.2L V8 models, the PCV valve is located on the valve cover. On the 5.4L V8 model, the PCV valve is located on the top of the intake manifold.

2   Disconnect the PCV valve electrical connector, if equipped.

3   Disconnect the PCV valve hose from the PCV valve (see illustration).

➡ **Note: If you have difficulty disconnecting the hose, information on quick-connect fittings can be found in Chapter 4, Section 4.**

4   On V6 and 4.6L, 5.0L, 6.2L V8 models, rotate the PCV valve counterclockwise and remove the valve. If you're replacing a PCV valve on a 5.4L V8 model, remove the fasteners securing the PCV valve, then remove the valve (see illustration).

5   Installation is the reverse of removal. Be sure to use a new O-ring.

22.3 Disconnect the PCV valve hose from the PCV valve

22.4 On 5.4L engines, remove the two fasteners securing the PCV valve

23 Spark plug check and replacement (see the Maintenance schedule for service intervals)

▶ **Refer to illustrations 23.2, 23.5a, 23.5b, 23.6a, 23.6b, 23.6c, 23.8, 23.9, 23.10a and 23.10b**

✲✲ CAUTION:

When removing the spark plugs on a 3.5L V6 or a 6.2L V8 engine, the engine should be WARM. Removing them on a hot or cold engine could gall the threads on the engine or the spark plugs.

✲✲ CAUTION:

Ford has issued a Technical Service Bulletin (TSB 08-7-6) stating that attempting to remove the spark plugs is likely to result in the extended electrode of the plug breaking off in the cylinder head. This TSB pertains to 4.6L three-valve engines built before 11/30/07, and 5.4L and 6.8L three-valve engines built before 10/9/07. Engine build date can be found on a label affixed to the left valve cover. We highly recommend entrusting this procedure to a Ford dealer service department or other qualified technician equipped with the necessary special tools. If you do decide to attempt spark plug replacement, we recommend that you obtain the Ford TSB (it can be obtained via internet search) and follow the procedure exactly.

1   The spark plugs are located in the cylinder heads.

2   In most cases, the tools necessary for spark plug replacement include a spark plug socket which fits onto a ratchet (spark plug sockets are padded inside to prevent damage to the porcelain insulators on the new plugs), various extensions and a gap gauge to check and adjust the gaps on the new plugs (see illustration). A torque wrench should be used to tighten the new plugs.

3   The best approach when replacing the spark plugs is to purchase the new ones in advance, adjust them to the proper gap and replace the plugs one at a time. When buying the new spark plugs, be sure to obtain the correct plug type for your particular engine. This information can be found in this Chapter's Specifications or in your owner's manual.

4   Allow the engine to cool completely before attempting to remove any of the plugs (except on 3.5L V6 or 6.2L V8 engines, which should be warm). These engines are equipped with aluminum cylinder heads, which can be damaged if the spark plugs are removed when the engine is hot. While you are waiting for the engine to cool, check the new plugs for defects and adjust the gaps.

➡ **Note: Extended ground electrode-type spark plugs, used on some V8 engines, are NOT adjustable. If the gap is out of specification, replace the spark plug.**

5   The gap is checked by inserting the proper-thickness gauge between the electrodes at the tip of the plug (see illustration). The gap between the electrodes should be the same as the one specified on the Vehicle Emissions Control Information label or in this Chapter's Specifications. The gauge should just slide between the electrodes with a slight amount of drag. If the gap is incorrect, use the adjuster on the gauge body to bend the curved side electrode slightly until the proper gap is obtained (see illustration). If the side electrode is not exactly over the center electrode, bend it with the adjuster until it is. Check for cracks in the porcelain insulator (if any are found, the plug should not be used).

➡ **Note: We recommend using a wire-type thickness gauge when checking platinum- or iridium-type spark plugs. Other types of gauges may scrape the thin coating from the electrodes, thus dramatically shortening the life of the plugs.**

6   V8 and OHC V6 engines are equipped with individual ignition coils which must be removed first to access the spark plugs (see illustrations). If you're working on a 3.7L V6, remove the upper intake manifold for access to the right-side spark plugs (see Chapter 2B). On

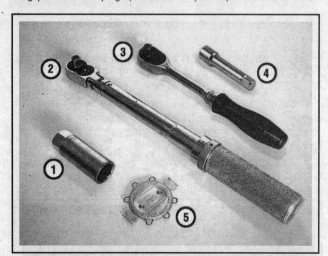

23.2 Tools required for changing spark plugs

1 *Spark plug socket* - This will have special padding inside to protect the spark plug porcelain insulator

2 *Torque wrench* - Although not mandatory, use of this tool is the best way to ensure that the plugs are tightened properly

3 *Ratchet* - Standard hand tool to fit the plug socket

4 *Extension* - Depending on model and accessories, you may need a longer extension and/or a universal joint to reach one or more of the plugs

5 *Spark plug gap gauge* - This gauge for checking the gap comes in a variety of styles. Make sure the gap for your engine is included

23.5a Spark plug manufacturers recommend using a wire-type gauge when checking the gap - if the wire doesn't slide between the electrodes with a slight drag, adjustment is required

23.5b To change the gap, bend the side electrode only, and be very careful not to crack or chip the porcelain insulator surrounding the center electrode

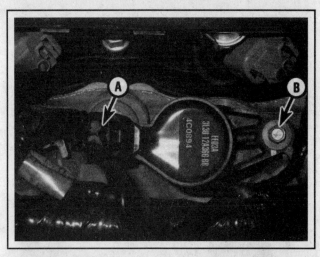

23.6a On models with individual ignition coils, disconnect the electrical connector (A), remove the mounting bolt (B) . . .

other V6 engines, remove the spark plug wire from one spark plug. Pull only on the boot at the end of the wire - do not pull on the wire. A plug wire removal tool should be used if available (see illustration).

➡ **Note: On 6.2L V8 engines, there are two sets of spark plugs. One set is mounted above the valve covers with individual coils, and another set of spark plugs is mounted in the cylinder heads near the exhaust manifold on each side, with spark plug wires leading from the coil-on-plug down to the lower set of spark plugs.**

7   If compressed air is available, use it to blow any dirt or foreign material away from the spark plug hole. The idea here is to eliminate the possibility of debris falling into the cylinder as the spark plug is removed.

8   Place the spark plug socket over the plug and remove it from the engine by turning it in a counterclockwise direction (see illustration).

23.6b . . . and the individual coil(s) to access the spark plug(s)

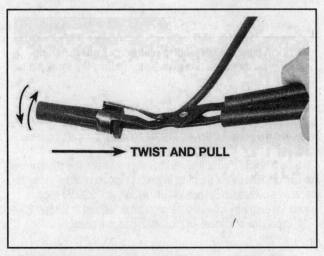

23.6c A tool like this one makes the job of removing the spark plug boot easier

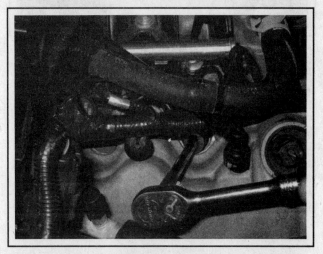

23.8 Use a socket and extension to unscrew the spark plugs

A normally worn spark plug should have light tan or gray deposits on the firing tip.

A carbon fouled plug, identified by soft, sooty, black deposits, may indicate an improperly tuned vehicle. Check the air cleaner, ignition components and engine control system.

An oil fouled spark plug indicates an engine with worn piston rings and/or bad valve seals allowing excessive oil to enter the chamber.

This spark plug has been left in the engine too long, as evidenced by the extreme gap- Plugs with such an extreme gap can cause misfiring and stumbling accompanied by a noticeable lack of power.

A physically damaged spark plug may be evidence of severe detonation in that cylinder. Watch that cylinder carefully between services, as a continued detonation will not only damage the plug, but could also damage the engine.

A bridged or almost bridged spark plug, identified by a build-up between the electrodes caused by excessive carbon or oil build-up on the plug.

23.9 Inspect the spark plug to determine engine running conditions

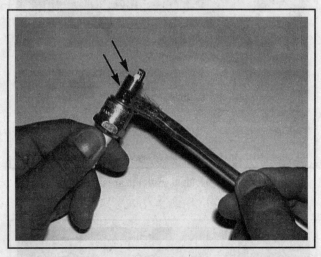

23.10a Apply a thin coat of anti-seize compound to the spark plug threads

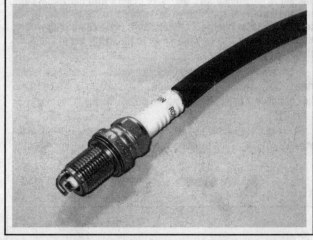

23.10b A length of snug-fitting rubber hose will save time and prevent damaged threads when installing the spark plugs

9   Compare the spark plug to those in the chart (see illustration) to get an indication of the general running condition of the engine.

10 Apply a small amount of anti-seize compound to the spark plug threads (see illustration). Install one of the new plugs into the hole until you can no longer turn it with your fingers, then tighten it with a torque wrench (if available) or the ratchet. It is a good idea to slip a short length of rubber hose over the end of the plug to use as a tool to thread it into place (see illustration). The hose will grip the plug well enough to turn it, but will start to slip if the plug begins to cross-thread in the hole - this will prevent damaged threads and the accompanying repair costs.

11 On 3.5L, 3.7L V6 and all V8 engines, before pushing the ignition coil onto the end of the plug, inspect the ignition coil following the procedures outlined in Section 24. On OHC V6 and 6.2L V8 engines, inspect the plug wire following the procedures outlined in Section 25.

12 Repeat the procedure for the remaining spark plugs.

24 Ignition coil check (3.5L and 3.7L V6, and V8 engines) (every 60,000 miles or 48 months)

1   Remove the ignition coils (see illustration 23.6a). Clean the coil(s) with a dampened cloth and dry them thoroughly.

2   Inspect each coil for cracks, damage and carbon tracking. If damage exists, replace the coil.

25 Spark plug wire check and replacement (OHC V6 and 6.2L V8 engines) (every 60,000 miles or 48 months)

1   The spark plug wires should be checked at the recommended intervals or whenever new spark plugs are installed.

2   Begin this procedure by making a visual check of the spark plug wires while the engine is running. In a darkened garage (make sure there is adequate ventilation) or at night, start the engine and observe each plug wire. Be careful not to come into contact with any moving engine parts. If possible, use an insulated or non-conductive object to wiggle each wire. If there is a break in the wire, you will see arcing or a small blue spark coming from the damaged area. Secondary ignition voltage increases with engine speed and sometimes a damaged wire will not produce an arc at idle speed. Have an assistant press the accelerator pedal to raise the engine speed to approximately 2000 rpm. Check the spark plug wires for arcing as stated previously. If arcing is noticed, replace all spark plug wires.

26 Differential lubricant change (every 60,000 miles or 48 months)

DRAIN

▶ **Refer to illustration 26.6, 26.8a, 26.8b, 26.8c and 26.10**

1   This procedure should be performed after the vehicle has been driven so the lubricant will be warm and therefore flow out of the differential more easily.

2   Raise the vehicle and support it securely on jackstands.

3   The easiest way to drain the differential(s) is to remove the lubricant through the filler plug hole with a suction pump. If the differential cover gasket is leaking, it will be necessary to remove the cover to drain the lubricant (which will also allow you to inspect the differential).

➡ **Note: If you're changing the front differential lubricant on a 4WD vehicle, simply remove the drain plug to drain the lubricant.**

Changing the lubricant with a suction pump

4   Remove the filler plug from the differential (see illustration 4.49).

5   Insert the flexible hose.

6   Work the hose down to the bottom of the differential housing and pump the lubricant out (see illustration).

Changing rear differential lubricant by removing the cover

7   Move a drain pan, rags, newspapers and wrenches under the vehicle.

8   Remove the bolts on the lower half of the cover. Loosen the bolts on the upper half and use them to loosely retain the cover. Allow the oil to drain into the pan, then completely remove the cover (see illustrations).

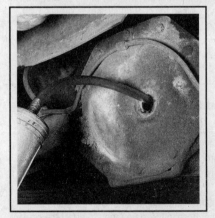

26.6 This is the easiest way to remove the differential lubricant - work the end of the hose to the bottom of the differential housing and draw out the old lubricant with a suction pump

26.8a Remove the bolts from the lower edge of the cover . . .

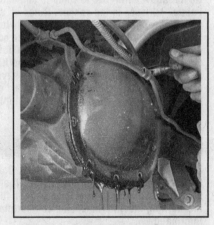

26.8b . . . then loosen the top bolts and let the lubricant drain

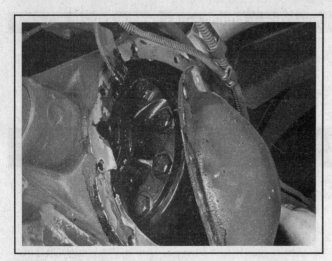

26.8c Once the lubricant has drained, remove the cover

26.10 Carefully scrape off the old material to ensure a leak-free seal

9 Using a lint-free rag, clean the inside of the cover and the accessible areas of the differential housing. As this is done, check for chipped gears and metal particles in the lubricant, indicating that the differential should be more thoroughly inspected and/or repaired.

10 Thoroughly clean the gasket mating surfaces of the differential housing and the cover plate. Use a gasket scraper or putty knife to remove all traces of the old gasket (see illustration).

11 Apply a thin layer of RTV sealant to the cover flange, then press a new gasket into position on the cover. Make sure the bolt holes align properly. Install the bolts and tighten them a little at a time, in a criss-cross pattern, to the torque listed in this Chapter's Specifications.

REFILL

12 Use a hand pump, syringe or funnel to fill the differential housing with the specified lubricant until it's level with the bottom of the filler plug hole.

13 Install the fill plug and tighten it securely.

27 Cooling system servicing (draining, flushing and refilling) (every 100,000 miles)

✸ WARNING:

Do not allow antifreeze to come in contact with your skin or painted surfaces of the vehicle. Rinse off spills immediately with plenty of water. Antifreeze is highly toxic if ingested. Never leave antifreeze lying around in an open container or in puddles on the floor; children and pets are attracted by its sweet smell and may drink it. Check with local authorities about disposing of used antifreeze. Many communities have collection centers which will see that antifreeze is disposed of safely. Never dump used antifreeze on the ground or pour it into drains.

✸ CAUTION:

Do not mix coolants of different colors. Doing so might damage the cooling system and/or the engine. The manufacturer specifies a gold colored coolant to be used in these systems. Read the warning label in the engine compartment for additional information.

➡ Note: Non-toxic antifreeze is now manufactured and available at local auto parts stores, but even this type must be disposed of properly.

1 Periodically, the cooling system should be drained, flushed and refilled to replenish the antifreeze mixture and prevent formation of rust and corrosion, which can impair the performance of the cooling system and cause engine damage. When the cooling system is serviced, all hoses and the expansion tank cap should be checked and replaced if necessary.

DRAINING

▶ Refer to illustrations 27.4

2 Apply the parking brake and block the wheels. If the vehicle has just been driven, wait several hours to allow the engine to cool down before beginning this procedure.

3 Once the engine is completely cool, remove the expansion tank cap.

4 Move a large container under the radiator drain to catch the coolant. Attach a length of hose to the drain fitting to direct the coolant into the container, then open the drain fitting (a pair of pliers may be required to turn it) (see illustration).

5 While the coolant is draining, check the condition of the radiator hoses, heater hoses and clamps (refer to Section 10 if necessary). Replace any damaged clamps or hoses.

27.4 The radiator drain fitting is located at the lower corner of the radiator

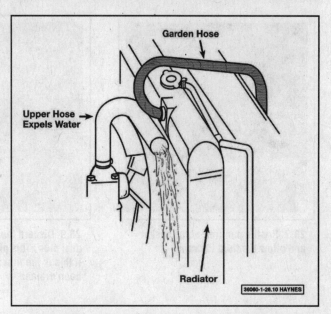

27.8 With the thermostat removed, disconnect the upper radiator hose and flush the radiator and engine block with a garden hose

FLUSHING

▶ **Refer to illustration 27.8**

6   Once the system has completely drained, remove the thermostat housing from the engine (see Chapter 3), then reinstall the housing without the thermostat. This will allow the system to be thoroughly flushed.

7   Disconnect the upper hose from the radiator.

8   Place a garden hose in the upper radiator inlet and flush the system until the water runs clear at the upper radiator hose (see illustration).

9   Severe cases of radiator contamination or clogging will require removing the radiator (see Chapter 3) and reverse flushing it. This involves inserting the hose in the bottom radiator outlet to allow the clean water to run against the normal flow, draining out through the top. A radiator repair shop should be consulted if further cleaning or repair is necessary.

10 When the coolant is regularly drained and the system refilled with the correct coolant mixture there should be no need to employ chemical cleaners or descalers.

REFILLING

11 Close and tighten the radiator drain.

12 Place the heater temperature control in the maximum heat position.

13 Slowly add new coolant (a 50/50 mixture of water and antifreeze) to the expansion tank until the level is at the COLD FILL RANGE mark on the expansion tank.

14 Leave the expansion tank cap off and run the engine in a well-ventilated area until the thermostat opens (coolant will begin flowing through the radiator and the upper radiator hose will become hot).

15 Turn the engine off and let it cool. Add more coolant mixture to bring the coolant level between the COLD FILL RANGE mark on the expansion tank.

16 Squeeze the upper radiator hose to expel air, then add more coolant mixture if necessary. Replace the expansion tank cap.

17 Start the engine, allow it to reach normal operating temperature and check for leaks. Also, set the heater and blower controls to the maximum setting and check to see that the heater output from the air ducts is warm. This is a good indication that all air has been purged from the cooling system.

28 Automatic transmission fluid and filter change (every 100,000 miles)

▶ **Refer to illustrations 28.7, 28.9, 28.10, 28.11 and 28.12**

1   At the specified intervals, the transmission fluid should be drained and replaced. Since the fluid will remain hot long after driving, perform this procedure only after the engine has cooled down completely.

2   Before beginning work, purchase the transmission fluid specified in *Recommended lubricants and fluids* in this Chapter's Specifications, a new filter and gasket. Never reuse the old filter or gasket!

3   Other tools necessary for this job include jackstands to support the vehicle in a raised position, a drain pan capable of holding at least eight quarts, newspapers and clean rags.

4   Raise the vehicle and support it securely on jackstands.

5   With the drain pan in place, remove the front and side transmis-

28.7 Pry the pan free of the gasket and allow the fluid to drain

28.9 Discard the factory-installed dust plug. This plug will be in the pan if this is the first time the fluid has been drained

28.10 Pull straight down on the filter to remove it

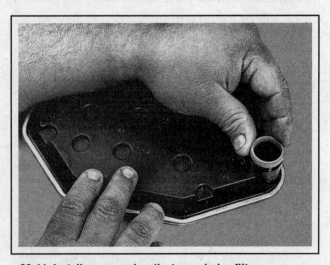

28.11 Install a new seal on the transmission filter

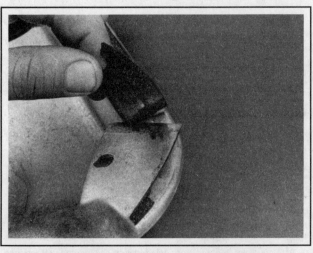

28.12 Be sure to clean all traces of the old gasket from the pan before installing a new one

sion pan mounting bolts.

6   Loosen the rear pan bolts approximately four turns.

7   Carefully pry the transmission pan loose with a screwdriver, allowing the fluid to drain (see illustration). Don't damage the pan or transmission gasket surfaces or leaks could develop.

8   Remove the remaining bolts, pan and gasket. Carefully clean the gasket surface of the transmission to remove all traces of the old gasket and sealant.

9   Drain the fluid from the transmission pan, clean it with solvent and dry it thoroughly.

➡ **Note: Upon initial service most transmissions will have plastic plug lying in the bottom of the pan. This plug was used to keep contamination out of the transmission while on the assembly line. Discard the factory-installed dust plug (see illustration).**

10 Remove the old filter from the transmission (see illustration). If the filter seal did not come out with the filter, remove it from the transmission being careful not to gouge the seal bore in anyway.

11 Install a new seal and filter (see illustration).

12 Make sure the gasket surface on the transmission pan is clean, then install a new gasket (see illustration). Put the pan in place against the transmission and install the bolts. Working around the pan, tighten each bolt a little at a time until the final torque figure listed in this Chapter's Specifications is reached. Don't overtighten the bolts!

13 Lower the vehicle and add four quarts of automatic transmission fluid through the filler tube (see Section 5).

14 With the transmission in Park and the parking brake set, run the engine at a fast idle, but don't race it.

15 Move the gear selector through each range and back to Park. Check the fluid level. Add fluid if needed to reach the correct level.

16 Check under the vehicle for leaks during the first few trips.

29 Transfer case lubricant change (4WD models) (every 100,000 miles)

1   Drive the vehicle for at least 15 minutes to warm the lubricant in the case. Perform this warm-up procedure with 4WD engaged, if possible. Use all gears, including Reverse, to ensure the lubricant is sufficiently warm to drain completely.

2   Raise the vehicle and support it securely on jackstands.

3   Remove the drain plug from the lower part of the case and allow the old lubricant to drain completely.

4   After the lubricant has drained completely, reinstall the plug and tighten it securely

5   Remove the filler plug from the case

6   Fill the case with the specified lubricant until it is level with the lower edge of the filler hole.

7   Install the filler plug and tighten it securely.

8   Drive the vehicle for a short distance and recheck the lubricant level. In some instances a small amount of additional lubricant will have to be added.

Specifications

Recommended lubricants and fluids

➡ **Note: Listed here are manufacturer recommendations at the time this manual was written. Manufacturers occasionally upgrade their fluid and lubricant specifications, so check with your local auto parts store for current recommendations.**

Engine oil	
Type	API "certified for gasoline engines," synthetic
Viscosity	SAE 5W-20
Fuel	Unleaded gasoline, 87 octane
Automatic transmission fluid*	
Four-speed transmission	MERCON® V automatic transmission fluid
Six-speed transmission	MERCON® LV automatic transmission fluid
Manual transmission lubricant*	MERCON® automatic transmission fluid
Transfer case (4WD)*	MERCON® automatic transmission fluid
Rear differential lubricant**	
2004 models	SAE 75W-90 Motorcraft High Performance Synthetic Rear Axle Lubricant or equivalent.
2005 and later models	SAE 75W-140 Motorcraft High Performance Synthetic Rear Axle Lubricant or equivalent.
Front differential lubricant (4WD)	SAE 75W-90 Motorcraft High Performance Synthetic Rear Axle Lubricant or equivalent.
Brake fluid	DOT 3 brake fluid
Clutch fluid	DOT 3 brake fluid
Engine coolant ***	Motorcraft Premium Gold Engine Coolant (yellow colored)
Power steering system	MERCON® automatic transmission fluid

*Caution: Be sure to use the correct type of transmission fluid. Do not mix MERCON® and MERCON® V.

**Traction-Lock (limited slip) differentials add 8oz. of friction modifier XL-3 or equivalent when lubricant is changed (2011 and later models use 4 oz. of modifier).

***Caution: Do not mix coolants of different colors. Doing so might damage the cooling system and/or the engine. The manufacturer specifies a gold colored coolant to be used in these systems.

Specifications (continued)

Recommended lubricants and fluids

➡ **Note: Listed here are manufacturer recommendations at the time this manual was written. Manufacturers occasionally upgrade their fluid and lubricant specifications, so check with your local auto parts store for current recommendations.**

Capacities*

Engine oil (including filter)	
V6 engines	6.0 quarts
V8 engines	
4.6L	6.0 quarts
5.0L	6.0 quarts
5.4L	7.0 quarts
6.2L	7.0 quarts
Cooling system	
Pushrod V6 engines	17.6 quarts
OHC V6 engines	
3.5L	16.5 quarts
3.7L	16.0 quarts
V8 engines	
4.6L	20.5 quarts
5.0L	17.0 quarts
5.4L	20.9 quarts
6.2L	19.5 quarts
Automatic transmission (dry fill)	
Four-speed transmission (2010 and earlier)	Up to 13.9 quarts
Six-speed transmission (2010 and earlier)	Up to 10.1 quarts
2011 and later	Up to 13 quarts

➡ **Note: Since this is a dry-fill specification, the amount required during a routine fluid change will be substantially less. The best way to determine the amount of fluid to add during a routine fluid change is to measure the amount drained. Begin the refill procedure by initially adding 1/3 of the amount drained. Then, with the engine running, add 1/2-pint at a time (cycling the shifter through each gear position between additions) until the level is correct. The correct fluid level should be checked at this time (see Section 4). It is important to not overfill the transmission.**

Manual transmission	Up to 3.75 quarts
Transfer case (4WD models)	Up to 2.9 quarts
Rear differential	
8.8/9.75 inch axle	Up to 5.5 pints
10.25 inch axle**	Up to 6.9 pints

All capacities approximate. Add as necessary to bring up to appropriate level.

**Traction-Lock (limited slip) differentials add 6.5 pints of SAE 75W-140 Motorcraft High Performance Synthetic Rear Axle and 8oz. of friction modifier XL-3 or equivalent when lubricant is changed (2011 and later models use 4 oz. of modifier).*

Ignition system

Spark plug type and gap	
Type	
2010 and earlier V6 engines	AGSF-34EE or equivalent
3.5L V6	CYFS-12-Y3 or equivalent
3.7L V6	CYFS12F-5 or equivalent

Spark plug type and gap (contined)

Type

4.6L V8	AGSF-32PM or equivalent
5.0L V8	CYFS-12Y or equivalent
5.4L V8 (2004)	PZT-2FE or equivalent
5.4L V8 (2005 and later)	PZT-2F or equivalent
6.2L V8	CYFS-12-FP or equivalent

Gap

V6 engines

2010 and earlier V6 engines	0.052 to 0.056 inch
3.5L V6	0.035 inch
3.7L V6	0.049 to 0.053 inch

V8 engines

4.6L V8	0.052 to 0.056 inch
5.0L V8	0.049 to 0.053 inch
5.4L V8	0.040 to 0.050 inch
6.2L V8	0.042 to 0.046 inch

V6 engines

36061-1-specs.B HAYNES

V8 engines

36061-1-specs.C HAYNES

Cylinder location and coil terminal identification - V6 engines
Pushrod V6 engines have a separate coil pack with plug wires leading to the spark plugs - OHC V6 engines have coil-on-plug ignition system

Cylinder locations - V8 engines

Engine firing order

V6 engines	1-4-2-5-3-6
V8 engines	
2010 and earlier V8 engines	1-3-7-2-6-5-4-8
5.0L V8 engine	1-5-4-8-6-3-7-2
6.2L V8 engine	1-3-7-2-6-5-4-8

Cooling system

Thermostat rating

Starts to open	188 to 195-degrees F
Fully open	208 to 215-degrees F

Brakes

Disc brake pad lining thickness (minimum)	1/16 inch
Parking brake shoe lining thickness (minimum)	1/32 inch

Torque specifications	Ft-lbs (unless otherwise indicated)

➡ **Note: One foot-pound (ft-lb) of torque is equivalent to 12 inch-pounds (in-lbs) of torque. Torque values below approximately 15 ft-lbs are expressed in inch-pounds, since most foot-pound torque wrenches are not accurate at these smaller values.**

Engine oil drain plug	
V6 engines	
2010 and earlier V6 engines	17
3.5L and 3.7L V6	20
V8 engines	
2010 and earlier V8 engines	120 in-lbs
5.0L V6	19
6.2L V8	17
Automatic transmission fluid pan bolts	120 in-lbs
Manual transmission	
Fill plug	35
Drain plug	35
Transfer case (4WD)	
Fill plug	18
Drain plug	18
Front axle (4WD)	
Cover bolts	24
Fill plug	18
Rear differential	
Cover bolts	33
Check/fill plug	22
Spark plugs	
V6 engines	132 in-lbs
V8 engines	
4.6L	132 in-lbs
5.0L	124 in-lbs
5.4L	25
6.2L	159 in-lbs
Drivebelt tensioner mounting bolt(s)	
V6 engines	
2010 and earlier V6 engines	41
3.5L and 3.7L V6	18
V8 engines	
2010 and earlier V8 engines	18
5.0L V8	35
6.2L V8	18
Wheel lug nuts	150

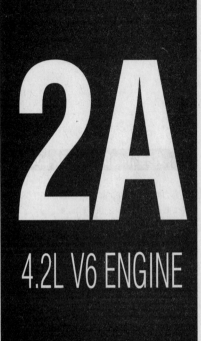

2A

4.2L V6 ENGINE

Section

1   General information
2   Repair operations possible with the engine in the vehicle
3   Top Dead Center (TDC) for number one piston - locating
4   Valve covers - removal and installation
5   Rocker arms and pushrods - removal, inspection and installation
6   Intake manifold - removal and installation
7   Exhaust manifolds - removal and installation
8   Cylinder heads - removal and installation
9   Timing chain cover - removal and installation
10 Timing chain and sprockets - inspection, removal and installation
11 Valve lifters - removal, inspection and installation
12 Camshaft, balance shaft and bearings - removal, inspection and installation
13 Oil pan - removal and installation
14 Oil pump - removal and installation
15 Crankshaft oil seals - replacement
16 Flywheel/driveplate - removal and installation
17 Engine mounts - check and replacement

Reference to other Chapters

CHECK ENGINE light on - See Chapter 6
Cylinder compression check - See Chapter 2D
Drivebelt check, adjustment and replacement - See Chapter 1
Engine - removal and installation - See Chapter 2D
Engine oil and filter change - See Chapter 1
Engine overhaul - general information - See Chapter 2D
Spark plug replacement - See Chapter 1
Water pump - replacement - See Chapter 3

1   General information

This Part of Chapter 2 is devoted to in-vehicle repair procedures for the 4.2L V6 engine. This engine design utilizes a cast-iron block with six cylinders arranged in a V-shape at a 90-degree angle between the two banks. The cylinder heads are also cast-iron and the block-mounted camshaft operates pushrods and rocker arms for valve actuation. The engine also features a balance shaft geared to the camshaft in the block.

Information concerning engine removal and installation and engine overhaul can be found in Part D of this Chapter. The following repair procedures are based on the assumption that the engine is installed in the vehicle. If the engine has been removed from the vehicle and mounted on a stand, many of the steps outlined in this Part of Chapter 2 will not apply.

2   Repair operations possible with the engine in the vehicle

Many major repair operations can be accomplished without removing the engine from the vehicle.

Clean the engine compartment and the exterior of the engine with some type of pressure washer before any work is done. It will make the job easier and help keep dirt out of the internal areas of the engine.

It may help to remove the hood to improve access to the engine as repairs are performed (refer to Chapter 11 if necessary).

If vacuum, exhaust, oil or coolant leaks develop, indicating a need for gasket or seal replacement, the repairs can generally be made with the engine in the vehicle. The intake and exhaust manifold gaskets, timing cover gasket, oil pan gasket, crankshaft oil seals and cylinder head gaskets are all accessible with the engine in place.

Exterior engine components, such as the intake and exhaust mani-

folds, the oil pan (and the oil pump), the water pump, the starter motor, the alternator, and the fuel system components can be removed for repair with the engine in place.

Since the cylinder heads can be removed without pulling the engine, valve component servicing can also be accomplished with the engine in the vehicle. Replacement of the timing chain and sprockets is also possible with the engine in the vehicle.

In extreme cases caused by a lack of necessary equipment, repair or replacement of piston rings, pistons, connecting rods and rod bearings is possible with the engine in the vehicle. However, this practice is not recommended because of the cleaning and preparation work that must be done to the components involved.

3   Top Dead Center (TDC) for number one piston - locating

▶ **Refer to illustration 3.6**

1   Top Dead Center (TDC) is the highest point in the cylinder that each piston reaches as it travels up-and-down when the crankshaft turns. Each piston reaches TDC on the compression stroke and again on the exhaust stroke, but TDC generally refers to piston position on the compression stroke. The timing marks on the crankshaft pulley installed on the front of the crankshaft are referenced to the number one piston at TDC on the compression stroke.

2   Positioning the piston(s) at TDC is an essential part of procedures such as timing chain and sprocket replacement.

3   In order to bring any piston to TDC, the crankshaft must be turned using one of the methods outlined below. When looking at the front of the engine, normal crankshaft rotation is clockwise.

❊❊ WARNING:

Before beginning this procedure, be sure to place the transmission in Neutral and remove the ignition key.

a) *The preferred method is to turn the crankshaft with a large socket and breaker bar attached to the crankshaft pulley bolt threaded into the front of the crankshaft.*

b) *A remote starter switch, which may save some time, can also be used. Attach the switch leads to the S (switch) and B (battery) terminals on the starter motor. Once the piston is close to TDC, use a socket and breaker bar as described in the previous paragraph.*

c) *If an assistant is available to turn the ignition switch to the Start position in short bursts, you can get the piston close to TDC without a remote starter switch. Use a socket and breaker bar as described in Paragraph a) to complete the procedure.*

4   Disable the ignition system by disconnecting the primary electrical connectors at the ignition coil pack (see Chapter 5). Disable the fuel pump (see Chapter 4, Section 2).

5   Remove the spark plugs and install a compression gauge in the number one cylinder. Turn the crankshaft clockwise as described in Step 3.

6 When the piston approaches TDC, compression will be noted on the compression gauge. Continue turning the crankshaft until the notch in the crankshaft damper is aligned with the TDC mark on the front cover (see illustration). At this point, number one cylinder is at TDC on the compression stroke. If the marks aligned but there was no compression, the piston was on the exhaust stroke. Continue rotating the crankshaft one complete revolution (360-degrees).

7 After the number one piston has been positioned at TDC on the compression stroke, TDC for any of the remaining cylinders can be located by turning the crankshaft and following the firing order (refer to the Specifications). Divide the crankshaft pulley into three equal sections with chalk marks at three points, each indicating 120-degrees of crankshaft rotation. Rotating the engine 120-degrees past TDC #1 will put the engine at TDC for cylinder no. 4.

3.6 Turn the crankshaft clockwise until the zero on the vibration damper scale is directly in line with the pointer

4 Valve covers - removal and installation

REMOVAL

▶ **Refer to illustration 4.2**

1 Disconnect the cable from the negative battery terminal (see Chapter 5, Section 1).

2 Remove the spark plug wire clips from the valve cover studs (see illustration). Be sure to mark them properly for correct reassembly.

3 Detach the spark plug wires from the plugs (see Chapter 1). Position the wires out of the way.

Left (driver's side) valve cover

▶ **Refer to illustration 4.4**

4 Remove the PCV vent tube (see illustration).

5 Remove the dipstick mounting bolt and lift the dipstick tube from the engine block.

6 Remove the engine lifting bracket from the cylinder head.

7 On some vehicles with cruise control, it may be necessary to disconnect the servo linkage at the throttle body and remove the servo bracket.

Right (passenger's side) valve cover

8 Remove the air filter housing duct (see Chapter 4).

9 Remove the PCV valve hose and electrical connector (see Chapter 6).

10 Remove the engine lifting bracket from the cylinder head.

Both valve covers

11 Remove the valve cover bolts (see illustration 4.4), then remove the valve cover from the cylinder head.

➡ **Note: If the cover is stuck to the cylinder head, bump one end with a wood block and a hammer to jar it loose. If that doesn't work, try to slip a flexible putty knife between the cylinder head and cover to break the gasket seal. Don't pry at the cover-to-cylinder head joint or damage to the sealing surfaces may occur (leading to oil leaks in the future).**

Some valve covers are made of plastic - be extra careful when tapping or pulling on them. On some models, the valve cover bolts stay with the valve cover. Do not attempt to remove them completely.

4.2 Remove the spark plug wire clips

4.4 Detach the crankcase vent tube (A) - B indicates two of the valve cover bolts

INSTALLATION

12 The mating surfaces of each cylinder head and valve cover must be perfectly clean when the covers are installed. Use a gasket scraper to remove all traces of sealant and old gasket material. If there's sealant or oil on the mating surfaces when the cover is installed, oil leaks may develop.

13 Clean the mounting bolt threads with a die to remove any corrosion and restore damaged threads. Make sure the threaded holes in the cylinder head are clean - run a tap into them to remove corrosion and restore damaged threads. Apply a small amount of light oil to the bolt threads.

14 Using a new gasket, carefully position the cover on the cylinder head and install the bolts/nuts.

15 Tighten the bolts in three or four steps to the torque listed in this Chapter's Specifications. Plastic valve covers are easily damaged, so don't overtighten the bolts!

16 The remaining installation steps are the reverse of removal.

17 Start the engine and check carefully for oil leaks as the engine warms up.

---

5 Rocker arms and pushrods - removal, inspection and installation

REMOVAL

▸ **Refer to illustrations 5.2 and 5.4**

1 Remove the valve cover(s) from the cylinder head(s) (see Section 4).

2 Beginning at the front of one cylinder head, remove the rocker arm fulcrum bolts (see illustration). Store them separately in marked containers to ensure that they will be reinstalled in their original locations.

➡ **Note: If the pushrods are the only items being removed, loosen each bolt just enough to allow the rocker arms to be rotated to the side so the pushrods can be lifted out.**

3 Lift off the rocker arms and fulcrums. Store them in the marked containers with the bolts (they must be reinstalled in their original locations).

4 Remove the pushrods and store them separately to make sure they don't get mixed up during installation (see illustration).

INSPECTION

▸ **Refer to illustration 5.7**

5 Check each rocker arm for wear, cracks and other damage, especially where the pushrods and valve stems contact the rocker arm faces.

6 Make sure the hole at the pushrod end of each rocker arm is open.

7 Check each rocker arm pivot area and fulcrum for wear, cracks and galling (see illustration). If the rocker arms are worn or damaged, replace them with new ones and use new fulcrums as well.

8 Inspect the pushrods for cracks and excessive wear at the ends. Roll each pushrod across a piece of plate glass to see if it's bent (if it wobbles, it's bent).

INSTALLATION

9 Lubricate the lower end of each pushrod with clean engine oil or

5.2 The rocker arm fulcrum bolts may not have to be completely removed in all cases - loosen them several turns and see if the rocker arms can be pivoted out of the way to allow pushrod removal

5.4 A perforated cardboard box can be used to store the pushrods to ensure that they are reinstalled in their original locations - note the label indicating the front of the engine

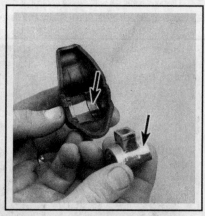

5.7 Check for wear on the rocker arm and fulcrum contact areas

moly-base grease and install them in their original locations. Make sure each pushrod seats completely in the lifter.

10 Apply moly-base grease to the ends of the valve stems and the upper ends of the pushrods before positioning the rocker arms and fulcrums.

11 Apply moly-base grease to the fulcrums to prevent damage to the mating surfaces before engine oil pressure builds up. Set the rocker arms and guides in place, then install the fulcrums and bolts. Tighten the rocker arm bolts to the Specifications listed in this Chapter.

12 Install the valve covers.

13 The remainder of installation is the reverse of removal.

---

6   Intake manifold - removal and installation

✳✳ WARNING:

Wait until the engine is completely cool before beginning this procedure.

REMOVAL

1 Relieve the fuel pressure and remove the air filter housing (see Chapter 4).

2 Disconnect the cable from the negative battery terminal (see Chapter 5, Section 1).

3 Drain the cooling system (see Chapter 1).

Upper intake manifold

▶ **Refer to illustration 6.14**

4 Disconnect the heater hose clamps and position the heater hoses off to the side (see Chapter 3).

5 Disconnect the EGR module vacuum hose and the EGR module connector (see Chapter 6).

6 Remove the EGR pipe from the EGR module (see Chapter 6).

7 Disconnect the electronic throttle body connector (see Chapter 4).

8 Disconnect the EVAP line from the upper intake manifold (see Chapter 4).

9 Disconnect the Fuel Rail Pressure Temperature (FRPT) sensor connector (see Chapter 6) and the fuel injection harness connectors from the fuel injectors (see Chapter 4).

10 Disconnect the vacuum hose connector and the brake booster vacuum hose from the rear of the upper intake manifold.

11 Remove the PCV hoses from the rear of the upper intake manifold (see Chapter 6).

12 Disconnect the PCV valve hoses from the valve covers and remove them from the engine (see Chapter 6).

13 Remove the mounting bolts from the upper intake manifold.

14 Cover the air intake passages with a shop towel (see illustration) to prevent anything from falling inside the engine.

Lower intake manifold

▶ **Refer to illustration 6.19**

15 Disconnect the Intake Manifold Runner Control (IMRC) connector (see Chapter 6).

16 Remove the fuel rail (see Chapter 4).

17 Remove the upper radiator hose and the bypass hose (see Chapter 3).

18 Remove the lower intake manifold mounting bolts. Loosen the intake manifold mounting bolts in 1/4-turn increments until they can be removed by hand (see illustration 6.27). Not all bolts are easily noticed; there are 14 in all, six long ones and eight short ones. Keep track of which ones go where.

19 The intake manifold will probably be stuck to the cylinder heads and force may be required to break the gasket seal. A prybar can be positioned under the cast-in lug (see illustration) to pry up the front of the intake manifold, but make sure all bolts have been removed first!

✳✳ CAUTION:

Don't pry between the engine block and intake manifold or the cylinder heads and intake manifold or damage to the gasket sealing surfaces may occur, leading to vacuum and oil leaks.

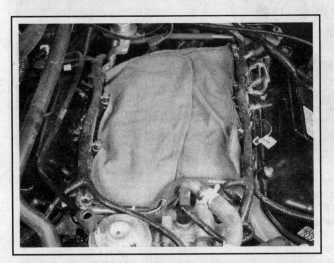

6.14 Cover the air intake with a shop towel to prevent debris from falling into the engine

6.19 Pry against a casting protrusion to break the intake manifold loose

INSTALLATION

Lower intake manifold
▶ Refer to illustrations 6.20, 6.23, 6.24 and 6.27

✲✲ CAUTION:

The mating surfaces of the cylinder heads, engine block and manifold must be perfectly clean when the manifold is installed. Gasket removal solvents in aerosol cans are available at most auto parts stores and may be helpful when removing old gasket material that's stuck to the cylinder heads and manifold (since the manifold is made of aluminum, aggressive scraping can cause damage). Be sure to follow directions printed on the container.

20 Use a gasket scraper to remove all traces of sealant and old gasket material (see illustration), then clean the mating surfaces with lacquer thinner or acetone. If there's old sealant or oil on the mating surfaces when the manifold is installed, oil or vacuum leaks may develop. When working on the cylinder heads and block, cover the lifter valley with shop rags to keep debris out of the engine. Use a vacuum cleaner to remove any gasket material that falls into the intake ports in the cylinder heads.

21 Use a tap of the correct size to chase the threads in the bolt holes, then use compressed air (if available) to remove the debris from the holes.

✲✲ WARNING:

Wear safety glasses or a face shield to protect your eyes when using compressed air!

Remove excessive carbon deposits and corrosion from the exhaust and coolant passages in the cylinder heads and manifold.

22 Make a final inspection of the gasket surfaces before installing the manifold.

23 Apply a 1/8-inch wide bead of RTV sealant to the front and rear of the block surface and install the rubber front and rear manifold seals (see illustration).

➡ **Note: This sealant sets up in 15 minutes. Do not take longer to install and tighten the manifold once the sealant is applied, or leaks may occur.**

24 Apply a small dab of RTV at the four corners where the side gaskets will fit against the end seals. Position the side gaskets on the cylinder heads, over the alignment studs. The upper side of each gasket will have a TOP or THIS SIDE UP label stamped into it to ensure correct installation (see illustration).

25 Make sure all intake port openings, coolant passage holes and bolt holes are aligned correctly.

26 Carefully set the manifold in place while the sealant is still wet.

✲✲ CAUTION:

Don't disturb the gaskets. Make sure the end seals haven't been disturbed.

27 Lightly oil the manifold bolts, install them and tighten them to the torque listed in this Chapter's Specifications, following the recommended sequence (see illustration). Work up to the final torque in three steps.

➡ **Note: Install the lower intake manifold bolts into their original positions. The long bolts are installed into bolt positions 1, 2, 3, 4, 11 and 12.**

28 The remaining installation steps are the reverse of removal. Install the upper intake manifold (see Steps 29 through 32).

Upper intake manifold
▶ Refer to illustration 6.30

29 Install 6 new intake manifold gasket seals into the runners of the upper intake manifold.

30 Install the upper intake manifold onto the lower intake manifold and tighten the bolts to the torque listed in this Chapter's Specifications following the correct sequence (see illustration).

31 The remaining installation steps are the reverse of removal. Refill the cooling system (see Chapter 1).

32 Start the engine and check carefully for oil and coolant leaks at the intake manifold joints.

6.20 After covering the lifter valley, use a gasket scraper to remove all traces of sealant and old gasket material from the cylinder head and intake manifold mating surfaces

6.23 Install the rubber end seals over a thin bead of RTV sealant, then apply a thin bead on top

6.24 Apply a dab of RTV sealant to the corners where the engine block, cylinder heads and intake manifold converge, then position the side gaskets in place and apply an additional bead of RTV sealant where the end seals and intake manifold gaskets meet

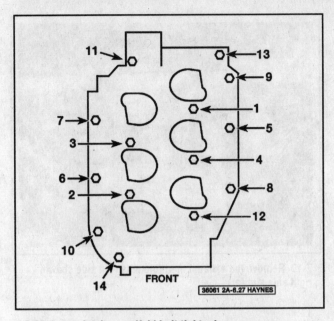

6.27 Lower intake manifold bolt tightening sequence

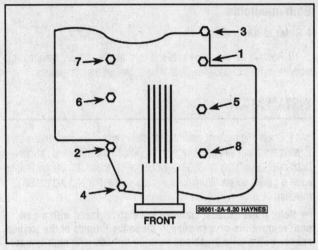

6.30 Upper intake manifold bolt tightening sequence

7 Exhaust manifolds - removal and installation

REMOVAL

▶ **Refer to illustration 7.5**

1   Disconnect the cable from the negative battery terminal (see Chapter 5, Section 1)

2   Raise the vehicle and support it securely on jackstands.

3   Disconnect the oxygen sensor electrical connector(s) (see Chapter 6).

4   Working under the vehicle, apply penetrating oil to the exhaust Y-pipe-to-manifold studs and nuts (they're usually rusty).

5   Remove the nuts holding the exhaust Y-pipe to the exhaust manifolds (see illustration).

Right (passenger's side) manifold

6   Disconnect the EGR pipe from the exhaust manifold (see Chapter 6).

7   Remove the engine lifting bracket.

Left (driver's side) manifold

▶ **Refer to illustration 7.9**

8   Remove the engine lifting bracket.

9   Remove the nut holding the oil dipstick tube support at the front of the manifold, then pull the dipstick tube up and out of the oil pan (see illustration).

7.5 From below, remove the two exhaust Y-pipe-to-manifold nuts

7.9 Remove the nut and pull the oil dipstick tube out

Both manifolds

▶ **Refer to illustration 7.10**

10 Remove the mounting nuts and separate the exhaust manifold(s) from the cylinder head (see illustration). Remove the old gaskets.

INSTALLATION

11 Check the exhaust manifold for cracks and make sure all the stud threads are clean and undamaged. The exhaust manifold and cylinder head mating surfaces must be clean before the manifolds are reinstalled - use a gasket scraper to remove all carbon deposits and old gasket material.

➡ **Note: If the exhaust manifold is being replaced with a new one, remove the oxygen sensor. Clean the threads of the oxygen sensor with a wire brush and coat the threads with high-temperature anti-seize compound before transferring the sensor to the new exhaust manifold.**

12 Position the exhaust manifold and new gasket on the cylinder head and install the mounting nuts.

13 When tightening the nuts, tighten the center pair first, the front pair, then the rear pair, and be sure to use a torque wrench. Tighten the bolts in three equal steps until the torque listed in this Chapter's Speci-

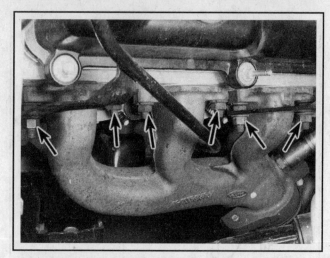

7.10 Remove the exhaust manifold nuts (left side shown, right side similar)

fications is reached.

14 The remaining installation steps are the reverse of removal.

15 Start the engine and check for exhaust leaks.

8 Cylinder heads - removal and installation

❄ **CAUTION:**

The engine must be completely cool when the cylinder heads are removed. Failure to allow the engine to cool off could result in cylinder head warpage.

REMOVAL

1 Relieve the fuel pressure (see Chapter 4), then disconnect the cable from the negative battery terminal (see Chapter 5, Section 1).

2 Remove the valve covers (see Section 4).

3 Remove the pushrods and rocker arms (see Section 5).

4 Remove the upper intake manifold and the lower intake manifold (see Section 6).

5 Unbolt the exhaust manifold(s) (see Section 7).

6 Remove the drivebelt and the drivebelt tensioner (see Chapter 1).

Left (driver's side) cylinder head

7 Remove the air conditioning compressor and position the compressor off to the side without disconnecting the refrigerant lines (see Chapter 3).

8 Remove the air conditioning compressor/power steering pump bracket from the cylinder head and position the assembly out of the way. DO NOT disconnect the hoses!

9 Disconnect any electrical connectors from the cylinder head and mark them with tape for correct reassembly.

Right (passenger's side) cylinder head

10 Remove the drivebelt idler pulley from the bracket.

11 Remove the alternator (see Chapter 5). Unbolt the alternator bracket.

12 Disconnect any electrical connectors from the cylinder head and mark them with tape for correct reassembly.

Both cylinder heads

▶ **Refer to illustration 8.14**

13 Loosen the cylinder head bolts in 1/4-turn increments until they can be removed by hand. Work from bolt-to-bolt in a pattern that's the reverse of the tightening sequence.

➡ **Note: Head bolts should not be reused. Remove the bolts and discard them - new bolts must be used when installing the cylinder head(s).**

14 Lift the cylinder head(s) off the engine. If resistance is felt, DO NOT pry between the cylinder head and engine block as damage to the mating surfaces will result. To dislodge the cylinder head, place a wood block against the end of it and strike the wood block with a hammer or pry against a casting protrusion (see illustration). Store the cylinder heads on blocks of wood to prevent damage to the gasket sealing surfaces.

❄ **CAUTION:**

Do not slide the heads across the floor or workbench, as the aluminum is easily gouged.

15 Cylinder head disassembly and inspection procedures must be performed by a qualified automotive machine shop.

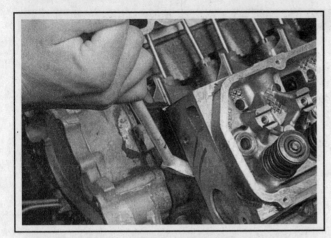

8.14 Using a prybar, carefully lever it against a casting protrusion to lift the cylinder head and break the gasket seal

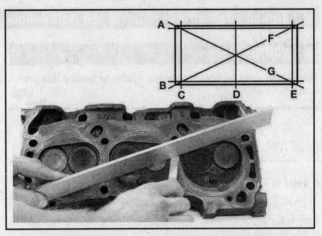

8.17 Check the cylinder head and block surfaces for flatness with a straightedge - if a feeler gauge in excess of the Specification fits under it, have the head machined

8.19 Locating dowels are used to position the gaskets on the engine block - make sure the mark (circled) is correctly oriented

8.22 Cylinder head bolt tightening sequence

INSTALLATION

▶ **Refer to illustrations 8.17, 8.19 and 8.22**

16 The mating surfaces of the cylinder heads and engine block must be perfectly clean when the cylinder heads are installed. Use a gasket scraper to remove all traces of carbon and old gasket material, then clean the mating surfaces with lacquer thinner or acetone. If there's oil on the mating surfaces when the cylinder heads are installed, the gaskets may not seal correctly and leaks may develop. When working on the engine block, cover the lifter valley with shop rags to keep debris out of the engine. Use a vacuum cleaner to remove any debris that falls into the valley or intake ports.

17 Check the engine block and cylinder head mating surfaces for nicks, deep scratches and other damage. If damage is slight, it can be removed with a file - if it's excessive, machining may be the only alternative. Do not use a rotary abrasive tool or wire brush on the aluminum cylinder heads. Use a straightedge and feeler gauges to check for warpage (see illustration). If the warpage is beyond Specifications, have the head machined at an automotive machine shop.

18 Use a tap of the correct size to chase the threads in the cylinder head bolt holes. Dirt, corrosion, sealant and damaged threads will affect

torque readings.

19 Position the new gasket(s) over the dowel pins in the engine block (see illustration). Make sure it's facing the right way.

20 Carefully position the cylinder head(s) on the engine block without disturbing the gasket(s).

21 Before installing the new cylinder head bolts, lightly oil the threads.

22 Install the bolts (long bolts inside, short bolts outside row) and tighten them finger tight. Follow the recommended sequence and tighten the bolts, in the recommended steps, to the torque listed in this Chapter's Specifications (see illustration).

⁕⁕ CAUTION:

When following the torque sequence, at Step 4, do not loosen all the bolts at the same time or the gasket will not seal properly. Loosen the first bolt in the sequence, tighten it to the final torque then go on to the next bolt in the sequence, loosening and tightening the bolts until the sequence is completed.

23 The remaining installation steps are the reverse of removal.

24 Change the engine oil and filter and refill the cooling system (see Chapter 1), then start the engine and check carefully for oil and coolant leaks.

9 Timing chain cover - removal and installation

※ WARNING:

The engine must be completely cool before beginning this procedure.

REMOVAL

▶ **Refer to illustration 9.10**

1 Drain the cooling system (see Chapter 1). Remove the engine cooling fan and water pump (see Chapter 3). Disconnect the radiator and heater hoses.

2 Drain the engine oil and remove the oil filter (see Chapter 1).

3 Remove the crankshaft pulley (see Section 15).

4 Remove the drivebelt idler pulleys.

9.10 Gently tap the timing chain cover loose with a soft-face hammer

5 Unbolt and remove all accessory brackets attached to the timing chain cover. When unbolting the power steering pump (see Chapter 10), tie it aside with the hoses still connected. On air-conditioned models, remove the air conditioning compressor/power steering pump assembly and bracket (see Chapter 3).

6 Position the number one piston at TDC on the compression stroke (see Section 3).

7 Disconnect the electrical connector at the Camshaft Position (CMP) sensor and remove the sensor (see Chapter 6).

8 Disconnect the knock sensor and Crankshaft Position (CKP) sensor electrical connectors (see Chapter 6).

9 Remove the front oil pan-to-timing chain cover bolts (see Section 13).

10 Remove the bolts and separate the timing chain cover from the engine block. If it's stuck, tap it gently with a soft-face hammer (see illustration).

※ CAUTION:

DO NOT use excessive force or you may crack the cover. If the cover is difficult to remove, double check to make sure all of the bolts have been removed.

INSTALLATION

▶ **Refer to illustrations 9.11, 9.13, 9.16 and 9.18**

11 Use a gasket scraper to remove all traces of old gasket material and sealant from the cover, oil pan and engine block, then clean them with lacquer thinner or acetone (see illustration).

12 Inspect the oil pump (see Section 14).

13 Inspect the gear and intermediate shaft inside the timing chain cover (see illustration).

14 While the cover is off the engine, it's a good idea to install a new crankshaft front seal (see Section 15). Lubricate the front crankshaft oil seal lip with engine oil.

9.11 Scrape the old gasket and sealant from the block and cover, then clean the surfaces thoroughly

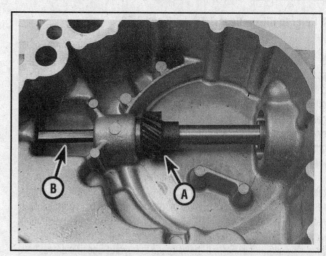

9.13 While the cover is off, inspect the camshaft position sensor driven gear (A) and the shaft (B)

9.16 With the new cover gasket on the engine, apply a small bead of RTV sealant along the pan-to-cover flange, and a small bead on each side where the pan, cover and block meet

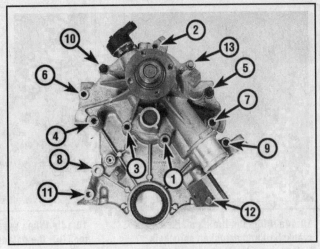

9.18 Timing chain cover bolt tightening sequence

15 Apply a small bead of RTV sealant along the oil pan-to-block joints.

16 Install the front cover gasket on the block and press it into place. Then again apply a small bead of RTV sealant to the block-to-pan joints and along the front edge of the oil pan (see illustration).

17 Slide the front cover onto the engine. The dowel pins will position it correctly. Don't damage the crankshaft front oil seal and make sure the gasket remains in place.

18 Install the bolts finger tight. Follow the correct sequence (see

illustration) and tighten them to the torque listed in this Chapter's Specifications only after the water pump has been installed (some of the water pump bolts also hold the timing chain cover in place).

➡ **Note: When installing the water pump, be sure to coat the threads of the water pump bolts with sealant.**

19 Install the oil pan bolts (see Section 13).

20 Install the remaining parts in the reverse order of removal.

21 Add engine oil and coolant (see Chapter 1).

22 Run the engine and check for leaks.

---

10 Timing chain and sprockets - inspection, removal and installation

INSPECTION

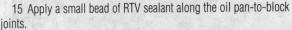

▶ **Refer to illustration 10.4**

1 Disconnect the cable from the negative battery terminal (see Chapter 5, Section 1)

2 Refer to Section 3 and position the number one piston several degrees before TDC on the compression stroke.

3 Remove the right valve cover (see Section 4).

4 Loosen the number one cylinder rocker arms and turn them out of the way, then attach a dial indicator to the cylinder head with the plunger in-line with and resting on the pushrod (see illustration).

5 Remove the timing chain cover (see Section 9).

6 Temporarily remove the timing chain and sprockets to remove the chain tensioner (see below).

7 Temporarily install the timing chain and sprockets without the tensioner and slip the timing chain cover and vibration damper in place to provide timing marks.

8 Turn the crankshaft clockwise until the number one piston is at TDC (see Section 3). This will take up the slack on the right side of the chain.

10.4 Install a dial indicator to measure timing chain deflection - use a short length of vacuum hose to hold the plunger on the pushrod (rocker arm removed), if necessary, so it doesn't slip off (typical)

10.14a Align the timing marks on the crankshaft and camshaft sprockets before removing the sprockets from the shafts

10.14b When the marks are aligned for TDC, the balance shaft keyway will point straight up

10.15 Remove the camshaft sprocket bolt without turning the engine

10.16 Compress the timing chain tensioner with a screwdriver and insert a drill bit or punch as a retaining pin

10.17 Remove the camshaft sprocket and chain from the camshaft

9 Zero the dial indicator.

10 Slowly turn the crankshaft counterclockwise until the slightest movement is seen on the dial indicator. Stop and note how far the number one piston has moved away from TDC by looking at the ignition timing marks.

11 If the mark has moved more than 6 degrees, install a new timing chain and sprockets.

REMOVAL

▶ **Refer to illustrations 10.14a, 10.14b, 10.15, 10.16 and 10.17**

12 Position the number one piston at TDC on the compression stroke (see Section 3).

13 Remove the timing chain cover (see Section 10). Try to avoid turning the crankshaft during vibration damper removal.

14 Make sure the crankshaft, camshaft and balance shaft sprocket timing marks are aligned (see illustrations). If they aren't, install the vibration damper bolt and use it to turn the crankshaft clockwise until all marks are aligned.

➡ **Note: When all marks are aligned, the crankshaft keyway is straight up, the camshaft keyway is straight down, and the balance shaft keyway is straight up.**

15 Remove the camshaft sprocket mounting bolt and camshaft position sensor drive gear (see illustration).

✴✴ CAUTION:

Do not allow the crankshaft to be turned from TDC while removing the camshaft sprocket bolt.

16 Compress the timing chain tensioner with a screwdriver and insert a drill bit, punch or Allen wrench as a retaining pin to hold it in the retracted position (see illustration).

17 Pull the camshaft sprocket/chain off the camshaft (see illustration).

➡ **Note: The crankshaft sprocket will slide off with the chain and camshaft sprocket.**

18 If you intend to remove the tensioner assembly, remove the two bolts holding it to the block.

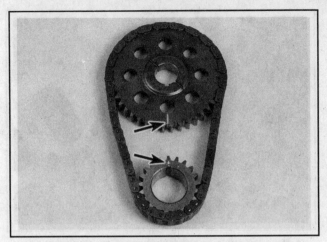

10.20 Assemble the chain and both sprockets so the marks are aligned, then slip the assembly onto the crankshaft and camshaft

10.22 Align the keyway on the camshaft position sensor drive gear with the Woodruff key on the camshaft

INSTALLATION

▶ **Refer to illustrations 10.20 and 10.22**

19 Turn the crankshaft until the key is facing up (12 o'clock position).

20 Drape the chain over the camshaft sprocket and turn the sprocket until the timing mark faces down (6 o'clock position). Position the chain over the camshaft and crankshaft sprockets with their timing marks aligned, then slip both sprockets onto the camshaft and crankshaft (see illustration).

21 When correctly installed, a straight line should pass through the center of the balance shaft gear, the camshaft, the camshaft timing mark (in the 6 o'clock position), the crankshaft timing mark (in the 12 o'clock position) and the center of the crankshaft (see illustrations 10.14a and 10.14b). DO NOT proceed until the valve timing is correct!

22 Install the camshaft position sensor drive gear (see illustration).

23 Apply a non-hardening thread locking compound to the threads and install the camshaft sprocket bolt. Tighten the bolt to the torque listed in this Chapter's Specifications.

24 Remove the retaining pin from the timing chain tensioner. Reinstall the remaining parts in the reverse order of removal.

11 Valve lifters - removal, inspection and installation

REMOVAL

▶ **Refer to illustrations 11.3a, 11.3b, 11.4a and 11.4b**

1 Remove the upper and lower intake manifold (see Section 6).

2 Remove the rocker arms and pushrods (see Section 5).

3 Before removing the lifters, arrange to store them in a clearly labeled box to ensure that they're reinstalled in their original locations. Remove the lifter guide plates (see illustrations).

4 There are several ways to extract the lifters from the bores. Spe-

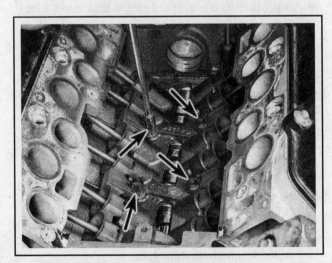

11.3a Remove the lifter guide plate bolts

11.3b Be sure to store the lifters in an organized manner to make sure they're reinstalled in their original locations

11.4a If the lifters are difficult to remove, you may have to remove them with a special puller . . .

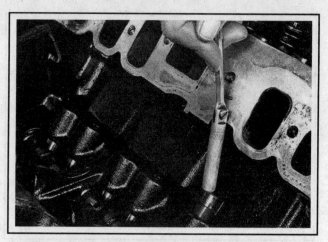

11.4b . . . or you may be able to remove the lifters with a magnet

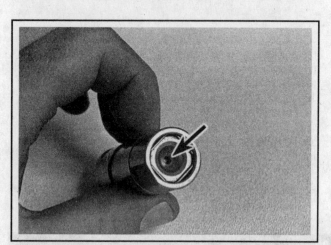

11.6 Inspect the pushrod seat in the top of each lifter for wear

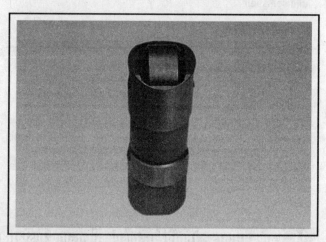

11.7 The roller must turn freely - check for wear and excessive play as well

cial tools designed to grip and remove lifters are manufactured by many tool companies and are widely available (see illustration), but may not be needed in every case. On newer engines without a lot of varnish buildup, the lifters can often be removed with a small magnet (see illustration) or even with your fingers. A machinist's scribe with a bent end can be used to pull the lifters out by positioning the point under the retainer ring in the top of each lifter.

☀ CAUTION:

Don't use pliers to remove the lifters unless you intend to replace them with new ones (along with the camshaft). The pliers may damage the precision machined and hardened lifters, rendering them useless. On engines with a lot of sludge and varnish, work the lifters up and down, using carburetor cleaner spray to loosen the deposits.

INSPECTION

◆ **Refer to illustrations 11.6 and 11.7**

5   Clean the lifters with solvent and dry them thoroughly without mixing them up.

6   Check each lifter wall and pushrod seat for scuffing, score marks and uneven wear. If the lifter walls are damaged or worn (which isn't very likely), inspect the lifter bores in the engine block as well. If the pushrod seats (see illustration) are worn, check the pushrod ends.

7   Check the roller carefully for wear and damage and make sure they turn freely without excessive play (see illustration).

8   If any lifters are found to be defective, they can be replaced with new ones without having to replace the camshaft (unlike conventional, non-roller lifters), but if the camshaft is being replaced due to high mileage, all the lifters should be replaced as well.

INSTALLATION

9   The original lifters, if they're being reinstalled, must be returned to their original locations. Coat them with moly-base grease or engine assembly lube.

10 Install the lifters in the bores.

11 Install the guide plates and tighten the bolts to the torque listed in this Chapter's Specifications.

12 Install the pushrods and rocker arms.

13 Install the intake manifold and valve covers.

14 Change the engine oil and filter (see Chapter 1).

12 Camshaft, balance shaft and bearings - removal, inspection and installation

CAMSHAFT LOBE LIFT CHECK

1 In order to determine the extent of cam lobe wear, the lobe lift should be checked prior to camshaft removal. Refer to Section 4 and remove the valve covers. The rocker arms must also be removed (see Section 5), but leave the pushrods in place.

2 Position the number one piston at TDC on the compression stroke (see Section 3).

3 Beginning with the number one cylinder, mount a dial indicator on the engine and position the plunger in-line with and resting on the first pushrod (see illustration 10.4).

4 Zero the dial indicator, then very slowly turn the crankshaft in the normal direction of rotation until the indicator needle stops and begins to move in the opposite direction. The point at which it stops indicates maximum cam lobe lift.

5 Record this figure for future reference, then reposition the piston at TDC on the compression stroke.

6 Move the dial indicator to the remaining number one cylinder pushrod and repeat the check. Be sure to record the results for each valve.

7 Repeat the check for the remaining valves. Since each piston must be at TDC on the compression stroke for this procedure, work from cylinder-to-cylinder following the firing order sequence (see Section 3).

8 After the check is complete, compare the results to the Specifications. If camshaft lobe lift is less than specified, cam lobe wear has occurred and a new camshaft should be installed.

REMOVAL

▶ **Refer to illustrations 12.11, 12.12 and 12.13**

9 Refer to the appropriate Sections and remove the pushrods, the valve lifters and the timing chain and camshaft sprocket. The radiator should be removed also (see Chapter 3). You also may have to remove the air conditioning condenser and the grille as well, but wait and see if the camshaft can be pulled out of the engine.

10 Check the camshaft end play with a dial indicator aligned with the front of the camshaft. Insert the camshaft sprocket bolt and use it to pull the camshaft fore and aft. If the play is greater than specified, replace the thrust plate with a new one when the camshaft is reinstalled.

11 Slide the larger balance shaft drive gear from the end of the camshaft (see illustration).

12 Remove the camshaft thrust plate bolts. A T-30 Torx bit is required. Remove the thrust plate and the spacer ring (see illustration).

13 Carefully pull the camshaft out. Support the cam so the lobes don't nick or gouge the bearings as it's withdrawn (see illustration).

INSPECTION

▶ **Refer to illustration 12.15**

14 After the camshaft has been removed, clean it with solvent and dry it, then inspect the bearing journals for uneven wear, pitting and evidence of seizure. If the journals are damaged, the bearing inserts in

12.11 Slide the balance shaft drive gear from the camshaft

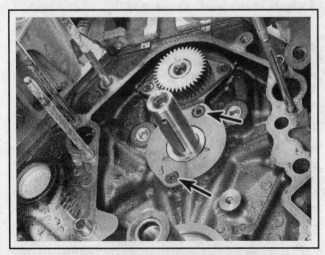

12.12 T-30 Torx screws retain the camshaft thrust plate - remove the thrust plate and spacer (at center of plate)

12.13 Carefully guide the camshaft out of the engine block to avoid nicking the bearings with the lobes

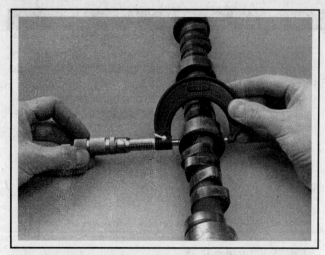

12.15 The camshaft bearing journal diameters are checked to pinpoint excessive wear and out-of-round conditions

12.17 Remove the balance shaft thrust plate bolts . . .

12.18 . . . and guide the balance shaft out with one hand supporting the shaft inside the engine's valley

the engine block are probably damaged as well. Both the camshaft and bearings will have to be replaced. Replacement of the camshaft bearings requires special tools and techniques which place it beyond the scope of the home mechanic. The engine block will have to be removed from the vehicle and taken to an automotive machine shop for this procedure.

15 Measure the bearing journals with a micrometer (see illustration) to determine whether they are excessively worn or out-of-round.

16 Inspect the camshaft lobes for heat discoloration, score marks, chipped areas, pitting and uneven wear. If the lobes are in good condition and if the lobe lift measurements are as specified, you can reuse the camshaft.

BALANCE SHAFT

▶ **Refer to illustrations 12.17 and 12.18**

17 Remove the bolts holding the balance shaft thrust plate (see illustration).

18 Carefully guide the balance shaft out of the block (see illustration).

➡ **Note: There is very little to go wrong with the balance shaft or its bearings, which are pressed into the front and rear of the block like camshaft bearings. If abnormal wear is noticed on either bearings or the front and rear balance shaft journals, the bearings must be replaced at an automotive machine shop, and a new balance shaft installed. The balance shaft gear can be replaced without replacing the balance shaft, but requires a machine shop press to replace it or the thrust plate on the balance shaft.**

19 When reinstalling the balance shaft, lubricate the front and rear journals and the back of the thrust plate with camshaft installation or engine assembly lube, and line the gear's keyway at the 12 o'clock position. Torque the thrust plate bolts to Specifications listed in this Chapter.

INSTALLATION

▶ **Refer to illustrations 12.20 and 12.21**

20 Lubricate the camshaft bearing journals and cam lobes with camshaft installation lube (see illustration).

21 Slide the camshaft into the engine. Support the cam near the engine block and be careful not to scrape or nick the bearings. Align the camshaft keyway straight down (6 o'clock position) and the balance shaft drive gear (on the camshaft) should align perfectly with the smaller gear on the balance shaft. Align their marks (see illustration).

22 Apply moly-base grease or engine assembly lube to both sides of the thrust plate, then position it on the engine block with the oil grooves in (against the engine block). Install the bolts and tighten them to the torque listed in this Chapter's Specifications.

23 Refer to the appropriate Sections and install the lifters, pushrods, rocker arms, timing chain/sprocket, timing chain cover and valve covers.

24 The remaining installation steps are the reverse of removal.

25 Before starting and running the engine, change the oil and install a new oil filter and refill the cooling system (see Chapter 1).

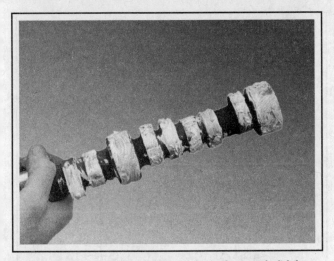

12.20 Apply camshaft installation lube to the camshaft lobes and journals prior to installation

12.21 Align the marks on the balance shaft drive gear on the camshaft (A) and the balance shaft driven gear (B) above it

13 Oil pan - removal and installation

REMOVAL

▶ **Refer to illustration 13.8**

1 Disconnect the cable from the negative battery terminal (see Chapter 5, Section 1)
2 Remove the oil dipstick (see Section 7).
3 Drain the engine oil and remove the oil filter (see Chapter 1).

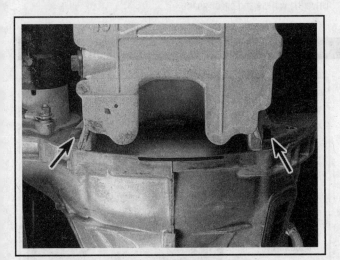

13.8 Remove the two oil pan-to-transmission bolts

4 Raise the vehicle and place it securely on jackstands.
5 Remove the crossmember bolts and the crossmember.
6 Remove the engine mount through-bolts (see Section 17).
7 Raise the engine about two inches with an engine hoist properly attached to the engine lifting brackets (see Chapter 2D).

✳ CAUTION:

Do not use a jack under the oil pan itself, it is cast-aluminum and can be damaged easily.

8 Remove the oil pan-to-transmission bolts (see illustration).
9 Remove the oil pan-to-engine bolts.
10 Remove the oil pan. It may be necessary to break the seal of the pan with a thin putty knife, but do not pry between the pan and block or the pan's sealing edge could be gouged, leading to oil leaks later. Empty any residual oil from the oil pan, and clean it out with solvent.

INSTALLATION

▶ **Refer to illustrations 13.13 and 13.16**

11 Use a gasket scraper or putty knife to remove all traces of old gasket material and sealant from the pan and engine block. Remove the oil pan rubber seal at the rear main seal housing and clean any sealant residue with lacquer thinner.
12 Clean the mating surfaces with lacquer thinner or acetone. Make sure the bolt holes in the engine block are clean.

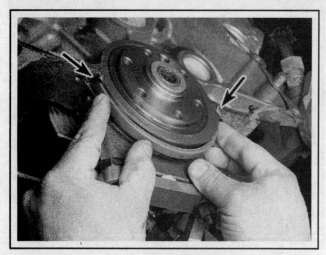

13.13 Press the new rear rubber seal onto the rear main cap and place a dab of RTV on each side

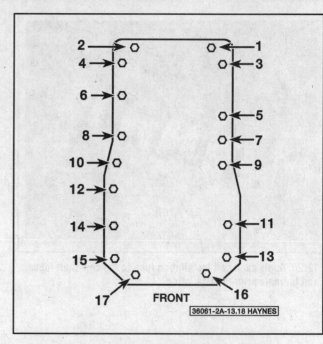

13.16 Oil pan bolt tightening sequence

13 Use a dab of gasket adhesive to hold the rear rubber seal in the rear main cap, using a small screwdriver to force the new seal tightly into the groove (see illustration). Stick the side gaskets in place on the engine block with a few dabs of adhesive and tuck the front and rear tabs into the slots in the ends of the front and rear rubber seals. Apply a dab of RTV sealant to the four corners where the side gaskets meet the end seals.

14 Make two alignment dowels by cutting off the heads of two long bolts that fit the holes in the block. Slot the ends of the "studs" with a hacksaw and install one at the front of the block and one at the rear.

15 Apply a bead of RTV sealant on the block and front cover, and a small dab at each corner of the rubber rear seal.

✱ CAUTION:

The oil pan must be installed within 15 minutes or the sealant will "set up" then harden and must be cleaned off and new sealant applied.

16 Carefully position the pan against the engine block and install the bolts finger tight. When all of the pan-to-engine bolts are started, tighten the bolts to the torque listed in this Chapter's Specifications in two steps, removing the two alignment studs and replacing them with pan bolts. Follow the correct sequence (see illustration). After the pan-to-engine bolts are tightened, install and tighten the pan-to-transmission bolts.

17 The remaining steps are the reverse of removal.

✱ CAUTION:

Don't forget to add engine oil and install a new oil filter (see Chapter 1).

18 Start the engine and check carefully for oil leaks at the oil pan. Drive the vehicle and check again.

14 Oil pump - removal and installation

▶ **Refer to illustrations 14.2, 14.10 and 14.11**

1 Remove the oil filter (see Chapter 1).

2 Remove the oil pump cover and O-ring, then remove the gears from the cavity in the timing chain cover (see illustration). Discard the O-ring.

3 Clean and inspect the oil pump cavity. If the oil pump gear pocket in the timing chain cover is damaged or worn, replace the timing chain cover.

4 Remove all traces of gasket material from the oil pump cover.

5 To remove the pressure relief valve, first remove the timing chain cover from the engine (see Section 9). Drill a hole in the plug, then pry it out or remove it with a slide hammer and screw adapter. Remove the spring and valve from the bore.

6 Remove all metal chips from the bore and the valve, then check them carefully for wear, score marks and galling. If the bore is worn or

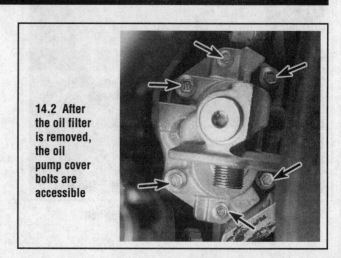

14.2 After the oil filter is removed, the oil pump cover bolts are accessible

14.10 To detach the oil pickup tube, remove the nut and bolts

14.11 Install a new O-ring lubricated with clean oil before reinstalling the oil pump

damaged, a new timing chain cover will be required. The valve should fit in the bore with no noticeable side play or binding.

7   If the spring appears to be fatigued or collapsed, replace it with a new spring.

8   Apply clean engine oil to the valve and install it in the bore, small end first. Insert the spring, then install a new plug. Carefully tap it in until it's 0.010-inch below the machined surface of the cover.

9   Install the intermediate shaft (see Section 9) and the camshaft position sensor (see Chapter 6).

10 The oil pump pickup tube is inside the oil pan. For access, remove the oil pan (see Section 13). Remove the pick-up tube nut and the two mounting bolts (see illustration). When reinstalling it, replace the gasket at the front.

11 Installation is the reverse of removal. Fill the oil pump with clean engine oil before installation. Install a new cover O-ring (see illustration) and tighten the bolts to the torque listed in this Chapter's Specifications in a criss-cross pattern. Use a new pick-up tube gasket and tighten the mounting bolts securely.

15 Crankshaft oil seals - replacement

FRONT SEAL - TIMING CHAIN COVER IN PLACE

▶ **Refer to illustrations 15.5 and 15.7**

1   Disconnect the cable from the negative battery terminal (see Chapter 5, Section 1)

2   Remove the engine cooling fan (see Chapter 3).

3   Remove the drivebelt (see Chapter 1).

4   Unbolt and remove the crankshaft pulley. Remove the bolt from the front of the crankshaft, then use a puller to detach the crankshaft pulley.

✷ CAUTION:

Don't use a puller with jaws that grip the outer edge of the damper. The puller must be the type that utilizes bolts to apply force to the damper hub only.

Clean the crankshaft nose and the seal contact surface on the pulley with lacquer thinner or acetone. Leave the Woodruff key in place in the crankshaft keyway.

➡ **Note: Lock the crankshaft pulley in place with a special strap-wrench designed for this purpose.**

5   Carefully remove the seal from the timing chain cover with a screwdriver or seal removal tool (see illustration). Be careful not to

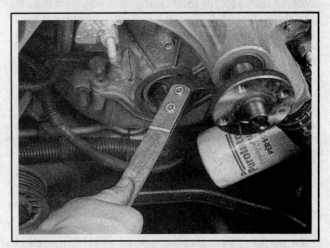

15.5 Use a screwdriver or seal removal tool (shown) to work the seal out of the timing chain cover - be very careful not to damage the cover or nick the crankshaft!

damage the cover or scratch the wall of the seal bore. If the engine has accumulated a lot of miles, apply penetrating oil to the seal-to-cover joint and allow it to soak in before attempting to remove the seal.

6   Check the seal bore and crankshaft, as well as the seal contact surface on the vibration damper for nicks and burrs. Position the new seal in the bore with the open end of the seal facing IN. A small amount

15.7 Clean the bore, then apply a small amount of oil to the outer edge of the new seal and drive it squarely into the opening with a large socket and a hammer - don't damage the seal in the process and make sure it's completely seated

15.15 The new seal can also be driven in carefully with the cover off the engine - be sure to support the cover from below with a wood block to prevent damage to the cover

15.17 If you're very careful not to damage the crankshaft or the seal bore, the rear seal can be pried out with a screwdriver - normally a special puller is used for this procedure

of oil applied to the outer edge of the new seal will make installation easier - don't overdo it!

7   Drive the seal into the bore with a seal driver or a large socket and hammer until it's completely seated (see illustration). If you're using a socket, select one that's the same outside diameter as the seal.

8   Apply moly-base grease or clean engine oil to the seal contact surface of the crankshaft pulley and coat the keyway (groove) with a thin layer of RTV sealant.

9   Install the pulley on the end of the crankshaft. The keyway in the pulley bore must be aligned with the Woodruff key in the crankshaft nose. If the pulley can't be seated by hand, tap it into place with a soft-face hammer or slip a large washer over the bolt, install the bolt and tighten it to press the pulley into place. Remove the large washer, then install the bolt and tighten it to the torque listed in this Chapter's Specifications.

10 Install the remaining parts removed for access to the seal.

11 Start the engine and check for leaks at the seal-to-cover joint.

FRONT SEAL - TIMING CHAIN COVER REMOVED

▶ **Refer to illustration 15.15**

12 Remove the timing chain cover (see Section 9).

13 Use a punch or screwdriver and hammer to drive the seal out of the cover from the back side. Support the cover as close to the seal bore as possible. Be careful not to distort the cover or scratch the wall of the seal bore. If the engine has accumulated a lot of miles, apply penetrating oil to the seal-to-cover joint on each side and allow it to soak in before attempting to drive the seal out.

14 Clean the bore to remove any old seal material and corrosion. Support the cover on blocks of wood and position the new seal in the bore with the open end of the seal facing IN. A small amount of oil applied to the outer edge of the new seal will make installation easier - don't overdo it!

15 Drive the seal into the bore with a seal driver or a large socket and hammer until it's completely seated (see illustration). If you're using a socket, select one that's the same outside diameter as the seal.

REAR MAIN SEAL

▶ **Refer to illustration 15.17**

16 Refer to Chapter 7 and remove the transmission, then remove the flywheel or driveplate and the rear cover plate from the engine (see Section 16).

17 The old seal can be removed by prying it out with a screwdriver (see illustration) or by making one or two small holes in the seal flange with a sharp pick, then using a screw-in type slide-hammer puller. Be sure to note how far the seal is recessed into the bore before removing it; the new seal will have to be recessed an equal amount.

✳✳ CAUTION:

Be very careful not to scratch or otherwise damage the crankshaft or the bore in the housing or oil leaks could develop!

---

18 Clean the crankshaft and seal bore with lacquer thinner or acetone. Check the seal contact surface very carefully for scratches and nicks that could damage the new seal lip and cause oil leaks. If the crankshaft is damaged, the only alternative is a new crankshaft.

19 Make sure the bore is clean, then apply a thin coat of engine oil to the outer edge of the new seal. Apply moly-based grease to the seal lips. The seal must be pressed squarely into the bore, a special seal installation tool is highly recommended. Hammering it into place is not recommended.

20 Reinstall the engine rear cover plate, the flywheel or driveplate and the transmission.

16 Flywheel/driveplate - removal and installation

▶ **Refer to illustrations 16.3, 16.4a and 16.4b**

1   Raise the vehicle and support it securely on jackstands, then refer to Chapter 7 and remove the transmission. If it's leaking, now would be a very good time to replace the front pump seal/O-ring (automatic transmission only).

2   Remove the pressure plate and clutch disc (see Chapter 8) (manual transmission equipped vehicles). Now is a good time to check/ replace the clutch components and pilot bearing.

3   Look for factory paint marks that indicate flywheel-to-crankshaft alignment. If they aren't there, use a center-punch or paint to make alignment marks on the flywheel/driveplate and crankshaft to ensure correct alignment during reinstallation (see illustration).

4   Remove the bolts that secure the flywheel/driveplate to the crankshaft (see illustration). If the crankshaft turns, use a flywheel-holding tool or wedge a screwdriver through the starter opening to jam the flywheel.

➡ **Note: On manual-shift transmission flywheels, there are two extra threaded holes. Insert two bolts in the holes and tighten them evenly from side to side to force the flywheel off the crankshaft (see illustration).**

5   Remove the flywheel/driveplate from the crankshaft. Since the flywheel is fairly heavy, be sure to support it while removing the last bolt.

❊❊ WARNING:

The flywheel is heavy and the ring gear teeth may be sharp, wear gloves to protect your hands.

6   Clean the flywheel with brake cleaner to remove grease and oil. Inspect the surface for cracks, rivet grooves, burned areas and score marks. Light scoring can be removed with emery cloth. Check for cracked and broken ring gear teeth. Lay the flywheel on a flat surface and use a straightedge to check for warpage.

7   Clean and inspect the mating surfaces of the flywheel/driveplate and the crankshaft. If the crankshaft rear seal is leaking, replace it before reinstalling the flywheel/driveplate.

8   Position the flywheel/driveplate against the crankshaft. Be sure to align the marks made during removal. Note that some engines have an alignment dowel or staggered bolt holes to ensure correct installation. Before installing the bolts, apply Teflon thread sealant to the threads.

9   Use a flywheel holding tool or wedge a screwdriver through the starter motor opening to keep the flywheel/driveplate from turning as you tighten the bolts to the torque listed in this Chapter's Specifications.

10   The remainder of installation is the reverse of the removal procedure.

16.3 Mark the position of the flywheel to preserve alignment

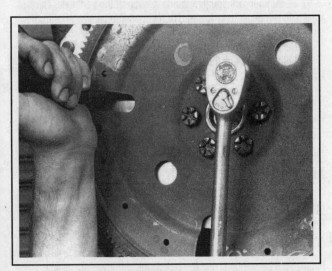

16.4a On automatic transmission driveplates, insert a prybar through a hole to keep the crankshaft from turning when loosening/tightening the bolts

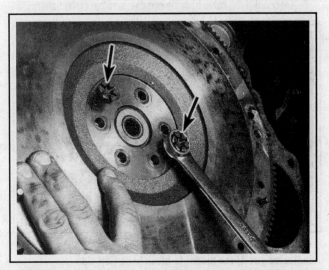

16.4b On manual transmission flywheels, use two bolts in the threaded holes to force the flywheel from the crankshaft

17 Engine mounts - check and replacement

.1   There are three powertrain mounts on the vehicles covered by this manual; left and right engine mounts attached to the engine block and to the frame and a rear mount attached to the transmission and the frame. The rear transmission mount is covered in Chapter 7. Engine mounts seldom require attention, but broken or deteriorated mounts should be replaced immediately or the added strain placed on the driveline components may cause damage or wear.

CHECK

2   During the check, the engine must be raised slightly to remove the weight from the mounts.

3   Raise the vehicle and support it securely on jackstands, then position a jack under the engine oil pan. Place a large wood block between the jack head and the oil pan, then carefully raise the engine just enough to take the weight off the mounts.

※ WARNING:

DO NOT place any part of your body under the engine when it's supported only by a jack!

4   Check for relative movement between the inner and outer portions of the mount (use a large screwdriver or prybar to attempt to move the mounts). If movement is noted, lower the engine and tighten the mount fasteners.

5   Check the mounts to see if the rubber is cracked, hardened or separated from the metal casing which would indicate a need for replacement.

6   Rubber preservative should be applied to the mounts to slow deterioration.

REPLACEMENT

7   Disconnect the cable from the negative terminal of the battery

17.13 Remove the engine mount through-bolts (A) - B indicates one of the mount-to-block bolts (left side shown here)

(see Chapter 5, Section 1).

8   Remove the engine cooling fan and shroud (see Chapter 3).

※ CAUTION:

Raising the engine with the cooling fan in place may damage the viscous clutch.

9   Raise the front of the vehicle and support it securely on jackstands.

10   Remove the engine cooling fan and the shroud (see Chapter 3).

11   Remove the starter (see Chapter 5) for right side engine mount replacement.

12   Support the engine with a lifting device from above.

※ CAUTION:

Do not connect the lifting device to the intake manifold.

Raise the engine just enough to take the weight off the engine mounts. If you're removing the driver's side engine mount, removal of the oil filter will be necessary.

2WD models

▶ **Refer to illustration 17.13**

13   Remove the engine mount-to-frame support bracket through-bolt (see illustration).

14   Remove the mount-to-engine block bolts, then remove the mount and the heat shield, if equipped.

15   Place the heat shield and the new mount in position, install the mount-to-engine block bolts and tighten all the bolts securely.

4WD models

16   Remove the engine skidplate.

17   Use a floor jack and jackstands to support the front axle. The front axle will be partially lowered to make additional clearance for the engine mount removal.

18   Remove the front crossmember (see Chapter 10).

19   Remove the bolts that attach the front axle to the frame (see Chapter 10).

20   Remove the engine mount-to-frame support bracket through-bolt.

21   Remove the engine mount to engine support bracket bolt and nuts.

22   Install the engine mount onto the engine support bracket and tighten the bolts securely.

All models

23   After the engine mounts have been installed onto the engine, lower the engine while guiding the engine mount and through-bolt into the frame support bracket. Install the through-bolt nut and tighten it securely.

24   The remainder of the installation is the reverse of removal. Remove the engine hoist and the jackstands and lower the vehicle.

Specifications

General

Displacement	4.2 liters (256 cubic inches)
Cylinder numbers (front-to-rear)	
Left (driver's) side	4-5-6
Right side	1-2-3
Firing order	1-4-2-5-3-6

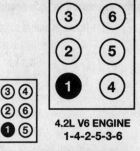

Cylinder and coil terminal locations - 4.2L V6 engine

4.2L V6 ENGINE
1-4-2-5-3-6

36061-1-specs.B HAYNES

Camshaft and lifters

Lobe lift	
Intake	0.24 inch
Exhaust	0.26 inch
Lobe wear limit	0.005 inch
Endplay	0.001 to 0.006 inch
Journal diameter (all)	2.0505 to 2.0515 inches
Journal-to-bearing (oil) clearance	0.001 to 0.003 inch
Journal runout limit	0.002 inch
Journal out-of-round limit	0.001 inch

Torque specifications*   Ft-lbs (unless otherwise indicated)

➡ **Note: One foot-pound (ft-lb) of torque is equivalent to 12 inch-pounds (in-lbs) of torque. Torque values below approximately 15 ft-lbs are expressed in inch-pounds, since most foot-pound torque wrenches are not accurate at these smaller values.**

Alternator bracket bolts	35
Air conditioning and power steering pump bracket	
Bolts	35
Nuts	18
Balance shaft thrust plate bolts	96 in-lbs
Camshaft sprocket bolt	33
Camshaft thrust plate bolts	96 in-lbs
Crankshaft pulley bolt	118
Crossmember bolts	66
Cylinder head bolts (oiled) (see illustration 8.22)	
Step 1	15
Step 2	30
Step 3	37

Step 4 - Loosen each bolt three 3 turns and then re-tighten it to the proper torque figure shown below (DO NOT loosen all the bolts at the same time. Work on one bolt at a time, in sequence. Remember, each bolt must be loosened 3 turns before making the final torque).

Long bolts	
Step 1	33
Step 2	Tighten an additional 180-degrees
Short bolts	
Step 1	18
Step 2	Tighten an additional 180-degrees
Drivebelt idler pulley bolt(s)	41
Exhaust manifold nuts	18
Flywheel/driveplate bolts	59

Torque specifications*   **Ft-lbs (unless otherwise indicated)**

➡ Note: One foot-pound (ft-lb) of torque is equivalent to 12 inch-pounds (in-lbs) of torque. Torque values below approximately 15 ft-lbs are expressed in inch-pounds, since most foot-pound torque wrenches are not accurate at these smaller values.

Intake manifold bolts	
Lower intake manifold-to-cylinder head (see illustration 6.27)	
Step 1	44 in-lbs
Step 2	89 in-lbs
Upper intake manifold-to-lower intake manifold (see illustration 6.30)	
Step 1	53 in-lbs
Step 2	89 in-lbs
Oil pan-to-block bolts	89 in-lbs
Oil pan-to-transmission bolts	25
Oil pan baffle bolts/nuts	24
Oil pump screen nuts	
Oil pump screen-to-main bearing cap nut	24
Oil pump screen-to-engine block nuts	18
Oil pump and filter body-to-front cover	
8-mm bolts	
2004 through 2006	18
2007 on	21
6-mm bolts	89 in-lbs
Rocker arm fulcrum bolts	
Step 1	44 in-lbs
Step 2	24
Timing chain cover-to-block bolts (see illustration 9.18)	
Bolt number 12 (capscrew)	89 in-lbs
Bolts 1 through 11 and 13	21
Oil pan-to-timing chain cover bolts	89 in-lbs
Timing chain tensioner bolts	96 in-lbs
Valve cover bolts	89 in-lbs
Valve lifter guide plate bolts	108 in-lbs

* Refer to Part D for additional specifications.

2B

3.5L AND 3.7L V6 ENGINES

Section

1   General information
2   Repair operations possible with the engine in the vehicle
3   Valve clearance - check and adjustment
4   Valve covers - removal and installation
5   Intake manifold(s) - removal and installation
6   Exhaust manifolds - removal and installation
7   Crankshaft pulley and crankshaft front seal - replacement
8   Cylinder heads - removal and installation
9   Engine front cover - removal and installation
10 Timing chain and sprockets - inspection, removal and installation
11 Camshaft and tappets - removal, inspection and installation
12 Oil pan - removal and installation
13 Oil pump - removal and installation
14 Driveplate - removal and installation
15 Turbocharger(s) (3.5L engine) - removal and installation
16 Rear main oil seal - replacement
17 Engine mounts - check and replacement

Reference to other Chapters

CHECK ENGINE light on - See Chapter 6
Cylinder compression check - See Chapter 2D
Drivebelt check, adjustment and replacement - See Chapter 1
Engine - removal and installation - See Chapter 2D
Engine oil and filter change - See Chapter 1
Engine overhaul - general information - See Chapter 2D
Spark plug replacement - See Chapter 1
Water pump - replacement - See Chapter 3

1 General information

This Part of Chapter 2 is devoted to in-vehicle repair procedures for the 3.5L and 3.7L V6 engines. These engines utilize a cast-aluminum block with six cylinders arranged in a V-shape at a 90-degree angle between the two banks. The cylinder heads are also cast-aluminum and the valve actuation is via two overhead camshafts in each cylinder head (one for the intake valves and one for the exhaust valves). The principle differences are that the 3.5L engine is equipped with direct injection of fuel into the cylinders and the use of two turbochargers, while the

3.7L engine does not have direct injection or turbochargers, but does have larger displacement. Information concerning engine removal and installation and engine overhaul can be found in Part D of this Chapter. The following repair procedures are based on the assumption that the engine is installed in the vehicle. If the engine has been removed from the vehicle and mounted on a stand, many of the steps outlined in this Part of Chapter 2 will not apply.

2 Repair operations possible with the engine in the vehicle

Many major repair operations can be accomplished without removing the engine from the vehicle.

Clean the engine compartment and the exterior of the engine with some type of pressure washer before any work is done. It will make the job easier and help keep dirt out of the internal areas of the engine.

It may help to remove the hood to improve access to the engine as repairs are performed (refer to Chapter 11 if necessary).

If vacuum, exhaust, oil or coolant leaks develop, indicating a need for gasket or seal replacement, the repairs can generally be made with the engine in the vehicle. The intake and exhaust manifold gaskets, timing cover gasket, oil pan gasket, crankshaft oil seals and cylinder head gaskets are all accessible with the engine in place.

Exterior engine components, such as the intake and exhaust mani-

folds, the oil pan (and the oil pump), the water pump, the starter motor, the alternator, and the fuel system components can be removed for repair with the engine in place.

Since the cylinder heads can be removed without pulling the engine, valve component servicing can also be accomplished with the engine in the vehicle. Replacement of the timing chain and sprockets is also possible with the engine in the vehicle.

In extreme cases caused by a lack of necessary equipment, repair or replacement of piston rings, pistons, connecting rods and rod bearings is possible with the engine in the vehicle. However, this practice is not recommended because of the cleaning and preparation work that must be done to the components involved.

3 Valve clearance - check and adjustment

▸ Refer to illustrations 3.5 and 3.8

➡ **Note: The engine must be cold before checking the valve clearances.**

➡ **Note: Checking and, if necessary, adjusting the valve clearance is only necessary after replacement of the camshaft(s) or other valve-related parts, or if the valvetrain is making excessive noise.**

1 Disconnect the cable from the negative terminal of the battery (see Chapter 5).

2 Remove the spark plugs (see Chapter 1).

3 Remove the valve covers (see Section 4).

4 Using a socket and a breaker bar on the crankshaft pulley center bolt, rotate the engine until the cam lobes on the cylinder to be checked are pointing away from the tappets.

5 Measure the clearance of the indicated valves with a feeler gauge (see illustration). Record each measurement and compare your measurements with the desired valve clearance found in this Chapter's Specifications. Note which are out of specification, as this data will be used later to determine the required replacement tappets.

3.5 Measure the clearance for each valve with a feeler gauge of the specified thickness - if the clearance is correct, you should feel a slight drag on the gauge as you pull it out

6 Repeat Steps 4 and 5 until the clearances for all valves have been measured.

7 If a clearance is out of specification, the tappet must be replaced with a new tappet that has a different thickness head to correct the clearance. Refer to Section 11 and remove the camshafts to access the tappets.

8 Mark the lifters that are to be replaced, and record which valve they came from. Use a micrometer to measure the thickness of the head of the lifter, making sure the measurement is precise and on the center projection on the underside of the lifter (see illustration).

9 To calculate the correct thickness for a replacement lifter that will place the valve clearance within the specified value, use the following formula:

$N = R + (M1 - M2)$
N = thickness of new tappet
R = thickness of old tappet
$M1$ = measured valve clearance
$M2$ = standard valve clearance

10 Lifters are marked on the underside as to their size. A marking of 3.310 on the underside of the lifter indicates a thickness value of 3.31 mm, or 0.13 inch.

11 Mark the new lifters as to their destination, lubricate them with

3.8 Use a micrometer to measure the thickness of the head of the tappet

engine assembly lube and install them. After replacing the lifters, refer to Section 11 to reinstall the camshafts and Section 10 to reinstall the timing chains, then re-check the valve clearances.

4 Valve covers - removal and installation

REMOVAL

1 If you're going to be removing the left valve cover on a 3.5L engine, relieve the fuel system pressure (see Chapter 4).

2 Disconnect the cable from the negative battery terminal (see Chapter 5, Section 1).

3 Remove the engine cover, if equipped.

4 Remove the ignition coils from the cover to be removed (see Chapter 5).

Left (driver's side) valve cover

♦ **Refer to illustration 4.5**

5 Disconnect the vent tube from the valve cover (see illustration).

6 Remove the dipstick.

7 If you're working on a 3.7L engine, remove the air intake duct and the air filter housing cover (see Chapter 4).

3.5L engine

8 Remove the nuts securing the charge air cooler bracket from the cylinder head.

9 Disconnect the two turbocharger regulator tubes and set them aside.

10 Remove the high-pressure fuel pump (see Chapter 4).

Right (passenger's side) valve cover

♦ **Refer to illustration 4.13**

11 Remove the air filter housing duct (see Chapter 4).

12 If you're working on a 3.7L engine, remove the upper intake manifold (see Section 5).

13 Detach the PCV hose from the valve cover (see illustration).

4.5 Detach the vent tube from the valve cover

4.13 Detach the PCV hose from the valve cover

4.14 Disconnect the electrical connectors from the VCT oil control solenoids in each valve cover

4.15 Valve cover fasteners

4.17 Check the spark plug tube seals, VCT solenoid seals and valve cover gasket. If they are in good condition they can be reused

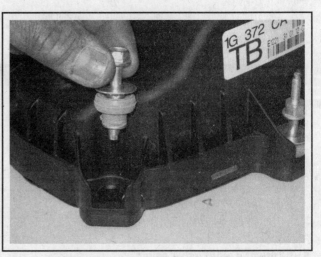

4.18 Check the bolt seals - replace them if they're not in good condition

Both valve covers

▶ **Refer to illustrations 4.14 and 4.15**

14 Disconnect the two electrical connectors at the valve cover for the VCT solenoids, being careful not to twist the solenoids (see illustration).

15 Remove the valve cover fasteners, then separate the wiring/clips and remove the valve cover from the cylinder head (see illustration). Use hand-pressure to wiggle the valve cover from the cylinder head.

✳✳ CAUTION:

If that doesn't work, do not use a hammer. Try to slip a flexible putty knife between the cylinder head and cover to break the gasket seal. Don't pry at the cover-to-cylinder head joint or damage to the sealing surfaces may occur (leading to oil leaks in the future).

INSTALLATION

▶ **Refer to illustrations 4.17, 4.18, 4.19 and 4.21**

16 The mating surfaces of each cylinder head and valve cover must be perfectly clean when the covers are installed. Remove all traces of sealant and old gasket material, then clean the mating surfaces with brake cleaner. If there's sealant or oil on the mating surfaces when the cover is installed, oil leaks may develop.

17 Inspect the spark plug seals, the seals for the VCT solenoids and the valve cover gasket (see illustration). Do not replace them unless necessary.

18 Make sure the bolt seals are in good condition, too (see illustration).

19 Apply a bead of RTV sealant to the joints where the engine front cover meets the cylinder head and install the valve cover within four minutes (see illustration).

4.19 Apply RTV sealant to the seams where the front cover meets the cylinder head

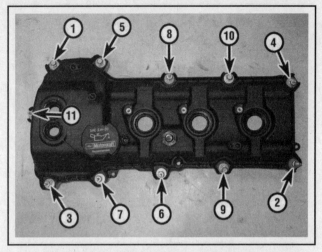

4.21 Valve cover bolt tightening sequence (left side shown, right side similar)

20 Carefully position the cover on the cylinder head and install the bolts.

21 Tighten the bolts a little at a time, in the proper sequence (see illustration), to the torque listed in this Chapter's Specifications.

22 The remaining installation steps are the reverse of removal.

23 Start the engine and check carefully for oil leaks as the engine warms up.

5 Intake manifold(s) - removal and installation

3.5L ENGINE

Removal

1 Disconnect the cable from the negative battery terminal (see Chapter 5, Section 1).

2 Remove the engine cover.

3 Remove the air filter housing and hoses (see Chapter 4).

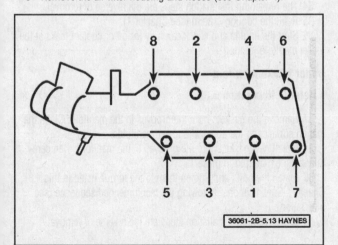

5.12 Intake manifold bolt tightening sequence - 3.5L V6 engine

4 Remove the three bolts and the engine cover bracket from the intake manifold.

5 Loosen the large hose clamp securing the hose to the charge air controller and remove the hose from the throttle body.

6 Disconnect the electrical connector at the throttle body.

7 Disconnect the PCV electrical connector.

8 Disconnect the brake booster vacuum hose from the intake manifold, then disconnect the MAP sensor and the EVAP canister purge valve connectors.

9 Disconnect the turbocharger vacuum regulator hose from the intake manifold, then release the pushpin securing the turbocharger vacuum regulator to the intake manifold.

10 Remove the manifold mounting bolts and detach the manifold from the engine.

➡ **Note: Do not use a hammer, and once the manifold is off, cover the intake ports of the engine with clean shop rags.**

Installation

◆ **Refer to illustration 5.12**

11 Remove the old gaskets from the manifold. Clean the manifold and cylinder head mating surfaces.

12 Install the new manifold gaskets to the grooves in the manifold. Install the manifold and bolts. Tighten the bolts in the indicated sequence to the torque listed in this Chapter's Specifications (see illustration).

13 The remainder of the installation is the reverse of removal.

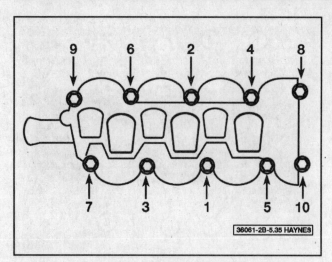

5.33 Lower intake manifold bolt tightening sequence - 3.7L V6 engine

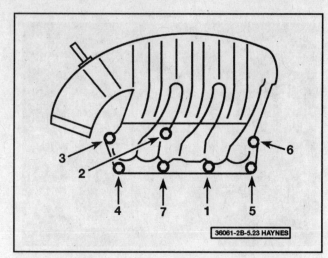

5.39 Upper intake manifold bolt tightening sequence - 3.7L V6 engine

3.7L ENGINE

Removal

14 If you're going to be removing the lower intake manifold, relieve the fuel system pressure (see Chapter 4).

15 Disconnect the cable from the negative battery terminal (see Chapter 5, Section 1).

Upper intake manifold

16 Remove the air filter housing and hoses (see Chapter 4).

17 Remove the PCV tube from the manifold.

18 Disconnect the electrical connector from the throttle body (see Chapter 4).

19 Disconnect the EVAP tube and the EVAP canister purge valve electrical connector (see Chapter 4).

20 Disconnect the vacuum hose connector and the brake booster vacuum hose from the rear of the upper intake manifold.

21 Disconnect the PCV valve hoses from the valve covers and remove them from the engine (see Chapter 6).

22 Remove the upper intake support bracket from the right cylinder head.

23 Remove the mounting bolts from the upper intake manifold, then lift the upper manifold off of the lower manifold.

24 Cover the air intake passages with a shop towel to prevent tools or debris from falling inside the engine.

Lower intake manifold

> **※ WARNING:**
>
> **Wait until the engine is completely cool before beginning this procedure.**

25 Remove the upper intake manifold.

26 Drain the cooling system (see Chapter 1).

27 Cover the drivebelt with plastic wrap, then remove the thermostat housing (see Chapter 3). Disconnect the heater hose from the manifold.

28 Detach the fuel line from the fuel rail (see Chapter 4).

29 Disconnect the electrical connectors from the injectors.

30 Loosen the intake manifold mounting bolts in 1/4-turn increments in the reverse of the tightening sequence (see illustration 5.33) until they can be removed by hand.

Installation

Lower intake manifold

▶ **Refer to illustration 5.33**

31 Remove the gaskets from the grooves in the manifold. Clean the manifold and cylinder head mating surfaces.

32 Install new gaskets into the grooves in the manifold, then carefully set the manifold in place.

33 Install the bolts and tighten them to the torque listed in this Chapter's Specifications, following the recommended sequence (see illustration).

34 The remaining installation steps are the reverse of removal.

35 Refill the cooling system (see Chapter 1).

36 Start the engine and check carefully for oil or coolant leaks at the intake manifold joints.

Upper intake manifold

▶ **Refer to illustration 5.39**

37 Remove the gaskets from the grooves in the manifold. Clean the mating surfaces of the upper and lower manifolds.

38 Install new gaskets into the grooves in the manifold, then carefully set the manifold in place.

39 Install the bolts and tighten them to the torque listed in this Chapter's Specifications, following the recommended sequence (see illustration).

40 The remaining installation steps are the reverse of removal.

6   Exhaust manifolds - removal and installation

REMOVAL

▶ **Refer to illustrations 6.5 and 6.9**

1   Disconnect the cable from the negative battery terminal (see Chapter 5, Section 1)

2   Loosen the wheel lug nuts on the side of the vehicle from which the exhaust manifold is to be removed, then raise the vehicle and support it securely on jackstands.

3   Disconnect the oxygen sensor electrical connectors (see Chapter 6).

4   Working under the vehicle, apply penetrating oil to the exhaust Y-pipe-to-manifold (or turbocharger) studs and nuts (they're usually rusty).

5   Remove the nuts holding the exhaust Y-pipe to the exhaust manifolds or turbochargers (see illustration).

6   Remove the wheel and the inner fender liner.

7   On 3.5L engines, remove the turbocharger (see Section 15).

8   On 3.7L engines, remove the two bolts and remove the exhaust manifold heat shield.

9   Remove the manifold mounting nuts and detach the manifold from the cylinder head (see illustration).

➡ **Note: The manufacturer recommends removing the exhaust manifold mounting studs from the cylinder heads and installing new studs.**

10   Remove the exhaust gaskets and clean the gasket surfaces on the manifold and cylinder heads.

INSTALLATION

➡ **Note: The manufacturer recommends removing the exhaust mounting studs from the cylinder heads and installing new studs.**

11   Check the exhaust manifold for cracks and make sure all the stud threads are clean and undamaged. The exhaust manifold and cylinder head mating surfaces must be clean before the manifolds are reinstalled.

12   Position the exhaust manifold and new gasket over the studs on the cylinder head and install the mounting nuts.

13   When tightening the nuts, tighten the center pair first, then the front pair, then the rear pair, to the torque listed in this Chapter's Specifications is reached.

14   The remaining installation steps are the reverse of removal.

15   Start the engine and check for exhaust leaks.

6.5 From below, remove the two exhaust Y-pipe-to-manifold nuts (left side shown, right side similar)

6.9 Exhaust manifold upper mounting nuts (three more below) (right-side exhaust manifold shown, left side similar)

7   Crankshaft pulley and crankshaft front seal - replacement

REPLACEMENT WITH TIMING CHAIN COVER IN PLACE

1   Disconnect the cable from the negative battery terminal (see Chapter 5, Section 1)

2   Remove the drivebelt (see Chapter 1).

3   On 3.5L engines, remove the air filter housing pipe and the turbocharger pipes.

4   Secure the crankshaft from rotating with a strap or chain wrench (wrap a length of rag or old drivebelt around the pulley to protect it). Remove the bolt from the front of the crankshaft, then use a three-jaw puller to detach the crankshaft pulley.

✳ CAUTION:

Don't use a puller with jaws that grip the outer edge of the damper. The puller must be the type that applies force to the damper hub only.

Clean the crankshaft nose and the seal contact surface on the pulley with RTV remover. Leave the Woodruff key in place in the crankshaft keyway.

5   Carefully remove the seal from the timing chain cover with a screwdriver or seal removal tool. Be careful not to damage the cover or scratch the wall of the seal bore. If the engine has accumulated a lot of miles, apply penetrating oil to the seal-to-cover joint and allow it to soak in before attempting to remove the seal.

6   Check the seal bore and crankshaft, as well as the seal contact surface on the pulley for nicks and burrs. Position the new seal in the bore with the open end of the seal facing IN. A film of engine oil applied to the outer edge of the new seal will make installation easier.

7   Drive the seal into the bore with a seal driver or a large socket and hammer until it's completely seated. If you're using a socket, select one that's the same outside diameter as the seal.

8   Apply clean engine oil to the seal contact surface of the crankshaft pulley and coat the keyway (groove) with a thin layer of RTV sealant.

9   Install the pulley on the end of the crankshaft. The keyway in the pulley bore must be aligned with the Woodruff key in the crankshaft nose. If the pulley can't be seated by hand, tap it into place with a soft-face hammer or slip a large washer over the bolt, install the bolt and tighten it to press the pulley into place. Remove the large washer, then install the bolt and tighten it in Steps to the torque listed in this Chapter's Specifications.

10 Install the remaining parts removed for access to the seal.

11 Start the engine and check for leaks.

REPLACEMENT WITH ENGINE FRONT COVER REMOVED

12 Remove the engine front cover (see Section 9).

13 Use a punch or screwdriver and hammer to drive the seal out of the cover from the back side. Support the cover as close to the seal bore as possible, using blocks of wood. Be careful not to distort the cover or scratch the wall of the seal bore. If the engine has accumulated a lot of miles, apply penetrating oil to the seal-to-cover joint on each side and allow it to soak in before attempting to drive the seal out.

14 Clean the bore to remove any old seal material and corrosion. Support the cover on blocks of wood and position the new seal in the bore with the open end of the seal facing IN. A film of oil applied to the outer edge of the new seal will make installation easier.

15 Drive the seal into the bore with a seal driver or a large socket and hammer until it's completely seated. If you're using a socket, select one that's the same outside diameter as the seal.

16 Reinstall the engine front cover and crankshaft pulley (see Steps 8 and 9).

17 Start the engine and check for leaks.

8   Cylinder heads - removal and installation

❋❋ WARNING:

Wait until the engine is completely cool before beginning this procedure.

REMOVAL

1   Relieve the fuel system pressure (see Chapter 4), then disconnect the cable from the negative battery terminal (see Chapter 5, Section 1).

2   Drain the cooling system (see Chapter 1).

3   Remove the intake manifold(s) (see Section 5).

4   Remove the exhaust manifold (see Section 6).

5   Remove the valve covers (see Section 4).

6   Remove the camshafts and tappets (see Section 11).

7   Remove the drivebelt and the drivebelt tensioner (see Chapter 1).

8   Remove the two Camshaft Position (CMP) sensors at the rear of each cylinder head. Disconnect any other electrical connectors from the cylinder head and mark them with tape for correct reassembly.

9   Loosen the cylinder head bolts in 1/4-turn increments until they can be removed by hand. Work from bolt-to-bolt in a pattern that's the reverse of the tightening sequence (see illustration 8.18).

➡ **Note: Remove the bolts and discard them - new bolts must be used when installing the cylinder head(s).**

10 Lift the cylinder head(s) off the engine. If resistance is felt, DO NOT pry between the cylinder head and engine block as damage to the mating surfaces will result. To dislodge the cylinder head, place a wood block against the end of it and strike the wood block with a hammer or pry against a casting protrusion. Store the cylinder heads on blocks of wood to prevent damage to the gasket sealing surfaces.

11 Cylinder head disassembly and inspection procedures should be performed by a qualified automotive machine shop.

INSTALLATION

▶ **Refer to illustrations 8.13 and 8.18**

12 The mating surfaces of the cylinder heads and engine block must be perfectly clean when the cylinder heads are installed.

❋❋ CAUTION:

Do not use a scraper of any kind or abrasive discs to remove old gasket material, as the block, heads and intake manifold(s) are aluminum. Cover all openings with shop rags to keep debris out of the engine. Use a vacuum cleaner to remove any debris that falls into the valley or intake ports.

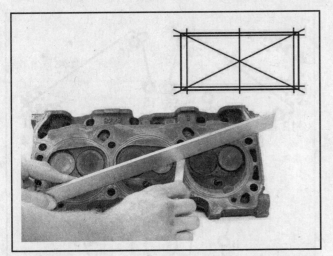

8.13 Check the cylinder head and block surfaces for flatness with a straightedge

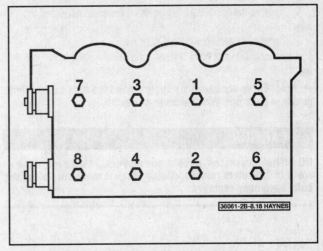

8.18 Cylinder head bolt tightening sequence

13 Check the engine block and cylinder head mating surfaces for nicks, deep scratches and other damage. If damage is slight, it can be removed with a file - if it's excessive, machining may be the only alternative. Use a straightedge and feeler gauges to check for warpage (see illustration). If the warpage is beyond Specifications, have the head machined at an automotive machine shop.

14 Use a tap of the correct size to chase the threads in the block head bolt holes. Dirt, corrosion, sealant and damaged threads will affect torque readings.

15 Position the new gasket(s) over the dowel pins in the engine block. Make sure it's facing the right way. If the cylinder head is to be replaced, a new secondary timing chain tensioner will be required.

16 Carefully position the cylinder head(s) on the engine block without disturbing the gasket(s).

17 Before installing the new cylinder head bolts, lightly oil the threads.

18 Install the bolts and tighten them finger tight. Tighten the bolts, in the recommended sequence, to the torque listed in this Chapter's Specifications (see illustration).

19 The remaining installation steps are the reverse of removal.

20 Change the engine oil and filter and refill the cooling system (see Chapter 1), then start the engine and check carefully for oil and coolant leaks.

9 Engine front cover - removal and installation

▶ Refer to illustration 9.5

✸ WARNING:

The engine must be completely cool before beginning this procedure.

REMOVAL

1 Drain the cooling system and engine oil, and remove the oil filter (see Chapter 1).

2 If you're working on a 3.5L engine, remove the intake manifold (see Section 5).

3 Remove the valve covers (see Section 4).

4 Remove the crankshaft pulley (see Section 7).

5 Remove the drivebelt tensioner (see Chapter 1) and remove all accessory brackets attached to the timing chain cover (see illustration).

9.5 Remove the drivebelt, the idler pulley (indicated), alternator and crankshaft pulley

6   Remove the alternator bolt and swing the alternator out of the way.

7   Remove the water pump (see Chapter 3).

8   Remove the front cover bolts and separate the cover from the engine block.

➡ **Note: There are seven pry spots around the front cover. Work gently at each one until the cover comes off.**

✳ CAUTION:

DO NOT use excessive force or you may crack the cover. If the cover is difficult to remove, double check to make sure all of the bolts have been removed.

INSTALLATION

▶ **Refer to illustration 9.14**

9   Clean the gasket mating surfaces with brake system cleaner.

10   While the cover is off the engine, it's a good idea to install a new crankshaft front seal (see Section 7). There is also a radial seal in the center of the front cover. Install a new radial seal before mounting the front cover.

11   Apply a 1/8-inch bead of RTV sealant to the mating surface of the cover.

12   Apply a 3/16-inch bead of sealant to the areas where the oil pan and cylinder heads meet the engine block.

13   Slide the front cover onto the engine. The dowel pins will position it correctly.

14   Install the bolts finger tight. The first Stage is placement of bolts 1, 2, 7, 8, 15, 17, 18, 19, 20 and 21. Following the correct sequence (see illustration), tighten them to the torque listed in this Chapter's Specifications within ten minutes of installation. The remaining bolts

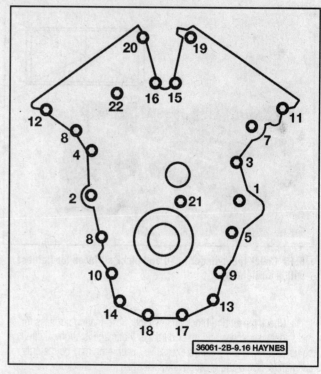

9.14 Engine front cover bolt locations - see this Chapter's Specifications for the tightening sequence

must be tightened within 35 minutes.

15   Install the remaining parts in the reverse order of removal.

16   Install a new oil filter, then add engine oil and coolant (see Chapter 1).

17   Run the engine and check for leaks.

10 Timing chain and sprockets - removal and installation

✳ CAUTION:

These engines are difficult to work on and require some special tools. On any procedure involving the timing chains, the Steps must be read carefully and disassembly must proceed using the special tools, otherwise damage to the engine will result.

✳ CAUTION:

Because this is an "interference" engine design, if the timing chain has broken, there will be damage to the valves (and possibly the pistons) and will require removal of the cylinder heads.

✳ CAUTION:

The timing system is complex. Severe engine damage will occur if you make any mistakes. Do not attempt this procedure unless you are highly experienced with this type of repair. If you are at all unsure of your abilities, consult an expert. Double-check all your work and be sure everything is correct before you attempt to start the engine.

REMOVAL

▶ **Refer to illustrations 10.5 and 10.10**

1   Disconnect the cable from the negative battery terminal (see Chapter 5, Section 1).

2   Remove the valve covers (see Section 4).

3   Remove the engine front cover (see Section 9).

4   Turn the engine clockwise until the VCT units (camshaft sprockets) on each intake camshaft are positioned at 90-degrees (12 o'clock)

10.5 Remove three of the camshaft cap bolts to remove the valvetrain oil tubes

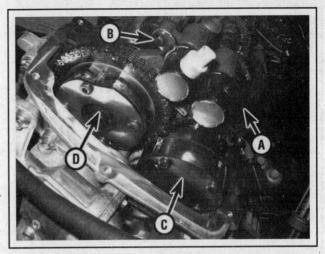

10.10 Remove the VCT oil control solenoid mounting bolts (A and B) - (C) is the exhaust VCT unit and (D) is the intake VCT unit

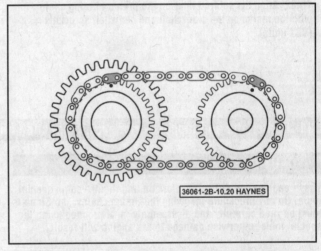

10.20 Align the colored links of the secondary timing chain with the marks on the back of the sprockets (VCT units)

in relation to the top surface of the cylinder heads.

5   Remove the bolts that secure the valvetrain oil tubes to each cylinder head (see illustration).

6   Install the special camshaft locking tools (303-1248), with the tools holding the flats on each camshaft.

7   If you can't see the timing marks on the timing chain, add a paint dot to align with the marks on the VCT units and the crankshaft timing sprocket.

8   Remove the two bolts and the primary timing chain tensioner arm, then unbolt and remove the two tensioners.

9   Remove the mounting bolts and the lower-left chain guide, then the lower right chain guide.

10 Remove the bolts securing the VCT solenoids to the cylinder heads (see illustration). You may have to twist or wiggle the solenoids to disengage them.

➡ **Note: The intake solenoids are white, the exhaust solenoids are black.**

11 Keep the VCT solenoids in clean plastic sandwich bags, marked with their destination.

12 Remove the primary timing chain.

13 The two camshafts on each cylinder head are jointly driven by a smaller secondary timing chain.

14 Depress and lock the secondary chain tensioner on each bank, using the factory tool (303-1530) inserted in the large hole at the camshaft first bearing cap, or a length of threaded rod and nuts to hold the tensioner down, by pushing from the camshaft bearing cap.

15 With the camshafts still locked at TDC, remove the mounting bolts from the VCT units (camshaft sprockets), and remove the sprockets and secondary timing chains from the camshafts.

16 If the primary timing chain sprocket (at the center of the front of the block) is to be replaced, remove the nine bolts securing the plate that mounts the gear to the front of the block.

INSTALLATION

▶ **Refer to illustrations 10.20 and 10.22**

17 If the primary chain gear and its plate were removed, clean the mounting surface and the block and install the sprocket and plate with

a new gasket. Prepare the primary chain tensioners by pushing in the release button and compressing the plunger until a nail or large paper clip can be inserted to hold the plunger.

18 If the secondary timing chain tensioners were removed, they cannot be reused. New tensioners must be installed.

✳✳ WARNING:

Do not remove the plastic clip that is keeping the new tensioner compressed.

19 The tensioner is installed to the correct depth when you hear a "snap" sound. Install the tensioner shoe. The plastic clip can now be removed with pliers.

20 Align the colored links with the marks on the VCT units and install the chain on the backside of the VCT units (see illustration). Align the two VCT units with the dowel pins on the front of the camshafts.

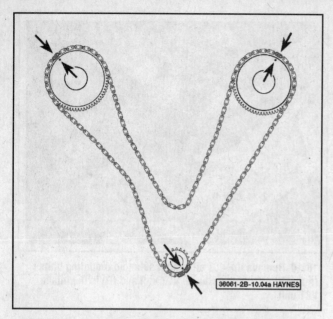

10.22 Align the colored links on the primary timing chain with the marks on the crankshaft and camshaft sprockets (VCT units)

21 New bolts must be used to install the VCT units. Tighten the bolts to the torque listed in this Chapter's Specifications.

22 When the secondary chains and VCT units are installed and aligned, install the primary timing chain, aligning the colored links with the marks on the sprockets (see illustration). When all components are installed and aligned, pull the pins holding back the two primary chain tensioners.

23 Reinstall the remaining parts in the reverse order of removal.

24 Carefully rotate the crankshaft by hand through at least two full revolutions (use a socket and breaker bar on the crankshaft pulley center bolt).

❋❋ CAUTION:

If you feel any resistance, STOP! There is something wrong - most likely, valves are contacting the pistons. You must find the problem before proceeding.

25 Install a new oil filter, then add engine oil and coolant (see Chapter 1).

26 Run the engine and check for leaks.

11 Camshafts and tappets - removal, inspection and installation

❋❋ CAUTION:

These engines are difficult to work on and require some special tools. On any procedure involving the timing chains, the Steps must be read carefully and disassembly must proceed using the special tools, otherwise damage to the engine will result.

❋❋ CAUTION:

Because this is an "interference" engine design, if the timing chain has broken, there will be damage to the valves (and possibly the pistons) and will require removal of the cylinder heads.

❋❋ CAUTION:

The timing system is complex. Severe engine damage will occur if you make any mistakes. Do not attempt this procedure unless you are highly experienced with this type of repair. If you are at all unsure of your abilities, consult an expert. Double-check all your work and be sure everything is correct before you attempt to start the engine.

REMOVAL

1 Before removing the camshafts, check the valve clearances (see Section 3).

2 Refer to Section 10 and remove the primary timing chain and camshaft VCT units.

3 Loosen the camshaft cap and "mega-cap" mounting bolts and remove the caps.

❋❋ CAUTION:

Keep the caps in order and don't mix them up.

Remove the camshafts from the cylinder head.

4 With the camshafts removed, the tappets can be removed using a magnet.

❋❋ CAUTION:

They must be stored in an egg carton or other divided and marked container, so they can be restored to their original locations during reassembly.

INSPECTION

▶ **Refer to illustrations 11.7a and 11.7b**

5 After the camshafts have been removed, clean them with solvent, then inspect the bearing journals for uneven wear and pitting. If the journals are damaged, the bearing saddles in the cylinder heads and caps are probably damaged as well. The head and camshaft caps will have to be replaced.

6 Measure the bearing journals with a micrometer and compare to

11.7a Lobe lift can be obtained by measuring camshaft lobe height . . .

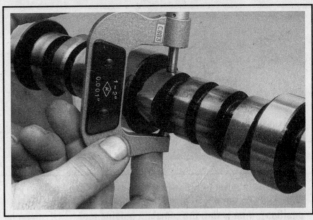

11.7b . . . and by measuring the camshaft base circle - the difference between the two measurements equals lobe lift

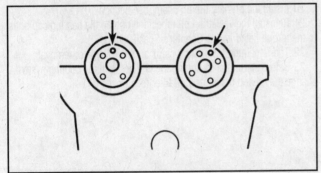

11.13a When installing the left (driver's) side cylinder head camshafts, position the dowel pins like this

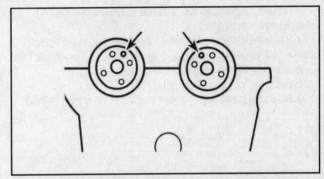

11.13b When installing the right (passenger's) side cylinder head camshafts, position the dowel pins like this

the Specifications in this Chapter to determine whether they are excessively worn or out-of-round.

7   Measure the camshaft lobe height and the base circle (see illustrations). The difference between the two measurements is the lobe lift (lobe height - base circle = lobe lift). Record this figure for future reference and repeat the check on the remaining camshaft lobes. Compare the results to the values listed in this Chapter's Specifications.

8   Inspect the camshaft lobes for heat discoloration, score marks, chipped areas, pitting and uneven wear. If the lobes are in good condition and if the lobe lift measurements are as specified, you can reuse the camshafts.

INSTALLATION

▶ **Refer to illustrations 11.13a, 11.13b, 11.14, 11.17a and 11.17b**

9   Rotate the crankshaft counterclockwise and position the keyway in the 9 o'clock position (this is the neutral position).

10   Lubricate the tappets with clean engine oil and reinstall them in their original locations. If any valve clearances were out-of-specification, replace the tappet(s) with new ones of the proper thickness to achieve the desired clearance.

11   At the front of each camshaft, there are two grooves to hold seals. Obtain new seals and install them in the camshaft grooves.

➥ **Note: The split where the ends of each seal come together must face UP (12 o'clock position) on the camshafts when they are installed.**

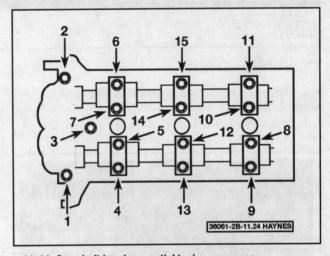

11.14 Camshaft bearing cap tightening sequence

12   Lubricate the camshaft bearing journals and cam lobes with moly-based grease or camshaft installation lubricant.

13   Position the camshafts in the cylinder head in their neutral positions (see illustrations).

14   Install the camshaft bearing caps (in their original locations), and tighten the bolts, in sequence, to the torque listed in this Chapter's Specifications (see illustration).

15   Recheck the valve clearances (see Section 3). Since the crankshaft is in the neutral position, the camshafts can be turned without the

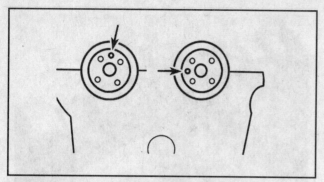

11.17a Rotate the left (driver's) side cylinder head camshafts so the dowel pins are positioned like this (TDC position), then install the camshaft holding tool

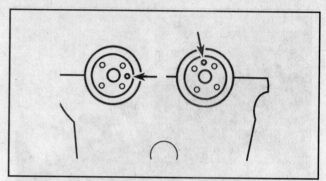

11.17b Rotate the right (passenger's) side cylinder head camshafts so the dowel pins are positioned like this (TDC position), then install the camshaft holding tool

valves contacting the pistons.

16 Remove the camshaft cap bolts that secure the valvetrain oil tubes. Remove the oil tubes.

17 Rotate the camshafts to position the dowel pins in their proper positions for installing the VCT units and secondary timing chains (see illustrations). Install the camshaft holding tools.

18 Install the VCT units (see Section 10).

19 Rotate the crankshaft clockwise to position the keyway in the 11

o'clock position.

20 Install the primary timing chain (see Section 10).

21 Reinstall the valvetrain oil tubes and tighten the bearing cap bolts to the torque listed in this Chapter's Specifications.

22 The remaining installation steps are the reverse of removal.

23 Before starting and running the engine, refill the cooling system, change the oil and install new oil filter (see Chapter 1).

12 Oil pan - removal and installation

REMOVAL

▶ **Refer to illustration 12.10**

1 Disconnect the cable from the negative battery terminal (see Chapter 5, Section 1).

2 Remove the oil dipstick.

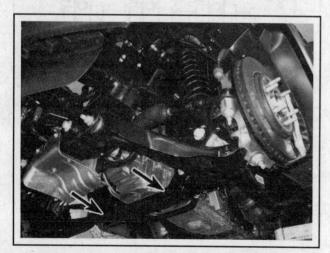

12.10 Remove the crossmember mounting fasteners

3 Drain the engine oil and remove the oil filter (see Chapter 1).

4 Raise the vehicle and support it securely on jackstands. On 4WD models, strap the front differential to a sturdy jack, remove the bushing bolts and lower the front axle enough to allow clearance for oil pan removal (see Chapter 8).

5 Disconnect the oxygen sensor harness clips and the starter motor harness clips from the oil pan. Position the harness out of the way.

6 Disconnect the alternator harness from the engine front cover.

7 Remove the under-vehicle splash shield by twisting the quarter-turn fasteners counterclockwise.

8 On models with an air dam below the radiator, remove the two bolts and the air dam.

9 On models with a skid-plate, remove the mounting bolts and the skid-plate.

10 Remove the nuts/bolts securing the crossmember below the oil pan, and remove the crossmember (see illustration).

11 Remove the front cover-to-oil pan bolts.

12 Remove the oil pan-to-transmission bolts.

13 Remove the oil pan-to-engine block bolts.

14 Loosen the following bolts 3/16-inch: the four upper bellhousing bolts, the bellhousing bolt above the starter motor, the two mounting bolts on the left side of the bellhousing, and the two nuts in the center of the transmission crossmember. Move the transmission rearward as allowed by the loosened fasteners.

15 There are two notches at the top rear corners of the oil pan where a large screwdriver can safely be used to pry the pan loose.

INSTALLATION

▶ **Refer to illustration 12.19**

✳✳ **CAUTION:**

✳✳ **CAUTION:**

Do not use abrasive discs or scrapers on either the engine or the pan mounting surfaces. The aluminum components can easily be gouged, leading to oil leakage.

16 Clean the surfaces of the pan, the engine, front cover and transmission of all traces of RTV sealant.

17 Apply a 7/32-inch (5.5 mm) bead of RTV sealant at the junctures of the rear main seal housing and the block, and also where the pan meets the front cover.

18 Apply a 1/8-inch (3 mm) bead of RTV sealant around the inner perimeter of the oil pan's mounting surface and install the oil pan. Install the four corner bolts within four minutes of applying the RTV sealant. Install and tighten the remaining bolts within an hour.

19 When all of the pan-to-engine bolts are started, tighten the bolts, in sequence, to the torque listed in this Chapter's Specifications (see illustration). After the pan-to-engine bolts are tightened, install and tighten the pan-to-transmission bolts, and all fasteners loosened in Step 14.

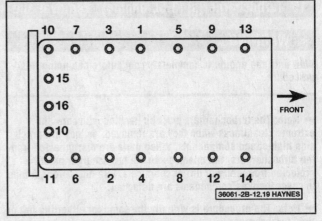

12.19 Oil pan-to-engine bolt tightening sequence

20 The remaining steps are the reverse of removal.

✳✳ **CAUTION:**

Don't forget to add engine oil and install a new oil filter (see Chapter 1), but wait at least 90 minutes before doing so.

21 Start the engine and check carefully for oil leaks at the oil pan.

13 Oil pump - removal and installation

1 Drain the oil and remove the oil filter (see Chapter 1).
2 Remove the engine front cover (see Section 9).
3 Remove the oil pan (see Section 12).
4 Remove the primary timing chain (see Section 10).
5 Slide the crankshaft sprocket from the crankshaft.
6 Remove the three fasteners and the oil pump pickup and screen assembly.

7 Remove the three oil pump mounting bolts and remove the oil pump.
8 Installation is the reverse of removal. After bolting the oil pump in place, reinstall the oil pump pickup tube and screen with a new O-ring.

14 Driveplate - removal and installation

1 Raise the vehicle and support it securely on jackstands, then refer to Chapter 7B and remove the transmission. If it's leaking, now would be a very good time to replace the front pump seal/O-ring.

2 Look for factory paint marks that indicate driveplate-to-crankshaft alignment. If they aren't there, use a center-punch or paint to make alignment marks on the driveplate and crankshaft to ensure correct alignment during reinstallation.

3 Remove the bolts that secure the driveplate to the crankshaft. If the crankshaft turns, use a flywheel holding tool or wedge a screwdriver in the ring gear teeth to jam the driveplate.

4 Remove the driveplate from the crankshaft.

5 Check for cracked and broken ring gear teeth.

6 Clean and inspect the mating surfaces of the driveplate and the crankshaft. If the crankshaft rear seal is leaking, replace it before reinstalling the driveplate (see Section 16).

7 Position the driveplate against the crankshaft, but make sure the crankshaft sensor ring is positioned between the driveplate and the engine. Be sure to align the marks made during removal. Note that some engines have an alignment dowel or staggered bolt holes to ensure correct installation.

8 Tighten the bolts to the torque listed in this Chapter's Specifications.

9 The remainder of installation is the reverse of the removal procedure.

15 Turbocharger(s) (3.5L engine) - removal and installation

✳✳ WARNING:

Wait until the engine is completely cool before beginning this procedure.

➡ **Note: The turbochargers must be handled with care and extreme cleanliness when they are removed, as they are precision high-speed components. When parts are disconnected from the turbochargers, the openings on the turbocharger must be protected from entry of dirt or chemicals. Use high-strength tape to cover them as components are detached.**

➡ **Note: The procedure is virtually the same for either the left or right turbocharger.**

1 The engine must be cold before removing the turbocharger(s). Before disconnecting any hoses, pipes or connections from the turbocharger, remove the heat insulation material.

2 Drain the cooling system (see Chapter 1).

3 When removing the right-hand turbocharger, first remove the drivebelt and the air conditioning compressor from the block (see Chapter 3). Support the compressor out of the way with a length of wire or rope.

✳✳ WARNING:

Don't disconnect the refrigerant lines.

4 To disconnect the Y-pipe and catalytic converters, support the transmission with a suitable jack and remove the transmission mount/ mount retainer and the crossmember. On 4WD models, raise the transfer case, remove the insulator, retainer plate and crossmember.

5 Remove the Y-pipe and converter assembly, then reinstall the transmission insulator, retainer plate and crossmember, tightening the fasteners just snug.

6 Disconnect the vacuum hose at the wastegate. Tag and disconnect the two other vacuum hoses, and the coolant pipe connection.

7 Disconnect the electrical connector at the turbocharger bypass valve.

8 Disconnect the tube that feeds oil into the top of the center bearing housing for cooling, and disconnect the pipe leading from the bottom of the center bearing housing to return oil to the engine's oil pan.

9 Disconnect and remove the duct from the air cleaner housing to the turbocharger, then tape the openings.

10 Remove the exhaust heat shield (if equipped) attached to the frame.

11 Tape off any openings on the turbocharger assembly. Remove the mounting bolt from the turbocharger-to-block bracket while holding the turbocharger. Remove the turbocharger.

12 Installation is the reverse of removal, noting the following:

  a) *Use new gaskets at the turbo-to-exhaust junction on each side, and new gaskets where the oil supply and return pipes connect to the turbocharger housing.*

  b) *Use anti-seize compound on the **new** turbocharger-to-exhaust manifold bolts, and on the Y-pipe-to turbocharger junctions.*

  c) *Tighten all fasteners to the torque listed in this Chapter's Specifications.*

  d) *Refill and bleed the cooling system and install a new oil filter and fresh engine oil.*

16 Rear main oil seal - replacement

1 Remove the transmission (see Chapter 7B).

2 Remove the driveplate (see Section 14).

3 The old seal can be removed by prying it out with a screwdriver or by making one or two small holes in the seal flange with a sharp pick, then using a screw-in type slide-hammer puller. Be sure to note how far the seal is recessed into the bore before removing it; the new seal will have to be recessed an equal amount.

✳✳ CAUTION:

Be very careful not to scratch or otherwise damage the crankshaft or the bore in the housing, or oil leaks could develop!

4 The seal installation can be performed more easily by unbolting and removing the seal retainer plate. Remove all the mounting bolts, then use two of the retainer-to-oil pan bolts and start them into the two threaded holes in the retainer plate. Tightening these two bolts alternately will push the retainer from the engine. Remove all traces of RTV sealant. Apply a 3/16-inch bead of RTV where the block and oil pan flanges meet.

5 Install the retainer to the engine and install all the bolts within 10 minutes of applying the sealant.

6 Make sure the bore is clean, then apply a film of clean engine oil to the outer edge and the lips of the new seal. The seal must be pressed squarely into the bore; a special seal installation tool is highly recommended. Hammering it into place is not recommended.

7 Reinstall the driveplate, making sure the crankshaft sensor ring is between the crankshaft and the driveplate.

8 Reinstall the transmission (see Chapter 7B).

17 Engine mounts - check and replacement

➡ **Note:** The tightening torque required for installing the engine mount through-bolts is considerable. Make sure you have access to a high-torque torque wrench before beginning.

➡ **Note:** The following is the factory-recommended procedure, using an engine support fixture from above. With some creativity and depending on tool selection, it may be possible to replace the engine mounts without performing some of the steps listed here.

1   There are three powertrain mounts on the vehicles covered by this manual; left and right engine mounts attached to the engine block and the frame, and a rear mount attached to the transmission and the transmission crossmember. The rear transmission mount is covered in Chapter 7. Engine mounts seldom require attention, but broken or deteriorated mounts should be replaced immediately or the added strain placed on the driveline components may cause damage or wear.

CHECK

2   During the check, the engine must be raised slightly to remove the weight from the mounts.

3   Raise the vehicle and support it securely on jackstands.

4   Position a jack under the engine oil pan. Place a large wood block between the jack head and the oil pan, then carefully raise the engine just enough to take the weight off the mounts.

✳✳ **WARNING:**

 DO NOT place any part of your body under the engine when it's supported only by a jack!

5   Check for relative movement between the inner and outer portions of the mount (use a large screwdriver or prybar to attempt to move the mounts). If movement is noted, lower the engine and tighten the mount fasteners.

6   Check the mounts to see if the rubber is cracked, hardened or separated from the metal casing which would indicate a need for replacement.

REPLACEMENT

♦ Refer to illustrations 17.17a and 17.17b

✳✳ **CAUTION:**

Use only hand tools to either remove or install the engine mount through-bolts.

➡ **Note:** A high amount of torque must be employed to remove/install the engine mounts. Unless you have the proper tools, you may not be able to fully tighten the fasteners, which is an unsafe condition. Have the job done at a shop or dealership.

7   Disconnect the cable from the negative terminal of the battery (see Chapter 5, Section 1).

8   Raise the front of the vehicle and support it securely on jackstands. Remove the hood (see Chapter 11).

9   Remove the intake manifold (see Section 6).

10   On 3.5L models, remove the high-pressure fuel pump (see Chapter 4).

11   On 3.5L models, remove the two nuts securing the charge air cooler's tube bracket, and release the coolant hose from the clip on the valve cover.

12   Remove the cowl panel (see Chapter 11) and the air deflector over the radiator (see Chapter 3).

13   Remove the under-vehicle splash shield.

14   Loosen, but don't remove, the nuts on the transmission mount crossmember (see Chapter 7).

15   Attach lifting eyes at the right-front and left-rear of the engine. Support the engine with a crane or a lifting device such as an engine support fixture.

✳✳ **CAUTION:**

Raise the engine just enough to take the weight off the engine mounts.

17.17a Right-side engine mount details

A   Mount-to-frame fasteners
B   Through-bolt
C   Bracket-to-engine bolts (two indicated here)

17.17b Left-side engine mount details

A   Mount-to-frame fasteners
B   Through-bolt
C   Bracket-to-engine bolts

16 On 4WD models, place a floor jack under the front differential and chain or otherwise securely retain the differential to the jack. Raise the front axle slightly, and remove the differential mounting bushing bolts, then lower the differential for room to access the engine mounts. Remove the front driveshaft (see Chapter 8).

17 Remove the engine mount through-bolt (see illustrations).

18 Remove the bracket-to-engine block bolts, then remove the bracket.

19 Remove the three bolts securing the mount insulator to the frame rail.

20 Install the new engine mount, tightening the bolts to the torque

listed in this Chapter's Specifications.

21 Install the engine mount onto the engine support bracket and tighten the bolts securely, then install the mount through-bolts, using thread locking compound on the threads.

22 The remainder of the installation is the reverse of removal. Remove the engine hoist and the jackstands and lower the vehicle.

> ❈❈ **CAUTION:**
>
> **Be sure to tighten the nuts at the transmission crossmember.**

Specifications

General

Displacement	
3.5L engine	214 cubic inches
3.7L engine	226 cubic inches
Cylinder numbers (front-to-rear)	
Left (driver's) side	4-5-6
Right side	1-2-3
Firing order	1-4-2-5-3-6
Cylinder head warpage limit	
Lengthwise	0.003 inch
Widthwise	0.002 inch

36061-1-specs.B HAYNES

Cylinder locations

Camshaft

Lobe lift (intake and exhaust)	
3.5L engine	0.373 inch
3.7L engine	0.390 inch
Lobe wear limit	0.0024 inch
Endplay	
Standard	0.001 to 0.006 inch
Service limit	0.0074 inch
Journal diameter	
First journal	1.535 to 1.536 inches
Intermediate journals	1.021 to 1.022 inches
Journal-to-bearing (oil) clearance	0.0029 inch
Journal runout limit	0.0015 inch

Torque specifications*	Ft-lbs (unless otherwise indicated)

→ **Note: One foot-pound (ft-lb) of torque is equivalent to 12 inch-pounds (in-lbs) of torque. Torque values below approximately 15 ft-lbs are expressed in inch-pounds, since most foot-pound torque wrenches are not accurate at these smaller values.**

Variable Camshaft Timing (VCT) unit (camshaft sprocket) bolt (new)
Step 1	30
Step 2	Loosen one full turn
Step 3	18
Step 4	Tighten an additional 180 degrees

Camshaft cap bolts (see illustration 11.14)
Step 1	71 in-lbs
Step 2	Tighten an additional 45 degrees
Step 3	Loosen bolts 8 through 11
Step 4	Repeat Steps 1 and 2 on bolts 8 through 11

Crankshaft pulley bolt
Step 1	89
Step 2	Loosen one turn
Step 3	37
Step 4	Tighten an additional 90 degrees

Crossmember bolts   66

Cylinder head bolts (new, oiled) (in sequence - see illustration 8.18)
Step 1	177 in-lbs
Step 2	26
Step 3	Tighten an additional 90 degrees
Step 4	Tighten an additional 90 degrees
Step 5	Tighten an additional 45 degrees
M6 bolt at front of cylinder head	89 in-lbs

Drivebelt tensioner pulley mounting bolt(s)   18

Exhaust manifold nuts
Step 1	168 in-lbs
Step 2	18

Exhaust manifold studs   106 in-lbs
Driveplate bolts   59

Intake manifold bolts
3.5L engine (see illustration 5.12)
Step 1	89 in-lbs
Step 2	Tighten an additional 45 degrees

3.7L engine
Lower intake manifold-to-cylinder
heads (see illustration 5.33)   89 in-lbs
Upper intake manifold-to-lower intake manifold (see illustration 5.39)
Step 1	89 in-lbs
Step 2	Tighten an additional 45 degrees

Oil pan-to-block bolts   89 in-lbs
Oil pump screen nuts-to-engine block nuts   89 in-lbs
Oil pump mounting bolts   89 in-lbs
Oil filter adapter bolt
Step 1	89 in-lbs
Step 2	Tighten an additional 45 degrees

Torque specifications*	Ft-lbs (unless otherwise indicated)

Engine front cover-to-block bolts (see illustration 9.14)

Bolt numbers 1, 2, 7, 8, 15, 17, 18, 19, 20, 21

Step 1	89 in-lbs
Step 2	177 in-lbs
Step 3	Tighten an additional 45 degrees
Step 4, bolt 21	177 in-lbs
Step 5, bolt 21	Tighten an additional 90 degrees

Bolts 3, 4, 5, 6, 9, 10, 11, 12, 13, 14, 16, 22

Step 1	89 in-lbs
Step 2	177 in-lbs
Step 3	Tighten an additional 45 degrees
Step 4, bolt 22	89 in-lbs
Step 5, bolt 22	Tighten an additional 45 degrees
Oil pan-to-timing chain cover bolts	89 in-lbs

Engine mount fasteners

Through-bolts	258
Mount bracket-to-engine block bolts	46
Mount-to-frame bolts	129
Timing chain tensioner bolts	96 in-lbs
Turbocharger-to-exhaust manifold bolts	24
Turbocharger bracket-to-block bolts	89 in-lbs
Turbocharger bracket-to-turbocharger bolt	159 in-lbs
Valve cover bolts	89 in-lbs

Variable Camshaft Timing oil control solenoid bolts

Step 1	71 in-lbs
Step 2	Tighten an additional 20 degrees

*Refer to Part D for additional specifications.

2C

V8 ENGINES

Section

1   General information
2   Repair operations possible with the engine in the vehicle
3   Top Dead Center (TDC) for number one piston - locating
4   Valve covers - removal and installation
5   Intake manifold - removal and installation
6   Exhaust manifolds - removal and installation
7   Crankshaft pulley and front oil seal - removal and installation
8   Timing chain cover - removal and installation
9   Timing chains, tensioners and sprockets - removal, inspection
    and installation
10 Rocker arms and valve lash adjusters - removal, inspection
    and installation
11 Variable Camshaft Timing (VCT) system - general information
12 Camshaft(s) - removal, inspection and installation
13 Cylinder heads - removal and installation
14 Oil pan - removal and installation
15 Oil pump - removal and installation
16 Flywheel/driveplate - removal and installation
17 Rear main oil seal - replacement
18 Engine mounts - check and replacement

Reference to other Chapters

CHECK ENGINE light on - See Chapter 6

1 General information

This Part of Chapter 2 is devoted to in-vehicle repair procedures for the 4.6L, 5.0L, 5.4L and 6.2L Single Overhead Camshaft (SOHC) engines. There are two versions of the 4.6L engine: Two-valve combustion chamber design and three-valve combustion chamber design. All 5.4L engines use three-valve combustion chambers. The two-valve 4.6L engine and the 5.4L engine have aluminum cylinder heads and a cast iron block. The three-valve 4.6L engine has aluminum heads and an aluminum block. The 5.0L (four-cam) engine has an aluminum block and heads and four valves per cylinder, and the 6.2L has aluminum heads with one camshaft per head and two valves per cylinder on a cast-iron block. Information concerning engine removal and installation can be found in Part D of this Chapter.

These engines are an interference design. In the event the timing chain breaks, the pistons will contact the valves and cause damage.

2 Repair operations possible with the engine in the vehicle

Many major repair operations can be accomplished without removing the engine from the vehicle.

If possible, clean the engine compartment and the exterior of the engine with some type of pressure washer before any work is started. It will make the job easier and help keep dirt out of the internal areas of the engine.

It may help to remove the hood to improve access to the engine as repairs are performed (see Chapter 11).

If vacuum, exhaust, oil or coolant leaks develop, indicating a need for gasket or seal replacement, the repairs can generally be made with the engine in the vehicle. The intake and exhaust manifold gaskets, timing cover gasket, oil pan gasket, crankshaft oil seals and cylinder head gaskets are all accessible with the engine in place.

Exterior engine components, such as the intake and exhaust manifolds, the oil pan, the water pump, the starter motor, the alternator and the fuel system components can be removed for repair with the engine in place.

The manufacturer recommends that the engine be removed from the vehicle to remove the cylinder heads.

Replacement of the timing chain and sprockets and oil pump is possible with the engine in the vehicle.

3 Top Dead Center (TDC) for number one piston - locating

▶ **Refer to illustration 3.1**

Refer to Chapter 2, Part A for the TDC locating procedure, but use the illustration provided with this Section for the appropriate reference marks and the following exceptions:

a) *Remove the ignition coils (see Chapter 5).*

b) *Remove the spark plugs and install a compression gauge in the number one cylinder. Turn the crankshaft clockwise with a socket and breaker bar.*

c) *When the piston approaches TDC, compression will be noted on the compression gauge. Continue turning the crankshaft until the notch in the crankshaft pulley is aligned with the TDC mark on the front cover (see illustration). At this point, number one cylinder is at TDC on the compression stroke.*

d) *On engines without TDC marks, remove the right-side valve cover and rotate the engine until the valves of Number 1 cylinder are closed. This is approximately TDC.*

e) *After the number one piston has been positioned at TDC on the compression stroke, TDC for any of the remaining cylinders can be located by turning the crankshaft in 90-degree increments and following the firing order (refer to the Specifications). Divide the crankshaft pulley into four equal sections with chalk marks at four points, each indicating 90-degrees of crankshaft rotation.*

3.1 When placing the engine at Top Dead Center (TDC), align the notch in the crankshaft pulley with the TDC indicator on the timing chain cover (5.4L engine shown)

4 Valve covers - removal and installation

REMOVAL

1 If you're removing the right (passenger's side) valve cover on a 2008 and earlier model, have the refrigerant recovered by an automotive air conditioning specialist before beginning this procedure.

2 Disconnect the cable from the negative battery terminal (see Chapter 5). Remove the air filter housing and intake air duct (see Chapter 4).

3 If you're removing the left valve cover, remove the air intake duct and, if necessary, the air filter housing (see Chapter 4).

4 If a PCV hose or tube is connected to the valve cover that you're removing, disconnect it (see Chapter 6). If the PCV valve is electrically-heated, disconnect the electrical connector from the PCV valve.

5 Remove the ignition coils from the valve cover that you're removing (see Chapter 5).

6 If a wiring harness is routed across a valve cover, disconnect the harness electrical connectors. Detach the pin-type wiring harness retainers from the valve cover studs and harness brackets, and set the harness aside. Disconnect the fuel injector harness from the injectors and position the harness off to the side (see Chapter 4).

4.6L engines

Right (passenger's side) valve cover

7 On 2008 and earlier models, remove the Powertrain Control Module (PCM) (see Chapter 6).

8 Remove the transmission fluid dipstick tube mounting bolt and position the tube off to the side.

9 On 2009 and later models, disconnect the electrical connector from the Variable Camshaft Timing (VCT) solenoid (see Chapter 6).

10 On 2008 and earlier models, remove the accumulator bracket bolts and position the assembly off to the side (see Chapter 3).

11 Loosen the valve cover bolts/studs and remove the valve cover. Follow the reverse of the tightening sequence (see illustration 4.39a). If it's stuck, tap it with a hammer and block of wood to dislodge it.

➡ **Note: Make sure that the bolts are stored or labeled correctly so they can be reinstalled in their original locations.**

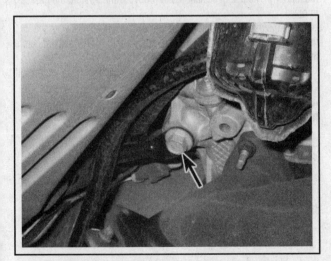

4.23 Location of the transmission fluid dipstick tube retaining bolt

Left (driver's side) valve cover

12 On 2008 and earlier models, remove the EGR valve (see Chapter 6).

13 Remove the oil dipstick tube mounting bolt and position the dipstick tube off to the side.

14 On 2009 and later models, disconnect the electrical connector from the Variable Camshaft Timing (VCT) solenoid(s) (see Chapter 6).

15 On 2008 and earlier models, remove the bolts from the power steering fluid reservoir support bracket and position the assembly off to the side (see Chapter 10).

16 Loosen the valve cover bolts/studs and remove the cover. Follow the reverse of the tightening sequence (2008 and earlier models, see illustration 4.39b; 2009 and later models, see illustration 4.39f). If it's stuck, tap it with a hammer and block of wood to dislodge it.

➡ **Note: Make sure the bolts are stored or labeled correctly so they can be reinstalled in their original locations.**

5.4L engines

Right (passenger's side) valve cover

▶ **Refer to illustration 4.23**

17 Disconnect the electrical connector from the Variable Camshaft Timing (VCT) control solenoid (see Chapter 6). On 2009 and later models, disconnect the electrical connector(s) from the PCM and set the harness aside.

2008 and earlier models

18 Remove the Powertrain Control Module (PCM) (see Chapter 6).

19 Disconnect the vacuum line connector. Label the vacuum lines for correct reassembly.

20 Remove the air conditioning compressor manifold tube and disconnect the evaporator inlet tube fitting (see Chapter 3).

21 Remove the air conditioning accumulator (see Chapter 3).

22 Remove the battery cover (see Chapter 5).

23 Remove the transmission fluid dipstick tube mounting bolt and position the tube off to the side (see illustration).

All models

24 Loosen the valve cover bolts/studs and remove the valve cover. Follow the reverse of the tightening sequence (2007 and earlier models, see illustration 4.39c; 2008 and later models, see illustration 4.39e). If it's stuck, tap it with a hammer and block of wood to dislodge it.

➡ **Note: Make sure the bolts are stored or labeled correctly so they can be reinstalled in their original locations.**

Left (driver's side) valve cover

▶ **Refer to illustrations 4.29a and 4.29b**

25 Disconnect the electrical connector from the Variable Camshaft Timing (VCT) control solenoid(s) (see Chapter 6).

26 Disconnect the intake manifold vacuum hose from the brake booster (see Chapter 9), then disconnect the vacuum tube from the support bracket and the stud on the valve cover. On 2009 and later models, remove the oil dipstick and squeeze the clips securing the dipstick tube. Remove the tube.

27 Disconnect the electrical connector from the radio interference capacitor.

4.29a Location of the two forward mounting nuts on the power steering fluid reservoir support bracket

4.29b The lower support bracket mounting bolt is hidden from view

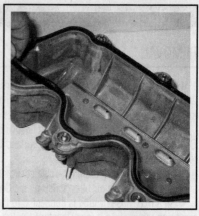

4.36 Make sure the gasket is pushed all the way into the groove in the valve cover

4.37 Apply a dab of RTV sealant to the mating joints between the timing chain cover and the cylinder head before installing the valve cover (4.6L engine shown)

28 Remove the oil dipstick tube mounting bolt and position the dipstick tube off to the side.

29 On 2008 and earlier models, remove the bolts from the power steering fluid reservoir support bracket and position the assembly off to the side (see illustrations).

30 Loosen the valve cover bolts/studs and remove the valve cover. Follow the reverse of the tightening sequence (2007 and earlier models, see illustration 4.39d; 2008 and later models, see illustration 4.39f). If it's stuck, tap it with a hammer and block of wood to dislodge it.

5.0L and 6.2L engines

31 If you're removing the left valve cover on a 5.0L engine, remove the engine oil dipstick, then depress the tabs and pull the dipstick tube from the valve cover.

32 If you're working on a 6.2L engine, detach the spark plug wires from the ignition coils and the clips on the valve cover.

33 Disconnect the electrical connectors from the Variable Camshaft Timing (VCT) oil control solenoid(s).

34 Remove the valve cover bolts, following the reverse of the tightening sequence (see illustrations 4.39g or 4.39h), then remove the valve cover.

INSTALLATION

▶ **Refer to illustrations 4.36, 4.37, 4.39a, 4.39b, 4.39c, 4.39d, 4.39e, 4.39f, 4.39g and 4.39h**

35 The mating surfaces of each cylinder head and valve cover must be perfectly clean when the valve covers are installed. Remove all traces of sealant. If there's old sealant or oil on the mating surfaces when the valve cover is installed, oil leaks may develop.

36 Install a new valve cover gasket in the cover's groove. Make sure the gasket is pushed all the way into the groove in the valve cover (see illustration). The use of sealant in the groove will help hold the gasket in place.

37 At the mating joint (two spots per cylinder head) between the timing chain cover and cylinder head, apply a dab of RTV sealant before installing the valve cover (see illustration).

38 Carefully position the valve cover on the cylinder head and install the studs and bolts.

➡ **Note: Install the covers within five minutes of applying the RTV sealant.**

39 Tighten the fasteners, in sequence, to the torque listed in this Chapter's Specifications (see illustrations).

40 The remainder of installation is the reverse of removal.

41 Start the engine and check for oil leaks as the engine warms up.

42 If it was discharged, have the air conditioning system evacuated, charged and leak checked by the shop that discharged it.

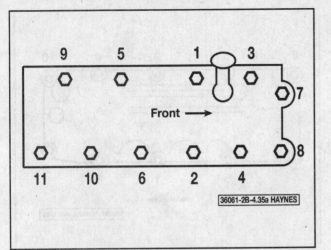

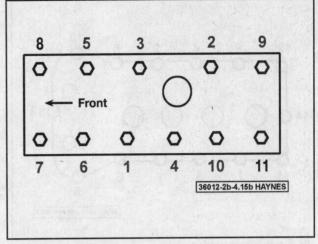

4.39a Right valve cover bolt tightening sequence (2008 and earlier 4.6L engines)

4.39b Left valve cover bolt tightening sequence (2008 and earlier 4.6L engines)

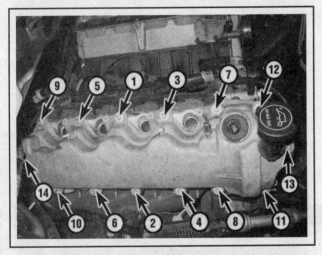

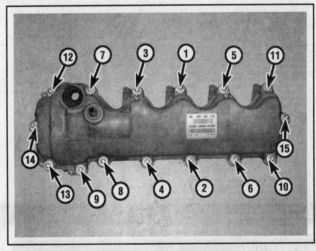

4.39c Right valve cover bolt tightening sequence (2007 and earlier 5.4L engines)

4.39d Left valve cover bolt tightening sequence (2007 and earlier 5.4L engines)

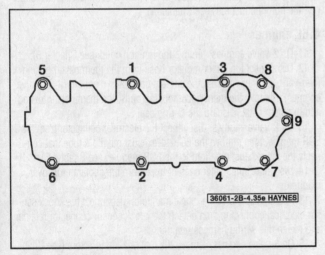

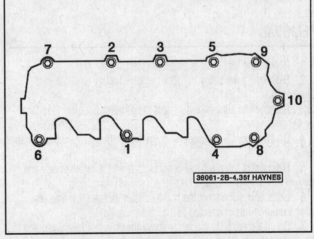

4.39e Right valve cover bolt tightening sequence (2009 and later 3-valve 4.6L and 2008 and later 5.4L engines)

4.39f Left valve cover bolt tightening sequence (2009 and later 3-valve 4.6L and 2008 and later 5.4L engines)

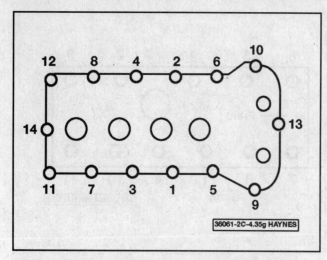

4.39g Valve cover bolt tightening sequence (5.0L engine)

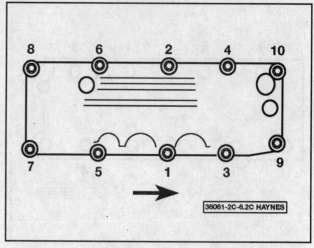

4.39h Valve cover bolt tightening sequence (6.2L engine)

5   Intake manifold - removal and installation

❋❋ WARNING:

Wait until the engine is completely cool before beginning this procedure.

REMOVAL

1   Relieve the fuel system pressure (see Chapter 4).

2   Disconnect the cable from the negative battery terminal (see Chapter 5).

3   Remove the air intake duct and the air filter housing (see Chapter 4).

4   On all except 5.0L models, drain the cooling system (see Chapter 1).

5   Disconnect the electrical connectors from the throttle body and the fuel injectors (see Chapter 4).

6   Label and disconnect the brake booster vacuum line and any other vacuum lines connected to the intake manifold.

7   On all except 5.0L models, remove the drivebelt (see Chapter 1), the alternator (see Chapter 5) and the alternator mounting bracket.

8   On models with an electrically heated PCV valve, disconnect the electrical connector from the PCV valve.

9   Disconnect the crankcase ventilation hose from the valve cover and from the intake manifold (see Chapter 6).

10 Disconnect the electrical connector and the EVAP purge line from the EVAP canister purge valve (see Chapter 6). Disconnect the fuel supply line from the fuel rail (see Chapter 4).

4.6L engines

11 On 2-valve engines, remove the ignition coils (see Chapter 5).

12 Disconnect the upper radiator hose from the thermostat housing (two-valve engines) or from the coolant crossover manifold (three-valve engines). Remove the thermostat housing bolts, the thermostat housing and the thermostat. Discard the O-ring seal.

13 On 2-valve engines, disconnect the electrical connector from the EGR module, then remove the EGR-to-exhaust manifold tube that connects the left exhaust manifold to the EGR module (see Chapter 6).

14 Disconnect the heater coolant hose from the coolant crossover manifold.

15 At the back end of the intake manifold, disconnect the knock sensor electrical connector, then detach the knock sensor connector retainer and the engine wiring harness retainer.

16 On 3-valve engines, remove the fuel rail and injectors (see Chapter 4).

17 On 2004 and 2005 models, disconnect the electrical connector from the Intake Manifold Tuning (IMT) valve (see Chapter 6).

5.30 Coolant crossover tube mounting bolt locations (5.4L engine)

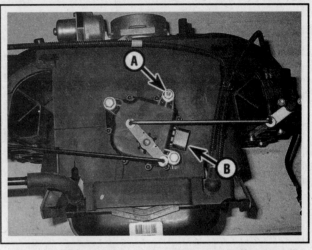

5.35 The manifold will have to be moved forward a little to access the nut retaining the wiring harness to this stud (A) on the CMCV. (B) indicates where the CMCV connector plugs in

18 Disconnect the electrical connector from the Injection Pressure (IPR) sensor (see Chapter 6).

19 On 2008 and earlier models, remove the power steering reservoir and brackets (see Chapter 10) and move it out of the way.

20 Loosen the intake manifold bolts and nuts in 1/4-turn increments, following the reverse order of the tightening sequence (see illustration 5.63a), until they can be removed by hand. Proceed to Step 58.

5.4L engines

2008 and earlier models

▶ **Refer to illustrations 5.30 and 5.35**

21 Disconnect the upper radiator hose from the thermostat housing and disconnect the heater hose from the coolant crossover assembly (see Chapter 3).

22 On 2004 models, disconnect the Injection Pressure (IPR) sensor connector (see Chapter 6). On 2005 through 2008 models, disconnect the Fuel Rail Pressure and Temperature (FRPT) sensor connector (see Chapter 6).

23 Disconnect the engine oil pressure sensor (see Chapter 2C).

24 Disconnect the electrical connector from the left (driver's) side Camshaft Position (CMP) sensor (see Chapter 6).

25 Disconnect the electrical connector from the left (driver's) side Variable Camshaft Timing (VCT) solenoid (see Chapter 6).

26 Disconnect the electrical connector from the left side (driver's) side radio ignition interference capacitor.

27 Disconnect the wiring harness retainers from the left side valve cover (see Section 4) and set the harness aside.

28 Disconnect the brake booster vacuum hose from the intake manifold vacuum line.

29 Loosen the intake manifold bolts and nuts in 1/4-turn increments, following the reverse order of the tightening sequence (see illustration 5.63b), until they can be removed by hand.

30 Unbolt the coolant crossover assembly and remove it (see illustration).

31 Disconnect the electrical connector from the Charge Motion Control Valve (CMCV).

32 Disconnect the intake manifold vacuum line from the valve cover stud and from the support bracket.

33 Reposition the intake manifold assembly forward, then disconnect the electrical connector from the Cylinder Head Temperature (CHT) sensor (see Chapter 6).

34 Disconnect the electrical connectors from the two knock sensors (see Chapter 6).

35 Remove the nut and detach the wiring harness retainer from the CMCV stud at the rear of the manifold (see illustration).

36 Disconnect the electrical connector from the right oxygen sensor (see Chapter 6) and detach the electrical sensor retainer. Proceed to Step 58.

2009 and later models

37 Disconnect the upper radiator hose from the thermostat housing.

38 Disconnect the heater hose from the coolant crossover assembly.

39 Remove the air intake resonator assembly from the air intake duct adapter, then remove the adapter (see Chapter 4).

40 Disconnect the electrical connectors from the four left (driver's) side ignition coils and from the left Variable Camshaft Timing (VCT) solenoid(s) (see Chapter 6), then detach the wiring harness from the left valve cover studs.

41 Disconnect the intake manifold vacuum line from the brake booster vacuum hose.

42 Disconnect the intake manifold vacuum line from the left valve cover stud and from the support bracket at the rear of the left cylinder head.

➡ **Note: The intake manifold vacuum line must be removed with the intake manifold as a single assembly.**

43 Loosen the intake manifold bolts and nuts in 1/4-turn increments, following the reverse order of the tightening sequence (see illustration 5.63b), until they can be removed by hand.

44 Unbolt the coolant crossover assembly and remove it.

45 Position the intake manifold vacuum line under the wiring harness and reposition the intake manifold assembly forward to access the wiring harness retainers.

46 Disconnect the two engine wiring harness retainers from the rear of the manifold.

47 Disconnect the electrical connector from the Cylinder Head Temperature (CHT) harness.

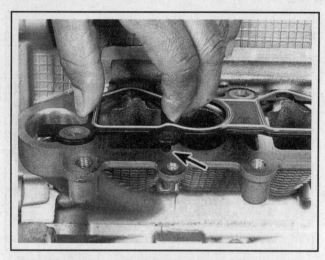

5.61a Install the new intake manifold gaskets and position the locating tabs in the holes in the cylinder head casting (4.6L engine)

5.61b On 5.4L engines, the locating pins on the gaskets fit into holes in the intake manifold

48 Proceed to Step 58.

➡ **Note:** The intake manifold vacuum line must be removed with the intake manifold as a single assembly.

5.0L and 6.2L engines

49 On 6.2L models, remove the throttle body (see Chapter 4).

50 Detach the electrical harness where it attaches to the valve covers or intake manifold, then disconnect the electrical connectors at the ignition coils.

51 On 6.2L models, remove the ignition coils.

52 On 6.2L models, remove the alternator and the alternator support bracket (see Chapter 5).

53 On 6.2L models, remove the thermostat housing (see Chapter 3).

54 Disconnect the EVAP tube (quick-connect) and the PCV hose.

55 On 5.0L engines, remove the fuel injector insulators and disconnect the purge valve electrical connector. Disconnect the fuel injector connectors and the wiring harness at the rear of the intake manifold.

56 Release the heater hose from its clip and set it aside.

57 Remove the intake manifold bolts and remove the intake manifold with the fuel rail still attached. On 5.0L engines, there are four fuel rail bolts and six intake manifold bolts. On 6.2L engines, there are 12 intake mounting bolts and four fuel rail bolts.

All engines

58 The manifold may be stuck to the cylinder heads and force may be required to break the gasket seal(s). A prybar can be used to pry up the manifold, but make sure all fasteners have been removed first!

✳✳ CAUTION:

Don't pry between the engine block and manifold or the cylinder heads, or damage to the gasket sealing surface may occur, leading to vacuum and oil leaks. Pry only at a manifold protrusion.

59 Remove the intake manifold gaskets and clean all traces of gasket or sealant material from the sealing surfaces of the cylinder heads and intake manifold.

✳✳ CAUTION:

The mating surfaces of the cylinder heads, engine block and intake manifold must be perfectly clean. Do not use metal scrapers, wire brushes, power abrasive discs or other abrasive means to clean sealing surfaces; these tools can scratch and gouge gasket surfaces, which creates leak paths. Instead, use gasket removal solvents, which are available at most auto parts stores, and may be helpful when removing old gasket material that's stuck to the cylinder heads and intake manifold. Since the cylinder heads are aluminum and the intake manifold is aluminum or plastic, aggressive scraping can cause damage! Follow the directions printed on the container, and use only a plastic-tipped scraper, not a metal one. While the manifold is removed, cover the open engine areas with shop rags to keep debris out of the engine. Use a vacuum cleaner to remove any debris that falls into the intake ports in the cylinder heads.

INSTALLATION

▶ **Refer to illustrations 5.61a, 5.61b, 5.63a, 5.63b, 5.63c and 5.63d**

60 If you are replacing the manifold, transfer all components to the new unit.

61 On 4.6L engines, install the gaskets on the cylinder heads. Make sure the alignment pins are properly engaged with their corresponding holes in the cylinder head (see illustration). On 5.4L engines, attach the gaskets to the intake manifold (see illustration). On 5.0L and 6.2L engines, install new O-ring type intake manifold gaskets into their grooves in the manifold.

62 Carefully set the intake manifold in place.

63 Install the intake manifold bolts and, following the recommended tightening sequence (see illustrations), tighten them to the torque listed in this Chapter's Specifications.

64 The remainder of installation is the reverse of removal.

65 Refill the cooling system (see Chapter 1). Start the engine and check carefully for coolant leaks.

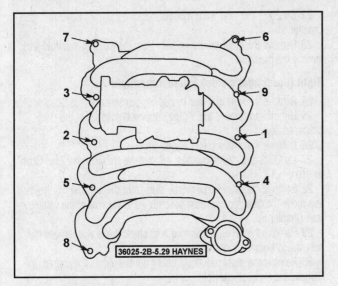

5.63a Intake manifold bolt tightening sequence (4.6L engine)

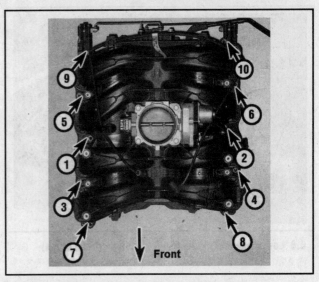

5.63b Intake manifold bolt tightening sequence (5.4L engine)

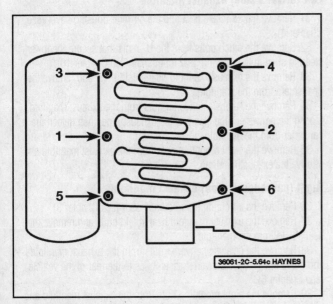

5.63c Intake manifold bolt tightening sequence (5.0L engine)

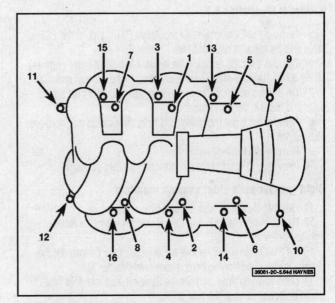

5.63d Intake manifold bolt tightening sequence (6.2L engine)

6   Exhaust manifolds - removal and installation

REMOVAL

1   If you're working on a 6.2L model, relieve the fuel system pressure (see Chapter 4). If you're working on a 5.0L model, have the air conditioning system discharged at an automotive air conditioning system facility.

2   Disconnect the cable from the negative battery terminal (see

Chapter 5).

3   Raise the vehicle and support it securely on jackstands. Remove the inner splash shield from the fenderwell (see Chapter 11).

4   Working under the vehicle, apply penetrating oil to the exhaust pipe-to-manifold studs and nuts (they're usually corroded or rusty). On 4.6L engines, also apply penetrating oil to the EGR pipe fitting on the left exhaust manifold.

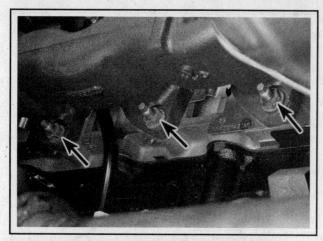

6.8 Lower exhaust manifold nut locations (4.6L engine)

4.6L engines

Left (driver's side) exhaust manifold

▶ **Refer to illustration 6.8**

5   Remove the Exhaust Gas Recirculation (EGR) pipe at the EGR valve and the exhaust manifold (see Chapter 6).

6   Remove the nuts retaining the exhaust Y-pipe (2-valve engines) or the dual-catalyst Y-pipe (3-valve engines) to the exhaust manifold.

7   On 3-valve engines, remove the exhaust manifold heat shield bolts and remove the heat shield.

8   Remove the eight mounting nuts from the exhaust manifold (see illustration).

9   Remove the exhaust manifold.

10 Remove and discard the old exhaust manifold gasket(s).

Right (passenger's side) exhaust manifold

11 Remove the starter (see Chapter 5).

12 Remove the nuts retaining the exhaust Y-pipe to the exhaust manifold.

13 On 3-valve engines, remove the drivebelt (see Chapter 1), then remove the air conditioning compressor (see Chapter 3).

14 On 3-valve engines, remove the three exhaust manifold heat shield bolts and remove the heat shield.

15 Remove the eight mounting nuts from the exhaust manifold. Remove the exhaust manifold.

5.4L engine

Left (driver's side) exhaust manifold

16 Remove the front and rear heated oxygen sensors (see Chapter 6).

17 Unbolt and remove the Y-pipe support bracket from the crossmember.

18 On 2009 and later models, remove the air intake duct and the air filter housing cover (see Chapter 4).

19 On 2009 and later models, remove the pinch bolts from the U-joints that secure the lower steering shaft to the steering gear input shaft (see Chapter 10).

20 Remove the catalytic converter nuts from the exhaust manifolds and pull the catalytic converter flanges off their studs on the exhaust manifolds.

21 Remove the heat shield mounting bolts and remove the heat shield from the exhaust manifold.

22 On 2009 and later 4WD models, remove the front driveshaft (see Chapter 8).

23 Remove the eight mounting nuts from the exhaust manifold and remove the manifold.

Right (passenger's side) exhaust manifold

24 Remove the front and rear heated oxygen sensors (see Chapter 6).

25 Unbolt and remove the Y-pipe support bracket from the crossmember.

26 Remove the starter (see Chapter 5).

27 On 2008 and earlier models, remove the stabilizer bar (see Chapter 10).

28 Remove the catalytic converter nuts from the exhaust manifolds and move the catalytic converter assemblies to the rear of the vehicle (see Chapter 6).

29 Remove the exhaust manifold heat shield bolts and remove the heat shield from the manifold.

30 Remove the eight mounting nuts from the exhaust manifold. Remove the exhaust manifold.

5.0L engine

Left (driver's side) exhaust manifold

31 Remove the air intake duct and the air filter housing cover (see Chapter 4).

32 Remove the pinch bolts from the U-joints that secure the lower steering shaft to the steering gear input shaft (see Chapter 10).

33 Remove the exhaust manifold heat shield bolts and remove the heat shield from the manifold.

34 Remove the catalytic converter nuts from the exhaust manifold, loosen the converter pipe clamp at the exhaust pipe, then detach the converter from the manifold.

35 Remove the eight mounting nuts from the exhaust manifold and remove the exhaust manifold.

Right (passenger's side) exhaust manifold

36 Remove the air conditioning compressor (see Chapter 3).

37 Remove the exhaust manifold heat shield bolts and remove the heat shield from the manifold.

38 Remove the catalytic converter nuts from the exhaust manifolds and move the catalytic converter assemblies to the rear of the vehicle (see Chapter 6).

39 Remove the eight mounting nuts from the exhaust manifold and remove the exhaust manifold.

6.2L engine

40 Remove the intake manifold (see Section 5).

41 Suspend the engine from above with an engine support fixture or hoist. It will be necessary to bolt on a support bracket (tool no. 303-1507 or equivalent) to the front of the engine between the cylinder banks.

42 Remove the catalytic converter nuts from both exhaust manifolds.

43 Loosen, but don't remove, the transmission-to-crossmember nuts.

44 Remove the right-side engine mount-to-frame nuts and the left side engine mount through-bolt.

45 If you're working on a 4WD model, remove the front driveshaft (see Chapter 8).

Left (driver's side) exhaust manifold

46 Remove the pinch bolts from the U-joints that secure the lower steering shaft to the steering gear input shaft (see Chapter 10).

47 Using the engine support fixture or hoist, raise the engine slightly.

48 Remove the exhaust manifold heat shield bolts and remove the heat shield from the manifold.

49 Remove the eight mounting nuts from the exhaust manifold and remove the exhaust manifold.

Right (passenger's side) exhaust manifold

50 Remove the starter (see Chapter 5).

51 Unbolt the air conditioning compressor and position it aside.

✳✳ WARNING:

Don't disconnect the refrigerant lines.

52 Using the engine support fixture or hoist, raise the engine slightly.

53 Remove the exhaust manifold heat shield bolts and remove the heat shield from the manifold.

54 Remove the eight mounting nuts from the exhaust manifold and remove the exhaust manifold.

INSTALLATION

55 The manufacturer recommends that, when an exhaust manifold is removed, all exhaust manifold studs be removed and discarded and replaced with new studs. Use a little anti-seize on the studs, and tighten the new studs to the torque listed in this Chapter's Specifications

56 Inspect the exhaust manifolds for cracks. If you're using the old exhaust manifold studs, make sure the stud threads are clean and undamaged. The exhaust manifold and cylinder head mating surfaces must be clean before the exhaust manifolds are reinstalled - use a gasket scraper to remove all carbon deposits.

57 Position a new gasket in place and slip the exhaust manifold over the studs on the cylinder head. Install the mounting nuts. When tightening the mounting nuts, work from the rear to the front, alternating between top and bottom rows. Tighten the bolts in three equal steps to the torque listed in this Chapter's Specifications.

58 The remainder of installation is the reverse of removal. On 4.6L engines, when reconnecting the EGR pipe to the left manifold, use a slight amount of anti-seize compound on the threads. Start the engine and check for exhaust leaks.

59 If you're working on a 5.0L model, have the air conditioning system recharged by the shop that discharged it.

---

7 Crankshaft pulley and front oil seal - removal and installation

REMOVAL

◆ **Refer to illustrations 7.5, 7.6 and 7.7**

1 Disconnect the cable from the negative battery terminal (see Chapter 5).

2 Remove the drivebelt (see Chapter 1).

3 On 2010 and earlier models, remove the engine cooling fan and shroud assembly (see Chapter 3).

4 Raise the vehicle and support it securely on jackstands.

5 Use a breaker bar and socket to remove the crankshaft pulley center bolt (see illustration).

➡ **Note: It will be necessary to lock the pulley in position using a strap or chain wrench. Wrap a shop rag or a piece of drivebelt material around the pulley before installing the special tool.**

6 On models with threaded holes in the pulley, use a bolt-type puller to remove the pulley (see illustration). On models without threaded holes, remove the pulley from the crankshaft with a three-jaw puller that grabs the inner portion of the hub.

✳✳ CAUTION:

An adapter should be used between the puller bolt and the crankshaft (to prevent damage to the bore and threads in the end of the crankshaft).

7.5 Wrap a shop rag or a piece of drivebelt material around the pulley before installing the strap wrench

7.6 Remove the crankshaft pulley with a puller that bolts to the pulley hub (2009 and earlier models)

7.7 Pry out the oil seal with a special seal removal tool - be careful to not damage the crankshaft or the bore while using the special tool

7.9 There is a special tool for installing the front oil seal into the timing chain cover - if the tool is not available, a large socket (the same diameter as the seal) can be used to drive the seal into place

7.10 Inspect the crankshaft pulley for signs of damage or excessive wear

1   Oil seal surface
2   Woodruff keyway

7   Use a seal puller to remove the crankshaft front oil seal (see illustration).

8   Clean the seal bore and check it for nicks or gouges. Also, examine the area of the hub that rides in the seal for signs of abnormal wear or scoring.

INSTALLATION

◆ **Refer to illustrations 7.9 and 7.10**

➡ **Note: On 5.0L and 6.2L engines, a new bolt must be used when reinstalling the crankshaft pulley.**

9   Coat the lip of the new seal with clean engine oil and drive it into the bore with a seal driver or a large socket slightly smaller in diameter than the seal (see illustration). The open side of the seal faces into the engine.

10   Lubricate the oil seal contact surface of the crankshaft pulley hub (see illustration) with multi-purpose grease or clean engine oil. Apply a dab of RTV sealant to the front end of the keyway in the crankshaft pulley before installation.

11   Install the crankshaft pulley with a special installation tool, available at most auto parts stores. Do not use a hammer to install the pulley. Install the center bolt and tighten it to the torque listed in this Chapter's Specifications.

12   The remainder of installation is the reverse of removal.

8   Timing chain cover - removal and installation

⁂ **WARNING:**

Wait until the engine is completely cool before beginning this procedure.

➡ **Note: The timing chain cover is also referred to as the engine front cover.**

REMOVAL

◆ **Refer to illustration 8.18**

1   Disconnect the cable from the negative battery terminal (see Chapter 5).

2   Drain the engine oil and remove the oil filter (see Chapter 1). On 5.0L engines, drain the cooling system (see Chapter 1).

3   Remove the engine cooling fan (see Chapter 3).

4   Remove the drivebelt (see Chapter 1) and the water pump pulley (see Chapter 3).

5   Remove the crankshaft pulley and front oil seal (see Section 7).

6   Remove both valve covers (see Section 4).

7   Remove the nut from the transmission fluid cooler line bracket and remove the bracket from the lower timing chain cover.

8   Remove the nut from the power steering pressure hose bracket and move the pressure hose off to the side (see Chapter 10).

9   Remove the power steering pump pulley (see Chapter 10). Drain the power steering fluid, remove the mounting bolts and position the power steering pump off to the side (see Chapter 10).

8.18 Separate the timing chain cover from the engine, using a soft-faced hammer if necessary to break the gasket seal

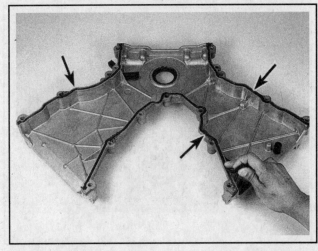

8.20 Install three new gaskets into the grooves in the back of the timing chain cover

10 If you're working on a 5.0L engine, remove the thermostat housing and water pump.

11 Remove the drivebelt tensioner (see Chapter 1) and the drivebelt idler pulleys from the timing chain cover.

12 On 2010 and earlier models, disconnect the electrical connector to the Crankshaft Position (CKP) sensor (see Chapter 6).

13 On 2010 and earlier models, remove the Camshaft Position (CMP) sensors (see Chapter 6).

14 Remove the radio ignition interference capacitors from the left and right sides of the upper timing chain cover.

15 On 2008 and earlier 4.6L 2-valve models, remove the air conditioning manifold tube support bracket and position the assembly off to the side (see Chapter 3).

16 Remove the four front oil pan bolts (see Section 14).

➡ **Note: Two of the fasteners are usually studs, which also should be removed.**

17 Remove the timing chain cover-to-engine block bolts. Note the locations of studs and different-length bolts so they can be reinstalled in their original locations.

18 Separate the timing chain cover from the engine block (see illustration). If it's stuck, tap it gently with a soft-face hammer to break the gasket bond.

❊❊ CAUTION:

DO NOT use excessive force or you may crack the cover. If the cover is difficult to remove, make sure all of the bolts and studs have been removed.

INSTALLATION

▶ **Refer to illustrations 8.20, 8.21, 8.23a and 8.23b**

19 Clean the mating surfaces of the timing chain cover, engine block and cylinder heads to remove all traces of old gasket material, oil and dirt.

8.21 Apply a bead of RTV sealant to the mating junctions of the oil pan-to-engine block and cylinder head-to-engine block

❊❊ WARNING:

Be careful when cleaning any of the aluminum components. Use of a metal scraper could cause scratches or gouges that could lead to an oil leak later.

20 Install new gaskets into the grooves of the timing chain cover (see illustration).

21 Apply a 1/8-inch bead of RTV sealant to the junctions of the oil pan-to-engine block and the cylinder head-to-engine block (see illustration). Apply a small dab of RTV where the timing chain cover and engine block meet, and where the timing chain cover and cylinder heads meet at the valve cover surfaces.

22 Lubricate the timing chains and the lip of the crankshaft front oil seal with clean engine oil.

23 Install the timing chain cover on the engine, within five minutes of applying the RTV sealant. Position the bottom/front edge of the timing chain cover flush with the front edge of the oil pan and tilt the top of

8.23a Timing chain cover bolt tightening sequence (4.6L, 5.4L and 5.0L engines)

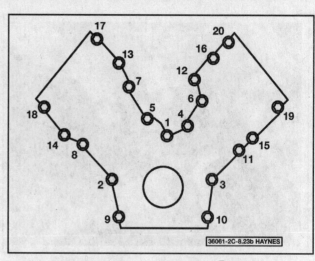

8.23b Timing chain cover bolt tightening sequence (6.2L engine)

the cover into place against the engine. Do not press the cover straight in against the engine or the sealant may be scraped off the front of the oil pan and cause a leak. Tighten the timing chain cover-to-engine block bolts in the recommended sequence (see illustrations), to the torque listed in this Chapter's Specifications. Tighten the timing chain

cover-to-oil pan bolts (and studs if applicable).

24 Install the remaining parts in the reverse order of removal.

25 Add the proper type and quantity of engine oil (see Chapter 1). On 5.0L models, also refill the cooling system (see Chapter 1). Run the engine and check for leaks.

9 Timing chains, tensioners and sprockets - removal, inspection and installation

⁂ CAUTION:

These engines are difficult to work on and require special tools. On any procedure involving timing chain, camshaft(s) or cylinder head removal, the steps must be read carefully and disassembly must proceed using the special tools, otherwise damage to the engine could result.

⁂ CAUTION:

The timing system is complex. Severe engine damage will occur if you make any mistakes. Do not attempt this procedure unless you are highly experienced with this type of repair. If you are at all unsure of your abilities, consult an expert. Double-check all your work and be sure everything is correct before you attempt to start the engine.

⁂ CAUTION:

Because this is an interference engine design, if the chain has broken, there will be damage to the valves (and possibly the pistons), and removal of the cylinder heads will be required.

REMOVAL

▶ **Refer to illustration 9.3**

1 Disconnect the cable from the negative battery terminal (see Chapter 5).

9.3 These engines have two long timing chains with two main tensioners (4.6L shown, other V8 engines similar)

2 Remove the spark plugs (see Chapter 1) and position the number one cylinder on TDC (see Section 3).

3 Remove the valve covers (see Section 4) and the timing chain cover (see Section 8). Two long timing chains connect the crankshaft to the camshafts (see illustration).

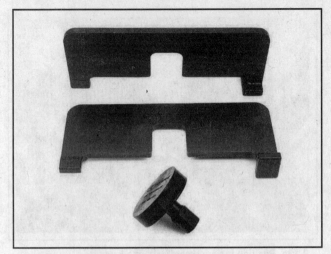

9.5 The special camshaft-locking tools attach to the camshaft and cylinder head and prevent the camshaft from rotating (4.6L and 5.4L engine tools shown)

9.6a To remove the timing chain tensioner, remove the two bolts from the tensioner . . .

9.6b . . . and detach the guide from the dowel at the opposite end

9.8 Remove the stationary chain guide mounting bolts

2-valve 4.6L engine

▶ **Refer to illustrations 9.5, 9.6a, 9.6b and 9.8**

4   Remove the Crankshaft Position (CKP) sensor toothed-wheel by sliding it off the end of the crankshaft nose. Note its installed direction to make sure it's reinstalled the same way.

5   Turn the crankshaft so the timing mark on the right (passenger's) side camshaft sprocket is approximately in the 11 o'clock position and the mark on the left camshaft sprocket is approximately in the 12 o'clock position. With the engine in this position, install special camshaft positioning/locking tools to hold the camshafts in this position (see illustration).

6   Remove the right side timing chain tensioner (see illustrations).

7   Remove the right timing chain from the crankshaft and camshaft sprockets.

8   Remove the timing chain stationary guide (see illustration).

9   Remove the left side timing chain tensioner. Lift the chain off the camshaft sprocket and the crankshaft sprocket.

10 Remove the left side timing chain stationary guide.

11 If the camshaft sprockets are to be replaced, unscrew the bolts and remove the sprockets (see Section 12).

➡ **Note: Note the location and direction of any spacers on the crankshaft or camshafts, but do not remove the spacers unless necessary.**

9.12 Remove the CKP sensor toothed wheel

9.13a Position the crankshaft with the keyway in the 12 o'clock position

9.13b Positions for the intake (A) and exhaust (B) lobes for cylinder number one

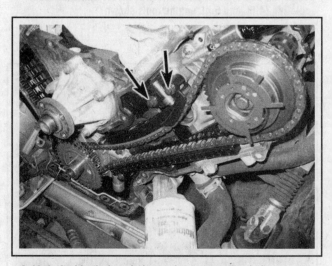

9.16 Left side timing chain tensioner mounting bolt locations - typical

3-valve 4.6L and 5.4L engines

▶ **Refer to illustrations 9.12, 9.13a, 9.13b, 9.16 and 9.17**

12 Remove the Crankshaft Position (CKP) sensor toothed wheel (see illustration) by sliding it off the end of the crankshaft nose. Note the direction of the teeth on the wheel to insure correct reassembly (the wheel is marked "front").

13 Rotate the crankshaft and position the crankshaft keyway in the 12 o'clock position (see illustrations).

14 Remove the rocker arms from the designated cylinders (see Steps 5 and 6 in Section 10).

15 Rotate the crankshaft CLOCKWISE and position the crankshaft keyway in the 6 o'clock position. Remove the remaining rocker arms (see Step 7 in Section 10) from the cylinder heads.

16 Remove the left side timing chain tensioner (see illustration) and the timing chain tensioner guide.

17 Remove the right side timing chain tensioner (see illustration) and the timing chain tensioner guide.

18 Remove the right timing chain from the crankshaft and camshaft sprockets.

19 Remove the left timing chain from the crankshaft and camshaft sprockets, by slipping the chain off the camshaft sprocket and under the crankshaft sprocket.

20 Remove the timing chain stationary guides.

21 The camshafts can now be removed, if desired (see Section 12).

5.0L V8 engines

▶ **Refer to illustration 9.24**

➡ **Note: The 5.0L engine has a similar valvetrain design to the previous V8 engines, but is equipped with four camshafts; two in each cylinder head, one for the intake and one for the exhaust. The valves are actuated by roller rocker arms that are stabilized by hydraulic lash adjusters.**

22 Use the special tool to rotate the crankshaft during this procedure (see illustration 9.57).

23 Rotate the engine clockwise until the crankshaft keyway is straight up (12 o'clock). The marked sides of the camshafts ("data matrix" marks, etched into the shafts just behind the no. 1 bearing cap) must face up. If they do not, rotate the engine 360 degrees clockwise.

9.17 Right side timing chain tensioner mounting bolt locations

9.24 Use the tensioner arm to compress the tensioner and insert a drill bit or paper clip to hold it in the retracted position (5.0L and 6.2L engines)

24 Push in on the right (passenger's side) primary chain tensioner arm to compress the plunger in the tensioner (one at each side of the engine). Keep it depressed until you can insert a large paper clip or drill bit in the hole in the tensioner (see illustration). Repeat for the tensioner on the other side.

25 Turn the crankshaft just a little, if necessary, to provide some slack in the timing chain.

26 Remove the right-side tensioner, then the tensioner arm and the stationary chain guide.

27 Remove the right-side primary timing chain.

28 Remove the three bolts securing each VCT (sprocket) assembly to the right-side intake and exhaust camshafts.

✳✳ CAUTION:

Don't allow the shafts to turn as this is done. Place a large wrench on the flats of the camshaft while using a ratchet and socket to remove the VCT assembly mounting bolts.

29 Slide the VCT units forward 5/64-inch (2 mm).

30 Push down on the right-side secondary chain tensioner while twisting the plastic guide on the top of the tensioner until it is positioned 90-degrees to the timing chain. The VCT assemblies and secondary chain can now be removed.

✳✳ CAUTION:

Don't mix up the VCT units; they are not interchangeable.

31 Rotate the engine counterclockwise with the special tool until the crankshaft's keyway is in the 9 o'clock position and repeat the procedure to remove the left-side timing components.

6.2L V8 engines

32 Remove the lower set of spark plug wires and the lower set of spark plugs (these engines have two plugs per cylinder).

33 Rotate the engine until the intake valve for cylinder Number 1 is open. Working on the left (driver's side) cylinder head, remove the ten intake rocker shaft mounting bolts and the shaft. Number the rocker

arms (if they are not marked already), so they can be reinstalled in the same locations.

34 Rotate the engine clockwise until the exhaust valve for cylinder Number 1 is open. Working on the left (driver's side) cylinder head, remove the ten exhaust rocker shaft mounting bolts and the shaft. Number the rocker arms (if they are not marked already), so they can be reinstalled in the same locations.

35 Rotate the engine clockwise until the intake valve for cylinder Number 1 is closed. Working on the right (passenger's side) cylinder head, remove the ten intake rocker shaft mounting bolts and the shaft. Number the rocker arms (if they are not marked already), so they can be reinstalled in the same locations.

36 Rotate the engine clockwise until the exhaust valve for cylinder Number 1 is closed. Working on the right (passenger's side) cylinder head, remove the ten exhaust rocker shaft mounting bolts and the shaft. Number the rocker arms (if they are not marked already), so they can be reinstalled in the same locations.

37 Rotate the engine clockwise until the crankshaft keyway is at the 11 o'clock position.

38 Push in on the right (passenger's side) primary chain tensioner arm to compress the plunger in the tensioner (one at each side of the engine). Keep it depressed until you can insert a large paper clip or drill bit in the hole in the tensioner (see illustration 9.24). Repeat for the tensioner on the other side.

39 Turn the crankshaft just a little, if necessary, to provide some slack in the timing chain.

40 Remove the right-side tensioner, then the tensioner arm and the stationary chain guide.

41 Remove the right-side primary timing chain.

42 Repeat Steps 38 through 41 on the left-side timing chain tensioner, guide and chain.

INSPECTION

▶ **Refer to illustrations 9.45a, 9.45b and 9.45c**

43 Inspect the individual sprocket teeth and keyways for wear and damage.

44 Check the chain for cracked plates, and pitted or worn rollers. Check the wear surface of the chain guides for wear and damage.

9.45a Check the condition of the tensioner seal (4.6L and 5.4L engines)

9.45b Install a special tool (A) onto the plunger and tensioner side rail (B) to lock the plunger in the retracted position (4.6L and 5.4L engines)

Replace any worn or defective parts with new ones.

※※ CAUTION:

If excessive plastic material is missing from the chain guides, the oil pan should be removed and cleaned of all debris (see Section 13). Check the oil pick-up tube screen, too.

45 Check the timing chain tensioners:
  a) *Check the condition of the tensioner seal (see illustration). Make sure the seal is intact and not broken, chipped or damaged.*
  b) *Check the condition of the plunger. Depress the plunger to make sure it moves freely.*
  c) *On 4.6L and 5.4L engines, compress the tensioner in a vise and lock it in the retracted position using a special retainer clip (see illustration).*
  d) *On 5.0L and 6.2L engines, remove the plastic oil filter in the center hole of the VCT assemblies. Install new filters with the wide end out.*
  e) *The tensioners on 5.0L and 6.2L engines can be kept in the retracted position with a drill bit or paper clip. Compress the tensioner in a vise and place the drill bit or paper clip into the lock pin hole to hold it in the compressed position (see illustration).*

※※ CAUTION:

Compress only the round plunger on the tensioner and not the ratchet mechanism.

INSTALLATION

※※ CAUTION:

Before starting the engine, carefully rotate the crankshaft by hand through at least two full revolutions (use a socket and breaker bar on the crankshaft pulley center bolt). If you feel any resistance, STOP! There is something wrong - most likely, valves are contacting the pistons. You must find the problem

before proceeding. Check your work and see if any updated repair information is available.

46 Install the timing chain stationary guides for both sides, and tighten the bolts to the torque listed in this Chapter's Specifications.
47 Install the crankshaft sprocket on the crankshaft with the timing marks facing forward.

2-valve 4.6L engine

▶ **Refer to illustrations 9.49 and 9.50**

48 The two timing chains should have colored links on each chain. If no colored links are present, purchase timing chains equipped with colored links.
49 Install the left timing chain, aligning the colored link with the dimple on the camshaft sprocket (see illustration). Loop the timing chain under the crankshaft sprocket and align the colored link with the alignment mark on the crankshaft sprocket.
50 Install the right chain, aligning its colored links with the marks on the camshaft and crankshaft sprockets (see illustration).
51 The steps for installing the timing chain tensioners/guides are the same for both sides; either side can be done first. Before assembling the tensioner with the chain guide, compress the tensioner and lock it in

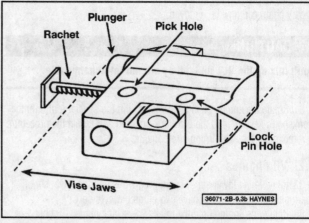

9.45c Timing chain tensioner details (5.0L and 6.2L engines)

9.49 Align the colored link at the lower end of the chain with the timing mark on the crankshaft sprocket - both chains are aligned here

9.50 When installing the timing chain, align one of the colored links on the timing chain with the dimple on the camshaft sprocket

this position with a retainer clip (see illustration 9.45b).

➡ **Note: The left side tensioner guide has an identification bump next to the dowel hole.**

52 Remove the slack from the chain, install the timing chain guide and install the tensioner in the retracted position. Tighten the bolts to the torque listed in this Chapter's Specifications. Repeat for the other chain.

53 Remove the retainer clip and apply pressure against the tensioner chain guide so the tensioner fully extends against the chain guide and all slack is removed from the chain.

54 Recheck all the timing marks to make sure they are still in alignment (see illustration 9.49).

55 Install the rocker arms and valve lash adjusters (see Section 10).

3-valve 4.6L and 5.4L engines

▶ **Refer to illustrations 9.57, 9.59a, 9.59b and 9.61**

56 Install the camshafts (see Section 12) if they were removed.

✳✳ CAUTION:

Do NOT install the rocker arms at this time. The rocker arms will be installed as a final step when the timing chains and tensioners have been installed.

---

57 On 5.4L engines, use the special tool (see illustration) to position the crankshaft keyway in the 10 o'clock position; this is the TDC number 1 position. On 3-valve 4.6L engines, install the crankshaft sprocket (if removed) with the flange facing out and the timing mark at 6 o'clock (see illustration 9.49); if the timing mark is not at 6 o'clock, rotate the crankshaft as necessary to put the mark at 6 o'clock.

58 The timing chains should have three colored links on each chain. If no colored links are present, purchase timing chains equipped with colored links.

59 Loop the left side timing chain under the crankshaft sprocket and align the colored link with the alignment mark on the crankshaft sprocket (see illustration). Install the timing chain over the camshaft sprocket, aligning the two bright links with the L on the sprocket (see illustration).

➡ **Note: The slack side of the chain should be below the tensioner arm dowel on the block.**

9.57 This tool slips over the end of the crankshaft and engages with the dowel pin on the right (passenger's) side of the engine on 4.6L and 5.4L engines (on 5.0L engines, the same tool is used to rotate the crankshaft)

9.59a Colored link on the timing chain aligned with the mark on the crankshaft sprocket (right timing chain shown, left timing chain similar)

9.59b Align the L on the left camshaft sprocket (A) with the two colored links (B) on the timing chain

9.61 Align the I on the right camshaft sprocket (A) with the two colored links (B) on the timing chain

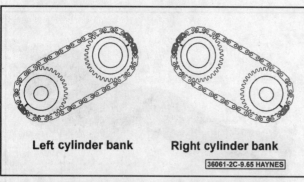

Left cylinder bank   **Right cylinder bank**

36061-2C-9.65 HAYNES

9.65 Secondary timing chain alignment marks (as viewed from the back sides of the VCT units) - 5.0L engine

60 Install the left timing chain tensioner guide. Before assembling the tensioner with the chain guide, compress the tensioner and lock it in this position with a retainer clip (see illustration 9.45b). Install the tensioner and tighten the bolts to the torque listed in this Chapter's Specifications. Remove the retainer clip to apply force against the tensioner chain guide so the tensioner fully extends against the chain guide, and all slack is removed from the chain.

61 Loop the right side timing chain under the crankshaft sprocket and align the colored link with the alignment mark on the crankshaft sprocket (see illustration 9.59a). Install the timing chain over the camshaft sprocket, aligning the two colored links with the I on the camshaft sprocket (see illustration).

➡ **Note: The slack side of the chain should be above the tensioner arm dowel on the block.**

62 Install the right timing chain tensioner guide. Before assembling the tensioner with the chain guide, compress the tensioner and lock it in this position with a retainer clip (see illustration 9.45b). Install the tensioner, tighten the bolts to the torque listed in this Chapter's Specifications and remove the retainer clip to apply force against the tensioner chain guide so the tensioner fully extends against the chain guide and all slack is removed from the chain.

63 Recheck all the timing marks to make sure they are still in alignment.

64 Install the rocker arms (see Section 10).

5.0L engine

▶ **Refer to illustration 9.65**

65 Align the marks on the back sides of the intake and exhaust VCT assemblies with the marks on the secondary chains (see illustration). The intake VCT mark must line up between two colored links, while the exhaust VCT mark must align directly with its colored link. Position the VCT assemblies aligned with their camshafts, but not engaged fully (5/64-inch [2 mm] from fully engaged). The exhaust VCT unit should be positioned with its timing mark for the primary chain in the 11 o'clock position; if necessary, turn the camshaft(s) slightly to allow engagement of the VCT units.

66 Rotate the secondary chain tensioner back 1/4-turn, then push the VCT units so they are completely seated on the camshafts.

67 Hold the camshafts from turning by placing a wrench on their flats, then install and tighten the new VCT bolts to the torque listed in this Chapter's Specifications.

68 Install the left-side primary timing chain with its colored link aligning with the mark on the VCT assembly and the crankshaft sprocket.

69 Install the secondary chain guide, tensioner arm and tensioner.

70 Remove the pin holding the tensioner in the retracted position.

71 Using the special tool (see illustration 9.57), turn the crankshaft clockwise 1/4 turn and position the keyway in the 12 o'clock position.

72 Align the marks on the back sides of the intake and exhaust VCT assemblies with the marks on the secondary chains (see illustration 9.65). The intake VCT mark must line up between two colored links, while the exhaust VCT mark must align directly with its colored link. Position the VCT assemblies aligned with their camshafts, but not engaged fully (5/64-inch [2 mm] from fully engaged). The exhaust VCT unit should be positioned with its timing mark for the primary chain in the 1 o'clock position; if necessary, turn the camshaft(s) slightly to allow engagement of the VCT units.

73 Rotate the secondary chain tensioner back 1/4-turn, then push the VCT units so they are completely seated on the camshafts.

74 Hold the camshafts from turning by placing a wrench on their flats, then install and tighten the new VCT bolts to the torque listed in this Chapter's Specifications.

75 Install the right-side primary timing chain with its colored link aligning with the mark on the VCT assembly and the crank-

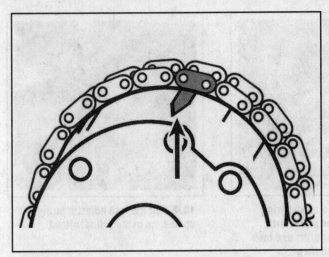

9.78 On 6.2L engines, align the colored link with the groove in the VCT unit (sprocket)

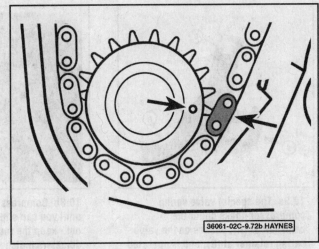

9.79 On 6.2L engines, align the colored link with the mark on the crankshaft sprocket

shaft sprocket. Install the secondary chain guide, tensioner arm and tensioner.

76 Remove the pin holding the tensioner in the retracted position.

6.2L engines

▶ **Refer to illustrations 9.78 and 9.79**

77 Install the camshaft VCT units (sprockets), if removed.

78 Install the left-side timing chain, making sure a colored link in the timing chain align with the marks on the VCT unit (see illustration).

79 Engage the crankshaft sprocket with the chain, aligning the colored link on the chain with the mark on the sprocket, then install the sprocket onto the crankshaft.

➡ **Note: Make sure the crankshaft keyway is in the 11 o'clock position.**

80 Install the secondary chain guide, tensioner arm and tensioner.

81 Remove the pin holding the tensioner in the retracted position.

82 Engage the right-side timing chain with the crankshaft sprocket, aligning a colored link on the chain with the mark on the sprocket.

83 Loop the chain over the right-side VCT unit, aligning the other colored link with the mark on the VCT unit.

84 Install the secondary chain guide, tensioner arm and tensioner.

85 Remove the pin holding the tensioner in the retracted position.

86 Double-check to make sure all of the timing marks and colored links are in proper alignment.

87 Lubricate the camshafts and valve stems with camshaft installation lubricant or clean engine oil.

88 Turn the crankshaft clockwise so the intake cam lobe for cylinder

number 1 is pointing toward the roller of the intake rocker arm (when it is installed) - so as to ensure the number one cylinder intake valve will be fully opened when the rocker shaft is installed.

89 Working on the left (driver's side) cylinder head, install the intake rocker shaft (see Section 10).

90 Turn the crankshaft clockwise so the exhaust cam lobe for cylinder number 1 is pointing toward the roller of the exhaust rocker arm (when it is installed) - so as to ensure the number one cylinder exhaust valve will be fully opened when the rocker shaft is installed.

91 Working on the left (driver's side) cylinder head, install the exhaust rocker shaft (see Section 10).

92 Turn the crankshaft clockwise so the intake cam lobe for cylinder number 1 is pointing away the roller of the intake rocker arm (when it is installed) - so as to ensure the number one cylinder intake valve will be fully closed when the rocker shaft is installed.

93 Working on the right-side cylinder head, install the intake rocker shaft (see Section 10).

94 Turn the crankshaft clockwise so the exhaust cam lobe for cylinder number 1 is pointing away from the roller of the exhaust rocker arm (when it is installed) - so as to ensure the number one cylinder exhaust valve will be fully closed when the rocker shaft is installed.

95 Install the right-side exhaust rocker shaft (see Section 10).

All engines

96 Slowly rotate the crankshaft in the normal direction of rotation (clockwise) at least two revolutions and again bring the engine to TDC. If you feel any resistance, stop and find out why.

97 The remainder of installation is the reverse of removal.

10 Rocker arms and valve lash adjusters - removal, inspection and installation

✱✱ CAUTION:

These engines are difficult to work on and require special tools for many procedures. On any procedure involving timing chain, camshaft or cylinder head removal, the steps must be read carefully and disassembly must proceed using the special tools, otherwise damage to the engine could result.

REMOVAL

1 Remove the valve cover(s) (see Section 4).

2-valve 4.6L engine

▶ **Refer to illustrations 10.3a, 10.3b and 10.4**

2 Because of the interference design of these engines, the rocker

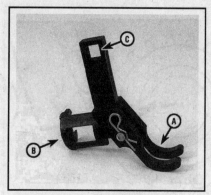

10.3a The special valve spring compressor hooks under the camshaft at (A), pushes on the valve spring retainer at (B), and is operated by a ratchet or breaker bar placed at (C)

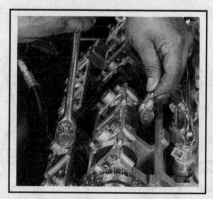

10.3b Compress the valve spring until you can slip the rocker arm out - keep the rocker arms and lash adjusters matched to their original locations

10.4 Pull the lash adjuster straight up and out of the cylinder head

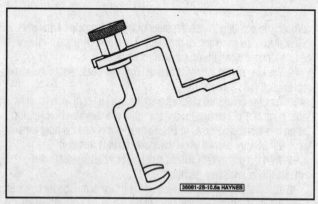

10.6a Use a special tool to compress the valve springs and remove the rocker arms (3-valve 4.6L and 5.4L engines)

arms must be removed before the timing chains and the camshafts are removed. The pistons must be positioned off TDC before compressing the valve springs to remove the rocker arms or lash adjusters. Compress the valve springs on one cylinder at a time. For whatever cylinder you are removing the rocker arms from, remove the spark plug and insert a long dowel (hold onto it) to see how far the piston is from the top of its travel. If necessary, turn the crankshaft until the dowel indicates the piston is down at least an inch or two from TDC.

3   Install a valve spring compressor and compress the spring enough to remove the rocker arm (see illustrations) on each cylinder. Camshaft rocker arms and hydraulic lash adjusters MUST be reinstalled with the same camshaft lobe that they were removed from. Label and store all components to avoid confusion during reassembly.

⁂ CAUTION:

A valve spring spacer should be inserted into the coils of the spring before compressing it. If the spacer isn't in place between one of the valve spring coils, the spring can be compressed too far and the valve seal may be damaged.

4   Remove the hydraulic lash adjuster (see illustration). If there are many miles on the vehicle, the adjusters may have become varnished and difficult to remove. Apply a little penetrating oil around the lash

adjuster to help loosen the varnish.

➡ **Note: Keep the rocker arm and lash adjuster for each valve together in a marked plastic sandwich bag.**

3-valve 4.6L and 5.4L engines

▶ **Refer to illustrations 10.6a, 10.6b and 10.6c**

5   Because of the interference design of these engines, the rocker arms must be removed before the timing chains and camshafts are removed. This will be accomplished in two stages. In the first stage, certain valve springs on designated cylinders must be compressed and the rocker arms removed to prevent any valve-to-piston contact during the repair procedure. Position the number one cylinder slightly advanced from TDC number 1 and follow the procedure carefully using the special tools (see Step 6). In the second stage, the engine will be rotated 180-degrees CLOCKWISE (crankshaft keyway in the 6 o'clock position) and the remaining rocker arms removed (see Step 7).

6   Stage 1: Position the engine at TDC number 1 (see Section 3), then continue to rotate the engine until the crankshaft keyway is in the 12 o'clock position and remove the rocker arms from the designated cylinders:

a) *Working on the right cylinder head, install a special valve spring compressing tool onto the indicated valve springs (see illustration), compress the springs and remove the rocker arms (see illustration).*

⁂ CAUTION:

Do not allow the valve spring keepers to fall off the valve stems or the valves will release and drop down into the cylinders.

b) *Working on the left cylinder head, install a special valve spring compressing tool onto the indicated valve springs (see illustration 10.6a), compress the springs and remove the rocker arms (see illustration).*

⁂ CAUTION:

Do not allow the valve spring keepers to fall off the valve stems or the valves will release and drop down into the cylinders.

10.6b With the crankshaft keyway positioned at 12 o'clock (just past TDC for cylinder number one), the exhaust rocker arm can be removed from cylinder number 1, the intake rocker arms from cylinder number 4 . . .

10.6c . . . and cylinder number 5, and the exhaust rocker arm from cylinder number 8

7   Stage 2: Rotate the engine 180-degrees CLOCKWISE until the crankshaft keyway is in the 6 o'clock position. Install the valve spring compressing tool onto the remaining valve springs, compress the springs and remove the remaining rocker arms. Camshaft rocker arms MUST be reinstalled with the same camshaft lobe that they were removed from. Label and store all components to avoid confusion during reassembly.

8   Remove the timing chains (see Section 9) and the camshafts from the cylinder heads (see Section 12) to access the hydraulic lash adjusters.

9   Remove the hydraulic lash adjusters. The hydraulic lash adjusters must be reinstalled in their original locations. Label and store all components to avoid confusion during reassembly.

5.0L engine

10 Remove the camshaft that operates the roller followers being serviced (see Section 12). Separate the hydraulic lash adjusters from the clips that secure them to the roller followers.

➡ Note: Store the parts so that each lash adjuster is with its original roller follower.

6.2L engine

➡ Note: On 6.2L engines, the manufacturer refers to the variable timing device on the front of the camshafts as a camshaft phaser-and-sprocket. 6.2L engines have rocker arms mounted on two shafts, one for the intake valve and one for the exhaust.

11 Remove the lower eight spark plugs.

Left (driver's side) rocker arms

12 Rotate the crankshaft clockwise until the intake valve on cylinder Number 6 is open. Remove the 10 bolts and the intake rocker shaft assembly. Keep the rockers in position and number them if they aren't already.

13 Rotate the crankshaft clockwise until the exhaust valve on cylinder Number 6 is open. Remove the 10 bolts and the exhaust rocker shaft assembly.

Right (passenger's side) rocker arms

14 Rotate the crankshaft clockwise until the intake valve on cylinder Number 1 is closed. Remove the 10 bolts and the right-side intake rocker shaft assembly.

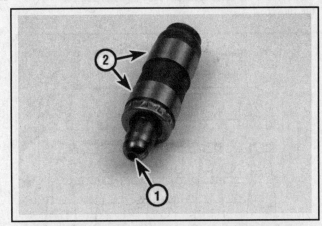

10.16 Inspect the lash adjuster for signs of excessive wear or damage, such as pitting, scoring or signs of overheating (bluing or discoloration), where the tip contacts the camshaft follower (1) and the side surfaces that contact the lifter bore in the cylinder head (2)

15 Rotate the crankshaft clockwise until the exhaust valve on cylinder Number 1 is closed. Remove the 10 bolts and the exhaust rocker shaft assembly.

INSPECTION

▶ Refer to illustrations 10.16 and 10.18

16 Inspect each adjuster carefully for signs of wear or damage. The areas of possible wear are the ball tip that contacts the cam follower and the sides of the adjuster that contact the bore in the cylinder head (see illustration). Since the lash adjusters frequently become clogged as mileage increases, we recommend replacing them if you're concerned about their condition or if the engine is exhibiting valve tapping noises.

17 A thin wire or paper clip can be placed in the oil hole to move the plunger and make sure it's not stuck.

➡ Note: The lash adjuster must have no more than 1/16-inch of total plunger travel.

It's recommended that if replacement of any of the adjusters is necessary, that the entire set be replaced. This will avoid the need to repeat the repair procedure as the others require replacement in the future.

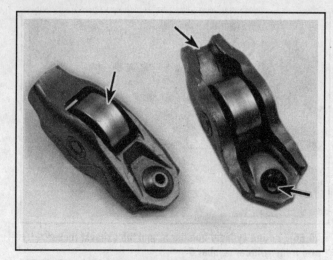

10.18 Check the roller surface of the rocker arms and the areas where the valve stem and lash adjuster contact the rocker

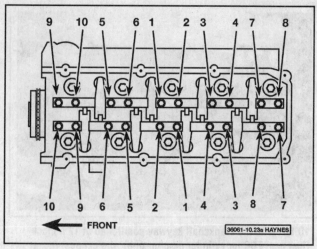

10.24 Left cylinder head intake (top) and exhaust (bottom) rocker shaft bolt tightening sequence (6.2L engine)

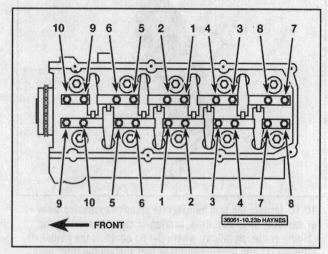

10.26 Right cylinder head intake (bottom) and exhaust (top) rocker shaft bolt tightening sequence (6.2L engine)

18 Inspect the rocker arms for signs of wear or damage. The areas of wear are the ball socket that contacts the lash adjuster and the roller where the follower contacts the camshaft (see illustration).

INSTALLATION

➡ **Note: When re-starting the engine after replacing the adjusters, the adjusters will normally make some tapping noises, until all the air is bled from them. After the engine is warmed-up, raise the speed from idle to 3,000 rpm for one minute. Stop the engine and let it cool down. All of the noise should be gone when it is restarted.**

All except 6.2L engine

19 Before installing the lash adjusters, bleed as much air as possible out of them. Stand the adjusters upright in a container of oil. Use a thin wire or paper clip to work the plunger up and down. This primes the adjuster and removes most of the air. Leave the adjusters in the oil until ready to install (just be sure not to mix them up).

20 Lubricate the valve stem tip, rocker arm, and lash adjuster bore with clean engine oil.

21 Install the lash adjusters and, with the valve spring depressed (4.6L/5.4L engines), install each rocker arm.

22 The remainder of installation is the reverse of removal.

6.2L engine

23 Clean, then lubricate the rocker arms and shafts with clean engine oil before installation.

Left (driver's side) rocker arms

▶ **Refer to illustration 10.24**

24 Rotate the engine clockwise to position the left-side camshaft's intake lobe for cylinder Number 6 so that the intake valve would be opened fully if the rocker shafts were tightened down. Install the left-side intake rocker arms and rocker shaft. Install all the bolts hand tight, then tighten them, in sequence, to the torque listed in this Chapter's Specifications (see illustration).

25 Rotate the engine clockwise to position the left-side camshaft's exhaust lobe for cylinder Number 6 so that the exhaust valve would be opened fully if the rocker shafts were tightened down. Install the left-side intake rocker arms and rocker shaft. Install all the bolts hand tight, then tighten them, in sequence, to the torque listed in this Chapter's Specifications (see illustration 10.24).

Right (passenger's side) rocker arms

▶ **Refer to illustration 10.26**

26 Rotate the engine clockwise to position the right-side camshaft's intake lobe for cylinder Number 1 so that the intake valve would be closed if the rocker shafts were tightened down. Install the right-side intake rocker arms and rocker shaft. Install all the bolts hand tight, then tighten them, in sequence, to the torque listed in this Chapter's Specifications (see illustration).

27 Rotate the engine clockwise to position the right-side camshaft's exhaust lobe for cylinder Number 1 so that the exhaust valve would be closed if the rocker shafts were tightened down. Install the right-side exhaust rocker arms and rocker shaft. Install all the bolts hand tight, then tighten them, in sequence, to the torque listed in this Chapter's Specifications (see illustration 10.26).

28 The remainder of installation is the reverse of removal.

11 Variable Camshaft Timing (VCT) system - general information

1   The Variable Camshaft Timing (VCT) system consists of a VCT solenoid (or a pair of VCT solenoids on DOHC engines) mounted on the front of each cylinder head over the camshaft(s), a Camshaft Position (CMP) sensor with a trigger wheel and a variable camshaft timing sprocket mounted on each camshaft. When oil flow is sent to the timing sprockets by way of the VCT solenoids, the phasing of the camshafts is altered, thereby advancing or retarding the actuation of the valves. The Variable Camshaft Timing (VCT) system oil control solenoid replace-

ment procedure is in Chapter 6. The VCT units, sometimes called camshaft phasers, are removed and installed in Section 9 of this Chapter.

2   The Variable Camshaft Timing (VCT) system should be diagnosed by a dealer service department or other qualified automotive repair facility. The VCT system is controlled and monitored by the Powertrain Control Module (PCM), thereby requiring a specialized scan tool for diagnostics.

12 Camshaft(s) - removal, inspection and installation

✳ CAUTION:

These engines are difficult to work on and require special tools for many procedures. On any procedure involving timing chain, camshaft or cylinder head removal, the steps must be read carefully and disassembly must proceed using the special tools, otherwise damage to the engine could result.

REMOVAL

▶ **Refer to illustration 12.3**

1   Remove the valve covers (see Section 4), and the timing chain cover (see Section 8).

2   Remove the timing chains (see Section 9) and the rocker arms (see Section 10).

3   Measure the thrust clearance (endplay) of the camshaft(s) with a dial indicator (see illustration). If the clearance is greater than the value listed in this Chapter's Specifications, replace the camshaft and/or the cylinder head.

2-valve 4.6L engines

▶ **Refer to illustration 12.5**

4   Remove the camshaft sprockets. It will be necessary to lock the camshaft in position using a special tool before loosening the camshaft sprocket bolt.

✳ CAUTION:

Don't mix up the sprockets. Make an identification mark on each sprocket using paint to insure correct reassembly.

5   These engines have two camshaft cap clusters for each camshaft. The configuration of the two cap clusters are different and must be placed in their original locations. Mark the camshaft cap clusters with a front and rear indication, for both the left and right cylinder heads.

➡ **Note: Two bolts used on one camshaft cluster are different than the others; be sure they go back in the same locations on reassembly (see illustration).**

6   It's IMPORTANT to loosen the bearing cap bolts only 1/4-turn at

12.3 Camshaft endplay can be checked by setting up a dial indicator off the front of the camshaft and prying the camshaft gently forward and back

12.5 2-valve 4.6L engines are equipped with camshaft cap clusters rather than individual bearing caps that hold the camshaft in place on the cylinder head. Note the position of the two different bolts

12.9 A special tool bolted to the cylinder head locks the camshaft sprocket in position (3-valve 4.6L and 5.4L engines)

12.21a Areas to look for excessive wear or damage on the camshafts are the bearing surfaces and the camshaft lobes

a time, following the reverse of the tightening sequence (see illustration 12.28c), until they can be removed by hand.

7 Remove the caps and lift the camshaft off the cylinder head. You may have to tap lightly under the camshaft caps to jar them loose. Don't mix up the camshafts or any of the components. They must all go back on the same positions, and on the same cylinder head they were removed from.

8 Repeat this procedure for removal of the remaining camshaft.

3-valve 4.6L and 5.4L engines

▸ **Refer to illustration 12.9**

9 Remove the camshaft sprockets. It will be necessary to lock the camshaft in position using a special tool before loosening the camshaft sprocket bolt (see illustration).

✳ CAUTION:

Don't mix up the sprockets. Make an identification mark on each sprocket using paint to insure correct reassembly.

10 Working on the right (passenger's) side cylinder head, remove the camshaft cap bolts. It's IMPORTANT to loosen the bearing cap bolts only 1/4-turn at a time, following the reverse of the tightening sequence (see illustration 12.28d), until they can be removed by hand.

➡ **Note: Lift the front thrust camshaft cap straight up and even to prevent side-loading.**

11 Working on the left (driver's) side cylinder head, remove the camshaft cap bolts. It's IMPORTANT to loosen the bearing cap bolts only 1/4-turn at a time, following the reverse of the tightening sequence (see illustration 12.28d), until they can be removed by hand.

➡ **Note: Lift the front thrust camshaft cap straight up and even to prevent side-loading.**

12 Remove the caps and lift the camshaft off the cylinder head. You may have to tap lightly under the camshaft caps to jar them loose.

13 Don't mix up the camshafts or any of the components. They must all go back on the same positions, and on the same cylinder head they were removed from.

14 Repeat this procedure for removal of the remaining camshaft.

5.0L and 6.2L engines

15 Remove the VCT assembly from the front end of each camshaft.

16 Hold the flats of the camshaft with a wrench while using a ratchet and socket to remove the VCT mounting bolts (see Section 9).

17 On 5.0L engines, remove the larger camshaft cap (mega-cap) at the front first. Loosen and remove the remainder of the bearing cap bolts, 1/4-turn at a time, in the reverse of the tightening sequence (see illustration 12.28e), and remove the caps.

18 On 6.2L engines, loosen and remove the camshaft bearing cap bolts 1/4-turn at a time in the reverse of the tightening sequence (see illustration 12.28f).

19 Lift the camshafts out of their bearing saddles and set the cams aside.

20 Keep the camshafts clean and mark them with paint to indicate left or right and intake or exhaust.

INSPECTION

▸ **Refer to illustrations 12.21a, 12.21b, 12.22a, 12.22b, 12.22c, 12.23a, 12.23b and 12.25**

21 Visually examine the cam lobes and bearing journals for score marks, pitting, galling and evidence of overheating (blue, discolored areas). Look for flaking of the hardened surface of each lobe (see illustrations).

22 Using a micrometer, measure the diameter of each camshaft journal and the lift of each camshaft lobe (see illustrations). Compare your measurements with this Chapter's Specifications, and if the diameter of any one of these is less than specified, replace the camshaft.

23 Check the oil clearance for each camshaft journal as follows:

a) *Clean the bearing surfaces and the camshaft journals with lacquer thinner or acetone.*

b) *Carefully lay the camshaft(s) in place in the cylinder head. Don't install the rocker arms or lash adjusters and don't use any lubrication.*

c) *Lay a strip of Plastigage on each journal (see illustration).*

d) *Install the camshaft bearing caps.*

e) Tighten the cap bolts, a little at a time, to the torque listed in this Chapter's Specifications.

➡ **Note: Don't turn the camshaft while the Plastigage is in place.**

f) Remove the bolts and detach the caps.
g) Compare the width of the crushed Plastigage (at its widest point) to the scale on the Plastigage envelope (see illustration).
h) If the clearance is greater than specified, and the diameter of any journal is less than specified, replace the camshaft. If the journal diameters are within specifications but the oil clearance is too great, the cylinder head is worn and must be replaced.

24 Scrape off the Plastigage with your fingernail or the edge of a credit card - don't scratch or nick the journals or bearing surfaces.

25 Finally, check the timing chain tensioner oil feed tube and reservoir before installing the cam caps (see illustration). It must be absolutely clean and free of all obstructions or it will affect the operation of the timing chain tensioner.

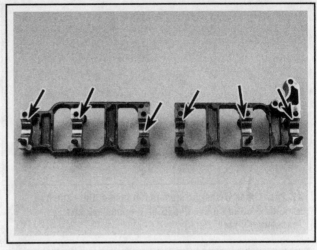

12.21b Inspect the bearing surfaces of the camshaft bearing caps for signs of excessive wear, damage or overheating

12.22a Measure the camshaft bearing journal diameter

12.22b Measure the camshaft lobe at its greatest dimension

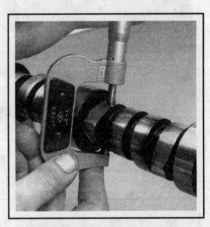

12.22c Subtract the camshaft lobe diameter at its smallest dimension to obtain the lobe lift specification

12.23a Lay a strip of Plastigage on each of the camshaft journals

12.23b Compare the width of the crushed Plastigage to the scale on the envelope to determine the oil clearance

12.25 Oil is delivered to the timing chain tensioner by a feed tube (1) and reservoir (2) in the cylinder head (4.6L and 5.4L engines shown)

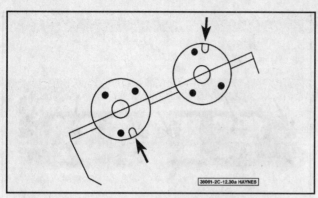

12.28a These U-shaped slots in the face of the camshaft should be oriented like this (5.0L engines - right [passenger's-side] bank)

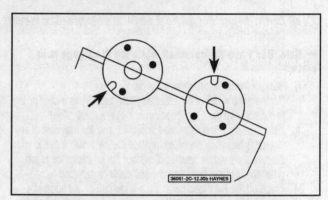

12.28b These U-shaped slots in the face of the camshaft should be oriented like this (5.0L engines - left [driver's-side] bank)

12.28c The camshaft cap cluster bolt tightening sequence - notice that each cap cluster (two total) is tightened separately and has its own sequence (2-valve 4.6L engines)

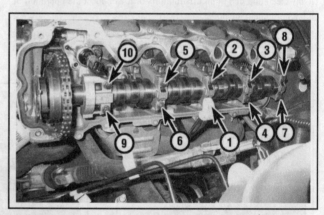

12.28d Camshaft cap bolt tightening sequence - notice that there are five separate camshaft caps for each camshaft (3-valve 4.6L and 5.4L engines)

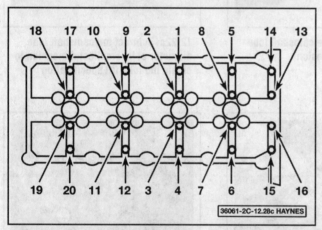

12.28e Camshaft cap bolt tightening sequence (5.0L engine)

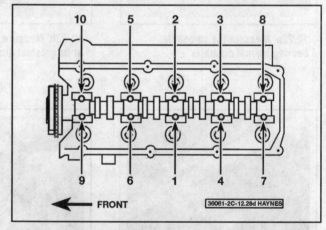

12.28f Camshaft cap bolt tightening sequence (6.2L engine)

INSTALLATION

◆ **Refer to illustrations 12.28a, 12.28b, 12.28c, 12.28d, 12.28e and 12.28f, 12.30a and 12.30b**

26 If the lash adjusters and/or camshaft followers have been removed, install them in their original locations (see Section 10).

27 Apply moly-base grease or camshaft installation lube to the camshaft lobes and bearing journals, then install the camshaft(s).

28 Install the camshaft caps in the correct locations, and loosely install all the bolts. Align the camshaft sprockets before tightening the cap bolts (see Section 9). On 5.0L engines, rotate the camshafts to their Neutral position before proceeding with installation of the VCT assemblies and timing chains (see illustrations). On all engines, follow the correct bolt-tightening sequence (see illustrations), and tighten the bolts to the torque listed in this Chapter's Specifications.

29 Install the timing chain(s) (see Section 9).

30 The remainder of installation is the reverse of removal.

13 Cylinder heads - removal and installation

✲✲ CAUTION:

These engines are difficult to work on and require special tools for many procedures. On any procedure involving timing chains, the steps must be read carefully and disassembly must proceed using the special tools, otherwise damage to the engine could result.

✲✲ CAUTION:

The engine must be completely cool when the cylinder heads are removed. Failure to allow the engine to cool off could result in cylinder head warpage.

➡ **Note: The manufacturer recommends that the engine be removed from the vehicle to perform this procedure (see Chapter 2D).**

REMOVAL

1 Relieve the fuel system pressure (see Chapter 4)
2 Disconnect the cable from the negative battery terminal (see Chapter 5).
3 Drain the cooling system (see Chapter 1).
4 Remove the valve covers (see Section 4).
5 Remove the intake manifold (see Section 5).
6 Remove the engine from the vehicle (see Chapter 2D).
7 Remove the exhaust manifolds (see Section 6).
8 Remove the timing chains, tensioners and sprockets (see Section 9).
9 Remove the camshafts (see Section 12).
10 Following the reverse of the tightening sequence (see illustration 13.19a, 13.19b or 13.19c), use a breaker bar to remove the cylinder head bolts. Loosen the bolts in sequence 1/4-turn at a time.
11 Lift the cylinder head(s) off the engine. If resistance is felt, place a

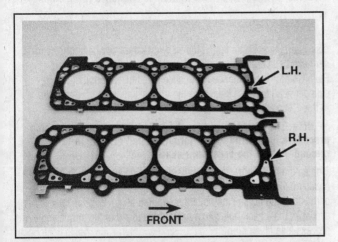

13.17 Identify the left and right cylinder head gaskets, the shapes are different and cannot be interchanged (4.6L and 5.4L engines)

wood block against the end and strike the wood block with a hammer.

✲✲ CAUTION:

The cylinder heads are aluminum; store them on wood blocks to prevent damage to the gasket sealing surfaces.

12 If the head sticks, use a pry bar at the corners of the cylinder head-to-engine block mating surface to break the cylinder head gasket seal. Do not pry between the cylinder head and engine block in the gasket sealing area.
13 Remove the cylinder head gasket(s). Before removing, note which gasket goes on which side (they are different and cannot be interchanged).

INSTALLATION

▶ **Refer to illustrations 13.17, 13.18, 13.19a, 13.19b, 13.19c and 13.19d**

✲✲ CAUTION:

New cylinder head bolts must be used for reassembly. Failure to use new bolts may result in cylinder head gasket leakage and engine damage.

14 The mating surfaces of the cylinder heads and engine block must be perfectly clean when the cylinder heads are installed. Use a gasket scraper to remove all traces of carbon and old gasket material, then clean the mating surfaces with silicone gasket remover and a plastic scraper. If there's oil on the mating surfaces when the cylinder heads are installed, the gaskets may not seal correctly and leaks may develop. When working on the engine block, cover the open areas of the engine with shop rags to keep debris out during repair and reassembly. Use a vacuum cleaner to remove any debris that falls into the cylinders.

✲✲ CAUTION:

Do not use abrasive wheels or metal scrapers on the heads or block surface; use a plastic scraper and chemical gasket remover, or the head gasket surfaces could have future leaks.

15 Check the engine block and cylinder head mating surfaces for nicks, deep scratches and other damage.
16 Use a tap of the correct size to chase the threads in the cylinder head bolt holes. Dirt, corrosion, sealant and damaged threads will affect torque readings.
17 Make sure the new gaskets are installed on the correct cylinder banks (see illustration). They are not interchangeable.
18 Position the new gasket(s) over the alignment dowels (see illustration) in the engine block.
19 Carefully position the cylinder heads on the engine block without

13.18 Position the gaskets on the correct cylinder banks, then push them down over the alignment dowels

13.19a Cylinder head bolt-tightening sequence - 4.6L/5.4L engines (left cylinder head shown)

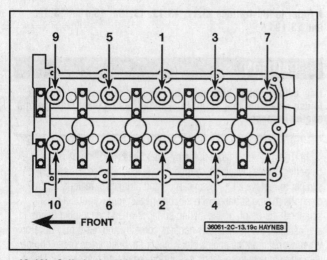

13.19b Cylinder head bolt-tightening sequence (5.0L engine)

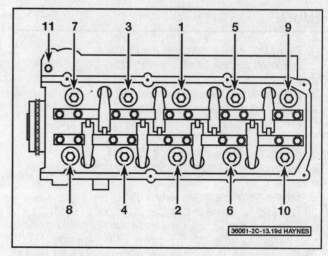

13.19c Cylinder head bolt-tightening sequence (6.2L engine)

13.19d Mark each cylinder head bolt with a paint stripe and, using a breaker bar and socket, tighten the bolts in sequence to the correct torque angle

disturbing the gaskets. Install the NEW cylinder head bolts (the cylinder head bolts are torque-to-yield design and they cannot be reused). Following the recommended sequence (see illustrations), tighten the cylinder head bolts, in stages, to the torque and angle of rotation listed in this Chapter's Specifications.

➡ **Note: The method used for the cylinder head bolt tightening procedure is referred to as "torque-angle" or "torque-to-yield" method. Follow the procedure exactly.**

Tighten the bolts in the first step using a torque wrench, then use a breaker bar and a special torque-angle gauge (available at most auto parts stores) to tighten the bolts the required angle. If the adapter is not available, mark each bolt with a paint stripe to aid in the torque angle process (see illustration).

20 The remainder of installation is the reverse of removal.

21 Change the engine oil and filter and refill the cooling system (see Chapter 1), then start the engine and check carefully for oil and coolant leaks.

14 Oil pan - removal and installation

REMOVAL

▶ **Refer to illustrations 14.5 and 14.8**

1 Disconnect the cable from the negative battery terminal (see Chapter 5).

2 Raise the vehicle and support it securely on jackstands.

3 Drain the engine oil and remove the oil filter (see Chapter 1).

4 Remove the skid plate, if equipped.

5 Remove the front crossmember (see illustration).

6 On 2010 and earlier 4WD models, remove the front axle assembly (see Chapter 8). On 2011 and later 4WD models, support the front differential with a floor jack and chain the differential to the jack, then remove the front axle support bushing bolts and lower the front axle. Make sure that no vacuum lines or wiring are stretched while lowering or raising the front axle.

7 Remove the oil level dipstick. On 2011 and later models, remove the front stabilizer bar bracket bolts and lower the stabilizer bar. Disconnect or unclip any hoses or wiring harness attached to the oil pan rail.

8 Remove the oil pan mounting bolts (see illustration).

9 Carefully separate the oil pan from the engine block. Don't pry between the engine block and oil pan or damage to the sealing surfaces may result and oil leaks could develop. Instead, dislodge the oil pan with a large rubber mallet or a wood block and a hammer.

INSTALLATION

▶ **Refer to illustration 14.12**

10 Use a gasket scraper or putty knife to remove all traces of old gasket material and sealant from the pan and engine block.

> ✱✱ **CAUTION:**
>
> **Be careful not to gouge the oil pan or block, or oil leaks could develop later.**

11 Clean the mating surfaces with RTV gasket remover. Make sure the bolt holes in the engine block are clean.

12 Apply a bead of RTV sealant to the four corner seams where the rear seal retainer meets the engine block, and where the front cover meets the engine block (see illustration).

➡ **Note: You must work fast to secure the oil pan to the engine within 5 minutes of applying the RTV.**

13 Carefully position the oil pan against the engine block and install the bolts finger tight. Make sure the gaskets haven't shifted, then tighten the bolts to the torque listed in this Chapter's Specifications. Start at the center of the oil pan and work out toward the ends in a spiral pattern.

14 The remainder of installation is the reverse of removal.

> ✱✱ **CAUTION:**
>
> **Allow at least 90 minutes for the RTV to dry, then refill the engine with oil before starting it (see Chapter 1).**

15 Start the engine and check carefully for oil leaks at the oil pan. Drive the vehicle and check again.

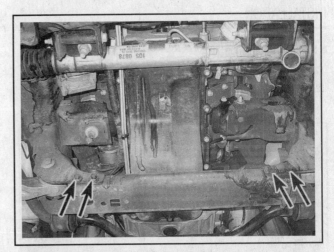

14.5 Crossmember mounting bolt locations (5.4L engine shown)

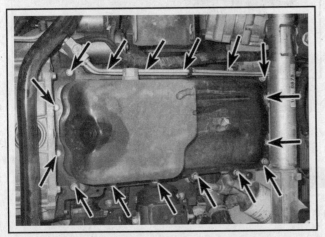

14.8 Remove the bolts from around the perimeter of the oil pan (5.4L engine shown)

14.12 Apply a bead of RTV sealant at the junctions of the front cover-to-engine block and the rear seal retainer-to-engine block before installing the oil pan

15 Oil pump - removal and installation

➡ **Note: The oil pump is available as a complete replacement unit only. No service parts or repair specifications are available from the manufacturer.**

REMOVAL

▶ **Refer to illustrations 15.3 and 15.5**

1 Raise the vehicle and support it securely on jackstands.
2 Drain the engine oil (see Chapter 1).
3 On all except 5.0L models, remove the oil pan (see Section 14). On all models, remove the two bolts that attach the oil pump pick-up tube to the oil pump (see illustration).
4 Remove the timing chain cover, timing chains, chain guides and crankshaft sprocket (see Section 9).
5 Remove the oil pump mounting fasteners (see illustration) and separate the pump from the engine block. On 5.0L and 6.2L models, the oil pump is mounted with four fasteners, two bolts and two stud-bolts. Note the location of the studs.

INSTALLATION

▶ **Refer to illustration 15.6**

6 Inspect the O-ring gasket on the pick-up tube (see illustration). If it's damaged, replace it.

7 Install the oil pump to the engine and tighten the bolts to the torque listed in this Chapter's Specifications.

➡ **Note: Prime the oil pump prior to installation. Pour clean oil into the pick-up port and turn the pump by hand.**

8 The remainder of installation is the reverse of removal.
9 Fill the engine with the correct type and quantity of oil. Start the engine and check for leaks.

15.3 Remove the two bolts retaining the pickup tube to the oil pump

15.5 Remove the oil pump mounting bolts and detach the oil pump from the engine block (4.6L engine shown)

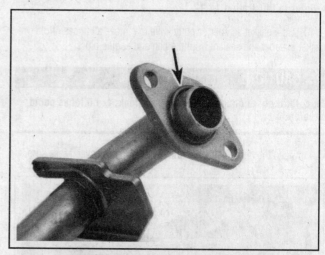

15.6 Before bolting the pickup tube back into the oil pump, inspect the O-ring and replace it if necessary

16 Flywheel/driveplate - removal and installation

This procedure is essentially the same as for the V6 engine. Refer to Part A of this Chapter and follow the procedure outlined there. However, use the bolt torque value listed in this Chapter's Specifications.

17 Rear main oil seal - replacement

▶ Refer to illustration 17.7

➡ **Note: Rear main oil seal replacement is a time-consuming job requiring several special tools; read through the procedure and obtain the necessary tools before beginning.**

1   Disconnect the cable from the negative battery terminal (see Chapter 5).

2   Raise the vehicle and support it securely on jackstands.

3   Remove the transmission (see Chapter 7).

4   Remove the flywheel/driveplate (see Section 16). Remove the toothed-wheel (used by the CKP sensor) between the crankshaft and driveplate.

5   Use a special tool and remove the crankshaft rear oil slinger.

6   Use a special tool and remove the rear main oil seal from the retainer.

✳✳ CAUTION:

To prevent an oil leak after the new seal is installed, be very careful not to scratch or otherwise damage the crankshaft sealing surface or the bore in the engine block.

7. Clean the crankshaft and seal bore in the retainer thoroughly and de-grease these areas with brake system cleaner. Check the seal contact surface on the crankshaft very carefully for scratches or nicks that could damage the new seal lip and cause oil leaks (see illustration). Lubricate the lip of the new seal and the outer diameter of the crankshaft with engine oil. Make sure the edges of the new oil seal are not rolled over.

8   Position the new seal onto the crankshaft.

➡ **Note: When installing the new seal, if so marked, the words THIS SIDE OUT on the seal must face out, toward the rear of the engine.**

17.7 Inspect the seal contact surface on the crankshaft for signs of excessive wear or grooves (seal retainer removed for clarity)

Use a special rear main oil seal installation tool to drive the seal in place. Make sure the seal is not off-set; it must be flush along the entire circumference of the seal retainer. An alternative method is to remove the seal retainer plate, and replace the seal on the bench, then apply a new gasket and RTV to the seal retainer plate and install it within five minutes of applying the RTV.

9   Use a special tool and install the crankshaft rear oil slinger.

10 The remainder of installation is the reverse of removal.

18 Engine mounts - check and replacement

▶ Refer to illustrations 18.1a and 18.1b

This procedure is essentially the same as for the V6 engine. Refer to Part A and follow the procedure outlined there, but refer to the accompanying illustrations for this Section.

➡ **Note: The amount of bolt installation torque applied to engine mounts in the covered trucks is substantial. Before beginning, make sure you have the proper tools and torque wrench that can tighten to the correct Specifications.**

18.1a With the engine raised slightly, remove the right side engine mount through-bolt

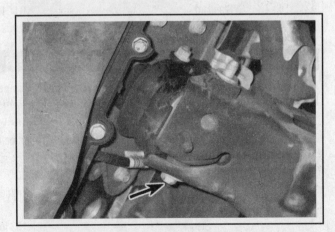

18.1b Left side engine mount through-bolt location

Specifications

General

Displacement

4.6L engine	281 cubic inches
5.0L engine	302 cubic inches
5.4L engine	330 cubic inches
6.2L engine	379 cubic inches

Cylinder numbers (front to rear)

Right side	1-2-3-4
Left (driver's) side	5-6-7-8

Firing order

4.6L and 5.4L	1-3-7-2-6-5-4-8
5.0L and 6.2L	1-5-4-8-6-3-7-2

36061-1-specs.C HAYNES

Cylinder locations

Camshaft

Lobe lift

4.6L (2-valve)	0.256 inch
4.6L (3-valve) and 5.4L	0.217 inch
5.0L	
Intake	0.207 inch
Exhaust	0.216 inch
6.2L	
Intake	0.315 inch
Exhaust	0.309 inch

Allowable lobe lift loss

4.6L (2-valve and 3-valve)	0.000 inch
5.0L	Not available
5.4L and 6.2L	0.005 inch
Endplay	0.001 to 0.007 inch

Journal diameter

4.6L (2-valve)	1.061 to 1.062 inches
4.6L (3-valve), 5.0L, 5.4L, and 6.2L	1.126 to 1.127 inches

Bearing inside diameter

4.6L (2-valve)	1.063 to 1.064 inches
4.6L (3-valve) , 5.0L, 5.4L, and 6.2L	1.128 to 1.129 inches

Journal-to-bearing (oil) clearance

Standard	0.001 to 0.003 inch
Service limit	0.002 inch maximum

Torque specifications   Ft-lbs (unless otherwise indicated)

➡ Note: One foot-pound (ft-lb) of torque is equivalent to 12 inch-pounds (in-lbs) of torque. Torque values below approximately 15 ft-lbs are expressed in inch-pounds, since most foot-pound torque wrenches are not accurate at these smaller values.

Accessory drivebelt pulley bolt(s)	18
Camshaft sprocket/Variable Camshaft Timing (VCT) unit bolt*	
4.6L/5.4L engines	
Step 1	30
Step 2	Tighten an additional 90-degrees
5.0L engine	
Step 1	133 in-lbs
Step 2	Tighten an additional 90-degrees

Torque specifications   **Ft-lbs (unless otherwise indicated)**

➡ **Note: One foot-pound (ft-lb) of torque is equivalent to 12 inch-pounds (in-lbs) of torque. Torque values below approximately 15 ft-lbs are expressed in inch-pounds, since most foot-pound torque wrenches are not accurate at these smaller values.**

Camshaft sprocket/Variable Camshaft Timing (VCT) unit bolt* (continued)

6.2L engine

Step 1	80 in-lbs
Step 2	Tighten an additional 90-degrees

Camshaft cap bolts

4.6L and 5.4L   89 in-lbs

5.0L and 6.2L

Step 1	53 in-lbs
Step 2	Tighten an additional 45 degrees

Rocker shaft bolts (6.2L)

Step 1	89 in-lbs
Step 2	177 in-lbs
Step 3	Tighten an additional 60 degrees

Coolant crossover assembly bolts   89 in-lbs

Cylinder head bolts*

4.6L and 5.4L

Step 1	30
Step 2	Tighten an additional 90-degrees
Step 3	Tighten an additional 90-degrees

5.0L

Step 1	18
Step 2	30
Step 3	Tighten an additional 90-degrees
Step 4	Tighten an additional 90-degrees

6.2L

Step 1, M12 bolts	18
Step 2, M12 bolts	44
Step 3, M12 bolts	Tighten an additional 90-degrees
Step 4, M12 bolts	Tighten an additional 90-degrees
Step 5, M8 bolts	177 in-lbs
Step 6, M8 bolts	Tighten an additional 45-degrees

Crankshaft pulley-to-crankshaft bolt

2010 and earlier models

Step 1	66
Step 2	Loosen one full turn
Step 3	37
Step 4	Tighten an additional 90-degrees

2011 and later models*

Step 1	103
Step 2	Loosen one full turn
Step 3	74
Step 4	Tighten an additional 90-degrees

Crossmember mounting bolts

4.6L, 5.0L and 6.2L	66
5.4L	75

Drivebelt tensioner bolts   18

Exhaust manifold studs

4.6L and 5.4L	106 in-lbs
5.0L and 6.2L	18

Use new bolts

Torque specifications   Ft-lbs (unless otherwise indicated)

➡ **Note:** One foot-pound (ft-lb) of torque is equivalent to 12 inch-pounds (in-lbs) of torque. Torque values below approximately 15 ft-lbs are expressed in inch-pounds, since most foot-pound torque wrenches are not accurate at these smaller values.

Exhaust manifold-to-cylinder head nuts
4.6L
    2008 and earlier   18
    2009 and later
        Step 1   159 in-lbs
        Step 2   177 in-lbs
5.4L   18
5.0L and 6.2L
    Step 1   18
    Step 2   24
Exhaust pipe-to-exhaust manifold nuts   30
Catalytic converter-to-exhaust manifold
  bolts (5.0L and 6.2L)   30
Flywheel/driveplate bolts   59
Intake manifold-to-cylinder head bolts
    4.6L and 5.4L   89 in-lbs
    5.0L and 6.2L
        Step 1 (manifold bolts)   89 in-lbs
        Step 2 (manifold bolts)   Tighten an additional 45 degrees
        Step 3 (fuel rail bolts)   89 in-lbs
        Step 4 (fuel rail bolts)   Tighten an additional 90 degrees
Oil pan-to-engine block bolts
    4.6L and 5.4L
        Step 1   18 in-lbs
        Step 2   15
        Step 3   Tighten an additional 60-degrees
    5.0L and 6.2L
        Step 1   18 in-lbs
        Step 2   89 in-lbs
        Step 3   Tighten an additional 45-degrees
Oil pan-to-rear main seal retainer bolts   15
Oil filter adapter bolts   18
Oil pump-to-engine block mounting bolts
    4.6L and 5.4L   89 in-lbs
    5.0L
        Step 1 (in the following sequence:
            Lower bolt   89 in-lbs
            Upper stud bolt   18
            Upper bolt   89 in-lbs
            Lower stud bolt   177 in-lbs
        Step 2 (in the following sequence:
            Lower bolt   Tighten an additional 45-degrees
            Upper stud bolt   Tighten an additional 75-degrees
            Upper bolt   Tighten an additional 45-degrees
            Lower stud bolt   Tighten an additional 60-degrees
    6.2L
        Step 1 (all fasteners)   18 in-lbs
        Step 2 (two upper bolts)   89 in-lbs
        Step 3 (two lower stud bolts)   177 in-lbs
        Step 4 (two upper bolts)   Tighten an additional 45-degrees
        Step 5 (two lower stud bolts)   Tighten an additional 60-degrees
Oil pick-up screen-to-engine block bolt   18
Oil pick-up tube-to-oil pump bolts   89 in-lbs
Rear main seal retainer-to-engine block bolts   89 in-lbs
Use new bolts

Torque specifications　　　　**Ft-lbs (unless otherwise indicated)**

➡ Note: One foot-pound (ft-lb) of torque is equivalent to 12 inch-pounds (in-lbs) of torque. Torque values below approximately 15 ft-lbs are expressed in inch-pounds, since most foot-pound torque wrenches are not accurate at these smaller values.

Timing chain cover bolts
    4.6L
        Step 1   15
        Step 2   Tighten an additional 60 degrees
    5.0L
        Cover-to-cylinder block and heads
            Step 1   18
            Step 2   Tighten an additional 60 degrees
        Oil pan-to-cover
            Step 1   89 in-lbs
            Step 2   Tighten an additional 45-degrees
    5.4L (see illustration 8.23)
        Step 1, Bolts 1 through 15   18
        Step 2, Bolts 6 and 7   35
    6.2L
        Cover-to-cylinder block and heads
            Step 1   89 in-lbs
            Step 2   177 in-lbs
            Step 3   Tighten an additional 45-degrees
        Oil pan-to-cover
            Step 1   89 in-lbs
            Step 2   Tighten an additional 45-degrees
Timing chain stationary guide bolts   89 in-lbs
Timing chain tensioner bolts   18
Valve cover bolts   89 in-lbs

Use new bolts

Notes

2D

GENERAL ENGINE OVERHAUL PROCEDURES

Section

1   General information - engine overhaul
2   Oil pressure check
3   Cylinder compression check
4   Vacuum gauge diagnostic checks
5   Engine rebuilding alternatives
6   Engine removal - methods and precautions
7   Engine - removal and installation
8   Engine overhaul - disassembly sequence
9   Pistons and connecting rods - removal and installation
10   Crankshaft - removal and installation
11   Engine overhaul - reassembly sequence
12   Initial start-up and break-in after overhaul

Reference to other Chapters

CHECK ENGINE light on - See Chapter 6

1 General information - engine overhaul

▶ **Refer to illustrations 1.1, 1.2, 1.3, 1.4, 1.5 and 1.6**

Included in this portion of Chapter 2 are general information and diagnostic testing procedures for determining the overall mechanical condition of your engine.

The information ranges from advice concerning preparation for an overhaul and the purchase of replacement parts and/or components to detailed, step-by-step procedures covering removal and installation.

The following Sections have been written to help you determine whether your engine needs to be overhauled and how to remove and install it once you've determined it needs to be rebuilt. For information concerning in-vehicle engine repair, see Chapter 2A, 2B or 2C.

The Specifications included in this Part are general in nature and include only those necessary for testing the oil pressure and checking the engine compression. Refer to Chapter 2A, 2B or 2C for additional engine Specifications.

It's not always easy to determine when, or if, an engine should be completely overhauled, because a number of factors must be considered.

High mileage is not necessarily an indication that an overhaul is needed, while low mileage doesn't preclude the need for an overhaul. Frequency of servicing is probably the most important consideration.

An engine that's had regular and frequent oil and filter changes, as well as other required maintenance, will most likely give many thousands of miles of reliable service. Conversely, a neglected engine may require an overhaul very early in its service life.

Excessive oil consumption is an indication that piston rings, valve seals and/or valve guides are in need of attention. Make sure that oil leaks aren't responsible before deciding that the rings and/or guides are bad. Perform a cylinder compression check to determine the extent of the work required (see Section 3). Also check the vacuum readings under various conditions (see Section 4).

Check the oil pressure with a gauge installed in place of the oil pressure sending unit and compare it to this Chapter's Specifications (see Section 2). If it's extremely low, the bearings and/or oil pump are probably worn out.

Loss of power, rough running, knocking or metallic engine noises, excessive valve train noise and high fuel consumption rates may also point to the need for an overhaul, especially if they're all present at the same time. If a complete tune-up doesn't remedy the situation, major mechanical work is the only solution.

An engine overhaul involves restoring the internal parts to the specifications of a new engine. During an overhaul, the piston rings are replaced and the cylinder walls are reconditioned (rebored and/or honed) (see illustrations 1.1 and 1.2). If a rebore is done by an automotive machine shop, new oversize pistons will also be installed. The main bearings, connecting rod bearings and camshaft bearings are generally replaced with new ones and, if necessary, the crankshaft may be reground to restore the journals (see illustration 1.3). Generally, the valves are serviced as well, since they're usually in less-than-perfect condition at this point. While the engine is being overhauled, other components, such as the distributor, starter and alternator, can be rebuilt as well. The end result should be similar to a new engine that will give many trouble free miles.

➡ **Note: Critical cooling system components such as the hoses, drivebelts, thermostat and water pump should be replaced with new parts when an engine is overhauled. The radiator should be checked carefully to ensure that it isn't clogged or leaking (see Chapter 3). If you purchase a rebuilt engine or short block, some rebuilders will not warranty their engines unless the radiator has been professionally flushed. Also, we don't recommend overhauling the oil pump - always install a new one when an engine is rebuilt.**

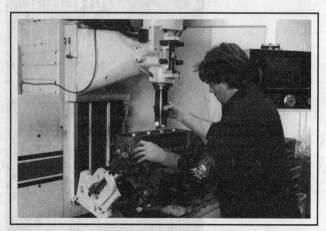

1.1 An engine block being bored. An engine rebuilder will use special machinery to recondition the cylinder bores

1.2 If the cylinders are bored, the machine shop will normally hone the engine on a machine like this

1.3 A crankshaft having a main bearing journal ground

1.4 A machinist checks for a bent connecting rod, using specialized equipment

1.5 A bore gauge being used to check the main bearing bore

1.6 Uneven piston wear like this indicates a bent connecting rod

Overhauling the internal components on today's engines is a difficult and time-consuming task which requires a significant amount of specialty tools and is best left to a professional engine rebuilder (see illustrations 1.4, 1.5 and 1.6). A competent engine rebuilder will handle the inspection of your old parts and offer advice concerning the reconditioning or replacement of the original engine, never purchase parts or have machine work done on other components until the block has been thoroughly inspected by a professional machine shop. As a general rule, time is the primary cost of an overhaul, especially since

the vehicle may be tied up for a minimum of two weeks or more. Be aware that some engine builders only have the capability to rebuild the engine you bring them while other rebuilders have a large inventory of rebuilt exchange engines in stock. Also be aware that many machine shops could take as much as two weeks time to completely rebuild your engine depending on shop workload. Sometimes it makes more sense to simply exchange your engine for another engine that's already rebuilt to save time.

2 Oil pressure check

♦ **Refer to illustrations 2.2a, 2.2b and 2.2c**

1   Low engine oil pressure can be a sign of an engine in need of rebuilding. A "low oil pressure" indicator (often called an "idiot light") is not a test of the oiling system. Such indicators only come on when the oil pressure is dangerously low. Even a factory oil pressure gauge in the instrument panel is only a relative indication, although much better for driver information than a warning light. A better test is with a

mechanical (not electrical) oil pressure gauge.

2   Locate the oil pressure sending unit:

a) On 4.2L V6 engines, the oil pressure sending unit is located on the front left side of the engine block near the front cover (see illustration).

b) On all other engines, the oil pressure sending unit is located near the lower left side of the engine on the oil filter adapter (see illustrations).

2.2a On 4.2L V6 engines, the oil pressure sending unit is located on the left side of the engine block near the front cover

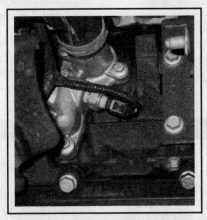

2.2b Oil pressure sending location - 4.6L and 5.4L V8 engines

2.2c Oil pressure sending unit location - 3.7L V6 engine shown, 3.5L V6 engine and 5.0L and 6.2L V8 engines similar

3   Unscrew and remove the oil pressure sending unit and screw in the hose for your oil pressure gauge. If necessary, install an adapter fitting. Use Teflon tape or thread sealant on the threads of the adapter and/or the fitting on the end of your gauge's hose.

4   Connect an accurate tachometer to the engine, according to the tachometer manufacturer's instructions.

5   Check the oil pressure with the engine running (normal operating temperature) at the specified engine speed, and compare it to this Chapter's Specifications. If it's extremely low, the bearings and/or oil pump are probably worn out.

3   Cylinder compression check

▶ **Refer to illustration 3.6**

1   A compression check will tell you what mechanical condition the upper end of your engine (pistons, rings, valves, head gaskets) is in. Specifically, it can tell you if the compression is down due to leakage caused by worn piston rings, defective valves and seats or a blown head gasket.

➡ **Note: The engine must be at normal operating temperature and the battery must be fully charged for this check.**

2   Begin by cleaning the area around the spark plugs before you remove them (compressed air should be used, if available). The idea is to prevent dirt from getting into the cylinders as the compression check is being done.

3   On all except the 6.2L V8 engine, remove all of the spark plugs from the engine (see Chapter 1). If you're working on a 6.2L V8, remove the ignition coils and the upper 8 spark plugs. If you're working on a 4.2L V6 engine, disconnect the primary (low voltage) wires from the coil pack.

4   Block the throttle wide open.

5   Disconnect the fuel pump electrical connector (see Chapter 4, Section 2).

6   Install a compression gauge in the spark plug hole (see illustration).

7   Crank the engine over at least seven compression strokes and watch the gauge. The compression should build up quickly in a healthy engine. Low compression on the first stroke, followed by gradually increasing pressure on successive strokes, indicates worn piston rings. A low compression reading on the first stroke, which doesn't build up during successive strokes, indicates leaking valves or a blown head gasket (a cracked head could also be the cause). Deposits on the undersides of the valve heads can also cause low compression. Record the highest gauge reading obtained.

8   Repeat the procedure for the remaining cylinders and compare the results to this Chapter's Specifications.

9   Add some engine oil (about three squirts from a plunger-type oil can) to each cylinder, through the spark plug hole, and repeat the test.

10 If the compression increases after the oil is added, the piston rings are definitely worn. If the compression doesn't increase signifi-

3.6 Use a compression gauge with a threaded fitting for the spark plug hole, not the type that requires hand pressure to maintain the seal

cantly, the leakage is occurring at the valves or head gasket. Leakage past the valves may be caused by burned valve seats and/or faces or warped, cracked or bent valves.

11 If two adjacent cylinders have equally low compression, there's a strong possibility that the head gasket between them is blown. The appearance of coolant in the combustion chambers or the crankcase would verify this condition.

12 If one cylinder is slightly lower than the others, and the engine has a slightly rough idle, a worn lobe on the camshaft could be the cause.

13 If the compression is unusually high, the combustion chambers are probably coated with carbon deposits. If that's the case, the cylinder head(s) should be removed and decarbonized.

14 If compression is way down or varies greatly between cylinders, it would be a good idea to have a leak-down test performed by an automotive repair shop. This test will pinpoint exactly where the leakage is occurring and how severe it is.

4   Vacuum gauge diagnostic checks

▶ **Refer to illustrations 4.4 and 4.6**

1   A vacuum gauge provides inexpensive but valuable information about what is going on in the engine. You can check for worn rings or cylinder walls, leaking head or intake manifold gaskets, incorrect carburetor adjustments, restricted exhaust, stuck or burned valves, weak valve springs, improper ignition or valve timing and ignition problems.

2   Unfortunately, vacuum gauge readings are easy to misinterpret, so they should be used in conjunction with other tests to confirm the diagnosis.

3   Both the absolute readings and the rate of needle movement are important for accurate interpretation. Most gauges measure vacuum in inches of mercury (in-Hg). The following references to vacuum assume the diagnosis is being performed at sea level. As elevation increases (or atmospheric pressure decreases), the reading will decrease. For every 1,000 foot increase in elevation above approximately 2,000 feet, the

gauge readings will decrease about one inch of mercury.

4   Connect the vacuum gauge directly to the intake manifold vacuum, not to ported (throttle body) vacuum (see illustration). Be sure no hoses are left disconnected during the test or false readings will result.

5   Before you begin the test, allow the engine to warm up completely. Block the wheels and set the parking brake. With the transmission in Park, start the engine and allow it to run at normal idle speed.

✳ WARNING:

Keep your hands and the vacuum gauge clear of the fans.

6   Read the vacuum gauge; an average, healthy engine should normally produce about 17 to 22 in-Hg with a fairly steady needle (see illustration). Refer to the following vacuum gauge readings and what they indicate about the engine's condition:

7   A low steady reading usually indicates a leaking gasket between the intake manifold and cylinder head(s) or throttle body, a leaky vac-

4.4 A simple vacuum gauge can be handy in diagnosing engine condition and performance

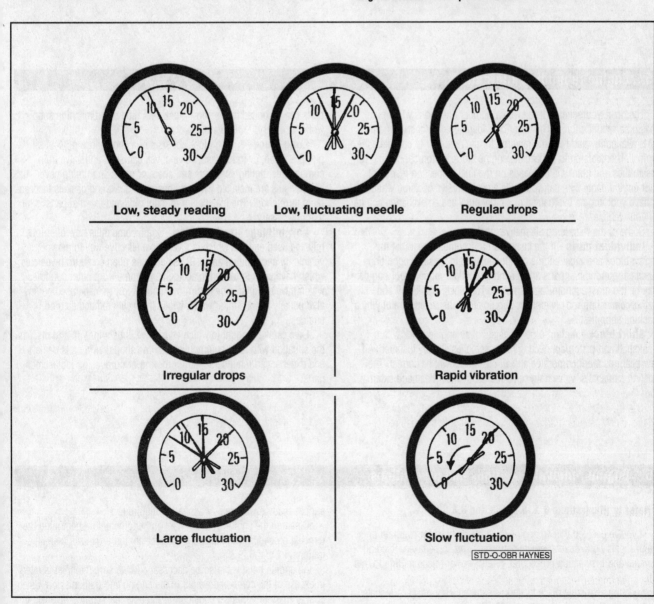

4.6 Typical vacuum gauge readings

uum hose, late ignition timing or incorrect camshaft timing. Check ignition timing with a timing light and eliminate all other possible causes, utilizing the tests provided in this Chapter before you remove the timing chain cover to check the timing marks.

8 If the reading is three to eight inches below normal and it fluctuates at that low reading, suspect an intake manifold gasket leak at an intake port or a faulty fuel injector.

9 If the needle has regular drops of about two-to-four inches at a steady rate, the valves are probably leaking. Perform a compression check or leak-down test to confirm this.

10 An irregular drop or down-flick of the needle can be caused by a sticking valve or an ignition misfire. Perform a compression check or leak-down test and read the spark plugs.

11 A rapid vibration of about four in-Hg vibration at idle combined with exhaust smoke indicates worn valve guides. Perform a leak-down test to confirm this. If the rapid vibration occurs with an increase in engine speed, check for a leaking intake manifold gasket or head gasket, weak valve springs, burned valves or ignition misfire.

12 A slight fluctuation, say one inch up and down, may mean ignition problems. Check all the usual tune-up items and, if necessary, run the engine on an ignition analyzer.

13 If there is a large fluctuation, perform a compression or leakdown test to look for a weak or dead cylinder or a blown head gasket.

14 If the needle moves slowly through a wide range, check for a clogged PCV system, incorrect idle fuel mixture, throttle body or intake manifold gasket leaks.

15 Check for a slow return after revving the engine by quickly snapping the throttle open until the engine reaches about 2,500 rpm and let it shut. Normally the reading should drop to near zero, rise above normal idle reading (about 5 in-Hg over) and return to the previous idle reading. If the vacuum returns slowly and doesn't peak when the throttle is snapped shut, the rings may be worn. If there is a long delay, look for a restricted exhaust system (often the muffler or catalytic converter). An easy way to check this is to temporarily disconnect the exhaust ahead of the suspected part and redo the test.

5 Engine rebuilding alternatives

The do-it-yourselfer is faced with a number of options when purchasing a rebuilt engine. The major considerations are cost, warranty, parts availability and the time required for the rebuilder to complete the project. The decision to replace the engine block, piston/connecting rod assemblies and crankshaft depends on the final inspection results of your engine. Only then can you make a cost effective decision whether to have your engine overhauled or simply purchase an exchange engine for your vehicle.

Some of the rebuilding alternatives include:

Individual parts - If the inspection procedures reveal that the engine block and most engine components are in reusable condition, purchasing individual parts and having a rebuilder rebuild your engine may be the most economical alternative. The block, crankshaft and piston/connecting rod assemblies should all be inspected carefully by a machine shop first.

Short block - A short block consists of an engine block with a crankshaft and piston/connecting rod assemblies already installed. All new bearings are incorporated and all clearances will be correct. The existing camshafts, valve train components, cylinder head and external parts can be bolted to the short block with little or no machine shop work necessary.

Long block - A long block consists of a short block plus an oil pump, oil pan, cylinder head, valve cover, camshaft and valve train components, timing sprockets and chain or gears and timing cover. All components are installed with new bearings, seals and gaskets incorporated throughout. The installation of manifolds and external parts is all that's necessary.

Low mileage used engines - Some companies now offer low mileage used engines which is a very cost effective way to get your vehicle up and running again. These engines often come from vehicles which have been in totaled in accidents or come from other countries which have a higher vehicle turn over rate. A low mileage used engine also usually has a similar warranty like the newly remanufactured engines.

Give careful thought to which alternative is best for you and discuss the situation with local automotive machine shops, auto parts dealers and experienced rebuilders before ordering or purchasing replacement parts.

6 Engine removal - methods and precautions

⬥ **Refer to illustrations 6.1, 6.2, 6.3 and 6.4**

If you've decided that an engine must be removed for overhaul or major repair work, several preliminary steps should be taken. Read all removal and installation procedures carefully prior to committing to this job.

Locating a suitable place to work is extremely important. Adequate work space, along with storage space for the vehicle, will be needed. If a shop or garage isn't available, at the very least a flat, level, clean work surface made of concrete or asphalt is required.

Cleaning the engine compartment and engine before beginning the removal procedure will help keep tools clean and organized (see illustrations 6.1 and 6.2).

An engine hoist will also be necessary. Make sure the hoist is rated in excess of the combined weight of the engine and transmission. Safety is of primary importance, considering the potential hazards involved in removing the engine from the vehicle.

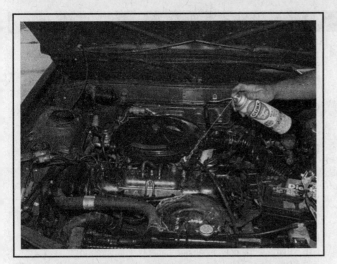

6.1 After tightly wrapping water-vulnerable components, use a spray cleaner on everything, with particular concentration on the greasiest areas, usually around the valve cover and lower edges of the block. If one section dries out, apply more cleaner

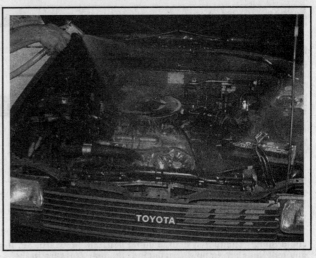

6.2 Depending on how dirty the engine is, let the cleaner soak in according to the directions and hose off the grime and cleaner. Get the rinse water down into every area you can get at; then dry important components with a hair dryer or paper towels

6.3 Get an engine stand sturdy enough to firmly support the engine while you're working on it. Stay away from three-wheeled models: they have a tendency to tip over more easily, so get a four-wheeled unit.

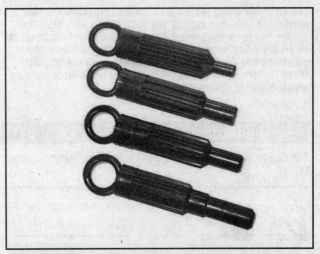

6.4 A clutch alignment tool is necessary if you plan to install a rebuilt engine equipped with a manual transmission

If you're a novice at engine removal, get at least one helper. One person cannot easily do all the things you need to do to remove a big heavy engine and transmission assembly from the engine compartment. Also helpful is to seek advice and assistance from someone who's experienced in engine removal.

Plan the operation ahead of time. Arrange for or obtain all of the tools and equipment you'll need prior to beginning the job (see illustrations 6.3 and 6.4). Some of the equipment necessary to perform engine removal and installation safely and with relative ease are (in addition to a vehicle hoist and an engine hoist) a heavy duty floor jack (preferably fitted with a transmission jack head adapter), complete sets of wrenches and sockets as described in the front of this manual, wooden blocks, plenty of rags and cleaning solvent for mopping up spilled oil, coolant and gasoline.

Plan for the vehicle to be out of use for quite a while. A machine shop can do the work that is beyond the scope of the home mechanic. Machine shops often have a busy schedule, so before removing the engine, consult the shop for an estimate of how long it will take to rebuild or repair the components that may need work.

7 Engine - removal and installation

▶ Refer to illustrations 7.6, 7.12, 7.29a, 7.29b, 7.30, 7.32a and 7.32b

✳ WARNING 1:

Gasoline is extremely flammable, so take extra precautions when you work on any part of the fuel system. Don't smoke or allow open flames or bare light bulbs near the work area, and don't work in a garage where a gas-type appliance (such as a water heater or clothes dryer) is present. Since gasoline is carcinogenic, wear fuel-resistant gloves when there's a possibility of being exposed to fuel, and, if you spill any fuel on your skin, rinse it off immediately with soap and water. Mop up any spills immediately and do not store fuel-soaked rags where they could ignite. The fuel system is under constant pressure, so, if any fuel lines are to be disconnected, the fuel pressure in the system must be relieved first (see Chapter 4 for more information). When you perform any kind of work on the fuel system, wear safety glasses and have a Class B type fire extinguisher on hand.

✳ WARNING 2:

The air conditioning system is under high pressure. DO NOT loosen any fittings or remove any components until after the system has been discharged. Air conditioning refrigerant should be properly discharged into an EPA-approved container at a dealer service department or an automotive air conditioning repair facility. Always wear eye protection when disconnecting air conditioning system fittings.

✳ WARNING 3:

The engine must be completely cool before beginning this procedure.

REMOVAL

1 Have the air conditioning system discharged by an automotive air conditioning technician.

2 Relieve the fuel system pressure (see Chapter 4).

3 Disconnect the cable from the negative battery terminal (see Chapter 5, Section 1).

4 Remove the fender splash shields and the hood (see Chapter 11). Cover the fenders and cowl using special pads. An old bedspread or blanket will also work.

5 On manual transmission models, remove the clutch fluid reservoir and secure it off to the side without disconnecting the hydraulic line.

6 Remove the cowl extension panel (see illustration).

7 Remove the intake ducts and the air filter housing (see Chapter 4).

8 Remove the Powertrain Control Module (PCM) (see Chapter 6).

9 Remove the intake manifold(s) (see Chapter 2A, 2B or 2C).

10 Remove the power steering fluid reservoir and position it off to the side.

11 Remove the battery and the battery tray (see Chapter 5).

12 Clearly label and disconnect all vacuum lines, emissions hoses, wiring harness connectors, ground straps and fuel lines between the engine and the chassis. Masking tape and/or a touch up paint applicator work well for marking items (see illustration). Take instant photos or sketch the locations of components and brackets.

13 Remove the drivebelt (see Chapter 1).

14 Remove the power steering pump (see Chapter 10).

15 Remove the radiator support cover (see Chapter 3).

16 Remove the air conditioning lines from the condenser and the manifold and tube assembly at the rear of the engine compartment (see Chapter 3). Remove the air conditioning manifold and tube bracket.

17 Raise the vehicle and support it securely on jackstands.

18 Drain the cooling system (see Chapter 1).

19 Drain the engine oil (see Chapter 1).

20 Detach the lower radiator hose from the engine (see Chapter 3).

21 Lower the vehicle and detach the heater hoses at the firewall (see

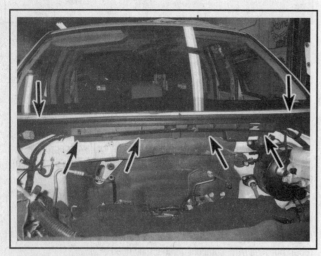

7.6 Remove the cowl extension panel mounting bolts

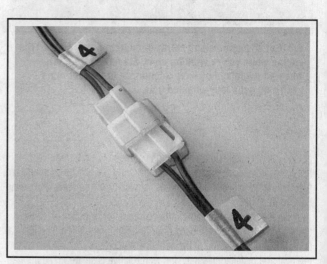

7.12 Label both ends of each wire and hose before disconnecting it

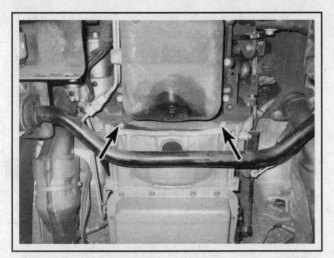

7.29a Remove the inspection cover bolts and separate the cover from the bellhousing

7.29b Also, remove this rubber plug from the left rear of the engine block . . .

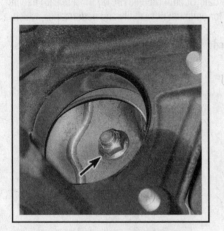

7.30 . . . for access to the torque converter nuts

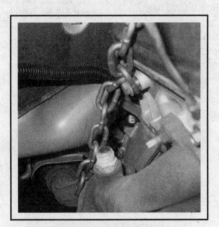

7.32a Attach the chain to the threaded boss on the cylinder head

7.32b Raise the engine using the engine hoist

Chapter 3). Also, remove the upper radiator hose.

22 If you're working on a 3.5L V6 engine, remove the turbocharger intake and outlet tubes.

23 Remove the cooling fan(s) and shroud(s) (see Chapter 3).

24 Remove the radiator (see Chapter 3).

25 Remove the air conditioning compressor (see Chapter 3).

26 Remove the oil filter (see Chapter 1).

27 Unplug the upstream oxygen sensor electrical connector(s).

28 Detach the heat shields, exhaust brackets and the exhaust pipes from the exhaust manifolds (see Chapter 4).

29 If you're working on a model with an automatic transmission, remove the inspection cover from the bellhousing on the transmission (see illustration). Also remove the rubber plug from the left rear part of the engine block (see illustration).

30 On automatic transmission models, remove the torque converter nuts (see illustration). Turn the crankshaft with a wrench to bring each nut into view.

31 Remove the starter motor (see Chapter 5).

32 Roll the engine hoist into position and attach the chain or sling to the engine (see illustrations). Take up the slack in the sling or chain, but don't lift the engine.

> ✳ **WARNING:**
>
> **DO NOT place any part of your body under the engine when it's supported only by a hoist or other lifting device.**

33 If you're working on a 5.4L V8 mated to a manual transmission, remove the transmission (see Chapter 7A) and the clutch pressure plate and disc (see Chapter 8).

34 Remove the engine mount through-bolts (see Chapter 2A, 2B or 2C).

35 Support the transmission with a floor jack. Be sure to place a piece of wood on the jack head to protect the transmission.

36 Recheck to be sure nothing is still connecting the engine to the vehicle. Disconnect anything still remaining.

37 Raise the engine slightly and inspect it thoroughly once more to

make sure that nothing is still attached, then slowly raise the engine out of the engine compartment. Check carefully to make sure nothing is hanging up.

38 It may be necessary to tilt or turn the engine as it is being raised.

⁂ WARNING:

Don't place any part of your body under the engine or between the engine and the vehicle.

39 Remove the flywheel/driveplate (see Chapter 2A, 2B or 2C) and mount the engine on an engine stand.

40 Inspect the engine mounts (see Chapter 2A, 2B or 2C) and transmission mount (see Chapter 7A). If they're worn or damaged, replace them.

INSTALLATION

41 Install the flywheel/driveplate (see Chapter 2A, 2B or 2C).

42 If you're working on a vehicle with manual transmission, install the clutch and pressure plate (see Chapter 8). Now is a good time to install a new clutch.

43 If you're working on a model with an automatic transmission, lubricate the torque converter hub with multi-purpose grease.

44 Carefully lower the engine into the engine compartment and engage it with the engine mounts and the transmission (except for 5.4L V8 engines mated to a manual transmission). If you're working on a vehicle with an automatic transmission, guide the torque converter into the crankshaft following the procedure outlined in Chapter 7B.

45 If you're working on a model with a 5.4L V8 engine and manual transmission, install the transmission (see Chapter 7A). Apply a dab of high-temperature grease to the input shaft and guide it into the crankshaft pilot bearing until the bellhousing is flush with the engine block.

46 Install the transmission-to-engine bolts and tighten them securely.

⁂ CAUTION:

DO NOT use the bolts to force the transmission and engine together!

47 Reinstall the remaining components in the reverse order of removal.

48 Add coolant, oil and transmission fluid as needed (see Chapter 1).

49 Reconnect the battery, run the engine and check for leaks and proper operation of all accessories, then install the hood and test drive the vehicle. The Powertrain Control Module (PCM) must relearn its idle and fuel trim strategy for optimum driveability and performance, which may take a few trips.

50 Have the air conditioning system recharged by the shop that discharged it.

8 Engine overhaul - disassembly sequence

1   It's much easier to remove the external components if it's mounted on a portable engine stand. A stand can often be rented quite cheaply from an equipment rental yard. Before the engine is mounted on a stand, the flywheel/driveplate should be removed from the engine.

2   If a stand isn't available, it's possible to remove the external engine components with it blocked up on the floor. Be extra careful not to tip or drop the engine when working without a stand.

3   If you're going to obtain a rebuilt engine, all external components must come off first, to be transferred to the replacement engine. These components include:

Clutch and flywheel (models with manual transmission)
Driveplate (models with automatic transmission)
Ignition system components
Emissions-related components
Engine mounts and mount brackets
Engine rear cover (spacer plate between flywheel/driveplate and engine block)
Intake/exhaust manifolds

Fuel injection components
Oil filter
Spark plugs
Thermostat and housing assembly
Water pump

➡ **Note: When removing the external components from the engine, pay close attention to details that may be helpful or important during installation. Note the installed position of gaskets, seals, spacers, pins, brackets, washers, bolts and other small items.**

4   If you're going to obtain a short block (assembled engine block, crankshaft, pistons and connecting rods), then remove the timing chain, cylinder head, oil pan, oil pump pick-up tube, oil pump and water pump from your engine so that you can turn in your old short block to the rebuilder as a core. See *Engine rebuilding alternatives* for additional information regarding the different possibilities to be considered.

9 Pistons and connecting rods - removal and installation

REMOVAL

▶ **Refer to illustrations 9.1, 9.3 and 9.4**

➡ **Note: Prior to removing the piston/connecting rod assemblies, remove the cylinder head and oil pan (see Chapter 2A, 2B or 2C).**

1   Use your fingernail to feel if a ridge has formed at the upper limit of ring travel (about 1/4-inch down from the top of each cylinder). If carbon deposits or cylinder wear have produced ridges, they must be completely removed with a special tool (see illustration). Follow the manufacturer's instructions provided with the tool. Failure to remove the ridges before attempting to remove the piston/connecting rod assemblies may result in piston breakage.

2   After the cylinder ridges have been removed, turn the engine so the crankshaft is facing up.

3   Before the main bearing cap assembly and connecting rods are removed, check the connecting rod endplay with feeler gauges. Slide them between the first connecting rod and the crankshaft throw until the play is removed (see illustration). Repeat this procedure for each connecting rod. The endplay is equal to the thickness of the feeler gauge(s). Check with an automotive machine shop for the endplay service limit (a typical end play limit should measure between 0.005 to 0.015 inch [0.127 to 0.381 mm]). If the play exceeds the service limit, new connecting rods will be required. If new rods (or a new crankshaft) are installed, the endplay may fall under the minimum allowable. If it does, the rods will have to be machined to restore it. If necessary, consult an automotive machine shop for advice.

4   Check the connecting rods and caps for identification marks. If they aren't plainly marked, use paint or marker to clearly identify each rod and cap (1, 2, 3, etc., depending on the cylinder they're associated with) (see illustration).

5   Remove the connecting rod cap bolts evenly.

➡ **Note: Obtain new bolts for final installation, but save the old bolts for the oil clearance check that will be performed later.**

6   Remove the number one connecting rod cap and bearing insert. Don't drop the bearing insert out of the cap.

7   Remove the bearing insert and push the connecting rod/piston assembly out through the top of the engine. Use a wooden or plastic hammer handle to push on the upper bearing surface in the connecting rod. If resistance is felt, double-check to make sure that all of the ridge was removed from the cylinder.

8   Repeat the procedure for the remaining cylinders.

9   After removal, reassemble the connecting rod caps and bearing inserts in their respective connecting rods and install the cap bolts finger tight. Leaving the old bearing inserts in place until reassembly will help prevent the connecting rod bearing surfaces from being accidentally nicked or gouged.

10 The pistons and connecting rods are now ready for inspection and overhaul at an automotive machine shop.

9.1 Before you try to remove the pistons, use a ridge reamer to remove the raised material (ridge) from the top of the cylinders

9.3 Checking the connecting rod endplay (side clearance)

9.4 If the connecting rods and caps are not marked, mark the caps to the rods by cylinder number (for example, this would be the No. 4 connecting rod)

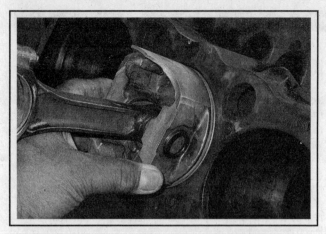

9.13 Install the piston ring into the cylinder then push it down into position using a piston so the ring will be square in the cylinder

9.14 With the ring square in the cylinder, measure the ring end gap with a feeler gauge

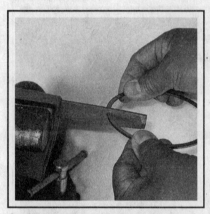

9.15 If the ring end gap is too small, clamp a file in a vise as shown and file the piston ring ends - be sure to remove all raised material

9.19a Installing the oil ring spacer in the piston oil ring groove

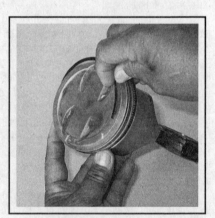

9.19b DO NOT use a piston ring installation tool when installing the oil control side rails (oil rings)

PISTON RING INSTALLATION

▶ **Refer to illustrations 9.13, 9.14, 9.15, 9.19a, 9.19b and 9.22**

11 Before installing the new piston rings, the ring end gaps must be checked. It's assumed that the piston ring side clearance has been checked and verified correct.

12 Lay out the piston/connecting rod assemblies and the new ring sets so the ring sets will be matched with the same piston and cylinder during the end gap measurement and engine assembly.

13 Insert the top (number one) ring into the first cylinder and square it up with the cylinder walls by pushing it in with the top of the piston (see illustration). The ring should be near the bottom of the cylinder, at the lower limit of ring travel.

14 To measure the end gap, slip feeler gauges between the ends of the ring until a gauge equal to the gap width is found (see illustration). The feeler gauge should slide between the ring ends with a slight amount of drag. A typical ring gap should fall between 0.010 and 0.020 inch [0.25 to 0.50 mm] for compression rings and up to 0.030 inch [0.76 mm] for the oil ring steel rails. If the gap is larger or smaller than specified, double-check to make sure you have the correct rings before proceeding.

15 If the gap is too small, it must be enlarged or the ring ends may come in contact with each other during engine operation, which can cause serious damage to the engine. If necessary, increase the end gaps by filing the ring ends very carefully with a fine file. Mount the file in a vise equipped with soft jaws, slip the ring over the file with the ends contacting the file face and slowly move the ring to remove material from the ends. When performing this operation, file only by pushing the ring from the outside end of the file towards the vise (see illustration).

16 Excess end gap isn't critical unless it's greater than 0.040 inch (1.01 mm). Again, double-check to make sure you have the correct ring type.

17 Repeat the procedure for each ring that will be installed in the first cylinder and for each ring in the remaining cylinders. Remember to keep rings, pistons and cylinders matched up.

18 Once the ring end gaps have been checked/corrected, the rings can be installed on the pistons.

19 The oil control ring (lowest one on the piston) is usually installed first. It's composed of three separate components. Slip the spacer/expander into the groove (see illustration). If an anti-rotation tang is used, make sure it's inserted into the drilled hole in the ring groove. Next, install the upper side rail in the same manner (see illustration). Don't use a piston ring installation tool on the oil ring side rails, as they may be damaged. Instead, place one end of the side rail into the

groove between the spacer/expander and the ring land, hold it firmly in place and slide a finger around the piston while pushing the rail into the groove. Finally, install the lower side rail.

20 After the three oil ring components have been installed, check to make sure that both the upper and lower side rails can be rotated smoothly inside the ring grooves.

21 The number two (middle) ring is installed next. It's usually stamped with a mark which must face up, toward the top of the piston. Do not mix up the top and middle rings, as they have different cross-sections.

➡ **Note: Always follow the instructions printed on the ring package or box - different manufacturers may require different approaches.**

22 Use a piston ring installation tool and make sure the identification mark is facing the top of the piston, then slip the ring into the middle groove on the piston (see illustration). Don't expand the ring any more than necessary to slide it over the piston.

23 Install the number one (top) ring in the same manner. Make sure the mark is facing up. Be careful not to confuse the number one and number two rings.

24 Repeat the procedure for the remaining pistons and rings.

INSTALLATION

25 Before installing the piston/connecting rod assemblies, the cylinder walls must be perfectly clean, the top edge of each cylinder bore must be chamfered, and the crankshaft must be in place.

26 Remove the cap from the end of the number one connecting rod (refer to the marks made during removal). Remove the original bearing inserts and wipe the bearing surfaces of the connecting rod and cap with a clean, lint-free cloth. They must be kept spotlessly clean.

Connecting rod bearing oil clearance check

▶ **Refer to illustrations 9.30, 9.35, 9.37 and 9.41**

27 Clean the back side of the new upper bearing insert, then lay it in place in the connecting rod.

28 Make sure the tab on the bearing fits into the recess in the rod. Don't hammer the bearing insert into place and be very careful not to nick or gouge the bearing face. Don't lubricate the bearing at this time.

29 Clean the back side of the other bearing insert and install it in the rod cap. Again, make sure the tab on the bearing fits into the recess in the cap, and don't apply any lubricant. It's critically important that the mating surfaces of the bearing and connecting rod are perfectly clean and oil free when they're assembled.

30 Position the piston ring gaps at intervals around the piston as shown (see illustration).

31 Lubricate the piston and rings with clean engine oil and attach a piston ring compressor to the piston. Leave the skirt protruding about 1/4-inch to guide the piston into the cylinder. The rings must be compressed until they're flush with the piston.

32 Rotate the crankshaft until the number one connecting rod journal is at BDC (bottom dead center) and apply a liberal coat of engine oil to the cylinder walls.

33 With the weight designation mark on top of the piston facing the front (timing chain end) of the engine, gently insert the piston/connecting rod assembly into the number one cylinder bore and rest the bottom edge of the ring compressor on the engine block. Install the pistons with the cavity mark(s) facing toward the timing chain.

34 Tap the top edge of the ring compressor to make sure it's contact-

9.22 Use a piston ring installation tool to install the number 2 and the number 1 (top) compression rings - be sure the directional mark on the piston ring(s) is facing toward the top of the piston

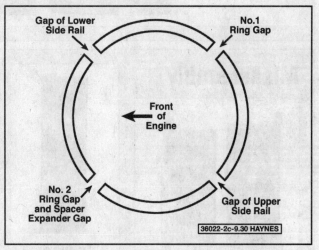

9.30 Position the piston ring end gaps as shown here before installing the piston/connecting rod assemblies into the engine

A	Top compression ring gap	D	Lower oil ring gap
B	Second compression ring	E	Oil ring spacer gap
C	Upper oil ring gap		

ing the block around its entire circumference.

35 Gently tap on the top of the piston with the end of a wooden or plastic hammer handle (see illustration) while guiding the end of the connecting rod into place on the crankshaft journal. The piston rings may try to pop out of the ring compressor just before entering the cylinder bore, so keep some downward pressure on the ring compressor. Work slowly, and if any resistance is felt as the piston enters the cylinder, stop immediately. Find out what's hanging up and fix it before proceeding. Do not, for any reason, force the piston into the cylinder - you might break a ring and/or the piston.

36 Once the piston/connecting rod assembly is installed, the connecting rod bearing oil clearance must be checked before the rod cap is

ENGINE BEARING ANALYSIS

Debris

Babbitt bearing embedded with debris from machinings

Microscopic detail of debris

Microscopic detail of gouges

Overplated copper alloy bearing gouged by cast iron debris

Aluminum bearing embedded with glass beads

Microscopic detail of glass beads

Damaged lining caused by dirt left on the bearing back

Misassembly

Result of a lower half assembled as an upper - blocking the oil flow

Excessive oil clearance is indicated by a short contact arc

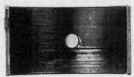

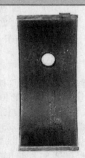

Polished and oil-stained backs are a result of a poor fit in the housing bore

Result of a wrong, reversed, or shifted cap

Overloading

Damage from excessive idling which resulted in an oil film unable to support the load imposed

Damaged upper connecting rod bearings caused by engine lugging; the lower main bearings (not shown) were similarly affected

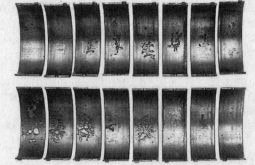

The damage shown in these upper and lower connecting rod bearings was caused by engine operation at a higher-than-rated speed under load

Misalignment

A warped crankshaft caused this pattern of severe wear in the center, diminishing toward the ends

A poorly finished crankshaft caused the equally spaced scoring shown

A tapered housing bore caused the damage along one edge of this pair

A bent connecting rod led to the damage in the "V" pattern

Lubrication

Result of dry start: The bearings on the left, farthest from the oil pump, show more damage

Result of a low oil supply or oil starvation

Severe wear as a result of inadequate oil clearance

Corrosion

Microscopic detail of corrosion

Corrosion is an acid attack on the bearing lining generally caused by inadequate maintenance, extremely hot or cold operation, or inferior oils or fuels

Microscopic detail of cavitation

Example of cavitation - a surface erosion caused by pressure changes in the oil film

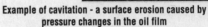

Damage from excessive thrust or insufficient axial clearance

Bearing affected by oil dilution caused by excessive blow-by or a rich mixture

9.35 Use a plastic or wooden hammer handle to push the piston into the cylinder

9.37 Place Plastigage on each connecting rod bearing journal parallel to the crankshaft centerline

9.41 Use the scale on the Plastigage package to determine the bearing oil clearance - be sure to measure the widest part of the Plastigage and use the correct scale; it comes with both standard and metric scales

permanently installed.

37 Cut a piece of the appropriate size Plastigage slightly shorter than the width of the connecting rod bearing and lay it in place on the number one connecting rod journal, parallel with the journal axis (see illustration).

38 Clean the connecting rod cap bearing face and install the rod cap. Make sure the mating mark on the cap is on the same side as the mark on the connecting rod (see illustration 9.4).

39 Install the old rod bolts, at this time, and tighten them to the torque listed in this Chapter's Specifications.

➡ **Note: Use a thin-wall socket to avoid erroneous torque readings that can result if the socket is wedged between the rod cap and the bolt. If the socket tends to wedge itself between the fastener and the cap, lift up on it slightly until it no longer contacts the cap. DO NOT rotate the crankshaft at any time during this operation.**

40 Remove the fasteners and detach the rod cap, being very careful

not to disturb the Plastigage. Discard the cap bolts at this time as they cannot be reused.

➡ **Note: You MUST use new connecting rod bolts.**

41 Compare the width of the crushed Plastigage to the scale printed on the Plastigage envelope to obtain the oil clearance (see illustration). The connecting rod oil clearance is usually about 0.001 to 0.002 inch. Consult an automotive machine shop for the clearance specified for the rod bearings on your engine.

42 If the clearance is not as specified, the bearing inserts may be the wrong size (which means different ones will be required). Before deciding that different inserts are needed, make sure that no dirt or oil was between the bearing inserts and the connecting rod or cap when the clearance was measured. Also, recheck the journal diameter. If the Plastigage was wider at one end than the other, the journal may be tapered. If the clearance still exceeds the limit specified, the bearing will have to be replaced with an undersize bearing.

✳✳ CAUTION:

When installing a new crankshaft always use a standard size bearing.

Final installation

43 Carefully scrape all traces of the Plastigage material off the rod journal and/or bearing face. Be very careful not to scratch the bearing - use your fingernail or the edge of a plastic card.

44 Make sure the bearing faces are perfectly clean, then apply a uniform layer of clean moly-base grease or engine assembly lube to both of them. You'll have to push the piston into the cylinder to expose the face of the bearing insert in the connecting rod.

45 Slide the connecting rod back into place on the journal, install the rod cap, install the new bolts and tighten them to the torque listed in this Chapter's Specifications.

✳✳ CAUTION:

Install new connecting rod cap bolts. Do NOT reuse old bolts - they have stretched and cannot be reused (see Step 5).

46 Repeat the entire procedure for the remaining pistons/connecting rods.

47 The important points to remember are:

a) *Keep the back sides of the bearing inserts and the insides of the connecting rods and caps perfectly clean when assembling them.*

b) *Make sure you have the correct piston/rod assembly for each cylinder.*

c) *The mark on the piston must face the front (timing chain end) of the engine.*

d) *Lubricate the cylinder walls liberally with clean oil.*

e) *Lubricate the bearing faces when installing the rod caps after the oil clearance has been checked.*

48 After all the piston/connecting rod assemblies have been correctly installed, rotate the crankshaft a number of times by hand to check for any obvious binding.

49 As a final step, check the connecting rod endplay, as described in Step 3. If it was correct before disassembly and the original crankshaft and rods were reinstalled, it should still be correct. If new rods or a new crankshaft were installed, the endplay may be inadequate. If so, the rods will have to be removed and taken to an automotive machine shop for resizing.

10 Crankshaft - removal and installation

REMOVAL

▶ **Refer to illustrations 10.1, 10.3 and 10.4**

➡ **Note: The crankshaft can be removed only after the engine has been removed from the vehicle. It's assumed that the flywheel or driveplate, crankshaft pulley, timing chain, oil pan, oil pump body, oil filter and piston/connecting rod assemblies have already been removed. The rear main oil seal retainer must be unbolted and separated from the block before proceeding with crankshaft removal.**

1   Before the crankshaft is removed, measure the endplay. Mount a dial indicator with the indicator in line with the crankshaft and just touching the end of the crankshaft as shown (see illustration).

2   Pry the crankshaft all the way to the rear and zero the dial indicator. Next, pry the crankshaft to the front as far as possible and check the reading on the dial indicator. The distance traveled is the endplay. A typical crankshaft endplay will fall between 0.003 to 0.010 inch (0.076 to 0.254 mm). If it is greater than that, check the crankshaft thrust surfaces for wear after it's removed. If no wear is evident, new main bearings should correct the endplay.

a) *On 4.2L V6 engines, the crankshaft thrust bearings are located in the upper number 3 crankshaft saddle and the lower number 3 crankshaft main bearing cap.*

b) *On 4.6L V8 engines, the crankshaft thrust washer is located on the back of the number 5 main bearing journal saddle and the thrust bearing is located in the number 5 main bearing cap.*

c) *On 5.4L V8 engines, the crankshaft thrust washers are located in the number 5 main bearing journal saddle and the number 5 main bearing cap.*

d) *On 3.5L and 3.7L V6 engines, the thrust bearings are installed at the number 4 crankshaft saddle and bearing cap.*

e) *On 5.0L and 6.2L V8 engines, the thrust bearings are installed at number 5 crankshaft saddle and bearing cap.*

➡ **Note: When installing thrust washers, make sure the grooves in the washer face the crankshaft.**

3   If a dial indicator isn't available, feeler gauges can be used. Gently pry the crankshaft all the way to the front of the engine. Slip feeler gauges between the crankshaft and the front face of the thrust bearing or washer to determine the clearance (see illustration).

4   Loosen the main bearing cap bolts 1/4-turn at a time each, until

10.1 Checking crankshaft endplay with a dial indicator

10.3 Checking the crankshaft endplay with feeler gauges at the thrust bearing journal

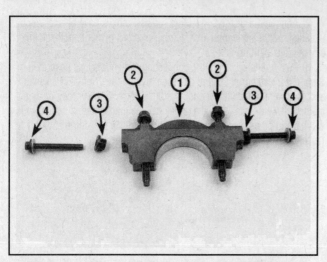

10.4 2005 and later 4.6L V8 engines use main bearing caps that use jack screws in addition to the main bearing cap bolts and side bolts

1	Main bearing cap	3	Jack screws
2	Main bearing bolts	4	Side bolts

10.17 Place the Plastigage onto the crankshaft bearing journal as shown

they can be removed by hand. On V8 models, follow the reverse of the tightening sequence (see illustrations 10.19a and 10.19b).

➡ **Note 1: 2005 and later 4.6L V8 engines are equipped with jack screws in addition to the vertical and horizontal main bearing bolts (see illustration). The jack screws have left-hand threads and must be turned counterclockwise to slightly sink them into the main bearing caps to allow cap removal.**

➡ **Note 2: Some 2004 4.6L engines may be equipped with jack screws, too.**

5 Remove the main bearing caps. Gently tap the main bearing cap with a soft-face hammer. Pull the main bearing cap straight up and off the cylinder block. Try not to drop the bearing inserts if they come out with the assembly.

6 Carefully lift the crankshaft out of the engine. It may be a good idea to have an assistant available, since the crankshaft is quite heavy and awkward to handle. With the bearing inserts in place inside the

engine block and main bearing caps, reinstall the main bearing cap assembly onto the engine block and tighten the bolts finger tight. Make sure the caps are in the exact order they were removed with the arrow pointing toward the front (timing chain and front cover) of the engine.

INSTALLATION

7 Crankshaft installation is the first step in engine reassembly. It's assumed at this point that the engine block and crankshaft have been cleaned, inspected and repaired or reconditioned.

8 Position the engine block with the bottom facing up.

9 Remove the mounting bolts and lift off the main bearing caps.

10 If they're still in place, remove the original bearing inserts from the block and from the main bearing cap assembly. Wipe the bearing surfaces of the block and main bearing cap assembly with a clean, lint-free cloth. They must be kept spotlessly clean. This is critical for determining the correct bearing oil clearance.

MAIN BEARING OIL CLEARANCE CHECK

◆ **Refer to illustrations 10.17, 10.19a, 10.19b, 10.19c, 10.19d, 10.19e, 10.19f, 10.19g and 10.21**

11 Without mixing them up, clean the back sides of the new upper main bearing inserts (with grooves and oil holes) and lay one in each main bearing saddle in the engine block. Each upper bearing (engine block) has an oil groove and oil hole in it.

✳ CAUTION:

The oil holes in the block must line up with the oil holes in the engine block inserts.

The thrust washer or thrust bearing insert must be installed in the correct location.

➡ **Note: The oil grooves in the thrust washers must face toward the front of the engine.**

Clean the back sides of the lower main bearing inserts and lay them in the corresponding location in the main bearing cap assembly. Make sure the tab on the bearing insert fits into the recess in the block or main bearing cap assembly.

✳ CAUTION:

Do not hammer the bearing insert into place and don't nick or gouge the bearing faces. DO NOT apply any lubrication at this time.

12 Clean the faces of the bearing inserts in the block and the crankshaft main bearing journals with a clean, lint-free cloth.

13 Check or clean the oil holes in the crankshaft, as any dirt here can go only one way - straight through the new bearings.

14 Once you're certain the crankshaft is clean, carefully lay it in position in the cylinder block.

15 Before the crankshaft can be permanently installed, the main bearing oil clearance must be checked.

16 Cut several strips of the appropriate size of Plastigage. They must be slightly shorter than the width of the main bearing journal.

17 Place one piece on each crankshaft main bearing journal, parallel with the journal axis as shown (see illustration).

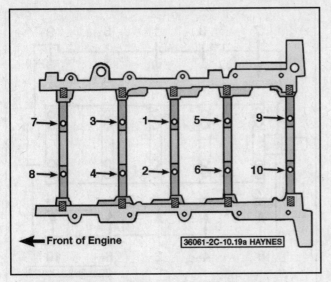

10.19a Main bearing cap bolt tightening sequence
(4.6L/5.4L V8 engines)

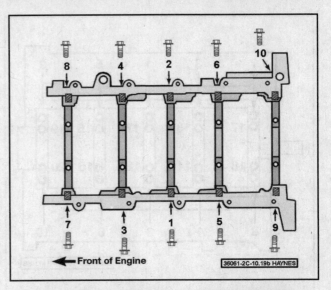

10.19b Main bearing cap side (horizontal) bolt tightening
sequence (4.6L/5.4L V8 engines). Note: *This sequence also
applies to the jack screws on 2005 and later 4.6L engines*

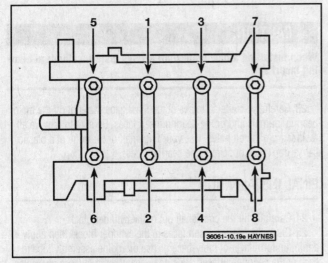

10.19c Main cap bolt tightening sequence - 3.5L/
3.7L V6 engines

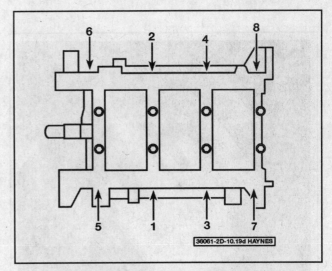

10.19d Side bolt tightening sequence - 3.5L/3.7L V6 engines

18 Clean the faces of the bearing inserts in the main bearing cap
assembly. Hold the bearing inserts in place and install the assembly
onto the crankshaft and cylinder block. DO NOT disturb the Plastigage.

19 Apply clean engine oil to all bolt threads prior to installation, then
install all bolts finger-tight. On 4.2L V6 engines, tighten the main bearing caps starting with the center cap and working out. On V8 engines
and 3.5L/3.7L V6 engines, tighten the bearing cap assembly bolts in the
sequence shown (see illustrations) progressing in steps, to the torque
listed in this Chapter's Specifications. DO NOT rotate the crankshaft at
any time during this operation.

➡ **Note: The V8 engines and 3.5L/3.7L V6 engines are equipped
with side bolts, but it isn't necessary to install them for the oil
clearance check.**

20 Remove the bolts in the reverse order of the tightening sequence
and carefully lift the main bearing caps straight up and off the block. Do
not disturb the Plastigage or rotate the crankshaft. If the main bearing
cap assembly is difficult to remove, tap it gently from side-to-side with

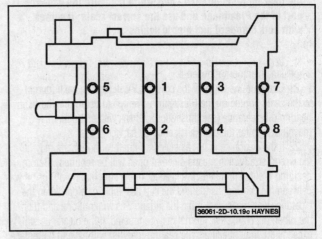

10.19e Main cap support, bolt tightening sequence -
3.5L/3.7L V6 engines

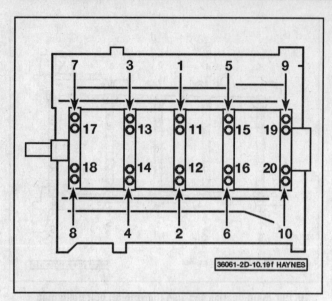

10.19f Main cap bolt tightening sequence - 5.0L and 6.2L V8 engines

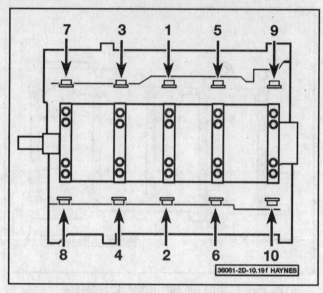

10.19g Side bolt tightening sequence - 5.0L and 6.2L V8 engines

10.21 Use the scale on the Plastigage package to determine the bearing oil clearance - be sure to measure the widest part of the Plastigage and use the correct scale; it comes with both standard and metric scales

a soft-face hammer to loosen it.

21 Compare the width of the crushed Plastigage on each journal to the scale printed on the Plastigage envelope to determine the main bearing oil clearance (see illustration). Check with an automotive machine shop for the crankshaft endplay service limits.

22 If the clearance is not as specified, the bearing inserts may be the wrong size (which means different ones will be required). Before deciding if different inserts are needed, make sure that no dirt or oil was between the bearing inserts and the cap assembly or block when the clearance was measured. If the Plastigage was wider at one end than the other, the crankshaft journal may be tapered. If the clearance still exceeds the limit specified, the bearing insert(s) will have to be replaced with an undersize bearing insert(s).

❊❊ CAUTION:

When installing a new crankshaft always install a standard bearing insert set.

23 Carefully scrape all traces of the Plastigage material off the main bearing journals and/or the bearing insert faces. Be sure to remove all residue from the oil holes. Use your fingernail or the edge of a plastic card - don't nick or scratch the bearing faces.

FINAL INSTALLATION

24 Carefully lift the crankshaft out of the cylinder block.

25 Clean the bearing insert faces in the cylinder block, then apply a thin, uniform layer of moly-base grease or engine assembly lube to each of the bearing surfaces. Be sure to coat the thrust faces as well as the journal face of the thrust bearing.

26 Make sure the crankshaft journals are clean, then lay the crankshaft back in place in the cylinder block.

27 Clean the bearing insert faces and apply the same lubricant to them. Clean the engine block and the main bearing caps thoroughly. The surfaces must be free of oil residue.

28 On V6 engines, apply a bead of RTV sealant to the engine block on the rear main bearing cap parting line. Be sure the main bearing cap is installed within four minutes after the RTV sealant is applied.

29 Prior to installation, apply clean engine oil to all bolt threads wiping off any excess, then install all bolts finger-tight.

30 Tighten the main bearing caps. On pushrod V6 engines, start with the center bearing cap bolts and work out. On V8 models and OHC V6 engines, follow the correct torque sequence (see illustrations 10.19a through 10.19g). Tighten the bolts to the torque listed in this Chapter's Specifications.

➡ **Note: On 4.6L V8 engines, tighten the main bearing cap (vertical) bolts first, then tighten the jack screws (on models so equipped) against the block by turning them clockwise (they have left hand threads, so turning them clockwise will back them out against the block), then install and tighten the side bolts.**

31 Recheck the crankshaft endplay with a feeler gauge or a dial indicator. The endplay should be correct if the crankshaft thrust faces aren't worn or damaged and if new bearings have been installed.

32 Rotate the crankshaft a number of times by hand to check for any obvious binding. It should rotate with a running torque of 50 in-lbs or less. If the running torque is too high, correct the problem at this time.

33 Install the new rear main oil seal (see Chapter 2A, 2B or 2C).

11 Engine overhaul - reassembly sequence

1   Before beginning engine reassembly, make sure you have all the necessary new parts, gaskets and seals as well as the following items on hand:

Common hand tools
A 1/2-inch drive torque wrench
New engine oil
Gasket sealant
Thread locking compound

2   If you obtained a short block it will be necessary to install the cylinder head, the oil pump and pick-up tube, the oil pan, the water pump, the timing chain and cover, and the valve covers (see Chapter 2A, 2B or 2C). In order to save time and avoid problems, the external components must be installed in the following general order:

Water pump
Exhaust manifolds
Lower intake manifold (3.7L V6 engine)*
Fuel injection components
Emission control components
Spark plug wires and spark plugs
Ignition coils or coil packs
Oil filter
Engine mounts and mount brackets
Clutch and flywheel (manual transmission)
Driveplate (automatic transmission)

* The intake manifold on V8 engines and the upper intake manifold on 3.7L V6 engines will be installed after the engine is installed.

12 Initial start-up and break-in after overhaul

❄ WARNING:

Have a fire extinguisher handy when starting the engine for the first time.

1   Once the engine has been installed in the vehicle, double-check the engine oil and coolant levels.

2   With the spark plugs out of the engine and the ignition system and fuel pump disabled, crank the engine until oil pressure registers on the gauge or the light goes out.

3   Install the spark plugs, hook up the plug wires and restore the ignition system and fuel pump functions.

4   Start the engine. It may take a few moments for the fuel system to build up pressure, but the engine should start without a great deal of effort.

5   After the engine starts, it should be allowed to warm up to normal operating temperature. While the engine is warming up, make a thorough check for fuel, oil and coolant leaks.

6   Shut the engine off and recheck the engine oil and coolant levels.

7   Drive the vehicle to an area with minimum traffic, accelerate from 30 to 50 mph, then allow the vehicle to slow to 30 mph with the throttle closed. Repeat the procedure 10 or 12 times. This will load the piston rings and cause them to seat properly against the cylinder walls. Check again for oil and coolant leaks.

8   Drive the vehicle gently for the first 500 miles (no sustained high speeds) and keep a constant check on the oil level. It is not unusual for an engine to use oil during the break-in period.

9   At approximately 500 to 600 miles, change the oil and filter.

10 For the next few hundred miles, drive the vehicle normally. Do not pamper it or abuse it.

11 After 2,000 miles, change the oil and filter again and consider the engine broken in.

GLOSSARY

B

Backlash - The amount of play between two parts. Usually refers to how much one gear can be moved back and forth without moving the gear with which it's meshed.

Bearing Caps - The caps held in place by nuts or bolts which, in turn, hold the bearing surface. This space is for lubricating oil to enter.

Bearing clearance - The amount of space left between shaft and bearing surface. This space is for lubricating oil to enter.

Bearing crush - The additional height which is purposely manufactured into each bearing half to ensure complete contact of the bearing back with the housing bore when the engine is assembled.

Bearing knock - The noise created by movement of a part in a loose or worn bearing.

Blueprinting - Dismantling an engine and reassembling it to EXACT specifications.

Bore - An engine cylinder, or any cylindrical hole; also used to describe the process of enlarging or accurately refinishing a hole with a cutting tool, as to bore an engine cylinder. The bore size is the diameter of the hole.

Boring - Renewing the cylinders by cutting them out to a specified size. A boring bar is used to make the cut.

Bottom end - A term which refers collectively to the engine block, crankshaft, main bearings and the big ends of the connecting rods.

Break-in - The period of operation between installation of new or rebuilt parts and time in which parts are worn to the correct fit. Driving at reduced and varying speed for a specified mileage to permit parts to wear to the correct fit.

Bushing - A one-piece sleeve placed in a bore to serve as a bearing surface for shaft, piston pin, etc. Usually replaceable.

C

Camshaft - The shaft in the engine, on which a series of lobes are located for operating the valve mechanisms. The camshaft is driven by gears or sprockets and a timing chain. Usually referred to simply as the cam.

Carbon - Hard, or soft, black deposits found in combustion chamber, on plugs, under rings, on and under valve heads.

Cast iron - An alloy of iron and more than two percent carbon, used for engine blocks and heads because it's relatively inexpensive and easy to mold into complex shapes.

Chamfer - To bevel across (or a bevel on) the sharp edge of an object.

Chase - To repair damaged threads with a tap or die.

Combustion chamber - The space between the piston and the cylinder head, with the piston at top dead center, in which air-fuel mixture is burned.

Compression ratio - The relationship between cylinder volume (clearance volume) when the piston is at top dead center and cylinder volume when the piston is at bottom dead center.

Connecting rod - The rod that connects the crank on the crankshaft with the piston. Sometimes called a con rod.

Connecting rod cap - The part of the connecting rod assembly that attaches the rod to the crankpin.

Core plug - Soft metal plug used to plug the casting holes for the coolant passages in the block.

Crankcase - The lower part of the engine in which the crankshaft rotates; includes the lower section of the cylinder block and the oil pan.

Crank kit - A reground or reconditioned crankshaft and new main and connecting rod bearings.

Crankpin - The part of a crankshaft to which a connecting rod is attached.

Crankshaft - The main rotating member, or shaft, running the length of the crankcase, with offset throws to which the connecting rods are attached; changes the reciprocating motion of the pistons into rotating motion.

Cylinder sleeve - A replaceable sleeve, or liner, pressed into the cylinder block to form the cylinder bore.

D

Deburring - Removing the burrs (rough edges or areas) from a bearing.

Deglazer - A tool, rotated by an electric motor, used to remove glaze from cylinder walls so a new set of rings will seat.

E

Endplay - The amount of lengthwise movement between two parts. As applied to a crankshaft, the distance that the crankshaft can move forward and back in the cylinder block.

F

Face - A machinist's term that refers to removing metal from the end of a shaft or the face of a larger part, such as a flywheel.

Fatigue - A breakdown of material through a large number of loading and unloading cycles. The first signs are cracks followed shortly by breaks.

Feeler gauge - A thin strip of hardened steel, ground to an exact thickness, used to check clearances between parts.

Free height - The unloaded length or height of a spring.

Freeplay - The looseness in a linkage, or an assembly of parts, between the initial application of force and actual movement. Usually perceived as slop or slight delay.

Freeze plug - See Core plug.

G

Gallery - A large passage in the block that forms a reservoir for engine oil pressure.

Glaze - The very smooth, glassy finish that develops on cylinder walls while an engine is in service.

H

Heli-Coil - A rethreading device used when threads are worn or damaged. The device is installed in a retapped hole to reduce the thread size to the original size.

I

Installed height - The spring's measured length or height, as installed on the cylinder head. Installed height is measured from the spring seat to the underside of the spring retainer.

J

Journal - The surface of a rotating shaft which turns in a bearing.

K

Keeper - The split lock that holds the valve spring retainer in position on the valve stem.

Key - A small piece of metal inserted into matching grooves machined into two parts fitted together - such as a gear pressed onto a shaft - which prevents slippage between the two parts.

Knock - The heavy metallic engine sound, produced in the combustion chamber as a result of abnormal combustion - usually detonation. Knock is usually caused by a loose or worn bearing. Also referred to as detonation, pinging and spark knock. Connecting rod or main bearing knocks are created by too much oil clearance or insufficient lubrication.

L

Lands - The portions of metal between the piston ring grooves.

Lapping the valves - Grinding a valve face and its seat together with lapping compound.

Lash - The amount of free motion in a gear train, between gears, or in a mechanical assembly, that occurs before movement can begin. Usually refers to the lash in a valve train.

Lifter - The part that rides against the cam to transfer motion to the rest of the valve train.

M

Machining - The process of using a machine to remove metal from a metal part.

Main bearings - The plain, or babbitt, bearings that support the crankshaft.

Main bearing caps - The cast iron caps, bolted to the bottom of the block, that support the main bearings.

O

O.D. - Outside diameter.

Oil gallery - A pipe or drilled passageway in the engine used to carry engine oil from one area to another.

Oil ring - The lower ring, or rings, of a piston; designed to prevent excessive amounts of oil from working up the cylinder walls and into the combustion chamber. Also called an oil-control ring.

Oil seal - A seal which keeps oil from leaking out of a compartment. Usually refers to a dynamic seal around a rotating shaft or other moving part.

O-ring - A type of sealing ring made of a special rubberlike material; in use, the O-ring is compressed into a groove to provide the sealing action.

Overhaul - To completely disassemble a unit, clean and inspect all parts, reassemble it with the original or new parts and make all adjustments necessary for proper operation.

P

Pilot bearing - A small bearing installed in the center of the flywheel (or the rear end of the crankshaft) to support the front end of the input shaft of the transmission.

Pip mark - A little dot or indentation which indicates the top side of a compression ring.

Piston - The cylindrical part, attached to the connecting rod, that moves up and down in the cylinder as the crankshaft rotates. When the fuel charge is fired, the piston transfers the force of the explosion to the connecting rod, then to the crankshaft.

Piston pin (or wrist pin) - The cylindrical and usually hollow steel pin that passes through the piston. The piston pin fastens the piston to the upper end of the connecting rod.

Piston ring - The split ring fitted to the groove in a piston. The ring contacts the sides of the ring groove and also rubs against the cylinder wall, thus sealing space between piston and wall. There are two types of rings: Compression rings seal the compression pressure in the combustion chamber; oil rings scrape excessive oil off the cylinder wall.

Piston ring groove - The slots or grooves cut in piston heads to hold piston rings in position.

Piston skirt - The portion of the piston below the rings and the piston pin hole.

Plastigage - A thin strip of plastic thread, available in different sizes, used for measuring clearances. For example, a strip of plastigage is laid across a bearing journal and mashed as parts are assembled. Then parts are disassembled and the width of the strip is measured to determine clearance between journal and bearing. Commonly used to measure crankshaft main-bearing and connecting rod bearing clearances.

Press-fit - A tight fit between two parts that requires pressure to force the parts together. Also referred to as drive, or force, fit.

Prussian blue - A blue pigment; in solution, useful in determining the area of contact between two surfaces. Prussian blue is commonly used to determine the width and location of the contact area between the valve face and the valve seat.

R

Race (bearing) - The inner or outer ring that provides a contact surface for balls or rollers in bearing.

Ream - To size, enlarge or smooth a hole by using a round cutting tool with fluted edges.

Ring job - The process of reconditioning the cylinders and installing new rings.

Runout - Wobble. The amount a shaft rotates out-of-true.

S

Saddle - The upper main bearing seat.

Scored - Scratched or grooved, as a cylinder wall may be scored by abrasive particles moved up and down by the piston rings.

Scuffing - A type of wear in which there's a transfer of material between parts moving against each other; shows up as pits or grooves in the mating surfaces.

Seat - The surface upon which another part rests or seats. For example, the valve seat is the matched surface upon which the valve face rests. Also used to refer to wearing into a good fit; for example, piston rings seat after a few miles of driving.

Short block - An engine block complete with crankshaft and piston and, usually, camshaft assemblies.

Static balance - The balance of an object while it's stationary.

Step - The wear on the lower portion of a ring land caused by excessive side and back-clearance. The height of the step indicates the ring's extra side clearance and the length of the step projecting from the back wall of the groove represents the ring's back clearance.

Stroke - The distance the piston moves when traveling from top dead center to bottom dead center, or from bottom dead center to top dead center.

Stud - A metal rod with threads on both ends.

T

Tang - A lip on the end of a plain bearing used to align the bearing during assembly.

Tap - To cut threads in a hole. Also refers to the fluted tool used to cut threads.

Taper - A gradual reduction in the width of a shaft or hole; in an engine cylinder, taper usually takes the form of uneven wear, more pronounced at the top than at the bottom.

Throws - The offset portions of the crankshaft to which the connecting rods are affixed.

Thrust bearing - The main bearing that has thrust faces to prevent excessive endplay, or forward and backward movement of the crankshaft.

Thrust washer - A bronze or hardened steel washer placed between two moving parts. The washer prevents longitudinal movement and provides a bearing surface for thrust surfaces of parts.

Tolerance - The amount of variation permitted from an exact size of measurement. Actual amount from smallest acceptable dimension to largest acceptable dimension.

U

Umbrella - An oil deflector placed near the valve tip to throw oil from the valve stem area.

Undercut - A machined groove below the normal surface.

Undersize bearings - Smaller diameter bearings used with re-ground crankshaft journals.

V

Valve grinding - Refacing a valve in a valve-refacing machine.

Valve train - The valve-operating mechanism of an engine; includes all components from the camshaft to the valve.

Vibration damper - A cylindrical weight attached to the front of the crankshaft to minimize torsional vibration (the twist-untwist actions of the crankshaft caused by the cylinder firing impulses). Also called a harmonic balancer.

W

Water jacket - The spaces around the cylinders, between the inner and outer shells of the cylinder block or head, through which coolant circulates.

Web - A supporting structure across a cavity.

Woodruff key - A key with a radiused backside (viewed from the side).

Specifications

General

Displacement
3.5L V6 engine	214 cubic inches
3.7L V6 engine	226 cubic inches
4.2L V6 engine	256 cubic inches
4.6L V8 engine	281 cubic inches
5.0L V8 engine	302 cubic inches
5.4L V8 engine	330 cubic inches
6.2L V8 engine	379 cubic inches

Bore and stroke
3.5L V6 engine	3.64 X 3.41 inches
3.7L V6 engine	3.76 X 3.41 inches
4.2L V6 engine	3.81 X 3.74 inches
4.6L V8 engine	3.55 X 3.54 inches
5.0L V8 engine	3.63 X 3.65 inches
5.4L V8 engine	3.55 X 4.17 inches
6.2L V8 engine	4.01 X 3.74 inches

Cylinder compression	Lowest cylinder must be within 75 percent of highest cylinder

Oil pressure (engine at operating temperature)
3.5L/3.7L V6 engines	30 psi @ 1,500 rpm
4.2L V6 engine	40 to 125 psi @ 2,500 rpm
4.6L/5.4L V8 engines	40 to 75 psi @ 2,000 rpm
5.0L V8 engine	10 to 15 psi @ idle
6.2L V8 engine	8 psi @ idle

Torque specifications   Ft-lbs (unless otherwise indicated)

➡ **Note: One foot-pound (ft-lb) of torque is equivalent to 12 inch-pounds (in-lbs) of torque. Torque values below approximately 15 ft-lbs are expressed in inch-pounds, since most foot-pound torque wrenches are not accurate at these smaller values.**

Flywheel/driveplate mounting bolts	See Chapter 2A, 2B or 2C
Torque converter nuts	27
Connecting rod bearing cap bolts*	

3.5L/3.7L V6 engines
Step 1	17
Step 2	32
Step 3	Tighten an additional 90-degrees

4.2L V6 engine
Step 1	18
Step 2	33
Step 3	Tighten an additional 105-degrees

4.6L/5.4L V8 engines
Step 1	32
Step 2	Tighten an additional 105-degrees

5.0L V8 engine
Step 1	177 in-lbs
Step 2	28
Step 3	Tighten an additional 105-degrees

Use new connecting rod bolts

Torque specifications   **Ft-lbs (continued) (unless otherwise indicated)**

➡ Note: One foot-pound (ft-lb) of torque is equivalent to 12 inch-pounds (in-lbs) of torque. Torque values below approximately 15 ft-lbs are expressed in inch-pounds, since most foot-pound torque wrenches are not accurate at these smaller values.

Connecting rod bearing cap bolts* (continued)
    6.2L V8 engine
        Step 1   177 in-lbs
        Step 2   32
        Step 3   Tighten an additional 135-degrees
Main bearing cap bolts (tighten the bolts in the order listed here)
    3.5L and early-build 3.7L engines (engine code 1G 372 BA)
        Vertical cap bolts
               Step 1   44
               Step 2   Tighten an additional 90-degrees
        Side bolts
               Step 1, side bolts (new)   33
               Step 2, side bolts   Tighten an additional 90-degrees
        Bearing cap support bolts
               Step 1   177 in-lbs
               Step 2   Tighten an additional 180-degrees
    3.7L V6 engine, late-build (engine code 1G 372 CA)
        Vertical cap bolts
               Step 1   24
               Step 2   Tighten an additional 135-degrees
        Side bolts
               Step 1, side bolts (new)   18
               Step 2, side bolts   Tighten an additional 180-degrees
        Bearing cap support bolts
               Step 1   177 in-lbs
               Step 2   Tighten an additional 180-degrees
    4.2L V6 engine
        Step 1   41
        Step 2   Tighten an additional 90-degrees
    4.6L/5.4L V8 engines
        Main bolts (vertical bolts) (see illustration 10.19a)
               Step 1   30
               Step 2   Tighten an additional 90-degrees
        Jack screws (2005 and later 4.6L V8 engines**)
               Step 1   44 in-lbs
               Step 2   89 in-lbs
        Side bolts (horizontal bolts) (see illustration 10.19b)
               2004 4.6L V8 and all 5.4L V8 engines
                   Step 1   22
                   Step 2   Tighten an additional 90-degrees
               2005 and later 4.6L V8 engines   15
* Use new connecting rod bolts
** And 2004 models so equipped

Torque specifications (continued)   Ft-lbs (unless otherwise indicated)

➡ **Note: One foot-pound (ft-lb) of torque is equivalent to 12 inch-pounds (in-lbs) of torque. Torque values below approximately 15 ft-lbs are expressed in inch-pounds, since most foot-pound torque wrenches are not accurate at these smaller values.**

Main bearing cap bolts (tighten the bolts in the order listed here)
    5.0L V8 engine
        Vertical bolts

Step 1, bolts 1 through 20	177 in-lbs
Step 2, bolts 1 through 10	30
Step 3, bolts 11 through 20	48
Step 4, bolts 1 through 20	Tighten an additional 90-degrees

        Side bolts (new)

Step 1	89 in-lb
Step 2	22
Step 3	Tighten an additional 60-degrees

    6.2L V8 engine
        Vertical bolts

Step 1, bolts 1 though 10	26
Step 2, bolts 1 through 10	26
Step 3, bolts 1 through 10	Tighten an additional 90-degrees
Step 4, bolts 11 through 20	26
Step 5, bolts 11 through 20	48
Step 6, bolts 11 through 20	Tighten an additional 90-degrees

        Side bolts

Step 1	177 in-lbs
Step 2	26
Step 3	Tighten an additional 60-degrees

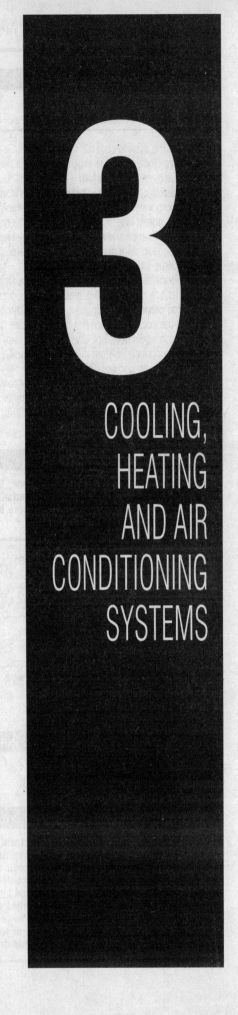

3

COOLING, HEATING AND AIR CONDITIONING SYSTEMS

Section

1   General information
2   Antifreeze - general information
3   Thermostat - check and replacement
4   Engine cooling fan - check and replacement
5   Coolant expansion tank - removal and installation
6   Radiator - removal and installation
7   Water pump - check
8   Water pump - replacement
9   Coolant temperature indicator - check
10 Blower motor resistor and blower motor - replacement
11 Heater/air conditioner control assembly - removal and installation
12 Heater core - replacement
13 Air conditioning and heating system - check and maintenance
14 Air conditioning compressor - removal and installation
15 Air conditioning accumulator - removal and installation
16 Air conditioning condenser - removal and installation
17 Air conditioning pressure cycling switch and high-pressure
    cutoff switch - replacement
18 Air conditioning orifice tube - removal and installation

Reference to other Chapters

Coolant level check - See Chapter 1
Cooling system check - See Chapter 1
Cooling system servicing (draining, flushing and refilling) - See Chapter 1
Drivebelt check, adjustment and replacement - See Chapter 1
Underhood hose check and replacement - See Chapter 1

1   General information

ENGINE COOLING SYSTEM

The cooling system consists of a radiator, an expansion tank, a pressure cap (located on the expansion tank), a thermostat, a cooling fan and clutch, and a belt-driven water pump.

The radiator cooling fan is mounted on the front of the water pump. The fan incorporates a fluid drive fan clutch, which saves horsepower and reduces noise. When the engine is cold, the fluid in the clutch offers little resistance and allows the fan to freewheel. As the engine heats up and reaches a predetermined temperature, the fluid in the clutch thickens and drives the fan.

The expansion tank, referred to by the manufacturer as a degas bottle, functions somewhat differently than a conventional recovery tank. Designed to separate any trapped air in the coolant, it is connected directly to the cooling system and has a pressure cap on top. The radiator on these models does not have a pressure cap. When the thermostat is closed, no coolant flows in the expansion tank, but when the engine is fully warmed up, coolant flows from the top of the radiator through a small hose that enters the top of the expansion tank, where the air separates and the coolant falls into the tank, and is then fed to the cooling system through a larger hose connected to a fitting on the lower radiator hose.

✳ WARNING:

Unlike a conventional coolant recovery tank, the pressure cap on the expansion tank should never be opened after the engine has warmed up, because of the danger of severe burns caused by steam or scalding coolant.

Coolant in the left side of the radiator circulates through the lower radiator hose to the water pump, where it is forced through coolant passages in the cylinder block. The coolant then travels up into the cylinder head, circulates around the combustion chambers and valve seats, travels out of the cylinder head past the open thermostat into the upper radiator hose and back into the radiator.

When the engine is cold, the thermostat restricts the circulation of coolant to the engine. When the minimum operating temperature is reached, the thermostat begins to open, allowing coolant to return to the radiator.

TRANSMISSION COOLING SYSTEMS

Vehicles with an automatic transmission are equipped with a transmission fluid cooler located inside the radiator. Hot transmission fluid is directed to the cooler by lines and hoses attached to the radiator; but actually, they are connected to the cooler inside. The cooler is like a small radiator within the radiator. Once cooled, the fluid is directed back to the transmission. Some models are also equipped with an additional (auxiliary) external transmission oil cooler that is located in front of the air conditioning condenser and the radiator.

For more information on external transmission oil coolers, refer to Chapter 7B.

HEATING SYSTEM

The heating system consists of the heater controls, the heater core, the heater blower assembly (which houses the blower motor and the blower motor resistor), and the hoses connecting the heater core to the engine cooling system. Hot engine coolant is circulated through the heater core. When the heater mode is activated, a flap door opens to expose the heater box to the passenger compartment. A fan switch on the heater controls activates the blower motor, which forces air through the core, heating the air.

AIR CONDITIONING SYSTEM

The air conditioning system consists of the condenser, which is mounted in front of the radiator and the external transaxle fluid cooler (if equipped), the evaporator case assembly under the dash, a compressor mounted on the engine, and the plumbing connecting all of the above components.

A blower fan forces the warmer air of the passenger compartment through the evaporator core (sort of a radiator-in-reverse), transferring the heat from the air to the refrigerant. The liquid refrigerant boils off into low pressure vapor, taking the heat with it when it leaves the evaporator.

2   Antifreeze - general information

▶ **Refer to illustration 2.5**

✳ WARNING:

Do not allow antifreeze to come in contact with your skin or painted surfaces of the vehicle. Rinse off spills immediately with plenty of water. Antifreeze is highly toxic if ingested. Never leave antifreeze lying around in an open container or in puddles on the floor; children and pets are attracted by its sweet smell and may drink it. Check with local authorities about disposing of used antifreeze. Many communities have collection centers which will see that antifreeze is disposed of safely. Never dump used antifreeze on the ground or pour it into drains.

✳ CAUTION:

Do not mix coolants of different colors. Doing so might damage the cooling system and/or the engine. The manufacturer specifies either a green colored coolant or a yellow colored coolant to be used in these systems. Read the warning label in the engine compartment for additional information.

➡ **Note: Non-toxic antifreeze is now manufactured and available at local auto parts stores, but even this type must be disposed of properly.**

The cooling system should be filled with a water/ethylene glycol based antifreeze solution, which will prevent freezing down to at least -20-degrees F. It also provides protection against corrosion and increases the coolant boiling point. The manufacturer recommends that the correct type of coolant be used and strongly urges that coolant types not be mixed (see Chapter 1).

Drain, flush and refill the cooling system at least every other year (see Chapter 1). The use of antifreeze solutions for periods of longer than two years is likely to cause damage and encourage the formation of rust and scale in the system.

Before adding antifreeze to the system, inspect all hose connections. Antifreeze can leak through very minute openings.

The exact mixture of antifreeze to water, which you should use, depends on the relative weather conditions. The mixture should contain at least 40-percent antifreeze, but should never contain more than 60-percent antifreeze. Consult the mixture ratio chart on the container before adding coolant.

Hydrometers are available at most auto parts stores to test the coolant (see illustration).

※ WARNING:

Do not remove the expansion tank cap, drain the coolant or perform any service procedures on the cooling system until the engine has cooled completely.

2.5 Use a hydrometer (available at auto parts stores) to test the condition of your coolant

3   Thermostat - check and replacement

CHECK

1   Before assuming the thermostat is to blame for a cooling system problem, check the coolant level, drivebelt tension (see Chapter 1) and temperature gauge operation.

2   If the engine seems to be taking a long time to warm up, based on heater output or temperature gauge operation, the thermostat is probably stuck open. Replace the thermostat with a new one.

3   If the engine runs hot, use your hand to check the temperature of the upper radiator hose. If the hose isn't hot, but the engine is, the thermostat is probably stuck closed, preventing the coolant inside the engine from escaping to the radiator. Replace the thermostat.

※ CAUTION:

Don't drive the vehicle without a thermostat. The computer may stay in open loop and emissions and fuel economy will suffer.

4   If the upper radiator hose is hot, it means that the coolant is flowing and the thermostat is open. Consult the *Troubleshooting* section at the front of this manual for cooling system diagnosis.

REPLACEMENT

※ WARNING:

Wait until the engine is completely cool before beginning this procedure.

➡ **Note: Cover the drivebelts with kitchen plastic-wrap. If coolant gets on the belts it can ruin them.**

5   Disconnect the cable from the negative battery terminal (see Chapter 5, Section 1).

6   Drain the cooling system (see Chapter 1). If the coolant is relatively new and still in good condition, save it and reuse it.

7   On 5.4L engine models, remove the air inlet duct to the air cleaner housing. On all other models, remove the air duct between the air cleaner housing and the throttle body if necessary (see Chapter 4).

8   On 4.2L and 4.6L V6, 5.4L and 6.2L V8 engines, follow the upper radiator hose to the thermostat housing. On 3.7L and 3.7L V6, and 5.0L V8 engines, follow the lower radiator hose to the thermostat housing.

9   Loosen the hose clamp by squeezing the ends together. Hose clamp pliers work best, but regular pliers will work also. If the radiator hose is stuck, grasp it near the end with a pair of adjustable pliers and twist it to break the seal, then pull it off. If the hose is old or if it has deteriorated, cut it off and install a new one.

10 If the outer surface of the thermostat housing cover, which mates with the hose, is already corroded, pitted, or otherwise deteriorated, it might be damaged even more by hose removal. If it is, replace the thermostat housing cover.

V6 models

11 Remove the fasteners and detach the thermostat cover. If the cover is stuck, tap it with a soft-face hammer to jar it loose. Be prepared for some coolant to spill as the gasket seal is broken.

12 Note how the thermostat is installed with emphasis on the position of the small jiggle valve and then remove the thermostat by twisting it.

13 Carefully remove all traces of old gasket material and sealant from the housing and cover with a gasket scraper, if applicable.

14 Position the thermostat into the housing cover, with the jiggle valve at the top, then turn it clockwise or counterclockwise to lock it in place. The jiggle valve must end up in either the 11 o'clock or 1 o'clock position. Using a new gasket, install the housing cover and tighten the bolts to the torque listed in this Chapter's Specifications.

3.15 Remove the thermostat housing cover mounting bolts (V8 model shown)

3.16 Thermostat details on the V8 engine

1	*Thermostat housing*	3	*Thermostat*
2	*O-ring seal*	4	*Jiggle valve*

V8 models

♦ **Refer to illustrations 3.15 and 3.16**

15 Remove the fasteners and detach the thermostat housing cover (see illustration). If the cover is stuck, tap it with a soft-face hammer to jar it loose. Be prepared for some coolant to spill as the seal is broken.

➡ **Note: On 4.6L engine models, remove the small bracket that is attached to the thermostat cover before removing it.**

16 Note how the thermostat is installed, then remove it from the housing (see illustration).

17 Install the thermostat into the housing, then install a new O-ring seal.

18 Install the thermostat housing cover and tighten the bolts to the torque listed in this Chapter's Specifications. .

All models

19 Reattach the radiator hose to the thermostat housing cover. Make sure that the hose clamp still holds tight. If it doesn't, replace it.

20 Refill the cooling system (see Chapter 1) and reconnect the battery (see Chapter 5, Section 1).

21 Start the engine and allow it to reach normal operating temperature, then check for leaks and proper thermostat operation (as described in Steps 2 through 4).

---

4   Engine cooling fan - check and replacement

CHECK

✳✳ WARNING 1:

While checking the fan, make sure that the engine is NOT started. If it is, you could be severely injured.

✳✳ WARNING 2:

Before the fan clutch operation can be checked in Step 5, the engine must be warmed up to its normal operating temperature and then turned off. Even though the engine won't be running during this check, it's HOT! Make sure that you don't touch the engine itself during this check, or you could be burned.

✳✳ WARNING 3:

Keep hands, tools and clothing away from the fan when the engine is running. To avoid injury or damage DO NOT operate the engine with a damaged fan. Do not attempt to repair fan blades - replace a damaged fan with a new one.

1 Symptoms of fan clutch failure are continuous noisy operation, looseness, vibration and/or silicone fluid leaking from the clutch.

Cold engine checks

2 Rock the fan back and forth by hand to check for excessive bearing play.

3 With the engine cold, turn the blades by hand. The fan should turn freely.

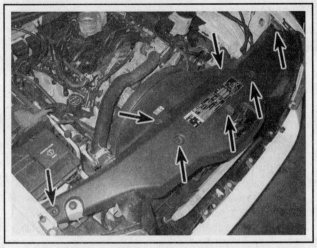

4.7 Release the locking pins to remove the radiator cover

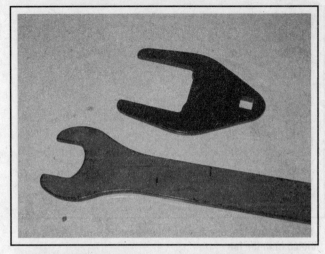

4.10a Typical fan wrench set - the large wrench spans the four pulley mounting bolts

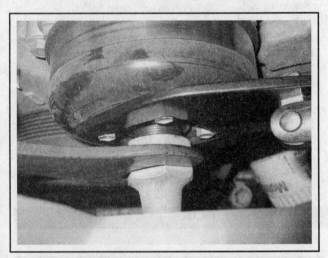

4.10b Hold the pulley while turning the large fan clutch nut counterclockwise to remove it

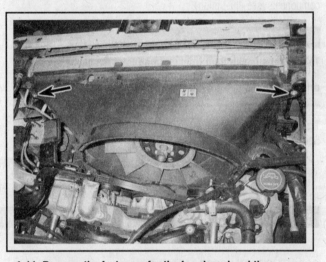

4.11 Remove the fasteners for the fan shroud and then remove it with the fan and clutch assembly

4   Visually inspect for substantial fluid leakage from the fan clutch assembly, a deformed bi-metal spring or grease leakage from the cooling fan bearing. If any of these conditions exist, replace the fan clutch.

Hot engine check

5   Start the engine and allow it to warm up to its normal operating temperature. When the engine is fully warmed up, turn off the ignition switch. Turn the fan by hand. Some resistance should be felt. If the fan turns easily, replace the fan clutch.

REMOVAL AND INSTALLATION

2004 through 2009 models

▶ Refer to illustrations 4.7, 4.10a, 4.10b, 4.11 and 4.12

6   On 5.4L engine models, remove the air inlet duct to the air cleaner housing. On all other models, remove the air duct between the air cleaner housing and the throttle body (see Chapter 4).

7   Remove the radiator cover by removing the pin-type retainers (see illustration).

8   On 5.4L engine models, remove the air cleaner housing bracket.

9   On V8 engine models, detach the battery cable harness from the radiator shroud.

10 A fan wrench set, available at most auto parts stores, is needed to remove the cooling fan assembly (see illustrations). Remove the fan and clutch assembly and let it rest within the fan shroud.

❋❋❋ CAUTION:

Don't allow the fan to fall forward into the radiator.

---

11 Remove the fan shroud mounting bolts and then carefully remove it and the fan and clutch assembly from the engine compartment (see illustration).

➥ **Note: If the upper radiator hose is making removal difficult, consider disconnecting it and moving it aside (see Section 6).**

4.12 Remove the four mounting bolts and separate the fan clutch from the fan

12 If you're going to replace the fan or the clutch, unbolt the two components (see illustration).

❊❊ CAUTION:

To prevent silicone fluid from draining from the clutch assembly into the fan drive bearing and ruining the lubricant, keep the drive unit in the upright position (as if it were installed).

Tighten the fan mounting bolts to the torque listed in this Chapter's Specifications.

13 Installation is the reverse of removal. Tighten the shroud fasteners securely.

2010 and later models

➡ **Note: For troubleshooting the engine cooling fan assembly, a professional scan tool will help.**

14 Disconnect the cable from the negative battery terminal (see Chapter 5).

15 Remove the air intake duct (see Chapter 4).

16 Detach the retainer for the power steering fluid cooler hose from the fan motor and shroud assembly.

17 Detach the retainer from the power steering fluid reservoir stud bolt.

18 Detach the wiring harness retainer from the left side of the fan motor and shroud assembly.

19 Detach the two retainers for the alternator battery harness from the top of the cooling motor and shroud assembly.

20 Detach the wiring harness retainer from the right side of the fan motor and shroud assembly.

21 Disconnect the electrical connectors from both cooling fan motors.

22 Detach the three cooling fan motor harness retainers.

23 Remove the four battery junction box bracket bolts.

24 Remove the power steering fluid reservoir stud bolt and set the reservoir aside.

25 Remove the two bolts that secure the cooling fan motor and shroud assembly and lift the assembly out of the engine compartment.

26 If you're only removing the fan shroud assembly to access some other component(s), no further disassembly is necessary. If you're replacing a fan or motor, proceed to the next step.

27 Unbolt the motor that you're replacing from the shroud.

28 Remove the fastener that secures the fan to the motor.

29 Installation is the reverse of removal.

5   Coolant expansion tank - removal and installation

2004 THROUGH 2008 MODELS

♦ **Refer to illustration 5.2**

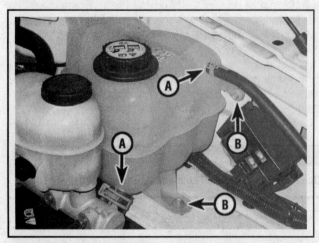

5.2 Remove the spring clamps from the expansion tank hoses (A) and carefully twist the coolant hoses off. Remove the mounting bolts (B) to remove the tank

❊❊ WARNING:

Wait until the engine is completely cool before beginning this procedure.

1   Drain the cooling system (see Chapter 1). If the coolant is in good condition, save it and reuse it.

2   Disconnect the expansion tank hoses (see illustration).

3   Remove the expansion tank mounting bolts (see illustration 5.2). Lift the tank out of the engine compartment.

4   Installation is the reverse of removal. Refill the cooling system with the proper type and concentration of antifreeze (see Chapter 1).

2009 AND LATER MODELS

❊❊ CAUTION:

Treat the cap of the expansion tank bottle like you would a hot radiator cap!

5   The coolant expansion tank is an integral part of the air filter lower housing. See Chapter 4, Section 9, for the replacement procedure.

6 Radiator - removal and installation

☀ WARNING:

Wait until the engine is completely cool before beginning this procedure.

➡ **Note: A special tool, available at most auto parts stores, is necessary to disconnect the transmission oil cooler lines from the radiator.**

REMOVAL

▸ **Refer to illustrations 6.4a, 6.4b, 6.9a, 6.9b, and 6.11**

1 On 2009 and later models, have the air conditioning system refrigerant discharged and recovered by a licensed air conditioning technician.

2 Drain the cooling system (see Chapter 1). If the coolant is relatively new and in good condition, save it and reuse it.

3 On 2004 through 2008 5.4L engine models, remove the inlet duct to the air cleaner housing. On 2004 through 2008 4.6L engine models, remove the air cleaner housing (see Chapter 4). On all 2009 and later models, remove the coolant expansion tank/air filter lower housing (see Chapter 4).

4 Disconnect the upper and lower radiator hoses and the expansion tank hose from the radiator (see illustrations). Loosen the hose clamps by squeezing the ends together. Hose clamp pliers work best, but regular pliers will work also.

➡ **Note: On 2011 and later models, the lower radiator hose is attached to the radiator with a spring clip. Separate the hose from the radiator by prying the clip up and remove the hose.**

If any hose is stuck, grasp it near the end with a pair of adjustable pliers and twist it to break the seal, then pull it off. If any hose is old or deteriorated, cut it off and install a new one.

5 Remove the cooling fan(s) and fan shroud (see Section 4). On 2011 and later models equipped with a power steering cooler, separate the power steering fluid hoses from the power steering cooler that is part of the condenser assembly. From below, remove the pushpins and quarter-turn fasteners and remove the lower air deflector.

6 On 2009 and later models, release the clamp and disconnect the hose from the power steering cooler (see Chapter 10).

7 On 2009 and later models, remove the bolt and nut that secure the upper and lower air conditioning condenser fittings. Discard the old gasket seals and O-rings.

8 On 2009 and later models, release the two pin-type retainers from the left air deflector, three from the right deflector and three from the lower deflector, then remove all three deflectors.

9 On models with automatic transmissions, disconnect the oil cooler lines from the radiator (see illustrations).

➡ **Note: If you are replacing the radiator, make sure the new radiator has this type of line fitting. It may be necessary to remove the fittings from the old radiator and transfer them to the new one.**

10 On 2009 and later models, disconnect the electrical connector from the horn, then detach the retainers for the ambient temperature sensor and the wiring harness for the horn and ambient temperature sensor.

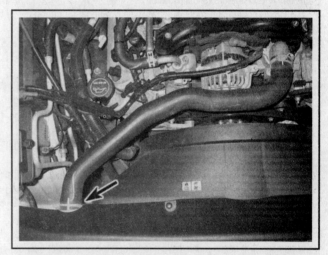

6.4a Release the clamp for the upper radiator hose and then separate it from the radiator

6.4b Remove the lower radiator hose (A) and the expansion tank hose (B) from the radiator

6.9a Remove the secondary plastic clip on the line and move it back. Install the tool onto the line and push it into the fitting . . .

6.9b . . . then remove the line from the fitting by pulling it straight out

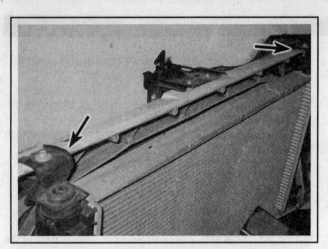

6.11 Remove the two brackets that secure the top of the radiator (2004 through 2008 unit shown)

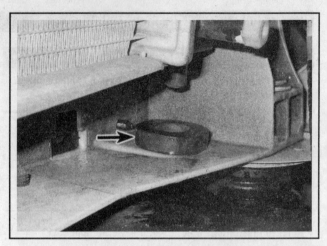

6.16 Be sure to check the rubber insulators before installing the radiator

11 On 2004 through 2008 models, remove the radiator mounting brackets and insulators (see illustration).

12 On 2009 and later models, remove the two upper mounting bracket bolts, then lift the condenser and radiator out of the engine compartment as a single assembly. Disconnect the two transmission fluid cooler hoses from the radiator, then release the lock tabs and separate the radiator from the condenser.

13 On 2011 and later models, pull the condenser assembly toward the front to separate it from the radiator. From the engine compartment, remove the two bolts securing the top of the radiator to the radiator support.

14 Carefully lift the radiator from the engine compartment. Don't spill coolant on the vehicle or scratch the paint. The rubber insulators that help secure the bottom of the radiator may stick to the radiator when it's removed. They will need to be returned to their original positions during installation.

15 Remove bugs and dirt from the radiator with compressed air and a soft brush. Don't bend the cooling fins. Inspect the radiator for leaks and damage. If it needs repair, have a radiator shop or a dealer service department do the work.

INSTALLATION

▶ **Refer to illustration 6.16**

16 Inspect the rubber insulators (where the bottom of the radiator mounts in the engine compartment and in the top mounting brackets) for cracks and deterioration (see illustration). Make sure that they're free of dirt and gravel. When installing the radiator, make sure that it's correctly seated on the insulators before fastening the top brackets.

17 Installation is otherwise the reverse of the removal procedure. After installation, fill the cooling system with the correct mixture of antifreeze and water (see Chapter 1). Reconnect the battery (see Chapter 5, Section 1).

18 Start the engine and check for leaks. Allow the engine to reach normal operating temperature, indicated by the upper radiator hose becoming hot. Recheck the coolant level and add more if required.

19 If you're working on a model equipped with an automatic transmission, check and add ATF fluid as needed (see Chapter 1).

7 Water pump - check

▶ **Refer to illustration 7.2**

1 A failure in the water pump can cause serious engine damage due to overheating.

2 If a failure occurs at the pump seal, coolant will leak from the weep hole(s) on the water pump (see illustration).

3 Using a flashlight, look for traces of coolant residue or dried coolant tracks around the weep hole(s). If the seal has leaked, it should be very apparent.

4 If the water pump shaft bearings fail, there may be a howling sound near the water pump while it's running. With the engine off, shaft wear can be felt if the water pump pulley is rocked up-and-down. Don't mistake drivebelt slippage, which causes a squealing sound, for water pump bearing failure.

5 A quick water pump performance check is to put the heater on. If the pump is failing, it won't be able to efficiently circulate hot water all the way to the heater core as it should.

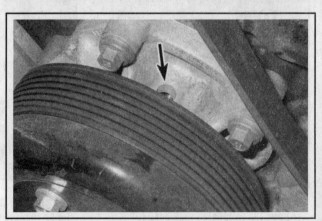

7.2 The weep hole location on a V8 model (there's usually one on the underside of the pump, too) - V6 models are similar

8 Water pump - replacement

2010 AND EARLIER MODELS

▶ **Refer to illustration 8.4**

> ✳✳ **CAUTION:**
>
> **Treat the cap of the expansion tank bottle like you would a hot radiator cap!**

1 Disconnect the cable from the negative battery terminal (see Chapter 5, Section 1).

2 Drain the cooling system (see Chapter 1).

3 On 2004 through 2009 models, remove the engine cooling fan and shroud (see Section 4). On 2010 models, remove the air intake duct (see Chapter 4).

4 Loosen the water pump pulley bolts, then remove the drivebelt (see Chapter 1) and the water pump pulley.

➡ **Note: Loosen the pulley bolts while the drivebelt is still installed; it will make pulley removal easier (see illustration).**

V6 models

▶ **Refer to illustration 8.7**

5 Remove the support bracket (if equipped) for the air conditioning compressor.

6 Remove the heater hose fitting (on the top) and the lower radiator hose from the water pump.

7 Remove the water pump mounting bolts and remove the pump from the engine (see illustration). If the water pump is stuck, gently tap it with a soft-faced hammer to break the seal.

8 Clean the bolt threads and the threaded holes in the engine; removing any corrosion and sealant. Remove all traces of old gasket material from the sealing surfaces.

V8 models

▶ **Refer to illustrations 8.9 and 8.10**

9 Remove the water pump mounting bolts (see illustration).

10 Clean the O-ring surfaces on the pump and the housing (see illustration).

8.4 Loosen (but don't remove) the water pump pulley mounting bolts with the drivebelt installed

8.7 Water pump mounting bolt locations (pushrod V6 engine shown)

8.9 Water pump mounting bolts (one hidden from view) - V8 engines

8.10 Inspect the pump cavity for dirt or signs of pitting

11 If you're installing the old pump, install a new O-ring.

12 Clean the bolt threads and the threaded holes in the engine removing any corrosion or debris.

All models

13 Compare the new pump to the old one to make sure that they're identical.

14 On V6 models, apply a thin film of RTV sealant to hold the new gasket in place during installation.

✳✳ CAUTION:

Make sure that the gasket is correctly positioned on the water pump and the engine block surface is clean and free of old gasket material.

15 Carefully mate the pump with the water pump housing.

16 Install the water pump bolts and tighten them to the torque listed in this Chapter's Specifications.

17 The remainder of installation is the reverse of removal.

18 Tighten the water pump pulley mounting bolts to the torque listed in this Chapter's Specifications.

19 Refill the cooling system (see Chapter 1). Reconnect the battery (see Chapter 5, Section 1).

20 Operate the engine and thoroughly check for leaks.

2011 AND LATER MODELS

21 Remove the air cleaner pipe (see Chapter 4).

22 Loosen the fasteners securing the water pump pulley (see illustration 8.4).

23 Remove the drivebelt (see Chapter 1).

24 Remove the water pump pulley.

25 On 5.0L V8 models, remove the thermostat housing (see Section 3), then disconnect the heater outlet hose from the water pump.

26 Remove the water pump mounting bolts.

27 Clean the O-ring surfaces on the pump and the housing.

28 If you're installing the old pump, install a new O-ring.

29 Clean the bolt threads and the threaded holes in the engine removing any corrosion or debris.

30 Remove the air cleaner tube (see Chapter 4).

31 Loosen the fasteners securing the water pump pulley.

32 Remove the drivebelt (see Chapter 1).

33 Remove the water pump pulley.

34 Compare the new pump to the old one to make sure that they're identical.

35 Carefully mate the pump with the water pump housing.

36 Install the water pump bolts and tighten them to the torque listed in this Chapter's Specifications. Don't overtighten the water pump bolts; doing so will damage the pump.

37 The remainder of installation is the reverse of removal. Tighten the water pump pulley mounting bolts to the torque listed in this Chapter's Specifications. Refill the cooling system (see Chapter 1). Reconnect the battery (see Chapter 5, Section 1).

38 Operate the engine and thoroughly check for leaks.

9   Coolant temperature indicator - check

✳✳ WARNING:

Wait until the engine is completely cool before beginning this procedure.

1   The coolant temperature indicator system consists of a temperature gauge on the dash and a sensor mounted on the engine. On all models, a Cylinder Head Temperature (CHT) sensor (see Chapter 6), which is an information sensor for the Powertrain Control Module (PCM), provides a signal to the PCM which controls and actuates the temperature gauge.

➡ **Note: Models equipped with a Message Center may also advise that you check the instrument panel gauges to alert you of a possible malfunction.**

2   If an overheating indication has occurred, first check the coolant level in the system (see Chapter 1) and that the coolant mixture is correct (see Section 2). Also, refer to the *Troubleshooting* section at the beginning of this book before assuming that the temperature indicator is faulty.

3   Start the engine and warm it up for 10 minutes. If the temperature gauge has not moved from the C position, check the wiring harness connections going to the instrument cluster.

4   If there is a problem with the CHT sensor, it is very likely that the CHECK ENGINE light will be illuminated and the sensor or circuit will need repair (see Chapter 6).

10 Blower motor resistor and blower motor - replacement

✳✳ WARNING:

The models covered by this manual are equipped with Supplemental Restraint Systems (SRS), more commonly known as airbags. Always disarm the airbag system before working in the vicinity of any airbag system component to avoid the possibility of accidental deployment of the airbag, which could cause personal injury (see Chapter 12). Do not use a memory saving device to preserve the PCM's memory when working on or near the airbag system components.

BLOWER MOTOR RESISTOR

▶ **Refer to illustration 10.2**

1   Remove the glove box (see Chapter 11).

2   Disconnect the electrical connector from the blower motor resistor (see illustration).

3   Remove the blower motor resistor mounting screws and remove the resistor from the housing.

10.2 Location of the blower motor resistor

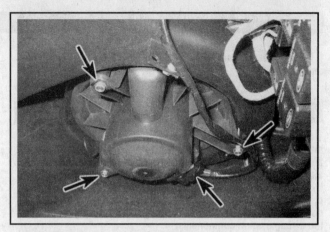

10.7 Blower motor mounting fasteners and electrical connector

4   Installation is the reverse of removal.

BLOWER MOTOR

▶ **Refer to illustration 10.7**

5   Remove the right kick panel (see Chapter 11, Section 24).

6   Move the carpet under the blower motor aside.
7   Disconnect the blower motor electrical connector (see illustration).
8   Remove the blower motor mounting screws and remove the blower motor (see illustration 10.7).
9   Installation is the reverse of removal.

11 Heater/air conditioner control assembly - removal and installation

▶ **Refer to illustrations 11.3 and 11.4**

✳✳ WARNING:

The models covered by this manual are equipped with Supplemental Restraint Systems (SRS), more commonly known as airbags. Always disarm the airbag system before working in the vicinity of any airbag system component to avoid the possibility of accidental deployment of the airbag, which could cause personal injury (see Chapter 12). Do not use a memory saving device to preserve the PCM's memory when working on or near the airbag system components.

1   Disconnect the cable from the negative battery terminal (see Chapter 5, Section 1).
2   Remove the instrument panel center bezel (see Chapter 11).
3   Disconnect the connectors from the back of the control assembly and the other connectors so that the bezel can be removed completely from the vehicle (see illustration).
4   Remove the heater/air conditioner control assembly retaining screws and remove it from the center bezel (see illustration).
5   Installation is the reverse of removal. Reconnect the battery (see Chapter 5, Section 1).

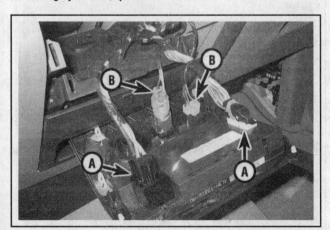

11.3 Disconnect the electrical connectors from the control assembly (A) and from the center bezel (B)

11.4 Mounting screws for the control assembly

12 Heater core - replacement

◆ Refer to illustrations 12.5, 12.6, 12.9a, 12.9b, 12.12, 12.13 and 12.14

✳✳ WARNING 1:

The models covered by this manual are equipped with Supplemental Restraint Systems (SRS), more commonly known as airbags. Always disarm the airbag system before working in the vicinity of any airbag system component to avoid the possibility of accidental deployment of the airbag, which could cause personal injury (see Chapter 12). Do not use a memory saving device to preserve the PCM's memory when working on or near the airbag system components.

✳✳ WARNING 2:

The air conditioning system is under high pressure. DO NOT loosen any fittings or remove any components until after the system has been discharged. Air conditioning refrigerant must be properly discharged into an EPA-approved container at a dealer service department or an automotive air conditioning repair facility. Always wear eye protection when disconnecting air conditioning system fittings.

✳✳ WARNING 3:

Wait until the engine is completely cool before beginning this procedure.

➡ Note 1: A spring-lock coupling tool is necessary to detach the evaporator lines at the heater core housing.

➡ Note 2: Heater core replacement is a difficult procedure which involves removing the instrument panel. Unless you have considerable mechanical experience, it is advisable to have this procedure performed by a qualified technician.

1   Have the air conditioning system discharged by a dealer service department or an automotive air conditioning shop before proceeding (see **Warning** above).

2   Disconnect the cable from the negative battery terminal (see Chapter 5, Section 1).

3   Drain the cooling system (see Chapter 1).

4   Remove the air conditioning accumulator (see Section 15).

5   Disconnect the evaporator lines and heater hoses from the evaporator/heater core housing at the firewall in the engine compartment (see illustration). Plug all open lines and fittings to prevent contamination of heating and cooling and air conditioning systems.

➡ Note: Squeeze the plastic tabs on the heater hose fittings to release the hose.

6   Pull the carpet up and release the fasteners for the heater outlet duct and then remove it (see illustration).

7   Remove the instrument panel (see Chapter 11).

8   Remove the mounting fastener for the fuse/relay box and move it aside (see illustration 12.9b).

9   Remove the evaporator/heater core housing mounting fasteners (see illustrations).

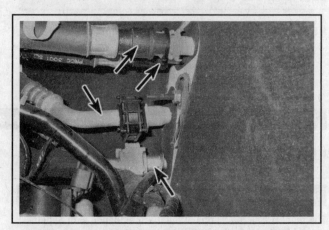

12.5 Press the plastic tabs on the heater hose fittings to release the heater hoses. Use a spring-lock coupling tool to disconnect the evaporator lines after removing the plastic fitting covers

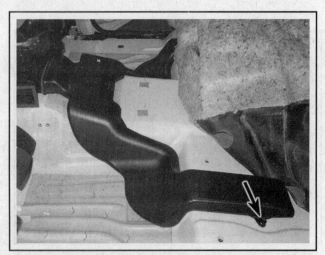

12.6 The heater outlet duct can easily be removed by pulling up the carpet and removing the fasteners (one hidden)

12.9a Mounting fasteners for the evaporator/heater core housing within the engine compartment

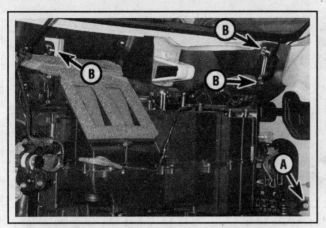

12.9b Remove the mounting bolt for the junction box (A) and move it aside. Then remove the evaporator/heater core housing mounting fasteners and bracket (B)

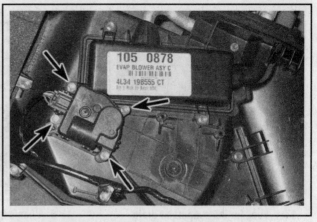

12.12 The temperature blend door actuator mounting fasteners

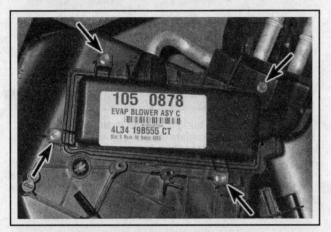

12.13 The heater core cover mounting fasteners

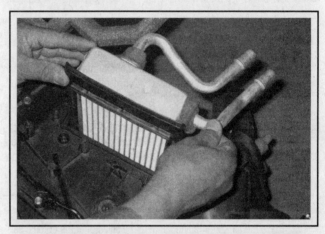

12.14 Carefully remove the heater core from the housing by pulling it straight up

10 Disconnect any electrical connectors and anything else that may be attached to the housing and carefully pull the housing away from the firewall and then lift it out from the passenger compartment.

11 Remove the insulating panel seal from around the heater core and evaporator inlet and outlet tubes.

12 Remove the temperature blend door actuator (see illustration).

13 Remove the heater core cover (see illustration).

14 Pull the heater core from the housing (see illustration).

15 Installation is the reverse of removal. Reconnect the battery (see Chapter 5, Section 1).

16 Refill the cooling system (see Chapter 1). Have the air conditioning system recharged and leak-tested by the shop that discharged it.

13 Air conditioning and heating system - check and maintenance

▶ **Refer to illustration 13.1**

❋❋ **WARNING:**

The air conditioning system is under high pressure. Do not loosen any hose fittings or remove any components until after the system has been discharged by a dealer service department or service station. Always wear eye protection when disconnecting air conditioning system fittings.

1   The following maintenance checks should be performed on a regular basis to ensure the air conditioner continues to operate at peak efficiency.

a) Check the compressor drivebelt. If it's worn or deteriorated, replace it (see Chapter 1).

b) Check the drivebelt tension and, if necessary, adjust it (see Chapter 1).

c) Check the system hoses. Look for cracks, bubbles, hard spots and deterioration. Inspect the hoses and all fittings for oil bubbles and seepage. If there's any evidence of wear, damage or leaks, replace the hose(s).

d) Inspect the condenser fins for leaves, bugs and other debris. Use a fin comb or compressed air to clean the condenser.

e) Make sure the system has the correct refrigerant charge.

f) Check the evaporator housing drain tube (see illustration) for blockage.

13.1 Look for the evaporator drain hose on the firewall, directly behind the engine's right (passenger's side) bank

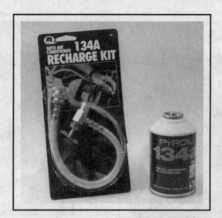

13.9 A basic R-134a charging kit is available at most auto parts stores ñ it must say R-134a (not R-12) on the kit and on the can of refrigerant

13.12 Always add refrigerant to the low side of the air conditioning system

2   It's a good idea to operate the system for about 10 minutes at least once a month, particularly during the winter. Long term non-use can cause hardening, and subsequent failure, of the seals.

3   Because of the complexity of the air conditioning system and the special equipment necessary to service it, in-depth troubleshooting and repairs are not included in this manual. However, simple checks and component replacement procedures are provided in this Chapter.

4   The most common cause of poor cooling is simply a low system refrigerant charge. If a noticeable drop in cool air output occurs, the following quick check will help you determine if the refrigerant level is low.

CHECKING THE REFRIGERANT CHARGE

5   Warm the engine up to normal operating temperature.

6   Place the air conditioning temperature selector at the coldest setting and the blower at the highest setting. Open the vehicle doors (to make sure the air conditioning system doesn't cycle off as soon as it cools the passenger compartment).

7   With the compressor engaged, the clutch will make an audible click and the center of the clutch will rotate. If the compressor discharge line (the small-diameter pipe) feels warm and the compressor inlet pipe (the large-diameter pipe) feels cool, the system is properly charged.

8   Place a thermometer in the dashboard vent nearest the evaporator and operate the system until the indicated temperature is around 40 to 45 degrees F. If the ambient (outside) air temperature is very high, say 110 degrees F, the duct air temperature may be as high as 60 degrees F, but generally the air conditioning is 30 to 40 degrees F cooler than the ambient air.

➥ **Note: Humidity of the ambient air also affects the cooling capacity of the system. Higher ambient humidity lowers the effectiveness of the air conditioning system.**

ADDING REFRIGERANT

◆ **Refer to illustrations 13.9, 13.12 and 13.15**

9   Buy an automotive air conditioning system charging kit at an auto parts store. A charging kit includes a can of refrigerant, a tap valve and a short section of hose that can be attached between the tap valve and the system low side service valve (see illustration). Because one can of refrigerant may not be sufficient to bring the system charge up to the proper level, it's a good idea to buy an additional can. Make sure that one of the cans contains red refrigerant dye. If the system is leaking, the red dye will leak out with the refrigerant and help you pinpoint the location of the leak.

✳✳ CAUTION:

There are two types of refrigerant used in automotive systems; R-12 - which has been widely used on earlier models and the more environmentally-friendly R-134a used in all models covered by this manual. These two refrigerants (and their appropriate refrigerant oils) are not compatible and must never be mixed or components will be damaged. Use only R-134a refrigerant in the models covered by this manual.

10 Hook up the charging kit by following the manufacturer's instructions.

✳✳ WARNING:

DO NOT attempt to hook the charging kit hose to the system high side! The fittings on the charging kit are designed to fit only on the low side of the system.

11 Back off the valve handle on the charging kit and screw the kit onto the refrigerant can, making sure first that the O-ring or rubber seal inside the threaded portion of the kit is in place.

✳✳ WARNING:

Wear protective eyewear when dealing with pressurized refrigerant cans.

12 Remove the dust cap from the low-side charging connection and attach the quick-connect fitting on the kit hose (see illustration).

13 Warm up the engine and turn on the air conditioner. Keep the charging kit hose away from the fan and other moving parts.

➥ **Note: The charging process requires the compressor to be running. Your compressor may cycle off if the pressure is low due to a low charge. If the clutch cycles off, you can pull the low-pressure cycling switch plug and attach a jumper wire. This will keep the compressor ON.**

14 Turn the valve handle on the kit until the stem pierces the can, then back the handle out to release the refrigerant. You should be able to hear the rush of gas. Add refrigerant until the compressor discharge line (the small-diameter pipe) feels warm and the compressor inlet pipe (the large-diameter pipe) feels cool. Allow stabilization time between each addition.

15 If you have an accurate thermometer, place it in the center air conditioning vent (see illustration) and note the temperature of the air coming out of the vent. A fully-charged system which is working correctly should cool down to about 40 degrees F. Generally, an air conditioning system will put out air that is 30 to 40 degrees F cooler than the ambient air. For example, if the ambient (outside) air temperature is very high (over 100 degrees F), the temperature of air coming out of the registers should be 60 to 70 degrees F.

16 When the can is empty, turn the valve handle to the closed position and release the connection from the low-side port. Replace the dust cap.

13.15 Insert a thermometer in the center vent, turn on the air conditioning system and wait for it to cool down; depending on the humidity, the output air should be 30 to 40 degrees cooler than the ambient air temperature

❄❄ WARNING:

Never add more than two cans of refrigerant to the system.

17 Remove the charging kit from the can and store the kit for future use with the piercing valve in the UP position, to prevent inadvertently piercing the can on the next use.

HEATING SYSTEMS

18 If the carpet under the heater core is damp, or if antifreeze vapor or steam is coming through the vents, the heater core is leaking. Remove it (see Section 12) and install a new unit (most radiator shops will not repair a leaking heater core).

19 If the air coming out of the heater vents isn't hot, the problem could stem from any of the following causes:

   a) *The thermostat is stuck open, preventing the engine coolant from warming up enough to carry heat to the heater core. Replace the thermostat (see Section 3).*

   b) *There is a blockage in the system, preventing the flow of coolant through the heater core. Feel both heater hoses at the firewall. They should be hot. If one of them is cold, there is an obstruction in one of the hoses or in the heater core, or the heater control valve is shut. Detach the hoses and back flush the heater core with a water hose. If the heater core is clear but circulation is impeded, remove the two hoses and flush them out with a water hose.*

   c) *If flushing fails to remove the blockage from the heater core, the core must be replaced (see Section 12).*

ELIMINATING AIR CONDITIONING ODORS

▶ **Refer to illustration 13.23**

20 Unpleasant odors that often develop in air conditioning systems are caused by the growth of a fungus, usually on the surface of the evaporator core. The warm, humid environment there is a perfect breeding ground for mildew to develop.

21 The evaporator core on most vehicles is difficult to access, and dealership service departments have a lengthy, expensive process for eliminating the fungus by opening up the evaporator case and using a powerful disinfectant and rinse on the core until the fungus is gone. You can service your own system at home, but it takes something much

13.23 Remove the glove box (see Chapter 11) and insert the nozzle of the disinfectant through the air recirculation door

stronger than basic household germ-killers or deodorizers.

22 Aerosol disinfectants for automotive air conditioning systems are available in most auto parts stores, but remember when shopping for them that the most effective treatments are also the most expensive. The basic procedure for using these sprays is to start by running the system in the RECIRC mode for ten minutes with the blower on its highest speed. Use the highest heat mode to dry out the system and keep the compressor from engaging by disconnecting the wiring connector at the compressor (see Section 14).

23 Make sure that the disinfectant can comes with a long spray hose. Point the nozzle through the air recirculation door, just above the blower motor section of the housing (see illustration), and spray according to the manufacturer's recommendations. Follow the manufacturer's recommendations for the length of spray and waiting time between applications.

❄❄ CAUTION:

Be careful not to let the spray hose get caught in the blower motor fan.

24 Once the evaporator has been cleaned, the best way to prevent the mildew from coming back again is to make sure your evaporator housing drain tube is clear (see illustration 13.1).

14 Air conditioning compressor - removal and installation

✳ WARNING:

The air conditioning system is under high pressure. DO NOT loosen any fittings or remove any components until after the system has been discharged. Air conditioning refrigerant should be properly discharged into an EPA-approved container at a dealer service department or an automotive air conditioning repair facility. Always wear eye protection when disconnecting air conditioning system fittings.

➡ **Note:** If you are replacing the compressor due to internal damage, you must also replace the accumulator (see Section 15) and the evaporator orifice tube (see Section 16).

REMOVAL

1   Have the air conditioning system discharged by a dealer service department or by an automotive air conditioning shop before proceeding (see **Warning** above).

2   Remove the drivebelt (see Chapter 1).

V6 models

3   Remove the air duct between the air cleaner housing and the throttle body (see Chapter 4). On 3.5L V6 models, remove the right hand turbocharger bypass hose and the right hand turbocharger-to-charge air cooler (see Chapter 2B).

4   Disconnect the electrical connector from the compressor clutch field coil.

5   Disconnect the compressor inlet and outlet line manifold from the compressor. Remove and discard the old O-rings.

6   Remove the power steering bracket fasteners, then move the bracket and reservoir aside.

7   Remove the compressor mounting bolts and carefully remove the compressor.

V8 models

▸ **Refer to illustration 14.11**

8   Loosen the right front wheel lug nuts. Raise the vehicle and support it securely on jackstands.

9   On 4WD models, remove the engine cooling fan (see Section 4) and the skid plate under the engine, if equipped.

10   Remove the right front wheel and inner fender splash shield (see Chapter 11).

11   Disconnect the electrical connector from the compressor clutch field coil (see illustration).

12   Disconnect the Crankshaft Position (CKP) sensor connector and

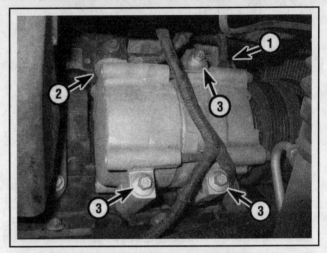

14.11 Air conditioning compressor details on the V8 engine

1   *Compressor clutch field coil electrical connector*
2   *Compressor inlet and outlet line manifold (the mounting bolt is out of view on the top - not the fastener on the side in this photo)*
3   *Compressor mounting bolts*

position the harness aside (see Chapter 6).

13   Disconnect the compressor inlet and outlet line manifold from the compressor (see illustration 14.11). Remove and discard the old O-rings.

14   Remove the compressor mounting bolts and remove the compressor (see illustration 14.11).

INSTALLATION

15   If a new compressor is being installed, follow the directions with the compressor regarding the draining of excess oil prior to installation.

16   The clutch may have to be transferred from the original compressor to the replacement.

17   Before reconnecting the inlet and outlet lines to the compressor, replace all manifold O-rings and lubricate them with the appropriate refrigerant oil.

18   Installation is otherwise the reverse of removal.

19   Replace the accumulator (see Section 15) and the orifice tube (see Section 18) if necessary (see **Note** above).

20   Have the system evacuated, recharged and leak tested by the shop that discharged it.

15 Air conditioning accumulator - removal and installation

▶ Refer to illustrations 15.4a and 15.4b

❋ WARNING:

The air conditioning system is under high pressure. DO NOT loosen any fittings or remove any components until after the system has been discharged. Air conditioning refrigerant should be properly discharged into an EPA-approved container at a dealer service department or an automotive air conditioning repair facility. Always wear eye protection when disconnecting air conditioning system fittings.

➡ **Note: A spring lock coupling tool is necessary to remove the accumulator.**

1   Have the air conditioning system discharged by a dealer service department or by an automotive air conditioning shop before proceeding (see **Warning** above).
2   Remove the battery and the battery tray (see Chapter 5).
3   Remove the PCM and the PCM mounting bracket (see Chapter 6).

4   Disconnect the condenser line from the accumulator and the evaporator line from the line coupling at the firewall (see illustrations). Remove and discard the O-rings. Plug all open lines and fittings to prevent contamination of the air conditioning system.

➡ **Note: Remove the plastic clip on the line coupling before installing the spring lock coupling tool.**

5   Remove the accumulator mounting bolts and remove the accumulator (see illustration 15.4a).
6   Install new O-rings on all fittings and coat them with the appropriate refrigerant oil. If you are installing a replacement accumulator, drill a 1/2 inch hole in the accumulator and drain the oil into a measuring cup. Add the measured amount plus 2 ounces of refrigerant oil to the replacement accumulator.
7   Tighten the line fitting at the accumulator to the torque listed in this Chapter's Specifications.
8   Installation is otherwise the reverse of removal.
9   Take the vehicle to the shop that discharged it and have the system evacuated, leak tested and recharged.

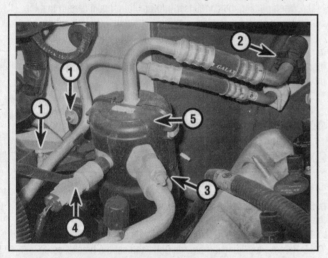

15.4a Air conditioning accumulator details:

1   *Mounting fasteners*
2   *Line coupling for accumulator inlet line*
3   *Line fitting for accumulator outlet line*
4   *Cycling switch electrical connector*
5   *Accumulator*

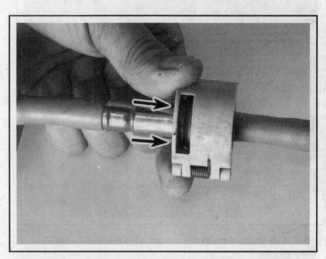

15.4b To separate the lines at the coupling, install the tool, push it towards the female fitting until you can see the coupling through the window in the tool, then pull the lines apart

16 Air conditioning condenser - removal and installation

❋ WARNING:

The air conditioning system is under high pressure. DO NOT loosen any fittings or remove any components until after the system has been discharged. Air conditioning refrigerant should be properly discharged into an EPA-approved container at a dealer service department or an automotive air conditioning repair facility. Always wear eye protection when disconnecting air conditioning system fittings.

➡ **Note: If you are replacing the condenser due to damage, the accumulator should be replaced as well, if the condenser had been damaged for a significant length of time (see Section 15).**

1   Have the air conditioning system discharged by a dealer service department or by an automotive air conditioning shop before proceeding (see the **Warning** above).

16.6 To disconnect the condenser line fittings, hold the line fitting (A) with a open-end wrench and loosen the tube nut (B) with a flare nut wrench to avoid damaging it

16.7 The condenser mounting bracket bolt locations

16.9 The lower condenser mount with insulator - right side shown

2004 THROUGH 2008 MODELS

▶ **Refer to illustrations 16.6, 16.7 and 16.9**

2   Remove the radiator cover (see illustration 4.7).

3   Remove the transmission oil cooler and place it aside (see Chapter 7B). It isn't necessary to disconnect the hoses, but it's a good idea to wrap the cooler in a towel to prevent damage.

4   Remove the hood latch bracket and place it aside.

5   Remove the flexible air deflector on the right side of the condenser.

6   Disconnect the refrigerant inlet and outlet lines from the condenser (see illustration). Plug or cap all open line fittings to prevent dirt or contamination from entering the system.

7   Remove the condenser mounting bracket bolts and then carefully remove the condenser by moving it forward and clearing the condenser lines through the radiator support (see illustration).

8   If you're going to install a new condenser, pour two ounces of the appropriate refrigerant oil directly into the condenser prior to installing it.

9   When placing the condenser into position, make certain that the condenser is seated in the lower mounts correctly (see illustration).

10 Before reconnecting the refrigerant lines to the condenser, be sure to coat a pair of new O-rings with the appropriate refrigerant oil and install them in the refrigerant line fittings. Tighten the condenser line fittings and mounting bolts securely.

11 Installation is otherwise the reverse of removal.

12 Have the system evacuated, recharged and leak tested by the shop that discharged it.

2009 AND LATER MODELS

13 Remove the pin-type retainers and remove the upper sight shield, both side air deflector-to-headlight panels, and the side deflector from the condenser bracket.

14 Remove the horn assembly (see Chapter 12).

15 Remove four junction bracket bolts and set the bracket aside.

16 Remove the pin-type retainers and remove the radiator lower air deflector.

17 Remove the refrigerant inlet fitting bolt and the outlet fitting nut and disconnect the fittings from the condenser. Remove and discard the O-ring and gasket seals.

18 Plug or cap all open line fittings to prevent dirt or contamination from entering the system.

19 Remove the ambient temperature sensor retainer from the condenser support.

20 Remove the hood latch cable retainer from the condenser bracket.

21 Remove the power steering cooler line clip from the top of the condenser bracket.

22 Remove the transmission cooler line retainers from the condenser bracket. Loosen the two transmission cooler line clamps and disconnect the cooler lines from the transmission cooler.

23 Remove the two radiator bolts and two cooling fan shroud bolts.

24 Release the two power steering cooler hose clamps, then disconnect the hoses from the condenser core.

25 Release the two condenser core lower retaining clips.

26 Carefully move the radiator core slightly toward the rear, then carefully remove the condenser by moving it forward and pulling it out.

27 If you are going to install a new condenser, pour two ounces of appropriate refrigerant oil directly into the condenser prior to installing it.

28 When placing the condenser into position, make certain that the condenser is seated correctly and that the two lower retaining clips are secure.

29 Before installing the refrigerant lines, install new O-rings and gasket seals and coat them with the appropriate refrigerant oil. Tighten the bolts and nuts securely.

30 Installation is otherwise the reverse of removal.

31 Have the system evacuated, recharged and leak tested by the shop that discharged it.

17 Air conditioning pressure cycling switch and high-pressure cutoff switch - replacement

▶ Refer to illustrations 17.1a and 17.1b

➡ **Note 1: Since both switches are threaded onto Schrader valves, it isn't necessary to discharge the air conditioning system to remove them.**

➡ **Note 2: The pressure cycling switch detects low refrigerant line pressure at 21 to 23 psi, switches the A/C compressor off, then back on again at 42 psi. If the pressure increases over 435 to 475 psi, the high-pressure cut-off switch will turn the A/C compressor off.**

1 Unplug the electrical connector from the switch (see illustrations).

2 Unscrew the switch from the Schrader valve.

3 Lubricate the switch O-ring with clean refrigerant oil of the correct type.

4 Screw the new switch onto the threads until hand tight, then tighten it securely.

5 Reconnect the electrical connector.

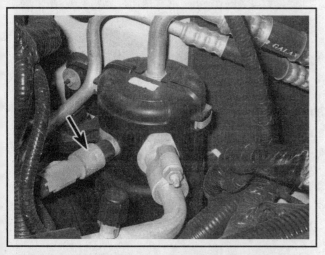

17.1a Disconnect the air conditioning pressure cycling switch connector, then remove it with an open-end wrench from the fitting on the accumulator

17.1b The air conditioning high pressure cut-off switch is removed the same way as the pressure cycling switch. It is mounted to a high pressure A/C line

18 Air conditioning orifice tube - removal and installation

▶ Refer to illustrations 18.2 and 18.3

✳✳ WARNING:

The air conditioning system is under high pressure. DO NOT loosen any hose fittings or remove any components until the system has been discharged. Air conditioning refrigerant should be properly discharged into an EPA-approved recovery/recycling unit by a dealer service department or an automotive air conditioning repair facility. Always wear eye protection when disconnecting air conditioning system fittings.

➡ Note: The orifice tube is located in the condenser-to-evaporator line. The orifice tube changes the high-pressure liquid refrigerant into a low-pressure liquid.

1   Have the air conditioning system discharged by a dealer service department or by an automotive air conditioning shop before proceeding (see the **Warning** above).

2   Disconnect the refrigerant line that houses the orifice tube (see illustration). Use an open-end wrench on the stationary fitting and a flare nut wrench to avoid rounding off the tube nut.

3   Remove the orifice tube from the line with a pair of needle-nose pliers (see illustration). If it's really stuck (or breaks off), special extractor tools are available at most auto parts stores.

4   Installation is the reverse of removal. Be sure to remove and discard the old O-rings and replace them with new ones.

5   Take the vehicle back to the shop that discharged it. Have the system evacuated, recharged and leak tested.

18.2 The orifice tube can be removed by opening this high-pressure A/C line and carefully pulling it out of the line with needle nose pliers

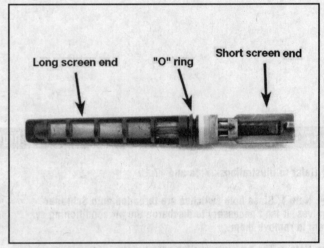

18.3 The orifice tube is equipped with a tapered mesh screen that must be clean and free of damage (typical shown)

Specifications

General

Expansion tank cap pressure rating	16 psi
Thermostat rating (opening to fully open temperature range)	188-195 to 208-215 degrees F
Cooling system capacity	See Chapter 1
Refrigerant type	R-134a
Refrigerant capacity	Refer to HVAC specification tag

Torque specifications   Ft-lbs (unless otherwise indicated)

➡ **Note: One foot-pound (ft-lb) of torque is equivalent to 12 inch-pounds (in-lbs) of torque. Torque values below approximately 15 ft-lbs are expressed in inch-pounds, since most foot-pound torque wrenches are not accurate at these smaller values.**

Accumulator line fitting fastener	71 in-lbs
Condenser inlet and outlet line tube nuts	18
Fan assembly-to-clutch bolt	
2004 through 2006	156 in-lbs
2007 on	
V6 engines (2007 and 2008)	156 in-lbs
V8 engines (2007 through 2009)	62 in-lbs
Coolant crossover pipe	
3.5L V6	
Step 1	89 in-lbs
Step 2	Tighten an additional 45-degrees
Thermostat housing cover bolts	
4.2L V6 engine	
Step 1	71 in-lbs
Step 2	Tighten an additional 60-degrees
3.5L and 3.7L V6 engines	89 in-lbs
V8 engines	
2-valve 4.6L engines	18
All others	89 in-lbs
Thermostat housing-to-block bolts	
3.5L and 3.6L V6 engines	
Step 1	71 in-lbs
Step 2	Tighten an additional 45-degrees
Water pump bolts	
4.2L V6 engine	21
3.5L and 3.7L V6 engines	
Step 1	89 in-lbs
Step 2	Tighten an additional 45-degrees
V8 engines	
4.6L and 5.4L models	18
5.0L models	
Step 1	177 in-lbs
Step 2	Tighten an additional 60-degrees
6.2L models	
Step 1	177 in-lbs
Step 2	Tighten an additional 45-degrees
Water pump pulley bolts	18

Notes

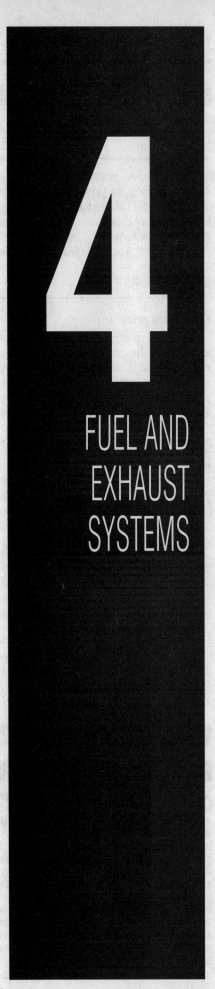

4

FUEL AND EXHAUST SYSTEMS

Section

1   General information
2   Fuel pressure relief procedure
3   Fuel pump/fuel pressure - check
4   Fuel lines and fittings - general information
5   Fuel tank - removal and installation
6   Fuel tank - cleaning and repair
7   Fuel pump/fuel level sensor - removal and installation
8   Fuel pump and fuel level sensor - replacement
9   Air intake duct and air filter housing - removal and installation
10 Sequential Multiport Fuel Injection (SFI) system -
    general information
11 Fuel injection system - check
12 Throttle body - removal and installation
13 Fuel rail and injectors - removal and installation
14 High-pressure fuel pump (3.5L V6 engine) - removal and installation
15 Exhaust system servicing - general information

Reference to other Chapters

Air filter replacement - See Chapter 1
CHECK ENGINE light on - See Chapter 6
Exhaust system check - See Chapter 1
Fuel filter replacement - See Chapter 1
Fuel system check - See Chapter 1
Underhood hose check and replacement - See Chapter 1

1 General information

SEQUENTIAL MULTIPORT FUEL INJECTION (SFI) SYSTEM

The fuel system consists of the Powertrain Control Module (PCM), the fuel pump relay, the Inertia Fuel Shutoff (IFS) switch, the Fuel Pump Driver Module (FPDM), the fuel tank, the electric in-tank fuel pump/fuel level sensor, the fuel rail pressure sensor, the fuel rail and fuel injectors, the air filter housing and the electronic throttle body. For a more detailed description of the SFI system, refer to Section 10.

FUEL PUMP CIRCUIT

Fuel pump relay

The fuel pump relay is equipped with a primary and secondary voltage circuit. The primary circuit is controlled by the PCM and the secondary circuit is linked directly to battery voltage from the ignition switch. With the ignition switch ON (engine not running), the PCM will ground the relay for one second. During cranking, the PCM grounds the fuel pump relay as long as the Camshaft Position (CMP) sensor sends its position signal (see Chapter 6). If there are no reference pulses, the fuel pump will shut off after two or three seconds.

Inertia Fuel Shutoff (IFS) switch

The Inertia Fuel Shutoff (IFS) switch disables the fuel pump circuit in the event of a collision. The IFS switch is located behind the right (passenger side) kick panel, ahead of the fuse and relay box. Here's how it works: A cylindrical magnet inside the switch has a steel ball sitting on top of it. Under normal driving conditions, the magnetic attraction between the magnet and the ball holds the ball in position on top of the magnet. When a collision occurs, the steel ball breaks away from the magnet, rolls up a conical ramp and strikes a target plate, which opens the switch electrical contacts and the fuel pump circuit. Once the IFS switch is open, you must manually reset it (see Section 3).

Fuel pump

Fuel is circulated from the fuel tank to the fuel injection system through a metal line running along the underside of the vehicle. An electric fuel pump/fuel level sensor is located inside the fuel tank. The fuel pump/fuel level sensor assembly consists of the pump, the fuel level sensor, an inlet filter (sometimes referred to as a sock or strainer), a check valve to maintain pressure after the pump is shut off and a pressure relief valve to protect the pump from overpressurization in the event of a blocked fuel line. But what sets this pump apart from conventional in-tank pumps is its variable speed capability. The PCM controls fuel pressure by controlling the speed (rpm) of the pump. The PCM alters the fuel pressure by controlling the duty cycle of the Fuel Pump Driver Module (FPDM), which in turn controls the speed of the fuel pump by modulating the voltage to the fuel pump.

The turbocharged 3.5L OHC V6 uses a second fuel pump mounted near the fuel rail that is driven by the intake camshaft of the left cylinder bank. The pump is of a high-pressure design because this engine injects fuel directly into the combustion chamber (called Direct Injection). The tank module supplies fuel to the high-pressure pump.

EXHAUST SYSTEM

The exhaust system includes the exhaust manifolds, the catalytic converters (or catalysts), the mufflers and the exhaust pipes connecting all of these components together.

The catalytic converters, which are installed in the exhaust system, are emission-control devices that reduce the three principal tailpipe pollutants: hydrocarbons (HC), carbon monoxide (CO) and oxides of nitrogen (NOx). For more information about how catalysts work, refer to Chapter 6.

On most models, there are two catalytic converters; one per cylinder bank. The inlet and outlet exhaust pipes are welded onto each catalyst assembly. A crossover pipe connects the outlet pipes of the two catalyst assemblies. The rest of the exhaust system consists of a single intermediate pipe and a muffler and tailpipe that are welded into one single assembly.

On some models, there are four catalysts (upstream and downstream catalysts in each exhaust pipe). Each catalyst assembly includes an inlet pipe, the upstream catalyst, a connecting pipe, the downstream catalyst and the outlet pipe, all of which is welded together into a single assembly. A crossover pipe connects the outlet pipes of the two catalyst assemblies. The rest of the exhaust system consists of a single intermediate pipe and the (welded together) muffler/tailpipe assembly.

2 Fuel pressure relief procedure

❊❊❊ WARNING:

Gasoline is extremely flammable, so take extra precautions when you work on any part of the fuel system. Don't smoke or allow open flames or bare light bulbs near the work area, and don't work in a garage where a gas-type appliance (such as a water heater or a clothes dryer) is present. Since gasoline is carcinogenic, wear fuel-resistant gloves when there's a possibility of being exposed to fuel, and, if you spill any fuel on your skin, rinse it off immediately with soap and water. Mop up any spills immediately and do not store fuel-soaked rags where they could ignite. The fuel system is under constant pressure, so, if any fuel lines are to be disconnected, the fuel pressure in the system must be relieved first. When you perform any kind of work on the fuel system, wear safety glasses and have a Class B type fire extinguisher on hand.

➡ **Note: After the fuel pressure has been relieved, it's a good idea to lay a shop towel over any fuel connection to be disassembled, to absorb the residual fuel that may leak out when servicing the fuel system.**

2010 AND EARLIER MODELS

▶ **Refer to illustrations 2.1 and 2.2**

1 Remove the splash shield, which is located on the left frame rail, below the driver's door (see illustration).

2 Disconnect the fuel pump electrical connector (see illustration).

2.1 To detach the fuel pump electrical connector shield, remove these two bolts

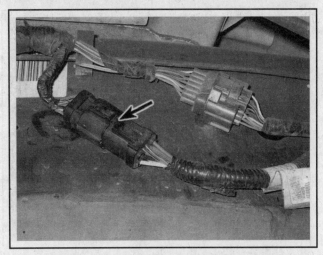

2.2 To disconnect the fuel pump connector, depress this release tab and pull the two halves of the connector apart

2011 AND LATER MODELS

3   Disconnect the electrical connector from the Fuel Pump Control Module (FPCM), which is located on the frame rail above the spare tire.

ALL MODELS

4   Start the engine and allow it to idle until it stalls.

5   After the engine stalls, crank the engine for about 5 seconds to make sure fuel pressure in the fuel rail is released.

6   Turn the ignition switch to OFF, then disconnect the cable from the negative terminal of the battery (see Chapter 5, Section 1) before performing any work on the fuel system.

3.5L V6 MODELS

✻✻ WARNING:

The fuel delivery system on 2011 and later 3.5L V6 models is made up of a low-pressure system and a high-pressure system. Once the pressure on the low-pressure side of the system has been relieved, wait at least two hours before loosening any fuel line fittings between the high-pressure fuel pump and the fuel rails.

7   Before loosening any fittings on the high-pressure side of the fuel system (from the high-pressure fuel pump to the fuel rails), wear full-face protection and thick leather gloves, cover the fitting being loosened with a rag, and loosen threaded fittings slowly so as to allow the pressure to seep out gradually instead of forcefully.

8   Properly dispose of fuel-soaked rags.

---

3   Fuel pump/fuel pressure - check

✻✻ WARNING:

Gasoline is extremely flammable, so take extra precautions when you work on any part of the fuel system. See the Warning in Section 2.

PRELIMINARY CHECKS

1   If you suspect insufficient fuel delivery check the following items first:

a) Check the battery and make sure that it's fully charged (see Chapter 5).

b) Check the fuel filter for obstructions (see Chapter 1).

c) Inspect the fuel line and quick-connect fittings (see Section 4). Verify that the problem is not simply a leak in a line.

2   Verify that the fuel pump actually runs. Remove the fuel filler cap and have an assistant turn the ignition switch to ON while you listen carefully for the sound of the fuel pump operating. You should hear a brief whirring noise (for about one second) as the pump comes on and pressurizes the system. If the fuel pump makes no sound, check the fuel pump relay fuse, the fuel pump relay and the Inertia Fuel Shutoff (IFS) switch (see Step 5). On 2011 and later 3.5L V6 models, there is a pressure sensor that maintains the correct output from the high-pressure fuel pump. If a code is set for the sensor, remove the intake manifold to access the sensor (see Chapter 2B).

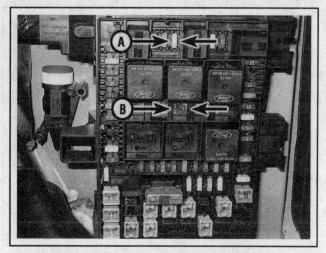

3.3 On 2008 and earlier models, the fuel pump relay fuse (A) and the fuel pump relay (B) are located in the passenger compartment fuse and relay box, which is located behind the right kick panel (for help with removing the kick panel, see Chapter 11, Section 24)

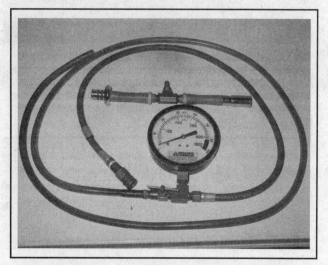

3.11 A typical fuel pressure gauge, with hoses and fittings suitable for tee-ing into the fuel system between the fuel delivery line and the fuel rail

Fuel pump electrical circuit check

▶ **Refer to illustration 3.3**

3   If the pump does not turn on, check the fuel pump relay fuse and the fuel pump relay. On 2008 and earlier models, these are both located in the passenger compartment fuse and relay box, which is located behind the right (passenger side) kick panel (see illustration).

➡ **Note: The fuel pump relay is built into the GEM board and cannot be removed. Consult with a dealer parts department before replacing it with a new component.**

On 2009 and later models, the fuse and relay are located in the Battery Junction Box at the front of the engine compartment.

4   If the fuse and relay are good, but the fuel pump still doesn't operate, inspect the fuel pump circuit.

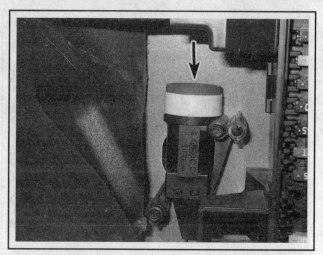

3.7 To reset the Inertia Fuel Shutoff (IFS) switch, depress the large button on top

Resetting the Inertia Fuel Shutoff (IFS) switch

▶ **Refer to illustration 3.7**

➡ **Note: The IFS switch is located in the lower right front corner of the passenger compartment, between the fuse and relay box and the firewall.**

5   To access the IFS switch, remove the right kick panel from the passenger's footwell (see Chapter 11).

6   Make sure that the ignition switch is turned to OFF.

7   Reset the IFS switch by pushing the large button on top of the switch (see illustration).

8   Run the test in Step 2 again. If the pump still doesn't run, check the fuel pump wiring harness for a loose connector or damaged wiring, or have the fuel pump circuit diagnosed by a professional.

9   If the fuel pump runs, but a fuel system problem persists, proceed to the fuel pump pressure check.

FUEL PUMP PRESSURE CHECK

▶ **Refer to illustrations 3.11 and 3.13**

➡ **Note: Before proceeding, obtain a fuel pressure gauge capable of measuring fuel pressure well above the specified operating range of the fuel system you're going to test, and you'll also need fittings suitable for tee-ing the gauge into the fuel system between the fuel delivery line and the fuel rail.**

10 Relieve the fuel system pressure (see Section 2).

11 In addition to a fuel pressure gauge capable of reading fuel pressure up to 50 psi, you'll need a hose and an adapter suitable for tee-ing into the fuel system at the quick-connect fitting between the fuel delivery hose and the fuel rail (see illustration).

12 Disconnect the quick-connect fitting at the connection between the fuel delivery hose and the fuel rail (if you're unfamiliar with quick-connect fittings, refer to Section 4).

13 Tee in the fuel pressure gauge between the fuel delivery hose and the fuel rail (see illustration).

14 Turn off all the accessories, then start the engine and let it idle. The fuel pressure should be within the operating range listed in this

Chapter's Specifications. If the pressure reading is within the specified range, the system is operating correctly.

15 If the fuel pressure is higher than specified, then the pump, the Fuel Pump Driver Module (FPDM), the Powertrain Control Module (PCM) or the circuit connecting these components is probably defective. But checking this circuit is beyond the scope of the home mechanic, so have the circuit checked by a professional.

16 If the fuel pressure is lower than specified, inspect the fuel delivery lines and hoses for an obstruction or a kink. Also inspect all fuel delivery line and hose quick-connect fittings for leaks. Replace the fuel filter (see Chapter 1) and re-check the pressure. If the lines, hoses, connections and the fuel filter are all in good shape, remove the fuel pump/ fuel level sensor assembly (see Section 7) and inspect the fuel pump inlet strainer for restrictions. If everything else is okay, replace the fuel pump (see Section 8).

17 Turn the ignition switch to OFF, wait five minutes and recheck the pressure on the gauge. Compare the reading with the hold pressure listed in this Chapter's Specifications. If the hold pressure is less than specified:

    a) *The fuel delivery line or a quick-connect fitting might be leaking.*
    b) *A fuel injector (or injectors) may be leaking.*
    c) *The fuel pump might be defective.*

18 After the testing is complete, relieve the fuel pressure (see Section 2), remove the fuel pressure gauge and reconnect the fuel delivery line to the fuel rail (see Section 4 if you're unfamiliar with quick-connect fittings)

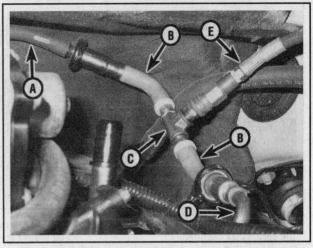

3.13 Here's a typical setup for tee-ing into the fuel system between the fuel delivery hose and the fuel rail:

A	*Fuel delivery hose*	D	*Fuel rail delivery pipe*
B	*Adapter hoses*	E	*Hose to fuel pressure gauge*
C	*Tee-fitting*		

4 Fuel lines and fittings - general information

✳ WARNING:

Gasoline is extremely flammable, so take extra precautions when you work on any part of the fuel system. See the Warning in Section 2.

1 Always relieve the system fuel pressure before servicing fuel lines or fittings (see Section 2).

2 The fuel supply line extends from the fuel tank to the engine compartment. The EVAP purge line extends from the EVAP canister, which is located behind the fuel tank, up to the purge valve, which is located on the firewall in the engine compartment. Anytime you raise the vehicle for underbody service, inspect the lines underneath the vehicle for leaks, kinks and dents.

3 The fuel and EVAP lines are secured to the underbody with plastic and metal clips. To disengage the fuel or EVAP lines from either type of clip, simply pull the line(s) straight out of the clip. To replace a damaged plastic clip, simply disengage the fuel and/or EVAP lines, then pull the clip out of its mounting bracket. To replace a damaged metal clip, disengage the fuel and/or EVAP lines, then unbolt the clip.

STEEL TUBING

4 If it's necessary to replace a fuel line or EVAP line, use steel tubing that complies with the manufacturer's specifications, or its equivalent.

5 Don't use copper or aluminum tubing to replace steel tubing. These materials cannot withstand normal vehicle vibration.

6 Because steel fuel lines are under high pressure when the engine is running, they require special consideration:

    a) *Inspect all O-rings for cuts, cracks and deterioration. If an O-ring is torn, cracked, hardened or otherwise damaged, replace it.*
    b) *If the lines are replaced, always use original equipment parts, or parts that meet the original equipment standards specified in this Section.*
    c) *Never allow metal lines to chafe against the frame. Maintain a minimum of 1/4-inch clearance around a line to prevent contact with the frame.*

7 If you find dirt in the system during disassembly, disconnect the fuel supply line and then blow it out with compressed air. And be sure to inspect the fuel filter (see Chapter 1) and the fuel pump inlet strainer for contamination (see Section 7).

FLEXIBLE HOSES

✳ CAUTION:

Use only original equipment replacement hoses or their equivalent. Unapproved hose material might fail when subjected to the fuel pressure at which this system operates.

8 Don't route fuel hose within four inches of any part of the exhaust system or within ten inches of the catalytic converter. Never allow rubber hoses to chafe against the frame. Maintain a minimum of 1/4-inch clearance around a hose to prevent contact with the frame.

9 If a hose is equipped with quick-connect fittings, the quick-connect fittings cannot be serviced separately. If the fitting or hose is damaged, replace the entire fuel hose assembly. Do not attempt to repair fuel hoses.

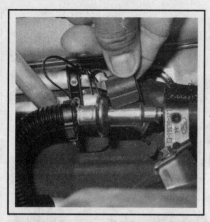

4.17 Remove the safety clamp from the spring lock coupling

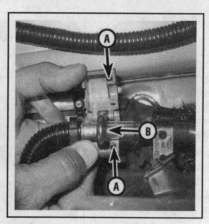

4.19a Place the spring-lock coupling tool around the coupling and close it so the lip (A) of the tool is flush against the garter spring housing (B) . . .

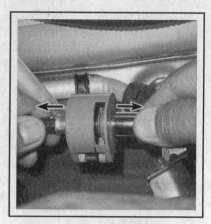

4.19b . . . push the spring-lock coupling tool toward the garter housing until the garter spring is disengaged, then pull the fuel lines apart

REPLACING FUEL LINES AND HOSES AND EVAP LINES

10 If a fuel line or hose or an EVAP line is damaged, replace it with factory replacement parts. Do not substitute fuel lines or hoses or EVAP lines of inferior quality. They might not be suitable for, and might fail when subjected to, the operating pressure of this system.

11 Always relieve the fuel system pressure before replacing fuel or EVAP lines (see Section 2).

12 Always disconnect the cable from the negative terminal of the battery (see Chapter 5, Section 1) before replacing fuel or EVAP lines.

13 Remove all clips that secure the fuel or EVAP line to the vehicle body. Pay close attention to all clips; they not only secure the fuel line and hoses, they also route them correctly. The hoses and line must be reattached to their respective clips when reassembled.

14 Be sure to use the correct tool and the correct procedure when disconnecting any fuel or EVAP couplings or fittings.

DISCONNECTING AND CONNECTING FUEL LINE AND EVAP LINE FITTINGS

Spring-lock couplings

▶ **Refer to illustrations 4.17, 4.19a, 4.19b, 4.19c and 4.19d**

15 The fuel supply line utilizes spring lock couplings at some connections such as the fuel rail and the fuel filter. The male side of the coupling, which is sealed by two O-rings, is simply the end of a fuel line with a flared end. The male side of the coupling is inserted into the female side of the coupling, which is secured by a garter spring that prevents unintentional disconnection by gripping the flared end of the male side of the coupling. On some of these fittings on some models, a safety clamp provides additional security. These clamps are often tethered to the female side of the coupling so that you don't lose them while the coupling is disconnected.

16 BEFORE DISCONNECTING SPRING-LOCK COUPLINGS, ALWAYS RELIEVE SYSTEM FUEL PRESSURE (see Section 2), then DISCONNECT THE CABLE FROM THE NEGATIVE BATTERY TERMINAL (see Chapter 5, Section 1).

17 Remove the safety clamp (see illustration).

18 If you're using a clamshell-type tool, install the tool over the coupling. Other types of release tools simply fit over the fuel line.

➡ **Note: These tools are available at most auto parts stores. They come in a variety of sizes, so it's a good idea to purchase a set of them to be sure you'll have the right size.**

19 Push the coupling tool firmly toward the garter spring housing to disengage the garter spring from the flared end of the female side of the connection (see illustrations). Then pull the two fuel lines apart to disengage the tool from the garter spring, open and remove the tool and disconnect the lines.

20 Before reconnecting the coupling, wipe off the ends of both fuel lines with a clean cloth. Inspect the condition of the O-rings and the garter spring. If either O-ring or the garter spring is damaged or worn, replace it. Also inspect the inside of the female side of the fitting and make sure it's clean.

21 Lubricate the O-rings with some clean engine oil, then press the two sides of the connection together until the flared end of the male side of the fitting is locked into place by the garter spring. Pull on the coupling to verify that it's fully engaged.

22 When you have verified that the coupling is reconnected, install the safety clamp.

23 Reconnect the cable to the negative battery terminal (see Chapter 5, Section 1).

24 Turn the ignition key to ON (not START) and re-pressurize the fuel system (see Section 2), which will take a moment, then check for fuel leakage around the coupling. If there are no signs of leaks, start the engine and check again.

Quick-connect couplings

25 Besides spring-lock couplings, the vehicles covered by this manual also use various types of quick-connect couplings to connect fuel lines, EVAP lines and PCV lines. After you locate the coupling, determine which type it is, then use whichever of the following procedures that applies to that particular style of coupling.

26 There are several types of quick-connect couplings in use on these vehicles. If you're in need of a replacement, take it with you to the auto parts store or dealer parts department. If you show the counterperson the coupling, retainer and/or O-ring and tell them the location of the coupling, they will be able to determine which part you need.

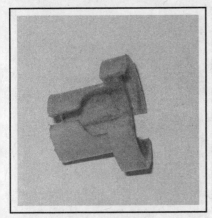

4.19c This type of spring-lock coupling tool can be used in places where access to the fitting is limited. To use it . . .

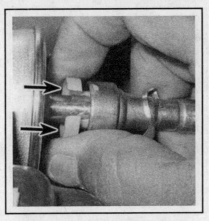

4.19d . . . slip it over the line, press it into the coupling and pull the lines apart

4.30 Using a screwdriver, carefully lever the locking tab up to its RELEASED position

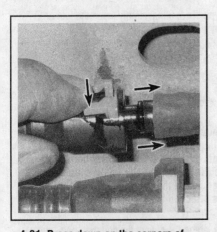

4.31 Press down on the corners of the locking tab to release it, push the fuel line into the coupling to release it from the retainer, then pull the fuel line out of the coupling

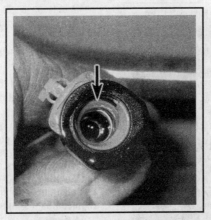

4.32 Inspect the condition of the O-ring inside the coupling. If the O-ring is cracked, torn or deteriorated, replace the coupling

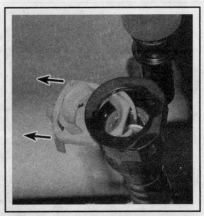

4.33 Inspect the condition of the retainer. If it's damaged, pull it out of the coupling, discard it and install a new retainer

27 Also, at the time of publication, the O-rings inside the following quick-connect couplings were not available separately from the coupling themselves. So if an O-ring is damaged, you must replace the coupling (which also includes the fuel hose or line to which it's permanently attached). And if one of these couplings is damaged, you cannot repair it. So, whether you're replacing a coupling because the O-ring is damaged or because the coupling itself is damaged, you must replace the coupling, and the fuel line to which it's permanently connected, as a single assembly.

28 Always relieve the system fuel pressure before disconnecting fuel line couplings (see Section 2).

29 Always disconnect the cable from the negative battery terminal before disconnecting fuel lines (see Chapter 5, Section 1).

Type 1

▶ Refer to illustrations 4.30. 4.31, 4.32 and 4.33

➡ **Note: The retainer clip for a Type 1 quick-connect coupling can be replaced separately, but the rest of the assembly (the coupling, O-ring and fuel hose or line to which the coupling is attached, must be replaced as a single assembly).**

30 Pull up the locking tab to the RELEASE position (see illustration).

31 Press down the corners of the locking tab to release it, push the fuel or EVAP line into the coupling to disengage it from the retainer, then pull the fuel line out of the coupling (see illustration).

32 Inspect the condition of the coupling and the O-ring inside (see illustration). If the coupling is damaged or if the O-ring inside the coupling is cracked, torn or deteriorated, replace the coupling.

33 Inspect the condition of the retainer (see illustration). If the retainer is damaged, remove it from the coupling and install a new retainer. (It's not a bad idea to replace the retainer anytime that you disconnect this type of coupling because retainers are inexpensive but critical parts.)

34 Before reconnecting the coupling to the fuel or EVAP line, apply a dab or two of clean engine oil to the end of the fuel line.

35 To connect the coupling, insert the fuel or EVAP line into the coupling until the fuel line clicks into place.

36 Verify that the coupling is fully connected by trying to pull the fuel or EVAP line and the coupling apart. If the coupling is fully connected, press down the locking tab to its LOCKED position.

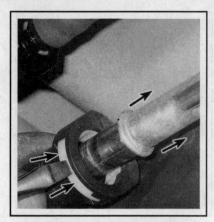

4.37 To disconnect a fuel line from this type of quick-connect coupling, depress the release button, then pull the fuel line out of the coupling

4.42a To disconnect this type of coupling, locate the brightly-colored locking tab on the side of the coupling . . .

4.42b . . . press it down firmly with the tip of a screwdriver and pull off the coupling

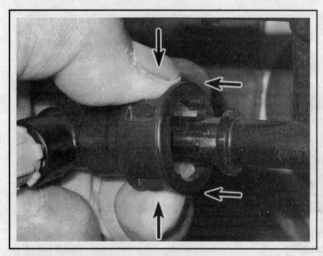

4.47 To disconnect this type of quick-connect coupling, depress the two release tabs on the top and bottom of the coupling and pull it off the pipe

Type II

▶ **Refer to illustration 4.37**

➡ **Note: This type of coupling has a brightly-colored, slender release button running along one side of the coupling body. You'll find this type of coupling used on both fuel and EVAP line connections anywhere from the fuel tank to the fuel and EVAP lines running under the vehicle. It's mainly used to connect EVAP lines together and to connect them to components such as the EVAP canister. If the coupling, the O-rings inside the coupling or the fuel hose or line to which the coupling is attached is damaged, they must be replaced as a single assembly.**

37 Press the button on the coupling and pull the fuel or EVAP line out of the coupling (see illustration).

38 Inspect the condition of the quick-connect coupling and the O-rings inside the coupling. If the coupling is damaged or if the O-rings are cracked, torn or deteriorated, replace the coupling and the EVAP line to which it's attached.

39 Apply a dab or two of clean engine oil to the fuel or EVAP line and to the O-rings inside the coupling.

40 To reconnect this type of coupling, simply insert the fuel or EVAP line into the coupling until it clicks into place.

41 Verify that the coupling is properly connected by trying to pull the coupling and the fuel or EVAP line apart.

Type III

▶ **Refer to illustrations 4.42a and 4.42b**

➡ **Note: This type of coupling has a brightly-colored locking tab on the side of the coupling body. It's used on some models to connect the PCV fresh air inlet and crankcase ventilation lines to the valve covers, the PCV valve and the intake manifold. If the coupling, the O-rings inside the coupling or the PCV line to which the coupling is attached is damaged, they must be replaced as a single assembly.**

42 Depress the locking tab on the side of the coupling body and disconnect the coupling (see illustrations).

43 Inspect the condition of the quick-connect coupling and the O-rings inside the coupling. If the coupling is damaged or if the O-rings are cracked, torn or deteriorated, replace the coupling and the EVAP line to which it's attached.

44 Apply a dab or two of clean engine oil to the O-rings inside the coupling.

45 To reconnect this type of coupling, release the locking tab by pushing it down again, then push the coupling onto the PCV pipe until the coupling clicks into place.

46 Verify that the coupling is properly connected by trying to pull the coupling and the EVAP line apart.

Type IV

▶ **Refer to illustration 4.47**

➡ **Note: This is another type of EVAP line quick-connect coupling that you'll find on some models. It's used to connect the EVAP purge line to the EVAP canister purge valve and to some other EVAP components. If the coupling, the O-rings inside the coupling or the fuel hose or line to which the coupling is attached is damaged, they must be replaced as a single assembly.**

47 To disconnect this type of quick-connect coupling, depress the two release tabs on the top and bottom of the fitting and pull it off the purge valve pipe (shown) or EVAP line (see illustration).

48 Inspect the condition of the quick-connect coupling and the O-rings inside the coupling. If the coupling is damaged or if the O-rings are cracked, torn or deteriorated, replace the coupling and the EVAP line to which it's attached.

49 Apply a dab or two of clean engine oil to the EVAP line and to the O-rings inside the coupling.

50 To reconnect this type of coupling, simply insert the EVAP line into the coupling, or push the coupling onto the EVAP line, until the line clicks into place.

51 Verify that the coupling is properly connected by trying to pull the coupling and the EVAP line apart.

5 Fuel tank - removal and installation

▶ **Refer to illustration 5.6, 5.7, 5.8, 5.11a, 5.11b, 5.13, 5.14a and 5.14b**

✳✳ WARNING:

Gasoline is extremely flammable, so take extra precautions when you work on any part of the fuel system. See the Warning in Section 2.

➡ **Note: Don't begin this procedure until the gauge indicates that the tank is empty or nearly empty. If the tank must be removed when it's full (for example, if the fuel pump malfunctions), siphon any remaining fuel from the tank prior to removal.**

1 Unless the vehicle has been driven far enough to completely empty the tank, it's critical to siphon the residual fuel out before removing the tank from the vehicle because this is a large tank and quite heavy when filled with fuel. The only way to siphon fuel from the tank is to withdraw it through the fuel filler neck hose (see Steps 8 and 9).

✳✳ WARNING:

DO NOT start the siphoning action by mouth! Use a siphoning kit (available at most auto parts stores).

2 Relieve the system fuel pressure (see Section 2).

3 Disconnect the cable from the negative terminal of the battery (see Chapter 5, Section 1).

4 Loosen the lug nuts for the left rear wheel. Raise the vehicle and support it securely on jackstands. Remove the left rear wheel.

5 If the vehicle is equipped with a skid plate, remove the four fuel tank skid plate mounting nuts and remove the skid plate.

6 Disconnect the quick-connect couplings for the fuel supply line and the EVAP canister purge line, both of which are located between the front of the fuel tank and the fuel filter (see illustration). If you're unfamiliar with these two types of quick-connect couplings, refer to Section 4.

7 Disconnect the quick-connect couplings for the fuel tank EVAP vent line and the EVAP canister purge line, both of which are located at the rear end of the fuel tank (see illustration). If you're unfamiliar with this type of quick-connect coupling, refer to Section 4.

8 Looking through the left rear wheelwell, locate the lower end of the metal fuel filler neck pipe (see illustration), loosen the hose clamp that secures the fuel filler neck hose to the filler neck pipe and pull off the hose.

9 If the fuel tank still contains more than a few gallons of fuel, siphon it out through the fuel filler neck hose at this time (see the **Warning** in Step 1). Simply run your siphoning hose through the fuel filler neck hose and into the tank. You might encounter some resistance

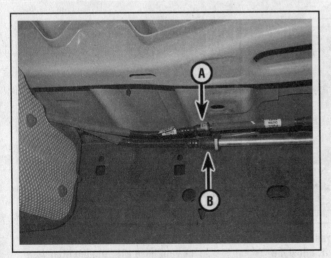

5.6 At the front of the fuel tank, disconnect the quick-connect couplings for the fuel supply line (A) and for the EVAP canister purge line (B) (see Section 4 if you don't know how to disconnect these two types of couplings)

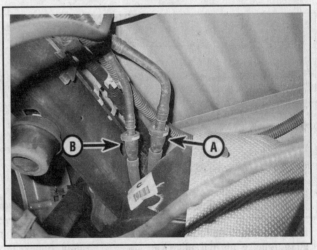

5.7 At the rear of the fuel tank, disconnect the quick-connect couplings for the EVAP vent line (A) and the EVAP canister purge line (B) (see Section 4 if you don't know how to disconnect this type of coupling)

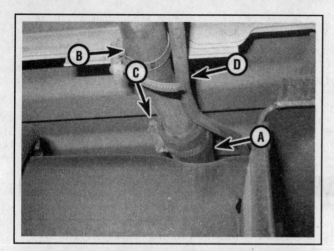

5.8 To disconnect the fuel filler neck hose (A) from the filler neck pipe (B), loosen this hose clamp (C) and pull off the hose. The smaller diameter pipe (D) is the vent pipe that directs vapors emitted during refueling back to the tank. The vent pipe is also connected to the top of the tank by a hose, but you can't access the hose clamp until you lower the tank a little

when the siphoning hose reaches the fuel tank because it must go through the filler pipe check valve, but the hose will push past the check valve as long as the hose diameter isn't too big. When you're done siphoning the fuel out of the tank, leave the siphon hose in place. Do NOT attempt to remove it until you have removed the fuel tank, because when you pull up on the siphoning hose it will snag at the spring-loaded check valve and could damage the valve if you use force to pull out the hose.

⁕⁕ WARNING:

If the fuel inside a full tank were to slosh around while lowering the tank and destabilize it, you could drop the tank and not only damage the tank but incur serious injuries to yourself.

10 Support the tank securely. Have at LEAST one assistant standing by to help out until the tank is on the floor.

⁕⁕ WARNING:

Do NOT attempt to lower the fuel tank by yourself. You could be seriously injured in the event that the tank gets out of control and falls on you.

11 Remove the bolts from the front and rear fuel tank straps (see illustrations), then allow the straps to swing down (they pivot from the other end) and disengage them from the crossmembers to which they're hooked.

12 Carefully and slowly lower the fuel tank just enough to access the electrical connectors and the hose that connects the filler neck vent pipe to the fuel tank.

⁕⁕ CAUTION:

Do NOT lower the fuel tank any more than absolutely necessary to access the connectors or you will damage the electrical harnesses and/or the hose that connects the filler neck vent pipe to the tank.

13 Disconnect the hose that connects the fuel tank filler neck vent pipe to the fuel tank (see illustration). This hose clamp is NOT a screw-type clamp. You must either pry the end loose or cut the clamp to remove it. Be careful not to damage the fuel tank filler neck vent hose.

14 Disconnect the electrical connectors from the fuel pump/fuel level and sending unit and from the Fuel Tank Pressure (FTP) sensor (see illustrations).

15 With the help of at least one assistant to help you steady the tank, carefully lower the tank to the floor.

16 If you're replacing the tank, or having it cleaned or repaired, refer to Section 6.

17 If you're going to remove the fuel pump/fuel level sensor, refer to Section 7.

18 Installation is the reverse of removal.

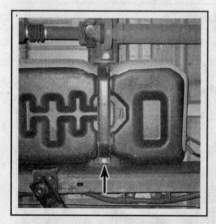

5.11a To detach the forward fuel tank strap, remove this bolt, allow the strap to swing down, then disengage the other end of the strap from the No. 3 crossmember and remove it

5.11b To detach the rear fuel tank strap, remove this bolt, allow the strap to swing down, then disengage the other end of the strap from the No. 4 crossmember and remove it

5.13 To disconnect the fuel tank filler neck vent hose (A) from the filler neck vent pipe (B), cut off this hose clamp (C) with a pair of diagonal cutters (this is not a screw-type clamp so the only way to remove it is to cut it off)

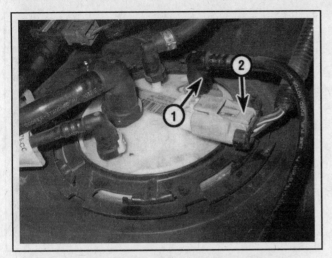

5.14a To disconnect the electrical connector from the fuel pump/fuel level sensor, push the red sliding lock (1) to the right, then depress the release tab (2) and pull off the connector

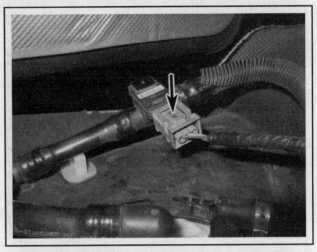

5.14b To disconnect the electrical connector from the Fuel Tank Pressure (FTP) sensor, depress the release tab on top and pull off the connector

6 Fuel tank - cleaning and repair

1 The fuel tanks installed in the vehicles covered by this manual are made of plastic and are not repairable.

2 If the fuel tank is removed from the vehicle, it should not be placed in an area where sparks or open flames could ignite the fumes coming out of the tank. Be especially careful inside a garage where a gas-type appliance is located, because it could cause an explosion.

7 Fuel pump/fuel level sensor - removal and installation

▶ Refer to illustrations 7.4, 7.5, 7.6a, 7.6b, 7.7, 7.8 and 7.11

✳✳ WARNING:

Gasoline is extremely flammable, so take extra precautions when you work on any part of the fuel system. See the Warning in Section 2.

1 Relieve the system fuel pressure (see Section 2).

2 Disconnect the cable from the negative battery terminal (see Chapter 5, Section 1).

3 Remove the fuel tank (see Section 5). Before removing the fuel pump module from the tank, first clean the tank surface thoroughly around the module, to prevent dirt or debris getting into the module opening of the tank.

4 Disconnect the fuel and EVAP line quick-connect couplings from the fuel pump/fuel level sensor (see illustration).

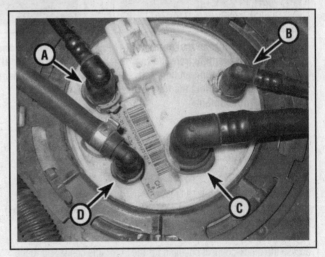

7.4 Disconnect the fuel and EVAP line quick-connect couplings (see Section 4) from the top of the fuel pump/fuel level sensor (typical):

A Fuel pump delivery line coupling
B EVAP line coupling
C EVAP line coupling
D EVAP line for fuel tank filler neck vent

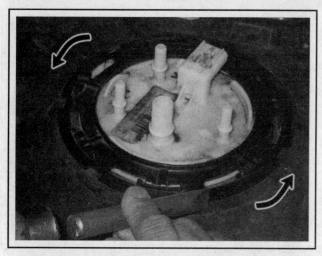

7.5 To unscrew the lock ring that secures the fuel pump/fuel level sensor, loosen it with a hammer and brass punch (don't use a steel punch, which might cause sparks)

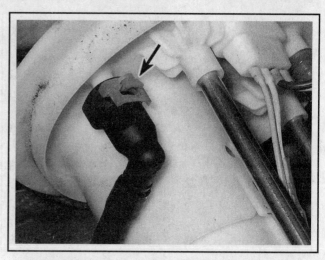

7.6a Lift up the fuel pump/fuel level sensor far enough to access this quick-connect coupling connected to the underside of the fuel pump mounting flange (this EVAP line is part of the plumbing inside the fuel tank for the EVAP fuel limit vent valve and for the fuel vapor vent valves)

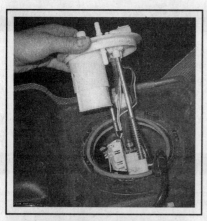

7.6b Carefully lift the fuel pump/fuel level sensor assembly from the fuel tank. Angle the pump/sending unit as necessary to protect the float arm and float from damage

7.7 Remove and discard the old O-ring type seal for the fuel pump/fuel level sensor

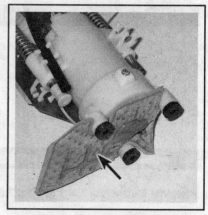

7.8 If you're going to install the old fuel pump, inspect the fuel inlet strainer. If it's slightly dirty, scrub it gently with a small brush and rinse it off with clean solvent. If the strainer is so dirty that you can't clean it, replace the fuel pump. The strainer cannot be removed

5   Using a hammer and a brass punch (do NOT use a steel punch!), loosen the fuel pump/fuel level sensor lock ring (see illustration). When the lock ring is loose enough, fully unscrew it.

6   Lift up the fuel pump/fuel level sensor assembly far enough to access the quick-connect coupling for the EVAP line connected to the underside of the fuel pump/fuel level sensor (see illustration). Disconnect the EVAP line's quick-connect coupling from the pump mounting flange (see Section 4), then carefully lift the fuel pump/fuel level sensor assembly out of the fuel tank (see illustration). (The EVAP hose connected to the underside of the pump flange is part of the plumbing inside the fuel tank for the fuel limit vent valve and fuel vapor vent valves. Neither the fuel limit vent valve, the fuel vapor vent valves nor

the plumbing for these EVAP components can be serviced separately from the fuel tank. If any one of these components fails, replace the fuel tank.)

7   Remove the old O-ring type seal (see illustration) and discard it.

8   If you're planning to reinstall the original fuel pump unit, inspect the condition of the fuel inlet strainer (see illustration). The strainer is a permanent part of the pump and cannot be removed. If it's only slightly dirty, try scrubbing it gently with a small brush, then rinse it off with clean solvent. But if the strainer is so dirty that it's obstructed - and you're unable to clean it - you must replace the pump. You can either purchase an entire new pump/sending unit assembly or remove the old fuel level sensor from this pump (see Section 8) and swap it onto a new

pump unit. Either way, the new pump will include a new strainer.

9   Clean the fuel pump mounting flange and the tank mounting surface, particularly the area where the O-ring type seal is installed.

10   Be sure to use a new O-ring type seal and apply a thin coat of heavy grease to the new seal ring to hold it in place while installing the fuel pump/fuel level sensor assembly.

11   After installing the fuel pump/fuel level sensor assembly in the fuel tank, make sure the alignment arrows on the pump mounting flange and on the top of the fuel tank (see illustration) are aligned.

12   Installation is otherwise the reverse of removal.

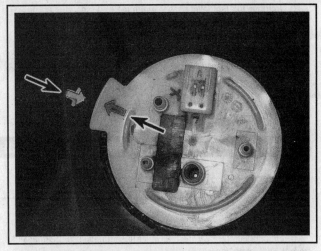

7.11 When installing the fuel pump/fuel level sensor, make sure the alignment arrows on the fuel pump mounting flange and on the top of the fuel tank are aligned

8   Fuel pump and fuel level sensor - replacement

▶ **Refer to illustrations 8.5 and 8.6**

✳ WARNING:

Gasoline is extremely flammable, so take extra precautions when you work on any part of the fuel system. See the Warning in Section 2.

1   Remove the fuel tank (see Section 5).

2   Remove the fuel pump/fuel level sensor from the tank (see Section 7).

3   Place the fuel pump/fuel level sensor on a clean workbench.

4   Note how the electrical wire for the fuel level sensor is bundled together with the wiring for the fuel pump and also note how the entire harness for both the pump and the sensor is routed. When you reassemble the pump and the sensor, the pump and sensor wiring harness MUST be routed exactly the same way for the pump and sensor to function properly.

5   Remove the heat shrink tubing from the electrical connector (see illustration) and disconnect the sensor electrical connector.

6   Note the location of the cable tie (see illustration) that secures the harness for the fuel pump and the fuel level sensor, then carefully cut the cable tie with a pair of diagonal cutters. Make SURE that you don't accidentally cut any of the wires!

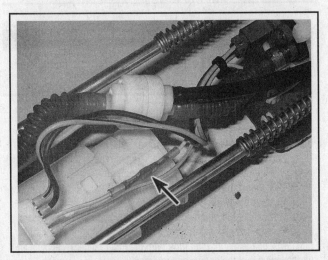

8.5 Remove the heat shrink tubing from the fuel level sensor electrical connector and disconnect the spade-type connector

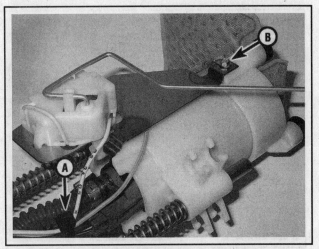

8.6 Cut this cable tie (A) and disengage the fuel level sensor wire from the fuel pump wiring harness. To detach the fuel level sensor from the fuel pump assembly, remove this mounting bolt (B)

7   Remove the fuel level sensor mounting bolt (see illustration 8.6) and remove the sensor from the fuel pump assembly.

8   No further disassembly of the fuel pump assembly is possible. You may now install the old fuel level sensor on a new fuel pump assembly or install a new fuel level sensor on the old fuel pump assembly.

9   Be sure to route the wiring harness for the fuel pump and the fuel level sensor exactly the same way that it was routed prior to disassembly, then secure it with a new cable tie in the same spot.

10   Installation is otherwise the reverse of removal.

9   Air intake duct and air filter housing - removal and installation

2004 THROUGH 2008 4.2L V6 AND 4.6L V8 MODELS

Air intake duct

1   Disconnect the PCV fresh air inlet hose (crankcase breather hose) from the air intake duct.

2   Loosen the hose clamp at the air filter housing end of the air intake duct and disconnect the intake duct from the filter housing.

3   Loosen the hose clamp at the throttle body end of the air intake duct, disconnect the intake duct from the throttle body and remove the duct.

4   Installation is the reverse of removal.

Air filter housing

5   Disconnect the electrical connector from the MAF sensor and detach the electrical connector retainer. (The connector is located on the underside of the filter housing assembly.)

6   To remove the air filter housing, disengage the filter housing locator pins and the fresh air inlet duct (on the upstream side of the filter housing) from their grommets.

7   Inspect the condition of the rubber grommets for the filter housing locator pins. If the grommets are cracked, torn or deteriorated, replace them.

8   If you want to disassemble the air filter housing to replace or inspect the air filter element, refer to Chapter 1.

9   If you want to disassemble the air filter housing to replace the Mass Air Flow (MAF) sensor, refer to Chapter 6.

10   Installation is the reverse of removal.

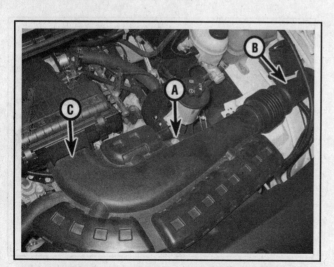

9.11 To detach the air intake duct on a 5.4L V8 model, remove this bolt (A), then pull the fresh air inlet end of the duct (B) out of the fender and pull the outlet end of the duct (C) out of the air filter housing

2004 THROUGH 2008 5.4L V8 MODELS

Air intake duct

▶ **Refer to illustration 9.11**

11   Remove the air intake duct retaining bolt (see illustration).

12   Pull the fresh air inlet end of the duct out of the fender.

13   Pull the outlet end of the duct out of the air filter housing.

14   Remove the air intake duct.

15   Installation is the reverse of removal.

Air filter housing

▶ **Refer to illustrations 9.17 and 9.20**

16   Remove the air intake duct (see Steps 11 through 14).

17   Disconnect the electrical connector from the MAF sensor (see illustration).

18   Disconnect the PCV fresh air inlet tube (crankcase ventilation hose) quick-connect coupling from the air filter housing.

19   Remove the four air filter housing mounting bolts.

20   Remove the air filter housing-to-throttle body seal (see illustration).

21   Inspect the condition of the air filter housing-to-throttle body seal. If it's cracked, torn or deteriorated, replace it.

22   Installation is the reverse of removal.

2009 AND LATER MODELS

☼☼ WARNING:

Wait until the engine is completely cool before beginning this procedure.

23   Drain the cooling system until the expansion tank is empty.

24   Disconnect the PCV fresh air inlet tube (crankcase ventilation hose) quick-connect coupling from the air intake duct.

25   Loosen both clamps securing the outlet pipe to the air cleaner cover and throttle body. Remove the outlet pipe.

26   Disconnect the electrical connector from the MAF sensor.

27   Remove the air filter element (see Chapter 1).

28   Disconnect the expansion tank overflow hose from the radiator.

29   Remove the expansion tank/air filter lower housing mounting bolts. Disengage the air inlet tube from the inner fender receptacle and lift the tank out of the engine compartment.

30   Installation is the reverse of removal.

31   Refill the cooling system with the proper type and concentration of antifreeze (see Chapter 1).

9.17 To detach the air filter housing from a 5.4L V8 engine, disconnect or remove the following:

1 *Mass Air Flow (MAF) sensor electrical connector (already disconnected in this photo)*
2 *Positive Crankcase Ventilation (PCV) fresh air inlet tube (crankcase ventilation hose) quick-connect coupling*
3 *Air filter housing mounting bolts*

9.20 Remove the air filter housing-to-throttle body seal and inspect the condition of the seal. If it's cracked, torn or deteriorated, replace it

10 Sequential Multiport Fuel Injection (SFI) system - general information

SEQUENTIAL MULTIPORT FUEL INJECTION (SFI) SYSTEM

All models are equipped with a Sequential Multiport Fuel Injection (SFI) system. The Powertrain Control Module (PCM) controls the fuel injectors, which inject fuel directly into the intake port of each cylinder in the engine firing order. When the engine is running, the PCM constantly monitors an array of engine operating conditions (cylinder head temperature, intake air temperature, mass of air moving through the intake system, engine rpm, load, etc.) and alters the pulse width of the injectors accordingly, delivering the right amount of fuel into the intake ports where it mixes with incoming air.

TORQUE BASED ELECTRONIC THROTTLE CONTROL (ETC) SYSTEM

In a conventional induction system with an accelerator cable, the position of the throttle plate inside the throttle body is determined by the position of the accelerator pedal, which is determined by your foot, isn't always appropriate to the prevailing operating conditions. For example, if you mash the accelerator pedal when the transmission is in high gear and the vehicle is cruising down the freeway under no load, it takes a moment for the PCM to downshift the transmission and spin up the engine speed so that it can respond to your new demand. The manufacturer claims that its Generation II (Gen II) Torque Based Electronic Throttle Control (ETC) system produces the ideal transmission output shaft torque because the position of the throttle plate inside the throttle body is no longer based solely on driver demand (the position of the accelerator pedal).

Electronic throttle body and Throttle Position (TP) sensors

Instead, the PCM-controlled electronic throttle body regulates the amount of air entering the intake manifold in response to driver demand and in response to the operating conditions. There is no accelerator cable or cruise control cable connected to the throttle body. Both of these functions are handled by the PCM. There is also no Idle Air Control (IAC) motor on the electronic throttle body. This function is also handled by the PCM, which opens the throttle plate slightly in response to any load imposed on the engine during idle or low-speed maneuvers.

The electronic throttle body uses two Throttle Position (TP) sensors (TP1 and TP2) because the monitor for this system requires a redundant TP sensor. TP1 has a negative slope (increasing angle, decreasing voltage) and TP2 has a positive slope (increasing angle, increasing voltage). When the engine is running, the negatively-sloped TP1 is used by the ETC system as the actual TP sensor and TP2 is used as a reference sensor by the monitor.

ELECTRONICALLY CONTROLLED RETURNLESS FUEL SYSTEM

In a conventional fuel system with a return line, a fuel pressure regulator maintains the pressure within the correct operating range. When the vehicle decelerates, intake manifold goes up and a vacuum hose between the intake manifold and the pressure regulator lifts the spring-loaded diaphragm inside the regulator, allowing excess fuel pressure to bleed off and the unused fuel to return to the fuel tank. When the vehicle accelerates again, intake manifold vacuum goes down and the spring inside the regulator closes the diaphragm, shutting off the return line and allowing fuel pressure to rise again. But all of the models covered by this manual use a returnless fuel system; there is no fuel pressure regulator and no fuel return line.

Fuel Pump Driver Module (FPDM)

In the type of returnless fuel system used by the vehicles covered by this manual, the PCM controls the fuel pressure by controlling the duty cycle of the Fuel Pump Driver Module (FPDM), which in turn controls the speed of the fuel pump by modulating the voltage to the fuel pump. The FPDM is located underneath the vehicle, on the crossmember immediately ahead of the spare tire. To replace the FPDM, refer to Chapter 6.

11 Fuel injection system - check

✳ WARNING:

Gasoline is extremely flammable, so take extra precautions when you work on any part of the fuel system. See the Warning in Section 2.

➡ **Note: The following procedure is based on the assumption that the fuel pump is working and the fuel pressure is adequate (see Section 3).**

PRELIMINARY CHECKS

1   Inspect all electrical connectors that are part of the SFI system. Loose electrical connectors and poor grounds can cause many problems that resemble more serious malfunctions.

2   Verify that the battery is fully charged. The Powertrain Control Module (PCM), the information sensors and the output actuators must receive adequate and stable voltage to function correctly.

3   Inspect the condition of the air filter element. A dirty or partially blocked filter will severely degrade performance and fuel economy (see Chapter 1).

4   Check the fuses that are related to the SFI system. If you find a blown fuse, replace it and note whether it blows again. If it does, look for a grounded or shorted wire in the harness for the relevant circuit (fuel pump, fuel injectors, etc.). For more information on fuses, refer to Chapter 12. For a complete guide to the fuses on your vehicle, refer to your owner's manual.

SYSTEM CHECKS

▶ **Refer to illustration 11.7**

5   Inspect the condition of any vacuum hoses connected to the intake manifold or to the throttle body.

6   Inspect the bore of the throttle body for dirt, carbon or other residue build-up, particularly around the throttle plate.

✳ CAUTION:

The bore inside the throttle bodies used on all vehicles covered in this manual is coated with a special film designed to protect the bore and throttle plate and to resist the accumulation of sludge. Do not attempt to clean the interior of the throttle body with carburetor or other spray cleaners. Cleaning the throttle body bore can damage the throttle body bore and impair performance.

11.7 Use an automotive stethoscope to listen to each injector. If an injector is working correctly, it should make a steady clicking sound that rises and falls in response to engine rpm

7   With the engine running, place an automotive stethoscope against each injector, one at a time, and listen for a clicking sound, indicating operation (see illustration). If you don't have a stethoscope, you can place the tip of a long screwdriver against the injector and listen through the handle.

8   If an injector isn't operating (not clicking), inspect the condition of the injector wiring harness. Make sure that the wiring is in good shape and that the injector electrical connector is correctly connected.

9   Any further diagnosis of the fuel injection system should be left to a professional service technician.

12 Throttle body - removal and installation

V6 MODELS AND 4.6L AND 5.0L V8 MODELS

1 Remove the air intake duct (see Section 9).

2 Disconnect the electronic throttle control electrical connector from the throttle body.

3 Remove the four throttle body mounting bolts and remove the throttle body.

4 Remove the old throttle body gasket. Inspect the condition of the gasket. If it's damaged, replace it. If it's undamaged, you can reuse it.

5 Installation is the reverse of removal. Be sure to use a new gasket, if necessary, and tighten the throttle body mounting bolts to the torque listed in this Chapter's Specifications.

5.4L AND 6.2L V8 MODELS

▶ **Refer to illustrations 12.8a, 12.8b, 12.9 and 12.10**

6 Remove the air intake duct and, on 5.4L models, the air filter housing (see Section 9).

7 On 2009 and later models, remove the clamp and mounting bolt and remove the intake resonator. Remove the four adapter mounting bolts and remove the air intake duct-to-throttle body adapter.

8 Disconnect the electrical connector(s) from the throttle body (see illustrations).

9 Remove the throttle body mounting bolts (see illustration), and remove the throttle body.

10 Remove and discard the old throttle body O-ring seal (see illustration).

11 Installation is the reverse of removal. Be sure to use a new O-ring seal and tighten the throttle body mounting bolts to the torque listed in this Chapter's Specifications.

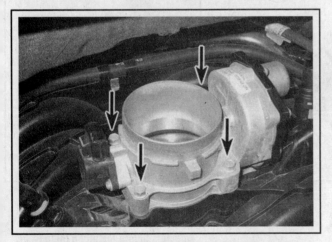

12.8a There are just two electrical connectors on the electronic throttle body used on 5.4L V8 models, the electronic throttle control connector (A) and the Throttle Position (TP) sensor connector (B). They both employ the same type of electrical connector

12.8b To disconnect the electronic throttle control electrical connector from the throttle body (or to disconnect the connector from the TP sensor), slide out the lock (1) (toward the harness), then depress the release tab (2) and pull off the connector

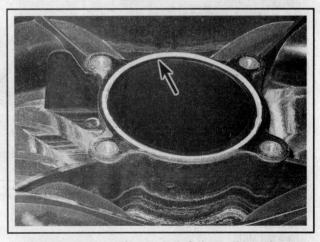

12.9 Throttle body mounting bolts (5.4L V8 engine)

12.10 Remove the old throttle body O-ring seal from the intake manifold and discard it. Always use a new O-ring seal when installing the throttle body

13 Fuel rail and injectors - removal and installation

1 Relieve the system fuel pressure (see Section 2).
2 Disconnect the cable from the negative battery terminal (see Chapter 5, Section 1).

4.2L V6 MODELS

▶ **Refer to illustrations 13.5, 13.7, 13.10a and 13.10b**

3 Disconnect the fuel supply line spring-lock coupling from the fuel rail. If you're unfamiliar with spring-lock couplings, see Section 4.
4 Disconnect the vacuum hose and the electrical connector from the Fuel Rail Pressure Temperature (FRPT) sensor.
5 Disconnect the electrical connectors from all six fuel injectors (see illustration).
6 Detach the injector wiring harness retainers from the fuel rail.
7 Remove the four fuel rail bolts (see illustration).

13.5 Disconnect all six electrical connectors from the fuel injectors (4.2L V6 models)

8 Remove the fuel rail and injectors as a single assembly.
9 Grasp each fuel injector firmly and pull it out of the fuel rail.
10 Remove the two old O-rings from each injector (see illustrations).
11 Install new O-rings on the fuel injectors.
12 Installation is the reverse of removal. Be sure to tighten the fuel rail mounting bolts to the torque listed in this Chapter's Specifications.

4.6L V8 MODELS

13 Remove the air intake duct (see Section 9).
14 Unscrew the threaded fitting at the upper end of the Exhaust Gas Recirculation (EGR) pipe and disconnect the pipe from the EGR module. Then loosen the threaded fitting at the lower end of the EGR pipe, at the exhaust manifold, and rotate the pipe out of the way (see Chapter 6).
15 Disconnect the power brake booster hose (see Chapter 9).
16 Disconnect the electrical connector from the Throttle Position (TP) sensor.
17 Disconnect the electronic throttle control electrical connector from the electronic throttle body.
18 Disconnect the electrical connector and vacuum hose from the Exhaust Gas Recirculation (EGR) module.
19 Disconnect both ends of the Positive Crankcase Ventilation (PCV) system's PCV fresh air inlet hose (crankcase breather hose) from the left valve cover and from the air intake duct.
20 Disconnect the PCV system's fresh air inlet hose from the right valve cover and remove the fresh air inlet hose. (You already disconnected the other end of this hose when you removed the air intake duct.)
21 On 2004 through 2006 models, disconnect the vacuum hose(s) from the throttle body spacer (see Chapter 2B).
22 On 2004 through 2006 models, disconnect the throttle body coolant hoses from the throttle body spacer.
23 On 2004 through 2006 models, remove the four throttle body spacer mounting bolts and remove the throttle body spacer and throttle body as a single assembly (it's not necessary to unbolt the throttle body from the throttle body spacer). Remove and discard the old throttle body

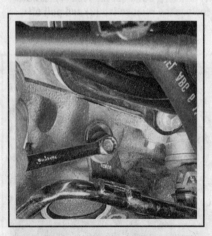

13.7 To detach the fuel rail assembly from a 4.2L V6 engine, remove all four fuel rail mounting bolts (two per side)

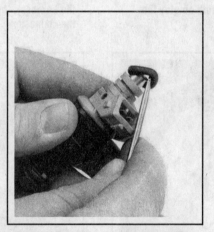

13.10a Remove the old O-ring from the upper end . . .

13.10b . . . and from the lower end of each fuel injector, then install new upper and lower O-rings on all injectors before installing them (4.2L V6 models)

13.36 Disconnect the electrical connector from the heated PCV valve (5.4L V8 models)

13.38 Disconnect the quick-connect coupling for the Vapor Management Valve (VMV) and set the VMV line aside (5.4L V8 models)

spacer gasket.

24 Disconnect the electrical connector from the Injection Pressure (IPR) sensor (2004 through 2006 models) or the injection pressure and temperature sensor (2007 and 2008 models).

25 Disconnect the electrical connectors from the eight fuel injectors.

26 Disconnect the vacuum connector from the IPR sensor.

27 Disconnect the fuel supply line spring-lock coupling from the fuel rail (see Section 4 if you're unfamiliar with spring-lock couplings).

28 Remove the four fuel rail mounting bolts and remove the fuel rail and injectors as a single assembly.

29 Remove the injectors from the fuel rail. If an injector sticks in its bore, work it out of the fuel rail by wiggling it from side-to-side while simultaneously pulling on it.

30 Remove the old upper and lower O-rings from each fuel injector and discard them (see illustrations 13.10a and 13.10b). Install new upper and lower O-rings on each injector.

31 Coat each upper injector O-ring with a small amount of clean engine oil, then install the injectors in the fuel rail.

32 Coat each lower injector O-ring with a small amount of clean engine oil, then install the fuel rail and injector assembly. Be sure to tighten the fuel rail mounting bolts to the torque listed in this Chapter's Specifications.

33 Installation is otherwise the reverse of removal.

5.4L V8 MODELS

▶ **Refer to illustrations 13.36, 13.38, 13.40, 13.42, 13.45, 13.46 and 13.47**

34 Remove the air intake duct and the air filter housing (see Section 9). On 2009 and later models, remove the four adapter bolts and remove the air intake-to-throttle body adapter.

35 Disconnect the EVAP purge line quick-connect coupling from the EVAP canister purge valve (see Section 24 in Chapter 6). If you're unfamiliar with quick-connect couplings, refer to Section 4.

36 Disconnect the electrical connector from the heated PCV valve (see illustration).

37 Disconnect the PCV hose from the PCV valve (see Section 22 in Chapter 1).

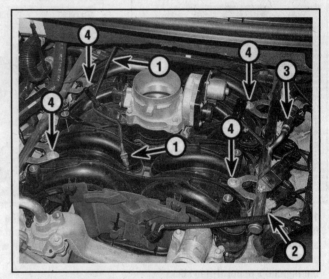

13.40 To detach the fuel rail from the intake manifold on a 5.4L V8 engine, disconnect or remove the following items:

1 *Vacuum line*
2 *Fuel injector electrical connector (just one injector connector shown here; but there are eight injector connectors, one for each injector)*
3 *Fuel supply line spring-lock coupling (see Section 4 if you need help)*
4 *Fuel rail assembly mounting bolts*

38 Disconnect the quick-connect coupling for the Vapor Management Valve (VMV) from the right side of the intake manifold (see illustration) and set the VMV line aside. If you're unfamiliar with quick-connect couplings, refer to Section 4.

39 Disconnect the electronic throttle control and the Throttle Position (TP) sensor electrical connectors from the throttle body (see illustrations 12.13a and 12.13b).

40 Disconnect the vacuum hose located near the rear of the right valve cover, if applicable (see illustration).

41 Disconnect the electrical connector and the vacuum hose from

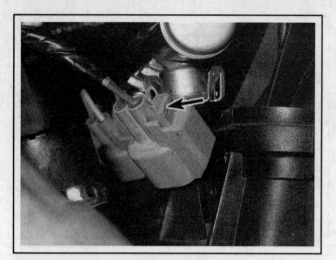

13.42 To disconnect an electrical connector from a fuel injector, depress this release tab and pull off the connector (5.4L V8 models)

13.45 To work the injectors loose from their bores, grasp the fuel rail firmly and carefully rock it from side-to-side while pulling up (5.4L V8 models)

13.46 To remove an injector from the fuel rail, spread these two retainers apart with a pair of needle-nose pliers and pull out the injector. If the injector's upper O-ring sticks in the injector mounting bore, simultaneously wiggle the injector from side-to-side while pulling on it (5.4L V8 models)

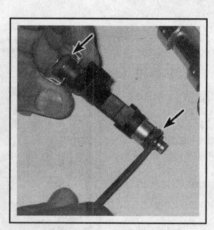

13.47 Remove the old upper and lower O-rings from each fuel injector and replace them with new ones (5.4L V8 models)

13.53 Fuel rail insulators (3.7L V6 engine)

the Fuel Rail Pressure Temperature (FRPT) sensor (see Chapter 6).

42 Disconnect the eight fuel injector electrical connectors (see illustration).

43 Disconnect the fuel supply line spring-lock coupling at the fuel rail (see illustration 13.40). If you're unfamiliar with spring-lock couplings, refer to Section 4 for help.

44 Remove the four fuel rail mounting bolts (see illustration 13.40).

45 Remove the fuel rail and the injectors as a single assembly (see illustration).

46 Remove the injectors from the fuel rail (see illustration).

47 Remove the two old O-rings from each injector (see illustration).

48 Install new O-rings on each injector, apply a little clean engine oil to each upper injector O-ring, then insert each injector into its mounting bore in the fuel rail.

49 Apply a little clean engine oil to each lower injector O-ring, then

install the fuel rail assembly. First, align the lower end of each injector with its bore in the intake manifold, then press down firmly on the fuel rail until all of the injectors are fully seated.

50 The remainder of installation is the reverse of removal. Be sure to tighten the fuel rail assembly mounting bolts to the torque listed in this Chapter's Specifications.

3.7L V6 AND 5.0L V8 MODELS

▶ Refer to illustrations 13.53, 13.54 and 13.55

51 If you're working on a 3.7L V6 model, remove the upper intake manifold (see Chapter 2B).

52 Detach the fuel feed line from the fuel rail (see Section 4).

53 Remove the fuel rail insulators (see illustration).

13.54 Depress the locking tab, then pull the electrical connector off the injector

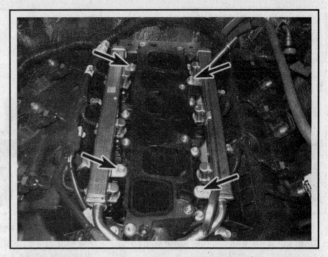

13.55 Fuel rail mounting bolts (3.7L V6 engine, others similar)

54 Disconnect the electrical connectors from the injectors (see illustration).

55 Remove the fuel rail mounting bolts (see illustration).

56 Remove the fuel rail and the injectors as a single assembly (see illustration 13.45).

57 Remove the injectors from the fuel rail (see illustration 13.46).

58 Remove the old O-rings from each injector (see illustration 13.47).

59 Install new O-rings on each injector, apply a little clean engine oil to each upper injector O-ring, then insert each injector into its mounting bore in the fuel rail.

60 Apply a little clean engine oil to each lower injector O-ring, then install the fuel rail assembly. First, align the lower end of each injector with its bore in the intake manifold, then press down firmly on the fuel rail until all of the injectors are fully seated.

61 The remainder of installation is the reverse of removal. Be sure to tighten the fuel rail assembly mounting bolts to the torque listed in this Chapter's Specifications.

6.2L V8 MODELS

62 Disconnect the air intake duct and adapter from the throttle body.

63 Detach the fuel feed line from the fuel rail (see Section 4).

64 Disconnect the electrical connectors and the spark plug wires from the ignition coils.

65 Disconnect the electrical connectors from the injectors (see illustration 13.54).

66 Remove the fuel rail and the injectors as a single assembly (see illustration 13.45).

67 Remove the injectors from the fuel rail (see illustration 13.46).

68 Remove the old O-rings from each injector (see illustration 13.47).

69 Install new O-rings on each injector, apply a little clean engine oil to each upper injector O-ring, then insert each injector into its mounting bore in the fuel rail.

70 Apply a little clean engine oil to each lower injector O-ring, then install the fuel rail assembly. First, align the lower end of each injector with its bore in the intake manifold, then press down firmly on the fuel rail until all of the injectors are fully seated.

71 The remainder of installation is the reverse of removal. Be sure to tighten the fuel rail assembly mounting bolts to the torque listed in this Chapter's Specifications.

3.5L V6 MODELS

▸ **Refer to illustration 13.86**

✳✳ WARNING:

Wait until the engine is completely cool before beginning this procedure.

✳✳ WARNING:

The fuel delivery system on these models is made up of a low-pressure system and a high-pressure system. Once the pressure on the low-pressure side of the system has been relieved, wait at least two hours before loosening any fuel line fittings between the high-pressure fuel pump and the fuel rail. Before loosening any fittings on the high-pressure side of the fuel system (from the high-pressure fuel pump to the fuel rails), wear full-face protection and thick leather gloves, cover the fitting being loosened with a rag, and loosen threaded fittings slowly so as to allow the pressure to seep out gradually instead of forcefully.

72 Drain the cooling system (see Chapter 1).

73 Remove the intake manifold (see Chapter 2B).

74 Detach the hoses from the thermostat housing, then remove the four bolts and detach the housing from the left cylinder head.

75 Remove the coolant pipe from between the cylinder heads.

➡ **Note: If necessary for clearance, remove the cooling fan assembly (see Chapter 3).**

76 Remove the bolts and detach the coolant crossover pipe from the rear of the cylinder heads.

77 Remove the high-pressure fuel tube bracket fasteners.

78 Unscrew the flare-nuts and detach the high-pressure fuel tube

13.86 To remove the Teflon sealing ring, cut it off with a hobby knife (be careful not to scratch the injector groove)

13.91 Slide the new Teflon seal onto the end of a socket that's the same diameter as the end of the fuel injector . . .

13.92 . . . align the socket with the end of the injector and slide the seal onto the injector and into its mounting groove

from the fuel rails and pump. Discard the high-pressure fuel tube - a new one must be installed on reassembly.

79 Disconnect the fuel injector harness electrical connectors.

80 Using compressed air, clean the valley between the cylinder banks.

81 Remove the fuel rail mounting bolts.

✳✳ CAUTION:

The manufacturer recommends that these bolts be replaced with new ones whenever they are removed.

82 Remove the left fuel rail and injectors, followed by the right fuel rail and injectors.

➡ **Note: The fuel injectors might come out with the fuel rail, but they will most likely stick in their bores in the cylinder heads. If they are difficult to remove a slide hammer and an adapter that grips the top of the injector might be required.**

83 Disconnect the electrical connectors from the injectors.

84 Remove the injector retaining clips. Discard the clips; the manufacturer recommends that they be replaced with new ones on installation.

85 Clean the injector bores in the cylinder head with a brush made for this purpose.

86 Remove the old combustion chamber Teflon sealing ring and the upper O-ring and support ring from each injector (see illustration).

✳✳ CAUTION:

Be extremely careful not to damage the groove for the seal or the rib in the floor of the groove. If you damage the groove or the rib, you must replace the injector.

87 Before installing the new Teflon seal on each injector, thoroughly clean the groove for the seal and the injector shaft. Remove all combustion residue and varnish with a clean shop rag.

Teflon seal installation using the special tools

88 The manufacturer recommends that you use special seal installation tools to install the Teflon lower seals on the injectors. Install the

special seal assembly cone on the injector, install the special sleeve on the injector and use the sleeve to push on the assembly cone, which pushes the Teflon seal into place on its groove. Do NOT use any lubricants to do so.

89 Pushing the Teflon seal into place in its groove expands it slightly. There is a sizing sleeve in the special tool set. Using a clockwise rotating motion of about 180 degrees, install the sleeve onto the injector and over the Teflon seal until the sleeve hits its stop, then carefully turn the sleeve counterclockwise as you pull it off the injector. The seal is now sized. Repeat this step for each injector.

➡ **Note: Install the injectors within 15 minutes of seal sizing (if they aren't installed, the seals could expand, necessitating re-sizing them again).**

Teflon seal installation without special tools

▶ **Refer to illustrations 13.91, 13.92, 13.93a and 13.93b**

90 If you don't have a special injector tool set, the Teflon seal can be installed using this method: First, find a socket that is equal or very close in diameter to the diameter of the end of the fuel injector.

91 Work the new Teflon seal onto the end of the socket (see illustration).

92 Place the socket against the end of the injector (see illustration) and slide the seal from the socket onto the injector. Do NOT use any lubricants to do so. Continue pushing the seal onto the injector until it seats into its mounting groove.

93 Because the inside diameter of the seal has to be stretched open to fit over the bore of the socket and the injector, its outside diameter is now slightly too large - it is no longer flush with the surface of the injector. It must be shrunk it back to its original size. To do so, push a piece of plastic tubing with an interference fit onto the end of the socket; a plastic straw that fits tightly on the injector will work. After pushing the plastic tubing onto the socket about an inch, snip off the rest of the tubing, then use the socket to push the tubing onto the end of the injector (see illustration) and slide it onto the injector until it completely covers the new seal (see illustration). Leave the tubing on for a few hours, then remove it. The seal should now be shrunk back its original outside diameter, or close to it.

➡ **Note: Install the injectors within 15 minutes of removing the straw (if they aren't installed, the seals could expand, necessitating re-sizing them again).**

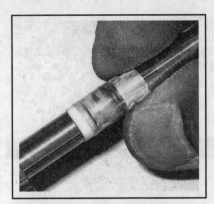

13.93a Use the socket to push a short section of plastic tubing onto the end of the injector and over the new seal . . .

13.93b . . . then leave the plastic tubing in place for several hours to compress the new seal

13.94 Note that the upper O-ring (1) is installed above the support ring (2)

Injector and fuel rail installation

▶ **Refer to illustration 13.94**

94 Install the new support ring at the upper end of the injector. Lubricate the new upper O-ring with clean engine oil and install it on the injector. Do NOT oil the new Teflon seal. Note that the seal is installed above the spacer (see illustration).

95 Thoroughly clean the injector bores with a small nylon brush.

96 Install the new compensation element and retaining ring to the bottom of each injector.

97 Install the fuel injectors in the cylinder head (NOT in the fuel rail). You should be able to push each assembled injector into its bore in the cylinder head. The bore is slightly tapered, so you will encounter some resistance as the Teflon seal nears the bottom of the bore. Press the injector into its bore until it stops, making sure to properly align the injector.

➡ **Note: Make sure the tang on the injector retaining clip engages with the groove in the fuel rail cup.**

98 Install a new spring steel retainer on each injector. Install the fuel rail, working it down evenly onto the injectors. Tighten the bolts a little at a time, starting from the center and working outwards, to the torque listed in this Chapter's Specifications.

99 Clean the high pressure fuel line fittings on the fuel rails, then apply a little clean engine oil to the threads. Install the new high-pressure fuel line, tightening the fittings in the sequence and to the torque listed in this Chapter's Specifications. Install a new high-pressure fuel sensor, if it was removed.

100 Install the thermostat housing and the coolant crossover pipe, tightening the bolts to the torque listed in the Chapter 3 Specifications.

101 The remainder of installation is the reverse of removal.

102 Refill the cooling system (see Chapter 1).

---

14 High-pressure fuel pump (3.5L V6 engine) - removal and installation

✳✳ WARNING:

Gasoline is extremely flammable. See Fuel system warnings in Section 2.

✳✳ WARNING:

Wait until the engine is completely cool before beginning this procedure.

✳✳ WARNING:

The fuel delivery system on these models is made up of a low-pressure system and a high-pressure system. Once the pressure on the low-pressure side of the system has been relieved, wait at least two hours before loosening any fuel line fittings between the high-pressure fuel pump and the fuel rail. Before loosening any fittings on the high-pressure side of the fuel system (from the high-pressure fuel pump to the fuel rails), wear full-face protection and thick leather gloves, cover the fitting being loosened with a rag, and loosen threaded fittings slowly so as to allow the pressure to seep out gradually instead of forcefully.

1 Relieve the fuel system pressure (see Section 2).

2 Remove the cover from the pump, mounted at the rear of the left valve cover.

3 Disconnect the electrical connector from the pump.

4 Detach the fuel feed line from the pump (see Section 4). Slowly and carefully loosen the high-pressure fuel line fitting from the pump and fuel rails. Discard the high-pressure fuel tube - a new one must be installed on reassembly.

5 Unscrew the pump mounting bolts 1/2 turn at a time until they are loose. Discard the bolts - new ones must be used on installation.

6 Remove the pump.

7 Remove the roller tappet from its bore and check it for wear. Replace it if necessary.

8 Remove the bolt and the pump mounting plate.

9 Look at the cam lobe that drives the pump - it must be at Bottom Dead Center (on it's base circle) before the pump can be installed. If it isn't positioned at BDC, turn the crankshaft with a wrench placed on the crankshaft pulley center bolt until it is.

10 Lubricate the roller tappet and its bore with clean engine oil, then install the tappet.

11 Lubricate the pump mounting plate seal with clean engine oil and install it.

12 Install and lubricate the pump O-rings with clean engine oil.

13 Using new bolts, install the pump, tightening the bolts in the sequence and to the torque listed in this Chapter's Specifications.

14 Clean the high pressure fuel line fittings on the fuel rails, then apply a little clean engine oil to the threads. Install the new high-pressure fuel tube, tightening the fittings in the sequence and to the torque listed in this Chapter's Specifications.

15 Connect the fuel feed line and electrical connector to the pump.

16 Install the pump cover.

15 Exhaust system servicing - general information

▶ **Refer to illustrations 15.1a, 15.1b and 15.1c**

✳✳ WARNING:

Inspection and repair of exhaust system components should be done only after enough time has elapsed after driving the vehicle to allow the system components to cool completely. Also, when working under the vehicle, make sure it is securely supported on jackstands.

1 The exhaust system consists of the exhaust manifolds, the catalytic converter, the muffler, the tailpipe and all connecting pipes, brackets, hangers and clamps. The exhaust system is suspended from the underside of the vehicle by a series of rubber hangers (see illustrations). Inspect these hangers periodically for cracks or other signs of deterioration, and replace them as necessary.

2 To keep the exhaust system safe and quiet, conduct regular inspections of the exhaust system anytime that you're servicing anything underneath the vehicle. Look for any damaged or bent parts, open seams, holes, loose connections, excessive corrosion or other defects which could allow exhaust fumes to enter the vehicle. Deteriorated exhaust system components should not be repaired; they should be replaced with new parts.

3 If the exhaust system components are extremely corroded or rusted together, you'll probably need welding equipment to remove them. The convenient way to accomplish this is to have a muffler repair shop remove the corroded sections with a cutting torch. If, however, you want to save money by doing it yourself (and you don't have a welding outfit with a cutting torch), simply cut off the old components with a hacksaw. If you have compressed air, special pneumatic cutting chisels can also be used. If you do decide to tackle the job at home, be sure to wear safety goggles to protect your eyes from metal chips and work gloves to protect your hands.

4 Here are some simple guidelines to follow when repairing the exhaust system:

a) Work from the back to the front when removing exhaust system components.

b) Apply penetrating oil to the exhaust system component fasteners to make them easier to remove.

c) Use new gaskets, hangers and clamps when installing exhaust systems components.

d) Apply anti-seize compound to the threads of all exhaust system fasteners during reassembly.

e) Be sure to allow sufficient clearance between newly installed parts and all points on the underbody to avoid overheating the floor pan and possibly damaging the interior carpet and insulation. Pay particularly close attention to the catalytic converter and heat shield.

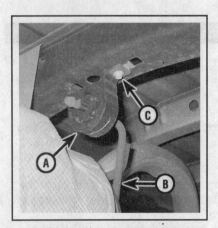

15.1a A typical exhaust system rubber hanger (A). To remove this type of hanger, support the exhaust pipe, disengage the exhaust pipe support rod (B), then remove the hanger mounting bolt (C) and disengage the other side of the hanger from the frame

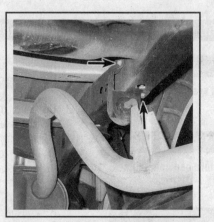

15.1b Another type of rubber exhaust hanger, which uses two mounting bolts. To replace it, support the exhaust system with a floor jack, then simply remove both bolts and pull the hanger off the exhaust pipe support rod

15.1c This type of rubber exhaust hanger has two support rods bolted to the transmission crossmember and a third rod welded to a bracket that's welded to the crossover pipe between the left and right catalytic converter assemblies. To replace it, support the crossover pipe with a floor jack, unbolt and remove the forward support rods, then pull the hanger off the crossover support rod

Specifications

Fuel pressure

2008 and earlier models	
Key on, engine off	35 to 45 psi
At idle	28 to 45 psi
2009 and 2010 models (at idle)	55 to 65 psi
2011 and later models (at idle)	
3.5L V6	62 to 73 psi
All others	51 to 62 psi
Fuel system hold pressure (after 5 minutes)	Less than 5-psi loss from indicated operating pressure

Torque specifications   Ft-lbs (unless otherwise indicated)

➡ **Note:** One foot-pound (ft-lb) of torque is equivalent to 12 inch-pounds (in-lbs) of torque. Torque values below approximately 15 ft-lbs are expressed in inch-pounds, since most foot-pound torque wrenches are not accurate at these smaller values.

Throttle body mounting bolts	
V6 engines	89 in-lbs
4.6L V8 engines	
2004 through 2008 (2-valve)	
Step 1	80 in-lbs
Step 2	Tighten an additional 90 degrees
2009 and later	
2-valve	
Step 1	89 in-lbs
Step 2	Tighten an additional 90 degrees
3-valve	89 in-lbs
5.0L V8 engines	
Step 1	89 in-lbs
Step 2	Tighten an additional 45-degrees
5.4L V8 engines	
Step 1	80 in-lbs
Step 2	Tighten an additional 90 degrees
6.2L V8 engines	
Step 1	106 in-lbs
Step 2	Tighten an additional 60-degrees
Fuel rail mounting bolts	
2010 and earlier models	89 in-lbs
2011 and later models	
3.5L V6 engine (replace with new ones)	
Step 1	89 in-lbs
Step 2	Tighten an additional 45 degrees
3.7L V6 engine	89 in-lbs
5.0L and 6.2L V8 engines	
Step 1	89 in-lbs
Step 2	Tighten an additional 90 degrees

Torque specifications (continued)   Ft-lbs (unless otherwise indicated)

➡ Note: One foot-pound (ft-lb) of torque is equivalent to 12 inch-pounds (in-lbs) of torque. Torque values below approximately 15 ft-lbs are expressed in inch-pounds, since most foot-pound torque wrenches are not accurate at these smaller values.

High-pressure fuel pump (3.5L V6 models)	
Mounting bolts (replace with new ones)	
Step 1	Tighten each bolt a little at a time until the pump is seated
Step 2	177 in-lbs
Step 3	Tighten an additional 45 degrees
Mounting plate bolt	89 in-lbs
High-pressure fuel tube flare nuts* (3.5L V6 models)	
Step 1	Hand tighten fitting to right-side fuel rail
Step 2	Hand tighten fitting to left-side fuel rail
Step 3	Hand tighten fitting to high-pressure pump
Step 4 (fitting to right-side fuel rail)	133 in-lbs
Step 5 (fitting to right-side fuel rail)	Tighten an additional 30 degrees
Step 6 (fitting to right-side fuel rail)	24
Step 7 (fitting to left-side fuel rail)	133 in-lbs
Step 8 (fitting to left-side fuel rail)	Tighten an additional 30 degrees
Step 9 (fitting to left-side fuel rail)	24
Step 10 (fitting to pump)	133 in-lbs
Step 11 (fitting to pump)	Tighten an additional 30 degrees
Step 12 (fitting to pump)	24
High-pressure fuel tube bracket (3.5L V6 models)	
Bolt	
Step 1	89 in-lbs
Step 2	Tighten an additional 45 degrees
Nut	71 in-lbs
High-pressure fuel sensor* (3.5L V6 models)	31

* Replace with a new one whenever removed. Lubricate threads with clean engine oil.

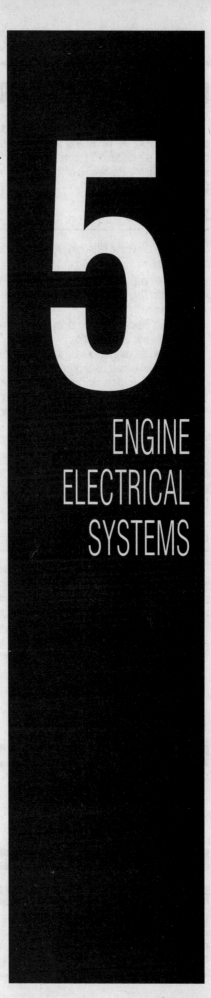

5

ENGINE ELECTRICAL SYSTEMS

Section

1   General information, precautions and battery disconnection
2   Battery - emergency jump starting
3   Battery - check and replacement
4   Battery cables - check and replacement
5   Ignition system - general information and precautions
6   Ignition system - check
7   Ignition coil(s) - replacement
8   Charging system - general information and precautions
9   Charging system - check
10   Alternator - removal and installation
11   Starting system - general information and precautions
12   Starter motor and circuit - in-vehicle check
13   Starter motor - removal and installation

Reference to other Chapters

Battery check, maintenance and charging - See Chapter 1
CHECK ENGINE light on - See Chapter 6
Drivebelt check, adjustment and replacement - See Chapter 1
Spark plug replacement - See Chapter 1

1   General information, precautions and battery disconnection

The engine electrical systems include all ignition, charging and starting components. Because of their engine-related functions, these components are discussed separately from body electrical devices such as the lights, the instruments, etc. (all of which are included in Chapter 12).

PRECAUTIONS

Always observe the following precautions when working on the electrical system:

a) *Be extremely careful when servicing engine electrical components. They are easily damaged if checked, connected or handled improperly.*

b) *Never leave the ignition switched on for long periods of time when the engine is not running.*

c) *Never disconnect the battery cables while the engine is running.*

d) *Maintain correct polarity when connecting battery cables from another vehicle during jump starting - see the "Booster battery (jump) starting" section at the front of this manual.*

e) *Always disconnect the negative battery cable from the battery before working on the electrical system, but read the following battery disconnection procedure first.*

It's also a good idea to review the safety-related information regarding the engine electrical systems located in the "Safety first!" section at the front of this manual, before beginning any operation included in this Chapter.

BATTERY DISCONNECTION

Several systems on the vehicle require battery power to be available at all times, either to ensure their continued operation (radio, alarm system, power door locks, windows, etc.) or to maintain control unit memories (the Powertrain Control Module and other modules) which would be lost if the battery were to be disconnected. Therefore, whenever the battery is to be disconnected, first note the following to ensure that there are no unforeseen consequences of this action:

a) *The engine management system's PCM might lose some of the information stored in its memory when the battery is discon-*

nected. This includes idling and operating values, any fault codes detected and system monitors required for emissions testing. Whenever the battery is disconnected, the computer might require a certain period of time to relearn these operating values (see Chapter 6 for more information about the engine management system and the PCM).

b) *On any vehicle with power door locks, it is a wise precaution to remove the key from the ignition and to keep it with you, so that it does not get locked inside if the power door locks should engage accidentally when the battery is reconnected!*

Devices known as "memory-savers" can be used to avoid some of the above problems. Precise details vary according to the device used. Typically, you plug it into the cigarette lighter and connect it to a spare battery. Then you disconnect the vehicle battery from the electrical system. The memory-saver passes sufficient current to maintain audio unit security codes, PCM memory values, etc. and it also maintains always-hot circuits such as the clock and radio memory.

✳✳ WARNING 1:

Some of these devices allow a considerable amount of current to pass, which can mean that many of the vehicle's systems are still operational when the main battery is disconnected. If a "memory-saver" is used, ensure that the circuit concerned is actually "dead" before carrying out any work on it!

✳✳ WARNING 2:

If work is to be performed around any of the airbag system components, the battery must be disconnected and a memory-saver device must NOT be used. If a memory-saver device is used, power will be supplied to the airbag and personal injury may result if the airbag is accidentally deployed.

To disconnect the battery for service procedures requiring power to be cut from the vehicle, peel back the insulator (if equipped), loosen the negative cable clamp nut and detach the cable from the negative battery terminal (see Section 3). Isolate the cable end to prevent it from coming into accidental contact with the battery post.

2   Battery - emergency jump starting

Refer to the "Booster battery (jump) starting" procedure at the front of this manual.

3   Battery - check and replacement

✳✳ WARNING:

Hydrogen gas is produced by the battery, so keep open flames and lighted cigarettes away from it at all times. Always wear eye protection when working around a battery. Rinse off spilled electrolyte immediately with large amounts of water.

CHECK

▶ **Refer to illustrations 3.1a, 3.1b and 3.1c**

1   A battery cannot be accurately tested until it is at or near a fully charged state. Disconnect the negative battery cable from the battery

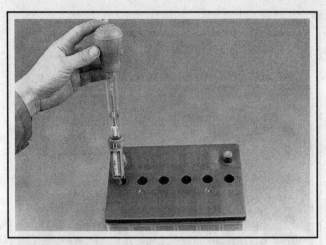

3.1a Use a battery hydrometer to draw electrolyte from the battery cell - this hydrometer is equipped with a thermometer to make temperature corrections

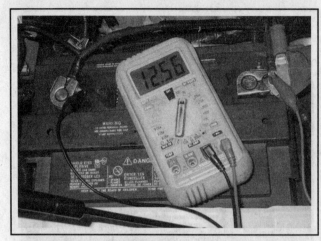

3.1b To test the open circuit voltage of the battery, connect the black probe of the voltmeter to the negative terminal and the red probe to the positive terminal of the battery. A fully charged battery should indicate about 12.5 volts

and perform the following tests:

a) *Battery state of charge test* - *Visually inspect the indicator eye (if equipped) on the top of the battery. If the indicator eye is dark in color, charge the battery as described in Chapter 1. If the battery is equipped with removable caps, check the battery electrolyte. The electrolyte level should be above the upper edge of the plates. If the level is low, add distilled water. DO NOT OVERFILL. The excess electrolyte may spill over during periods of heavy charging. Test the specific gravity of the electrolyte using a hydrometer (see illustration). Remove the caps and extract a sample of the electrolyte and observe the float inside the barrel of the hydrometer. Follow the instructions from the tool manufacturer and determine the specific gravity of the electrolyte for each cell. A fully charged battery will indicate approximately 1.270 (green zone) at 68-degrees F (20-degrees C). If the specific gravity of the electrolyte is low (red zone), charge the battery as described in Chapter 1.*

b) *Open circuit voltage test* - *Using a digital voltmeter, perform an open circuit voltage test (see illustration). Connect the negative probe of the voltmeter to the negative battery post and the positive probe to the positive battery post. The battery voltage should be greater than 12.5 volts. If the battery is less than the specified voltage, charge the battery before proceeding to the next test. Do not proceed with the battery load test until the battery is fully charged.*

c) *Battery load test* - *An accurate check of the battery condition can only be performed with a load tester (available at most auto parts stores). This test evaluates the ability of the battery to operate the starter and other accessories during periods of heavy amperage draw (load). Install a special battery load-testing tool onto the battery terminals (see illustration). Load test the battery according to the tool manufacturer's instructions. This tool utilizes a carbon pile to increase the load demand (amperage draw) on the battery. Maintain the load on the battery for 15 seconds and observe that the battery voltage does not drop below 9.6 volts. If the battery condition is weak or defective, the tool will indicate this condition immediately.*

➡ Note: Cold temperatures will cause the minimum voltage requirements to drop slightly. Follow the chart given in the tool

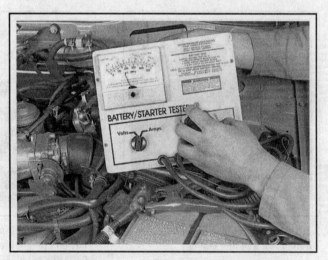

3.1c Some battery load testers are equipped with an ammeter which enables the battery load to be precisely dialed in, as shown - less expensive testers have a load switch and a voltmeter only

manufacturer's instructions to compensate for cold climates. Minimum load voltage for freezing temperatures (32 degrees F/0-degrees C) should be approximately 9.1 volts.

d) *Battery drain test* - *This test will indicate whether there's a constant drain on the vehicle's electrical system that can cause the battery to discharge. Make sure all accessories are turned off. If the vehicle has an underhood light, verify that it's working correctly, then disconnect it. Connect one lead of a digital ammeter to the disconnected negative battery cable clamp and the other lead to the negative battery post. A drain of approximately 100 milliamps or less is considered normal (due to the engine control compudigital clocks, digital radios and other components that normally cause a key-off battery drain). An excessive drain (approximately 500 milliamps or more) will cause the battery to discharge. The problem circuit or component can be located by removing the fuses, one at a time, until the excessive drain stops and normal drain is indicated on the meter.*

3.2 When disconnecting the cables from the battery terminals, ALWAYS disconnect the negative cable (1) first, then disconnect the positive cable (2)

3.4 Remove the battery cover . . .

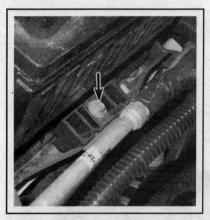

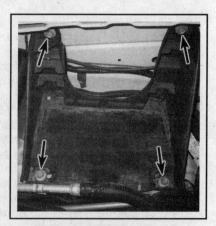

3.5 . . . then remove the battery hold-down bolt and clamp

3.6 A battery lifting strap like this one (available at most auto parts stores) makes removing and installing a heavy battery easier and safer

3.7 To detach the battery tray, remove these four bolts

REPLACEMENT

▶ **Refer to illustrations 3.2, 3.4, 3.5, 3.6 and 3.7**

✳✳ **CAUTION:**

Always disconnect the negative cable first and hook it up last or you might accidentally short the battery with the tool that you're using to loosen the cable clamps.

2   Loosen the cable clamp nut and disconnect the battery cable from the negative battery post (see illustration). Isolate the cable end to prevent it from accidentally coming into contact with the battery post.

3   Loosen the cable clamp nut and disconnect the battery cable from the positive battery post.

4   Remove the battery cover (see illustration).

5   Remove the battery hold-down clamp bolt (see illustration).

6   Lift out the battery (see illustration). Be careful - it's heavy. Battery lifting straps like the one shown in the accompanying illustration are available at most auto parts stores for a reasonable price. They make removing and installing the battery both easier and safer.

7   While that battery is out, inspect the battery tray for corrosion. If corrosion exists, clean the deposits with a mixture of baking soda and water to prevent further corrosion. Flush the area with plenty of clean water and dry thoroughly. If you need to remove the battery tray, release the wiring harness locators from the battery case. On 2004 through 2008 models, remove the four tray mounting bolts (see illustration) and lift out the tray. On 2009 and later models, remove the three tray mounting bolts and partially lift up the tray. Disconnect the washer electrical connector and the hose from the washer bottle and lift out the tray

8   If you are replacing the battery, make sure you replace it with a battery with identical dimensions, amperage rating, cold cranking rating, etc.

9   Installation is the reverse of removal.

10   After connecting the cables to the battery apply a light coating of petroleum jelly or grease to the connections to help prevent corrosion.

4 Battery cables - check and replacement

◆ Refer to illustrations 4.4a, 4.4b, 4.4c, 4.4d and 4.4e

1   Periodically inspect the entire length of each battery cable for damage, cracked or burned insulation and corrosion. Poor battery cable connections can cause starting problems and decreased engine performance.

2   Check the cable-to-terminal connections at the ends of the cables for cracks, loose wire strands and corrosion. The presence of white, fluffy deposits under the insulation at the cable terminal connection is a sign that the cable is corroded and should be replaced. Check the terminals for distortion, missing mounting bolts and corrosion.

3   When removing the cables always disconnect the negative cable from the negative battery post first and hook it up last or you might accidentally short the battery with the tool that you're using to loosen the cable clamps. Even if only the positive cable is being replaced, be sure to disconnect the negative cable from the negative battery post first (see Chapter 1 for further information regarding battery cable maintenance).

4   Disconnect the old cables from the negative (first) and positive (last) battery terminals (see Section 3) then disconnect them from the opposite end. Disconnect the ground cables from the firewall, the right upper control arm mounting bracket and the starter motor (see illustra-

tions). Then disconnect the positive cable from the alternator and from the starter solenoid (see illustrations). Note the routing of each cable to ensure correct installation, then detach any cable retaining clips or clamps and remove the cables.

5   If you are replacing either or both of the battery cables, take them with you when buying new cables. It is vitally important that you replace the cables with identical parts. Cables have characteristics that make them easy to identify. Positive cables are usually red and larger in cross-section; ground cables are usually black and smaller in cross-section.

6   Clean the threads of the starter solenoid or ground connection with a wire brush to remove rust and corrosion. Apply a light coat of battery terminal corrosion inhibitor or petroleum jelly to the threads to prevent future corrosion.

7   Attach the cable to the terminal and tighten the mounting nut/bolt securely.

8   Before connecting a new cable to the battery make sure that it reaches the battery post without having to be stretched.

9   After installing the cables connect the negative cable to the negative battery post.

4.4a One ground bolt is located on the firewall, behind the battery

4.4b Another ground bolt is located on the front side of the front mounting bracket for the right upper control arm

4.4c The third ground is secured to the lower starter mounting stud by this nut

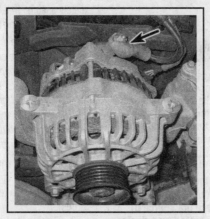

4.4d One positive battery cable is connected to the B+ terminal of the alternator

4.4e The other positive battery cable is connected to the B+ terminal on the starter motor solenoid

5 Ignition system - general information and precautions

GENERAL INFORMATION

4.2L V6 models

1   The ignition system consists of the ignition coil, the spark plug wires, the spark plugs and the Crankshaft Position (CKP) sensor. The ignition coil is located on the right valve cover. The coil, which is controlled by the Powertrain Control Module (PCM), fires two spark plugs simultaneously. For example, when it fires the plug in cylinder No. 1 (the right front cylinder) at Top Dead Center (TDC) on its compression stroke, it also fires the plug in cylinder No. 5, which is at TDC on its exhaust stroke. When it fires the plug in cylinder No. 4 at TDC on its compression stroke, it also fires the plug in cylinder No. 3 at TDC on its exhaust stroke. And when it fires the plug in cylinder No. 2 at TDC on its compression stroke, it also fires the plug in cylinder No. 6 at TDC on its exhaust stroke. Then when it fires the other three cylinders (Nos. 5, 3 and 6, respectively), it fires the plugs in cylinder Nos. 1, 4 and 2, respectively. So cylinder Nos. 1 and 5, 4 and 3, and 2 and 6 are referred to as companion cylinders. The simultaneous spark that goes to each companion cylinder is wasted; it doesn't do anything because there is no compression and no air/fuel mixture to ignite. This system is therefore generally referred to as a "waste spark" system. The CKP sensor provides base timing and crankshaft speed (rpm) signals to the PCM. For more information about the CKP sensor and the PCM, refer to Chapter 6. For more information about the spark plug wires and the spark plugs, refer to Chapter 1.

3.5L and 3.7L V6, and 4.6L, 5.0L and 5.4L V8 models

2   The ignition system consists of eight ignition coils, the spark plugs and the Crankshaft Position (CKP) sensor. The ignition coils are located on the valve covers, above each spark plug. This setup is generally referred to as a "coil-over-plug" system. Each coil is connected directly to the spark plug that it fires. There are no spark plug wires. The CKP sensor provides base timing and crankshaft speed (rpm) signals to the Powertrain Control Module (PCM). For more information about the CKP sensor and the PCM, refer to Chapter 6. For more information about the spark plugs, refer to Chapter 1.

6.2L V8 models

3   6.2L V8 engines have two sets of spark plugs, one row above the valve covers with coil-on-plug ignition and another row near the exhaust manifolds. The lower set of plugs is connected by plug wires to terminals on the individual coils.

PRECAUTIONS

4   When working on the ignition system take the following precautions:

a)   *Do not keep the ignition switch on for more than 10 seconds if the engine will not start.*

b)   *Always connect a tachometer in accordance with the manufacturer's instructions. Some tachometers may be incompatible with this ignition system. Consult an auto parts counterperson before buying a tachometer for use with this vehicle.*

c)   *Never allow the ignition coil terminals to touch ground. Grounding the coil could result in damage to the PCM and/or the ignition coil.*

d)   *Do not disconnect the battery when the engine is running.*

6 Ignition system - check

◆ **Refer to illustration 6.4**

✳ WARNING:

Because of the very high voltage generated by the ignition system, use extreme care when performing a procedure involving ignition components. This not only includes the coil and spark plugs, but related items connected to the system as well, such as the electrical connectors, tachometer and any test equipment.

➡ **Note: The ignition system components on these models are expensive and difficult to diagnose. In the event of ignition system failure, if the checks do not clearly indicate the source of the ignition system problem, have the vehicle tested by a dealer service department or other qualified repair facility.**

1   If a malfunction occurs and the vehicle won't start, do not immediately assume that the ignition system is causing the problem. First, check the following items:

a)   *Make sure the battery cable clamps, where they connect to the battery, are clean and tight.*

b)   *Test the condition of the battery (see Section 3). If it does not pass all the tests, replace it with a new battery.*

c)   *Check the ignition coil wiring and connections.*

d)   *Check the appropriate fuses in the fuse and relay box, which is located behind the right kick panel inside the vehicle (see Chapter 12). If they're burned, determine the cause and repair the circuit.*

2   If the engine turns over but won't start, make sure there is sufficient secondary ignition voltage to fire the spark plug. Obtain a calibrated ignition tester (such testers are available at most auto parts stores).

3   Disable the fuel injection system (see the fuel pressure relief procedure in Chapter 4). The fuel system must be disabled while checking the ignition system.

4   To test the spark on 3.5L and 3.7L V6 and 4.6L, 5.0L and 5.4L V8 engines, and the upper spark plugs on the 6.2L V8, remove an ignition coil (see Section 7), insert the tester into the boot on the coil, then clip the other end to a good ground or, depending on the type of tester being used, connect the other end to the spark plug (see illustration).

5   To test the spark on a 4.2L V6 or the lower spark plugs on a 6.2L V8, disconnect a spark plug wire from a spark plug, insert the tester into the spark plug wire boot and clip the other end to a good ground or, depending on the type of tester being used, connect the other end to the spark plug.

6   Crank the engine and watch the tester.

7   If the tester flashes (or sparks, depending on type), sufficient voltage is reaching the spark plug to fire it. Repeat the check on the remaining cylinders. Keep in mind that even if the coil is functioning normally and is firing the tester, one or more of the plugs themselves might be fouled, so remove, inspect and, if necessary, clean or replace the plugs (see Chapter 1).

8   If no sparks occur or if the spark is weak or intermittent, check for battery voltage to the primary terminal of the ignition coil. If there is no battery voltage at the coil primary terminal, have the ignition system checked out by a dealer service department or other qualified repair shop.

6.4 Here's the setup used for checking to see if the ignition coil is sending power to the spark plug. If the coil is delivering power, the tester will flash (or spark, depending on the type of tester being used) - coil-over-plug type ignition shown

A   Tester spark plug boot
B   Clear plastic tester body
C   Insert this end of tester into the spark plug boot
D   Ignition coil spark plug boot
E   Ignition coil

7   Ignition coil(s) - replacement

1   Disconnect the cable from the negative battery terminal (see Section 1).

4.2L V6 MODELS

2   Disconnect the electrical connector from the ignition coil.

3   Disconnect the spark plug wires from the ignition coil (see Chapter 1).

4   Remove the ignition coil mounting bolts and remove the coil from the valve cover.

5   Installation is the reverse of removal.

3.5L AND 3.7L V6, AND ALL V8 MODELS

▶ Refer to illustrations 7.6, 7.7, 7.8 and 7.9

➡ Note: This procedure applies to all eight ignition coils.

6   Disconnect the electrical connector from the ignition coil (see illustration).

➡ Note: If you're going to remove more than one ignition coil, mark each electrical connector with its corresponding coil to prevent mix-ups during reassembly.

7.6 To disconnect the electrical connector from an ignition coil on a 4.6L or 5.4L V8, depress this release tab, then pull off the connector

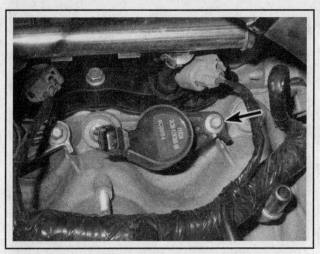

7.7 To detach the ignition coil on a 4.6L or 5.4L V8, remove the retaining bolt . . .

7.8 . . . then grasp the coil firmly and pull straight up

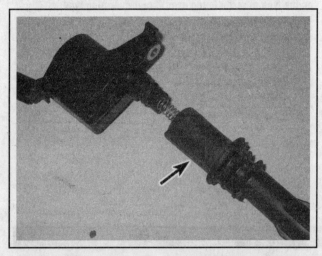

7.9 Inspect the condition of the rubber boot that insulates the connection between the ignition coil and the spark plug. If it's cracked, torn or otherwise deteriorated, replace it. To disconnect the boot, simply pull it off the coil (the spring, which carries the current to the plug, is a permanent part of the coil, so don't try to pull it off!)

7   Remove the ignition coil hold-down bolt (see illustration).

8   Grasp the ignition coil firmly and pull it straight up (see illustration).

9   Inspect the condition of the rubber boot that insulates the connection between the coil high-tension terminal and the spark plug (see illustration). If it's cracked, torn or otherwise deteriorated, replace it. Prior to installing the coil, coat the interior of the rubber boot with silicone dielectric compound.

10 Installation is otherwise the reverse of removal.

8   Charging system - general information and precautions

The charging system includes the alternator, a voltage regulator, a charge indicator or warning light, the battery, three fusible links and the wiring between all the components. The charging system supplies electrical power for the ignition system, the lights, the radio, etc. The alternator is driven by a drivebelt at the front of the engine.

The voltage regulator is located inside the alternator and is not separately serviceable. The voltage regulator limits the alternator's voltage to a preset value. This prevents power surges, circuit overloads, etc., during peak voltage output.

The charging system doesn't require much maintenance. However, you should inspect the drivebelt and battery at the intervals outlined in Chapter 1.

The charging system is protected by three large fusible links. In the event of charging system problems, check these fusible links for damage or broken contacts.

To protect the alternator and the charging system circuit, be very careful when making electrical connections:

  a) When reconnecting wires to the alternator from the battery, be sure to note the polarity.

  b) Before using arc welding equipment to repair any part of the vehicle, disconnect the wiring from the alternator and the cables from the battery.

  c) Never start the engine with a battery charger connected.

  d) Always disconnect both battery cables before using a battery charger.

  e) The alternator is turned by an engine drivebelt that could cause serious injury if your hands, hair or clothes become entangled in it with the engine running.

  f) Because the alternator is connected directly to the battery, it could arc or cause a fire if overloaded or shorted out.

9 Charging system - check

▶ **Refer to illustration 9.3**

1 If a malfunction occurs in the charging circuit, do not immediately assume that the alternator is causing the problem. First, check the following items:

  a) Make sure the battery cable clamps, where they connect to the battery, are clean and tight.

  b) Test the condition of the battery (see Section 3). If it does not pass all the tests, replace it with a new battery.

  c) Inspect the external alternator wiring and connections.

  d) Check the drivebelt tension and inspect the condition of the drivebelt (see Chapter 1).

  e) Make sure that the alternator mounting bolts are tight.

  f) Run the engine and verify that the alternator isn't making any abnormal noises.

  g) Check the fusible links in the charging system (see Chapter 12). If they're burned, determine the cause and repair the circuit.

  h) Check the charge light on the dash. It should illuminate when the ignition key is turned ON (engine not running). If it does not, check the circuit from the alternator to the charge light on the dash.

2 With the ignition key off, check the battery voltage with no accessories operating (see illustration 3.1b). It should be about 12.5 volts. (It might be slightly higher if the engine has been operating within the last hour.)

3 Start the engine and check the battery voltage again (see illustration). It should now be greater than the voltage indicated in Step 2, but not more than 15 volts. Turn on all the vehicle accessories (air conditioning, rear window defogger, blower motor, etc.) and increase the engine speed to 2,000 rpm - the voltage should not drop below the voltage indicated in Step 2.

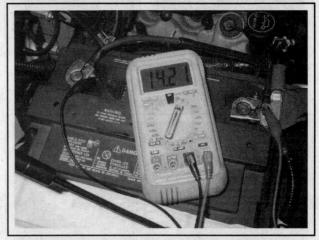

9.3 To measure charging voltage, attach the positive voltmeter lead to the battery's positive terminal and the negative lead to the negative battery terminal, then start the engine and record the voltage reading at idle

4 If the indicated voltage is greater than the specified charging voltage, replace the alternator.

5 If the indicated voltage reading is less than the specified charging voltage, the alternator is probably defective. Have the charging system checked at a dealer service department or other properly equipped repair facility.

➡ **Note: Many auto parts stores will bench test an alternator off the vehicle. Refer to your local auto parts store regarding their policy, many will perform this service free of charge.**

10 Alternator - removal and installation

1 Disconnect the cable from the negative terminal of the battery (see Section 1).

4.2L V6 MODELS

2 Remove the alternator drivebelt (see Chapter 1).

3 Disconnect the electrical connector from the alternator.

4 Remove the rubber weather boot from the alternator B+ terminal nut, remove the nut and disconnect the battery cable from the B+ terminal.

5 Remove the nut that attaches the air conditioning line bracket to the alternator and set the air conditioning line and bracket aside.

6 Remove the nut that attaches the alternator electrical harness bracket to the alternator and set the alternator harness and bracket aside.

7 Remove the two alternator stud bolts and remove the alternator.

8 Installation is the reverse of removal. Be sure to tighten the alternator mounting studs securely.

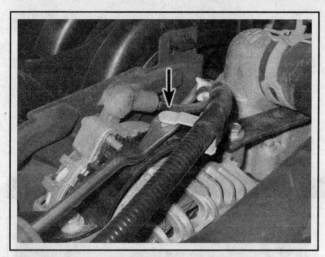

10.11 On a 4.6L or 5.4L V8 model, pry the alternator harness clip from the alternator support bracket

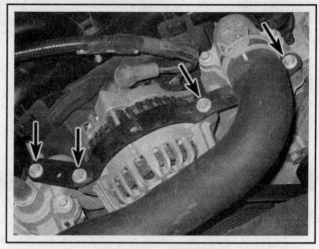

10.12 To detach the alternator support bracket on a 4.6L or 5.4L V8 model, remove these four bolts

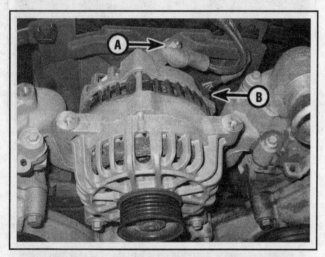

10.13 Remove the nut (A) that secures the battery cable to the alternator's B+ terminal and disconnect the cable from the terminal, then disconnect the electrical connector (B) from the alternator (4.6L and 5.4L V8 models)

10.14 To detach the alternator from a 4.6L or 5.4L V8 engine, remove these two bolts

4.6L AND 5.4L V8 MODELS

▶ Refer to illustrations 10.11, 10.12, 10.13 and 10.14

9　On 2009 and later models, remove the air intake duct (see Chapter 4).

10　Remove the alternator drivebelt (see Chapter 1).

11　Detach the alternator harness clip from the alternator support bracket (see illustration).

12　Remove the four alternator support bracket bolts (see illustration) and remove the bracket.

13　Remove the alternator B+ terminal nut and disconnect the battery cable from the B+ terminal, then disconnect the electrical connector from the alternator (see illustration).

14　Remove the two lower alternator mounting bolts (see illustration) and remove the alternator.

15　Installation is the reverse of removal. Be sure to tighten the alter-

nator mounting bolts and the support bracket bolts securely.

3.5L AND 3.7L V6, AND 5.0L AND 6.2L V8 MODELS

16　On 3.5L and 3.7L V6 and 6.2L V8 engines, remove the air intake duct (see Chapter 4).

17　On 3.5L V6 engines, remove the air cleaner pipe-to-turbocharger pipe and the turbocharger-to-charge air cooler pipe (see Chapter 2B).

18　Remove the drivebelt (see Chapter 1).

19　Remove the alternator B+ terminal nut and disconnect the battery cable from the B+ terminal, then disconnect the electrical connector from the alternator.

20　Remove the two alternator mounting fasteners and remove the alternator.

21　Installation is the reverse of removal. Be sure to tighten the alternator mounting fasteners securely.

11 Starting system - general information and precautions

The starting system consists of the battery, the ignition switch fuse, the ignition switch, the starter relay, the clutch start switch (manual transmissions), the Digital Transmission Range (DTR) sensor (automatic transmissions), the starter motor/solenoid assembly and the wiring connecting all of these components. The ignition switch fuse and starter relay are located in the fuse and relay box located behind the right kick panel inside the vehicle.

When the ignition key is turned to the START position, battery voltage is directed through the ignition switch fuse to the starter relay. The starter relay closes the starter control circuit, which runs through either the clutch start switch (manual transmission) or the DTR sensor (automatic transmission). If the clutch pedal is depressed or the transmission is in Neutral (manual transmission), or if the shift lever is in PARK or NEUTRAL (automatic transmission), battery voltage is sent to the starter solenoid, which engages the starter motor pinion gear with the flywheel/driveplate and the starter motor cranks the engine.

The starter motor on a vehicle equipped with a manual transmission can be operated only when the clutch pedal is depressed. The starter on a vehicle equipped with an automatic transmission can be operated only when the transmission selector lever is in PARK or NEUTRAL.

Always observe the following precautions when working on the starting system:

a) *Excessive cranking of the starter motor can overheat it and cause serious damage. Never operate the starter motor for more than 15 seconds at a time without pausing for at least two minutes to allow it to cool.*
b) *The starter is connected directly to the battery and could arc or cause a fire if mishandled, overloaded or short-circuited.*
c) *Always detach the cable from the negative battery terminal before working on the starting system.*

12 Starter motor and circuit in-vehicle check

▶ **Refer to illustrations 12.5 and 12.6**

1 If a malfunction occurs in the starting circuit, do not immediately assume that the starter is causing the problem. First, check the following items:

a) *Make sure that the battery cable clamps, where they connect to the battery terminals, are clean and tight.*
b) *Inspect the condition of the battery cables (see Section 4). Always replace defective battery cables with new ones.*
c) *Test the condition of the battery (see Section 3). If it does not pass all the tests, replace it with a new battery.*
d) *Inspect the condition of the starter solenoid wiring and connections. Refer to the wiring diagrams at the end of Chapter 12.*
e) *Make sure that the starter mounting bolts are tight.*
f) *Make sure the starter is receiving voltage on the S terminal (the small wire) of the starter solenoid when the ignition key is turned to Start.*
g) *Check the operation of the Digital Transmission Range (DTR) sensor (automatic transmission) or clutch start switch (manual transmission). Make sure that the shift lever is in PARK or NEUTRAL (automatic transmission) or the clutch pedal is pressed (manual transmission). The DTR sensor or clutch start switch must operate correctly to provide battery voltage to the ignition switch. To replace and/or adjust the DTR sensor, refer to Chapter 6. To replace and/or adjust the clutch start switch, refer to Chapter 8.*
h) *Check the operation of the starter relay. The starter relay is located in the fuse and relay box behind the right kick panel inside the vehicle. Refer to Chapter 12 for the relay testing procedure.*

2 If the starter does not actuate when the ignition switch is turned to the START position, check for battery voltage to the solenoid. Connect a test light or voltmeter to the starter solenoid positive terminal and have an assistant turn the ignition switch to the START position.

3 If there's no voltage at the solenoid, check the ignition switch fuse and the starter relay.

4 If there is voltage at the solenoid, but the starter motor does not operate, remove the starter (see Section 13) and bench test it (see Step 6).

12.5 To measure starter current draw with an inductive ammeter, simply hold the ammeter over the positive or negative cable (whichever cable has better clearance)

5 If the starter turns over slowly, check the starter cranking voltage and the current draw from the battery. This test must be performed with the starter assembly on the engine. Crank the engine over (for 10 seconds or less) and observe the battery voltage. It should not drop below 8.0 volts on manual transmission models or 8.5 volts on automatic transmission models. Also, observe the current draw using an ammeter (see illustration). It should not exceed 400 amps or drop below 250 amps.

✳ CAUTION:

The battery cables may be excessively heated because of the large amount of amperage being drawn from the battery. Discontinue the testing until the starting system has cooled down.

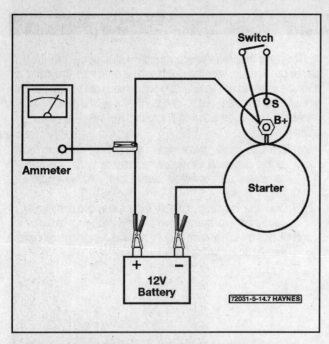

12.6 Starter motor bench testing details

If the starter motor cranking amp values are not within the correct range, replace it with a new unit. There are several conditions that may affect the starter cranking potential. The battery must be in good condition and the battery cold-cranking rating must not be under-rated for the particular application. Be sure to check the battery specifications carefully. The battery terminals and cables must be clean and not corroded. Also, in cases of extreme cold temperatures, make sure the battery and/or engine block is warmed before performing the tests.

6   If the starter is getting voltage but doesn't operate, remove the starter/solenoid assembly (see Section 13) and test it on the bench (see illustration). Most likely the solenoid is defective. In some rare cases, the engine might be seized, so be sure to try and rotate the crankshaft pulley (see Chapter 2A or 2B) before proceeding. With the starter/solenoid assembly mounted in a vise on the bench, install one jumper cable from the negative battery terminal to the body of the starter. Install the other jumper cable from the positive battery terminal to the B+ terminal on the starter. Install a starter switch and apply battery voltage to the solenoid S terminal (for 10 seconds or less) and see if the solenoid plunger, shift lever and overrunning clutch extends and rotates the pinion drive. If the pinion drive extends but does not rotate, the solenoid is operating but the starter motor is defective. If there is no movement but the solenoid clicks, the solenoid and/or the starter motor is defective. If the solenoid plunger extends and rotates the pinion drive, the starter/solenoid assembly is working properly.

13 Starter motor - removal and installation

▶ **Refer to illustrations 13.3, 13.4a and 13.4b**

1   Disconnect the cable from the negative battery terminal (see Section 1).
2   Raise the vehicle and support it securely on jackstands.
3   Disconnect the wiring from the terminals on the starter motor

solenoid (see illustration).
4   Disconnect the starter ground cable from the lower starter mounting stud, then remove the starter motor mounting fasteners (see illustrations) and detach the starter from the engine.
5   Installation is the reverse of removal.

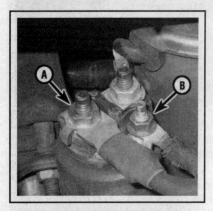

13.3 Remove nut A and disconnect the battery cable from the B+ terminal on the solenoid, then remove nut B and disconnect the starter cable from the S terminal on the solenoid

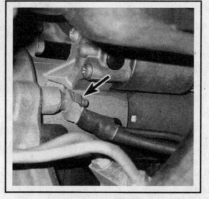

13.4a To disconnect the starter ground cable from the lower starter motor mounting stud, remove this nut and remove the cable

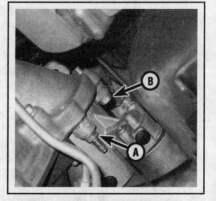

13.4b To detach the starter motor from the engine, remove the lower starter mounting bolt/stud (A) and the two mounting bolts (B) (upper mounting bolt not shown) - 5.4L V8 engine shown

Specifications

Charging system

Charging voltage   13.5 to 15 volts

6

EMISSIONS AND ENGINE CONTROL SYSTEMS

Section

1   General information
2   On-Board Diagnostic (OBD) system and trouble codes
3   Accelerator Pedal Position Sensors (APPS) - replacement
4   Camshaft Position (CMP) sensor - replacement
5   Crankshaft Position (CKP) sensor - replacement
6   Cylinder Head Temperature (CHT) sensor - replacement
7   Digital Transmission Range (DTR) sensor - replacement
8   Engine Oil Temperature (EOT) sensor - replacement
9   Injection Pressure (IPR) sensor/Fuel Rail Pressure
    Temperature (FRPT) sensor - replacement
10 Intake Air Temperature (IAT) sensor - replacement
11 Knock sensor(s) - replacements
12 Mass Airflow (MAF) sensor - replacement
13 Oxygen sensors - general information and replacement
14 Power Steering Pressure (PSP) switch - replacement
15 Throttle Position (TP) sensor - replacement
16 Transmission speed sensors - replacement
17 Powertrain Control Module (PCM) - removal and installation
18 Charge Motion Control Valve (CMCV) (5.4L V8 models) -
    removal and installation
19 Fuel Pump Driver Module (FPDM) - replacement
20 Intake Manifold Runner Control (IMRC) actuator - replacement
21 Intake Manifold Tuning (IMT) valve - replacement
22 Variable Camshaft Timing (VCT) oil control solenoid - replacement
23 Catalytic converters - general description, check and replacement
24 Evaporative emissions control (EVAP) system - general
    description and component replacement
25 Exhaust Gas Recirculation (EGR) system - general
    description and component replacement

Reference to other Chapters

Positive Crankcase Ventilation (PCV) system - component
    replacement - See Chapter 1

1 General information

▶ **Refer to illustration 1.6**

To minimize atmospheric pollution caused by evaporative emissions, unburned hydrocarbons and other exhaust gas pollutants, and to maintain good driveability and fuel economy, a number of emission control systems are utilized on the vehicles covered in this manual. They include the following systems:

Charge Motion Control Valve (CMCV) system (5.4L V8 models)
Electronic Fuel Injection (EFI) system
Exhaust Gas Recirculation (EGR) system (4.2L V6 and 2-valve 4.6L V8 models)
Evaporative Emissions Control (EVAP) system
Idle Air Control (IAC) system
Intake Manifold Runner Control (IMRC) system (4.2L V6 models)
Intake Manifold Tuning (IMT) system (2004 and 2005 4.6L V8 models)
On-Board Diagnostics (OBD-II) system
Positive Crankcase Ventilation (PCV) system
Catalytic converters

The Sections in this Chapter include general descriptions, checking procedures within the scope of the home mechanic and component replacement procedures (when possible) for each of the systems listed above.

Before assuming that an emissions control system is malfunctioning, check the fuel and ignition systems carefully. The diagnosis of some emission control devices requires specialized tools, equipment and training. If checking and servicing become too difficult or if a procedure is beyond your ability, consult a dealer service department or other repair shop. Remember, the most frequent cause of emissions problems is simply a loose or broken wire or vacuum hose, so always check the hose and wiring connections first.

This doesn't mean, however, that emissions control systems are particularly difficult to maintain and repair. You can quickly and easily perform many checks and do most of the regular maintenance at home with common tune-up and hand tools.

➡ **Note: Because of a Federally mandated warranty which covers the emissions control system components, check with your dealer about warranty coverage before working on any emissions-related systems. Once the warranty has expired, you may wish to perform some of the component checks and/or replacement procedures in this Chapter to save money.**

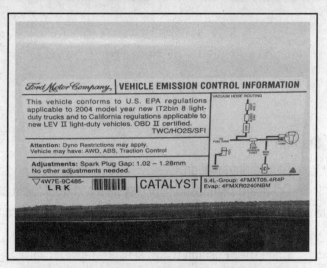

1.6 The Vehicle Emission Control Information (VECI) label contains such essential information as the types of emission control systems installed on the engine, and a vacuum diagram

Pay close attention to any special precautions outlined in this Chapter. It should be noted that the illustrations of the various systems may not exactly match the system installed on your vehicle because of changes made by the manufacturer during production or from year-to-year.

A Vehicle Emissions Control Information (VECI) label (see illustration) is attached to the underside of the hood. This label contains important emissions specifications and adjustment information. Part of this label, the vacuum hose routing diagram, provides a vacuum hose schematic with emissions components identified. When servicing the engine or emissions systems, always refer to the VECI label and the vacuum hose routing diagram on your vehicle for up-to-date information.

➡ **Note: When replacing control components on 2011 and later models, such as CMP or CKP sensors, a professional scan tool may be required to address what the manufacturer calls the Misfire Monitor Neutral Profile Correction.**

2 On-Board Diagnostic (OBD) system and trouble codes

SCAN TOOL INFORMATION

▶ **Refer to illustration 2.2**

1 Hand-held scanners are the most powerful and versatile tools for analyzing engine management systems used on later model vehicles.

➡ **Note: An aftermarket generic scanner should work with any model covered by this manual. Before purchasing a generic scan tool, verify that it will work properly with the OBD-II system you want to scan. If necessary, of course, you can always have the codes extracted by a dealer service department or an independent repair shop with a professional scan tool.**

2 With the arrival of the Federally mandated emission control system (OBD-II), specially designed aftermarket scanners have been developed. Several tool manufacturers have released OBD-II scan tools for the home mechanic (see illustration).

OBD SYSTEM GENERAL DESCRIPTION

3 All models are equipped with the second-generation on-board diagnostic (OBD-II) system. This system consists of an on-board computer known as the Powertrain Control Module (PCM), and information sensors, which monitor various functions of the engine and send data to the PCM. This system incorporates a series of diagnostic monitors

that detect and identify fuel injection and emissions control systems faults and store the information in the computer memory. This updated system also tests sensors and output actuators, diagnoses drive cycles, freezes data and clears codes.

4 This powerful diagnostic computer must be accessed using an OBD-II scan tool and the 16 pin Data Link Connector (DLC) located under the driver's dash area. The PCM is the brain of the electronically controlled fuel and emissions system. It receives data from a number of sensors and other electronic components (switches, relays, etc.). Based on the information it receives, the PCM generates output signals to control various relays, solenoids (fuel injectors) and other actuators. The PCM is specifically calibrated to optimize the emissions, fuel economy and driveability of the vehicle.

5 It isn't a good idea to attempt diagnosis or replacement of the PCM or emission control components at home while the vehicle is under warranty. Because of a Federally mandated warranty which covers the emissions system components and because any owner-induced damage to the PCM, the sensors and/or the control devices may void this warranty, take the vehicle to a dealer service department if the PCM or a system component malfunctions.

INFORMATION SENSORS

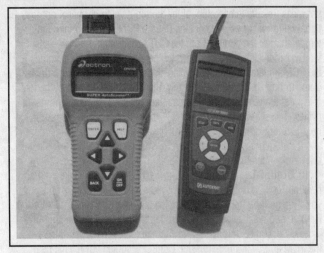

2.2 Scan tools like these from Actron and AutoXray are powerful and relatively inexpensive. They have a lot of features that were once found only on expensive professional scanners

➡ **Note: The following list provides a brief description of the function, operation and location of each of the important information sensors.**

6 **Accelerator Pedal Position Sensors (APPS)** - All vehicles covered by this manual are equipped with the Generation II (GEN II) Torque Based Electronic Throttle Control (ETC) system. The ETC system uses an electronic throttle body instead of a conventional cable-operated throttle body. The Powertrain Control Module (PCM) controls the position of the throttle plate with a solenoid that's located in the throttle body. The PCM's commands are based on the inputs that it receives from the APPS, all three of which are located inside a small plastic module, known as the Electronic Throttle Control (ETC) module, which is located at the top of the accelerator pedal assembly. The three APP sensors are referred to as APP1, APP2 and APP3. APP1 has a negative slope (increasing angle, decreasing voltage) and APP2 and APP3 both have a positive slope (increasing angle, increasing voltage). The PCM uses APP1 as the principal sensor for pedal position. Its signal is converted into a rotary angle (degrees of pedal travel) by the PCM, and then it's converted into "counts," which is the input used by the second-generation (Gen II) torque-based ETC system.

The ETC module is an integral component of the accelerator pedal assembly. If one APP sensor fails, you must replace the pedal and sensors as a single assembly.

7 **Camshaft Position (CMP) sensor** - The CMP sensor monitors the position of the camshaft(s) and tells the Powertrain Control Module (PCM) when the piston in the No. 1 cylinder is on its compression stroke. The PCM uses the CMP sensor signal to synchronize the sequential firing of the fuel injectors.

On 4.2L V6 models, the CMP sensor assembly looks similar to a distributor and is located on the timing chain cover in the same location where the distributor was once located. (the manufacturer refers to this distributor-like mechanism as the "camshaft synchronizer.") Inside the CMP sensor housing is a Hall Effect switching device that generates a square-wave pulse each time that a single vane mounted on the upper end of the camshaft synchronizer shaft passes by the sensor. When the metal vane passes by the CMP sensor, voltage goes low (less than 0.3 volt). When the vane isn't passing by the sensor, voltage goes high (5.0 volts). To the PCM, the switch to the low-voltage output as the vane

passes the sensor represents the piston in the No. 1 cylinder on its compression stroke.

On 4.6L and 5.4L V8 engines, the CMP sensor is a variable reluctance type sensor that generates an analog (sine wave) signal. On these models, both of which use Coil-On-Plug (COP) type ignition coils, the PCM also uses the CMP signal to select which coil to fire next. 4.6L V8 engines are equipped with one CMP sensor, which is located on the front of the left cylinder head.

On 3.5L and 3.7L OHC V6 engines, the CMP sensors are bolted to the back of the cylinder heads. There are two for each cylinder head and they are difficult to reach. On 5.4L V8 engines, which are equipped with Variable Camshaft Timing (VCT), there are two CMP sensors, one on the front of each cylinder head. The PCM uses the additional CMP sensor to identify the position of the camshaft on cylinder bank No. 2 (the left cylinder head). The manufacturer refers to this extra CMP sensor as "CMP2."

8 **Crankshaft Position (CKP) sensor** - The CKP sensor is a magnetic transducer and is the primary sensor that provides ignition information to the PCM. The PCM uses the CKP sensor to determine crankshaft position (which piston will be at TDC next) and crank speed (rpm), both of which it needs to synchronize the ignition system. A pulse wheel or tone wheel, which is mounted on the front of the crankshaft, has 35 teeth about 10 degrees apart, with one empty space for a missing tooth. Basic timing is set by the position of this missing tooth. The PCM uses the input generated by this missing tooth to synchronize the ignition system and to track the rotation of the crankshaft.

On 4.2L V6 engines, the CKP sensor is located on the front of the timing chain cover, at about 11 o'clock in relation to the crankshaft. The pulse wheel is mounted on the front end of the crankshaft, behind the damper pulley. On 4.6L and 5.4L V8 engines, the CKP sensor is mounted on the lower right side of the timing cover.

On 5.0L and 6.2L V8 engines, the CKP sensor is at the rear of the engine, where it reads signals from a toothed-wheel plate that is sandwiched between the crankshaft and the driveplate. On 3.7L and 3.5L OHC V6 engines, the CKP is located at the bottom-left at the rear of the engine. Remove the heat-shield on that side to access the sensor mounting bolt.

9 **Cylinder Head Temperature (CHT) sensor** - Unlike a conventional Engine Coolant Temperature (ECT) sensor, the CHT sen-

sor measures the temperature of the aluminum cylinder head, not the temperature of the engine coolant. But the PCM is able to infer the temperature of the coolant from the CHT sensor signal nonetheless. If the CHT indicates a cylinder head temperature of about 250 degrees F, the PCM initiates a fail-safe cooling strategy that allows you to drive home in limp-home mode. Basically, the PCM disables half of the fuel injectors. It alternates which injectors are disabled every 32 engine cycles. The cylinders that are not injected with fuel act as air pumps to help cool down the engine. If the CHT sensor indicates a temperature of about 330 degrees F. or higher, the PCM shuts down all of the injectors until the temperature goes below about 310 degrees F.

10 **Digital Transmission Range (DTR) sensor** - Like the Park/Neutral Position (PNP) switch that it replaces, the DTR sensor prevents you from starting the engine unless the automatic transaxle is in Park or Neutral, and it activates the back-up lights when you put the shift lever in Reverse. Unlike the PNP switch, however, the DTR sensor also tells the PCM and/or the Transmission Control Module (TCM) what gear the transaxle is in. The PCM uses this information to determine what gear the transaxle should be in and to determine when to upshift and downshift. If the DTR sensor fails, the PCM uses pressure switch data to calculate the correct shift lever position. The DTR sensor is mounted on the left side of the transmission.

11 **Engine Oil Temperature (EOT) sensor** - The EOT sensor measures the temperature of the engine oil. It's located on the right side of the oil pan, below the starter motor. The PCM uses the EOT sensor input for three purposes: To determine the condition of the oil; on models equipped with the Variable Camshaft Timing (VCT) system, to adjust VCT control gains and to adjust the logic for camshaft timing; and to reduce engine power by disabling some of the cylinders.

12 **Fuel Rail Pressure (FRP) sensor or Injection Pressure (IPR) sensor** - The FRP/IPR sensor monitors the difference in pressure between the fuel rail and the intake manifold, but does not measure the temperature of the fuel inside the fuel rail. The FRP/IPR sensor is used on 2005 4.2L V6, all 4.6L V8 engines and on 2004 5.4L V8 engines. All other engines covered by this manual are equipped with a Fuel Rail Pressure Temperature (FRPT) sensor (see Step 13).The FRP/IPR sensor has no integral fuel temperature sensor. On 4.2L V6 engines, the IPR sensor is located at the rear end of the left fuel rail. On 4.6L V8 engines, the FRP/IPR sensor is located at the front end of the left fuel rail. On 2004 5.4L V8 engines, the FRP/IPR sensor is located near the front end of the left fuel rail.

13 **Fuel Rail Pressure Temperature (FRPT) sensor** - The FRPT sensor, which is used on 2006 through 2008 4.2L V6 models and 2005 through 2008 5.4L V8 models, measures the pressure and the temperature of the fuel in the fuel rail. The FRPT sensor uses intake manifold vacuum as a reference to determine the pressure difference between the fuel rail and the intake manifold. The relationship between fuel pressure and fuel temperature is used to determine the likelihood of the presence of fuel vapor in the fuel rail. Both the pressure and temperature signals are used to control the speed of the fuel pump. The speed of the fuel pump controls the pressure inside the fuel rail in order to keep the fuel in a liquid state. Keeping the fuel in a liquid state increases the efficiency of the injectors because the higher fuel rail pressure allows a decrease in the injector pulse width (the interval of time during which the injector is open).

On 4.2L V6 engines, the FRPT sensor is located at the rear end of the left fuel rail. On 2005 through 2008 5.4L V8 engines, the FRPT sensor is located on the left fuel rail, just ahead of the fuel supply line pipe.

14 **Intake Air Temperature (IAT) sensor** - The IAT sensor is used by the PCM to calculate air density, which is one of the variables it must know in order to calculate injector pulse width and adjust igni-

tion timing (to prevent spark knock when intake air temperature is high). Like the ECT sensor, the IAT sensor is a Negative Temperature Coefficient (NTC) type thermistor, whose resistance decreases as the temperature increases. The IAT sensor is an integral component of the Mass Air Flow (MAF) sensor on all models. It cannot be serviced separately from the MAF sensor. For more information about the MAF sensor, refer to Step 16.

15 **Knock sensor** - The knock sensor monitors engine vibration caused by detonation. Basically, a knock sensor converts abnormal engine vibration to an electrical signal. When the knock sensor detects a knock in one of the cylinders, it signals the PCM so that the PCM can retard ignition timing accordingly. The PCM doesn't respond to the knock sensor's input when the engine is idling; it only responds when the engine reaches a specified speed.

On 4.2L V6 engines, the knock sensor is located on the rear end of the left cylinder head. On all other engines, the knock sensor(s) is/are located in the valley between the cylinder heads. You must remove the intake manifold to access the knock sensor(s) on these models.

16 **Mass Air Flow (MAF) sensor** - The MAF sensor is the principal means by which the PCM monitors intake airflow. It uses a hot-wire sensing element to measure the amount of air entering the engine. Air passing over the hot wire causes it to cool down. The hot wire's temperature is maintained at 392 degrees F above the ambient temperature by electrical current supplied to the wire and controlled by the PCM. A constantly "cold" wire located right next to the hot wire measures the ambient air temperature. As intake air passes through the MAF sensor and over the hot wire, it cools the wire, and the control system immediately corrects the temperature back to its constant value. The current required to maintain the specified constant temperature value is used by the PCM as an indicator of airflow.

On 2004 through 2008 4.2L V6 and 4.6L V8 models, the MAF sensor is located inside the air filter housing. On 5.4L V8 and all 2009 and later models, the MAF sensor is located on the right side of the air filter housing.

17 **Oxygen sensors** - Oxygen sensors generate a voltage signal that varies in accordance with the amount of oxygen in the exhaust stream. The PCM uses the data from the upstream oxygen sensor to calculate the injector pulse width. The downstream oxygen sensor monitors the oxygen content of the exhaust gases as they exit the catalytic converter. This information is used by the PCM to predict catalyst deterioration and/or failure. There are four oxygen sensors on all models. On 4.2L V6 models, the upstream oxygen sensors are located on the exhaust manifolds, above manifold flanges, and the downstream sensors are located on the catalysts. On 4.6L and 5.4L V8 models, the upstream oxygen sensors are located just below the exhaust manifold flanges and above the catalytic converters, and the downstream sensors are located in the exhaust pipes between the upstream and downstream catalysts.

18 **Power Steering Pressure (PSP) sensor** - The PSP sensor monitors the hydraulic pressure of the power steering fluid in the power steering system. The PSP sensor provides a voltage input to the PCM that varies in accordance with changes in the hydraulic pressure. The PCM uses the input signal from the PSP sensor to elevate the idle speed when the engine is already under some other load, such as the air conditioning compressor, while maneuvering the vehicle at low speed, such as parking or stop-and-go driving. The PSP sensor also signals the PCM to adjust the Electronic Pressure Control (EPC) pressure during high-load situations such as parking. The PSP sensor is located on the power steering system's high-pressure line, which is located between the power steering pump and the steering gear.

19 **Throttle Position (TP) Sensor** - The TP sensor, which is

located on the throttle body, is a rotary potentiometer, which is a type of variable resistor, that produces a variable voltage signal in proportion to the opening angle of the throttle plate. The PCM sends 5 volts to the TP sensor. As the plate opens and closes, the resistance of the TP sensor changes with it, altering the signal back to the PCM. The output voltage of the TP sensor is about 0.6 volt at idle (closed throttle plate) to 4.5 volts at wide-open throttle. This variable signal enables the PCM to calculate the position (opening angle) of the throttle plate. The PCM uses the TP sensor input, along with other sensor inputs, to adjust fuel injector pulse-width and ignition timing.

On all 3.5L, 3.7L and 4.2L V6 engines, 2004 4.6L V8 engines, all 5.0L V8 engines, 2004 5.4L V8 engines, and all 6.2L V8 engines, the TP sensor is an integral part of the electronic throttle body and is not serviceable separately from the throttle body. You can, however, replace the TP sensor on the electronic throttle bodies used on 2005 and 2006 4.6L and 2005 and later 5.4L V8 engines.

20 **Transmission speed sensors** - On vehicles with an automatic transmission, there are two speed sensors: the Turbine Shaft Speed (TSS) sensor and the Output Shaft Speed (OSS) sensor. Both sensors are located on the left side of the transmission. The TSS sensor provides the PCM with turbine shaft speed information, which the PCM uses to determine. The OSS sensor provides the PCM with output shaft speed information, which the PCM uses to determine transmission shift scheduling, Torque Converter Clutch (TCC) engagement scheduling and Electronic Pressure Control (EPC) pressure.

21 **Vehicle Speed Sensor (VSS)** - On vehicles with a manual transmission, the VSS provides information to the PCM to indicate vehicle speed. The VSS is a variable reluctance or Hall-Effect sensor that generates a waveform with a frequency that's proportional to the speed of the vehicle. If the vehicle is moving at a relatively low speed, the VSS generates a signal with a lower frequency. As the vehicle speed increases, the VSS generates a signal with a higher frequency. The PCM uses this information to determine when acceleration or deceleration occurs, so that it can alter parameters such as fuel injector pulse-width and ignition advance or retard. The VSS is located on the left side of the transmission extension housing (2WD models) or on the left side of the transfer case extension housing (4WD models).

OUTPUT ACTUATORS

➡ **Note: Based on the information it receives from the information sensors described above, the PCM adjusts fuel injector pulse width, idle speed, ignition spark advance, ignition coil dwell and EVAP canister purge operation. It does so by controlling the output actuators. The following list provides a brief description of the function, location and operation of each of the important output actuators.**

22 **Charge Motion Control Valve (CMCV)** - The CMCV, which is used on 5.4L V8 engines, provides more intake airflow to improve torque, lower emissions and increase performance. The CMCV system consists of the PCM-controlled CMCV on the intake manifold, a crank arm, a pair of actuating rods, and butterfly valves located inside the lower ends of the intake manifold runners. Below the specified rpm (1500 to 3000 rpm, depending on the model), the CMCV is not energized, the actuating rods are fully extended and the butterfly valves are closed. When the butterflies are closed, airflow through the intake runners is restricted, which decreases the amount of air that can move through the runners but increases the speed of the airflow, which improves torque, lowers emissions and increases performance. When engine speed reaches the threshold rpm level, the PCM energizes the CMCV and the crank arm on the actuator moves the actuating rods,

which open the butterfly valves inside the manifold. When the butterfly valves are opened, the intake airflow through the intake runners increases. The CMCV is located on the back (firewall) side of the intake manifold, so you must remove the intake manifold to replace the CMCV.

23 **Electronic Throttle Body** - All vehicles covered by this manual use an electronic throttle body. There is no accelerator cable, no cruise control cable and no Idle Air Control (IAC) motor. All of these functions are handled electronically by the Powertrain Control Module (PCM). The electronic throttle body is part of the manufacturer's Generation II (Gen II) Torque Based Electronic Throttle Control (ETC), which is a hardware and software strategy designed to deliver output shaft torque based on driver demand (the position of the accelerator pedal). Torque based ETC allows earlier upshifts and later downshifts, which improves shift quality, performance and high-altitude responsiveness, reduces emissions and saves fuel. For more information about the electronic throttle body, see Chapter 4.

24 **Evaporative Emission Control (EVAP) canister purge valve** - When the engine is cold or still warming up, no captive fuel vapors are allowed to escape from the EVAP canister. After the engine is warmed up, the PCM energizes the canister purge valve, which regulates the flow of these vapors from the canister to the intake manifold. The rate of the flow of vapors is regulated by the purge valve in response to commands from the PCM, which controls the duty cycle of the valve. The EVAP canister purge valve is located in the engine compartment, on the firewall, near the power brake booster. For more information about the EVAP system, see Section 24.

25 **Exhaust Gas Recirculation (EGR) valve** - When you pull a trailer, pass another vehicle or go up a steep hill, the temperature inside the combustion chambers heats up. When the temperature inside the combustion chambers reaches 2500 degrees F, the engine begins to produce oxides of nitrogen (NOx), which is an odorless, colorless and toxic gas that causes health problems for children, seniors, people with respiratory problems and people exercising outside on a smoggy day. The PCM-controlled EGR valve reduces NOx by introducing a controlled amount of spent exhaust gases into the intake manifold, which dilutes the air/fuel mixture, lowers combustion chamber temperatures and reduces the creation of NOx.

The typical Differential Pressure Feedback EGR (DPFE EGR) system consists of the EGR sensor, EGR vacuum regulator solenoid, EGR valve, orifice tube assembly, the Powertrain Control Module (PCM) and the electrical wiring and vacuum hoses connecting these components. A DPFE type EGR system measures the pressure drop across the metering orifice and sends an analog voltage feedback signal, between 0 and 5 volts, to the PCM that's proportional to the pressure drop. The PCM uses this feedback signal to constantly trim the pressure drop across the orifice in order to maintain the correct flow rate.

The manufacturer refers to the newest version of the DPFE EGR system as the EGR System Module (ESM) because everything except the EGR pipe itself has been combined into a single module. On 4.2L V6 models, the ESM is located on the right side of the intake manifold, between the throttle body and the plenum. On 2-valve 4.6L V8 models, the ESM is located at the left rear corner of the intake manifold. For more information about the EGR system, see Section 25.

26 **Fuel injectors** - The PCM opens the fuel injectors sequentially (in firing order sequence). The PCM also controls the pulse width, which is the interval of time during which each injector is open. The pulse width of an injector (measured in milliseconds) determines the amount of fuel delivered. For more information on the fuel delivery system and the fuel injectors, including injector replacement, refer to Chapter 4.

27 **Fuel Pump Driver Module (FPDM)** - The fuel systems used

on all vehicles covered by this manual are returnless, there is no intake-manifold-vacuum-actuated fuel pressure regulator and there is no fuel return line between the fuel rail and the fuel tank. Instead, system fuel pressure is controlled by the speed of the fuel pump. The PCM controls the duty cycle to the FPDM, which modulates the voltage to the fuel pump to maintain the correct fuel pressure. The FPDM is located under the vehicle, in the vicinity of the spare tire (which you must remove to access the FPDM). The FPDM is bolted to the crossmember immediately ahead of the spare tire.

28 **Fuel pump relay** - When grounded by the PCM, the fuel pump relay connects battery voltage to the fuel pump. The fuel pump relay provides battery voltage, through the Inertia Fuel Shutoff (IFS) switch, to the fuel pump. The fuel pump relay is located inside the fuse and relay box, which is located behind the right kick panel inside the vehicle.

29 **Ignition coils** - The ignition coils are triggered by the PCM. The ignition coils are mounted on the valve cover. Refer to Chapter 5 for more information on the ignition coils.

30 **Intake Manifold Runner Control (IMRC) actuator** - The IMRC actuator, which is used on 4.2L V6 engines, provides more intake airflow to improve torque, lower emissions and increase performance. The IMRC system consists of a PCM-controlled actuator on the intake manifold and butterfly valves located inside the lower ends of the intake manifold runners. Below the specified rpm (1500 to 3000 rpm, depending on the model), the IMRC actuator is not energized and the butterfly valves are closed. When the butterflies are closed, airflow through the intake runners is restricted, which decreases the amount of air that can move through the runners but increases the speed of the airflow, which improves torque, lowers emissions and increases performance. When engine speed reaches the threshold rpm level, the PCM energizes the IMRC actuator and the butterfly valves open. When the butterfly valves are opened, the intake airflow through the intake runners increases. The IMRC actuator is located on the back (firewall) side of the upper intake manifold, so you must remove the upper intake manifold to replace the actuator.

31 **Intake Manifold Tuning (IMT) valve** - The IMT valve, which is used on 2004 and 2005 4.6L V8 engines, controls the intake manifold dynamics. The IMT system consists of the PCM-controlled IMT valve, which is mounted on the front end of the intake manifold, and a flap inside the intake manifold. The IMT valve is not energized below about 2600 rpm, and the flap is closed, which prevents intake air from blending inside the intake manifold. When the engine speed reaches 2600 rpm, the IMT valve is energized by the PCM to move the flap to the open position. The flap opens up the end of the vertical separating wall at higher engine speeds to allow both sides of the manifold to blend together. The IMT valve's duty cycle is controlled by the PCM. When it initially energizes the IMT valve, the PCM does so at 100 percent duty cycle. Once the flap is fully opened, the PCM decreases the duty cycle to about 50 percent to keep the flap open.

32 **Variable Camshaft Timing (VCT) system** - The VCT system produces lower emissions, more power, better fuel efficiency and improved idle quality. There are several versions of the VCT system. The VCT system consists of a Camshaft Position (CMP) sensor and trigger wheel on each cylinder head and a PCM-controlled hydraulic positioning control solenoid on each head (in this manual we call this device the VCT oil control solenoid).

Here's how the VCT system works: Each CMP sensor's trigger wheel has four evenly-spaced teeth (equal to the number of cylinders in each head) and one extra tooth. The extra tooth between the evenly-spaced teeth represents the CMP sensor signal for that cylinder bank. The PCM also uses the signal from the Crankshaft Position (CKP) sensor for information on the crankshaft position and as a reference signal for the positioning signal from the CMP sensor.

The PCM doesn't enable the VCT system until the engine is warmed up and the operating conditions are right.

The PCM-controlled VCT oil control solenoid controls the flow of engine oil in the VCT actuator assembly, which is an integral component of the camshaft timing-chain sprocket. When the oil control solenoid is energized by the PCM, engine oil flows into the actuator assembly, which advances or retards the camshaft timing. One half of the actuator is connected to the timing chain and the other half is coupled to the camshaft. Oil chambers between the two halves couple the timing chain to the cam. When the flow of oil is shifted from one side of the chamber to the other, the differential change in oil pressure forces the camshaft to rotate in either an advance or retard position, depending on which way the oil flows. As the PCM alters the duty cycle of the solenoid valve, oil pressure/flow advances or retards the camshaft timing. When a fixed camshaft phase is called for, the PCM achieves a steady cam phase by oscillating the duty cycle of the oil control solenoid valve.

OBD-II DIAGNOSTIC TROUBLE CODES (DTCS) AND THE MALFUNCTION INDICATOR LIGHT (MIL)

33 To test the critical emission control components, circuit and systems on an OBD-II vehicle, the PCM runs a series of monitors during each vehicle trip. The monitors are a series of testing protocols used by the PCM to determine whether each monitored component, circuit or system is functioning satisfactorily. The monitors must be run in a certain order. An OBD-II trip consists of operating the vehicle (after an engine-off period) and driving it in such a manner that the PCM's monitors test all of the monitored components, circuits and systems at least once.

34 If the PCM recognizes a fault in some component, circuit or system while it's running the monitors, it stores a Diagnostic Trouble Code (DTC) and turns on the Malfunction Indicator Light (MIL) on the instrument cluster. A DTC can self-erase, but only after the MIL has been extinguished. For example, the MIL might be extinguished for a misfire or fuel system malfunction if the fault doesn't recur when monitored during the next three subsequent sequential driving cycles in which the conditions are similar to those under which the malfunction was first identified. (For other types of malfunctions, the criteria for extinguishing the MIL can vary.)

35 Once the MIL has been extinguished, the PCM must pass the diagnostic test for the most recent DTC for 40 warm-up cycles (80 warm-up cycles for the fuel system monitor and the misfire monitor). A warm-up cycle consists of the following chain of events:

The engine has been started and is running
The engine temperature rises by at least 40-degrees above its temperature when it was started
The engine coolant temperature crosses the 160-degree F mark
The engine is turned off after meeting the above criteria

OBTAINING DTCS

▶ **Refer to illustration 2.36**

36 Of course, if the MIL does NOT go out after several driving cycles, it's probably an indication that something must be repaired or replaced before the DTC can be erased and the MIL extinguished. This means that you will need to extract the DTC(s) from the PCM, make the

necessary repair or replace a component, then erase the DTC yourself. You can extract the DTCs from the PCM by plugging a generic OBD-II scan tool (see illustration 2.2) into the PCM's data link connector (see illustration), which is located under the left side of the dash. Plug the scan tool into the 16-pin data link connector (DLC), then follow the instructions included with the scan tool to extract all the diagnostic codes.

ERASE THE DTC(S), TURN OFF THE MIL AND VERIFY THE REPAIR

37 Once you've completed the repair or replaced the component, use your code reader or scan tool to erase the DTC(s) and turn off the MIL. On most tools, you simply press a button to erase DTCs and turn off the MIL, but on some tools you'll have to locate this function by using the menu on the tool's display. If it isn't obvious, follow the instructions that come with your tool.

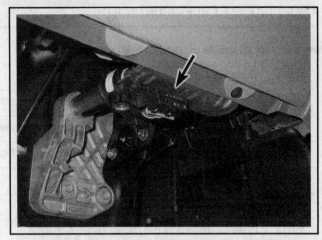

2.36 The 16-pin Data Link Connector (DLC) is located under the left side of the dash

OBD-II TROUBLE CODES

➡ **Note: Not all trouble codes apply to all models.**

Code	Probable cause
P0010	Intake camshaft position actuator circuit, open/short in Variable Cam Timing (VCT) circuit or solenoid (Bank 1)
P0011	Intake camshaft position timing over-advanced (Bank 1)
P0012	Variable cam timing over-retarded (Bank 1)
P0013	Exhaust cam position actuator circuit, open/short in VCT circuit or solenoid or open in VPWR circuit (Bank 1)
P0020	Intake camshaft position actuator circuit, open circuit (Bank 2)
P0021	Intake camshaft position timing over-advanced (Bank 2)
P0022	Intake camshaft position timing over-retarded (Bank 2)
P0040	Upstream oxygen sensors swapped from bank to bank (crossed wiring harnesses)
P0041	Downstream oxygen sensors swapped from bank to bank (crossed wiring harnesses)
P0053	Upstream oxygen sensor heater resistance, heater current requirements too low or too high (Bank 1)
P0054	Downstream oxygen sensor heater resistance, heater current requirements too low or too high (Bank 1)
P0055	Second downstream oxygen sensor heater resistance, heater current requirements too low or too high (Bank 1)
P0059	Upstream oxygen sensor heater resistance, heater current requirements too low or too high (Bank 2)
P0060	Downstream oxygen sensor heater resistance, heater current requirements too or too high (Bank 2)
P0061	Second downstream oxygen sensor heater resistance, heater current requirements too low or too high (Bank 2)
P0068	Throttle Position (TP) sensor inconsistent with Mass Air Flow sensor
P0102	Mass Air Flow (MAF) sensor circuit, low input
P0103	Mass Air Flow (MAF) sensor circuit, high input
P0104	Mass Air Flow (MAF) sensor circuit, intermittent or erratic

OBD-II TROUBLE CODES (CONTINUED)

→ **Note: Not all trouble codes apply to all models.**

Code	Probable cause
P0106	Barometric (BARO) pressure sensor circuit, performance problem
P0107	Barometric (BARO) pressure sensor/MAP sensor circuit, low voltage
P0108	Barometric (BARO) pressure sensor/MAP sensor circuit, high voltage
P0109	BARO sensor circuit intermittent
P0112	Intake Air Temperature (IAT) sensor circuit, low input
P0113	Intake Air Temperature (IAT) sensor circuit, high input
P0114	Intake Air Temperature (IAT) sensor circuit, intermittent or erratic
P0116	Engine Coolant Temperature (ECT) circuit range or performance problem
P0117	Engine Coolant Temperature (ECT) sensor circuit, low input
P0118	Engine Coolant Temperature (ECT) sensor circuit, high input
P0119	Engine Coolant Temperature (ECT) sensor circuit, intermittent or erratic
P0121	Throttle Position (TP) circuit, performance problem
P0122	Throttle Position (TP) sensor circuit, low input
P0123	Throttle Position (TP) sensor circuit, high input
P0125	Insufficient coolant temperature for closed loop fuel control
P0127	Intake air temperature too high
P0128	Coolant temperature below thermostat regulated temperature
P0148	Fuel delivery error
P0171	System too lean (Bank 1)
P0172	System too rich (Bank 1)
P0174	System too lean (Bank 2)
P0175	System too rich (Bank 2)
P0180	Engine Fuel Temperature (EFT) sensor A circuit, low input
P0181	Engine Fuel Temperature (EFT) sensor A circuit, range/performance problem
P0182	Engine Fuel Temperature (EFT) sensor A circuit, low input
P0183	Engine Fuel Temperature (EFT) sensor A circuit, high input
P0186	Engine Fuel Temperature (EFT) sensor B circuit, range/performance problem
P0187	Engine Fuel Temperature (EFT) sensor B circuit, low input
P0188	Engine Fuel Temperature (EFT) sensor B circuit, high input
P0190	Fuel Rail Pressure (FRP) sensor circuit malfunction
P0191	Fuel Rail Pressure (FRP) sensor circuit performance

Code	Probable cause
P0192	Fuel Rail Pressure (FRP) sensor circuit, low input
P0193	Fuel Rail Pressure (FRP) sensor circuit, high input
P0196	Engine Oil Temperature (EOT) sensor circuit, range/performance problem
P0197	Engine Oil Temperature (EOT) sensor circuit, low input
P0198	Engine Oil Temperature (EOT) sensor circuit, high input
P0201	Injector No. 1 circuit malfunction
P0202	Injector No. 2 circuit malfunction
P0203	Injector No. 3 circuit malfunction
P0204	Injector No. 4 circuit malfunction
P0205	Injector No. 5 circuit malfunction
P0206	Injector No. 6 circuit malfunction
P0207	Injector No. 7, circuit malfunction
P0208	Injector No. 8, circuit malfunction
P0217	Engine coolant over-temperature condition
P0218	Transmission Fluid Temperature (TFT), overheating condition
P0219	Engine over speed condition
P0221	Throttle Position (TP) sensor 2 circuit, range/performance problem
P0222	Throttle Position (TP) sensor 2 circuit, low input
P0223	Throttle Position (TP) sensor 2 circuit, high input
P0230	Fuel pump primary circuit malfunction
P0231	Fuel pump secondary circuit, low voltage
P0232	Fuel pump secondary circuit, high voltage
P0234	Supercharger overboost condition
P0243	Supercharger boost bypass solenoid, circuit malfunction
P0297	Vehicle over speed condition
P0298	Engine oil high-temperature condition
P0300	Random misfire detected
P0301	Cylinder No. 1, misfire detected
P0302	Cylinder No. 2, misfire detected
P0303	Cylinder No. 3, misfire detected
P0304	Cylinder No. 4, misfire detected
P0305	Cylinder No. 5, misfire detected
P0306	Cylinder No. 6, misfire detected
P0307	Cylinder No. 7, misfire detected

OBD-II TROUBLE CODES (CONTINUED)

➡ **Note: Not all trouble codes apply to all models.**

Code	Probable cause
P0308	Cylinder No. 8, misfire detected
P0310	Misfire detection monitor
P0315	PCM unable to learn crankshaft pulse wheel tooth spacing (exceeds allowable correction tolerances)
P0316	Misfire occurred during first 1000 engine revolutions
P0320	Ignition engine speed input, circuit malfunction
P0325	Knock sensor No. 1, circuit malfunction (Bank 1)
P0326	Knock sensor No. 1, circuit range or performance problem (Bank 1)
P0330	Knock sensor No. 2, circuit malfunction (Bank 2)
P0331	Knock sensor No. 2, circuit range or performance problem (Bank 2)
P0340	Camshaft Position (CMP) sensor, circuit malfunction (Bank 1)
P0345	Camshaft Position (CMP) sensor, circuit malfunction (Bank 2)
P0350	Ignition coil (undetermined), primary or secondary circuit malfunction
P0351	Ignition coil A, primary or secondary circuit malfunction
P0352	Ignition coil B, primary or secondary circuit malfunction
P0353	Ignition coil C, primary or secondary circuit malfunction
P0354	Ignition coil D, primary or secondary circuit malfunction
P0355	Ignition coil E, primary or secondary circuit malfunction
P0356	Ignition coil F, primary or secondary circuit malfunction
P0357	Ignition coil G, primary or secondary circuit malfunction
P0358	Ignition coil H, primary or secondary circuit malfunction
P0400	EGR flow failure (outside the minimum or maximum limits)
P0401	Exhaust Gas Recirculation (EGR) valve, insufficient flow detected
P0402	Exhaust Gas Recirculation (EGR) valve, excessive flow detected
P0403	EGR vacuum regulator solenoid, circuit malfunction (vehicles without electric EGR)
P0405	Differential Pressure Feedback (DPF) EGR sensor circuit, low voltage detected
P0406	Differential Pressure Feedback (DPF) EGR sensor circuit, high voltage detected
P0411	Secondary Air Injection (AIR) system, upstream flow
P0412	Secondary Air Injection (AIR) system, circuit malfunction
P0420	Catalyst system efficiency below threshold (Bank 1)
P0430	Catalyst system efficiency below threshold (Bank 2)
P0442	EVAP control system, small leak detected

Code	Probable cause
P0443	EVAP control system, canister purge valve, circuit malfunction
P0446	EVAP control system canister vent solenoid, circuit malfunction
P0451	EVAP system Fuel Tank Pressure (FTP) sensor, circuit out of range or performance problem
P0452	Fuel Tank Pressure (FTP) sensor circuit, low voltage detected
P0453	Fuel Tank Pressure (FTP) sensor circuit, high voltage detected
P0454	Fuel Tank Pressure (FTP) sensor, noisy circuit
P0455	EVAP control system, leak detected (no purge flow or large leak)
P0456	EVAP control system, very small leak detected
P0457	EVAP control system, leak detected (fuel filler neck cap loose or off)
P0460	Fuel level sensor, circuit malfunction
P0461	Fuel level sensor circuit, range or performance problem
P0462	Fuel level sensor circuit, low input
P0463	Fuel level sensor circuit, high input
P0480	Low Fan Control (LFC)/Fan Control No. 1 (FC1) primary circuit malfunction
P0481	High Fan Control (HFC)/Fan Control No. 3 (FC3) primary circuit malfunction
P0482	Medium Fan Control (MFC), primary circuit failure
P0500	Vehicle Speed Sensor (VSS) malfunction
P0501	Vehicle Speed Sensor (VSS), range or performance problem
P0503	Vehicle Speed Sensor (VSS), intermittent malfunction
P0504	Brake switch A/B correlation
P0505	Idle Air Control (IAC) system malfunction
P0506	Idle Air Control (IAC) system, rpm lower than expected
P0507	Idle Air Control (IAC) system, rpm higher than expected
P0511	Idle Air Control (IAC) system, circuit malfunction
P0512	Starter request circuit - shorted
P0532	Air Conditioning Pressure (ACP) sensor, high voltage detected
P0533	Air Conditioning Pressure (ACP) sensor, low voltage detected
P0534	Low air conditioning cycling period (frequent A/C compressor clutch cycling)
P0537	Air Conditioning Evaporator Temperature (ACET) circuit, low input
P0538	Air Conditioning Evaporator Temperature (ACET) circuit, high input
P0552	Power Steering Pressure (PSP) sensor circuit, low input
P0553	Power Steering Pressure (PSP) sensor circuit, high input
P0562	System voltage low
P0563	System voltage high

OBD-II TROUBLE CODES (CONTINUED)

➡ **Note: Not all trouble codes apply to all models.**

Code	Probable cause
P0572	Brake switch A circuit - low voltage detected
P0573	Brake switch A circuit - high voltage detected
P0602	Control module programming error
P0603	Powertrain Control Module (PCM) Keep-Alive-Memory (KAM) error
P0605	Powertrain Control Module (PCM) Read-Only-Memory (ROM) error
P0606	Powertrain Control Module (PCM) internal communication error
P0620	Alternator control circuit failure
P0622	Alternator field terminal circuit failure
P0625	Alternator field circuit - low voltage
P0626	Alternator field circuit - high voltage
P0645	Open or shorted Wide-Open Throttle A/C cutoff (WAC) circuit shorted or open or damaged WAC relay
P0660	Intake Manifold Tuning Valve (IMTV) control circuit open (Bank 1)
P0663	Intake Manifold Tuning Valve (IMTV) control circuit open (Bank 2)
P0701	Transmission control system - range or performance problem
P0702	Transmission control system - electrical problem detected
P0703	Brake switch circuit input malfunction
P0704	Clutch pedal position switch malfunction
P0705	Transmission Range (TR) sensor A circuit - malfunction
P0706	Transmission Range (TR) sensor A circuit - range or performance problem
P0707	Transmission Range (TR) sensor A circuit - low voltage
P0708	Transmission Range (TR) sensor A circuit - high voltage
P0709	Transmission Range (TR) sensor A circuit - intermittent failure
P0710	Transmission Fluid Temperature (TFT) sensor A circuit - malfunction
P0711	Transmission Fluid Temperature (TFT) sensor A circuit - range or performance problem
P0712	Transmission Fluid Temperature (TFT) sensor A circuit - low voltage
P0713	Transmission Fluid Temperature (TFT) sensor A circuit - high voltage
P0715	Transmission input/turbine shaft speed sensor A circuit - malfunction
P0717	Transmission input/turbine shaft speed sensor A circuit - no signal
P0718	Transmission input/turbine shaft speed sensor A circuit - intermittent
P0720	Insufficient input from Output Shaft Speed (OSS) sensor

P0721	Noise interference on Output Shaft Speed (OSS) sensor signal
P0722	No signal from Output Shaft Speed (OSS) sensor
P0723	Output Shaft Speed (OSS) sensor circuit, intermittent failure
P0729	Transmission gear 6 ratio error
P0731	Transmission gear 1 ratio error
P0732	Transmission gear 2 ratio error
P0733	Transmission gear 3 ratio error
P0734	Transmission gear 4 ratio error
P0735	Transmission gear 5 ratio error
P0740	Torque Converter Clutch (TCC) circuit - open
P0741	Torque Converter Clutch (TCC) circuit - performance
P0742	Torque Converter Clutch (TCC) circuit - stuck on
P0743	Torque Converter Clutch (TCC) system - electrical failure
P0744	Torque Converter Clutch (TCC) circuit - intermittent failure
P0748	Pressure control solenoid circuit A - electrical failure
P0750	Shift solenoid A - malfunction
P0751	Shift solenoid A - stuck off
P0752	Shift solenoid A - stuck on
P0753	Shift solenoid A - electrical failure
P0754	Shift solenoid A - intermittent
P0755	Shift solenoid B - malfunction
P0756	Shift solenoid B - stuck off
P0757	Shift solenoid B - stuck on
P0758	Shift solenoid B - electrical failure
P0759	Shift solenoid B - intermittent
P0760	Shift solenoid C - malfunction
P0761	Shift solenoid C - stuck off
P0762	Shift solenoid C - stuck on
P0763	Shift solenoid C - electrical failure
P0764	Shift solenoid C - intermittent
P0765	Shift solenoid D - malfunction
P0766	Shift solenoid D - stuck off
P0767	Shift solenoid D - stuck on
P0768	Shift solenoid D - electrical failure

OBD-II TROUBLE CODES (CONTINUED)

➡ **Note: Not all trouble codes apply to all models.**

Code	Probable cause
P0769	Shift solenoid D- intermittent
P0770	Shift solenoid E - malfunction
P0771	Shift solenoid E - stuck off
P0772	Shift solenoid E - stuck on
P0773	Shift solenoid E - electrical failure
P0774	Shift solenoid E - intermittent

3 Accelerator Pedal Position Sensors (APPS) - replacement

⬧ **Refer to illustration 3.3**

➡ **Note: The APP sensors are located inside the Electronic Throttle Control (ETC) module, and are not replaceable separately.**

1 Disconnect the cable from the negative battery terminal (see Chapter 5, Section 1).

2 Remove the knee bolster (see Chapter 11).

3 Disconnect the electrical connector from the ETC module (see illustration).

4 Remove the ETC module mounting nuts and bolts, then remove the ETC module and accelerator pedal (the "pedal and sensor assembly") from the rest of the accelerator pedal assembly (see illustration 3.3).

5 Installation is the reverse of removal.

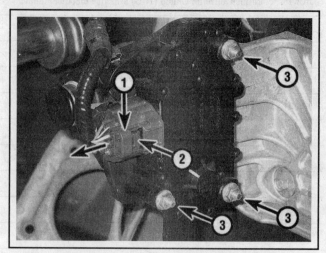

3.3 Slide the lock (1) away from the electrical connector, depress the release tabs (2) and pull off the connector. Remove these three nuts (3) and bolts to remove the ETC module and accelerator pedal as a single assembly (no further disassembly is possible)

4 Camshaft Position (CMP) sensor - replacement

4.2L V6 MODELS

CMP sensor

⬧ **Refer to illustrations 4.4 and 4.7**

✳ **WARNING:**

The engine must be completely cool before beginning this procedure.

➡ **Note: The CMP sensor is located on the upper part of the timing chain cover. It's mounted on the camshaft synchronizer, which looks like the lower part of a distributor, but is actually the drive unit for the sensor. If you're just replacing the CMP sensor, it's not necessary to remove the synchronizer. Simply remove the sensor mounting bolts from the sensor, detach it from the synchronizer and install the new sensor. However, some engine repair procedures, such as timing chain replacement, require removal of the synchronizer, in which case it will be necessary to align the synchronizer, which requires the use of a special tool. So if you're planning to remove or replace the synchronizer, read through the entire procedure and buy the special tool before you get started.**

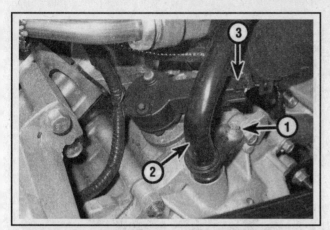

4.4 Remove this bolt (1), then pull the heater outlet pipe (2) out of the water pump. Depress the release tab (3) to disconnect the electrical connector from the CMP sensor (4.2L V6)

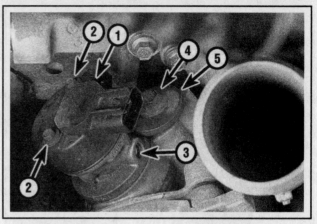

4.7 CMP sensor details

1	CMP sensor	4	Synchronizer hold-
2	Mounting bolts		down bolt
3	Synchronizer	5	Washer

1 Position the piston in the No. 1 cylinder at TDC (see Chapter 2A).

2 Disconnect the cable from the negative battery terminal (see Chapter 5, Section 1).

3 Drain the cooling system (see Chapter 1).

4 Disconnect the heater outlet pipe (see illustration). While the heater outlet pipe is removed, inspect the condition of the outlet pipe O-ring and replace it if it's cracked, torn, deteriorated or otherwise damaged (see Chapter 3).

5 Disconnect the electrical connector from the CMP sensor (see illustration 4.4).

6 If you're going to remove the synchronizer, mark the position of the CMP sensor electrical connector in relation to the timing cover so that the CMP sensor will be correctly oriented when it's reinstalled.

7 Remove the CMP sensor mounting bolts (see illustration) and remove the sensor from the synchronizer.

8 If you're removing or replacing the camshaft synchronizer, proceed to Step 10.

9 Installation is the reverse of removal.

Camshaft synchronizer

▶ **Refer to illustrations 4.12 and 4.14**

10 Remove the CMP sensor (see Steps 1 through 7).

11 Remove the camshaft synchronizer hold-down bolt and washer (see illustration 4.7) and pull the synchronizer straight up and out of the timing chain cover. Remove the oil pump intermediate shaft.

12 Place the special alignment tool on top of the camshaft synchronizer and align the vane of the synchronizer with the radial slot in the special tool (see illustration).

13 Turn the special tool on the cam synchronizer until the boss on the tool engages the notch on the synchronizer.

14 Lubricate the driven gear, thrust washer and bearing on the lower end of the synchronizer with clean engine oil. Then install the oil pump intermediate shaft on the lower end of the synchronizer and insert the synchronizer assembly into the engine, with the arrow on the special tool pointing 54-degrees from the engine's centerline (see illustration).

15 Turn the tool clockwise a little until the cam synchronizer engages the oil pump intermediate shaft. Push down on the synchronizer, slowly turning the tool until the driven gear on the lower end of the cam synchronizer engages with the drive gear on the camshaft.

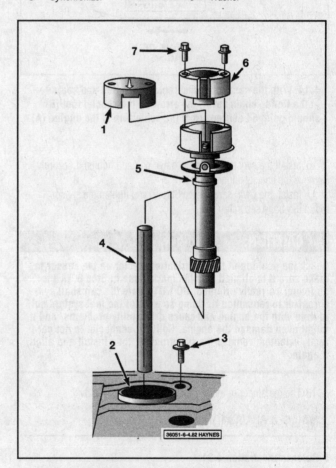

4.12 Exploded view of the CMP sensor and camshaft synchronizer assembly:

1	Synchronizer positioning tool
2	Timing chain cover
3	Synchronizer hold-down bolt
4	Oil pump intermediate shaft
5	Camshaft synchronizer
6	CMP sensor
7	CMP sensor mounting bolts

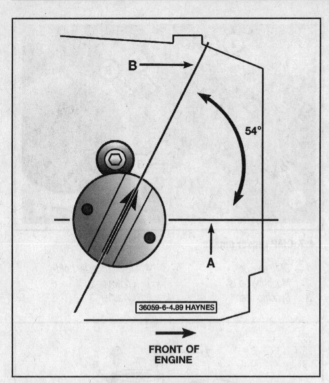

54°

B

A

36059-6-4.89 HAYNES

FRONT OF ENGINE

4.14 With the camshaft synchronizer installed and seated in the timing chain cover, the arrow on the special tool (B) should point 54 degrees from the centerline of the engine (A)

16 Install the synchronizer hold-down bolt and tighten it securely. Remove the special alignment tool.

17 Install the CMP sensor (see Step 9) and tighten the sensor mounting bolts securely.

⁕ CAUTION:

Check the position of the electrical connector on the sensor to make sure it is aligned with the mark made in Step 6. If it is no longer correctly oriented, DO NOT rotate the camshaft synchronizer to reposition it. Doing so will put the fuel system out of time with the engine and cause driveability problems, and it might even damage the engine. So if the connector is not correctly oriented, remove the synchronizer, then install and align it again.

18 The remainder of installation is the reverse of removal.

2-VALVE 4.6L V8 MODELS

▶ Refer to illustration 4.21

➡ Note: The CMP sensor is located on the front end of the left cylinder head.

19 Disconnect the cable from the negative battery terminal (see Chapter 5, Section 1).

20 Disconnect the electrical connector from the CMP sensor.

21 Remove the CMP sensor mounting bolt and remove the sensor from the cylinder head (see illustration).

22 Installation is the reverse of removal.

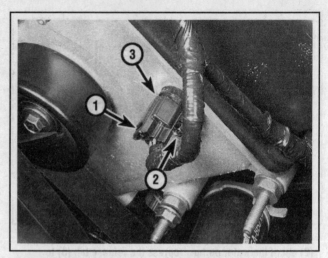

4.21 Depress this release tab (1), remove the sensor mounting bolt (2) and pull out the sensor (3)

5.4L AND 3-VALVE 4.6L V8 MODELS

▶ Refer to illustrations 4.24a, 4.24b, 4.25a and 4.25b

➡ Note: The two CMP sensors are located on the front end of the cylinder heads. The photos accompanying the removal procedure depict a CMP sensor being removed from the left cylinder head, but the removal procedure for the CMP sensor on the right head is identical.

23 Disconnect the cable from the negative battery terminal (see Chapter 5, Section 1).

24 Disconnect the electrical connector from the CMP sensor (see illustrations).

25 Remove the CMP sensor mounting bolt (see illustration) and remove the sensor from the cylinder head (see illustration).

26 Installation is the reverse of removal.

3.5L AND 3.7L V6 AND 5.0L V8 MODELS

➡ Note: The CMP sensors are located on the rear of the cylinder heads. There is a CMP sensor for each camshaft.

27 Disconnect the cable from the negative battery terminal (see Chapter 5, Section 1).

28 Disconnect the electrical connector from the CMP sensor.

29 Remove the CMP sensor mounting bolt and remove the sensor from the cylinder head. On 5.0L V8 models, one of the CMP sensors is located behind a heat-shield. Remove the heat-shield to gain access to the sensor mounting bolt.

30 Installation is the reverse of removal. Lubricate the sensor O-ring with clean engine oil before installation.

6.2L V8 MODELS

➡ Note: The CMP sensors are located on the rear of the cylinder heads just behind the intake manifold. There is a CMP sensor for each camshaft.

4.24a On 5.4L V8 engines, there is one CMP sensor on the front end of the left cylinder head . . .

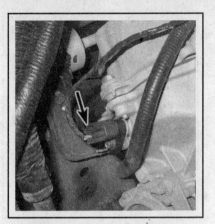

4.24b . . . and a second CMP sensor on the front end of the right cylinder head. To disconnect the electrical connector from either sensor, depress the release tab and pull off the connector

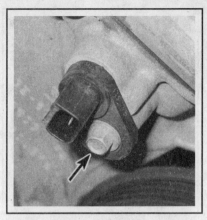

4.25a To detach a CMP sensor from either cylinder head on a 5.4L V8 engine, remove this bolt . . .

31 Disconnect the cable from the negative battery terminal (see Chapter 5, Section 1).
32 Disconnect the electrical connector from the CMP sensor.
33 Remove the CMP sensor mounting bolt and remove the sensor from the cylinder head.
34 Installation is the reverse of removal. Lubricate the sensor O-ring with clean engine oil before installation.

4.25b . . . then grasp the sensor firmly and pull it out of the head

5   Crankshaft Position (CKP) sensor - replacement

4.2L V6 MODELS

▶ **Refer to illustration 5.3**

➡ **Note:** The CKP sensor is located on the front of the engine block, at about 11 o'clock in relation to the crankshaft.

1 Disconnect the cable from the negative battery terminal (see Chapter 5, Section 1).
2 Raise the front of the vehicle and place it securely on jackstands.
3 Disconnect the electrical connector from the CKP sensor (see illustration).
4 Remove the CKP sensor mounting fasteners and remove the sensor from the timing chain cover.
5 Installation is the reverse of removal.

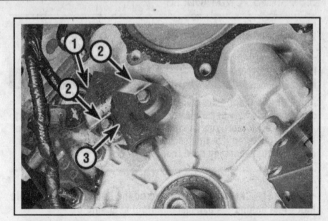

5.3 Disconnect the electrical connector (1) (hidden behind the small rock shield), then remove the sensor mounting bolts (2) and remove the sensor (3) from the timing cover (crankshaft pulley/damper and water pump housing removed for clarity)

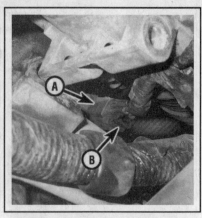

5.10 To disconnect the electrical connector (A) from the CKP sensor, depress this release tab (B) and pull off the connector

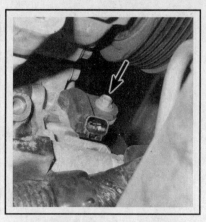

5.11 Remove this mounting bolt and pull out the sensor

5.15 Remove the fasteners securing the exhaust manifold heat shield

4.6L AND 5.4L V8 MODELS

▶ Refer to illustrations 5.10 and 5.11

➡ Note: The CKP sensor is located at the right front corner of the engine block.

6   Disconnect the cable from the negative battery terminal (see Chapter 5, Section 1).

7   Remove the accessory drivebelt (see Chapter 1).

8   Raise the front of the vehicle and place it securely on jackstands.

9   Loosen the air conditioning compressor bolts (see Chapter 3) and let the compressor drop down about an inch or so to allow access to the CKP sensor.

10 Disconnect the electrical connector from the CKP sensor (see illustration).

11 Remove the CKP sensor mounting bolt (see illustration) and remove the sensor from the block.

12 Installation is the reverse of removal.

3.5L AND 3.7L V6 MODELS

▶ Refer to illustration 5.15

❈❈ **CAUTION:**

According to the manufacturer, if you're replacing the old CKP sensor with a new sensor, the new unit must be re-initialized by a factory scan tool. You can remove and install the old CKP sensor, but if you replace this sensor at home, the engine may not run correctly when you start it up.

➡ Note: The CKP sensor is located on the left side of the engine block just behind the exhaust manifold heat shield.

13 Disconnect the cable from the negative battery terminal (see Chapter 5, Section 1).

14 On 3.5L engines, remove the left turbocharger (see Chapter 2B).

15 Remove the exhaust manifold heat shield (see illustration).

16 Remove the rubber grommet from the side of the engine block.

17 Disconnect the electrical connector from the CKP sensor.

18 Remove the CKP sensor mounting bolt and remove the sensor from the engine block.

19 Installation is the reverse of removal.

5.0L AND 6.2L V8 MODELS

❈❈ **CAUTION:**

According to the manufacturer, if you're replacing the old CKP sensor with a new sensor, the new unit must be re-initialized by a factory scan tool. You can remove and install the old CKP sensor, but if you replace this sensor at home, the engine may not run correctly when you start it up.

➡ Note: On 5.0L engines, the CKP sensor is located on the top of the engine block just behind the right cylinder head. On 6.2L engines, the CKP sensor is located on the back of the engine block under the intake manifold.

20 Disconnect the cable from the negative battery terminal (see Chapter 5, Section 1).

21 If you're working on a 6.2L engine, remove the intake manifold (see Chapter 2C).

22 Disconnect the electrical connector from the CKP sensor.

23 Remove the CKP sensor mounting bolt and remove the sensor from the engine block.

24 Installation is the reverse of removal.

❈❈ **CAUTION:**

On 6.2L engines, the new CKP sensor should be positioned into the fitting on the rear seal retainer plate and flush against the engine block before the mounting fastener is installed.

6   Cylinder Head Temperature (CHT) sensor - replacement

3.5L AND 4.2L V6 MODELS

➡ **Note:** The CHT sensor is located on the rear end of the left cylinder head. Because of the tight clearance between the cylinder heads and the firewall, the CHT sensor is easier to access from underneath the vehicle than from above.

1   Disconnect the cable from the negative battery terminal (see Chapter 5, Section 1).
2   Raise the front of the vehicle and place it securely on jackstands.
3   Disconnect the electrical connector from the CHT sensor.
4   Unscrew the CHT sensor with a wrench or socket and remove it.
5   Installation is the reverse of removal. Be sure to tighten the CHT sensor to the torque listed in this Chapter's Specifications.

4.6L AND 5.4L V8 MODELS

▸ **Refer to illustration 6.8**

✳ WARNING:

The engine must be completely cool before beginning this procedure.

➡ **Note:** The CHT sensor is located on the inner wall of the right (passenger's side) cylinder head. To access the CHT sensor, you must remove the intake manifold.

6   Relieve the fuel system pressure (see Chapter 4), then disconnect the cable from the negative battery terminal (see Chapter 5, Section 1).
7   On 2-valve 4.6L engines, remove the alternator (see Chapter 5). Remove the intake manifold (see Chapter 2C).
8   Disconnect the electrical connector from the CHT sensor (see illustration). Note that there are two electrical connectors for the CHT sensor, a bigger black connector at the main harness and a smaller white connector at the sensor itself. Unless you're replacing the pigtail that connects the CHT sensor to the main engine electrical harness, it's not necessary to disconnect the black connector.
9   Use the box end of a wrench or a suitable deep socket to loosen the CHT sensor, then unscrew and remove it.

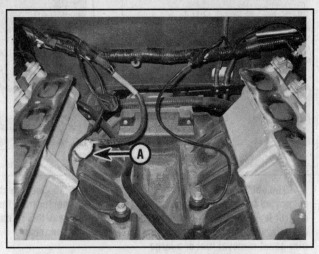

6.8 To disconnect the electrical connector (A) from the CHT sensor, depress this release tab and pull the connector off the sensor - typical

10 Installation is the reverse of removal. Be sure to tighten the CHT sensor to the torque listed in this Chapter's Specifications.

3.7L V6, 5.0L AND 6.2L V8 MODELS

➡ **Note:** On 3.7L engines, the CHT sensor is located under the lower intake manifold. On 5.0L and 6.2L engines, the CHT sensor is located under the intake manifold.

11 Disconnect the cable from the negative battery terminal (see Chapter 5, Section 1).
12 Remove the intake manifold (see Chapter 2B or 2C). On 3.7L engines remove the lower intake manifold (see Chapter 2B).
13 Disconnect the electrical connector from the CHT sensor.
14 Use the box end of a wrench or a suitable deep socket to loosen the CHT sensor, then unscrew and remove it.
15 Installation is the reverse of removal. Tighten the CHT sensor to the torque listed in this Chapter's Specifications.

7   Digital Transmission Range (DTR) sensor - replacement

▸ **Refer to illustrations 7.4, 7.5, 7.6, 7.7, 7.9, 7.11 and 7.14**

➡ **Note:** This procedure applies only to the DTR sensors used on 4R70E and 4R75E transmissions. It does not apply to the TR sensor (or PRNDL sensor) used on 6R80 transmissions; that device is an integral component of the valve body, and cannot be serviced at home.

➡ **Note:** The DTR sensor is located on the left side of the transmission.

➡ **Note:** If you're replacing the DTR sensor (not just removing and installing the same sensor on the same transmission), or if you're planning to remove the sensor to replace the transmission with a new or rebuilt unit, then you'll need the special DTR sensor alignment tool (307-351), or a suitable substitute, before beginning this procedure.

1   Put the shift lever in Neutral, then disconnect the cable from the negative battery terminal (see Chapter 5, Section 1).
2   Raise the vehicle and place it securely on jackstands.
3   On some 4WD models, it might be necessary to remove the front

7.4 The shift control cable is connected to a pin on the manual control lever. To disconnect the cable from the pin, pop it off with a trim panel removal tool or a large screwdriver

7.5 To disconnect the electrical connector from the DTR sensor, depress this release tab and pull off the connector

7.6 To detach the manual control lever from the manual selector shaft, remove this nut while holding the lever with pliers so it doesn't turn, then pull the manual control lever off the shaft

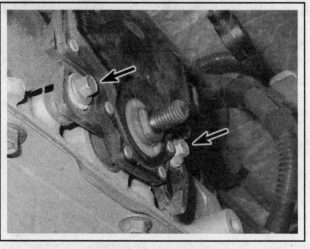

7.7 If you're removing and installing the same DTR sensor, mark the relationship of the sensor to the transmission case

7.9 To detach the DTR sensor from the transmission case, remove these two bolts

driveshaft or to disconnect one end of the driveshaft and push it aside (see Chapter 8).

4   Disconnect the shift control cable from the manual control lever (see illustration).

5   Disconnect the electrical connector from the DTR sensor (see illustration).

6   Remove the manual control lever nut and remove the manual control lever (see illustration).

7   If you're simply removing and installing the same DTR sensor, mark the relationship of the sensor to the transmission case (see illustration).

8   If you're replacing the DTR sensor, or removing the sensor to replace the transmission with a new or rebuilt unit, marking the sensor's position won't work. You must obtain a special manufacturer tool (307-351) to adjust the sensor when installing it.

9   Remove the DTR sensor mounting bolts (see illustration) and remove the DTR sensor.

➡ **Note: While the DTR sensor is removed, do NOT move the manual selector shaft from the Neutral position.**

10 If you or someone else accidentally moved the selector shaft while the DTR sensor was removed, you must put the manual selector shaft in the Neutral position before installing the DTR sensor. To do so, put a wrench on the two machined flats located at the base of the threaded part of the shaft and rotate the shaft through the gears in a clockwise direction until it stops. Then rotate the shaft counterclockwise three detent positions (three clicks). The selector shaft is now in the Neutral position.

11 Before installing the DTR sensor, make sure that the Neutral mark on the rotating part of the DTR sensor is aligned with the Neutral mark

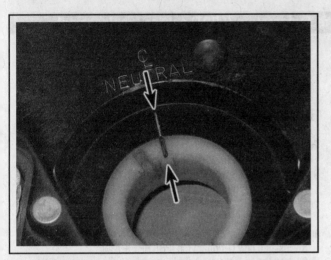

7.11 Before installing the DTR sensor, make sure that the Neutral mark on the rotating part of the sensor is aligned with the Neutral mark on the fixed part of the sensor. If the two marks are not aligned, turn the rotating part until they are

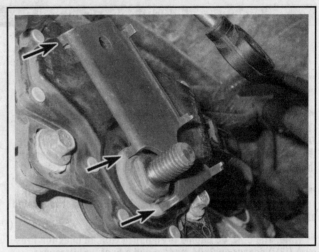

7.14 To install the special DTR sensor alignment tool, insert the three legs of the tool into their corresponding slots in the sensor, one at the top of, and two on the rotating part of, the sensor

on the fixed part of the sensor (see illustration). If the two marks are not aligned, turn the rotating part until the two marks are aligned.

12 Install the DTR sensor on the manual selector shaft and loosely install the sensor mounting bolts (see illustration 9.9).

13 If you're installing the old DTR sensor, align the marks that you made on the sensor and on the transmission case and hold the sensor

in this position while tightening the sensor mounting bolts securely.

14 If you're installing a new DTR sensor, install the special sensor alignment tool (see illustration), then tighten the sensor mounting bolts securely.

15 The remainder of installation is the reverse of removal.

8 Engine Oil Temperature (EOT) sensor - replacement

▶ **Refer to illustrations 8.4 and 8.5**

➡ **Note: The EOT sensor, which is used on 2004 through 2008 2-valve 4.6L V8 engines, is located on the right side of the engine oil pan.**

1 Disconnect the cable from the negative battery terminal (see Chapter 5, Section 1).

2 Drain the engine oil (see Chapter 1).

3 Raise the front of the vehicle and place it securely on jackstands.

4 Disconnect the electrical connector from the EOT sensor (see illustration).

5 Unscrew the EOT sensor (see illustration).

6 Installation is the reverse of removal. Be sure to tighten the EOT sensor to the torque listed in this Chapter's Specifications.

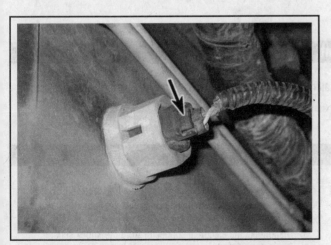

8.4 The EOT sensor is located on the side of the oil pan. To disconnect the electrical connector, depress this release tab and pull it off

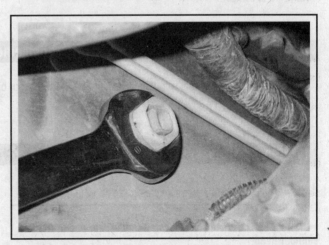

8.5 Use a wrench or a deep socket to unscrew the EOT sensor from the oil pan

9 Injection Pressure (IPR) sensor/Fuel Rail Pressure Temperature (FRPT) sensor - replacement

▶ **Refer to illustrations 9.3 and 9.8**

➡ **Note: This Section applies to 4.2L V6, 4.6L V8 and 5.4L V8 models only.**

➡ **Note: The 4.2L V6 engine is equipped with an Injection Pressure (IPR) sensor on 2005 models and a Fuel Rail Pressure Temperature (FRPT) sensor on 2006 through 2008 models. The IPR sensor and the FRPT sensor are located at the rear end of the left fuel rail.**

➡ **Note: The 4.6L V8 engine uses an Injection Pressure (IPR) sensor on 2004 through 2008 models. The IPR sensor is located at the front end of the left fuel rail.**

➡ **Note: The 5.4L V8 engine is equipped with an Injection Pressure (IPR) sensor on 2004 models and a Fuel Rail Pressure Temperature (FRPT) sensor on 2005 through 2008 models. The IPR sensor and the FRPT sensor are located on the left fuel rail, just in front of the fuel rail pipe for the fuel supply line connection.**

1   Relieve the fuel pressure in the fuel system (see Chapter 4).

2   Disconnect the cable from the negative battery terminal (see Chapter 5, Section 1).

3   Disconnect the electrical connector from the IPR/FRPT sensor (see illustration).

4   Disconnect the vacuum hose from the IPR/FRPT sensor (see illustration 9.3).

5   Remove the IPR/FRPT sensor mounting bolts (see illustration 9.3) and remove the sensor from the fuel rail.

6   Remove the old O-ring from the IPR/FRPT sensor (see illustration).

7   Carefully clean off the mating surfaces of the IPR/FRPT sensor and the fuel rail.

8   Install a new O-ring on the IPR/FRPT sensor.

9   Installation is the reverse of removal.

10 Start the engine and check for fuel leaks in the vicinity of the IPR/FRPT sensor.

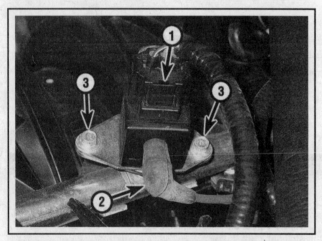

9.3 Depress this release tab (1) and disconnect the electrical connector, then disconnect the vacuum hose (2) from the sensor and remove the sensor mounting bolts (3) (5.4L V8 shown)

9.6 Remove the old O-rings from the IPR/FRPT sensor and replace them with new ones (5.4L V8 shown)

10 Intake Air Temperature (IAT) sensor - replacement

The IAT sensor is an integral part of the Mass Air Flow (MAF) sensor on all models covered by this manual. If the IAT sensor must be replaced, you must replace the MAF sensor (see Section 12).

11 Knock sensor(s) - replacement

4.2L V6 MODELS

➡ **Note: The knock sensor is located on the rear end of the left cylinder head.**

1   Disconnect the cable from the negative battery terminal (see Chapter 5, Section 1).

2   To access the knock sensor, remove the transmission bellhousing bolt that secures the fuel supply line bracket to the transmission bellhousing, then push the fuel supply line and bracket aside.

3   Disconnect the electrical connector from the knock sensor.

4   Remove the knock sensor mounting bolt and remove the knock sensor.

5   Installation is the reverse of removal. Be sure to tighten the knock

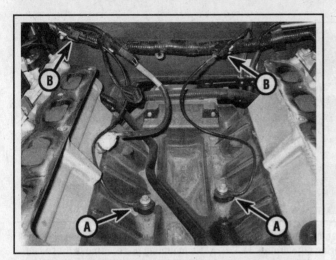

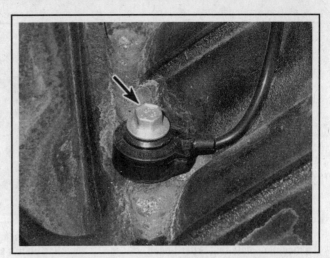

11.8 On 5.4L V8 engines, there are two knock sensors (A) and an electrical connector (B) for each sensor. On 4.6L V8 engines, there is only one knock sensor; it's located in the same spot on the right cylinder head as shown here (left arrows in this photo)

11.9 To detach a knock sensor from the engine block, remove this bolt

sensor to the torque listed in this Chapter's Specifications.

3.5L AND 3.7L V6, AND ALL V8 MODELS

▶ **Refer to illustrations 11.8 and 11.9**

➡ **Note: The knock sensor(s) is/are located in the valley between the cylinder heads, underneath the intake manifold, which must be removed to access the sensor(s). There is one knock sensor on 2-valve 4.6L engines. There are two knock sensors on all other engines.**

6 Relieve the fuel system pressure, then disconnect the cable from the negative battery terminal (see Chapter 5, Section 1).

7 Remove the intake manifold (see Chapter 2).

8 Depress the locking tab and disconnect the electrical connector from the knock sensor (see illustration).

9 Remove the knock sensor retaining bolt (see illustration) and remove the knock sensor.

10 Installation is the reverse of removal. Be sure to tighten the knock sensor retaining bolt to the torque listed in this Chapter's Specifications.

12 Mass Air Flow (MAF) sensor - replacement

2004 THROUGH 2008 4.2L V6 AND 4.6L V8 MODELS

▶ **Refer to illustrations 12.2, 12.4a, 12.4b and 12.5**

➡ **Note: The MAF sensor is located inside the air filter housing.**

1 Disconnect the cable from the negative battery terminal (see Chapter 5, Section 1).

2 Separate the two halves of the air filter housing (see Chapter 1). The MAF sensor is located inside the half of the air filter housing without the air filter element (see illustration).

3 Remove the grommet from the underside of the air filter housing where the electrical harness for the MAF sensor goes through the housing (see illustration 12.2).

12.2 The MAF sensor (A) is inside this half of the air filter housing. Before you can remove the MAF sensor from the housing, disengage the sensor wire harness grommet (B) from the underside of the housing

12.4a The MAF sensor is bolted to a mounting plate that is positioned inside the filter housing by these four retaining spring clips (assembly removed from filter housing for clarity)

12.4b After disengaging the sensor mounting plate's spring clips from the filter housing, carefully remove the sensor mounting plate and the sensor from the housing

12.5 To detach the MAF sensor from its mounting plate, remove these two bolts (4.6L V8 model shown; on V6 models, the mounting bolts are both on the same side instead of opposite corners)

4   The MAF sensor is bolted to a mounting plate that's positioned inside the filter housing by four retaining spring clips (see illustration). To disengage the MAF sensor mounting plate from the filter housing, carefully pry these plate retaining clips loose with a small screwdriver, then remove the mounting plate and MAF sensor as a single assembly (see illustration).

5   Detach the MAF sensor from the sensor mounting plate (see illustration).

6   Inspect the condition of the rubber grommet that seals the entry hole for the MAF sensor wiring harness on the underside of the filter housing. If it's cracked, torn or otherwise damaged, replace it.

7   Installation is the reverse of removal.

5.4L V8 AND ALL 2009 AND LATER MODELS

▶ **Refer to illustrations 12.9, 12.10 and 12.11**

➡ **Note: The MAF sensor is located on the right side of the air filter housing.**

8   Disconnect the cable from the negative battery terminal (see Chapter 5, Section 1).

9   Disconnect the electrical connector from the MAF sensor (see illustration).

10 Remove the MAF sensor mounting screws (see illustration) and remove the MAF sensor from the air filter housing.

11 If you're planning to install the old MAF sensor, inspect the condition of the rubber sealing ring at the sensor mounting flange (see illustration). If this seal is cracked, torn or deteriorated, replace the MAF sensor (or make your own sealing ring). At the time of publication, the manufacturer did not offer a replacement sealing ring for the MAF sensor on this model. The sealing ring is only available as part of a new MAF sensor.

12 Installation is the reverse of removal.

12.9 To disconnect the electrical connector from the MAF sensor, slide the lock (1) out of the connector, then depress the release tab (2) and pull off the connector (5.4L V8 model)

12.10 To detach the MAF sensor from the air filter housing, remove these two screws (5.4L V8 model)

12.11 After removing the MAF sensor, inspect the condition of this rubber sealing ring. If it's cracked, torn or deteriorated, replace the MAF sensor. The sealing ring is not available separately

13 Oxygen sensors - general information and replacement

GENERAL INFORMATION

1 Use special care when servicing an oxygen sensor:

a) *Oxygen sensors have a permanently attached pigtail and electrical connector that can't be removed from the sensor. Damage to or removal of the pigtail or the electrical connector will ruin the sensor.*

b) *Keep grease, dirt and other contaminants away from the electrical connector and the louvered end of the sensor.*

c) *Do not use cleaning solvents of any kind on an oxygen sensor or air/fuel ratio sensor.*

d) *Do not drop or roughly handle an oxygen sensor or air/fuel ratio sensor.*

e) *Be sure to install the silicone boot in the correct position to prevent the boot from melting and to allow the sensor to operate properly.*

REPLACEMENT

➡ **Note: Because it is installed in the exhaust manifold or catalytic converter, both of which contract when cool, an oxygen sensor might be very difficult to loosen when the engine is cold. Rather than risk damage to the sensor, start and run the engine for a minute or two, then shut it off. Be careful not to burn yourself during the following procedure.**

2 Disconnect the cable from the negative terminal of the battery (see Chapter 5, Section 1).

3 Raise the vehicle and place it securely on jackstands.

Upstream oxygen sensor

▸ **Refer to illustrations 13.4 and 13.5**

➡ **Note: There are two upstream oxygen sensors on all models. The upstream oxygen sensors are located on the exhaust manifolds, above the manifold flanges or below the exhaust manifold flanges at the upper ends of the catalytic converters.**

4 Trace the electrical lead from the upstream oxygen sensor to the electrical connector (see illustration) and disconnect it.

5 Using a special oxygen sensor socket, unscrew the sensor (see illustration).

6 After removing the old upstream oxygen sensor, clean the threads of the sensor bore in the exhaust manifold.

7 If you're going to install the old sensor, apply anti-seize compound to the threads of the sensor to facilitate future removal. If you're going to install a new oxygen sensor, it's not necessary to apply anti-seize compound to the threads. The threads on new sensors already have anti-seize compound on them.

8 Installation is otherwise the reverse of removal. Be sure to tighten the upstream sensor to the torque listed in this Chapter's Specifications.

Downstream oxygen sensor

▸ **Refer to illustration 13.9**

➡ **Note: There are two downstream oxygen sensors on all models. The downstream oxygen sensors are located on the catalytic converters or in the exhaust pipes between the upstream and downstream catalytic converters.**

9 Trace the electrical lead from the downstream oxygen sensor to the electrical connector and disconnect it (see illustration).

10 Unscrew and remove the downstream oxygen sensor (see illustration 13.9).

11 After removing the old downstream oxygen sensor, clean the threads of the sensor bore in the catalytic converter.

12 If you're going to install the old sensor, apply anti-seize compound to the threads of the sensor to facilitate future removal.

13 If you're going to install a new oxygen sensor, it's not necessary to apply anti-seize compound to the threads. The threads on new sensors already have anti-seize compound on them.

14 Installation is otherwise the reverse of removal. Be sure to tighten the downstream oxygen sensor to the torque listed in this Chapter's Specifications.

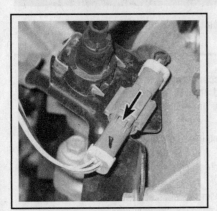

13.4 To disconnect the connector, depress this release tab and pull off the sensor half of the connector (5.4L V8 shown)

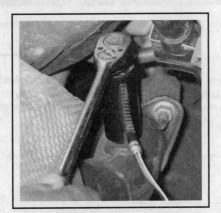

13.5 Use an oxygen sensor socket to unscrew either upstream oxygen sensor (upstream sensor for left cylinder bank on a 5.4L V8 model shown, upstream sensors on other models similar)

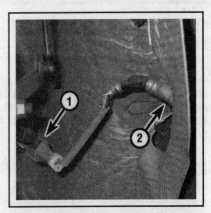

13.9 Trace the pigtail lead up to the electrical connector (1), disconnect the connector, then unscrew the oxygen sensor (2) from the catalyst (4.2L V6 models) or from the exhaust pipe just ahead of the downstream catalyst (4.6L and 5.4L V8 models, shown)

14 Power Steering Pressure (PSP) switch - replacement

▶ **Refer to illustration 14.3**

➡ **Note 1:** The PSP switch, which is used on 2004 through 2009 models, is located on the high-pressure power steering fluid line (which is located between the power steering pump and the steering gear).

➡ **Note 2:** The PSP switch may only be available as an integral component of the high-pressure power steering fluid line.

1   Disconnect the cable from the negative terminal of the battery (see Chapter 5, Section 1).

2   Raise the vehicle and place it securely on jackstands.

3   Disconnect the electrical connector from the PSP switch (see illustration).

4   If you were able to obtain a replacement PSP switch, place a drain pan directly underneath the old switch, and have some shop rags and your new PSP switch handy. Unscrew the PSP switch with a wrench or a deep socket, then immediately screw in the new switch to prevent loss of power steering fluid.

5   If you were unable to obtain a replacement PSP switch, drain the power steering fluid from the power steering system, or siphon it out of the power steering fluid reservoir, then remove the old high-pressure line and install a new high-pressure line and PSP switch assembly (see Chapter 10).

6   Installation is the reverse of removal. If you replaced just the PSP switch, be sure to tighten it securely.

7   Refill the power steering system (see Chapter 1), then bleed the power steering system as described in Chapter 10.

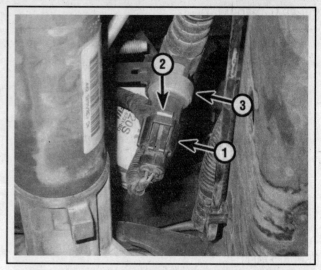

14.3 To disconnect the electrical connector (1) from the PSP switch (3), depress this release tab (2) and pull off the connector

15 Throttle Position (TP) sensor - replacement

ALL 4.2L V6 MODELS AND 2004 4.6L AND 5.4L V8 MODELS

➡ **Note:** The TP sensor is not removable on any 4.2L V6 model or on 2004 4.6L or 5.4L V8 models. If the TP sensor must be replaced on one of these models, you must replace the electronic throttle body assembly (see Chapter 4), which includes a new TP sensor.

2005 AND 2006 4.6L AND 2005 THROUGH 2008 5.4L V8 MODELS

▶ **Refer to illustrations 15.2, 15.3 and 15.4**

※※ **CAUTION:**

This procedure applies only to TP sensor replacement, NOT to removing and installing the old TP sensor. If you remove the TP sensor from the throttle body on one of these models, the manufacturer recommends installing a NEW TP sensor, not the old unit.

➡ **Note:** The photos accompanying this section depict the down-draft throttle body used on 5.4L V8 models. 4.6L V8 models use a side-draft throttle body, but the TP sensor shown here is similar.

1   Disconnect the cable from the negative battery terminal (see Chapter 5, Section 1).

2   Disconnect the electrical connector from the TP sensor (see illustration).

3   Remove the TP sensor mounting screws (see illustration) and remove the TP sensor from the throttle body.

※※ **CAUTION:**

The manufacturer-recommended technique for removing these screws is to loosen them one or two turns by hand, then removing them the rest of the way with a high-speed power driver. If this method is not followed, the screws may break.

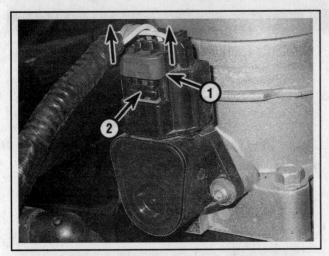

15.2 To disconnect the electrical connector, slide the red lock (1) away from the connector (toward the wire harness), then depress the release tab (2) and pull off the connector

15.3 To detach the TP sensor from the throttle body, remove these two screws (one screw not visible in this photo). Be sure to use the factory-recommended method for removing these screws

4   When installing the new TP sensor, make sure that the tip of the throttle plate shaft is aligned with the recessed area in the rotary part of the sensor. Note the two flat sides in this recessed area. The throttle plate shaft's flat tip must fit between these two flats (see illustration).

5   Installation is otherwise the reverse of removal. Be sure to use NEW sensor mounting screws and tighten them securely.

⁂ CAUTION:

The manufacturer states that the screws must be installed with a hand tool only, not a power driver.

2009 AND LATER 5.4L V8 MODELS

⁂ CAUTION:

You must not use a power tool to remove the TP sensor mounting screws on these models. Instead, you'll need an 1100-watt heat gun and either a digital temperature laser or an infrared thermometer. Attempting to remove the TP sensor mounting screws with a power tool instead of using the following procedure could result in damage to the throttle body, the TP sensor or the sensor mounting screws.

6   Disconnect the cable from the negative battery terminal (see Chapter 5).

7   Disconnect the electrical connector from the TP sensor.

8   Position the heat gun about an inch from the throttle body and apply heat to the throttle body. Monitor the temperature with a digital temperature laser or an infrared thermometer; after about three minutes, the upper TP sensor bolt should be about 130 degrees F.

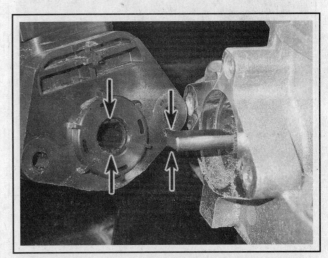

15.4 When installing a new TP sensor, make sure that the two flat sides of the throttle plate shaft are aligned with the two flats in the rotary part of the sensor

9   Use a hand tool to remove and discard the screw farthest from the heat source, then remove and discard the other screw. Remove and discard the TP sensor.

10 Installation is the same as earlier models (see Steps 4 and 5). Be sure to use new TP sensor fasteners.

3.5L AND 3.7L V6 AND 5.0L AND 6.2L V8 MODELS

➡ Note: The TP sensor is an integral component of the electronic throttle body, and is not separately serviceable. If you need to replace the TP sensor, you must replace the throttle body (see Chapter 4).

16 Transmission speed sensors - replacement

1   Disconnect the cable from the negative battery terminal (see Chapter 5, Section 1).

2   Raise the vehicle and place it securely on jackstands.

AUTOMATIC TRANSMISSIONS

➡ **Note: The automatic transmission speed sensors are located on the left side of the transmission. The front sensor is the Turbine Shaft Speed (TSS) sensor and the rear sensor is the Output Shaft Speed (OSS) sensor.**

Turbine Shaft Speed (TSS) sensor

▶ **Refer to illustrations 16.3 and 16.4**

3   Disconnect the electrical connector from the TSS sensor (see illustration).

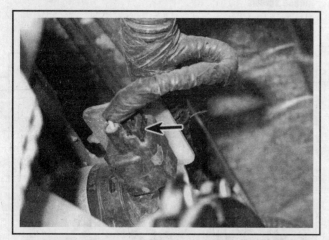

16.3 To disconnect the electrical connector from the TSS sensor, depress this release tab and pull off the connector

4   Remove the TSS sensor retaining bolt (see illustration).

5   Remove the old O-ring from the TSS sensor (see illustration 16.9) and install a new O-ring on the sensor.

6   Installation is the reverse of removal. Be sure to tighten the TSS sensor retaining bolt securely.

Output Shaft Speed (OSS) sensor

▶ **Refer to illustrations 16.7 and 16.9**

7   Disconnect the electrical connector from the OSS sensor (see illustration).

8   Remove the OSS sensor retaining bolt (see illustration 16.7).

9   Remove the old O-ring from the OSS sensor (see illustration) and install a new O-ring on the sensor.

10 Installation is the reverse of removal. Be sure to tighten the OSS sensor retaining bolt securely.

MANUAL TRANSMISSIONS - VEHICLE SPEED SENSOR (VSS)

➡ **Note: On 2WD models, the VSS is located on the left side of the extension housing, just behind the transmission-to-extension housing mounting flange. On 4WD models, the VSS is located on the left side of the transfer case extension housing, just behind the transfer case-to-extension housing mounting flange.**

11 Disconnect the electrical connector from the VSS.

12 Remove the VSS mounting bolt and remove the VSS sensor from the transmission extension housing (2WD models) or transfer case extension housing (4WD models).

13 Remove and discard the old VSS O-ring.

14 Install a new O-ring on the VSS.

15 Installation is the reverse of removal. Be sure to tighten the VSS mounting bolt securely.

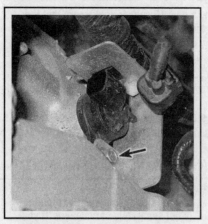

16.4 To detach the TSS sensor from the transmission, remove the sensor retaining bolt

16.7 Disconnect the electrical connector (1) and remove the OSS sensor retaining bolt (2)

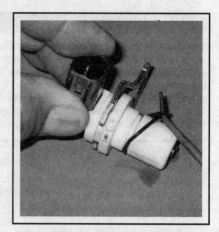

16.9 Remove the old O-ring from the OSS sensor and install a new O-ring (TSS sensor and O-ring identical)

17 Powertrain Control Module (PCM) - removal and installation

2004 AND 2005 MODELS

▶ **Refer to illustrations 17.2, 17.3 and 17.4**

✳ CAUTION:

To avoid electrostatic discharge damage to the PCM, handle the PCM only by its case. Do not touch the electrical terminals during removal and installation. If available, ground yourself to the vehicle with an anti-static ground strap, available at computer supply stores.

➡ **Note:** The Powertrain Control Module (PCM) is located in the engine compartment, at the right end of the firewall.

1 Disconnect the cable from the negative battery terminal (see Chapter 5, Section 1).

2 Disconnect the three large electrical connectors from the PCM (see illustration).

3 Remove the PCM mounting bolts (see illustration) and carefully remove the PCM from its mounting bracket.

✳ CAUTION:

Avoid static electricity damage to the computer by grounding yourself to the vehicle body before touching the PCM and using a special anti-static pad on which to store the PCM it is removed.

4 If you need to access something behind the PCM, such as the air conditioning evaporator hose fittings, remove the PCM mounting bracket (see illustration).

5 Installation is the reverse of removal.

2006 AND LATER MODELS

6 On these models you can remove and install the PCM but you cannot replace it. On 2006 and later models, a factory diagnostic scan tool is required to retrieve programming information from the old PCM so that this information can be loaded into the new PCM. On 2007 and later models, the tool is also needed to reprogram all keys after installing a new PCM. You can set the PCM aside or even remove it to access some other component, but you will not have the tools at home to reprogram the PCM and the keys after installing a new unit. Take the vehicle to a dealer service department or other qualified repair shop if the PCM requires replacement.

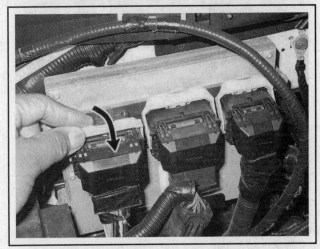

17.2 To disconnect the three electrical connectors from the PCM, flip each hinged connector lock forward, then carefully pull off each connector

17.3 To detach the PCM from its mounting bracket, remove these four bolts

17.4 To detach the PCM mounting bracket, remove these three bolts

18 Charge Motion Control Valve (CMCV) (5.4L V8 models) - removal and installation

◆ Refer to illustrations 18.2a and 18.2b

➡ **Note: The CMCV is used only on 5.4L V8 engines. The CMCV is located on the backside of the intake manifold (facing toward the firewall).**

1 Remove the intake manifold (see Chapter 2C).
2 Disconnect the outer ends of the CMCV actuator rods from the small actuator arms on the intake manifold (see illustrations).

3 Remove the CMCV mounting bolts and remove the CMCV from the intake manifold. Note the locations of the bolts; the one with the stud must go back into the same location, as it is the mounting point for a large wiring harness.

4 Installation is the reverse of removal.

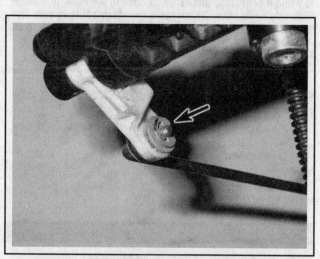

18.2a The CMCV actuator assembly (IMRC actuator assembly similar)

| A | Actuator | C | Actuator rods |
| B | Electrical terminal | D | Actuator arms |

18.2b Each of the CMCV actuator rods is retained to its crank arm on the intake manifold by a small E-clip

19 Fuel Pump Driver Module (FPDM) - replacement

◆ Refer to illustration 19.3

➡ **Note: The FPDM is located underneath the vehicle, on the crossmember just in front of the spare tire, which you'll need to remove to access the FPDM.**

1 Raise the rear of the vehicle and place it securely on jackstands.
2 Remove the spare tire (refer to your owner's manual, if necessary).
3 Disconnect the electrical connector from the FPDM (see illustration).
4 Remove the FPDM mounting bolts (see illustration 19.3) and remove the FPDM.
5 Installation is the reverse of removal.

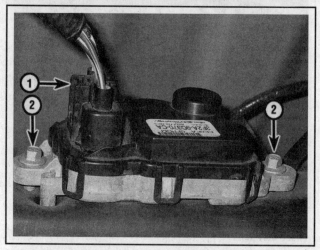

19.3 Depress this release tab (1) and pull off the electrical connector. Remove the mounting bolts (2) to remove the FPDM from the crossmember

20 Intake Manifold Runner Control (IMRC) actuator - replacement

➡ Note: Only 4.2L V6 engines are equipped with the IMRC actuator. The IMRC actuator is located on the backside of the intake manifold (facing toward the firewall). You will have to remove the intake manifold to access the IMRC actuator.

1 Remove the intake manifold (see Chapter 2A).
2 Disconnect the electrical connector from the IMRC actuator.

3 Disengage the outer ends of the two IMRC actuator rods from the actuator arms on the intake manifold (see illustration 18.2b).
4 Remove the three IMRC actuator mounting bolts and remove the IMRC actuator.
5 Installation is the reverse of removal.

21 Intake Manifold Tuning (IMT) valve - replacement

➡ Note: The IMT system is used only on 2004 and 2005 4.6L V8 models. The IMT valve is located on the front end of the intake manifold. You will have to remove the intake manifold to replace the IMT valve.

1 Remove the intake manifold (see Chapter 2C).

2 Disconnect the electrical connector from the IMT valve.
3 Remove the IMT valve mounting bolts and remove the IMT valve.
4 Remove the old O-ring from the IMT valve and install a new O-ring on the valve.
5 Installation is the reverse of removal.

22 Variable Camshaft Timing (VCT) oil control solenoid - replacement

3-VALVE 4.6L AND 5.4L V8 MODELS

▶ Refer to illustrations 22.3, 22.4 and 22.5

➡ Note: The VCT oil control solenoids (there are two, one per cylinder head) are located at the front end of each valve cover.

1 Disconnect the cable from the negative battery terminal (see Chapter 5, Section 1).
2 If you're removing the VCT oil control solenoid from the left valve cover, unbolt the power steering fluid reservoir and reservoir support bracket assembly (see *Valve covers - removal and installation* in Chapter 2C) and set the reservoir and support bracket aside. It's not neces-

sary to detach the power steering reservoir from its support bracket nor is it necessary to disconnect either of the power steering fluid hoses.
3 Disconnect the electrical connector from the VCT oil control solenoid (see illustration).
4 Remove the grommet that seals the mounting hole for the VCT oil control solenoid (see illustration).
5 Remove the VCT oil control solenoid mounting bolt (see illustration) and remove the VCT oil control solenoid.

➡ Note: This will require a long Torx driver.

6 Installation is the reverse of removal. Be sure to tighten the bolt to the torque listed in this Chapter's Specifications.

22.3 To disconnect the electrical connector from the VCT oil control solenoid, depress this release tab and pull off the connector

22.4 To remove the VCT oil control solenoid's grommet from the valve cover, carefully pull it out with pliers

22.5 To detach the VCT oil control solenoid from the cylinder head, remove this bolt and pull out the solenoid

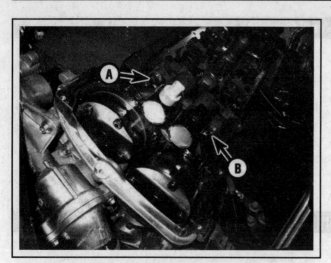

22.9 The mounting fasteners for the intake VCT (A) and the exhaust VCT (B) solenoids (3.7L V6 engine shown)

3.5L AND 3.7L V6, AND 5.0L AND 6.2L V8 MODELS

▶ Refer to illustration 22.9

➡ **Note: The VCT oil control solenoids are located under the valve covers; there is a VCT solenoid for each camshaft. The 3.5L and 3.7L V6 and 5.0L V8 each have four camshafts and four oil control solenoids. The 6.2L V8 has two camshafts and two oil control solenoids.**

7 Disconnect the cable from the negative battery terminal (see Chapter 5, Section 1).

8 Remove the right or left valve cover (see Chapter 2B or 2C).

9 Remove the fastener(s) securing the solenoids (see illustration).

10 Installation is the reverse of removal.

> ✳✳ **CAUTION:**
>
> **On 5.0L and 6.2L V8 engines, the pin in the center of the VCT solenoid must be fully depressed when installing the VCT solenoid. Failure to depress the pin could result in damage to the engine.**

11 Be sure to tighten the solenoid mounting fastener(s) to the tourque listed in this Chapter's Specifications.

---

23 Catalytic converters - general description, check and replacement

➡ **Note: Because of the Federally mandated extended warranty which covers emissions-related components such as the catalytic converter, check with a dealer service department before replacing the converter at your own expense.**

GENERAL DESCRIPTION

1 The catalytic converter is an emission control device installed in the exhaust system that reduces pollutants from the exhaust gas stream. There are two types of converters: The oxidation catalyst reduces the levels of hydrocarbon (HC) and carbon monoxide (CO) by adding oxygen to the exhaust stream to produce water vapor (H_2O) and carbon dioxide (CO_2). The reduction catalyst lowers the levels of oxides of nitrogen (NOx) by removing oxygen from the exhaust gases to produce nitrogen (N) and oxygen. These two types of catalysts are combined into a three-way catalyst that reduces all three pollutants.

2 The amount of oxygen entering the catalyst is critical to its operation because without oxygen it cannot convert harmful pollutants into harmless compounds. The catalyst is most efficient at capturing and storing oxygen when it converts the exhaust gases of an intake charge that's mixed at the ideal (stoichiometric) air/fuel ratio of 14.7:1. If the air/fuel ratio is leaner than stoichiometric for an extended period of time, the catalyst will store even more oxygen. But if the air/fuel ratio is richer than stoichiometric for any length of time, the oxygen content in the catalyst can become totally depleted. If this condition occurs, the catalyst will not convert anything!

3 Because the catalyst's ability to store oxygen is such an important factor in its operation, it can also be considered a factor in the catalyst's eventual inability to do its job. Catalysts do wear out. And one of the reasons that they do so is that they can no longer store oxygen. So the PCM monitors the oxygen content going into and coming out of the catalyst by comparing the voltage signals from the upstream and downstream oxygen sensors. When the catalyst is functioning correctly, there is very little oxygen to monitor at the outlet end of the catalyst because it's capturing, storing and releasing oxygen as needed to convert HC, CO and NOx into more benign substances. But as the catalyst ages, it slowly loses its ability to store oxygen, and the downstream oxygen sensor tells the PCM that the oxygen content in the catalyzed exhaust gases is going up. When the amount of oxygen exiting the catalyst reaches a specified threshold, the PCM stores a Diagnostic Trouble Code (DTC) and turns on the Malfunction Indicator Light (MIL).

CHECK

4 The equipment for testing a catalytic converter is expensive. If you suspect that the converter on your vehicle is malfunctioning, take it to a dealer or authorized emissions inspection facility for diagnosis and repair.

5 Whenever the vehicle is raised for servicing underbody components, inspect the converter for leaks, corrosion, dents and other damage. Inspect the welds/flange bolts that attach the front and rear ends of the converter to the exhaust system. If damage is discovered, the converter should be replaced.

6 Although catalytic converters don't break too often, they can become plugged. The easiest way to check for a restricted converter is to use a vacuum gauge to diagnose the effect of a blocked exhaust on intake vacuum.

a) *Connect a vacuum gauge to an intake manifold vacuum source (see Chapter 2).*

b) *Warm the engine to operating temperature, place the transaxle in Park (automatic) or Neutral (manual) and apply the parking brake.*

c) Note and record the vacuum reading at idle.
d) Quickly open the throttle to near full throttle and release it. Note and record the vacuum reading.
e) Perform the test three more times, recording the reading after each test.
f) If the reading after the fourth test is more than one in-Hg lower than the reading recorded at idle, the exhaust system may be restricted (the catalytic converter could be plugged or an exhaust pipe or muffler could be restricted).

REPLACEMENT

▶ **Refer to illustrations 23.9 and 23.10**

✳✳ **WARNING:**

Wait until the exhaust system is completely cool before beginning this procedure.

---

7   Raise the vehicle and place it securely on jackstands.
8   Disconnect the electrical connectors from the upstream and downstream oxygen sensors and remove the sensors so that neither of them is damaged when removing the catalyst assembly.
9   To separate the two catalyst assemblies from each other, loosen the clamp that secures the crossover pipe to the outlet pipe at the left catalyst assembly (see illustration). (The other end of the crossover pipe is welded to the right catalyst assembly.)
10   To disconnect the upper end of either catalyst assembly from the exhaust manifold, remove the pair of nuts that secure the upper mounting flange of the catalyst assembly to the exhaust manifold flange (see illustration).
11   Disengage the catalyst assembly from the exhaust manifold flange, from the crossover pipe (if you're removing the left catalyst assembly) and from the exhaust system behind the catalyst assembly.
12   Installation is the reverse of removal.

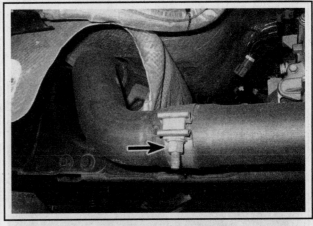

23.9 To separate the left and right catalyst assemblies from each other, loosen this nut on the clamp that secures the crossover pipe to the left catalyst assembly (5.4L V8 model shown, other models similar)

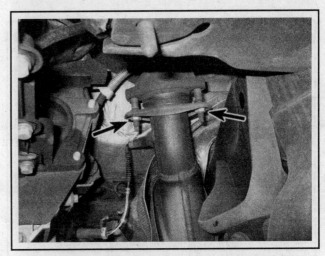

23.10 To disconnect either catalyst assembly from the exhaust manifold, remove these two nuts (5.4L V8 model shown, other models similar)

---

24 Evaporative emission control (EVAP) system - general description and component replacement

GENERAL DESCRIPTION

1   The Evaporative Emissions Control (EVAP) system absorbs fuel vapors (unburned hydrocarbons) and, during engine operation, releases them into the intake manifold from which they're drawn into the intake ports where they mix with the incoming air-fuel mixture.
2   The EVAP system consists of the EVAP canister, the vent solenoid, the filter tube, the dust separator and the canister purge valve. The EVAP canister, vent solenoid, filter tube and dust separator are located underneath the vehicle, above the spare tire (which you will have to remove to service any of these components). The EVAP canister purge valve is located in the engine compartment, on the firewall, near the brake fluid reservoir.

3   Other components in the EVAP system include the Fuel Tank Pressure (FTP) sensor, the Fuel Limit Vent Valve (FLVV) assembly, the fuel filler pipe check valve, the fuel filler neck cap and the EVAP system monitor.
4   The fuel filler neck cap prevents an overfilled tank from spilling out the filler neck and it prevents EVAP vapors from escaping out the filler neck to the atmosphere.
5   The FLVV assembly, which is mounted inside the fuel tank, controls the flow of fuel vapors entering the EVAP system, prevents the tank from overfilling during refueling and prevents liquid fuel from entering the EVAP lines if the vehicle gets out of control or rolls over. The FLVV cannot be serviced separately from the fuel tank.
6   The FTP sensor tells the PCM to energize the EVAP canister

24.9 To disconnect the electrical connector from the EVAP canister purge valve, depress this release tab and pull off the connector (2004 through 2008 model shown)

24.10a Disconnect the quick-connect couplings for the EVAP line going to the intake manifold (A) and for the EVAP line coming from the EVAP canister (B)

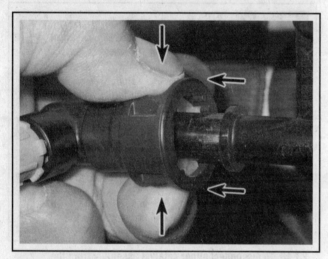

24.10b To disconnect the quick-connect coupling for the EVAP line coming from the EVAP canister, depress the two release tabs on the top and bottom of the coupling and pull it off the purge valve pipe

24.11 To disengage the EVAP canister purge valve from its mounting bracket, depress this release tab (A) with a small screwdriver and slide the purge valve out of the bracket

purge valve when the pressure inside the fuel tank is excessive. It also measures the (relative) vacuum conditions inside the fuel tank during an EVAP monitor test.

7   The EVAP system monitor is the test that the PCM runs to check the EVAP system and the fuel tank for leaks. This test is known as the "running loss system leak test." The EVAP system monitor runs this test as soon as the preconditions for purging have been met. There are two stages in the test. During the first stage the system monitor checks the EVAP system for big leaks. The EVAP canister vent solenoid is closed, but the canister purge valve stays open, which increases the (relative) vacuum in the EVAP system so that the FTP sensor can determine whether there is a leak somewhere in the system.

8   During the second stage of the running loss leak test, the canister purge valve closes and the FTP sensor monitors the "decay rate" (how long the system maintains an acceptable vacuum before leaking down) of the EVAP system. A slow decay rate indicates that there are no small leaks; a quick decay rate indicates that there's a small leak somewhere in the system.

COMPONENT REPLACEMENT

EVAP canister purge valve

▸ **Refer to illustrations 24.9, 24.10a, 24.10b and 24.11**

➡ **Note: On 2004 through 2008 models, the EVAP canister purge valve is located in the engine compartment, on the firewall, near the brake fluid reservoir. On 2009 and later models, the EVAP canister purge valve is mounted on the intake manifold.**

9   Disconnect the electrical connector from the EVAP canister purge valve (see illustration).

10 Disconnect the quick-connect couplings for the EVAP line coming from the EVAP canister and for the EVAP line going to the intake manifold (see illustrations). If you're unfamiliar with these types of quick-connect couplings, refer to "Fuel lines and fittings - general information" in Chapter 4.

11 Disengage the EVAP canister purge valve from its mounting bracket (see illustration) and remove it.

12 Installation is the reverse of removal.

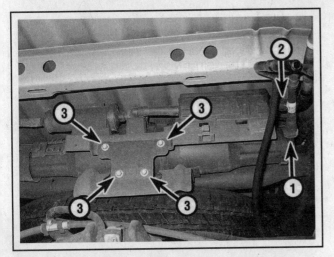

24.15a EVAP canister assembly details:

1   EVAP hose quick connect coupling (removed for clarity)
2   Fresh air inlet-hose
3   Mounting bracket bolts

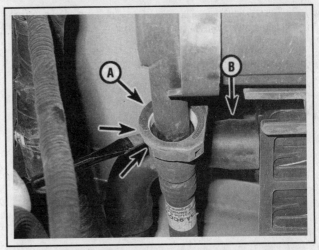

24.15b To disconnect the EVAP hose quick-connect coupling (A) from the EVAP canister, depress the release button with a small screwdriver and pull off the coupling. To disconnect the fresh air inlet hose (B) from the dust separator, pull it off the pipe on the separator

24.18 EVAP canister mounting bolt locations (the bolts are installed from above and are not visible in this photo)

24.19 To disconnect the connector from the vent solenoid, depress this release tab and pull off the connector

EVAP canister assembly

2004 through 2008 models

▶ **Refer to illustrations 24.15a, 24.15b, 24.18 and 24.19**

➡ **Note 1:** The EVAP canister assembly is located underneath the vehicle, above the spare tire. The canister assembly includes the EVAP canister, the canister heat shield, the dust separator, the canister vent solenoid, the filter tube, the hoses connecting all of these components and the large black plastic mounting bracket on which the canister and all of these components are mounted.

➡ **Note 2:** This procedure tells you how to remove the entire EVAP canister assembly, which includes not just the canister, but the canister vent solenoid, the filter tube and the dust separator.

13 Disconnect the cable from the negative battery terminal (see Chapter 5, Section 1).

14 Raise the rear of the vehicle and place it securely on jackstands.
15 Disconnect the EVAP hoses from the left end of the EVAP canister assembly (see illustrations).
16 Remove the four front canister mounting bolts from the EVAP canister's forward mounting bracket (see illustration 24.15a).
17 Remove the spare tire (refer to your owner's manual, if necessary).
18 Remove the four rear canister mounting bolts (see illustration).
19 Locate the electrical connector to the EVAP canister vent solenoid. The harness for this connector is routed across the top of the EVAP canister assembly. Trace the harness from the connector up to the pushpin retainer on top that secures the harness. When you have located the pushpin retainer, pull it up to detach it from the EVAP canister. Once the harness is detached from the EVAP canister, lower the canister assembly slightly, disconnect the electrical connector from the canister vent solenoid (see illustration), then remove the canister assembly.

20 The individual components of the assembly can now be inspected and, if necessary, replaced.

21 Installation is the reverse of removal.

2009 and later models

22 Disconnect the cable from the negative battery terminal (see Chapter 5, Section 1).

23 Raise the rear of the vehicle and place it securely on jackstands.

24 Disconnect the following quick-disconnect couplings:

a) *Fuel Tank Pressure (FTP) sensor and front vapor tube to EVAP canister.*

b) *Fuel tank supply tube-to-center fuel supply tube.*

c) *Front fuel supply tube-to-center fuel supply tube.*

d) *Front vapor tube-to-EVAP canister.*

25 Remove the vapor hose from the EVAP canister.

26 Disconnect the push pin retainer securing the center fuel supply tube to the frame.

27 Disconnect the electrical connector from the EVAP canister vent solenoid.

28 Remove the four canister mounting bolts and remove the canister assembly.

29 The individual components of the assembly can now be inspected, and, if necessary, replaced.

30 Installation is the reverse of removal.

---

25 Exhaust Gas Recirculation (EGR) system - general description and component replacement

→ **Note: Only 4.2L V6 and 2-valve 4.6L V8 engines are equipped with an EGR system.**

GENERAL DESCRIPTION

1 When you pull a trailer, pass another vehicle or go up a steep hill, the temperature inside the combustion chambers heats up. When the temperature inside the combustion chambers reaches 2500-degrees F., the engine begins to produce oxides of nitrogen (NOx), which is an odorless, colorless and toxic gas. The EGR system reduces NOx by introducing a controlled amount of spent exhaust gases into the intake manifold, which dilutes the air/fuel mixture, lowers combustion chamber temperatures and reduces the creation of NOx.

2 The EGR system, which is used on 4.2L V6 and 2-valve 4.6L V8 models, is the latest version of the manufacturer's Differential Pressure Feedback EGR (DPFE) system. A DPFE system consists of the Differential Pressure Feedback EGR sensor, the EGR Vacuum Regulator (EVR) solenoid, the EGR valve, the exhaust manifold-to-intake manifold pipe, the Powertrain Control Module (PCM) and the electrical wiring and vacuum hoses connecting these components.

3 The PCM relies on signals from the ECT, CHT, IAT, TP, MAF and CKP sensors to determine when the engine is fully warmed up, stabilized and running at a moderate load and rpm before it energizes the EGR system. The PCM does not turn on the EGR system at idle, or during extended wide-open-throttle conditions, or if it detects a failure of some EGR system component or the failure of some sensor input that it needs to control the EGR system.

4 The exhaust manifold-to-intake manifold pipe provides a path for the spent exhaust gases that are routed back through the intake manifold and into the combustion chambers. When the EGR valve is open, a metering orifice inside the exhaust manifold-to-intake manifold pipe produces a measurable pressure drop as the exhaust gases flow through it. A pair of pipes, one upstream and one downstream in relation to the orifice, send high and low pressure signals, respectively, to the DPFE sensor.

5 The DPFE sensor is a ceramic, capacitive-type pressure transducer that monitors the actual pressure drop (differential pressure) across the metering orifice and provides a proportional feedback signal between 0 and 5 volts to the PCM, which uses this signal to control the EGR flow rate.

6 The PCM calculates the correct amount of EGR flow for a given engine condition, uses the feedback signal from the DPFE sensor to determine the appropriate pressure drop across the metering orifice inside the exhaust manifold-to-intake manifold pipe that will create the correct flow, then outputs the appropriate signal to the EGR EVR solenoid.

7 The EGR EVR solenoid is controlled by a duty-cycle signal from the PCM that can be anywhere between 0 and 100 percent. The higher the duty cycle the greater the amount of vacuum diverted by the EVR solenoid to the EGR valve's vacuum diaphragm. When the vacuum signal through the EVR solenoid to the EGR valve diaphragm is strong enough to overcome the spring pressure that normally keeps the EGR valve closed, the EGR valve pintle lifts off its seat and allows exhaust gases to flow into the intake manifold.

8 The EGR system consists of the EGR system module and the exhaust manifold-to-intake manifold pipe. The EGR system module is similar to a DPFE-type EGR system described above, except that all of the DPFE system components are integrated into a single component.

9 The EGR transducer consists of a PCM-controlled solenoid and a backpressure transducer. When the PCM energizes the solenoid, no vacuum reaches the transducer; when the PCM de-energizes the solenoid, vacuum flows to the transducer. When exhaust backpressure reaches a specified threshold, it closes a bleed valve inside the transducer. When the bleed valve is closed by backpressure and the solenoid is de-energized by the PCM, vacuum flows through the transducer to operate the EGR valve. When exhaust backpressure has not fully closed the bleed valve and the PCM has de-energized the solenoid, a partial vacuum flows to the EGR valve, which reduces the amount of exhaust gases allowed to enter the engine.

COMPONENT REPLACEMENT

✳✳ WARNING:

Make sure that the engine is completely cooled off before beginning these procedures.

4.2L V6 MODELS

Exhaust manifold-to-EGR system module pipe

➡ **Note: The exhaust manifold-to-EGR system module pipe connects the right exhaust manifold to the mounting base of the EGR system module, which is bolted to the right side of the intake manifold.**

10 Unscrew the threaded fitting that connects the exhaust manifold-to-EGR system module pipe to the right exhaust manifold.

11 Unscrew the threaded fitting that connects the exhaust manifold-to-EGR system module pipe to the EGR system module.

12 Remove the exhaust manifold-to-EGR system module pipe.

13 Blow out the exhaust manifold-to-EGR system module pipe with compressed air.

14 Installation is the reverse of removal. Be sure to coat the threads of the fittings with anti-seize compound, then tighten the fittings securely.

EGR system module

15 Disconnect the cable from the negative battery terminal (see Chapter 5, Section 1).

16 Disconnect the vacuum connector from the EGR system module.

17 Disconnect the electrical connector from the EGR system module.

18 Remove the exhaust manifold-to-EGR system module pipe (see Steps 10 through 12).

19 Remove the two EGR system module mounting bolts and remove the EGR system module.

20 Remove and discard the old EGR system module gasket.

21 Clean off the gasket mating surfaces of the EGR system module and the intake manifold.

22 Installation is the reverse of removal. Be sure to use a new gasket and tighten the EGR system module mounting bolts to the torque listed in this Chapter's Specifications.

2-VALVE 4.6L V8 MODELS

Exhaust manifold-to-EGR system module pipe

➡ **Note: The exhaust manifold-to-EGR system module pipe connects the left exhaust manifold to the mounting base of the EGR system module, which is bolted to the left side of the intake manifold.**

23 Remove the nut that attaches the power brake booster vacuum hose to the EGR system module, detach the brake booster hose bracket from the module and set the booster hose and bracket aside.

24 Unscrew the threaded fitting that connects the exhaust manifold-to-EGR system module pipe to the left exhaust manifold.

25 Unscrew the threaded fitting that connects the exhaust manifold-to-EGR system module pipe to the EGR system module.

26 Remove the exhaust manifold-to-EGR system module pipe.

27 Blow out the exhaust manifold-to-EGR system module pipe with compressed air.

28 Installation is the reverse of removal. Be sure to coat the threads of the fittings with anti-seize compound, then tighten the fittings securely.

EGR system module

29 Disconnect the cable from the negative battery terminal (see Chapter 5, Section 1).

30 Disconnect the electrical connector from the EGR system module.

31 Disconnect the vacuum connector from the EGR system module.

32 Remove the exhaust manifold-to-EGR system module pipe (see Steps 23 through 26).

33 Remove the EGR system module mounting bolt and stud/bolt and remove the EGR system module.

34 Remove and discard the old EGR system module gasket.

35 Clean off the gasket mating surfaces of the EGR system module and the intake manifold.

36 Installation is the reverse of removal. Be sure to use a new gasket and tighten the EGR system module mounting bolts to the torque listed in this Chapter's Specifications.

Torque specifications   **Ft-lbs (unless otherwise indicated)**

→ **Note: One foot-pound (ft-lb) of torque is equivalent to 12 inch-pounds (in-lbs) of torque. Torque values below approximately 15 ft-lbs are expressed in inch-pounds, since most foot-pound torque wrenches are not accurate at these smaller values.**

Cylinder Head Temperature (CHT) sensor	
(all engines)	89 in-lbs
Engine oil temperature sensor (all engines)	15
Exhaust Gas Recirculation (EGR) valve (4.2L V6 and 2-valve 4.6L V8)	
EGR valve mounting bolts	18
Exhaust manifold-to-EGR valve tube	
fittings (both ends)	30
Fuel rail pressure sensor mounting bolts	
4.2L V6	44 in-lbs
4.6L and 5.4L V8	35 in-lbs
Knock sensor retaining bolt (all engines)	15
Oxygen sensors (all engines, all sensors)	34
Variable Camshaft Timing (VCT) oil control solenoid mounting bolt	
3.5L and 3.7L V6 engines	
Step 1	71 in-lbs
Step 2	Tighten an additional 20-degrees
4.6L and 5.4L V8 engines	44 in-lbs
5.0L and 6.2L V8 engines	
Step 1	89 in-lbs
Sep 2	Tighten an additional 45-degrees

7A

MANUAL
TRANSMISSION

Section

1   General information
2   Shift lever - removal and installation
3   Oil seal - replacement
4   Transmission mount - check and replacement
5   Manual transmission - removal and installation
6   Manual transmission overhaul - general information

Reference to other Chapters

Manual transmission lubricant - change - See Chapter 1
Manual transmission lubricant level - check - See Chapter 1

1 General information

Vehicles covered by this manual are equipped with either a five-speed manual or a four-speed automatic transmission. The M5OD is a fully-synchronized, five-speed manual transmission with an overdrive fifth gear. Information on the manual transmission is included in this Part of Chapter 7. Information on the automatic transmission can be found in Part B of this Chapter. You'll also find certain procedures common to both transmissions - such as oil seal replacement - in Part A. Information on the transfer case used on 4WD models can be found in Part C.

Depending on the expense involved in having a transmission overhauled, it might be a better idea to consider replacing it with either a used or rebuilt unit. Your local dealer or transmission shop should be able to supply information concerning cost, availability and exchange policy. Regardless of how you decide to remedy a transmission problem, you can still save a lot of money by removing and installing the unit yourself.

2 Shift lever - removal and installation

▶ **Refer to illustration 2.2a and 2.2b**

1   Remove the shift lever boot retainer clips and pull up the boot.
2   Remove the shift lever nut (see illustration) and install it onto the other side of the stud. Tighten the nut to remove the eccentric (see illustration) and lift up on the shift lever.

3   To remove the inner shift lever boot (the black rubber square-shaped boot below the shift lever), remove the four boot retaining screws (see illustration 2.2b) and replace it.
4   Installation is the reverse of removal. Be sure to tighten the nut on the shift lever eccentric stud securely.

2.2a To remove the shift lever, remove the nut and install it on the other side of the stud . . .

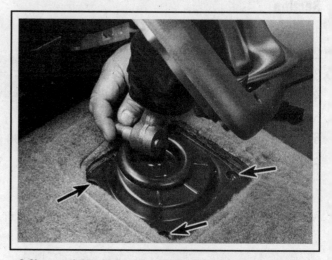

2.2b . . . tighten the nut to remove the eccentric stud and the shift lever; to remove the inner shift lever boot, remove the four screws

3 Oil seal - replacement

EXTENSION HOUSING SEAL

▶ **Refer to illustrations 3.4 and 3.5**

➡ **Note: This procedure applies to both manual and automatic transmissions.**

1   Oil leaks frequently occur due to wear of the extension housing oil seal or the transmission speed sensor seal. Replacement of these seals is relatively easy, since the repairs can usually be performed without removing the transmission from the vehicle.
2   If you suspect a leak at the extension housing seal, raise the vehicle and support it securely on jackstands. The extension housing

seal is located at the rear end of the transmission, where the driveshaft is attached. If the extension housing seal is leaking, transmission lubricant will be evident on the front of the driveshaft and may be dripping from the rear of the transmission.

3   Remove the driveshaft (see Chapter 8).
4   Using a soft-face hammer, carefully tap off the dust shield, if equipped. Be careful not to distort it. Using a screwdriver, pry bar or seal removal tool, carefully pry out the extension housing seal (see illustration). Do not damage the splines on the transmission output shaft.
5   Using a seal driver or a large deep socket, install the new extension housing seal (see illustration). Drive it into the bore squarely and make sure it's completely seated. Install the dust shield (if equipped) by

3.4 Remove the extension housing seal with a seal removal tool

3.5 Install the new extension housing seal with a seal driver or a large deep socket

carefully tapping it into place.

6   Lubricate the splines of the transmission output shaft and the outside of the driveshaft sleeve yoke with multi-purpose grease, then install the driveshaft (see Chapter 8). Be careful not to damage the lip of the new seal. Lower the vehicle.

TRANSMISSION SPEED SENSOR O-RING

7   The transmission speed sensor is located on the left side of the transmission extension housing (2WD models) or on the left side of the transfer case extension housing (4WD models). For information and O-ring replacement for the transmission speed sensor, see Chapter 6.

4   Transmission mount - check and replacement

CHECK

▶ **Refer to illustration 4.1**

1   Insert a large screwdriver or prybar into the space between the transmission and the crossmember and try to pry the transmission up (see illustration). If there is any separation of the rubber, the mount is worn out.

REPLACEMENT

▶ **Refer to illustrations 4.2 and 4.3**

2   Remove the nuts attaching the mount to the crossmember (see illustration).

4.1 To check the transmission mount, insert a prybar or large screwdriver and try to lever the transmission up and down; if the transmission is easily moved, look closely at the rubber insulator part of the mount - it's probably torn or cracked, and must be replaced

4.2 Remove the transmission mount-to-crossmember nuts

4.3 Remove the transmission mount bolts and remove the mount (crossmember removed for clarity)

3 Raise the transmission with a floor jack until the mount studs clear the crossmember, then remove the bolts attaching the mount to the transmission. Remove the mount (see illustration).

4 Installation is the reverse of the removal procedure. Be sure to tighten the nuts/bolts to the torque listed in this Chapter's Specifications.

5 Manual transmission - removal and installation

REMOVAL

▶ **Refer to illustrations 5.21, 5.22 and 5.24**

1 Disconnect the cable from the negative battery terminal (see Chapter 5, Section 1).

2 Place the transmission in NEUTRAL.

3 Remove the shift lever and inner shift lever boot (see Section 2).

4 Raise the vehicle and support it securely on jackstands.

5 Remove the driveshaft(s) (see Chapter 8).

6 Disconnect the clutch hydraulic line (see Chapter 8).

7 Remove the starter motor (see Chapter 5).

8 Remove the fuel line and harness bracket located on the top of the transmission.

9 Remove all exhaust components that will interfere with transmission removal (see Chapter 4).

10 Remove the exhaust hangers and the exhaust pipe heat shield(s).

➡ **Note: There are two exhaust heat shield bolts mounted on each side of the transmission crossmember.**

11 On 4WD models, remove the skid plate and transfer case (see Chapter 7C).

12 Disconnect the electrical connectors from the two upstream oxygen sensors and the two downstream oxygen sensors (see Chapter 6).

13 Disconnect the back-up light switch connector.

14 Disconnect the transmission speed sensor connector (see Chapter 6).

15 Remove the stabilizer bar and brackets (see Chapter 10).

16 Support the engine with a floor jack. Put a block of wood between the jack head and the engine oil pan to protect the pan.

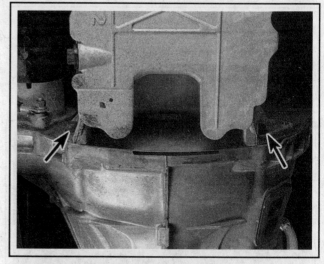

5.21 Remove the oil pan-to-transmission bolts

17 Remove the two transmission mount-to-crossmember nuts (see illustration 4.2).

18 Place a transmission jack or a floor jack under the transmission and secure the transmission to the jack with safety chains.

19 Raise the transmission slightly to take the weight off the crossmember, then remove the rear crossmember.

20 Remove the transmission mount (see Section 4).

21 Remove the oil pan-to-transmission bolts (see illustration).

5.22 The top transmission-to-engine bolts can be accessed using a special long extension attached to the ratchet wrench

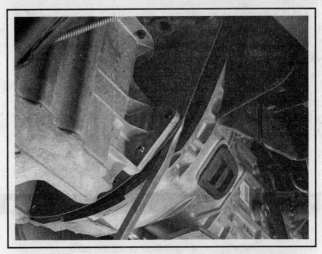

5.24 If the transmission input shaft hangs up on the clutch hub, the transmission may be difficult to separate from the engine; if this happens, carefully separate the two with a large prybar as shown

22 Remove the engine-to-transmission bolts (see illustration).

23 Remove the exhaust pipe-to-exhaust manifold nuts from both exhaust pipe flanges (see Chapter 4).

24 Make a final check that all wires have been disconnected from the transmission, then move the transmission and jack toward the rear of the vehicle until the transmission input shaft is clear of the clutch or clutch housing. If the transmission input shaft is difficult to disengage from the clutch hub, use a prybar to separate the transmission from the engine (see illustration). Keep the transmission level as you pull it to the rear.

25 Once the input shaft is clear, lower the transmission and remove it from under the vehicle.

✳✳ CAUTION:

Do not depress the clutch pedal while the transmission is out of the vehicle.

26 Inspect the clutch components. Generally speaking, new clutch components should always be installed whenever the transmission is removed (see Chapter 8).

INSTALLATION

27 Install the clutch components, if they were removed (see Chapter 8).

28 With the transmission secured to the jack, raise it into position behind the engine and carefully slide it forward, engaging the input shaft with the clutch plate hub. Do not use excessive force to install

the transmission - if the input shaft won't slide into place, readjust the angle of the transmission or turn the input shaft so the splines engage properly with the clutch.

29 Once the transmission is flush with the engine, install the transmission-to-engine and the oil pan-to-engine bolts. Tighten the bolts to the torque listed in this Chapter's Specifications.

✳✳ CAUTION:

Don't use the bolts to force the transmission and engine together. If the transmission doesn't slide up to the engine easily, find out what's wrong before proceeding.

30 Install the transmission mount and crossmember. Tighten all nuts and bolts to the torque listed in this Chapter's Specifications.

31 Remove the jacks supporting the transmission and the engine.

32 Install the various components removed previously. Refer to Chapter 7, Part C, for installation of the transfer case (if equipped), Chapter 8 for the installation of the driveshaft(s) and Chapter 4 for information regarding the exhaust system components. To connect the clutch hydraulic line and bleed the clutch hydraulic system, refer to Chapter 8.

33 Make a final check to verify all wires and hoses have been reconnected and the transmission has been filled with lubricant to the proper level (see Chapter 1). Lower the vehicle.

34 Install the inner shift lever boot, the shift lever and the outer boot (see Section 2).

35 Connect the negative battery cable. Road test the vehicle and check for leaks.

6   Manual transmission overhaul - general information

Overhauling a manual transmission is a difficult job for the do-it-yourselfer. It involves the disassembly and reassembly of many small parts. Numerous clearances must be precisely measured and, if necessary, changed with select fit spacers and snap-rings. As a result,

if transmission problems arise, it can be removed and installed by a competent do-it-yourselfer, but overhaul should be left to a transmission repair shop. Rebuilt transmissions may be available - check with your dealer parts department and auto parts stores. At any rate, the time and money involved in an overhaul is almost sure to exceed the cost of a rebuilt unit.

Nevertheless, it's not impossible for an inexperienced mechanic to rebuild a transmission if the special tools are available and the job is done in a deliberate step-by-step manner so nothing is overlooked.

The tools necessary for an overhaul include internal and external snap-ring pliers, a bearing puller, a slide hammer, a set of pin punches, a dial indicator and possibly a hydraulic press. In addition, a large, sturdy workbench and a vise or transmission stand will be required.

During disassembly of the transmission, make careful notes of how each piece comes off, where it fits in relation to other pieces and what holds it in place.

Before taking the transmission apart for repair, it will help if you have some idea what area of the transmission is malfunctioning. Certain problems can be closely tied to specific areas in the transmission, which can make component examination and replacement easier. Refer to the *Troubleshooting* section at the front of this manual for information regarding possible sources of trouble.

Torque specifications	Ft-lbs
Oil pan-to-transmission bolts	25
Transmission crossmember-to-chassis bolts	66
Transmission-to-engine bolts	44
Transmission mount-to-crossmember nuts	72
Transmission mount-to-transmission bolts	59

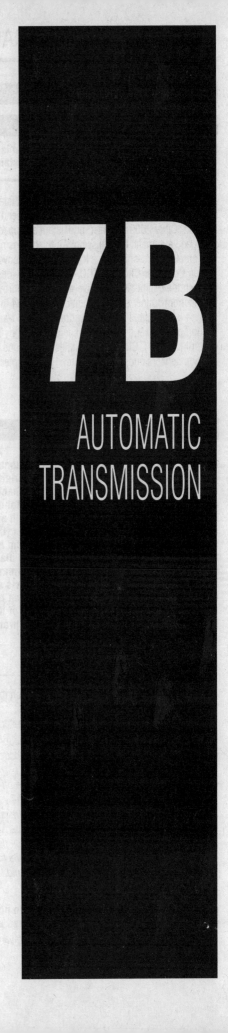

7B

AUTOMATIC TRANSMISSION

Section

1 General information
2 Diagnosis - general
3 Shift lever (center console models) - removal and installation
4 Shift cable - check, replacement and adjustment
5 Brake Transmission Shift Interlock (BTSI) system - description, check and replacement
6 Gear position indicator cable adjustment (models with a steering column-mounted shifter)
7 Transmission fluid cooler (2006 through 2008 models) - removal and installation
8 Automatic transmission - removal and installation
9 Automatic transmission overhaul - general information

Reference to other Chapters

Automatic transmission fluid and filter change - See Chapter 1
Automatic transmission fluid level check - See Chapter 1
Digital Transmission Range (DTR) sensor - description, adjustment and replacement - See Chapter 6
Oil seal - replacement - See Chapter 7A
Transmission mount - check and replacement - See Chapter 7A

1 General information

❋ CAUTION:

If a vehicle with an automatic transmission is disabled, do NOT tow it at speeds greater than 30 mph or distances over 50 miles.

All 2004 through 2008 and some 2009 and later models are equipped with either a 4R70E or 4R75E four-speed automatic transmission. Other 2009 and later models are equipped with the 6R80 six-speed automatic transmission. All three transmissions are equipped with an electronic-shift with a lock-up torque converter, known as a Torque Converter Clutch or TCC. The TCC provides a direct connection between the engine and the drive wheels for improved efficiency and fuel economy under certain conditions. On 2004 through 2008 models, shifting is controlled by the Powertrain Control Module (PCM), while shifting on 2009 and later models is controlled by the Transmission Control Module (TCM). Both modules use various engine and transmission sensors and output actuators (see Chapter 6). Downshifting is controlled by either the PCM or TCM in response to certain conditions. Each condition is listed in a specialized category: Coastdown, Torque Demand and Kickdown. Coastdown shifting occurs during a slow vehicle stop. Torque Demand occurs during part throttle acceleration under load. Kickdown occurs when the vehicle requires extra speed during passing or heavy acceleration.

Because of the complexity of the clutches and the electronic and hydraulic control systems, and because of the special tools and expertise needed to overhaul an automatic transmission, diagnosis and repair of this transmission should be handled by a dealer service department or a transmission repair shop. The procedures in this Chapter are limited to general diagnosis, routine maintenance and adjustment: replacing the shift lever, replacing and adjusting the shift cable, and similar jobs. Serious repair work, however, must be done by a transmission specialist. But if the transmission must be rebuilt or replaced, you can save money by removing and installing it yourself, so instructions for that procedure are included as well.

2 Diagnosis - general

➡ **Note: Automatic transmission malfunctions may be caused by five general conditions: poor engine performance, improper adjustments, hydraulic malfunctions, mechanical malfunctions or malfunctions in the computer or its signal network. Diagnosis of these problems should always begin with a check of the easily repaired items: fluid level and condition (Chapter 1), and shift cable adjustment. Next, perform a road test to determine if the problem has been corrected or if more diagnosis is necessary. If the problem persists after the preliminary tests and corrections are completed, additional diagnosis should be done by a dealer service department or transmission repair shop. Refer to the Troubleshooting section at the front of this manual for information on symptoms of transmission problems.**

PRELIMINARY CHECKS

1   Drive the vehicle to warm the transmission to normal operating temperature.

2   Check the fluid level as described in Chapter 1:

a) *If the fluid level is unusually low, add enough fluid to bring the level within the designated area of the dipstick, then check for external leaks (see below).*

b) *If the fluid level is abnormally high, drain off the excess, then check the drained fluid for contamination by coolant. The presence of engine coolant in the automatic transmission fluid indicates that a failure has occurred in the internal radiator walls that separate the coolant from the transmission fluid (see Chapter 3).*

c) *If the fluid is foaming, drain it and refill the transmission, then check for coolant in the fluid or a high fluid level.*

3   Check the engine idle speed.

➡ **Note: If the engine is malfunctioning, do not proceed with the preliminary checks until it has been repaired and runs normally.**

4   Inspect the shift cable (see Section 4). Make sure it's properly adjusted and operates smoothly.

FLUID LEAK DIAGNOSIS

5   Most fluid leaks are easy to locate visually. Repair usually consists of replacing a seal or gasket. If a leak is difficult to find, the following procedure may help.

6   Identify the fluid. Make sure it's transmission fluid and not engine oil or brake fluid (automatic transmission fluid is a deep red color).

7   Try to pinpoint the source of the leak. Drive the vehicle several miles, then park it over a large sheet of cardboard. After a minute or two, you should be able to locate the leak by determining the source of the fluid dripping onto the cardboard.

8   Make a careful visual inspection of the suspected component and the area immediately around it. Pay particular attention to gasket mating surfaces. A mirror is often helpful for finding leaks in areas that are hard to see.

9   If the leak still cannot be found, clean the suspected area thoroughly with a degreaser or solvent, then dry it.

10   Drive the vehicle for several miles at normal operating temperature and varying speeds. After driving the vehicle, visually inspect the suspected component again.

11   Once the leak has been located, the cause must be determined before it can be properly repaired. If a gasket is replaced but the sealing flange is bent, the new gasket will not stop the leak. The bent flange must be straightened.

12   Before attempting to repair a leak, check to make sure the following conditions are corrected or they may cause another leak.

➡ **Note: Some of the following conditions cannot be fixed without highly specialized tools and expertise. Such problems must be referred to a transmission repair shop or a dealer service department.**

Gasket leaks

13   Check the pan periodically. Make sure the bolts are tight, no bolts are missing, the gasket is in good condition and the pan is flat (dents in the pan may indicate damage to the valve body inside).

14 If the pan gasket is leaking, the fluid level or the fluid pressure may be too high, the vent may be plugged, the pan bolts may be too tight, the pan sealing flange may be warped, the sealing surface of the transmission housing may be damaged, the gasket may be damaged or the transmission casting may be cracked or porous. If sealant instead of gasket material has been used to form a seal between the pan and the transmission housing, it may be the wrong sealant.

Seal leaks

15 If a transmission seal is leaking, the fluid level or pressure may be too high, the vent may be plugged, the seal bore may be damaged, the seal itself may be damaged or improperly installed, the surface of the shaft protruding through the seal may be damaged or a loose bearing may be causing excessive shaft movement.

16 Make sure the dipstick tube seal is in good condition and the tube is properly seated. Periodically check the area around the speedometer gear or sensor for leakage. If transmission fluid is evident, check the O-ring for damage.

Case leaks

17 If the case itself appears to be leaking, the casting is porous and will have to be repaired or replaced.

18 Make sure the oil cooler hose fittings are tight and in good condition.

Fluid comes out vent pipe or fill tube

19 If this condition occurs, the transmission is overfilled, there is coolant in the fluid, the case is porous, the dipstick is incorrect, the vent is plugged or the drain back holes are plugged.

3 Shift lever (center console models) - removal and installation

1 Set the parking brake, then place the shift lever in the Neutral position.

2 Remove the center console side panels and top console shift cover (see Chapter 11).

3 Separate the shift cable end from the shift lever using a screwdriver or trim panel tool.

4 Disconnect the shift cable from the shift assembly mounting bracket.

5 Disconnect the shift lock solenoid electrical connector.

6 Remove the four bolts and remove the shift lever assembly from the floor.

7 Installation is the reverse of the removal procedure. Adjust the shift cable if necessary (see Section 4).

4 Shift cable - check, replacement and adjustment

※※ WARNING:

The models covered by this manual are equipped with a Supplemental Restraint System (SRS), more commonly known as airbags. Always disable the airbag system before working in the vicinity of any airbag system component to avoid the possibility of accidental deployment of the airbag(s), which could cause personal injury (see Chapter 12). Do not use a memory saving device to preserve the PCM or radio memory when working on or near airbag system components.

CHECK

1 Firmly apply the parking brake and try to momentarily operate the starter in each shift lever position. The starter should only operate when the manual shift lever is in the PARK or NEUTRAL positions. If the starter operates in any position other than PARK or NEUTRAL, adjust the shift cable (see later in this Section). If, after adjustment, the starter still operates in positions other than PARK or NEUTRAL, the Digital Transmission Range (DTR) sensor is defective (see Chapter 6).

REPLACEMENT

Steering column-mounted shifter

2 Make sure the manual shift lever is in the NEUTRAL position.

3 Raise the vehicle and place it securely on jackstands.

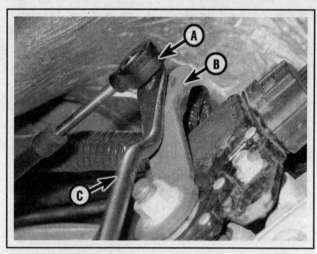

4.4 Pry the cable end (A) off the transmission shift lever (B) using a screwdriver or trim panel tool (C)

4.5 Use a screwdriver to lift the cable retainer to release it from the housing, then separate the shift cable from the transmission bracket

4.10 Disengage the shift cable (A) from the controller ballstud (B) under the steering column

4.11 Pry the cable housing off the steering column bracket in the direction of the arrow

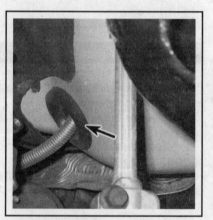

4.12 Remove the shift cable grommet from the firewall

2004 models

▶ **Refer to illustrations 4.4 and 4.5**

4 Working at the transmission, pry the cable end off the transmission shift lever using a screwdriver or panel tool (see illustration).

5 Release the cable retainer and separate the shift cable from the transmission bracket (see illustration).

2005 and later models

6 Working at the transmission, disconnect the shift cable from the transmission shift lever by pulling UP on the lock tab.

7 Release the cable retainer and separate the shift cable from the transmission bracket.

➡ **Note: 4.2L models are equipped with a bolt and nut mounted bracket on the side of the transmission.**

All models

▶ **Refer to illustrations 4.10, 4.11 and 4.12**

8 Lower the vehicle.

9 Working inside the passenger compartment, remove the knee bolster and the steering column covers (see Chapter 11).

10 Disengage the shift cable from the controller ballstud under the steering column (see illustration).

11 Pry the cable housing from the bracket under the steering column (see illustration).

12 Remove the shift cable grommet (see illustration) from the firewall.

13 Remove the shift cable through the hole in the firewall and toward the transmission.

14 Installation is the reverse of removal. Adjust the cable (see later in this Section).

Center console-mounted shifter

15 Place the shift lever in the NEUTRAL position.

16 Remove the center console side panels and top console shift cover (see Chapter 11).

17 Raise the vehicle and support it on jackstands.

2004 models

18 Working at the transmission, pry the cable end off the transmission shift lever (see illustration 4.4).

19 Disconnect the shift cable from the shift assembly mounting bracket (see illustration 4.5).

2005 and later models

20 Working at the transmission, disconnect the cable end from the transmission shift lever. Release the mechanism by rotating the lock upward and disconnect the lock (cable end) from the shift lever.

21 Separate the shift cable from the transmission bracket.

All center console models

22 Lower the vehicle.

23 Working inside the passenger's compartment, remove the shift cable from the selector shaft.

24 Release the cable retainer and separate the shift cable from transmission bracket.

25 Remove the shift cable grommet from the firewall.

26 Remove the shift cable through the hole in the firewall toward the transmission.

27 Installation is the reverse of removal. Adjust the cable (see below).

ADJUSTMENT

28 Working in the passenger's compartment, move the shift lever into the 1st position and back into the DRIVE position. Place a three-pound weight (approximate) on the lever to hold it in position, or have an assistant hold it there.

➡ Note: On center console types, it may be necessary to have an assistant apply slight pressure on the shift lever to keep it stationary.

29 Raise the vehicle and support it securely on jackstands.

Steering column-mounted shifter

2004 models

▶ Refer to illustration 4.32

30 Working at the transmission, pry the cable end off the transmission shift lever using a panel tool or screwdriver.

31 Move the manual shift lever to the FIRST gear position, then move it back two detent positions to the DRIVE position.

32 Slide the lock tab on the adjusting mechanism at the transmission bracket UP to release (see illustration). The cable should slide forward and backward through the adjuster.

33 Reattach the shift cable to the transmission shift lever and move the cable to adjust the position to the shift lever. The manual shift lever should remain stationary.

34 Slide the lock tab DOWN to lock the shift cable into position.

2005 and later models

➡ Note: The adjusting mechanism on 2005 and later models is built into the lock mechanism located on the cable end.

35 Working at the transmission, disconnect the shift cable from the transmission shift lever by pulling UP on the lock tab.

36 Move the manual shift lever to the FIRST gear position, then move it back two detent positions to the DRIVE position.

37 Reattach the shift cable to the transmission shift lever and lock the shift cable lock tab.

4.32 Use a screwdriver to pry the lock tab (A) on the adjusting mechanism in the direction of the arrow (B) to release the mechanism from the locked setting

Center console-mounted shifter

2004 models

38 Working at the transmission, pry the cable end off the transmission shift lever using a panel tool or screwdriver.

39 Move the manual shift lever to the FIRST gear position, then move it back two detent positions to the DRIVE position.

40 Slide the lock tab on the adjusting mechanism at the transmission bracket UP to release (see illustration 4.32). The cable should be able to move freely through the adjuster.

41 Reattach the shift cable to the transmission shift lever and move the cable to adjust the position to the transmission shift lever. The manual shift lever should remain stationary.

42 Slide the lock tab DOWN to lock the shift cable into position.

2005 and later models

➡ Note: The adjusting mechanism on 2005 and later models is built into the lock mechanism located on the cable end.

43 Working at the transmission, disconnect the cable end from the transmission shift lever. Release the mechanism by rotating the lock upward and disconnect the lock (cable end) from the transmission shift lever.

44 Install the shift cable onto the transmission shift lever and rotate the lock (cable end) down to lock the adjuster.

All models

45 Remove the jackstands and lower the vehicle.

46 Remove the weight from the manual shift lever, if used.

47 Move the manual shift lever through all gear positions and verify that the indicated positions correspond with the actual gear positions at the manual shift lever. Also verify that the engine will start only in PARK and NEUTRAL, and that the back-up lights come on when the manual shift lever is placed in REVERSE. If necessary, readjust the cable until these conditions are met. It may also be necessary to adjust the transmission range sensor (see Chapter 6).

5 Brake Transmission Shift Interlock (BTSI) system - description, check and replacement

❋❋ WARNING:

The models covered by this manual are equipped with a Supplemental Restraint System (SRS), more commonly known as airbags. Always disable the airbag system before working in the vicinity of any airbag system component to avoid the possibility of accidental deployment of the airbag(s), which could cause personal injury (see Chapter 12). Do not use a memory saving device to preserve the PCM or radio memory when working on or near airbag system components.

DESCRIPTION

1   The Brake Transmission Shift Interlock (BTSI) system is a solenoid-operated device, located behind the clockspring on the steering column (steering column type) or under the shift lever in the center console (center console type). The solenoid locks the shift lever into the PARK position when the ignition key is in the LOCK or ACCESSORY position. When the ignition key is in the RUN position, a magnetic holding device is energized. When the system is functioning correctly, the only way to unlock the shift lever and move it out of PARK is to depress the brake pedal. The BTSI system also prevents the ignition key from being turned to the LOCK or ACCESSORY position unless the shift lever is fully locked into the PARK position.

CHECK

2   Verify that the ignition key can be removed only in the PARK position.

3   When the shift lever is in the PARK position, you should be able to rotate the ignition key from OFF to LOCK. But when the shift lever is in any gear position other than PARK (including NEUTRAL), you should not be able to rotate the ignition key to the LOCK position.

4   You should not be able to move the shift lever out of the PARK position when the ignition key is turned to the OFF position.

5   You should not be able to move the shift lever out of the PARK position when the ignition key is turned to the RUN or START position until you depress the brake pedal.

6   You should not be able to move the shift lever out of the PARK position when the ignition key is turned to the ACC or LOCK position.

7   Once in gear, with the ignition key in the RUN position, you should be able to move the shift lever between gears, or put it into NEUTRAL or PARK, without depressing the brake pedal.

SOLENOID REPLACEMENT

8   Place the shift lever in Neutral, then disconnect the cable from the negative terminal of the battery (see Chapter 5, Section 1).

Steering column-mounted shifter

▶ Refer to illustrations 5.12 and 5.14

9   Remove the lower trim panel and the knee bolster (Chapter 11).

10 Remove the steering column covers (see Chapter 11).

11 Remove the steering wheel and the clockspring from the steering column (see Chapter 10).

12 Release the BTSI electrical connector (see illustration).

13 Remove the clockspring/steering column cover mounting bracket.

14 Carefully pull back the BTSI solenoid locking tab (see illustration) and separate the solenoid from the steering column.

15 Installation is the reverse of the removal.

Center console-mounted shifter

16 Disconnect the manual shift lever (see Section 3).

17 Working at the center console, disconnect the overdrive cancel button electrical connector. Cut the tie strap retaining the harness and separate the overdrive cancel button wiring from the console.

18 Remove the center console illumination bulb from the housing.

19 Disconnect the BTSI electrical connector. Cut the tie strap retaining the harness and separate the BTSI wiring from the console.

20 Remove the two mounting screws from the BTSI solenoid and separate the solenoid from the center console.

21 Installation is the reverse of removal.

5.12 Location of the Brake Transmission Shift Interlock (BTSI) solenoid connector

5.14 Remove the mounting plate for the clockspring/steering column covers (A - it's secured by three screws), then pry the tang (B) back and separate the solenoid from the column

SHIFT LOCK OVERRIDE FEATURE

▶ **Refer to illustration 5.22**

22 In the event the Brake Transmission Shift Interlock (BTSI) system fails and the shift lever cannot be moved out of gear, the system is equipped with an override feature. The BTSI system can be bypassed and the shift lever can be used in manual operation.

    a) On models with a steering column-mounted shifter, locate the round access plug under the steering column cover (see illustration) and remove the plug using a small-tipped screwdriver. Press the override button with a screwdriver, press the brake pedal and shift the column shift lever into NEUTRAL.

    b) On models with a center console-mounted shifter, remove the center console trim panels (see Chapter 11). Locate the white button alongside the BTSI solenoid on the driver's side of the center console, press the button and shift the console select lever into NEUTRAL.

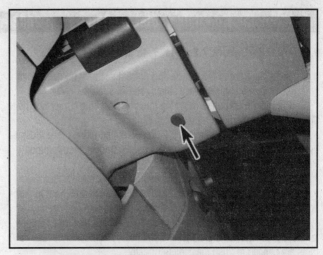

5.22 Location of the rubber plug for access to the Brake Transmission Shift Interlock (BTSI) system override button on steering column models

---

6   Gear position indicator cable adjustment (models with a steering column-mounted shifter)

▶ **Refer to illustration 6.7**

1 Remove the lower trim panel and the knee bolster (Chapter 11).

2 Remove the steering column covers (see Chapter 11).

3 Position the shift lever in the DRIVE position.

4 Move the shift lever until it stops (all the way to the 1st gear position) then move it back two detent positions to the DRIVE position.

5 Hang a three pound weight to the shift lever to maintain position.

6 Center the indicator needle (the pointer in the middle of the DRIVE position).

7 Rotate the adjuster (thumbwheel) on the bottom of the steering column (see illustration) to remove all slack from the adjuster cable. Make sure the indicator needle centers directly on the D.

6.7 Location of the gear position indicator adjuster (thumbwheel)

7 Transmission fluid cooler (2006 through 2008 models) - removal and installation

▶ Refer to illustrations 7.2, 7.4a, 7.4b and 7.5

1   Raise the front of the vehicle and place it securely on jackstands.

2   Remove the engine splash shield (see illustration).

3   Put a drain pan underneath the transmission fluid cooler line fittings to catch any spilled transmission fluid.

4   Disconnect the transmission fluid cooler line fittings (see illustrations) using a special transmission line quick-connect coupling tool. Plug the lines to prevent fluid spills.

5   Remove the transmission fluid cooler mounting bolts (see illustration) and remove the transmission fluid cooler. Be careful not to damage the fluid cooler tubes or fins or the condenser cooling fins.

6   If you removed the cooler in order to flush it after a transmission failure, have it flushed at a transmission shop. A number of special tools are needed to flush the cooler correctly.

7   Installation is the reverse of removal.

8   Check the transmission fluid level and add some if necessary (see Chapter 1).

7.2 Locations of the splash shield pin retainers

7.4a Locate the transmission fluid cooler lines (one at each end of the cooler) . . .

7.4b . . . and use a special quick-connect coupling tool to slide inside the fitting and release the line from the coupling

7.5 Location of the transmission fluid cooler mounting bolts

8 Automatic transmission - removal and installation

❈❈ CAUTION:

The transmission and torque converter must be removed as a single assembly. If you try to leave the torque converter attached to the driveplate, the converter driveplate, pump bushing and oil seal will be damaged. The driveplate is not designed to support the load, so none of the weight of the transmission should be allowed to rest on the plate during removal.

REMOVAL

▶ Refer to illustrations 8.9, 8.10, 8.11, 8.15 and 8.21

1   Put the manual shift lever in the NEUTRAL position.

2   Disconnect the cable from the negative terminal of the battery (see Chapter 5, Section 1).

3   Raise the vehicle and support it securely on jackstands.

4   Drain the transmission fluid (see Chapter 1), then reinstall the fluid pan.

5   Remove the fuel line bracket near the exhaust system (see Chapter 4).

6   Remove all exhaust components that will interfere with transmission removal (see Chapter 4).

7   Remove the exhaust pipe heat shield(s).

➡ **Note: There are two exhaust heat shield bolts mounted on each side of the transmission crossmember.**

8   Remove the shift cable from the transmission (see Section 4).

9   Remove the inspection cover (see illustration) at the bottom of the bellhousing.

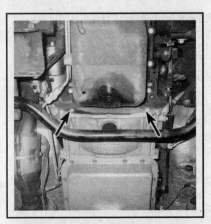

8.9 Location of the inspection cover mounting bolts

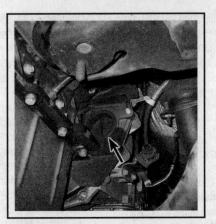

8.10 Location of the rubber inspection hole cover for access to the torque converter nuts

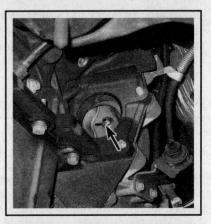

8.11 Remove the torque converter nut and rotate the engine to access the remaining torque converter nuts

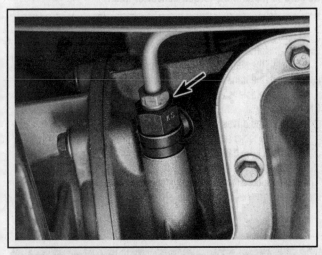

8.15 Disconnect the transmission fluid cooler line from the transmission using a flare-nut wrench on the tube nut. Hold the fitting with an open-end wrench to prevent it from turning

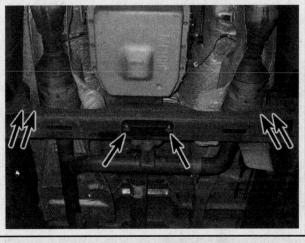

8.21 Location of the transmission crossmember mounting bolts and nuts

10 Remove the rubber plug at the left rear of the engine block (see illustration) and mark the relationship of the torque converter to the driveplate so they can be installed in the same position.

➡ **Note: Some V6 engines may not be equipped with a rubber plug. On these models, access the torque converter nuts through the inspection cover.**

11 Remove the driveplate-to-torque converter nuts (see illustration). Discard the nuts and replace them with new ones during installation.

12 Remove the starter motor (see Chapter 5).

13 Remove the driveshaft(s) (see Chapter 8).

14 On 4WD models, remove the skid plate and transfer case (see Chapter 7C).

15 On 2004 through 2008 models, disconnect the transmission oil cooler lines from the transmission (see illustration). On 2009 and later models, remove the transmission oil cooler line assembly mounting bolt and move the assembly aside; discard the two O-ring seals.

16 Remove the mounting bolt on the cylinder head and remove the transmission dipstick tube.

17 Disconnect the electrical connectors from the two upstream oxy-gen sensors and the two downstream oxygen sensors (see Chapter 6), the transmission speed sensor, the output shaft speed sensor, the Digital Transmission Range (DTR) sensor (see Chapter 6) and the solenoid body assembly.

18 Place a floor jack under the engine. Place a wood block between the jack head and the engine oil pan.

19 Place a transmission jack or a floor jack under the transmission and secure the transmission to the jack with safety chains.

20 Remove the bolts that attach the exhaust hanger and the transmission mount to the crossmember.

21 Raise the transmission slightly to take the weight off the crossmember, then remove the two center nuts and four outer bolts and remove the crossmember (see illustration).

22 Remove the nuts or bolts that attach the transmission isolator mount to the transmission, then remove the isolator mount.

23 On V6 models, remove the oil pan-to-transmission bolts (see Chapter 2A).

24 Remove the transmission-to-engine bolts. Be sure to note the length and the location of each bolt for correct reassembly.

25 Make a final check that all wires have been disconnected from the transmission, then move the transmission and jack toward the rear of the vehicle until the torque converter is separated from the driveplate. Secure the torque converter to the transmission so it won't fall out during removal.

INSTALLATION

26 Prior to installation, make sure the torque converter is securely engaged in the pump. If you've removed the converter, apply a small amount of transmission fluid on the torque converter rear hub, where the transmission front seal rides. Install the torque converter onto the front input shaft of the transmission while rotating the converter back and forth. It should engage into the transmission front pump in stages. To make sure the converter is fully engaged, lay a straightedge across the transmission-to-engine mating surface and make sure the converter lugs are at least 3/4-inch below the straightedge.

27 With the transmission secured to the jack, raise it into position. Be sure to keep it level so the torque converter doesn't fall out and disengage itself from the pump gear.

28 Turn the torque converter to line up the holes with the holes in the driveplate. The marks on the torque converter and driveplate made in Step 10 must line up.

29 Move the transmission forward carefully until the dowel pins on the engine are engaged with the holes on the transmission. Make sure the transmission mates with the engine with no gap. If there's a gap, make sure there are no wires or other objects pinched between the engine and transmission.

30 Install the transmission-to-engine bolts and tighten them to the torque listed in this Chapter's Specifications. As you're tightening the bolts, make sure that the engine and transmission mate completely at all points. If not, find out why. Never try to force the engine and transmission together with the bolts or you'll break the transmission case!

31 On V6 models, install the oil pan-to-transmission bolts and torque them to the Specifications listed in this Chapter.

32 Attach the exhaust pipes to the exhaust manifolds.

33 Attach the fuel line bracket and the exhaust pipe bracket. Tighten all bolts/nuts securely.

34 Install the transmission mount and crossmember and tighten the bolts/nuts securely.

35 Install the heat shield bolts and tighten them securely.

36 Remove the jacks supporting the transmission and the engine.

37 Plug in the heated oxygen sensor connectors.

38 On 2004 through 2008 models, attach the transmission oil cooler lines to the transmission. On 2009 and later models, install two new O-ring seals and attach the transmission oil cooler line assembly and mounting bolt. Tighten the bolt securely.

39 Attach the shift cable to the manual lever (see Section 4).

40 Install the torque converter nuts and tighten them to the torque listed in this Chapter's Specifications.

✷✷ CAUTION:

Be sure to install new torque converter nuts.

41 Install the transmission inspection cover and tighten the bolts securely. Install the rubber access plug.

42 Install the starter motor (see Chapter 5).

43 Install the transmission dipstick tube.

44 If the vehicle is equipped with 4WD, install the transfer case (see Chapter 7C).

45 Install the driveshaft(s) (see Chapter 8).

46 Remove jacks and jackstands and lower the vehicle.

47 Connect the transmission electrical connectors.

48 Attach the negative battery cable.

49 Fill the transmission with the specified fluid (see Chapter 1), run the engine and check for fluid leaks.

9 Automatic transmission overhaul - general information

In the event of a fault occurring, it will be necessary to establish whether the fault is electrical, mechanical or hydraulic in nature, before repair work can be contemplated. Diagnosis requires detailed knowledge of the transmission's operation and construction, as well as access to specialized test equipment, and so is deemed to be beyond the scope of this manual. It is therefore essential that problems with the automatic transmission are referred to a dealer service department or other qualified repair facility for assessment.

Note that a faulty transmission should not be removed before the vehicle has been assessed by a knowledgeable technician equipped with the proper tools, as troubleshooting must be performed with the transmission installed in the vehicle.

Specifications

General

Transmission fluid type	See Chapter 1

Torque specifications	Ft-lbs
Oil pan-to-transmission bolts (V6 models)	25
Torque converter nuts*	27
Transmission-to-engine bolts	35

*Install new torque converter nuts

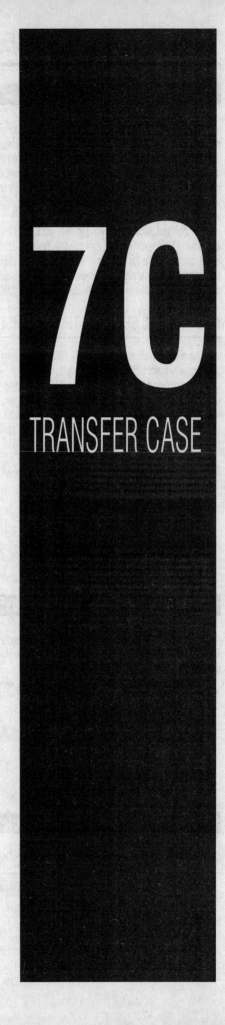

7C

TRANSFER CASE

Section

1 General information
2 Shift lever (manual-shift models) - removal and installation
3 Shift range selector switch (electric-shift models) - replacement
4 Electric shift motor (electric-shift models) - replacement
5 Oil seal - replacement
6 Transfer case - removal and installation

1   General information

Four-wheel drive (4WD) models are equipped with a Borg-Warner manual-shift or Borg Warner electric-shift transfer case mounted on the rear of the transmission. Drive is transmitted from the engine, through the transmission and the transfer case, to the front and rear differentials by driveshafts. From the front differential, drive is transmitted to the front wheels by the driveaxles and from the rear differential to the rear wheels by axleshafts (see Chapter 8).

We don't recommend trying to rebuild any of these transfer cases at home. They're difficult to overhaul without special tools, and rebuilt units are available for less than it would cost to rebuild your own. However, there are a number of components that you can check, adjust and/or replace - and those are the items covered in this Chapter.

MECHANICAL SHIFT-ON-THE-FLY (MSOF) SYSTEM

The mechanical shift-on-the-fly (MSOF) system allows the driver to manually select one of three ranges: 2WD High, 4WD High or 4WD Low. The driver can switch between 2WD High and 4WD High at speeds up to 55 mph (up to 45 mph at temperatures below 32 degrees F). 4WD Low can only be engaged or disengaged with the brake pedal depressed, the transmission in Neutral, and the speed under three mph (this is not a synchronized shift).

When shifting from 2WD High to 4WD High while the vehicle is moving, an electromagnetic clutch inside the transfer case brings the front driveline up to speed as follows: When the manual shift lever is moved from 2WD High to 4WD High, a 4WD indicator light is illuminated, and the 4WD electric clutch relay and electromagnetic clutch are energized. When the transfer is shifted into 4WD Low, an indicator is also illuminated. Both indicator lights are turned on by a 4WD indicator switch on the transfer case.

ELECTRONIC SHIFT-ON-THE-FLY (ESOF) SYSTEM

The electronic shift-on-the-fly (ESOF) system allows the driver the same three ranges (2WD High, 4WD High, 4WD Low) as the MSOF system, and the same rules apply for shifting from 2WD High to 4WD High, and for shifting to 4WD Low. However, the means by which a shift is initiated are electronic: When 4WD High is selected at a switch on the dash, the Powertrain Control Module (PCM) receives a voltage signal commanding it to energize the electromagnetic clutch inside the transfer case and the relays which energize the transfer case shift motor. When the shift motor reaches the correct position (determined by the position of contact plates which send inputs to the PCM), power to the shift relays and motor is cut. When the transfer case front and rear output shafts are turning at the same speed, a spring-loaded lock-up collar mechanically engages the mainshaft hub to the drive sprocket, the front axle collar is engaged and the electromagnetic clutch is de-energized.

2   Shift lever (manual-shift models) - removal and installation

1   Working on the small console that surrounds the manual shift lever for the 4WD system, pull up both sides evenly to separate it from the floor clips.
2   Remove the four shift lever boot retaining screws and lift the boot up to access the shift lever mounting bolt.
3   Remove the shift lever bolt and separate the shift lever from the transfer case.
4   Installation is the reverse of removal.

3   Shift range selector switch (electric-shift models) - replacement

2004 MODELS

1   Pry the shift range selector knob from the switch.
2   Unplug the electrical connector from the shift range selector switch.
3   Remove the two mounting screws.
4   Remove the shift range selector switch from the dash.
5   Installation is the reverse of removal.

2005 AND LATER MODELS

6   Pry the shift range selector switch from the instrument panel using a screwdriver or panel tool.
7   Unplug the electrical connector from the shift range selector switch.
8   Remove the shift range selector switch.
9   Installation is the reverse of removal.

4   Electric shift motor (electric shift models) - replacement

1   Turn the ignition key to the ON position (engine not running) and select 4WD High.

2   Turn the ignition key to the OFF position and shift the transmission into NEUTRAL.

3   Raise the vehicle and place it securely on jackstands.

4   Unplug the shift motor electrical connector.

5   Remove the bracket bolt and the three electric shift motor mount- ing bolts.

6   Remove the shifter shaft seal and replace it with a new seal.

7   Remove the electric shift motor.

8   Installation is the reverse of removal. Tighten the electric shift motor mounting bolts to the torque listed in this Chapter's Specifications.

5   Oil seal - replacement

▶ **Refer to illustrations 5.3 and 5.5**

➡ **Note: This procedure applies to the rear seal only; front seal replacement requires the removal and disassembly of the transfer case.**

1   Raise the vehicle and support it securely on jackstands.

2   Remove the rear driveshaft (see Chapter 8).

3   Pry out the seal with a screwdriver or a seal removal tool (see illustration). Don't damage the seal bore.

4   Lubricate the new seal lips with petroleum jelly or multi-purpose grease.

5   Drive the seal into place with a seal driver or large socket (see illustration). The outside diameter of the socket should be slightly smaller than the outside diameter of the seal.

6   The remainder of installation is the reverse of removal.

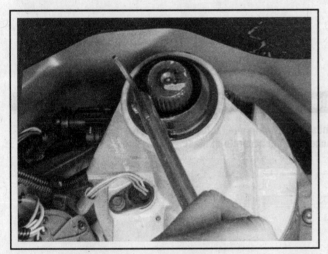

5.3 Pry out the rear transfer case seal with a seal removal tool or large screwdriver

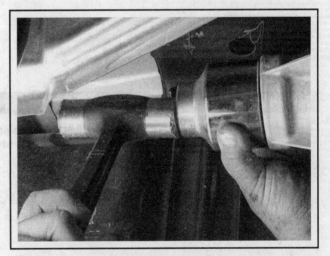

5.5 Drive the new rear transfer case seal into place with a seal driver or large socket

6   Transfer case - removal and installation

REMOVAL

1   Disconnect the cable from the negative terminal of the battery (see Chapter 5, Section 1).

2   Raise the vehicle and support it securely on jackstands.

3   Remove the transfer case skid plate bolts, then remove the skid plate.

4   Drain the transfer case lubricant (see Chapter 1).

5   Remove the front driveshaft shield, then remove the front and rear driveshafts (see Chapter 8).

6   Remove the transfer case vent tube.

Manual shift models

7   Disconnect the shift lever (see Section 2).

8   Disconnect the shift linkage from the shift bracket.

9   Disconnect the electrical connectors and detach the wiring harness.

Electric shift models

10   Disconnect the electrical connector for the electric shift motor (see Section 4).

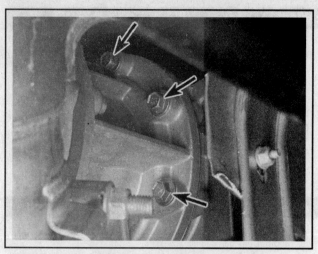

6.13 Remove the transfer case-to-transmission bolts

All models

▶ **Refer to illustration 6.13**

11 Unplug the electrical connector from the transmission speed sensor (see Chapter 6).

12 Support the transfer case with a jack - preferably a special jack made for this purpose. Safety chains or tie-downs will help steady the transfer case on the jack.

13 Remove the transfer case-to-transmission bolts (see illustration).

14 Make a final check that all wires and hoses have been disconnected from the transfer case, then move the transfer case and jack toward the rear of the vehicle until the transfer case is clear of the transmission. Keep the transfer case level as this is done. Once the input shaft is clear, lower the transfer case and remove it from under the vehicle.

INSTALLATION

15 Installation is the reverse of removal. Be sure to use new bolts and tighten the transfer case-to-transmission bolts gradually and evenly to the torque listed in this Chapter's Specifications.

16 Refill the transfer case with the proper lubricant (see Chapter 1).

Torque specification	Ft-lbs (unless otherwise indicated)

➡ **Note: One foot-pound (ft-lb) of torque is equivalent to 12 inch-pounds (in-lbs) of torque. Torque values below approximately 15 ft-lbs are expressed in inch-pounds, since most foot-pound torque wrenches are not accurate at these smaller values.**

Transfer case-to-transmission bolts	
2004 through 2008	35
2009 on	159 in-lbs
Electric shift motor-to-transfer case bolts	89 in-lbs

8

CLUTCH AND
DRIVELINE

Section

1 General information

2 Clutch - description and check

3 Clutch master cylinder - removal and installation

4 Clutch release cylinder - removal and installation

5 Clutch hydraulic system - bleeding

6 Clutch release bearing - removal, inspection and installation

7 Clutch components - removal, inspection and installation

8 Clutch pedal position switch - replacement

9 Driveshaft(s) - general information

10 Driveshaft(s) - removal and installation

11 Universal joints - replacement

12 Driveshaft slip yoke boot and center bearing - (two-piece driveshafts) - replacement

13 Front driveaxles (4WD models) - removal and installation

14 Driveaxle boot replacement (4WD models)

15 Rear axle - general information

16 Rear axle assembly - removal and installation

17 Rear axleshaft - removal and installtion

18 Rear axleshaft oil seal - replacement

19 Rear axleshaft bearing - replacement

20 Pinion oil seal - replacement

21 Front axle assembly (4WD models) - removal and installation

1 General information

The information in this Chapter deals with the components from the rear of the engine to the front wheels, except for the transmission and transfer case, which are dealt with in Chapter 7. For the purposes of this Chapter, these components are grouped into three categories - clutch, driveshaft(s) and axle(s).

Since nearly all the procedures covered in this Chapter involve working under the vehicle, make sure it's securely supported on sturdy jackstands or on a hoist where the vehicle can be easily raised and lowered.

2 Clutch - description and check

1 All vehicles with a manual transmission have a single dry plate, diaphragm spring-type clutch. The clutch disc has a splined hub which allows it to slide along the splines of the transmission input shaft. The clutch and pressure plate are held in contact by spring pressure exerted by the diaphragm in the pressure plate.

2 The clutch release system is operated by hydraulic pressure. The hydraulic release system consists of the clutch pedal, a master cylinder and a reservoir, a release (or slave) cylinder and the hydraulic line connecting the two components.

3 When the clutch pedal is depressed, a pushrod pushes against brake fluid inside the master cylinder, applying hydraulic pressure to the release cylinder, which pushes the release bearing against the diaphragm fingers of the clutch pressure plate.

4 Terminology can be a problem when discussing the clutch components because common names are in some cases different from those used by the manufacturer. For example, the driven plate is also called the clutch plate or disc, the clutch release bearing is sometimes called a throwout bearing, the release cylinder is sometimes called the slave cylinder.

5 Unless you're replacing components with obvious damage, do these preliminary checks to diagnose clutch problems:

a) *The first check should be of the fluid level in the master cylinder. If the fluid level is low, add fluid as necessary and inspect the hydraulic system for leaks. If the master cylinder reservoir is dry, bleed the system as described in Section 5 and recheck the clutch operation.*

b) *To check "clutch spin-down time," run the engine at normal idle speed with the transmission in Neutral (clutch pedal up - engaged). Disengage the clutch (pedal down), wait several seconds and shift the transmission into Reverse. No grinding noise should be heard. A grinding noise would most likely indicate a bad pressure plate or clutch disc.*

c) *To check for complete clutch release, run the engine (with the parking brake applied to prevent vehicle movement) and hold the clutch pedal approximately 1/2-inch from the floor. Shift the transmission between 1st gear and Reverse several times. If the shift is rough, component failure is indicated.*

d) *Visually inspect the pivot bushing at the top of the clutch pedal to make sure there's no binding or excessive play.*

3 Clutch master cylinder - removal and installation

REMOVAL

▶ **Refer to illustrations 3.1, 3.3, 3.5 and 3.7**

1 Working under the dash, disconnect the clutch master cylinder pushrod from the clutch pedal (see illustration).

2 Disconnect the clutch pedal position switch (see Section 8).

3 Remove the two clutch master cylinder reservoir push pins (see illustration).

4 Raise the vehicle and place it securely on jackstands.

5 Disconnect the clutch fluid hydraulic line from the transmission (see illustration). Have rags handy, as some fluid will be lost as the line is removed.

❋ CAUTION:

Don't allow brake fluid to come into contact with the paint - it will damage the finish. Also have a plug ready and immediately plug the line to prevent leakage.

3.1 To disconnect the clutch master cylinder pushrod from the pin on the clutch pedal lever, pry it off with a screwdriver

3.3 To detach the clutch master cylinder reservoir from the firewall, remove these two "push pins"

3.5 If you don't have a clutch coupling tool to disconnect the clutch fluid hydraulic line from the transmission, use a screwdriver instead - carefully push the spring-loaded transmission side of the coupling toward the transmission and simultaneously pull straight out on the hydraulic line side of the fitting

3.7 To detach the master cylinder from the firewall, rotate it clockwise 45-degrees and pull it out

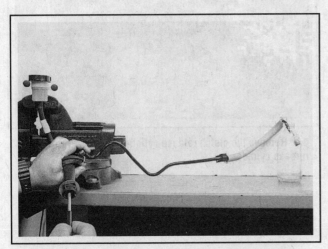

3.8a Secure the master cylinder reservoir in a bench vise as shown; put the release cylinder end of the hydraulic line in a container, fill the clutch master cylinder to the "Full" line . . .

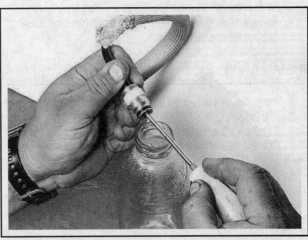

3.8d . . . depress and hold the clutch master cylinder pushrod, then have an assistant open the internal fitting of the male quick-connect coupling with a screwdriver - a stream of fluid will be ejected from the quick-connect coupling

6   Lower the vehicle.

7   To detach the master cylinder from the firewall, rotate the master cylinder clockwise 45-degrees (see illustration).

INSTALLATION

▶ **Refer to illustrations 3.8a and 3.8d**

❊❊ **WARNING:**

Wear eye protection when bleeding the master cylinder.

---

8   Before installing the clutch master cylinder, bleed it as follows:

a) *Secure the master cylinder reservoir in a bench vise (see illustration).*

b) *Fill the clutch master cylinder to the "Full" line.*

c) *Put the release cylinder end of the hydraulic line in a container of clean brake fluid.*

d) *Depress and hold the clutch master cylinder pushrod, then have an assistant open the internal fitting of the male quick-connect coupling, allowing fluid to flow out (see illustration).*

e) *When the stream of fluid subsides, release the internal fitting of the male quick-connect fitting, then release the master cylinder pushrod.*

f) *Repeat this procedure until a solid stream of brake fluid, with no air bubbles, is discharged from the quick-connect fitting. Check and refill the fluid reservoir, as necessary, during this procedure.*

9   Install the master cylinder in the firewall and lock it into place by rotating it 45-degrees counterclockwise (don't rotate it any further or you'll damage it).

10 Install the fluid reservoir, using new push pins.

11 Working inside the vehicle, connect the clutch pedal position switch and connect the clutch master cylinder pushrod to the clutch pedal.

12 Connect the hydraulic line to the transmission with the coupling tool.

13 Lower the vehicle and reactivate the air suspension system, if equipped.

14 Fill the clutch master cylinder reservoir with the fluid specified in Chapter 1 and bleed the clutch system (see Section 5).

4   Clutch release cylinder - removal and installation

REMOVAL

▶ **Refer to illustration 4.4**

1   Raise the vehicle and support it securely on jackstands.

2   Remove the clip and disconnect the hydraulic line at the transmission (see illustration 3.5). Have a small can and rags handy, as some fluid will be spilled as the line is removed. Plug the line to prevent excessive fluid loss and contamination.

3   Remove the transmission (see Chapter 7, Part A).

4   Remove the release cylinder mounting bolts (see illustration).

5   Remove the release cylinder.

INSTALLATION

6   Install the release cylinder into the transmission. Tighten the bolts to the torque listed in this Chapter's Specifications.

7   Install the transmission (see Chapter 7, Part A).

8   Connect the hydraulic line fitting to the transmission and install the clip.

9   Check the fluid level in the clutch fluid reservoir, adding brake fluid conforming to DOT 3 specifications until the level is correct.

10 Bleed the system as described in Section 5, then recheck the clutch fluid level.

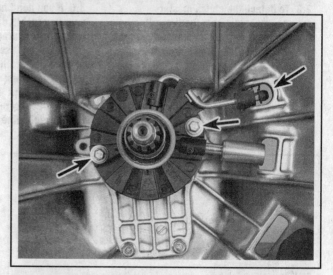

4.4 Remove the clutch release cylinder bolts and remove the release cylinder

5   Clutch hydraulic system - bleeding

1   Bleed the hydraulic system whenever any part of the system has been removed or the fluid level has fallen so low that air has been drawn into the master cylinder. The bleeding procedure is very similar to bleeding a brake system.

2   Fill the clutch master cylinder reservoir with new brake fluid conforming to DOT 3 specifications.

❊❊❊ CAUTION:

Do not re-use any of the fluid coming from the system during the bleeding operation or use fluid which has been inside an open container for an extended period of time.

3   Remove the cap from the bleeder valve and attach a length of clear hose to the valve. Place the other end of the hose into a container partially filled with clean brake fluid.

4   Have an assistant depress the clutch pedal and hold it. Open the bleeder valve on the hydraulic line, allowing fluid and any air to escape. Close the bleeder valve when the flow of fluid (and bubbles) ceases. Once closed, have your assistant release the pedal.

5   Continue this process until all air is evacuated from the system, indicated by a solid stream of fluid being ejected from the bleeder valve each time with no air bubbles. Keep a close watch on the fluid level inside the clutch master cylinder reservoir - if the level drops too far, air will get into the system and you'll have to start all over again.

➡ **Note: Wash the area with water to remove any excess brake fluid.**

6   Check the clutch fluid level again, and add some, if necessary, to bring it to the appropriate level. Check carefully for proper operation before placing the vehicle into normal service.

6 Clutch release bearing - removal, inspection and installation

The clutch release bearing and bearing hub are integral components of the clutch release cylinder. Replace the release cylinder as a single assembly (see Section 4).

7 Clutch components - removal, inspection and installation

WARNING:

Dust produced by clutch wear is hazardous to your health. DO NOT blow it out with compressed air and DO NOT inhale it. DO NOT use gasoline or petroleum-based solvents to remove the dust. Brake system cleaner should be used to flush the dust into a drain pan. After the clutch components are wiped clean with a rag, dispose of the contaminated rags and cleaner in a covered, marked container.

REMOVAL

Refer to illustration 7.4

1 Access to the clutch components is normally accomplished by removing the transmission, leaving the engine in the vehicle. If the engine is being removed for major overhaul, check the clutch for wear and replace worn components as necessary. However, the relatively low cost of the clutch components compared to the time and trouble spent gaining access to them warrants their replacement anytime the engine or transmission is removed, unless they are new or in near-perfect condition. The following procedures are based on the assumption the engine will stay in place.

2 Remove the transmission from the vehicle (see Chapter 7, Part A). Support the engine while the transmission is out. Preferably, an engine support fixture or a hoist should be used to support it from above.

3 To support the clutch disc during removal, install a clutch alignment tool through the clutch disc hub.

4 Carefully inspect the flywheel and pressure plate for indexing marks. The marks are usually an X, an O or a black mark. If they cannot be found, scribe or paint marks yourself so the pressure plate and the flywheel will be in the same alignment during installation (see illustration).

5 Turning each bolt a little at a time, loosen the pressure plate-to-flywheel bolts. Work in a criss-cross pattern until all spring pressure is relieved. Then hold the pressure plate securely and completely remove the bolts, followed by the pressure plate and clutch disc.

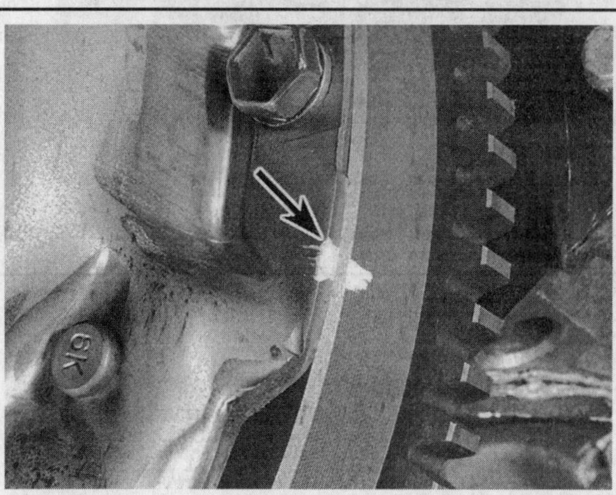

7.4 Mark the relationship of the pressure plate to the flywheel (if you're planning to re-use the old pressure plate)

INSPECTION

Refer to illustrations 7.8, 7.10a, 7.10b and 7.12

6 Ordinarily, when a problem occurs in the clutch, it can be attributed to wear of the clutch driven plate assembly (clutch disc). However, all components should be inspected at this time.

7 Inspect the flywheel for cracks, heat checking, grooves and other obvious defects. If the imperfections are slight, a machine shop can machine the surface flat and smooth, which is highly recommended regardless of the surface appearance. Refer to Chapter 2 for the flywheel removal and installation procedure.

8   Inspect the lining on the clutch disc. There should be at least 1/16-inch of lining above the rivet heads. Check for loose rivets, distortion, cracks, broken springs and other obvious damage (see illustration). As mentioned above, ordinarily the clutch disc is routinely replaced, so if in doubt about the condition, replace it with a new one.

9   The release bearing and release cylinder should also be replaced along with the clutch disc (see Section 4).

10   Check the machined surfaces and the diaphragm spring fingers of the pressure plate (see illustrations). If the surface is grooved or otherwise damaged, replace the pressure plate. Also check for obvious damage, distortion, cracking, etc. Light glazing can be removed with emery cloth or sandpaper. If a new pressure plate is required, new and re-manufactured units are available.

11   Check the pilot bearing in the end of the crankshaft for excessive

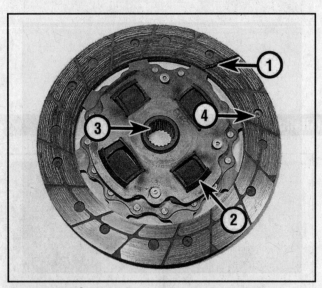

7.8 The clutch disc

1   **Lining** - this will wear down in use
2   **Springs or dampers** - check for cracking and deformation
3   **Splined hub** - the splines must not be worn and should slide smoothly on the transmission input shaft splines
4   **Rivets** - these secure the lining and will damage the flywheel or pressure plate if allowed to contact the surfaces

wear, scoring, dryness, roughness and any other obvious damage. If any of these conditions are noted, replace the bearing.

12   Removal can be accomplished with a slide hammer and puller attachment (see illustration), which are available at most auto parts stores or tool rental yards.

INSTALLATION

▶ **Refer to illustrations 7.13, 7.15a, 7.15b, 7.15c and 7.16**

13   To install a new pilot bearing, lightly lubricate the outside surface with grease, then drive it into the recess with a bearing driver or a socket (see illustration).

➡ **Note: The seal end of the bearing must be facing toward the transmission.**

14   Before installation, clean the flywheel and pressure plate machined surfaces with brake cleaner, lacquer thinner or acetone. It's important that no oil or grease is on these surfaces or the lining of the clutch disc. Handle the parts only with clean hands.

15   Adjust the clutch pressure plate before installing it onto the flywheel. Position the pressure plate in a hydraulic press. Apply pressure to the pressure plate until the adjusting ring is loose. Rotate the ring counterclockwise until the tension springs are compressed to the dimension listed in this Chapter's Specifications, then release the pressure on the diaphragm spring fingers (see illustrations).

16   Position the clutch disc and pressure plate against the flywheel with the clutch held in place with an alignment tool (see illustration). Make sure the disc is installed properly (most replacement clutch discs will be marked "flywheel side" or something similar - if not marked, install the clutch disc with the damper springs toward the transmission).

17   Tighten the pressure plate-to-flywheel bolts only finger tight, working around the pressure plate.

18   Center the clutch disc by ensuring the alignment tool extends through the splined hub and into the pilot bearing in the crankshaft. Wiggle the tool up, down or side-to-side as needed to center the disc. Tighten the pressure plate-to-flywheel bolts a little at a time, working in a criss-cross pattern to prevent distorting the cover. After all of the bolts are snug, tighten them to the torque listed in this Chapter's Specifications. Remove the alignment tool.

19   Install the clutch release bearing and release cylinder (see Section 4).

20   Install the transmission and all components removed previously.

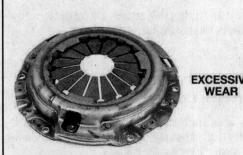

NORMAL FINGER WEAR   **EXCESSIVE FINGER WEAR**   **BROKEN OR BENT FINGERS**

EXCESSIVE WEAR

7.10a Replace the pressure plate if excessive wear or damage is noted

7.10b Inspect the pressure plate surface for excessive score marks, cracks and signs of overheating

7.12 A slide hammer with an internal puller attachment is handy for removing a pilot bearing

7.13 Tap the bearing into place with a bearing driver or a socket that is slightly smaller than the outside diameter of the bearing

7.15a Position the pressure plate on a hydraulic press and, using a suitable adapter, depress the diaphragm spring until the adjusting spring (arrow) moves freely

7.15b Using a screwdriver, move the adjusting spring counterclockwise . . .

7.15c . . . until the tension springs are compressed to the specified dimension

7.16 Center the clutch disc in the pressure plate with a clutch alignment tool

8   Clutch pedal position switch - replacement

1   Disconnect the clutch master cylinder pushrod from the clutch pedal (see illustration 3.1).

2   Unplug the electrical connector from the clutch pedal position switch.

3   Pull down the retaining clip underneath the switch, push the locking tabs together on top of the switch and slide off the plastic retainer.

4   Remove the switch.

5   Installation is the reverse of removal.

9   Driveshaft(s) - general information

1   A driveshaft is a tube that transmits power between the transmission or transfer case and the differential(s). Universal joints are located at either end of the driveshaft and allow the driveshaft to operate at different angles as the suspension moves.

2   Three different types of universal joints are used: single-cardan, double-cardan and constant velocity.

3   Some models have a two-piece driveshaft. The two driveshafts are connected at a center support bearing.

4   The rear driveshaft employs a splined yoke at the front, which slips into the extension housing of the transmission. The front driveshaft on 4WD models (and the rear half of the driveshaft on models with a two-piece driveshaft) incorporates a slip yoke as part of the shaft. This arrangement allows the driveshaft to alter its length during vehicle operation. On models with a one-piece rear driveshaft the slip yoke is splined to the transmission output shaft. An oil seal prevents fluid from leaking out of the extension housing and keeps dirt from entering the transmission or transfer case. If leakage is evident at the front of the

driveshaft, replace the extension housing oil seal (see Chapter 7).

5   The driveshaft assembly requires very little service. Factory U-joints are lubricated for life and must be replaced if problems develop. The driveshaft must be removed from the vehicle for this procedure. (Some aftermarket universal joints have grease fittings to allow periodic lubrication.)

6   Since the driveshaft is a balanced unit, it's important that no undercoating, mud, etc. be allowed to accumulate on it. When the vehicle is raised for service it's a good idea to clean the driveshaft and inspect it for any obvious damage. Also, make sure the small weights used to originally balance the driveshaft are in place and securely attached. Whenever the driveshaft is removed it must be reinstalled in the same relative position to preserve the balance.

7   Problems with the driveshaft are usually indicated by a noise or vibration while driving the vehicle. A road test should verify if the problem is the driveshaft or another vehicle component. Refer to the *Troubleshooting* section at the front of this manual.

10   Driveshaft(s) - removal and installation

➡ **Note: The manufacturer recommends replacing driveshaft fasteners with new ones when installing the driveshaft, if new fasteners are not available, coat the threads with a thread locking compound.**

REAR DRIVESHAFT

Removal

▶ **Refer to illustrations 10.2 and 10.3**

➡ **Note: Where a two-piece driveshaft is involved, the rear shaft must be removed before the front shaft.**

1   Raise the vehicle and support it securely on jackstands.

2   Use chalk or a scribe to "index" the relationship of the driveshaft to the differential axle assembly mating flange. This ensures correct alignment when the driveshaft is reinstalled (see illustration).

10.2 Mark the relationship of the rear driveshaft U-joint to the differential pinion flange

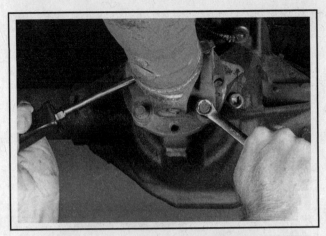

10.3 Insert a screwdriver through the U-joint to prevent the driveshaft from turning as you break loose the four U-joint-to-pinion flange bolts

3   Remove the bolts securing the driveshaft flange or universal joint clamps to the differential pinion flange (see illustration). Turn the driveshaft (or wheels) as necessary to bring the bolts into the most accessible position.

4   Pry the universal joint away from its mating flange and remove the shaft from the flange. Be careful not to let the caps fall off of the universal joint (which would cause contamination and loss of the needle bearings).

5   Lower the rear of the driveshaft. If the driveshaft is a one-piece unit, slide the front end of the driveshaft out of the transmission extension housing; if it's a two-piece driveshaft, mark the relationship of the center support bearing to the support bracket, then unbolt the center support bearing and slide the front end of the front driveshaft out of the extension housing.

6   Wrap a plastic bag over the extension housing and hold it in place with a rubber band. This will prevent loss of fluid and protect against contamination while the driveshaft is out.

Installation

7   Remove the plastic bag from the transmission or transfer case extension housing and wipe the area clean. Inspect the oil seal carefully. If it's leaking, now is the time to replace it (see Chapter 7).

8   Inspect the center support bearing, if equipped. If it's rough or noisy, replace it (see Section 12).

9   Insert the front end of the driveshaft assembly into the transmission or transfer case extension housing.

10 If the driveshaft is a one-piece unit, raise the rear of the driveshaft into position, checking to be sure the marks are in alignment. If not, turn the pinion flange until the marks line up.

11 If the driveshaft is a two-piece unit, raise the center support bearing and bolt it loosely into place, raise the rear end of the rear shaft into position and make sure the alignment marks are in alignment. If not, turn the pinion flange until they do.

12 Remove the tape securing the bearing caps and install the clamps, if equipped, and fasteners. Tighten these fasteners and the center support bearing bolts to the torque listed in this Chapter's Specifications.

FRONT (4WD)

Removal

➡ **Note: The front driveshaft on 2009 and later models uses CV joints instead of U-joints, but the removal procedure is essentially the same.**

13 Raise the vehicle and support it securely on jackstands.

14 If equipped, remove the driveshaft shield.

15 Use chalk or a scribe to mark the relationship of the driveshaft to the differential axle assembly mating flange (see illustration 10.2). This ensures correct alignment when the driveshaft is reinstalled.

16 Remove the bolts that secure the front end of the driveshaft to the differential mating flange.

17 Mark the relationship of the driveshaft to the transfer case flange. Unbolt the flange that secures the driveshaft universal joint to the transfer case, then remove the driveshaft.

Installation

18 Installation is the reverse of removal. If the shaft cannot be lined up due to the components of the differential or transfer case having been rotated, put the vehicle in Neutral or rotate one wheel to allow the original alignment to be achieved. Make sure the universal joint caps are properly placed in the flange seat. Tighten the fasteners to the torque listed in this Chapter's Specifications.

11   Universal joints - replacement

▶ **Refer to illustrations 11.2, 11.4 and 11.9**

➡ **Note: A press or large vise will be required for this procedure. It may be advisable to take the driveshaft to a local dealer service department, service station or machine shop where the universal joints can be replaced for you, normally at a reasonable charge.**

➡ **Note: The front driveshafts on 2009 and later models use CV joints instead of U-joints. These CV joints are not rebuildable; they must be replaced.**

1   Remove the driveshaft as outlined in Section 10.

2   Use a small pair of pliers to remove the snap-rings from the spider (see illustration).

3   Supporting the driveshaft, place it in position on a workbench equipped with a vise.

11.2 A pair of needle-nose pliers can be used to remove the universal joint snap-rings

11.4 To press the universal joint out of the driveshaft yoke, set it up in a vise with the small socket pushing the joint and bearing cap into the large socket

11.9 If the snap-ring will not seat in the groove, strike the yoke with a brass hammer - this will relieve the tension that has set up in the yoke and slightly spring the yoke ears (this should also be done if the joint feels tight when assembled)

4   Place a piece of pipe or a large socket, having an inside diameter slightly larger than the outside diameter of the bearing caps, over one of the bearing caps. Position a socket with an outside diameter slightly smaller than that of the opposite bearing cap against the cap (see illustration) and use the vise or press to force the bearing cap out (inside the pipe or large socket). Use the vise or large pliers to work the bearing cap the rest of the way out.

5   Transfer the sockets to the other side and press the opposite bearing cap out in the same manner.

6   Pack the new universal joint bearings with grease. Ordinarily, specific instructions for lubrication will be included with the universal joint servicing kit and should be followed carefully.

7   Position the spider in the yoke and partially install one bearing

cap in the yoke.

8   Start the spider into the bearing cap and then partially install the other cap. Align the spider and press the bearing caps into position, being careful not to damage the dust seals.

9   Install the snap-rings. If difficulty is encountered in seating the snap-rings, strike the driveshaft yoke sharply with a hammer. This will spring the yoke ears slightly and allow the snap-rings to seat in the groove (see illustration).

10 If equipped, install the grease fitting and fill the joint with grease. Be careful not to overfill the joint, as this could blow out the grease seals.

11 Install the driveshaft (see Section 10).

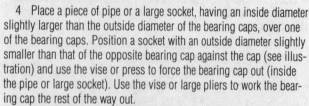

12   Driveshaft slip yoke boot and center bearing (two-piece driveshafts) - replacement

1   Raise the vehicle and place it securely on jackstands.
2   Remove the driveshaft (see Section 10).

SLIP YOKE BOOT

3   Put the driveshaft assembly on the bench and cut off the slip yoke boot clamps.

4   Mark the relationship of the slip yoke to the driveshaft. Separate the slip yoke from the splined stub shaft on the driveshaft.

5   Remove the driveshaft slip yoke boot. Inspect the boot for cracks and tears. If necessary, discard it and get a new one.

6   Inspect the slip yoke grease for signs of dirt or water contamination. If the grease is contaminated, pull off the slip yoke, clean off the old grease, and inspect the stub shaft and slip yoke splines for signs of excessive wear or corrosion. If the splines are damaged, replace the driveshaft with a new or rebuilt unit.

7   Install the center bearing, if removed (see below).

8   Slide the end of the new boot with the smaller opening onto the splined stub shaft. Push it on as far as it will go.

9   Attach the boot to the stub shaft with a new boot clamp. You'll need a special clamp crimping pliers, available at most auto parts stores, to crimp the new clamp.

10 Lubricate the stub shaft splines with high temperature grease and slide the slip yoke onto the splines, making sure the marks you made in Step 4 are in alignment.

11 Fill the slip yoke boot with about 10 grams of the same lubricant.

12 Slip the larger boot clamp onto the slip yoke.

13 Slip the boot onto the slip yoke, then adjust the distance from the weld bead on the driveshaft to the centerline of the U-joint to the dimension listed in this Chapter's Specifications.

14 Pry the lip of the boot open with a screwdriver to bleed air from the slip yoke boot, then install the large clamp and crimp it with suitable pliers.

15 Install the driveshaft (see Section 10).

CENTER BEARING

16 The center bearing is pressed onto the driveshaft and cannot be removed without a press and special adapter. Take the driveshaft to an automotive machine shop and have the old bearing pressed off and a new bearing installed. If the rubber support is damaged, have it replaced at this time as well.

17 Install the driveshaft (see Section 10).

13 Front driveaxles (4WD models) - removal and installation

REMOVAL

1 Loosen the wheel lug nuts, raise the vehicle and support it securely on jackstands, then remove the wheel. Remove the dust cap from the hub/wheel bearing.

2 Remove the driveaxle/hub nut from the axle and discard it.

3 Disconnect the vent and vacuum lines from the integrated wheel end, then remove the fasteners securing the integrated wheel end to the steering knuckle.

➡ **Note: The integrated wheel end is the device bolted to the steering knuckle that couples the driveaxles to the wheel hub when 4WD mode is engaged.**

4 Separate the upper control arm and tie-rod end from the steering knuckle (see Chapter 10).

5 Swing the knuckle/hub assembly out (away from the vehicle) until the end of the driveaxle is free of the hub.

6 Support the outer end of the driveaxle with a piece of wire to avoid unnecessary strain on the inner CV joint.

7 Remove the integrated wheel end from the driveaxle outboard end.

8 Mark the relationship of the inner CV joint to the flange, then remove the driveaxle flange bolts.

9 Carefully remove the driveaxle from the vehicle.

INSTALLATION

▸ **Refer to illustration 13.10**

10 Compress the integrated wheel end, then place caps on the vent and vacuum ports (see illustration).

11 Install the integrated wheel end on the driveaxle outboard end.

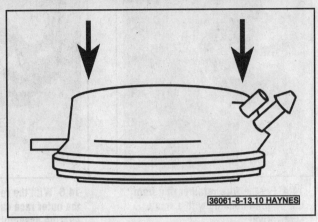

36061-8-13.10 HAYNES

13.10 Compress the integrated wheel end, then place caps on the vent and vacuum ports to keep it in a compressed state

12 The remainder of installation is the reverse of removal, with the following points:

a) *The upper balljoint-to-steering knuckle nut and the tie-rod end nut should not be reused. New ones should always be used. Be sure to tighten them to the torque listed in the Chapter 10 Specifications.*

b) *Tighten the driveaxle flange bolts, integrated wheel end fasteners and the driveaxle/hub nut to the torque listed in this Chapter's Specifications. Be sure to use a new driveaxle/hub nut.*

c) *Remove the caps from the vent and vacuum ports and connect the vent and vacuum lines to the integrated wheel end.*

d) *Install the wheel and lug nuts, lower the vehicle and tighten the lug nuts to the torque listed in the Chapter 1 Specifications.*

14 Driveaxle boot replacement (4WD models)

➡ **Note: If the CV joints exhibit signs of wear indicating need for an overhaul (usually due to torn boots), explore all options before beginning the job. Complete rebuilt driveaxles are available on an exchange basis, which eliminates much time and work. Whichever route you choose to take, check on the cost and availability of parts before disassembling the vehicle.**

INNER CV JOINT

Disassembly

▸ **Refer to illustrations 14.3, 14.4, 14.5, 14.7, 14.9, 14.10 and 14.11**

1 Remove the driveaxle from the vehicle (see Section 13).

2 Mount the driveaxle in a vise. The jaws of the vise should be lined with wood or rags to prevent damage to the axleshaft.

3 Cut the boot clamps from the boot and discard them (see illustration).

14.3 Cut off the boot clamps and discard them

14.4 Pry the wire retainer ring from the CV joint housing with a small screwdriver

14.5 With the retainer removed, the outer race can be pulled off the bearing assembly

14.7 Remove the snap-ring from the end of the axleshaft

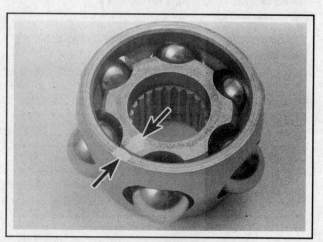

14.9 Make index marks on the inner race and cage so they'll both be facing the same direction when reassembled

14.10 Pry the balls from the cage with a screwdriver (be careful not to nick or scratch them)

4 Slide the boot back on the axleshaft and pry the wire ring ball retainer from the outer race (see illustration).

5 Pull the outer race off the inner bearing assembly (see illustration).

6 Wipe as much grease off the inner bearing as possible.

7 Remove the snap-ring from the end of the axleshaft (see illustration).

8 Slide the inner bearing assembly off the axleshaft.

9 Mark the inner race and cage to ensure that they are reassembled with the correct sides facing out (see illustration).

10 Pry the balls from the cage (see illustration). Be careful not to scratch the inner race, the balls or the cage.

11 Rotate the inner race 90-degrees, align the inner race lands with the cage windows and rotate the race out of the cage (see illustration).

Inspection

▶ **Refer to illustrations 14.12a and 14.12b**

12 Clean the components with solvent to remove all traces of grease. Inspect the cage and races for pitting, score marks, cracks and other signs of wear and damage. Shiny, polished spots are normal and will not adversely affect CV joint performance (see illustrations).

Reassembly

▶ **Refer to illustrations 14.14, 14.16, 14.17, 14.20, 14.22, 14.23 and 14.24**

13 Insert the inner race into the cage. Verify that the matchmarks are on the same side. However, it's not necessary for them to be in direct alignment with each other.

14 Press the balls into the cage windows with your thumbs (see illustration).

15 Wrap the axleshaft splines with tape to avoid damaging the boot.

16 Slide the small boot clamp and boot onto the axleshaft, then remove the tape (see illustration).

17 Install the inner race and cage assembly on the axleshaft with the larger diameter side or "bulge" of the cage facing the axleshaft end (see illustration).

18 Install the snap-ring (see illustration 14.7).

19 Fill the outer race with CV joint grease (normally included with the new boot kit).

20 Pack the inner race and cage assembly with grease, by hand, until grease is worked completely into the assembly (see illustration).

21 Slide the outer race down onto the inner race and install the wire ring retainer.

22 Wipe any excess grease from the axle boot groove on the outer race. Seat the small diameter of the boot in the recessed area on the axleshaft and install the clamp. Push the other end of the boot onto the outer race and move the race in-or-out to adjust the driveaxle to the proper length, as listed in this Chapter's Specifications (see illustration).

14.11 Tilt the inner race 90-degrees and rotate it out of the cage

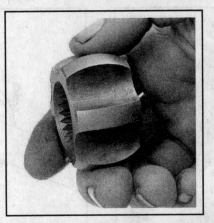

14.12a Inspect the inner race lands and grooves for pitting and score marks

14.12b Inspect the cage for cracks, pitting and score marks (shiny spots are normal and don't affect operation)

14.14 Press the balls into the cage through the windows

14.16 Wrap the splined area of the axle with tape to prevent damage to the boot, then install the small clamp and the boot

14.17 Install the inner race and cage assembly with the "bulge" facing the end of the axleshaft

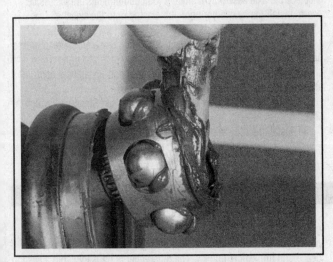

14.20 Pack grease into the bearing until it's completely full

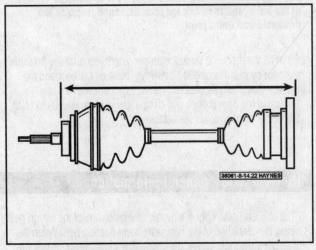

36061-8-14.22 HAYNES

14.22 Measure between the points indicated and move the inner CV joint in or out until the driveaxle is set to the length listed in this Chapter's Specifications

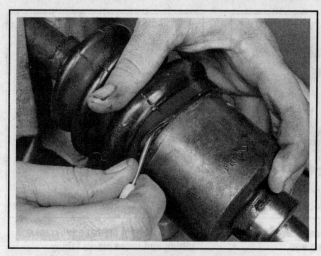

14.23 Equalize the pressure inside the boot by inserting a small screwdriver between the boot and the outer race

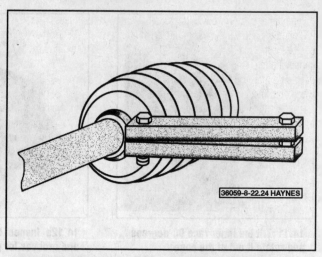

14.24 A special tool is required to crimp the boot clamps in place; tighten the bolt nearest the clamp until the ends of the tool touch - this tool is available at most auto parts stores (it generates much more clamping force than plier-type crimping tools)

OUTER CV JOINT AND BOOT

▶ **Refer to illustration 14.30**

➡ **Note: The outer CV joint is a non-serviceable item and is permanently retained to the driveaxle. If any damage or excessive wear occurs to the axle or the outer CV joint, the entire driveaxle assembly must be replaced (excluding the inner CV joint).**

26 Remove the driveaxle from the vehicle (see Section 13).

27 Mount the driveaxle in a vise. The jaws of the vise should be lined with wood or rags to prevent damage to the axleshaft.

28 Cut the boot clamps from both inner and outer boots and discard them (see illustration 14.3).

29 Remove the inner CV joint and boot (see Steps 4 through 11).

30 Remove the outer CV joint boot. Wash the outer CV joint assembly in solvent and inspect it as described in Step 12 (see illustration). Replace the axle assembly if any CV joint components are excessively worn. Install the new, outer boot and clamps onto the axleshaft (see illustration 14.16).

31 Repack the outer CV joint with CV joint grease and spread grease inside the new boot as well.

32 Position the outer boot on the CV joint and install new boot clamps (see illustration 14.24).

33 Reassemble the inner CV joint and boot (see Steps 13 through 24).

34 Install the driveaxle (see Section 13).

14.30 After the old grease has been rinsed away and the cleaning solvent has been blown out with compressed air, rotate the outer joint housing through its full range of motion and inspect the bearing surfaces for wear or damage - if any of the balls, the race or cage look damaged, replace the driveaxle and outer joint

23 With the driveaxle set to the proper length, equalize the pressure in the boot by inserting a dull screwdriver between the boot and the outer race (see illustration). Don't damage the boot with the tool.

24 Install the boot clamps and crimp them in place (see illustration).

25 Install the driveaxle (see Section 13).

15 Rear axle - general information

The rear axle assembly is a hypoid (the centerline of the pinion gear is below the centerline of the ring gear), semi-floating type. When the vehicle goes around a corner, the differential allows the outer rear tire to turn more quickly than the inner tire. The axleshafts are splined to the differential side gears, so when the vehicle goes around a corner, the inner tire, which turns more slowly than the outer tire, turns its side gear more slowly than the outer tire turns its side gear. The differential pinion gears roll around the slower side gear, driving the outer side gear - and tire - more quickly. The differential is housed within a casting (known as a "carrier") with a pressed steel cover. The steel axle tubes are pressed into and welded to the carrier.

An optional locking limited-slip rear axle is also available. This differential allows for normal operation until one wheel loses traction. A limited-slip unit is similar in design to a conventional differential, except for the addition - at either side of the differential side gears - of a series of alternating clutch friction discs and plates (not unlike a clutch pack on a motorcycle) which slow the rotation of the differential case when one wheel is on a firm surface and the other on a slippery one. The difference in wheel rotational speed produced by this condition applies additional force to the pinion gears and through the clutch fric-

tion discs, which are splined to the axleshafts, equalizes the rotation speed of the axleshaft driving the wheel with traction.

Due to the need for special tools and equipment, it is recommended that operations on these models be limited to those described in this Chapter. Where repair or overhaul is required, remove the axle assembly and take it to a rebuilder, or exchange it for a new or reconditioned unit. Always make sure that an axle unit is exchanged for one of identical type and gear ratio.

16 Rear axle assembly - removal and installation

REMOVAL

▶ **Refer to illustrations 16.6 and 16.10**

1   Raise the rear of the vehicle and support it with jackstands placed under the frame rails.

2   Remove the rear wheels.

3   Disconnect the driveshaft from the rear axle (see Section 10).

4   Disconnect the ABS sensor from the axle.

5   Disconnect the parking brake cable from the parking brake lever (see Chapter 9).

6   Unscrew the vent hose fitting to detach the brake line junction block from the axle tube (see illustration).

7   Disconnect the brake lines from the clips and brackets on the axle housing. Remove the rear brake calipers (see Chapter 9).

✳ CAUTION:

Tie the calipers up with wire to keep any strain off the brake lines.

8   Support the rear axle with a floor jack. If the rear differential is offset to one side, you'll have to use two jacks - one placed under each axle tube.

9   Remove the lower mounting bolts securing the rear shocks to the axle (see Chapter 10).

10   With the jack(s) supporting the axle, remove the nuts and U-bolts securing the axle to the springs (see illustration).

11   Lower the axle assembly and remove it from under the vehicle.

INSTALLATION

12   Installation is the reverse of the removal procedure.

13   Tighten the U-bolt nuts to the torque listed in the Chapter 10 Specifications. Tighten the caliper mounting bolts to the torque listed in the Chapter 9 Specifications. If necessary, check and fill the axle with the specified lubricant (see Chapter 1).

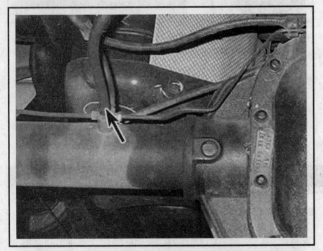

16.6 Disconnect the two rear brake lines, the axle vent tube and the rear brake hose from the junction block on top of the axle

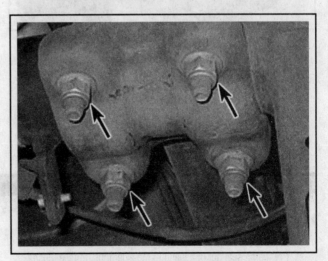

16.10 Remove the nuts and U-bolts securing the axle to the springs

17 Rear axleshaft - removal and installation

▶ **Refer to illustrations 17.3a, 17.3b and 17.4**

1   Raise the rear of the vehicle, support it securely on jackstands

17.3a Position a large screwdriver between the rear axle case and a ring gear bolt to keep the differential case from turning when removing the pinion shaft lock bolt

and block the front wheels. Remove the wheel and brake disc (see Chapter 9).

2   Remove the cover from the differential carrier and allow the lubricant to drain into a container.

3   Remove the lock bolt from the differential pinion shaft. Slide the notched end of the pinion shaft out of the differential case as far as it will go (see illustrations).

4   Push the outer (flanged) end of the axleshaft in and remove the C-lock from the inner end of the shaft (see illustration).

5   Withdraw the axleshaft, taking care not to damage the oil seal in the end of the axle housing as the splined end of the axleshaft passes through it.

6   Installation is the reverse of removal. The manufacturer recommends that a new pinion shaft lock bolt be used, but if one is not available, coat the threads with a non-hardening thread locking compound. Install the pinion shaft lock bolt and tighten it to the torque listed in this Chapter's Specifications.

7   Install the differential cover (see Chapter 1). Install the brake disc/caliper (see Chapter 9).

8   Refill the axle with the correct quantity and grade of lubricant (see Chapter 1). Tighten the wheel lug nuts to the torque listed in the Chapter 1 Specifications.

17.3b Rotate the differential case 180-degrees and slide the pinion shaft out of the case until the stepped part of the shaft contacts the ring gear

17.4 Push in on the axle flange and remove the C-lock from the inner end of the axleshaft

18 Rear axleshaft oil seal - replacement

▶ **Refer to illustrations 18.2 and 18.3**

1   Remove the axleshaft (see Section 17).

2   Pry the oil seal out of the end of the axle housing (see illustration).

3   Apply a film of multi-purpose grease to the oil seal recess and

tap the new seal evenly into place with a hammer and seal installation tool (see illustration) or a large socket so the lips are facing in and the metal face is visible from the end of the axle housing. When correctly installed, the face of the oil seal should be flush with the end of the axle housing.

4   Install the axleshaft (see Section 17).

18.2 Prying out the axleshaft oil seal with a seal removal tool

18.3 Using a seal driver to install the axleshaft oil seal - drive the seal in until it's flush with the bore

19 Rear axleshaft bearing - replacement

▶ **Refer to illustrations 19.2, 19.3 and 19.4**

1 Remove the axleshaft (see Section 17).

2 A bearing puller which grips the bearing from behind will be required for this job (see illustration).

3 Attach a slide hammer to the puller and extract the bearing from the axle housing (see illustration).

4 Clean out the bearing recess and drive in the new bearing with a bearing installer positioned against the outer bearing race (see illustration). Make sure the bearing is tapped in to the full depth of the recess.

5 Install a new oil seal (see Section 18), then install the axleshaft (see Section 17).

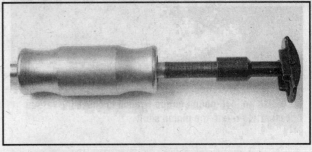

19.2 A typical slide hammer and axleshaft bearing remover attachment

19.3 Removing the axleshaft bearing with a slide hammer

19.4 Use a bearing driver or a large socket to tap the bearing evenly into the axle housing

20 Pinion oil seal - replacement

▶ **Refer to illustrations 20.3, 20.4, 20.5, 20.7, 20.8 and 20.9**

➡ **Note: This procedure applies to the front and rear pinion oil seals.**

1   Loosen the wheel lug nuts. Raise the front (for front differential) or rear (for rear differential) of the vehicle and support it securely on jackstands. Block the opposite set of wheels to keep the vehicle from rolling off the stands. Remove the wheels.

2   Disconnect the driveshaft from the differential pinion flange and support it out of the way with a piece of wire or rope (see Section 10).

3   Rotate the pinion a few times by hand. Use a beam-type or dial-type inch-pound torque wrench to check the torque required to rotate the pinion (see illustration). Record it for use later.

4   Mark the relationship of the pinion flange to the shaft then count and write down the number of exposed threads on the shaft (see illustration).

5   A special tool (available at most auto parts stores) or a chain wrench can be used to keep the companion flange from moving while the self-locking pinion nut is loosened. A screwdriver or long punch inserted through one of the holes in the flange can also be used to immobilize the flange (see illustration).

6   Remove the pinion nut.

7   Withdraw the flange. It may be necessary to use a two-jaw puller engaged behind the flange to draw it off. Do not attempt to pry or hammer behind the flange or hammer on the end of the pinion shaft (see illustration).

20.3 Use an inch-pound torque wrench to check the torque necessary to rotate the pinion shaft

20.4 Mark the relative positions of the pinion and flange before removing the nut

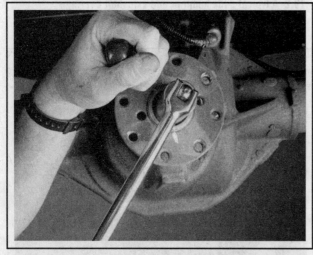

20.5 If you don't have a special flange holding tool to hold the pinion flange while loosening and backing off the pinion flange locknut, use a screwdriver inserted through a hole in the flange and jammed against the top of the reinforcing rib on the differential carrier

20.7 If the pinion flange is difficult to remove, pull it off with a two or three-jaw puller

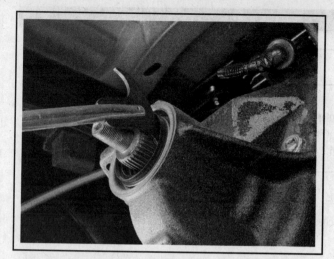

20.8 Pry out the old pinion seal with a seal removal tool

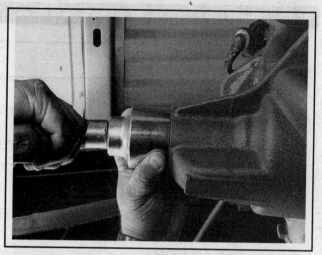

20.9 Lubricate the lips of the new pinion seal and seat it squarely in the bore, then drive it into the carrier with a seal driver or a large socket

8   Pry out the old seal and discard it (see illustration).

9   Lubricate the lips of the new seal and fill the space between the seal lips with wheel bearing grease, then tap it evenly into position with a seal installation tool or a large socket (see illustration). Make sure it enters the housing squarely and is tapped in to its full depth.

10 Install the pinion flange, lining up the marks made in Step 4. If necessary, tighten the pinion nut to draw the flange into place. Do not try to hammer the flange into position.

11 Apply a bead of RTV sealant to the ends of the splines visible in the center of the flange so oil will be sealed in.

12 Install the washer and a new pinion nut. Tighten the nut until the number of threads recorded in Step 4 are exposed.

13 Measure the torque required to rotate the pinion and tighten the nut in small increments (no more than 5 ft-lbs) until it matches the figure recorded in Step 3. To compensate for the drag of the new oil seal, the nut should be tightened a little more until the rotational torque of the pinion exceeds the earlier recording by 5 in-lbs.

14 Reinstall all components removed previously by reversing the removal Steps, tightening all fasteners to their specified torque values.

21 Front axle assembly (4WD models) - removal and installation

1   Loosen the wheel lug nuts, raise the front of the vehicle and support it securely on jackstands placed under the frame. Block the rear wheels to keep the vehicle from rolling off the stands. Remove the front wheels.

2   If equipped, remove the front skid plate.

3   Remove the front driveshaft (see Section 10).

4   Disconnect the front driveaxles from the axleshaft flanges. Sup-

port the driveaxles with wire or rope - don't let them hang by the outer CV joints.

5   Remove the front crossmember.

6   Support the front axle with a pair of floor jacks, then remove the upper, lower and axle tube mounting bolts

7   Lower the axle assembly and remove it from under the vehicle.

8   Installation is the reverse of removal. Be sure to tighten all fasteners securely.

Specifications

General

Clutch

Clutch fluid type	See Chapter 1
Pressure plate tension spring dimension (compressed)	0.55 inch

Driveaxles

Driveaxle length	
2004 through 2008 models	16.93 inches
2009 and later models	
Left driveaxle	16 inches
Right driveaxle	16.21 inches

Torque specifications   Ft-lbs (unless otherwise indicated)

➡ **Note: One foot-pound (ft-lb) of torque is equivalent to 12 inch-pounds (in-lbs) of torque. Torque values below approximately 15 ft-lbs are expressed in inch-pounds, since most foot-pound torque wrenches are not accurate at these smaller values.**

Clutch

Clutch pressure plate-to-flywheel bolts	41
Clutch release cylinder mounting bolts	17

Driveaxles

Driveaxle/hub nut	20
Driveaxle flange-to-axleshaft flange bolts	60
Integrated wheel end mounting fasteners	108 in-lbs

Driveshafts

Center support bearing	35
Front driveshaft-to-differential flange bolts (4WD models)	
2004 through 2008 models	76
2009 and later models	41
Front driveshaft-to-transfer case flange bolts (4WD models)	
2004 through 2008 models	76
2009 and later models	41
Rear driveshaft-to-differential flange bolts (2WD or 4WD models)	76

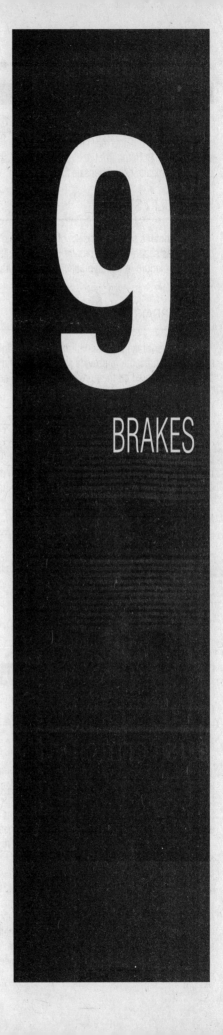

9

BRAKES

Section

1   General information
2   Anti-lock Brake System (ABS) - general information
3   Disc brake pads - replacement
4   Disc brake caliper - removal and installation
5   Brake disc - inspection, removal and installation
6   Parking brake shoes - replacement
7   Master cylinder - removal and installation
8   Brake hoses and lines - inspection and replacement
9   Brake hydraulic system - bleeding
10 Power brake booster - check, removal and installation
11 Adjustable brake pedal motor cable - replacement
12 Brake light switch - replacement

Reference to other Chapters

Brake check - See Chapter 1
Brake fluid level check - See Chapter 1

1   General information

The vehicles covered by this manual are equipped with hydraulically operated front and rear brake systems. The front and rear brakes are disc type. Both the front and rear brakes are self adjusting. The disc brakes automatically compensate for pad wear.

HYDRAULIC SYSTEM

The hydraulic system consists of two separate circuits. The master cylinder has separate reservoirs for the two circuits and, in the event of a leak or failure in one hydraulic circuit, the other circuit will remain operative.

POWER BRAKE BOOSTER

The power brake booster, utilizing engine manifold vacuum and atmospheric pressure to provide assistance to the hydraulically operated brakes, is mounted on the firewall in the engine compartment.

PARKING BRAKE

The parking brake mechanically operates the rear brakes only. The parking brake cables actuate a pair of parking brake shoes mounted inside the drum (hub) portion of each rear brake disc. The parking brake cable tension is adjusted automatically and requires no service.

SERVICE

After completing any operation involving disassembly of any part of the brake system, always test drive the vehicle to check for proper braking performance before resuming normal driving. When testing the brakes, perform the tests on a clean, dry, flat surface. Conditions other than these can lead to inaccurate test results.

Test the brakes at various speeds with both light and heavy pedal pressure. The vehicle should stop evenly without pulling to one side or the other.

Tires, vehicle load and wheel alignment are factors which also affect braking performance.

PRECAUTIONS

There are some general cautions and warnings involving the brake system on this vehicle:

a) *Use only brake fluid conforming to DOT 3 specifications.*
b) *The brake pads and linings are hazardous to your health if inhaled. Whenever you work on brake system components, clean all parts with brake system cleaner. Do not allow the fine dust to become airborne. Also, wear an approved filtering mask.*
c) *Safety should be paramount whenever any servicing of the brake components is performed. Do not use parts or fasteners which are not in perfect condition, and be sure that all clearances and torque specifications are adhered to. If you are at all unsure about a certain procedure, seek professional advice. Upon completion of any brake system work, test the brakes carefully in a controlled area before putting the vehicle into normal service. If a problem is suspected in the brake system, don't drive the vehicle until it's fixed.*

2   Anti-lock Brake System (ABS) - general information

GENERAL INFORMATION

▶ **Refer to illustration 2.2**

1   The anti-lock brake system is designed to maintain vehicle steerability, directional stability and optimum deceleration under severe braking conditions on most road surfaces. It does so by monitoring the rotational speed of each wheel and controlling the brake line pressure to each wheel during braking. This prevents the wheels from locking up.

2   The ABS system has three main components - the wheel speed sensors, the anti-lock brake control module and the hydraulic control unit (see illustration). Wheel speed sensors - one at each front wheel and another located on the rear differential - send a variable voltage signal to the control unit, which monitors these signals, compares them to its program and determines whether a wheel is about to lock up. When a wheel is about to lock up, the control unit signals the hydraulic unit to reduce hydraulic pressure (or not increase it further) at that wheel's brake caliper. Pressure modulation is handled by electrically-operated solenoid valves.

2.2 The hydraulic control unit for the Anti-lock Brake System is located in the left-front area of the engine compartment

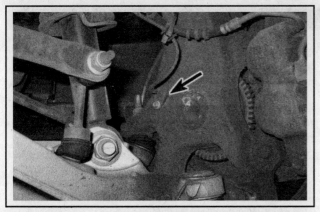

2.10 The location of the front wheel speed sensor on a 2WD model

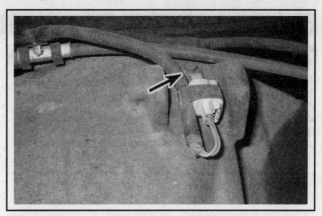

2.16 The rear wheel speed sensor is located on the differential

3   If a problem develops within the system, an ABS warning light will glow on the dashboard. Sometimes, a visual inspection of the ABS system can help you locate the problem. Carefully inspect the ABS wiring harness. Pay particularly close attention to the harness and connections near each wheel. Look for signs of chafing and other damage caused by incorrectly routed wires. If a wheel sensor harness is damaged, the sensor must be replaced.

※※ WARNING:

Do NOT try to repair an ABS wiring harness. The ABS system is sensitive to even the smallest changes in resistance. Repairing the harness could alter resistance values and cause the system to malfunction. If the ABS wiring harness is damaged in any way, it must be replaced.

※※ CAUTION:

Make sure the ignition is turned off before unplugging or reattaching any electrical connections.

DIAGNOSIS AND REPAIR

4   If a dashboard warning light comes on and stays on while the vehicle is in operation, the ABS system requires attention. Although special electronic ABS diagnostic testing tools are necessary to properly diagnose the system, you can perform a few preliminary checks before taking the vehicle to a dealer service department or other repair shop.

   a) *Check the brake fluid level in the reservoir.*
   b) *Verify that the computer electrical connectors are securely connected.*
   c) *Check the electrical connectors at the hydraulic control unit.*
   d) *Check the fuses.*
   e) *Follow the wiring harness to each wheel and verify that all connections are secure and that the wiring is undamaged.*

5   If the above preliminary checks do not rectify the problem, the vehicle should be diagnosed by a dealer service department or other qualified repair shop. Due to the complex nature of this system, all actual repair work must be done by a qualified automotive technician.

WHEEL SPEED SENSOR - REMOVAL AND INSTALLATION

Front wheel speed sensors

▶ **Refer to illustration 2.10**

4WD models

6   Loosen the wheel lug nuts, raise the vehicle and support it securely on jackstands. Remove the wheel.
7   Remove the brake disc (see Section 5).

All models

8   Make sure the ignition key is turned to the Off position.
9   Trace the wiring back from the sensor, detaching all brackets and clips while noting its correct routing, then disconnect the electrical connector.
10 Remove the mounting bolt and carefully pull the sensor out from the knuckle (see illustration).
11 Installation is the reverse of the removal procedure. Tighten the mounting bolt to the torque listed in this Chapter's Specifications.
12 On 4WD models, install the brake disc and caliper, tightening the caliper mounting bolts to the torque listed in this Chapter's Specifications.

➡ **Note: Bleeding won't be necessary unless the fluid hose was disconnected from the caliper. Install the wheel and lug nuts, tightening them securely. Lower the vehicle and tighten the lug nuts to the torque listed in the Chapter 1 Specifications.**

Rear wheel speed sensor

▶ **Refer to illustration 2.16**

13 The rear wheel speed sensor is located on the differential. Raise the rear of the vehicle and support it securely on jackstands.
14 Make sure the ignition key is turned to the Off position.
15 Trace the wiring back from the sensor, detaching all brackets and clips while noting its correct routing, then disconnect the electrical connector.
16 Remove the mounting bolt and carefully pull the sensor out from the differential (see illustration).
17 Installation is the reverse of the removal procedure. Tighten the mounting bolt to the torque listed in this Chapter's Spcifications.

3   Disc brake pads - replacement

※ WARNING:

Disc brake pads must be replaced on both wheels at the same time - never replace the pads on only one wheel. Also, the dust created by the brake system is harmful to your health. Never blow it out with compressed air and don't inhale any of it. An approved filtering mask should be worn when working on the brakes. Do not, under any circumstances, use petroleum-based solvents to clean brake parts. Use brake system cleaner only!

1   Remove the cap from the brake fluid reservoir.

FRONT DISC BRAKE PADS

▶ **Refer to illustrations 3.5 and 3.6a through 3.6p**

※ CAUTION:

Install new caliper slippers onto the caliper mounting bracket and new V-springs when installing new brake pads.

2   Loosen the wheel lug nuts, raise the front of the vehicle and support it securely on jackstands. Apply the parking brake.
3   Remove the wheels. Work on one brake assembly at a time, using the assembled brake for reference if necessary.
4   Inspect the brake disc carefully as outlined in Section 5. If machining is necessary, follow the information in that Section to remove the disc, at which time the pads can be removed as well.
5   Push the piston back into its bore to provide room for the new brake pads. A C-clamp can be used to accomplish this (see illustration). As the piston is depressed to the bottom of the caliper bore, the fluid in the master cylinder will rise. Make sure that it doesn't overflow. If necessary, remove some of the fluid.
6   Follow the accompanying photos (illustrations 3.6a through 3.6p), for the actual pad replacement procedure. Be sure to stay in order and read the caption under each illustration.
7   When reinstalling the caliper, be sure to tighten the mounting bolts to the torque listed in this Chapter's Specifications. After the job has been completed, firmly depress the brake pedal a few times to bring the pads into contact with the disc. Check the level of the brake fluid, adding some if necessary. Check the operation of the brakes carefully before placing the vehicle into normal service.

3.5 Before removing the caliper, be sure to depress the piston into the bottom of its bore in the caliper with a large C-clamp to make room for the new pads

3.6a Always wash the brakes with brake cleaner before disassembling anything

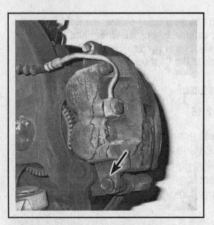

3.6b Remove the lower caliper mounting bolt . . .

3.6c . . . then swing the caliper up and use a piece of wire to tie it to the coil spring. Never let the caliper hang by the brake hose

3.6d Remove and discard the V-springs from the brake pads

3.6e Separate the inner pad from the caliper mounting bracket . . .

3.6f . . . then remove the outer pad from the caliper mounting bracket

3.6g Apply anti-squeal compound to the backs of the new pads

3.6h Remove and discard the spring clips from the upper and lower parts of the caliper mounting bracket

3.6i Inspect the caliper mounting bracket for burrs, deposits or other damage that may interfere with the brake pads moving properly during normal braking

3.6j Pull out both guide pins and clean them off, then apply a coat of high temperature grease to them Also, inspect the guide pin dust boots. Damaged dust boots must be replaced

3.6k Install new spring clips onto the mounting bracket

3.6l Install the inner pad

3.6m Install the outer pad

3.6n Install new V-springs

3.6o While holding the brake pads to the disc, swing the caliper into position

3.6p Install the lower bolt and tighten it to the torque listed in this Chapter's Specifications

3.11a Always wash the brakes with brake cleaner before disassembling anything

3.11b Loosen and remove the caliper guide pin bolts

3.11c Remove the caliper

REAR DISC BRAKE PADS

▶ **Refer to illustrations 3.11a through 3.11n**

❊❊❊ CAUTION:

Install new caliper slippers onto the caliper mounting bracket when installing new brake pads.

8   Loosen the wheel lug nuts, raise the rear of the vehicle and support it securely on jackstands. Block the wheels at the opposite end. Remove the wheels. Work on one brake assembly at a time, using the assembled brake for reference if necessary.

9   Inspect the brake disc carefully as outlined in Section 5. If

machining is necessary, follow the information in that Section to remove the disc, at which time the pads can be removed as well.

10 Push the piston back into its bore to provide room for the new brake pads. A C-clamp can be used to accomplish this (see illustration 3.5). As the piston is depressed to the bottom of the caliper bore, the fluid in the master cylinder will rise. Make sure that it doesn't overflow. If necessary, remove some of the fluid.

11 Follow the accompanying photos (illustrations 3.11a through 3.11n), for the actual pad replacement procedure. Be sure to stay in order and read the caption under each illustration.

12 When reinstalling the caliper, be sure to tighten the mounting bolts to the torque listed in this Chapter's Specifications. After the job has been completed, firmly depress the brake pedal a few times to bring the pads into contact with the disc. Check the level of the brake fluid, adding some if necessary. Check the operation of the brakes carefully before placing the vehicle into normal service.

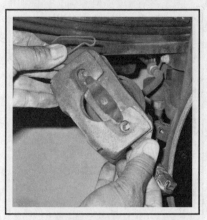

3.11d Unclip the outboard brake pad

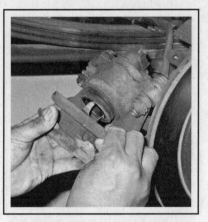

3.11e Remove the inboard brake pad

3.11f Never let the caliper hang by the brake hose - use a piece of wire to secure it, or place on the leaf spring

3.11g Remove the stainless steel slippers from the caliper mounting bosses

3.11h Install new slippers and make sure they are fully seated

3.11i Install the inner pad

3.11j If necessary, use a caliper piston tool to force the piston in until it is fully retracted (a C-clamp could also be used). As the piston is depressed to the bottom of the caliper bore, the fluid in the master cylinder will rise. Make sure that it doesn't overflow. If necessary, remove some of the fluid

3.11k Install the outer pad, making sure the projections on the pad backing plate and the spring arms engage properly with the caliper frame

3.11l Before installing the caliper, remove the caliper bushings from their boots and clean them. Inspect the boots for wear or damage. Replace any damaged parts. Coat the bushings with high-temperature grease and then reinstall them

3.11m Install the caliper, making sure the notches in the brake pads are aligned properly onto the slippers

3.11n Install the caliper mounting bolts and tighten them to the torque listed in this Chapter's Specifications

4   Disc brake caliper - removal and installation

❊❊ WARNING:

Dust created by the brake system is harmful to your health. Never blow it out with compressed air and don't inhale any of it. An approved filtering mask should be worn when working on the brakes. Do not, under any circumstances, use petroleum-based solvents to clean brake parts. Use brake system cleaner only.

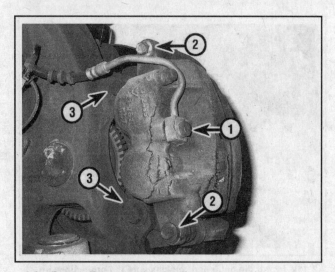

4.2a Front caliper mounting details

1   Inlet fitting and bolt
2   Caliper mounting bolts
3   Caliper mounting bracket bolts

➡ **Note: If replacement is indicated (usually because of fluid leakage), it is recommended that the calipers be replaced, not overhauled. New and factory rebuilt units are available on an exchange basis, which makes this job quite easy. Always replace the calipers in pairs - never replace just one of them.**

REMOVAL

▶ **Refer to illustrations 4.2a, 4.2b and 4.3**

1   Loosen the wheel lug nuts, raise the vehicle (front or rear) and place it securely on jackstands. Remove the wheels.

2   Remove the inlet fitting bolt and disconnect the brake hose from the caliper (see illustrations). Plug the brake hose to keep contaminants out of the brake system and to prevent losing any more brake fluid than is necessary.

➡ **Note: If the caliper is being removed for access to another component, don't disconnect the hose.**

3   Refer to Section 3 for the caliper removal procedure. If the caliper is being removed for access to another component, use a piece of wire to securely hang it out of the way (see illustration).

INSTALLATION

4   Install the caliper by reversing the removal procedure.

5   Bleed the brake circuit according to the procedure in Section 9. Make sure there are no leaks from the hose connections. Test the brakes carefully before returning the vehicle to normal service.

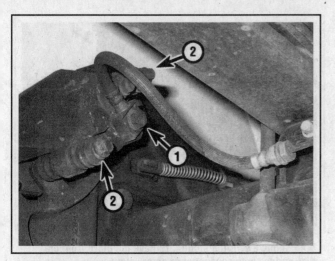

4.2b Rear caliper mounting details

1 *Inlet fitting and bolt*
2 *Caliper mounting bolts*

4.3 Hang the caliper with a wire. DON'T allow the caliper to hang by the brake hose! (typical shown)

5 Brake disc - inspection, removal and installation

✳✳ WARNING:

Dust created by the brake system is harmful to your health. Never blow it out with compressed air and don't inhale any of it. An approved filtering mask should be worn when working on the brakes. Do not, under any circumstances, use petroleum-based solvents to clean brake parts. Use brake system cleaner only.

INSPECTION

▶ **Refer to illustrations 5.3, 5.4a, 5.4b, 5.5a and 5.5b**

1 Loosen the wheel lug nuts, raise the vehicle and support it securely on jackstands and then remove the wheels. If you are working on a 4WD model, install the lug nuts to hold the disc in place against the hub flange.

➡ **Note: If the lug nuts don't contact the disc when screwed on all the way, install washers under them.**

2 Remove the brake caliper as outlined in Section 4. It isn't necessary to disconnect the brake hose. After removing the caliper bolts, suspend the caliper out of the way with a piece of wire (see illustration 4.3). On front disc brakes, remove the two caliper mounting bracket-to-steering knuckle bolts (see illustration 4.2a) and detach the mounting bracket.

3 Visually inspect the disc surface for score marks and other dam-

5.3 The brake pads on this vehicle were obviously neglected, as they wore down completely and cut deep grooves into the disc - wear this severe means the disc must be replaced

age. Light scratches and shallow grooves are normal after use and may not always be detrimental to brake operation, but deep scoring requires disc removal and refinishing by an automotive machine shop. Be sure to check both sides of the disc (see illustration). If pulsating has been noticed during application of the brakes, suspect disc runout.

5.4a Use a dial indicator and rotate the disc to check disc runout

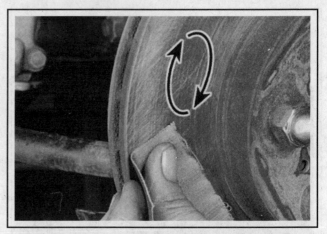

5.4b Using a swirling motion, remove the glaze from the disc surface with sandpaper or emery cloth

4   To check disc runout, place a dial indicator at a point about 1/2-inch from the outer edge of the disc (see illustration). Set the indicator to zero and turn the disc. The indicator reading should not exceed the specified allowable runout limit. If it does, the disc should be refinished by an automotive machine shop.

➡ **Note: The discs should be resurfaced regardless of the dial indicator reading, as this will impart a smooth finish and ensure a perfectly flat surface, eliminating any brake pedal pulsation or other undesirable symptoms related to questionable discs. At the very least, if you elect not to have the discs resurfaced, remove the glaze from the surface with emery cloth or sandpaper, using a swirling motion (see illustration).**

5   It's absolutely critical that the disc not be machined to a thickness under the specified minimum thickness. The minimum (or discard) thickness is cast or stamped into the inside of the disc (see illustration). The disc thickness can be checked with a micrometer (see illustration).

REMOVAL

▸ **Refer to illustrations 5.7 and 5.8**

➡ **Note: A new spindle nut is required for disc installation on 2008 and earlier 2WD models.**

6   If you haven't already done so, remove the brake caliper as outlined in Section 4. It isn't necessary to disconnect the brake hose. After removing the caliper bolts, suspend the caliper out of the way with a piece of wire (see illustration 4.3). On front disc brakes, remove the two caliper mounting bracket-to-steering knuckle bolts (see illustration 4.2a) and detach the mounting bracket.

7   If you're removing a rear disc, a front disc on a 2009 or later 2WD model, or a front disc on a 4WD model, remove the retaining washers that hold the disc in place (if equipped) and then remove the disc from the hub (see illustration).

8   If you are removing a front disc on a 2008 and earlier 2WD model, remove the brake disc/hub assembly by removing the spindle nut (see illustration).

✳ CAUTION:

Do not re-use the spindle nut; it must be replaced with a new one.

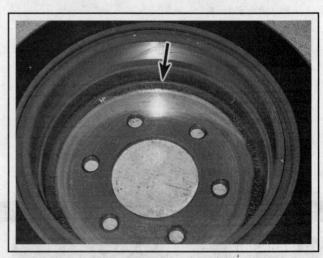

5.5a The minimum (discard) thickness of the brake disc is cast into the disc (rear disc shown, front similar)

INSTALLATION

9   Place the disc in position over the threaded studs (except for the front discs on 2WD models).

10   For front discs on 2WD models, reinstall the brake disc/hub assembly and tighten the new spindle nut to the torque listed in this Chapter's Specifications. Install the nut lock and a new cotter pin.

11   On front disc brakes, install the caliper mounting bracket, tightening the bolts to the torque value listed in this Chapter's Specifications.

12   Install the caliper and tighten the bolts to the torque listed in this Chapter's Specifications.

13   Install the wheel, then lower the vehicle to the ground. Tighten the lug nuts to the torque listed in the Chapter 1 Specifications. Depress the brake pedal a few times to bring the brake pads into contact with the disc. Bleeding won't be necessary unless the brake hose was disconnected from the caliper. Check the operation of the brakes carefully before driving the vehicle.

5.5b Use a micrometer to measure disc thickness

5.7 Use cutting pliers to remove any metal retaining washers from the wheel studs (if equipped)

5.8 When removing the front disc on a 2008 and earlier 2WD model, remove the cotter pin and nut lock, then remove the spindle nut and slide the disc off the spindle (when reinstalling the disc, be sure to use a new nut and cotter pin)

6   Parking brake shoes - replacement

▶ **Refer to illustrations 6.2, 6.3 and 6.6a through 6.6m**

⁜ **WARNING:**

Dust created by the brake system is harmful to your health. Never blow it out with compressed air and don't inhale any of it. An approved filtering mask should be worn when working on the brakes. Do not, under any circumstances, use petroleum-based solvents to clean brake parts. Use brake system cleaner only.

1   Release the parking brake.

2   Have an assistant pull the parking brake cable from under the left side of the vehicle (see illustration).

3   With the cable under tension from the assistant, insert a 5/32-inch drill bit into the control actuator to lock the assembly into position (see illustration).

4   Loosen the rear wheel lug nuts. Raise the vehicle and support it securely on jackstands. Remove the wheels. Be sure to block the front tires.

5   Remove the brake calipers (see Section 4) and the brake discs (see Section 5).

6.2 Have an assistant pull the parking brake cable until it stops . . .

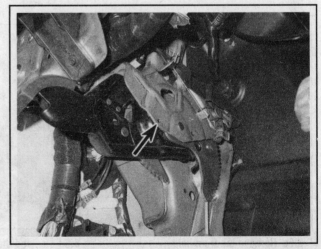

6.3 . . . then with the cable pulled, insert a 5/32-inch drill bit (or equivalent) into the hole on the control actuator to lock it into position

6   Clean the parking brake assembly with brake system cleaner before beginning any work. Follow illustrations 6.6a through 6.6m for replacement of the parking brake shoes. Be sure to stay in order and read the caption under each illustration.

7   Clean the brake disc/parking brake drum and check it for score marks, deep grooves, hard spots (which will appear as small discolored areas) and cracks. If the disc/drum is worn, scored or out-of-round, it can be resurfaced by an automotive machine shop.

8   After the shoes have been installed, turn the adjusting screw so the disc just fits over the new shoes. When the disc is installed, the shoes should not rub as the disc is turned. If you have a brake shoe adjusting gauge, adjust the diameter of the shoes to 0.02-inch less than that of the drum surface of the rear brake disc.

9   Repeat this procedure for the other parking brake assembly.

10 Install the brake discs (see Section 5) and the brake calipers (see Section 4).

11 Remove the rubber plug from the brake backing plate and, using a screwdriver or brake adjusting tool, turn the adjusting screw star wheel until the parking brake shoes start to drag as the disc is turned, then back off the star wheel until the shoes don't drag.

12 Install the rear wheels and lug nuts, lower the vehicle and tighten the lug nuts to the torque listed in the Chapter 1 Specifications.

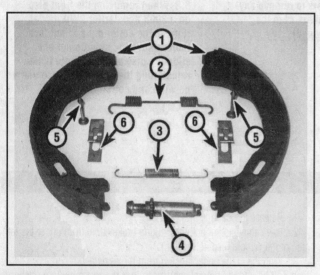

6.6a Parking brake shoes and component details

1	Parking brake shoes	4	Adjusting screw assembly
2	Retracting spring	5	Hold-down spring retainers
3	Adjusting screw spring	6	Hold-down clips

6.6b Wash down the brake assembly with brake cleaner; DO NOT blow it out with compressed air!

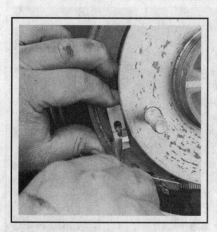

6.6c Remove the front hold-down clip . . .

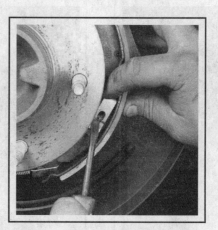

6.6d . . . and the rear hold-down clip

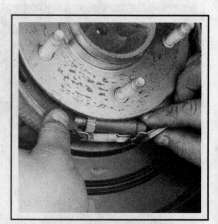

6.6e Remove the parking brake shoe adjuster . . .

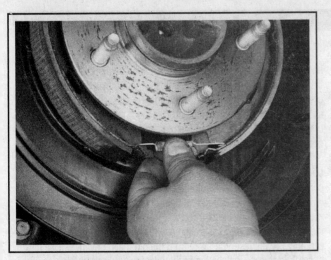

6.6f . . . remove the lower return spring

6.6g Spread the parking brake shoes as shown and lift off the parking brake shoe assembly; if you're replacing the old shoes, remove the upper return spring and transfer it to the new shoes

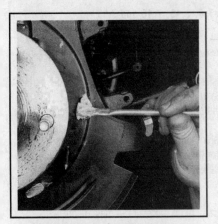

6.6h Lubricate the shoe contact points on the backing plate with high-temperature brake grease

6.6i With the upper return spring installed into the shoes as shown, spread the lower ends of the shoes apart and install the parking brake shoe assembly

6.6j Install the front shoe hold-down clip . . .

6.6k . . . and the rear shoe hold-down clip

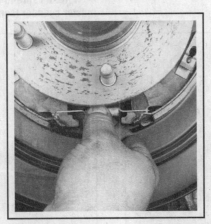

6.6l Install the lower return spring . . .

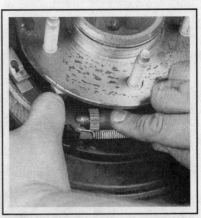

6.6m . . . and the adjuster (make sure the star wheel of the adjuster is pointing towards the front of the vehicle)

7 Master cylinder - removal and installation

REMOVAL

▶ **Refer to illustration 7.3**

1   The master cylinder is located in the engine compartment, mounted to the power brake booster.

2   Using a large syringe or equivalent, siphon the brake fluid from the master cylinder reservoir and dispose of it properly.

✵ CAUTION:

Brake fluid will damage paint. Cover all painted surfaces and avoid spilling fluid during this procedure.

3   Disconnect the electrical connector from the fluid level warning switch (see illustration).

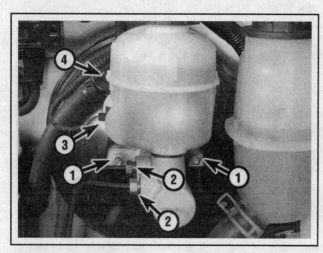

7.3 Master cylinder details

1   *Mounting nuts*
2   *Brake line fittings*
3   *Fluid level switch connector*
4   *Fluid reservoir*

4   Place rags under the fluid fittings and prepare caps or plastic bags to cover the ends of the lines once they are disconnected. Loosen the fittings at the ends of the brake lines where they enter the master cylinder. To prevent rounding off the corners on these nuts, the use of a flare-nut wrench, which wraps around the nut, is preferred. Pull the brake lines slightly away from the master cylinder and plug the ends to prevent contamination.

5   Remove the nuts attaching the master cylinder to the power booster. Pull the master cylinder off the studs and out of the engine compartment. Again, be careful not to spill the fluid as this is done.

6   If a new master cylinder is being installed and is not equipped with a reservoir, transfer the reservoir from the old master cylinder to the new one using new seals. Remove the reservoir retaining pins and carefully pry the reservoir away from the old master cylinder. Use clean brake fluid to ease installation of the new seals and reservoir.

INSTALLATION

▶ **Refer to illustrations 7.8, 7.13, 7.16 and 7.17**

7   Bench bleed the new master cylinder before installing it. Mount the master cylinder in a vise, with the jaws of the vise clamping on the mounting flange.

8   Attach a pair of master cylinder bleeder tubes to the outlet ports of the master cylinder (see illustration).

9   Fill the reservoir with brake fluid of the recommended type (see Chapter 1).

10 Slowly push the pistons into the master cylinder (a large Phillips screwdriver can be used for this) - air will be expelled from the pressure chambers and into the reservoir. Because the tubes are submerged in fluid, air can't be drawn back into the master cylinder when you release the pistons.

11 Repeat the procedure until no more air bubbles are present.

12 Remove the bleed tubes, one at a time, and install plugs in the open ports to prevent fluid leakage and air from entering. Install the reservoir cap.

13 Install the master cylinder over the studs on the power brake booster and tighten the attaching nuts only finger tight at this time.

➡ **Note: Be sure to install a new O-ring into the sleeve of the master cylinder (see illustration)**

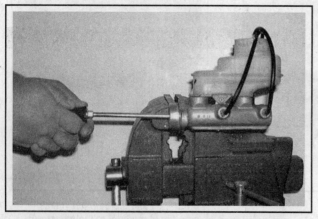

7.8 The best way to bleed air from the master cylinder before installing it on the vehicle is with a pair of bleeder tubes that direct brake fluid into the reservoir during bleeding

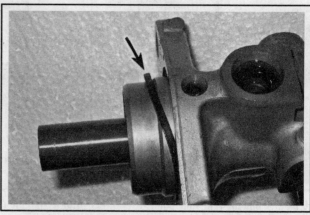

7.13 Be sure to install a new rubber O-ring on the master cylinder (typical shown)

7.16 Have an assistant depress the brake pedal and hold it down, then loosen the fitting nut, allowing the air and fluid to escape; repeat this procedure on both fittings until the fluid is clear of air bubbles

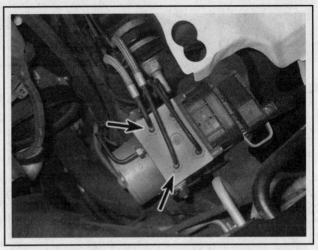

7.17 Loosen these fittings on the ABS hydraulic unit to bleed the lines coming from the master cylinder

14 Thread the brake line fittings into the master cylinder. Since the master cylinder is still a bit loose, it can be moved slightly in order for the fittings to thread in easily. Be careful not to cross-thread or strip the fittings as they are installed.

15 Fully tighten the mounting nuts, then the brake line fittings. Tighten the nuts to the torque listed in this Chapter's Specifications.

16 Fill the master cylinder reservoir with fluid, then bleed the master cylinder and the brake system as described in Section 9. To bleed the cylinder on the vehicle, have an assistant depress the brake pedal and hold the pedal to the floor. Loosen the fitting just enough to allow air and fluid to escape then tighten it lightly (see illustration). Repeat this procedure on both fittings until the fluid is clear of air bubbles and then tighten the fittings securely.

✻ CAUTION:

Have plenty of rags on hand to catch the fluid - brake fluid will ruin painted surfaces. After the bleeding procedure is completed, rinse the area under the master cylinder with clean water.

17 Repeat the previous procedure by opening the system at the line fittings which connect the master cylinder to the ABS hydraulic control unit. This step will remove any air that may have entered the lines when they were disconnected from the master cylinder (see illustration).

18 The remainder of installation is the reverse of removal. Test the operation of the brake system carefully before placing the vehicle into normal service.

✻ WARNING:

If you are in doubt about the effectiveness of the brake system, DO NOT OPERATE THE VEHICLE. On models equipped with ABS, it is possible for air to become trapped in the anti-lock brake system hydraulic control unit. If the brake pedal continues to feel spongy after repeated bleedings or the BRAKE or ANTI-LOCK light stays on, have the vehicle towed to a dealer service department or other qualified shop to be bled with the aid of a scan tool.

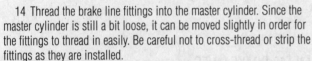

8   Brake hoses and lines - inspection and replacement

✻ WARNING:

If air has found its way into the hydraulic control unit, the system must be bled with the use of a scan tool. If the brake pedal feels spongy even after bleeding the brakes, or the ABS light on the instrument panel does not go off, or if you have any doubts whatsoever about the effectiveness of the brake system, have the vehicle towed to a dealer service department or other repair shop equipped with the necessary tools for bleeding the system.

1   About every six months, with the vehicle raised and placed securely on jackstands, the flexible hoses which connect the steel brake lines with the front and rear brake assemblies should be inspected

for cracks, chafing of the outer cover, leaks, blisters and other damage. These are important and vulnerable parts of the brake system and inspection should be complete. A light and mirror will be needed for a thorough check. If a hose exhibits any of the above defects, replace it with a new one.

FLEXIBLE HOSES

▶ **Refer to illustrations 8.3a and 8.3b**

2   If you're replacing a front hose, loosen the wheel lug nuts, raise the front of the vehicle and support it securely on jackstands. Clean all dirt away from the ends of the hose.

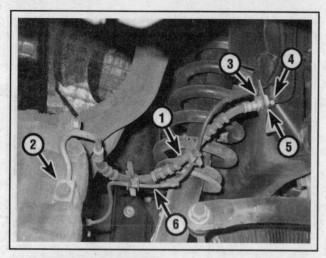

8.3a Front brake hose details

1 *Flexible hose*
2 *Brake hose fitting at caliper*
3 *Brake hose fitting*
4 *Steel brake line fitting-to-hose fitting*
5 *Brake hose fitting retaining clip*
6 *ABS wheel speed sensor harness*

3 To disconnect a front brake hose from the metal line, unscrew the steel brake line fitting with a flare-nut wrench. For front brake hoses, remove the clip that retains the fitting to the frame (see illustration).

4 Disconnect the hose from the caliper, discarding the sealing washers.

5 Using new sealing washers, attach the new brake hose to the caliper.

6 To reattach a brake hose to the junction, route the line to its original position. Make sure the hose isn't twisted, then attach it to the caliper by tightening the bolt securely.

7 Carefully check to make sure the suspension or steering components don't make contact with the hose. Have an assistant push down on the vehicle and also turn the steering wheel lock-to-lock during inspection.

8 Bleed the brake system (see Section 9).

8.3b Rear brake hose details

1 *Flexible hose*
2 *Brake hose fitting at caliper*
3 *Brake hose fitting*
4 *Steel brake line fitting to hose fitting*

METAL BRAKE LINES

9 To disconnect a metal brake line from any fitting, unscrew the metal tube nut with a flare nut.

10 When replacing brake lines, be sure to use the correct parts. Don't use copper tubing for any brake system components. Purchase steel brake lines from a dealer parts department or auto parts store.

11 Prefabricated brake lines, with the tube ends already flared and fittings installed, are available at auto parts stores and dealer parts departments. These lines can be bent to the proper shapes using a tubing bender.

12 When installing the new line make sure it's well supported in the brackets and has plenty of clearance between moving or hot components.

13 After installation, check the master cylinder fluid level and add fluid as necessary. Bleed the brake system as outlined in Section 9 and test the brakes carefully before placing the vehicle into normal operation.

9 Brake hydraulic system - bleeding

▶ **Refer to illustration 9.8**

❋❋ **WARNING:**

Wear eye protection when bleeding the brake system. If the fluid comes in contact with your eyes, immediately rinse them with water and seek medical attention.

➡ **Note: Bleeding the brake system is necessary to remove any air that's trapped in the system when it's opened during removal and installation of a hose, line, caliper, wheel cylinder or master cylinder.**

1 It will probably be necessary to bleed the system at all four brakes if air has entered the system due to low fluid level, or if the brake lines have been disconnected at the master cylinder.

2 If a brake line was disconnected only at a wheel, then only that caliper must be bled.

3 If a brake line is disconnected at a fitting located between the master cylinder and any of the brakes, that part of the system served by the disconnected line must be bled.

4 Remove any residual vacuum from the brake power booster by applying the brake several times with the engine off.

5 Remove the master cylinder reservoir cap and fill the reservoir with brake fluid. Reinstall the cap.

➡ **Note: Check the fluid level often during the bleeding operation and add fluid as necessary to prevent the fluid level from falling low enough to allow air bubbles into the master cylinder.**

6   Have an assistant on hand, as well as a supply of new brake fluid, an empty clear plastic container, a length of plastic, rubber or vinyl tubing to fit over the bleeder valve and a wrench to open and close the bleeder valve.

7   Beginning at the right rear wheel, loosen the bleeder screw slightly, then tighten it to a point where it's snug but can still be loosened quickly and easily.

8   Place one end of the tubing over the bleeder screw fitting and submerge the other end in brake fluid in the container (see illustration).

9   Have the assistant slowly depress the brake pedal and hold it in the depressed position.

10 While the pedal is held depressed, open the bleeder screw just enough to allow a flow of fluid to leave the valve. Watch for air bubbles to exit the submerged end of the tube. When the fluid flow slows after a couple of seconds, tighten the screw and have your assistant release the pedal.

11 Repeat Steps 9 and 10 until no more air is seen leaving the tube, then tighten the bleeder screw and proceed to the left rear wheel, the right front wheel and the left front wheel, in that order, and perform the same procedure. Be sure to check the fluid level in the master cylinder reservoir frequently.

12 Never use old brake fluid. It contains moisture which can boil, rendering the brake system inoperative.

13 Refill the master cylinder with fluid at the end of the operation.

14 Check the operation of the brakes. The pedal should feel solid when depressed, with no sponginess. If necessary, repeat the entire process.

9.8 When bleeding the brakes, a hose is connected to the bleed screw at the caliper and submerged in brake fluid - air will be seen as bubbles in the tube and container (all air must be expelled before moving to the next wheel)

✳✳ WARNING:

If you are in doubt about the effectiveness of the brake system, **DO NOT OPERATE THE VEHICLE**. On models equipped with **ABS**, it is possible for air to become trapped in the anti-lock brake system hydraulic control unit. If the brake pedal continues to feel spongy after repeated bleedings or the **BRAKE** or **ANTI-LOCK** light stays on, have the vehicle towed to a dealer service department or other qualified shop to be bled with the aid of a scan tool.

---

10 Power brake booster - check, removal and installation

OPERATING CHECK

1   Depress the brake pedal several times with the engine off and make sure that there is no change in the pedal reserve distance.

2   Depress the pedal and start the engine. If the pedal goes down slightly, operation is normal.

AIRTIGHTNESS CHECK

3   Start the engine and turn it off after one or two minutes. Depress the brake pedal several times slowly. If the pedal goes down farther the first time but gradually rises after the second or third depression, the booster is airtight.

4   Depress the brake pedal while the engine is running, then stop the engine with the pedal depressed. If there is no change in the pedal reserve travel after holding the pedal for 30 seconds, the booster is airtight.

REMOVAL AND INSTALLATION

▸ **Refer to illustrations 10.7, 10.8, 10.9 and 10.10**

5   Disassembly of the power unit requires special tools and is not ordinarily performed by the home mechanic. If a problem develops, it's recommended that a new or factory rebuilt unit be installed.

6   In the engine compartment, remove the nuts attaching the master cylinder to the booster and carefully pull the master cylinder forward until it clears the mounting studs. Be careful not to bend or kink the brake lines. On 2011 and later models, remove the coolant recovery tank and the air cleaner housing as an assembly (see Chapter 4).

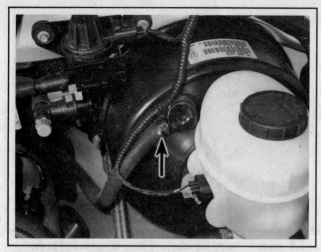

10.7 Disconnect the vacuum hose from the fitting on the power booster (don't pull the fitting out of the booster)

10.8 The location of the speed control deactivation switch

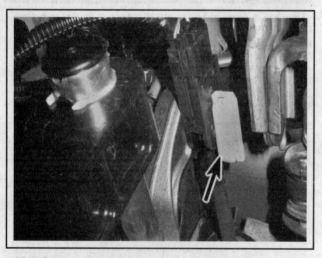

10.9 Remove the retaining pin cover to expose the retaining pin

10.10 To detach the power brake booster from the firewall, remove these four nuts

7   Disconnect the vacuum hose from the fitting on the power brake booster (see illustration).

8   On models without adjustable brake and accelerator pedals, rotate the speed control deactivation switch counterclockwise to remove it (see illustration).

9   Remove the retaining pin cover and the retaining pin and then disconnect the pushrod from the upper end of the brake pedal (see illustration).

10   Remove the nuts attaching the booster to the firewall (see illustration).

11   Carefully lift the booster unit away from the firewall and out of the engine compartment.

12   To install the booster, place it into position and tighten the retaining nuts to the torque listed in the Chapter's Specifications. Connect the pushrod to the brake pedal and install the retaining clip and cover.

13   Install the master cylinder. Reconnect the vacuum hose.

14   Carefully test the operation of the brakes before placing the vehicle in normal service.

11 Adjustable brake pedal motor cable - replacement

▶ **Refer to illustration 11.1**

1   Remove the motor cable by pulling the cable end from the brake pedal assembly, then removing the fasteners that attach the other end to the motor (see illustration).

2   Before installing the replacement cable, make certain that the accelerator pedal and brake pedal are at the same height. One method is to use the motor to set one pedal in the extreme upper or lower position, then disconnect the cable from that pedal. Perform the same procedure on the other pedal until the pedal heights match.

➡ **Note: Install the cable when the pedals are in the extreme upper or lower position only.**

3   With both pedals at the same height, install the cable ends firmly into place on the brake pedal assembly and the accelerator pedal assembly.

4   Confirm that the adjustable pedals are working correctly before placing the vehicle into normal service.

11.1 The end of the cable can be pulled directly away from the brake pedal assembly (lower arrow); the upper end must be unbolted from the motor

12 Brake light switch - replacement

2004 THROUGH 2008 MODELS

▶ **Refer to illustration 12.1**

1   Disconnect the electrical connector from the switch (see illustration).

2   Remove the retaining pin cover and pin to release the switch from the brake pedal arm (see illustrations 10.9 and 12.1).

3   Slide the bushing out and remove the brake light switch and the pushrod from the brake pedal.

4   To install the brake light switch, install the pushrod, the switch, the bushing, retaining pin and cover onto the brake pedal.

5   Connect the switch electrical connector.

2009 AND LATER MODELS

6   Disconnect the electrical connector from the switch.

7   Rotate the brake light switch clockwise about 1/8 turn and remove it from the bracket.

8   Installation is the reverse of removal.

12.1 Brake light switch details

1   *Electrical connector*
2   *Brake light switch*
3   *Retaining pin (shown with cover removed)*

Specifications

General

Brake fluid type	See Chapter 1

Disc brakes

Brake pad minimum thickness	See Chapter 1
Disc minimum thickness	Cast into disc
Minimum pad lining thickness	See Chapter 1
Disc lateral runout limit	0.003 inch

Parking brakes

Shoe lining minimum thickness	See Chapter 1

Torque specifications — Ft-lbs (unless otherwise indicated)

➥ **Note: One foot-pound (ft-lb) of torque is equivalent to 12 inch-pounds (in-lbs) of torque. Torque values below approximately 15 ft-lbs are expressed in inch-pounds, since most foot-pound torque wrenches are not accurate at these smaller values.**

Brake hose fitting bolt	
2008 and earlier models	26
2009 and later models	30
Caliper mounting bracket bolts (front)	
2008 and earlier models	148
2009 and 2010 models	136
2011 and later models	30
Caliper mounting bolts	
Front (guide pin bolts)	
2006 and earlier models	47
2007 through 2010	55
2011 and later	184
Rear	
2010 and earlier models	22
2011 and later models	24
Rear caliper support bracket mounting bolts	111
Master cylinder mounting nuts	18
Power brake booster mounting nuts	18
Spindle nut (2008 and earlier models only)	295
Wheel speed sensor mounting bolt	
2008 and earlier models	
Front	71 in-lbs
Rear	132 in-lbs
2009 and later models	
Front	150 in-lbs
Rear	133 in-lbs
Wheel lug nuts	See Chapter 1

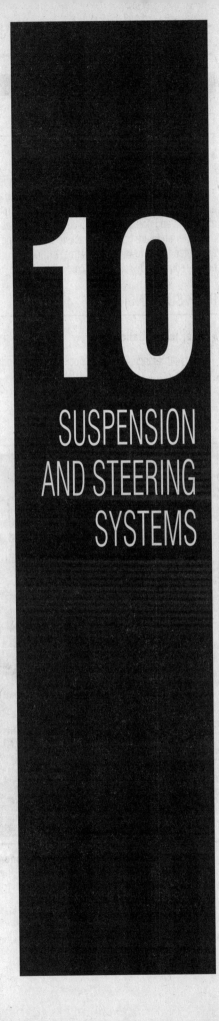

10

SUSPENSION
AND STEERING
SYSTEMS

Section

1   General information
2   Shock absorber/coil spring (front) - removal and installation
3   Stabilizer bar and bushings - removal and installation
4   Steering knuckle - removal and installation
5   Upper control arm - removal and installation
6   Lower control arm - removal and installation
7   Hub and bearing assembly - replacement
8   Balljoints - check and replacement
9   Shock absorbers (rear) - removal and installation
10   Leaf springs - removal and installation
11   Steering wheel - removal and installation
12   Steering column - removal and installation
13   Tie-rod ends - removal and installation
14   Steering gear boots - replacement
15   Steering gear - removal and installation
16   Power steering pump - removal and installation
17   Power steering system - bleeding
18   Power steering fluid cooler - removal and installation
19   Wheels and tires - general information
20   Wheel alignment - general information

Reference to other Chapters

Power steering fluid level check - See Chapter 1
Tire and tire pressure checks - See Chapter 1
Tire rotation - See Chapter 1

1 General information

FRONT SUSPENSION

▶ Refer to illustration 1.1

The front suspension system is fully independent (see illustration). The steering knuckles are connected to the upper and lower control arms by balljoints. The control arms are bolted to the frame. The shock absorbers and coil springs are integral assemblies (coil-over shock); the upper ends are bolted to brackets on the frame and the lower ends are bolted to the lower control arms. All models use a front stabilizer bar to reduce body roll during cornering.

REAR SUSPENSION

▶ Refer to illustration 1.2

The rear suspension uses shock absorbers and leaf springs (see

illustration). The forward end of each spring is attached to a bracket on each frame rail. The rear of each spring is shackled to a bracket on the side of the frame rail.

STEERING

All models are equipped with power-assisted rack-and-pinion steering systems. The steering gear is bolted to the crossmember and is connected to the steering knuckles by a pair of tie-rods.

2011 and later models may have either conventional hydraulic assist or a new system that utilizes an electric motor geared to the rack-and-pinion. A steering torque sensor determines when and how much the steering wheel and shaft are moved, and initiates the action of the steering gear. The electric motor is part of the rack-and-pinion and must be replaced as a unit, although replacement tie-rods, boots and tie-rod ends are available.

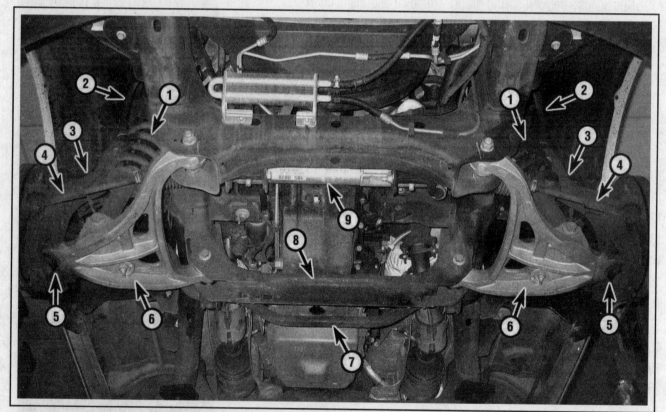

1.1 Front suspension and steering components (2WD model shown, 4WD model similar)

1 Shock absorber/coil spring assembly	4 Tie-rod end	7 Stabilizer bar
2 Upper control arm	5 Lower balljoint	8 Suspension crossmember
3 Steering knuckle	6 Lower control arm	9 Steering gear

PRECAUTIONS

Frequently, when working on the suspension or steering system components, you may come across fasteners which seem impossible to loosen. These fasteners on the underside of the vehicle are continually subjected to water, road grime, mud, etc., and can become rusted or frozen, making them extremely difficult to remove. In order to unscrew these stubborn fasteners without damaging them (or other components), be sure to use lots of penetrating oil and allow it to soak in for a while. Using a wire brush to clean exposed threads will also ease removal of the nut or bolt and prevent damage to the threads. Sometimes a sharp blow with a hammer and punch is effective in breaking the bond between a nut and bolt threads, but care must be taken to prevent the punch from slipping off the fastener and ruining the threads. Heating the stuck fastener and surrounding area with a torch sometimes helps too, but isn't recommended because of the obvious dangers associated with fire. Long breaker bars and extension, or cheater, pipes will increase leverage, but never use an extension pipe on a ratchet - the ratcheting mechanism could be damaged. Sometimes, turning the nut or bolt

in the tightening (clockwise) direction first will help to break it loose. Fasteners that require drastic measures to unscrew should always be replaced with new ones.

Since most of the procedures that are dealt with in this Chapter involve jacking up the vehicle and working underneath it, a good pair of jackstands will be needed. A hydraulic floor jack is the preferred type of jack to lift the vehicle, and it can also be used to support certain components during various operations.

✳✳ WARNING:

Never, under any circumstances, rely on a jack to support the vehicle while working on it. Also, whenever any of the suspension or steering fasteners are loosened or removed they must be inspected and, if necessary, replaced with new ones of the same part number or of original equipment quality and design. Torque specifications must be followed for proper reassembly and component retention. Never attempt to heat or straighten suspension or steering components. Instead, replace bent or damaged parts with new ones.

1.2 Rear suspension components

| 1 | Leaf springs | 2 | Shock absorber | 3 | Rear axle housing |

2 Shock absorber/coil spring (front) - removal and installation

➡ **Note: It is possible to replace the shocks or springs individually but the unit will have to be disassembled by a qualified repair shop with the proper equipment, and this will add considerable cost to the project. You can compare the cost of replacing the complete assemblies yourself to the cost of replacing individual components (with the help of a shop).**

REMOVAL

▶ **Refer to illustrations 2.2 and 2.4**

1 Loosen the front wheel lug nuts. Raise the vehicle and support it securely on jackstands. Remove the front wheels.

2 Remove the nuts that attach the upper end of the shock to the frame (see illustration).

3 Separate the tie-rod end from the steering knuckle and secure it aside (see Section 13).

4 Remove the fasteners attaching the lower end of the shock absorber to the lower control arm (see illustration).

5 Remove the shock absorber/coil spring assembly.

6 Inspect the shock absorber for leaking fluid, dents, cracks and other damage. Inspect the coil spring for chips and cracks which could cause premature failure. Inspect the spring seats for hardness and general deterioration. If any of the components of the assembly are worn or damaged, have the unit serviced by a qualified repair shop or replace it.

INSTALLATION

❋❋ **WARNING:**

The manufacturer states to discard removed suspension component fasteners (nuts and bolts) and replace them with new ones.

7 Installation is the reverse of removal. Be sure to tighten the fasteners to the torque listed in this Chapter's Specifications. Tighten the wheel lug nuts to the torque listed in the Chapter 1 Specifications.

➡ **Note: The shock absorber lower mounting fasteners should be tightened with the vehicle at normal ride height. This can be done after the vehicle has been lowered to the ground (on vehicles with adequate clearance), or can be simulated by raising the lower control arm with a floor jack.**

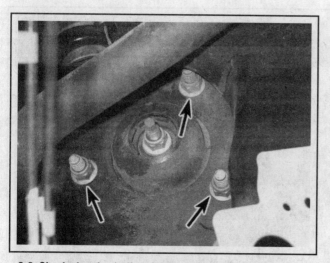

2.2 Shock absorber/coil spring upper mounting fasteners. DO NOT remove the damper rod nut in the middle

2.4 Shock absorber/coil spring lower mounting bolt - the nut is on the other side

3 Stabilizer bar and bushings - removal and installation

▶ **Refer to illustration 3.2**

❋❋ **WARNING:**

The manufacturer states to discard removed suspension component fasteners (nuts and bolts) and replace them with new ones.

1 Loosen the front wheel lug nuts. Raise the vehicle and support it securely on jackstands. Remove the front wheels.

2 On 2004 through 2006 models, remove the nuts from the sides of the stabilizer bar links (see illustration). On 2007 and later models, remove the nuts from the top of the stabilizer bar links. Detach the links from the arm.

➡ **Note: Hold the ballstud on the link with a wrench while removing the link nut. The link can be detached from the control arm in the same manner.**

3 Remove the stabilizer bar bushing bracket nuts.

4   Remove the stabilizer bar.

5   Remove the rubber bushings from the stabilizer bar.

6   Inspect the rubber bushings for cracks, tears and deterioration. If they're worn or damaged, replace them.

7   Check each stabilizer link for signs of excessive wear.

8   Installation is the reverse of removal. Be sure to tighten all fasteners to the torque values listed in this Chapter's Specifications.

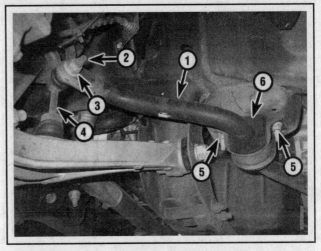

3.2 Stabilizer bar and link details (2004 through 2006 model shown)

1	Stabilizer bar	5	Stabilizer bar bushing
2	Link ballstud		bracket nuts
3	Link nut	6	Stabilizer bar bushings
4	Stabilizer bar link		

4   Steering knuckle - removal and installation

1   Apply the parking brake. Loosen the wheel lug nuts and the spindle nut (2WD models) or the driveaxle/hub nut (4WD models). Raise the front of the vehicle and support it securely on jackstands. Remove the wheel.

2   Remove the wheel speed sensor from the steering knuckle (see Chapter 9).

3   Remove the brake caliper and brake disc (see Chapter 9). Hang the caliper with a length of wire - don't let it hang by the brake hose.

4   Disconnect the tie-rod end from the steering knuckle (see Section 13).

5   On 4WD models, remove the driveaxle/hub nut.

6   Disconnect the upper and lower control arms from the steering knuckle (see Sections 5 and 6) and then remove the steering knuckle. The brake dust shield can also be removed if necessary.

7   On 4WD models, guide the driveaxle out of the hub, being careful to not overextend the inner CV joint. If the driveaxle is stuck in the hub splines, it will be necessary to use a puller to push the driveaxle out of the hub (see Chapter 8). Support the driveaxle with a length of wire - don't let it hang by the inner CV joint.

8   On 4WD models, remove the hub and bearing assembly from the knuckle, if necessary.

9   Installation is the reverse of removal. Tighten all suspension fasteners to the torque values listed in this Chapter's Specifications.

10 Tighten the spindle nut (2WD models) to the torque listed in the Chapter 9 Specifications or driveaxle/hub nut (4WD models) to the torque listed in the Chapter 8 Specifications.

11 Tighten the wheel lug nuts to the torque listed in the Chapter 1 Specifications.

5   Upper control arm - removal and installation

▶ **Refer to illustrations 5.4 and 5.5**

1   Loosen the wheel lug nuts, raise the front of the vehicle and support it securely on jackstands. Apply the parking brake. Remove the wheel.

2   Remove the wheel speed sensor from the steering knuckle (see Chapter 9).

3   Remove the shock absorber/coil spring (see Section 2).

4   Loosen the upper balljoint nut a few turns, then use a balljoint

5.4 Separate the upper control arm from the balljoint with a balljoint separator or a two-jaw puller

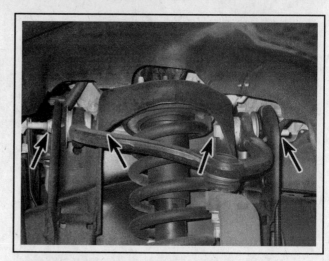

5.5 Remove the fasteners and lift the upper arm off the frame bracket

separator or puller to separate the balljoint from the steering knuckle (see illustration).

❊❊ CAUTION:

Don't allow the steering knuckle to fall outward, as the brake hose may be damaged. It's a good idea to wire the steering knuckle to the coil spring so this doesn't happen.

5   Remove the fasteners and detach the upper control arm from the frame (see illustration).

➡ **Note: When removing the right upper arm, remove the fastener for the small heat shield and move it aside.**

6   Inspect the bushings for wear and deterioration. If they're cracked or damaged, take the arm to an automotive machine shop and have new bushings installed.

7   Installation is the reverse of removal. Be sure to tighten all suspension fasteners to the torque listed in this Chapter's Specifications.

➡ **Note: The pivot bolt nuts should be tightened with the vehicle at normal ride height. This can be done after the vehicle has been lowered to the ground or simulated by raising the lower control arm with a floor jack.**

8   It's a good idea to have the wheel alignment checked and, if necessary, adjusted.

6   Lower control arm - removal and installation

▸ Refer to illustrations 6.5, 6.6a and 6.6b

❊❊ WARNING:

The manufacturer states to discard removed suspension component fasteners (nuts and bolts) and replace them with new ones.

1   Loosen the wheel lug nuts, raise the front of the vehicle and support it securely on jackstands. Apply the parking brake. Remove the wheel.

➡ **Note: On 4WD models, loosen the driveaxle/hub nut before raising the vehicle (see Chapter 8).**

2   On 4WD models, remove the steering knuckle (see Section 4).

3   Detach the stabilizer link from the lower control arm (see Section 3).

4   Remove the lower shock absorber/coil spring fasteners (see Section 2).

5   Loosen the lower balljoint nut a few turns, then use a balljoint separator or puller to separate the balljoint from the steering knuckle (see illustration).

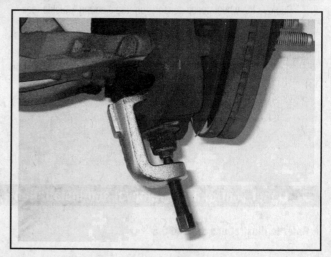

6.5 Separate the balljoint from the lower control arm using a puller or a tool like this

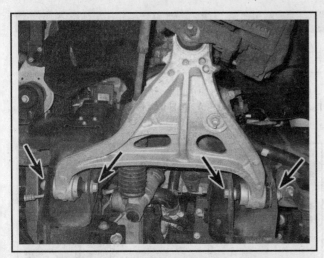

6.6a Location of the lower control arm front and rear pivot nuts/bolts

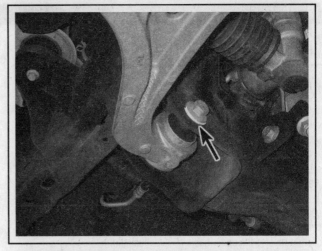

6.6b Mark the flange and frame bracket around all pivot bolts and nuts so that they can be installed in their original positions

6   Mark the position of the front and rear pivot fasteners (see illustrations).

7   Remove the pivot nuts and bolts from the control arm and then remove it from the frame.

8   Inspect the bushings for wear and deterioration. If they're cracked or damaged, take the control arm to an automotive machine shop and have new bushings installed.

9   Installation is the reverse of removal. Be sure to align the marks made in Step 6, and tighten all suspension fasteners to the torque listed in this Chapter's Specifications.

➡ **Note: The pivot bolt nuts should be tightened with the vehicle at normal ride height. This can be done after the vehicle has been lowered to the ground or simulated by raising the lower control arm with a floor jack.**

10   Have the wheel alignment checked and, if necessary, adjusted.

7   Hub and bearing assembly - replacement

✳✳ **WARNING:**

The manufacturer states to discard removed suspension component fasteners (nuts and bolts) and replace them with new ones.

➡ **Note: On 2WD models, the hub and wheel bearing is integrated with the front brake disc as a single assembly. At the time of this manual's writing, if the hub or wheel bearing is defective or worn, the entire assembly must be replaced.**

1   Apply the parking brake. Loosen the wheel lug nuts and the spindle nut (2WD) or the driveaxle/hub nut (4WD). Raise the front of the vehicle and support it securely on jackstands. Remove the wheel.

2   Remove the brake caliper and brake disc. Also remove the wheel speed sensor from the steering knuckle (see Chapter 9).

3   On 4WD models, remove the hub mounting bolts from the back of the steering knuckle.

4   If you're working on a 4WD model, remove the driveaxle/hub nut and push the driveaxle through the hub splines as the hub and bearing assembly is removed. If the driveaxle sticks in the hub, you'll have to push it out with a puller (see Chapter 8).

✳✳ **CAUTION:**

Be careful not to overextend the inner CV joint. Once the hub has been removed, support the outer end of the driveaxle with a length of wire or rope.

5   Installation is the reverse of removal, noting the following points:
   a) *Tighten the hub mounting bolts (4WD) to the torque listed in this Chapter's Specifications.*
   b) *When installing the brake disc on 2WD models, lube the inside of the bearing race to ease installation if necessary.*
   c) *Tighten the brake caliper mounting bracket bolts, caliper mounting bolts and the wheel speed sensor bolt to the torque listed in the Chapter 9 Specifications.*
   d) *Tighten the spindle nut (2WD models) to the torque listed in the Chapter 9 Specifications and the driveaxle/hub nut (4WD models) to the torque listed in the Chapter 8 Specifications.*
   e) *Tighten the wheel lug nuts to the torque listed in the Chapter 1 Specifications.*

8 Balljoints - check and replacement

CHECK

▶ **Refer to illustration 8.4**

1 Inspect the upper and lower balljoints for looseness whenever the vehicle is raised for any reason. You can check the balljoints with the suspension assembled as follows.

2 Raise the vehicle and support it securely on jackstands.

3 Wipe the balljoints clean and inspect the seals for cuts and tears. If a balljoint seal is damaged, replace the balljoint.

4 To check the upper balljoint, grab the upper control arm near the balljoint and attempt to move the arm up and down. Any noticeable play between the upper control arm and the steering knuckle indicates the need to replace the upper balljoint (see illustration).

5 To check the lower balljoint, attempt to move the wheel up and down while checking for play between the lower control arm and the steering knuckle. Any noticeable play indicates the need to replace the balljoint.

REPLACEMENT

6 The balljoints on these models are not serviceable. If the balljoint must be replaced, the control arm and balljoint must be replaced as a single assembly.

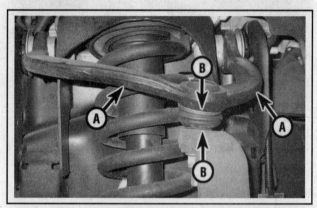

8.4 Grab the upper control arm (A) and attempt to move it up and down while checking for any movement between the control arm and the steering knuckle (B)

9 Shock absorbers (rear) - removal and installation

▶ **Refer to illustrations 9.2**

> ✳✳ **WARNING:**
> The manufacturer states to discard removed suspension component fasteners (nuts and bolts) and replace them with new ones.

1 Raise the rear of the vehicle, support it securely on jackstands and block the front wheels. Place a floor jack under the axle adjacent to the shock absorber being removed. Raise the jack just enough to take the load off the shock absorber.

2 Remove the nut and bolt securing the lower end of the shock absorber to the rear axle (see illustration).

3 Remove the nut and bolt securing the top of the shock absorber to the upper mounting bracket on the frame.

4 Installation is the reverse of the removal steps. Tighten the nuts and bolts to the torque listed in this Chapter's Specifications.

9.2 Shock absorber mounting fasteners

10 Leaf springs - removal and installation

REMOVAL

▶ **Refer to illustrations 10.5, 10.6 and 10.7**

> ✳✳ **WARNING:**
> The manufacturer states to discard removed suspension component fasteners (nuts and bolts) and replace them with new ones.

➡ **Note: Removal of the left-side leaf spring requires that the gas tank be lowered (see Chapter 4). Right-side spring removal requires that the muffler be removed (see Chapter 4).**

1 Loosen the rear wheel lug nuts. Raise the rear of the vehicle, support it securely on jackstands placed under the frame rails and block the front wheels. Remove the wheel.

2 If you're removing the right spring, remove the muffler; if you're removing the left spring, lower the gas tank (see Chapter 4).

3 Support the axle with a floor jack placed under the axle tube and

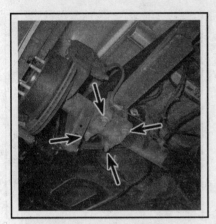

10.5 With the axle supported, remove the nuts from the U-bolts

10.6 To detach the rear end of the leaf spring from the spring shackle, remove the lower nut and bolt

10.7 To detach the front end of the leaf spring from its bracket, remove this nut and bolt

raise it slightly to take the weight of the axle.

4   Remove the rear shock lower fasteners (see Section 9).

5   Remove the nuts from the U-bolts, then remove the U-bolts and the spring plate from the spring (see illustration). Now lower the jack far enough to relieve tension on the spring.

➡ **Note: On 4WD models, note the position of the spacer between the axle and the spring.**

6   Remove the lower bolt and nut securing the shackle assembly to the frame bracket at the rear of the spring (see illustration).

7   Remove the spring hanger bolt and nut at the front of the spring (see illustration). Remove the spring.

8   Inspect the spring eye bushings for wear or distortion. If worn or damaged, have them replaced by an automotive machine shop or other qualified repair facility.

INSTALLATION

9   Install the spring in the front bracket. Tighten the bolt and nut finger-tight.

10   Place the spring shackle in the frame bracket. Install the bolt and nut and tighten them finger-tight.

11   Raise the axle into contact with the spring making sure they are positioned correctly. Install the U-bolts and nuts and tighten them to the torque listed in this Chapter's Specifications.

➡ **Note: On 4WD models, make certain that the spacer between the axle and the spring is in its original position.**

12   Install the wheel and lug nuts. Lower the vehicle to the ground and tighten the spring bracket bolt and nut and shackle-to-frame bracket bolt and nut to the torque values listed in this Chapter's Specifications.

11   Steering wheel - removal and installation

◗ **Refer to illustrations 11.3, 11.4, 11.6, 11.7 and 11.8**

✳✳ WARNING:

The models covered by this manual are equipped with Supplemental Restraint systems (SRS), more commonly known as airbags. Always disable the airbag system before working in the vicinity of any airbag system component to avoid the possibility of accidental deployment of the airbag, which could cause personal injury (see Chapter 12).

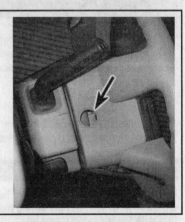

11.3 Pry off the covers on the sides of the steering wheel and remove the bolts that retain the airbag module (2008 and earlier models)

REMOVAL

1   Park the vehicle with the front wheels pointed straight ahead and the steering wheel centered. Disconnect the cable from the negative terminal of the battery (see Chapter 5).

2   Refer to Chapter 12 and disable the airbag system.

3   On 2004 through 2008 models, pry out the two small covers, one on each side of the steering wheel, and unscrew the two bolts that retain the airbag module (see illustration). On 2009 and later models, mounting pins on the left, right and lower center of the front side (steering wheel side) of the airbag module are secured by three wire clips mounted in the steering wheel. Each clip can be accessed through a small hole; one on each side of the steering wheel, and one on the underside. To disengage each mounting pin from its wire clip, insert a 3 mm hex key through each access hole, push the wire clip inward and simultaneously pull the airbag module away from the steering wheel.

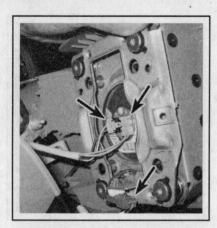

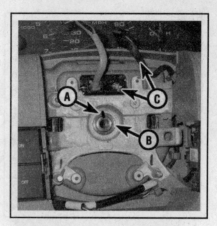

11.4 Disconnect the electrical connectors from the airbag module (squeeze the locking tabs on the sides of each connector, then pull the connectors out) and disconnect the horn connector below

11.6 Remove the steering wheel bolt and mark the relationship of the steering wheel to the steering shaft (A). Notice the keyed portion of the steering shaft to the steering wheel (B) and be sure to disconnect the electrical connector on the right side of the clockspring (C)

11.7 Use a puller to remove the steering wheel if it's stuck to the steering shaft. Be sure to place the steering wheel retaining bolt on the steering shaft before installing the puller

11.8 After centering the clockspring, make sure the alignment marks (A) on the clockspring align with the marks on the housing. To remove the clockspring, release the retaining clips (B)

4   Lift the airbag module off the steering wheel and disconnect the airbag and horn electrical connectors (see illustration).

※※ WARNING:

When handling the airbag module, hold it with the trim side facing away from you. Set the airbag module down in a safe location with the trim side facing up.

5   Unplug the electrical connector on the right side of the clockspring (see illustration 11.6).
6   Remove the steering wheel retaining bolt and mark the position of the steering wheel to the shaft, if marks don't already exist or don't line up (see illustration).

➡ Note: The steering wheel will only fit on one way, but marking it to the shaft will help during installation.

7   Lift the steering wheel off the shaft. If it's stuck and won't come off, reinstall the bolt finger-tight, then loosen it a few turns. Now use a two-jaw puller to break the bond between the steering wheel and the shaft (the puller screw must bear down on the steering wheel bolt so as not to damage the threads in the steering shaft) (see illustration). Finally, remove the bolt and take the wheel off the shaft.

※※ CAUTION:

Don't hammer on the shaft or the steering wheel in an attempt to dislodge the wheel!

※※ WARNING:

While the steering wheel is removed, do NOT turn the steering shaft. If the steering shaft is turned, the clockspring will be uncentered and the harness may break, rendering the airbag inoperative. If the clockspring is accidentally uncentered, it must be centered before installing the steering wheel.

8   Make sure the clockspring is centered, as follows: Verify that the front wheels are pointing straight ahead. Turn the clockspring housing counterclockwise by hand until it becomes hard to turn (don't apply too much force, though, because the cable could break). Turn the clockspring clockwise about 3 turns and align the marks (see illustration).
9   If it's necessary to remove the clockspring from the steering column, apply two pieces of tape across the hub of the clockspring to the housing to prevent it from rotating. Release the retaining clips (see illustration 11.8) and the electrical connectors from the bottom rear of the clockspring and then remove it. Reverse the removal procedure to install the clockspring, but be sure it is centered.

INSTALLATION

10 To install the wheel, align the mark on the steering wheel hub with the mark on the shaft and slide the wheel onto the shaft. Install the bolt and tighten it to the torque listed in this Chapter's Specifications.

11 The remainder of installation is otherwise the reverse of removal. Be sure the electrical connectors are securely connected to the airbag module and tighten the airbag module retaining bolts to the torque listed in this Chapter's Specifications.

---

12 Steering column - removal and installation

✳✳ WARNING:

The models covered by this manual are equipped with Supplemental Restraint systems (SRS), more commonly known as airbags. Always disable the airbag system before working in the vicinity of any airbag system component to avoid the possibility of accidental deployment of the airbag, which could cause personal injury (see Chapter 12).

REMOVAL

▶ **Refer to illustrations 12.4, 12.6a, 12.6b, 12.7, 12.8, and 12.9**

1 Park the vehicle with the wheels pointing straight ahead. Disconnect the cable from the negative terminal of the battery (see Chapter 5).

2 Remove the steering wheel (see Section 11). Place the ignition key in the LOCK position to prevent the steering shaft from turning.

✳✳ CAUTION:

If this is not done, the airbag clockspring could be damaged when the vehicle is put back into service.

3 Remove the knee bolster from under the steering column (see Chapter 11).

4 Remove the steering column panel from under the steering column (see illustration).

5 Remove the steering column covers (see Chapter 11).

6 Disconnect the electrical connectors for the steering column harness (see illustrations).

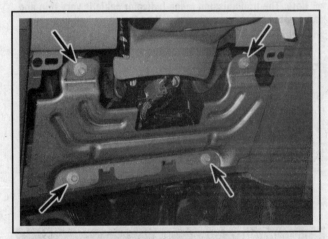

12.4 The steering column panel and mounting fasteners

12.6a Disconnect the electrical connectors (A) and detach all harnesses (B) from the bracket (typical)

12.6b Disconnect all electrical connectors (typical)

12.7 The transmission range indicator cable is near the shift cable on most models

12.8 Remove the pinch bolt for the intermediate shaft coupler

12.9 Typical steering column mounting nuts (left side shown, right side hidden)

7 On models with an automatic transmission, detach the shift cable (see Chapter 7B) and the transmission range indicator cable (see illustration).

→ **Note: The transmission range indicator cable is very thin and can easily be damaged. Do not pull on the cable and use care when removing it.**

8 Remove the intermediate shaft coupler bolt (see illustration) and discard it.

9 Remove the steering column mounting nuts (see illustration). Lower the column and pull it to the rear, making sure nothing is still connected. Separate the intermediate shaft from the steering shaft and remove the column.

INSTALLATION

10 Guide the steering column into position, connect the intermediate shaft, then install the mounting fasteners, but don't tighten them yet.

✳✳ WARNING:

If the front wheels were turned while the steering shaft was disconnected, the clockspring must be re-centered or it will be damaged when the vehicle is put back into service (see Section 11).

11 Install the pinch bolt, tightening it to the torque listed in this Chapter's Specifications.

✳✳ WARNING:

The manufacturer states that a new bolt should be installed during reassembly.

12 Tighten the column mounting fasteners to the torque listed in this Chapter's Specifications.

✳✳ WARNING:

The manufacturer recommends installing a new intermediate shaft coupler bolt.

13 The remainder of the installation is the reverse of removal.

13 Tie-rod ends - removal and installation

▶ **Refer to illustrations 13.2a, 13.2b and 13.3**

✳✳ WARNING:

The manufacturer states to discard removed suspension component fasteners (nuts and bolts) and replace them with new ones.

1 Loosen the wheel lug nuts, raise the vehicle and place it securely on jackstands. Remove the wheel.

2 Loosen the tie-rod end locknut and mark the position of the tie-rod end on the threaded portion of the tie-rod (see illustrations).

3 Loosen the nut from the tie-rod end balljoint stud, then separate the tie-rod end from the steering knuckle (see illustration). Remove the nut and detach the tie-rod end from the steering knuckle arm.

→ **Note: Hold the ballstud on the tie-rod end with the appropriate tool if it turns while removing the nut.**

4 Unscrew the old tie-rod end and install the new one. Make sure the new tie-rod end is aligned with the mark you made on the threads of the tie-rod.

5 Installation is the reverse of removal. Be sure to tighten the tie-rod end ballstud nut to the torque listed in this Chapter's Specifications. Tighten the locknut securely.

13.2a Loosen the tie-rod end locknut

13.2b Mark the position of the tie-rod end on the threaded portion of the tie-rod

13.3 With the ballstud nut loosened, separate the tie-rod end from the steering knuckle using a suitable tool or puller

14 Steering gear boots - replacement

▶ **Refer to illustration 14.4**

1 If a steering gear boot is torn, dirt and moisture can damage the steering gear. Replace it.

2 Loosen the wheel lug nuts, raise the vehicle and place it securely on jackstands. Remove the front wheels.

3 Remove the tie-rod end and locknut (see Section 13).

4 Remove the boot clamps (see illustration) and slide the boot off the tie-rod.

5 Installation is the reverse of removal. Be sure to use new clamps on the boot.

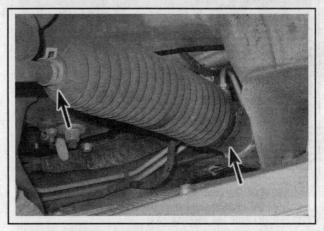

14.4 The outer clamp on the steering gear boot can be removed with pliers - the inner clamp must be cut off

15 Steering gear - removal and installation

CONVENTIONAL HYDRAULIC ASSIST STEERING

▶ **Refer to illustrations 15.4, 15.5, 15.6 and 15.8**

※※ WARNING 1:

The models covered by this manual are equipped with Supplemental Restraint systems (SRS), more commonly known as airbags. Always disable the airbag system before working in the vicinity of any airbag system component to avoid the possibility of accidental deployment of the airbag, which could cause personal injury (see Chapter 12).

※※ WARNING 2:

Make sure the steering column shaft is not turned while the steering gear is removed or you could damage the airbag system clockspring. To prevent the shaft from turning, turn the ignition key to the lock position before beginning work, and run the seat belt through the steering wheel and clip it into its latch.

1 Park the vehicle with the front wheels pointing straight ahead.

2 Loosen the wheel lug nuts. Raise the front of the vehicle and support it securely on jackstands. Apply the parking brake. Remove the wheels.

3 Remove the skid plate, if equipped.

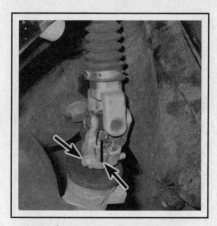

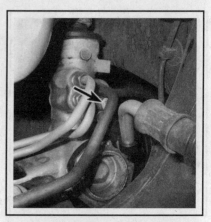

15.4 Mark the lower steering shaft U-joint and steering gear input shaft, then remove the pinch bolt

15.5 Oil drip tray mounting fasteners (2004 model shown - other models similar)

15.6 The pressure and return line fittings are held by a single fastener at the steering gear

15.8 Remove the steering gear bracket-to-crossmember fasteners (A), then remove the fasteners for the steering gear brackets (B) from the steering gear

4   Mark the relationship of the lower steering shaft U-joint to the steering gear input shaft, remove the U-joint pinch bolt and slide the U-joint up and off the input shaft (see illustration).

➡ **Note: If the U-joint won't slide all the way off the shaft, it can be detached after Step 8.**

5   Remove the oil drip tray (see illustration).

6   Disconnect the pressure and return lines from the steering gear and discard any O-ring seals (see illustration).

7   Disconnect the tie-rod ends from the steering knuckles (see Section 13).

8   On 2008 and earlier models, remove the steering gear bracket-to-crossmember fasteners, then remove the mounting brackets from the steering gear (see illustration).

➡ **Note: On 2009 and later models, the steering gear is bolted directly to the crossmember; there are no steering gear mounting brackets.**

9   Remove the steering gear assembly through the opening at the left wheel well.

10   Installation is the reverse of removal. Be sure to align the match-marks made in Step 4 and tighten all suspension and steering gear fasteners to the torque listed in this Chapter's Specifications. Also, use new O-rings when assembling the pressure and return lines to the steering gear. Tighten the wheel lug nuts to the torque listed in the Chapter 1 Specifications.

11   Refill the power steering fluid reservoir with the proper fluid (see Chapter 1), then bleed the power steering system when you're done (see Section 17).

ELECTRONIC POWER ASSIST STEERING

On 2011 and later models equipped with electronic power assist steering, the steering gear cannot be replaced at home because the new unit must be reprogrammed with a proprietary scan tool.

16 Power steering pump - removal and installation

▶ **Refer to illustrations 16.2, 16.3 and 16.6**

1   Remove the drivebelt (see Chapter 1).

2   Remove the power steering pump pulley. A special pulley removal tool, available at most auto parts stores, will be required for this (see illustration).

3   Position a drain pan under the power steering pump. Disconnect the pressure and feed hoses from the pump (see illustration). Plug the hoses to prevent contaminants from entering. Discard the seal from the pressure line - a new one should be used during installation.

4   Remove the pressure line mounting bracket and move the line away from the pump.

5   On 2004 through 2006 models, remove the four mounting fasteners and lift the pump from the mounting bracket. On 2007 and later models, remove the wiring harness retainer from the lower stub bolt,

16.2 Remove the pulley from the power steering pump with a pulley removal tool

16.3 Power steering pump details (2004 through 2006 models):

1   *Pressure line fitting*
2   *Feed line*
3   *Mounting bolts (two hidden from view)*

then remove the pressure line bracket mounting nut and bracket from the stud bolt. Remove the three mounting fasteners and lift the pump from the side of the engine. Take care not to spill fluid on the painted surfaces.

6   Installation is the reverse of removal. Use a new seal on the pressure line fitting. Tighten the pressure line fitting and the pump mounting bolts to the torque listed in this Chapter's Specifications. A special pulley installation tool, available at most auto parts stores, will be needed to press the pulley onto the pump shaft (see illustration).

7   Fill the power steering reservoir with the recommended fluid (see Chapter 1) and bleed the system following the procedure described in the next Section.

16.6 Press the pulley onto the shaft using a pulley installation tool - don't attempt to drive it on with a hammer or push it on with a traditional press!

17   Power steering system - bleeding

1   Following any operation in which the power steering fluid lines have been disconnected, the power steering system must be bled to remove all air and obtain proper steering performance.

2   With the front wheels in the straight ahead position, check the power steering fluid level and, if low, add fluid until it reaches the MIN mark on the reservoir.

3   Start the engine and allow it to run at fast idle. Recheck the fluid level and add more if necessary to reach the MIN mark on the reservoir.

4   Bleed the system by turning the wheels from side-to-side, without hitting the stops. This will work the air out of the system. Keep the reservoir full of fluid as this is done.

5   When the air is worked out of the system, return the wheels to the straight ahead position and leave the vehicle running for several more minutes before shutting it off.

6   Road test the vehicle to be sure the steering system is functioning normally and noise free.

7   Recheck the fluid level to be sure it's up near the MAX mark on the reservoir while the engine is at normal operating temperature. Add fluid if necessary (see Chapter 1).

18 Power steering fluid cooler - removal and installation

2004 THROUGH 2006 MODELS

▶ **Refer to illustration 18.3**

1   Raise the vehicle and place it securely on jackstands.
2   Place a drain pan below the power steering fluid cooler to collect dripping fluid.
3   Loosen the clamps and detach the hoses from the power steering fluid cooler (see illustration). Mark these hoses to insure correct reassembly. Plug the hoses to prevent leakage.
4   Loosen the mounting fasteners and detach the cooler from the crossmember (see illustration 18.3).
5   Installation is the reverse of the removal.
6   Add power steering fluid as necessary (see Chapter 1), then bleed the power steering system (see Section 17).

2007 AND 2008 MODELS

➡ **Note: On 2009 and later models, the power steering cooler is an integral part of the air conditioning condenser (see Chapter 3, Section 16).**

7   Remove the fluid from the power steering fluid reservoir
8   Raise the vehicle and support it securely on jackstands.
9   Place a drain pan under the left side of the steering gear assembly. Remove the pressure line mounting bolt, bracket and O-ring seals from the steering gear assembly.

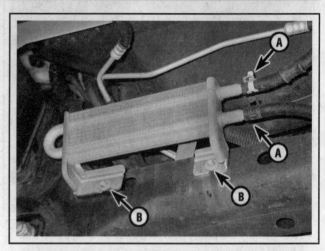

18.3 Remove the power steering fluid cooler hoses (A) and plug them immediately, then loosen the mounting fasteners (B) (2004 through 2006 models)

10   Loosen the clamp and detach the return line from the cooler hose assembly.
11   Detach the return line bracket-to-crossmember bolts.
12   Carefully remove the cooler assembly from the frame.
13   Installation is the reverse of removal.
14   Add power steering fluid (see Chapter 1), then bleed the power steering system (see Section 17).

19 Wheels and tires - general information

▶ **Refer to illustration 19.1**

All vehicles covered by this manual are equipped with metric-size steel belted radial tires (see illustration). These models require the specific tire size, speed rating, load range and construction type to insure the correct ride, handling, speedometer/odometer calibration, tire/body clearance, wheel bearing tolerance and brake cooling characteristics. Use of other size or type of tires may affect all/one of these conditions. Don't mix different types of tires, such as radials and bias belted, on the same vehicle as handling may be seriously affected. It's recommended that tires be replaced in pairs on the same axle, but if only one tire is being replaced, be sure it's the same size, structure and tread design as the other.

Because tire pressure has a substantial effect on handling and wear, the pressure on all tires should be checked at least once a month or before any extended trips (see Chapter 1).

Wheels must be replaced if they're bent, dented, leak air, have elongated bolt holes, are heavily rusted, out of vertical symmetry or if the lug nuts won't stay tight. Wheel repairs that use welding or peening are not recommended.

Tire and wheel balance is important to the overall handling, braking and performance of the vehicle. Unbalanced wheels can adversely affect handling and ride characteristics as well as tire life. Whenever a tire is installed on a wheel, the tire and wheel should be balanced by a shop with the proper equipment.

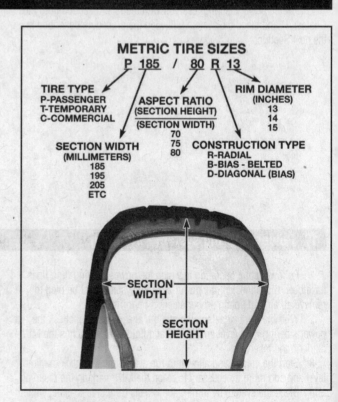

19.1 Metric tire size code

20 Wheel alignment - general information

♦ **Refer to illustration 20.1**

A wheel alignment refers to the adjustments made to the front and rear wheels so they're in proper angular relationship to the suspension and the ground (see illustration). Wheels that are out of proper alignment not only affect steering control, but also increase tire wear.

Getting the proper front and rear wheel alignment is a very exacting process, one in which complicated and expensive machines are necessary to perform the job properly. Because of this, you should have a technician with the proper equipment perform these tasks. We will, however, use this space to give you a basic idea of what is involved with front end alignment so you can better understand the process and deal intelligently with the shop that does the work.

Toe-in is the turning in of the front wheels. The purpose of a toe specification is to ensure parallel rolling of the front wheels. In a vehicle with zero toe-in, the distance between the front edges of the wheels will be the same as the distance between the rear edges of the wheels. The actual amount of toe-in is normally only a fraction of an inch. Toe-in adjustment is controlled by the tie-rod length. Incorrect toe-in will

cause the tires to wear improperly by making them scrub against the road surface.

Camber is the tilting of the front wheels from vertical when viewed from the front of the vehicle. When the wheels tilt out at the top, the camber is said to be positive (+). When the wheels tilt in at the top the camber is negative (-). The amount of tilt is measured in degrees from the vertical and this measurement is called the camber angle. This angle affects the amount of tire tread which contacts the road and compensates for changes in the suspension geometry when the vehicle is cornering or traveling over an undulating surface. Camber is adjusted by loosening the lower control arm-to-frame bolts and moving the arm in (to increase camber) or out (to decrease camber).

Caster is the tilting of the top of the front steering axis from the vertical. A tilt toward the rear is positive caster and a tilt toward the front is negative caster. Caster is also adjusted by loosening the lower control arm-to-frame bolts, but instead of moving the arm in or out, the outer end of the arm is moved toward the front (to increase caster) or toward the rear (to decrease caster).

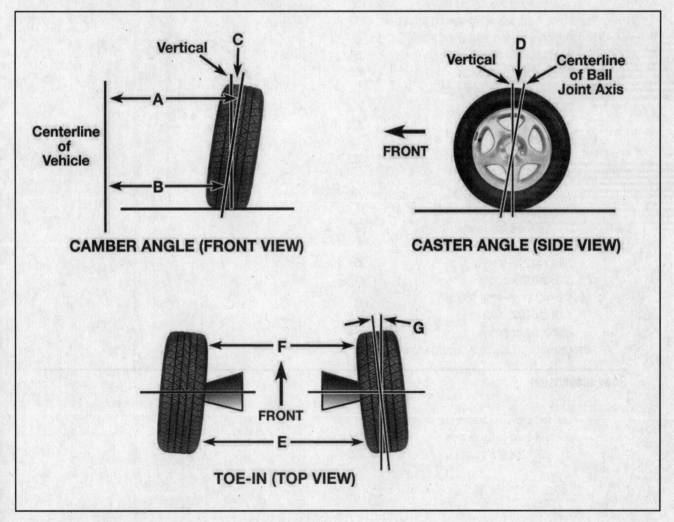

20.1 Front end alignment details

A minus B = C (degrees camber)
D = degrees caster

E minus F = toe-in (measured in inches)
G = toe-in (expressed in degrees)

Specifications

General

Power steering fluid type	See Chapter 1

Torque specifications | Ft-lbs

Front suspension

Front wheel hub/bearing assembly mounting bolts	
2008 and earlier models (4WD only)	148
2009 and later models (2WD and 4WD)	129
Lower control arm-to-frame nuts	
2WD	
2006 and earlier models	222
2007 and later models	258
4WD	
2004 and 2005 models	222
2006 and later models	258
Lower control arm balljoint-to-steering knuckle nut	111
Shock absorber-to-lower control arm nuts	
2008 and earlier models	351
2009 and later models	406
Shock absorber upper mounting nuts	
2008 and earlier models	35
2009 and later models	30
Stabilizer bar link nuts	
To control arm	66
To stabilizer bar	
2004 and 2005 models	98
2006 through 2008 models	18
2009 and later models	59
Stabilizer bar bracket-to-frame bolts	
2004 and 2005 models	35
2006 and later models	41
Upper control arm-to-frame bolt/nut	
2004 and 2005 models	114
2006 and later models	111
Upper control arm balljoint-to-steering knuckle nut	85

Rear suspension

Leaf spring	
Leaf spring-to-front bracket nut	
2006 and earlier models	222
2007 and later models	258

Torque specifications	**Ft-lbs (unless otherwise indicated)**

➡ **Note:** One foot-pound (ft-lb) of torque is equivalent to 12 inch-pounds (in-lbs) of torque. Torque values below approximately 15 foot-pounds are expressed in inch-pounds, because most foot-pound torque wrenches are not accurate at these smaller values.

Rear suspension (continued)

Leaf spring (continued)
 Shackle-to-frame nut

2008 and earlier models	98
2009 models	148
2010 and later models	136

 Shackle-to-spring nut

2008 and earlier	98
2009 models	148
2010 and later models	136

 U-bolt nuts
  2004 through 2006 models

Step 1 (in a crisscross pattern)	22
Step 2 (in a crisscross pattern)	85

  2007 and later models

Step 1 (in a crisscross pattern)	26
Step 2 (in a crisscross pattern)	52
Step 3 (in a crisscross pattern)	74
Step 4 (in a crisscross pattern)	98
Shock absorber mounting bolt/nut	66

Steering

Airbag module mounting screws* (2008 and earlier models)	89 in-lbs
Intermediate shaft coupler pinch bolt	22
Power steering fluid cooler bolts** (2008 and earlier models)	96 in-lbs
Power steering gear-to-lower shaft pinch bolt	22

Power steering pump pressure line fitting
 4.6L and 5.4L V8 engines

2008 and earlier models	48
2009 and later models	55
V6 engine models	15
Power steering pump mounting bolts	18

Steering wheel retainer bolt

2010 and earlier models	30
2011 and later models	35

Steering gear mounting bolts/nuts

2006 and earlier models	111
2007 and 2008 models	185
2009 and later models	325
Steering gear mounting bracket-to-crossmember bolt/nut***	76
Steering gear line fitting retainer bolt	17
Steering column mounting nuts	22
Steering column mounting bolts (2011 and later models)	21

Tie-rod end ballstud nuts

2006 and earlier models	111
2007 and later models	85

*Note: Modules on later models use mounting clips instead of screws.

**Note: The cooler on later models is an integral component of the air conditioning condenser.

***Note: Does not apply to 2009 and later models.

Notes

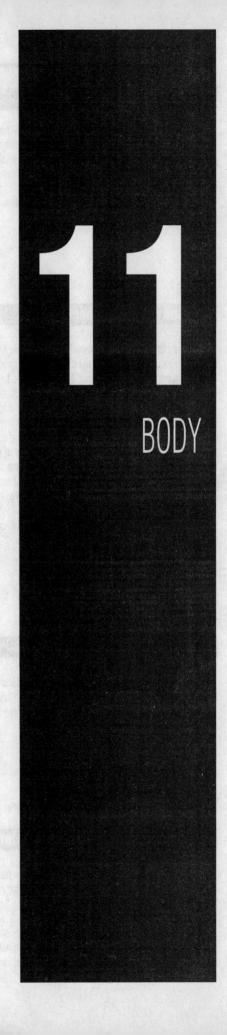

11

BODY

Section

1 General information
2 Body - maintenance
3 Vinyl trim - maintenance
4 Upholstery and carpets - maintenance
5 Body repair - minor damage
6 Body repair - major damage
7 Hinges and locks - maintenance
8 Windshield and fixed glass - replacement
9 Hood support struts - removal and installation
10 Hood - removal, installation and adjustment
11 Hood latch and release cable - removal and installation
12 Radiator grille - removal and installation
13 Bumpers - removal and installation
14 Front fender - removal and installation
15 Door trim panels - removal and installation
16 Door - removal, installation and adjustment
17 Door latch, lock cylinder and handle - removal and installation
18 Door window glass - removal and installation
19 Door window glass regulator - removal and installation
20 Mirrors - removal and installation
21 Tailgate - removal and installation
22 Tailgate latch and handle - removal and installation
23 Dashboard trim panels (2004 through 2008 models) - removal
    and installation
24 Dashboard trim panels (2009 and later models) - removal
    and installation
25 Instrument panel - removal and installation
26 Steering column covers - removal and installation
27 Seats - removal and installation
28 Cowl covers - removal and installation
29 Center console - removal and installation

1   General information

These models feature a body-on-frame construction. The frame is a ladder-type, consisting of two box sectioned steel side rails joined by crossmembers. The crossmembers are welded to the side rails, with the exception of the transmission and front suspension crossmembers, which are bolted in place for easy removal.

Certain components are particularly vulnerable to accident damage and can be unbolted and repaired or replaced. Among these parts are the body moldings, bumpers, hood, fenders, doors, tailgate and all glass.

Only general body maintenance practices and body panel repair procedures within the scope of the do-it-yourselfer are included in this Chapter.

2   Body - maintenance

1   The condition of your vehicle's body is very important, because the resale value depends a great deal on it. It's much more difficult to repair a neglected or damaged body than it is to repair mechanical components. The hidden areas of the body, such as the wheel wells, the frame and the engine compartment, are equally important, although they don't require as frequent attention as the rest of the body.

2   Once a year, or every 12,000 miles, it's a good idea to have the underside of the body steam cleaned. All traces of dirt and oil will be removed and the area can then be inspected carefully for rust, damaged brake lines, frayed electrical wires, damaged cables and other problems. The front suspension components should be greased after completion of this job.

3   At the same time, clean the engine and the engine compartment with a steam cleaner or water soluble degreaser.

4   The wheel wells should be given close attention, since undercoating can peel away and stones and dirt thrown up by the tires can cause the paint to chip and flake, allowing rust to set in. If rust is found, clean down to the bare metal and apply an anti-rust paint.

5   The body should be washed about once a week. Wet the vehicle thoroughly to soften the dirt, then wash it down with a soft sponge and plenty of clean soapy water. If the surplus dirt is not washed off very carefully, it can wear down the paint.

6   Spots of tar or asphalt thrown up from the road should be removed with a cloth soaked in solvent.

7   Once every six months, wax the body and chrome trim. If a chrome cleaner is used to remove rust from any of the vehicle's plated parts, remember that the cleaner also removes part of the chrome, so use it sparingly.

3   Vinyl trim - maintenance

Don't clean vinyl trim with detergents, caustic soap or petroleum-based cleaners. Plain soap and water works just fine, with a soft brush to clean dirt that may be ingrained. Wash the vinyl as frequently as the rest of the vehicle.

After cleaning, application of a high quality rubber and vinyl protectant will help prevent oxidation and cracks. The protectant can also be applied to weatherstripping, vacuum lines and rubber hoses (which often fail as a result of chemical degradation) and to the tires.

4   Upholstery and carpets - maintenance

1   Every three months remove the carpets or mats and clean the interior of the vehicle (more frequently if necessary). Vacuum the upholstery and carpets to remove loose dirt and dust.

2   Leather upholstery requires special care. Stains should be removed with warm water and a very mild soap solution. Use a clean, damp cloth to remove the soap, then wipe again with a dry cloth. Never use alcohol, gasoline, nail polish remover or thinner to clean leather upholstery.

3   After cleaning, regularly treat leather upholstery with a leather wax. Never use car wax on leather upholstery.

4   In areas where the interior of the vehicle is subject to bright sunlight, cover leather seats with a sheet if the vehicle is to be left out for any length of time.

5   Body repair - minor damage

See photo sequence

REPAIR OF MINOR SCRATCHES

1   If the scratch is superficial and does not penetrate to the metal of the body, repair is very simple. Lightly rub the scratched area with a fine rubbing compound to remove loose paint and built-up wax. Rinse the area with clean water.

2   Apply touch-up paint to the scratch, using a small brush. Continue to apply thin layers of paint until the surface of the paint in the scratch is level with the surrounding paint. Allow the new paint at least two weeks to harden, then blend it into the surrounding paint by rubbing with a very fine rubbing compound. Finally, apply a coat of wax to the scratch area.

3   If the scratch has penetrated the paint and exposed the metal of the body, causing the metal to rust, a different repair technique is required. Remove all loose rust from the bottom of the scratch with a pocket knife, then apply rust inhibiting paint to prevent the formation of rust in the future. Using a rubber or nylon applicator, coat the scratched area with glaze-type filler. If required, the filler can be mixed with thinner to provide a very thin paste, which is ideal for filling narrow scratches. Before the glaze filler in the scratch hardens, wrap a piece of smooth cotton cloth around the tip of a finger. Dip the cloth in thinner and then quickly wipe it along the surface of the scratch. This will ensure that the surface of the filler is slightly hollow. The scratch can now be painted over as described earlier in this Section.

REPAIR OF DENTS

4   When repairing dents, the first job is to pull the dent out until the affected area is as close as possible to its original shape. There is no point in trying to restore the original shape completely as the metal in the damaged area will have stretched on impact and cannot be restored to its original contours. It is better to bring the level of the dent up to a point which is about 1/8-inch below the level of the surrounding metal. In cases where the dent is very shallow, it is not worth trying to pull it out at all.

5   If the back side of the dent is accessible, it can be hammered out gently from behind using a soft-face hammer. While doing this, hold a block of wood firmly against the opposite side of the metal to absorb the hammer blows and prevent the metal from being stretched.

6   If the dent is in a section of the body which has double layers, or some other factor makes it inaccessible from behind, a different technique is required. Drill several small holes through the metal inside the damaged area, particularly in the deeper sections. Screw long, self-tapping screws into the holes just enough for them to get a good grip in the metal. Now the dent can be pulled out by pulling on the protruding heads of the screws with locking pliers.

7   The next stage of repair is the removal of paint from the damaged area and from an inch or so of the surrounding metal. This is done with a wire brush or sanding disk in a drill motor, although it can be done just as effectively by hand with sandpaper. To complete the preparation for filling, score the surface of the bare metal with a screwdriver or the tang of a file, or drill small holes in the affected area. This will provide a good grip for the filler material. To complete the repair, see the subsection on filling and painting later in this Section.

REPAIR OF RUST HOLES OR GASHES

8   Remove all paint from the affected area and from an inch or so of the surrounding metal using a sanding disk or wire brush mounted in a drill motor. If these are not available, a few sheets of sandpaper will do the job just as effectively.

9   With the paint removed, you will be able to determine the severity of the corrosion and decide whether to replace the whole panel, if possible, or repair the affected area. New body panels are not as expensive as most people think and it is often quicker to install a new panel than to repair large areas of rust.

10   Remove all trim pieces from the affected area except those which will act as a guide to the original shape of the damaged body, such as headlight shells, etc. Using metal snips or a hacksaw blade, remove all loose metal and any other metal that is badly affected by rust. Hammer the edges of the hole in to create a slight depression for the filler material.

11   Wire brush the affected area to remove the powdery rust from the surface of the metal. If the back of the rusted area is accessible, treat it with rust inhibiting paint.

12   Before filling is done, block the hole in some way. This can be done with sheet metal riveted or screwed into place, or by stuffing the hole with wire mesh.

13   Once the hole is blocked off, the affected area can be filled and painted. See the following subsection on filling and painting.

FILLING AND PAINTING

14   Many types of body fillers are available, but generally speaking, body repair kits which contain filler paste and a tube of resin hardener are best for this type of repair work. A wide, flexible plastic or nylon applicator will be necessary for imparting a smooth and contoured finish to the surface of the filler material. Mix up a small amount of filler on a clean piece of wood or cardboard (use the hardener sparingly). Follow the manufacturer's instructions on the package, otherwise the filler will set incorrectly.

15   Using the applicator, apply the filler paste to the prepared area. Draw the applicator across the surface of the filler to achieve the desired contour and to level the filler surface. As soon as a contour that approximates the original one is achieved, stop working the paste. If you continue, the paste will begin to stick to the applicator. Continue to add thin layers of paste at 20-minute intervals until the level of the filler is just above the surrounding metal.

16   Once the filler has hardened, the excess can be removed with a body file. From then on, progressively finer grades of sandpaper should be used, starting with a 180-grit paper and finishing with 600-grit wet-or-dry paper. Always wrap the sandpaper around a flat rubber or wooden block, otherwise the surface of the filler will not be completely flat. During the sanding of the filler surface, the wet-or-dry paper should be periodically rinsed in water. This will ensure that a very smooth finish is produced in the final stage.

17   At this point, the repair area should be surrounded by a ring of bare metal, which in turn should be encircled by the finely feathered edge of good paint. Rinse the repair area with clean water until all of the dust produced by the sanding operation is gone.

18   Spray the entire area with a light coat of primer. This will reveal any imperfections in the surface of the filler. Repair the imperfections with fresh filler paste or glaze filler and once more smooth the surface

These photos illustrate a method of repairing simple dents. They are intended to supplement Body repair - minor damage in this Chapter and should not be used as the sole instructions for body repair on these vehicles.

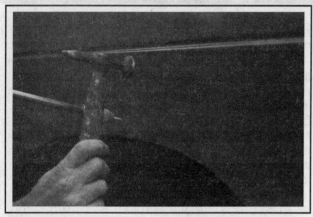

1 If you can't access the backside of the body panel to hammer out the dent, pull it out with a slide-hammer-type dent puller. Tap with a hammer near the edge of the dent to help 'pop' the metal back to its original shape, about 1/8-inch below the surface of the surrounding metal

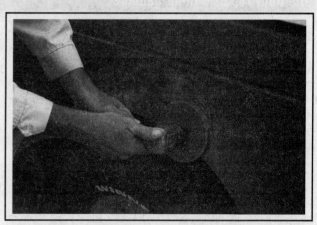

2 Using coarse-grit sandpaper, remove the paint down to the bare metal. Clean the repair area with wax/silicone remover.

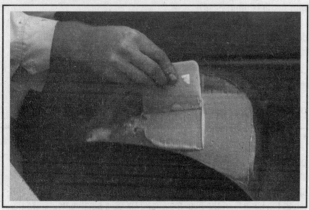

3 Following label instructions, mix up a batch of plastic filler and hardener, then quickly press it into the metal with a plastic applicator. Work the filler until it matches the original contour and is slightly above the surrounding metal

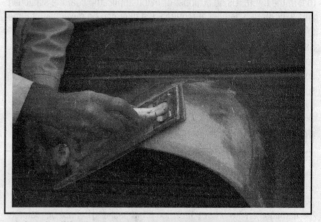

4 Let the filler harden until you can just dent it with your fingernail. File, then sand the filler down until it's smooth and even. Work down to finer grits of sandpaper - always using a board or block - ending up with 360 or 400 grit

5 When the area is smooth to the touch, clean the area and mask around it. Apply several layers of primer to the area. A professional-type spray gun is being used here, but aerosol spray primer works fine

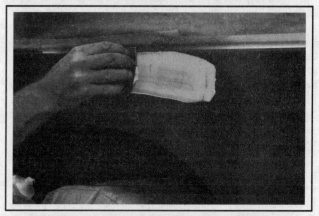

6 Fill imperfections or scratches with glazing compound. Sand with 360 or 400-grit and re-spray. Finish sand the primer with 600 grit, clean thoroughly, then apply the finish coat. Don't attempt to rub out or wax the repair area until the paint has dried completely (at least two weeks)

with sandpaper. Repeat this spray-and-repair procedure until you are satisfied that the surface of the filler and the feathered edge of the paint are perfect. Rinse the area with clean water and allow it to dry completely.

19 The repair area is now ready for painting. Spray painting must be carried out in a warm, dry, windless and dust free atmosphere. These conditions can be created if you have access to a large indoor work area, but if you are forced to work in the open, you will have to pick the day very carefully. If you are working indoors, dousing the floor in the work area with water will help settle the dust which would otherwise be in the air. If the repair area is confined to one body panel, mask off the surrounding panels. This will help minimize the effects of a slight mismatch in paint color. Trim pieces such as chrome strips, door handles, etc., will also need to be masked off or removed. Use masking tape and several thickness of newspaper for the masking operations.

20 Before spraying, shake the paint can thoroughly, then spray a test area until the spray painting technique is mastered. Cover the repair area with a thick coat of primer. The thickness should be built up using several thin layers of primer rather than one thick one. Using 600-grit wet-or-dry sandpaper, rub down the surface of the primer until it is very smooth. While doing this, the work area should be thoroughly rinsed with water and the wet-or-dry sandpaper periodically rinsed as well. Allow the primer to dry before spraying additional coats.

21 Spray on the top coat, again building up the thickness by using several thin layers of paint. Begin spraying in the center of the repair area and then, using a circular motion, work out until the whole repair area and about two inches of the surrounding original paint is covered. Remove all masking material 10 to 15 minutes after spraying on the final coat of paint. Allow the new paint at least two weeks to harden, then use a very fine rubbing compound to blend the edges of the new paint into the existing paint. Finally, apply a coat of wax.

6 Body repair - major damage

1   Major damage must be repaired by an auto body shop specifically equipped to perform these repairs. Most shops have the specialized equipment required to do the job properly.

2   If the damage is extensive, the frame must be checked for proper alignment or the vehicle's handling characteristics may be adversely affected and other components may wear at an accelerated rate.

3   Due to the fact that all of the major body components (hood, fenders, etc.) are separate and replaceable units, any seriously damaged components should be replaced rather than repaired. Sometimes the components can be found in a wrecking yard that specializes in used vehicle components, often at considerable savings over the cost of new parts.

7 Hinges and locks - maintenance

Once every 3000 miles, or every three months, the hinges and latch assemblies on the doors, hood and trunk should be given a few drops of light oil or lock lubricant. The door latch strikers should also be lubricated with a thin coat of grease to reduce wear and ensure free movement. Lubricate the door and trunk locks with spray-on graphite lubricant.

8 Windshield and fixed glass - replacement

Replacement of the windshield and fixed glass requires the use of special fast-setting adhesive/caulk materials and some specialized tools. It is recommended that these operations be left to a dealer or a shop specializing in glass work.

9 Hood support struts - removal and installation

▶ **Refer to illustration 9.2**

1   Open the hood and support it securely.

2   Using a small screwdriver, detach the retaining clips at both ends of the support strut. Then pry or pull sharply to detach it from the vehicle (see illustration).

3   Installation is the reverse of removal.

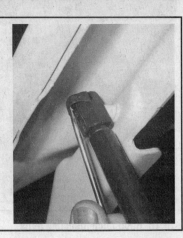

9.2 Use a small screwdriver to pry the clip out of its locking groove, then detach the end of the strut from the locating stud

10 Hood - removal, installation and adjustment

➡ **Note: The hood is heavy and somewhat awkward to remove and install - at least two people should perform this procedure.**

REMOVAL AND INSTALLATION

▶ **Refer to illustrations 10.3 and 10.4**

1 Use blankets or pads to cover the cowl area of the body and fenders. This will protect the body and paint as the hood is lifted off.

2 Disconnect any cables or wires that will interfere with removal.

3 Make marks or scribe a line around the hood hinge to ensure proper alignment during installation (see illustration).

4 Have an assistant support one side of the hood while you support the other. Simultaneously remove the hinge-to-hood bolts (see illustration).

5 Lift off the hood.

6 Installation is the reverse of removal.

ADJUSTMENT

▶ **Refer to illustrations 10.10 and 10.11**

7 Fore-and-aft and side-to-side adjustment of the hood is done by moving the hinge plate slot after loosening the bolts or nuts.

8 Scribe a line around the entire hinge plate so you can determine the amount of movement (see illustration 10.3).

9 Loosen the bolts or nuts and move the hood into correct alignment. Move it only a little at a time. Tighten the hinge bolts and carefully lower the hood to check the position.

10 If necessary after installation, the entire hood latch assembly can be adjusted up-and-down as well as from side-to-side on the radiator support so the hood closes securely and flush with the fenders. To make the adjustment, scribe a line or mark around the hood latch mounting bolts to provide a reference point, then loosen them and reposition the latch assembly, as necessary (see illustration). Following adjustment, retighten the mounting bolts.

11 Finally, adjust the hood bumpers on the radiator support so the hood, when closed, is flush with the fenders, and that the grille is supported by the lower bumpers (see illustration).

12 The hood latch assembly, as well as the hinges, should be periodically lubricated with white, lithium-base grease to prevent binding and wear.

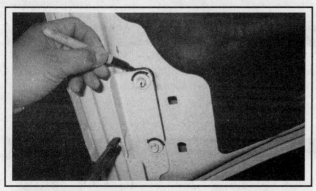

10.3 Before removing the hood, draw a mark around the hinge plates

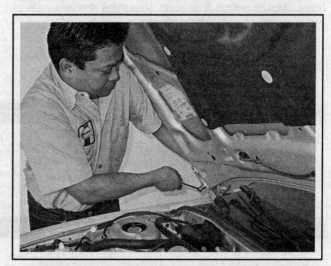

10.4 Support the hood with your shoulder while removing the hood bolts

10.10 Hood latch mounting bolts

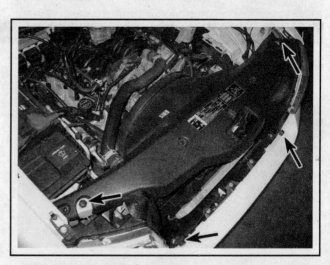

10.11 Hood adjustment bumpers

11 Hood latch and release cable - removal and installation

LATCH

1 Scribe a line around the latch to aid alignment when reinstalling the latch assembly.

2 Remove the latch retaining bolts securing the latch to the radiator support (see illustration 10.10) and remove the latch.

3 Disconnect the hood release cable by disengaging the cable from the back of the latch assembly.

4 Installation is the reverse of the removal procedure.

➡ **Note: Adjust the latch so the hood engages securely when closed and the hood bumpers are slightly compressed.**

CABLE

▶ **Refer to illustrations 11.5 and 11.8**

5 Remove the hood latch as described earlier in this Section, then detach the cable from the latch. Remove the radiator cover (see illustration).

6 Attach a length of wire to the end of the cable (in the engine compartment). This will be used to pull the new cable back into the engine compartment.

7 Working in the engine compartment, detach the cable from all of its retaining clips. It may be necessary to cut some of the clips to free the cable.

8 Working under the instrument panel, remove the left kick panel, then remove fastener and detach the hood release handle (see illustration). Dislodge the grommet and pull the cable through the firewall and into the cab.

9 Detach the wire from the old cable, then attach it to the end of the new cable.

➡ **Note: Make sure the new cable is equipped with a grommet.**

10 Pull the new cable through the firewall and into the engine compartment. Seat the grommet in the firewall.

11 The remainder of installation is the reverse of removal.

11.5 Release the locking pins to remove the radiator cover

11.8 Hood release handle mounting bolt

12 Radiator grille - removal and installation

▶ **Refer to illustration 12.2**

1 Open the hood.

2 Remove the mounting screws and nuts, then detach the grille assembly from the hood (see illustration).

3 Installation is the reverse of removal.

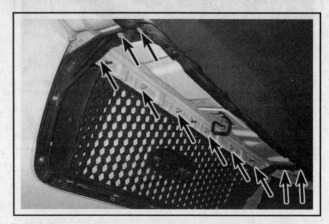

12.2 Remove the fasteners securing the grille to the hood

13 Bumpers - removal and installation

FRONT BUMPER

▶ **Refer to illustrations 13.3, 13.4, 13.6 and 13.7**

1 Loosen the front wheel lug nuts, raise the front of the vehicle and support it securely on jackstands. Apply the parking brake. Remove the front wheels.

2 Remove the inner fender splash shields (see illustration 14.2).

3 Remove the fasteners securing the upper bumper to the fender (see illustration).

4 Remove the upper bumper brace (see illustration).

5 Remove the headlight housings (see Chapter 12).

6 Remove the fasteners along the top of the upper bumper, then remove the upper bumper (see illustration).

7 With an assistant supporting the bumper, remove the nuts retaining the bumper to the brackets (see illustration).

8 Detach the bumper from the frame rails or brackets.

9 Installation is the reverse of removal.

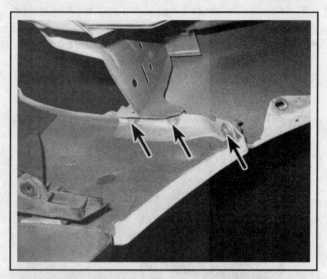

13.3 Remove the fasteners securing the upper bumper to the fender

13.4 Remove the fasteners, then remove the brace

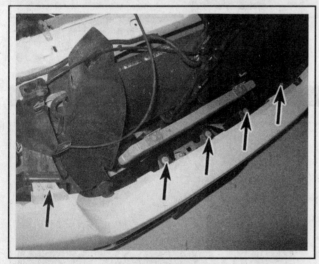

13.6 Remove the fasteners along the top of the upper bumper

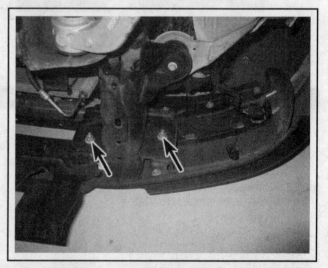

13.7 Remove the nuts retaining the bumper to the frame brackets

REAR BUMPER

▶ **Refer to illustration 13.11**

10 Unplug any electrical connectors which would interfere with bumper removal.

11 With an assistant supporting the bumper, remove the bolts retaining the bumper to the bumper arms (see illustration). Remove the bumper.

12 Installation is the reverse of removal.

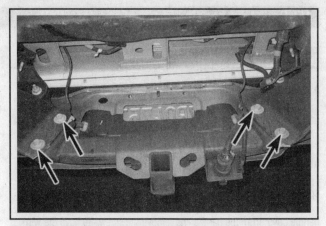

13.11 Remove the bolts retaining the bumper to the bumper arms

14 Front fender - removal and installation

▶ **Refer to illustrations 14.2, 14.4a, 14.4b and 14.5**

1 Raise the vehicle and support it securely on jackstands and remove the front wheel.

2 Remove the fasteners retaining the fender inner splash shield (see illustration).

3 Remove the headlight housing (see Chapter 12).

4 Remove the fender-to-rocker panel bolts and the fender-to-door pillar bolt (see illustrations).

5 Remove the fastener retaining the fender to the headlight housing opening and the fender upper mounting fasteners (see illustration).

6 Detach the fender. It's a good idea to have an assistant support the fender while it's being moved away from the vehicle to prevent damage to the surrounding body panels. If you're removing the right-side fender, disconnect the antenna (see Chapter 12).

7 Installation is the reverse of removal.

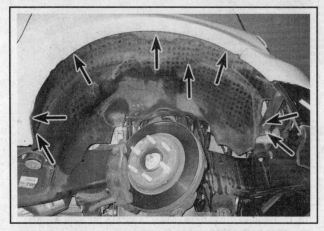

14.2 Location of the inner fender splash shield fasteners

14.4a Remove the two lower mounting bolts at the rear of the wheel opening . . .

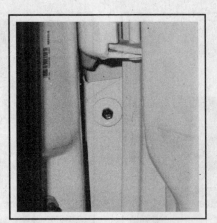

14.4b . . . and the fastener at the door pillar

14.5 Remove the remaining fender mounting bolts

15 Door trim panels - removal and installation

FRONT DOOR

▶ **Refer to illustrations 15.1a, 15.1b, 15.2, 15.3, 15.4 and 15.6**

1 Remove the fasteners securing the inside door handle (see illustrations).

2 Remove the inside door handle (see illustration).

3 Pry out the armrest switch control plate and disconnect the electrical connectors (see illustration).

4 Remove the speaker cover (see illustration), then remove the speaker (see Chapter 12).

5 On manual window equipped models, separate the window crank handle cover from the handle and remove the screw. Remove the window crank.

6 Remove the fasteners at the bottom of the door panel (see illustration). Pull upward to release the door panel hooks from the door.

7 Once all of the hooks are disengaged, raise the trim panel up and off the door. Disconnect any wiring harness connectors and remove the trim panel from the vehicle. For access to the inner door, carefully peel back the plastic watershield.

8 Installation is the reverse of removal.

REAR DOOR

▶ **Refer to illustrations 15.9, 15.10, 15.11 and 15.12**

9 Remove the door pillar trim covers (see illustration).

10 Remove the inside door handle (see illustration).

11 Pry out the armrest switch control plate and disconnect the electrical connector (see illustration).

12 Remove the fasteners securing the door panel (see illustration).

13 Pull upward to release the door panel hooks from the door.

14 Once all of the hooks are disengaged, raise the trim panel up and off the door. Disconnect any wiring harness connectors and remove the trim panel from the vehicle.

15 For access to the inner door, carefully peel back the plastic watershield.

16 Installation is the reverse of removal.

15.1a Remove the fastener cover to access the door handle mounting bolts (2010 and earlier models)

15.1b On 2011 and later models, the door handle retaining screw is accessed with a screwdriver while pulling on the handle

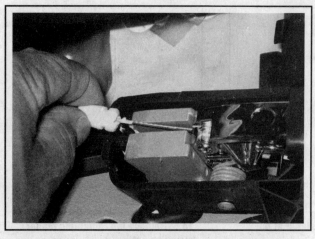

15.2 Remove the inside handle and detach the latch cable

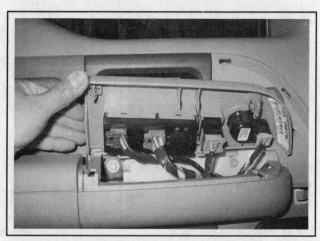

15.3 Pry out the armrest switch control plate and disconnect the electrical connectors

15.4 Using a trim stick, carefully remove the speaker cover

15.6 Remove the fasteners along the lower edge of the door

15.9 Remove both the left and right door pillar trim covers

15.10 Remove the fastener cover to access the door handle mounting bolts

15.11 Pry out the armrest switch control plate and disconnect the electrical connectors

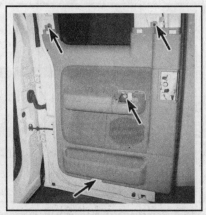

15.12 Remove the fasteners securing the door panel

16 Door - removal, installation and adjustment

➡ Note: The door is heavy and somewhat awkward to remove and install - at least two people should perform this procedure.

FRONT DOOR

▶ Refer to illustrations 16.1, 16.3a, 16.3b and 16.5

1 Disconnect the electrical connector in the door opening (see illustration).

2 Place a jack under the door or have an assistant on hand to support it when the hinge bolts are removed.

➡ Note: If a jack is used, place a few rags between it and the door to protect the door's painted surfaces.

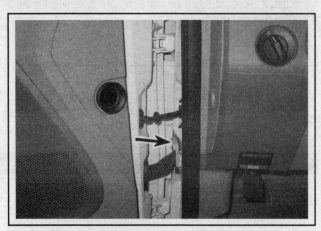

16.1 Flip the lever down, then disconnect the door's electrical harness from the A-pillar

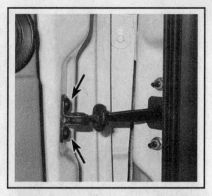

16.3a Remove the fasteners from the door stop strap

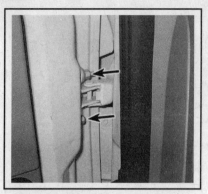

16.3b Mark their locations, then remove the door retaining bolt and nut at each hinge

16.5 Adjust the door lock striker by loosening the mounting screws and gently tapping the striker in the desired direction

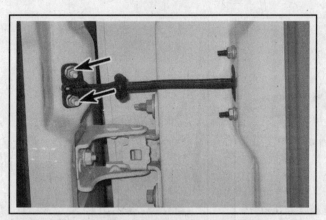

16.9 Remove the fasteners from the door stop strap

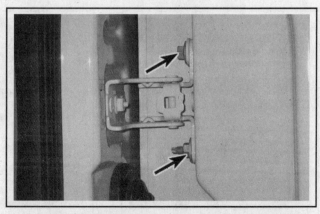

16.11 Mark their locations, then remove the door retaining bolt and nut at each hinge

3 Scribe around the mounting bolt/nut heads and hinges with a marking pen, remove the fasteners and carefully lift off the door (see illustrations).

4 Installation is the reverse of removal, making sure to align the hinge with the marks made during removal before tightening the bolts.

5 Following installation of the door, check the alignment and adjust the hinges, if necessary. Adjust the door lock striker, centering it in the door latch (see illustration).

REAR DOOR

▶ **Refer to illustrations 16.9 and 16.11**

6 Remove the door trim panel and water deflector (see Section 15).
7 Unplug all electrical connections, ground wires and harness retaining clips from the door.

➡ **Note: It is a good idea to label all connections to aid the reassembly process.**

8 Working through the door opening, detach the rubber conduit between the body and the door. Then pull wiring harness through the conduit hole and remove from the door.

9 Remove the screws securing the door stop (see illustration).

10 Mark around the door hinges with a pen or a scribe to facilitate realignment during reassembly.

11 Have an assistant hold the door, remove the hinge to door bolts (see illustration) and lift the door off.

12 Installation is the reverse of the removal.

13 Following installation of the door, check the alignment and adjust the hinges, if necessary. Adjust the door lock striker, centering it in the door latch.

17 Door latch, lock cylinder and handle - removal and installation

DOOR LATCH

▶ **Refer to illustrations 17.2**

1 Raise the window then remove the door trim panel and watershield as described in Section 15.

2 Remove the screws securing the latch to the door (see illustration).

3 Working through the large access hole, position the latch as necessary to disconnect the electrical connectors. Disengage the outside

door handle and outside lock cylinder-to-latch rods. Remove the latch assembly from the door.

4   Installation is the reverse of removal.

DOOR LOCK CYLINDER AND OUTSIDE HANDLE

▶ **Refer to illustrations 17.6 and 17.8**

5   To remove the outside handle and door lock cylinder assembly, raise the window and remove the door trim panel and watershield as described in Section 15.

6   Working through the access hole, detach the door handle and the lock cylinder actuating rods (see illustration).

7   Disconnect any electrical connectors which would interfere with removal.

8   Remove the remaining fasteners and remove the door handle and lock cylinder from the door (see illustration).

9   Installation is the reverse of removal.

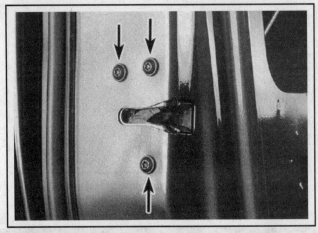

17.2 Remove the latch retaining screws from the end of the door

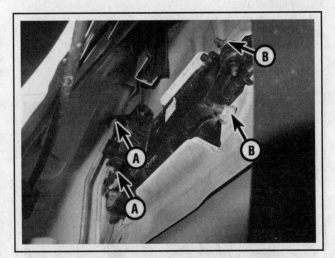

17.6 Detach the door handle and the lock cylinder actuating rods (A) and door handle mounting fasteners (B)

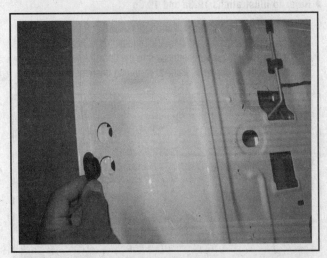

17.8 Remove the rubber plugs to access the remaining door handle fasteners

18 Door window glass - removal and installation

FRONT

▶ **Refer to illustration 18.4**

1   Remove the door trim panel and watershield (see Section 15).

2   Lower the window.

3   Pry the inner weather seal out of the door glass opening.

4   Raise the window for access to the glass retaining nuts, then remove the two nuts (see illustration).

5   Remove the window by tilting it forward, then lifting it out of the door.

6   To install, lower the glass into the door, slide it into position and install the nuts.

7   The remainder of installation is the reverse of removal.

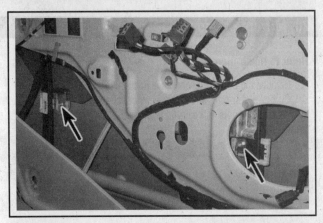

18.4 Remove the glass retaining nuts (speaker removed for clarity)

18.9 Remove the rear door glass retaining fasteners

REAR

▶ **Refer to illustration 18.9**

  8 Follow Steps 1 through 3.
  9 Raise the window for access to the glass retaining nuts, then remove the two fasteners (see illustration).
  10 Remove the window.
  11 Installation is the reverse of the removal procedure.

19 Door window glass regulator - removal and installation

▶ **Refer to illustrations 19.3a and 19.3b**

  1 Remove the door trim panel and watershield.
  2 Unbolt the window glass from the regulator (see Section 18). Push the glass all the way up and tape it to the door frame.
  3 Remove the window regulator-to-door and track mounting fasteners (see illustrations).
  4 On power window equipped models, unplug the electrical connector.
  5 Remove the regulator from the door.
  6 Installation is the reverse of removal.

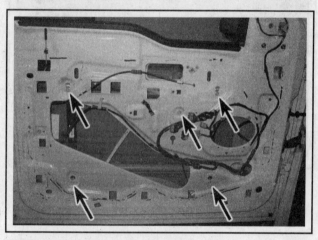

19.3a Window regulator-to-front door and track mounting fasteners

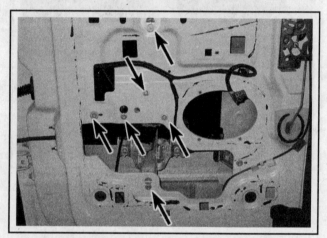

19.3b Window regulator-to-rear door and track mounting fasteners

20 Mirrors - removal and installation

▶ **Refer to illustration 20.3**

  1 Remove the door trim panel (see Section 15).
  2 On power mirrors, unplug the electrical connector.
  3 Remove the nuts and detach the mirror from the door (see illustration).
  4 Installation is the reverse of removal.

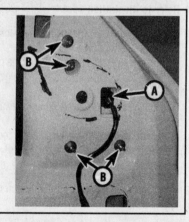

20.3 Disconnect the electrical connector (A) then detach the mirror retaining nuts (B)

21 Tailgate - removal and installation

▶ **Refer to illustrations 21.1 and 21.2**

1   Open the tailgate and detach the support cables (see illustration).
2   Lower the tailgate until the flat on the right side hinge-pin aligns with the slot in the hinge pocket. Lift the tailgate out of the pocket (see

illustration). With the help of an assistant to support the weight, withdraw the left hinge pin from the body and remove the tailgate from the vehicle.
3   Installation is the reverse of removal.

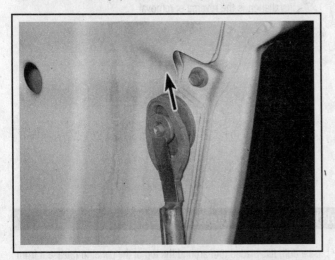

21.1 Lift the spring retainer up and slide the cable end off the pin

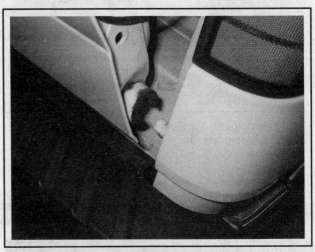

21.2 Align the flat on the right-side hinge pin with the slot in the hinge pocket and lift the tailgate off the vehicle

22 Tailgate latch and handle - removal and installation

▶ **Refer to illustration 22.1**

1   Lower the tailgate and remove the tailgate access cover (see illustration).

LATCH

▶ **Refer to illustration 22.2**

2   Remove the latch mounting fasteners (see illustration). It may be necessary to use an impact-driver to loosen them.
3   Disconnect the control rods from the latch and remove the latch from the door.
4   Installation is the reverse of removal.

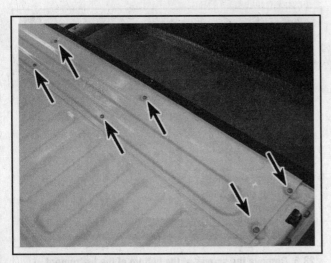

22.1 Remove the cover screws to access the inside of the tailgate

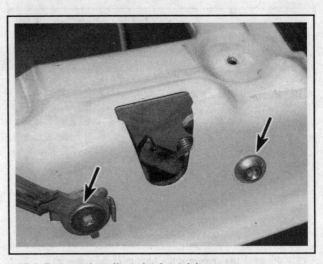

22.2 Remove the tailgate latch retaining screws

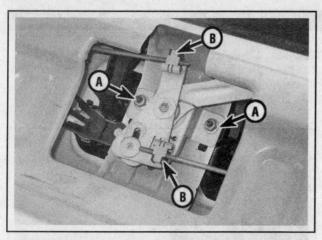

22.5 Disengage the handle-to-latch rods (A) and remove the handle retaining nuts (B)

HANDLE

▶ **Refer to illustration 22.5**

5 Disconnect the control rods (see illustration).

6 Detach the retaining nuts and remove the handle assembly from the tailgate.

7 Installation is the reverse of removal.

23 Dashboard trim panels (2004 through 2008 models) - removal and installation

✳✳ WARNING:

The models covered by this manual are equipped with Supplemental Restraint Systems (SRS), more commonly known as airbags. Always disable the airbag system before working in the vicinity of any airbag system component to avoid the possibility of accidental deployment of the airbags, which could cause personal injury (see Chapter 12).

1 Disconnect the cable from the negative battery terminal (see Chapter 5, Section 1).

KNEE BOLSTER

▶ **Refer to illustration 23.2**

2 Remove the screws at the bottom of the driver's knee bolster, then use a dull, flat-bladed tool around the top of the panel to release it from the clips at the top (see illustration).

3 Installation is the reverse of removal.

INSTRUMENT CLUSTER BEZEL

▶ **Refer to illustration 23.5**

4 Remove the knee bolster (see Step 2).

5 Remove the screws at the bottom of the instrument cluster bezel (see illustration), then use a trim stick or a dull, flat-bladed tool around the top of the panel to release it from the clips at the top. Disconnect the electrical connector, if equipped.

6 Installation is the reverse of removal.

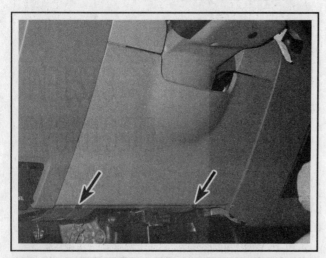

23.2 Remove the screws at the bottom of the driver's knee bolster

23.5 Remove the screws at the bottom of the instrument cluster bezel

INSTRUMENT PANEL CENTER BEZEL

▶ **Refer to illustration 23.7**

7   Use a flat-bladed tool around the panel to release it from the clips (see illustration).

8   Installation is the reverse of removal.

UPPER FINISH PANEL

▶ **Refer to illustration 23.10**

9   Remove the instrument center bezel (see Step 7).

10 Remove the screws at the bottom of the upper finish panel, then remove the panel (see illustration).

11 Installation is the reverse of removal.

GLOVE BOX

▶ **Refer to illustration 23.13**

12 Open the glove box door.

13 Press in on the two sides of the glove compartment bin and pull the door down until the bumpers on the bin have cleared the stops. Remove the fasteners at the bottom of the box (see illustration).

14 Installation is the reverse of removal.

CENTER BRACE COVER

▶ **Refer to illustration 23.15**

15 Remove the pushpin fasteners securing the center brace cover, then remove the cover (see illustration).

16 Installation is the reverse of removal.

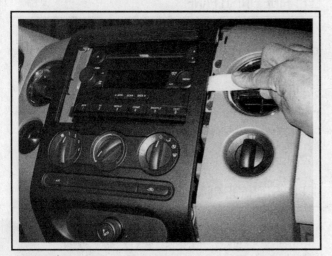

23.7 Using a trim stick, carefully pry around the panel to release it from the clips

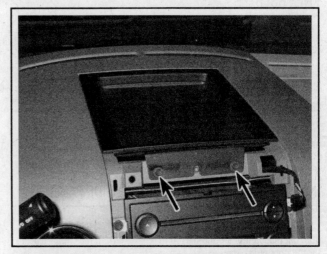

23.10 Remove the screws at the bottom of the upper finish panel

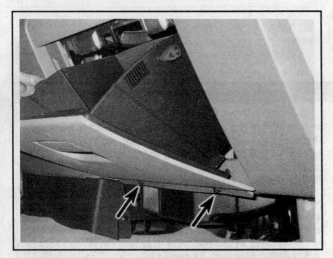

23.13 After the bumpers on the bin have cleared the stops, remove the fasteners at the bottom of the box

23.15 Remove the pushpin fasteners securing the center brace cover

24 Dashboard trim panels (2009 and later models) - removal and installation

❋ WARNING:

The models covered in this manual are equipped with Supplemental Restraint Systems (SRS), more commonly known as air bags. Always disable the airbag system before working in the vicinity of any airbag system component to avoid the possibility of accidental deployment of the airbags, which could cause personal injury (see Chapter 12).

1   Disconnect the cable from the negative battery terminal (see Chapter 5, Section 1).
2   If equipped, remove the center console (see Section 29).
3   If equipped, move the adjustable pedal assembly to the full forward position.
4   Move the steering wheel to the full down position.

KNEE BOLSTER

5   Remove the screws at the bottom of the driver's knee bolster, then use a dull, flat-bladed tool around the top to release it from the clips.
6   Installation is the reverse of removal.

INSTRUMENT CLUSTER FINISH PANEL

7   Remove the two upper screws. Carefully lower the finish panel and remove it.
8   Installation is the reverse of removal.

INSTRUMENT PANEL CENTER BEZEL SIDE PANELS

9   Remove the screw at the bottom of the left side panel, then use a dull, flat bladed tool around the top to release it from the clips. Repeat for the right side panel.
10   Installation is the reverse of removal.

INSTRUMENT PANEL CENTER BEZEL

11   Use a dull, flat bladed tool under the lower left side of the audio input jack cover to release it from the clips at the top and remove it.

Remove the lower center screw adjacent to the input jack.
12   Remove the mat from the upper trim panel.
13   Remove the screws securing the top of the upper trim panel to the center bezel.
14   Pull the center bezel forward to release it from the clips at each side.
15   Installation is the reverse of removal.

INSTRUMENT PANEL UPPER TRIM PANEL

16   Use a dull, flat bladed tool around the sides of the upper grille to remove it.
17   Remove the four screws, then remove the upper trim panel.
18   Installation is the reverse of removal.

LEFT SIDE FINISH PANEL

19   Use a dull, flat bladed tool around both sides of the side panel to release it from the clips on each side, then remove the panel.
20   Installation is the reverse of removal.

RIGHT SIDE FINISH PANEL

21   Remove the two lower screws at the bottom of the finish panel, then remove the panel.
22   Installation is the reverse of removal.

UPPER STORAGE COMPARTMENT

23   Remove the mat from the upper storage compartment.
24   Remove the two screws, then remove the upper storage compartment.
25   Installation is the reverse of removal.

LOWER STORAGE COMPARTMENT

26   Remove the four screws, then remove the lower storage compartment.
27   Installation is the reverse of removal.

25 Instrument panel - removal and installation

▶ Refer to the following illustrations 25.2, 25.7, 25.9a, 25.9b, 25.10, 25.13a, 25.13b, 25.13c, 25.13d and 25.13e

❋ WARNING:

The models covered by this manual are equipped with Supplemental Restraint Systems (SRS), more commonly known as airbags. Always disable the airbag system before working in the vicinity of any airbag system component to avoid the possibility of accidental deployment of the airbags, which could cause personal injury (see Chapter 12).

➡ Note 1: This is a difficult procedure for the home mechanic. There are many hidden fasteners, difficult angles to work in and many electrical connectors to tag and disconnect/connect. We recommend that this procedure be done only by an experienced do-it-yourselfer.

➡ Note 2: During removal of the instrument panel, make careful notes of how each piece comes off, where it fits in relation to other pieces and what holds it in place. If you note how each part is installed before removing it, getting the instrument panel back together again will be much easier.

➡ Note 3: It is not necessary, but it is suggested to remove both front seats to allow additional working space and lessen the chance of damage to the seats during this procedure.

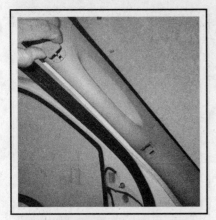

25.2 Remove the screw covers, then remove the A-pillar handle mounting fasteners

25.7 Use a flat-bladed tool or trim stick to remove the instrument panel end caps

25.9a Pry off the driver's and passenger's side scuff plates . . .

25.9b . . . and kick panels

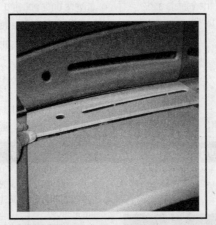

25.10 Using a flat-bladed tool or trim stick, carefully pry around the defrost grilles to release them from the clips

25.13a Remove the fasteners at the top of the instrument panel, on the right side . . .

1   Disconnect the cable from the negative battery terminal (see Chapter 5, Section 1). Turn the front wheels to the straight-ahead position and lock the steering column.

2   Remove the trim from the A-pillars (see illustration).

3   If equipped, remove the center console (see Section 29).

4   Remove the steering wheel (see Chapter 10).

5   On 2004 through 2008 models, remove the instrument bezel (see Section 23). On all models, remove the instrument cluster (see Chapter 12).

6   Remove the glove box, center brace cover, instrument panel center bezel and upper finish panel (see Section 23).

7   Remove the instrument panel end caps (see illustration).

8   Remove the screw and detach the hood release handle from the instrument panel.

9   Remove the side kick panels (see illustrations).

10 Remove the left and right side defrost grilles (see illustration).

11 Remove the pinch bolt and disconnect the steering column shaft (see Chapter 10).

12 Disconnect the instrument panel electrical connectors.

➡ **Note: A number of electrical connectors must be disconnected in order to remove the instrument panel. Most are designed so that they will only fit on the matching connector**

(male or female), but if there is any doubt, mark the connectors with masking tape and a marking pen before disconnecting them.

13 Remove the fasteners securing the instrument panel (see illustrations).

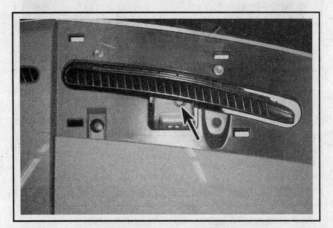

25.13b . . . and the left side

25.13c Remove both instrument panel center brackets

25.13d Remove the remaining fasteners . . .

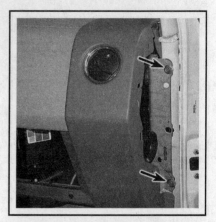

25.13e . . . from each end of the instrument panel

14 Pull the instrument panel towards the rear of the vehicle and detach any electrical connectors interfering with removal.

15 Once all the electrical connectors are detached, lift the instrument panel, pull it away from the windshield and take it out through the driver's door opening.

➡ **Note: This is a two-person job.**

16 Installation is the reverse of removal.

26 Steering column covers - removal and installation

▸ **Refer to illustrations 26.2 and 26.3**

⁂ WARNING:

The models covered by this manual are equipped with Supplemental Restraint Systems (SRS), more commonly known as airbags. Always disable the airbag system before working in the vicinity of any airbag system component to avoid the possibility of accidental deployment of the airbags, which could cause personal injury (see Chapter 12).

1 Remove the steering wheel (see Chapter 10).

2 Remove the fastener from the lower steering column cover (see illustration).

3 Separate the cover halves and remove the lower cover, then remove the fasteners securing the upper cover (see illustration).

4 Remove the upper cover.

5 Installation is the reverse of removal.

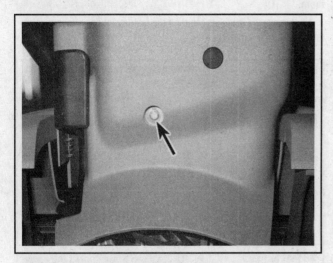

26.2 Remove the fastener from the bottom cover

26.3 Separate the two halves, then remove the two fasteners securing the upper cover

27 Seats - removal and installation

※ WARNING:

Some models are equipped with seat belt pre-tensioners, which are pyrotechnic (explosive) devices that tighten the seat belts during an impact of sufficient force. Always disable the airbag system before working in the vicinity of any restraint system component to avoid the possibility of accidental deployment of the airbag(s) and seat belt pre-tensioners, which could cause personal injury (see Chapter 12).

FRONT SEAT

▶ **Refer to illustration 27.3a and 27.3b**

1   Disconnect the cable from the negative battery terminal (see Chapter 5).

2   Position the seat all the way forward and all the way to the rear to access the front seat retaining bolts.

3   Detach any bolt trim covers and remove the retaining bolts (see illustrations).

4   Tilt the seat upward to access the underneath, then disconnect any electrical connectors and lift the seat from the vehicle.

5   Installation is the reverse of removal.

CENTER FRONT SEAT

▶ **Refer to illustrations 27.6 and 27.7**

6   Remove the center seat cushion (see illustration).

7   Remove the center seat retaining bolts, then disconnect any electrical connectors and lift the seat from the vehicle (see illustration).

8   Installation is the reverse of removal.

REAR SEAT

▶ **Refer to illustrations 27.9a, 27.9b, 27.10, 27.11, 27.12a and 27.12b**

9   At the top of the seat back, remove the seat belt cover (see illustrations).

27.3a Remove the bolts at the front . . .

27.3b . . . and the rear of the seat

27.6 Pull up at the front edge of the seat cushion and detach it from the center seat frame

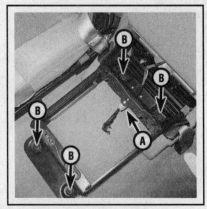

27.7 Disconnect the electrical connector (A), then remove the seat retaining bolts (B)

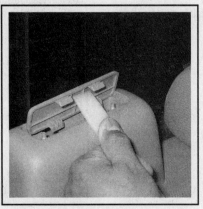

27.9a Using a flat-bladed tool or trim stick, carefully pry open the fastener cover . . .

27.9b . . . then remove the fasteners and the seat belt cover

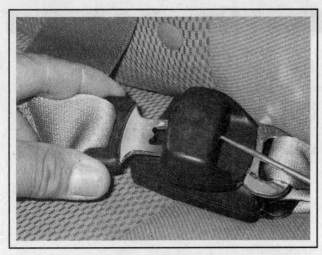

27.10 Insert a suitable tool into the latch to release the belt

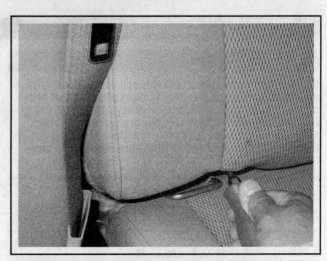

27.11 Using a screwdriver, release the seat back retaining clips from both the left and right side of the seat back

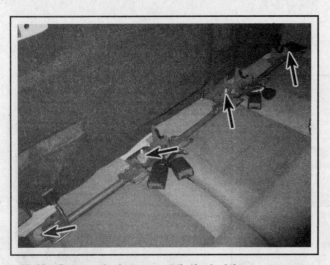

27.12a Remove the fasteners at the back of the seat cushion . . .

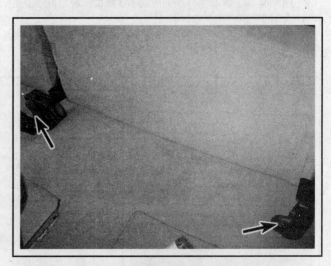

27.12b . . . then lift the seat cushions and remove the remaining fasteners

10 Using a suitable tool, release the seat belt buckle (see illustration).

11 Using a screwdriver, release the seat back retaining clips and remove the seat back (see illustration).

12 Remove the seat cushion mounting fasteners then remove the cushion (see illustrations).

13 Installation is the reverse of removal.

28 Cowl covers - removal and installation

◆ **Refer to illustrations 28.2, 28.3 and 28.4**

 1   Remove the windshield wiper arms (see Chapter 12).
 2   Remove the pushpin and release the clips on the left side cowl cover (see illustration).
 3   Disconnect the windshield washer hose (see illustration).
 4   Remove the screw and release the clips securing the right side cowl cover (see illustration).
 5   Installation is the reverse of removal.

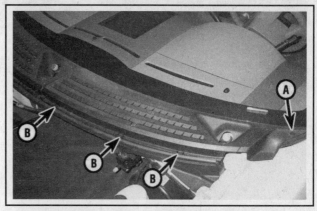

28.2 Remove the pushpin fastener (A), release the clips at the front edge of the cowl cover (B) and lift the cover from the cowl

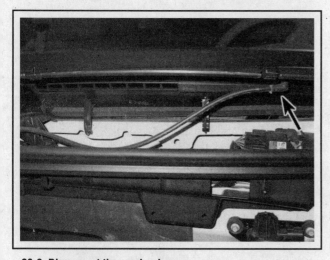

28.3 Disconnect the washer hose

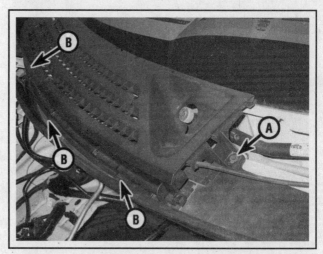

28.4 Remove the fastener (A), release the clips at the front edge of the right side cowl cover (B) and lift the cover from the cowl

29 Center console - removal and installation

 1   Remove the push pin fasteners securing the left and right floor trim panels at the front of the console. Remove the panels.
 2   Using a trim stick, carefully pry loose and remove the shifter trim panel.
 3   Disconnect the shifter cable (see Chapter 7, Part B), and the electrical connector.
 4   Remove the fasteners from the left and right sides of the floor console, then remove the console.
 5   Installation is the reverse of removal.

Notes

12

CHASSIS ELECTRICAL SYSTEM

Section

1   General information
2   Electrical troubleshooting – general information
3   Fuses and fusible links – general information
4   Circuit breakers – general information
5   Relays – general information and testing
6   Multi-function switch – replacement
7   Key lock cylinder and ignition switch – replacement
8   Instrument panel switches – replacement
9   Instrument cluster – removal and installation
10   Windshield wiper motor – replacement
11   Radio and speakers – removal and installation
12   Antenna and cables – replacement
13   Headlight housing – replacement
14   Headlight bulb – replacement
15   Headlights – adjustment
16   Bulb replacement
17   Horn – replacement
18   Adjustable accelerator and brake pedals – description and
     component replacement
19   Electric side view mirrors – general information
20   Cruise control system – general information
21   Power window system – description and check
22   Power door lock and keyless entry system – description and check
23   Daytime Running Lights (DRL) – general information
24   Airbag system – general information
25   Wiring diagrams – general information

1 General information

The electrical system is a 12-volt, negative ground type. Power for the lights and all electrical accessories is supplied by a lead/acid-type battery, which is charged by the alternator.

This Chapter covers repair and service procedures for the various electrical components not associated with the engine. Information on the battery, alternator, distributor and starter motor can be found in Chapter 5.

It should be noted that when portions of the electrical system are serviced, the cable should be disconnected from the negative battery terminal (see Chapter 5, Section 1) to prevent electrical shorts and/or fires.

2 Electrical troubleshooting - general information

▶ **Refer to illustrations 2.5a, 2.5b, 2.6 and 2.9**

A typical electrical circuit consists of an electrical component, any switches, relays, motors, fuses, fusible links or circuit breakers related to that component and the wiring and connectors that link the component to both the battery and the chassis. To help you pinpoint an electrical circuit problem, wiring diagrams are included at the end of this Chapter.

Before tackling any troublesome electrical circuit, first study the appropriate wiring diagrams to get a complete understanding of what makes up that individual circuit. Noting if other components related to the circuit are operating properly, for instance, can often narrow down trouble spots. If several components or circuits fail at one time, chances are the problem is in a fuse or ground connection, because several circuits are often routed through the same fuse and ground connections.

Electrical problems usually stem from simple causes, such as loose or corroded connections, a blown fuse, a melted fusible link or a failed relay. Visually inspect the condition of all fuses, wires and connections in a problem circuit before troubleshooting the circuit.

If test equipment and instruments are going to be utilized, use the diagrams to plan ahead of time where you will make the necessary connections in order to accurately pinpoint the trouble spot.

For electrical troubleshooting, you'll need a voltmeter, a circuit tes-

ter or a 12-volt bulb with a set of test leads; a continuity tester, which includes a bulb, battery and set of test leads; and a jumper wire, with a circuit breaker, which can be used to bypass electrical components (see illustrations). Before attempting to locate a problem with test instruments, use the wiring diagram(s) to decide where to make the connections.

VOLTAGE CHECKS

Voltage checks should be performed if a circuit is not functioning properly. Connect one lead of a circuit tester to either the negative battery terminal or a known good ground. Connect the other lead to a connector in the circuit being tested, preferably nearest to the battery or fuse (see illustration). If the bulb of the tester lights, voltage is present, which means that the part of the circuit between the connector and the battery is problem free. Continue checking the rest of the circuit in the same fashion. When you reach a point at which no voltage is present, the problem lies between that point and the last test point with voltage. Most of the time the problem can be traced to a loose connection.

➡ **Note: Keep in mind that some circuits receive voltage only when the ignition key is in the ACC (accessory) or ON/RUN position.**

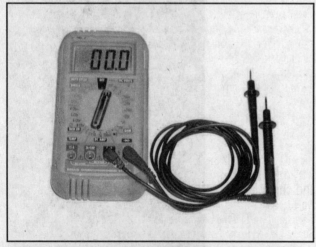

2.5a The most useful tool for electrical troubleshooting is a digital multimeter that can check volts, amps, and test continuity

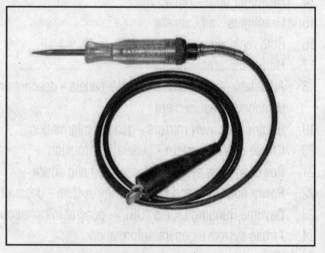

2.5b A simple test light is a very handy tool for testing voltage

2.6 To use a test light, clip the lead to a known good ground, then test connectors, wires or electrical sockets with the pointed probe. If the bulb lights, the circuit that you're testing has battery voltage

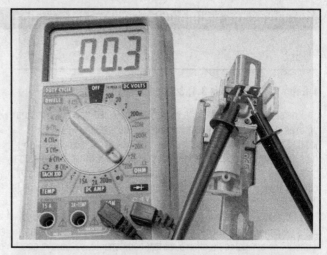

2.9 With a multimeter set to the ohm scale, you can check the resistance across two terminals. When checking for continuity, a low reading indicates continuity, a high reading or infinity indicates lack of continuity

FINDING A SHORT

One method of finding shorts in a live circuit is to remove the fuse and connect a test light in place of the fuse terminals (fabricate two jumper wires with small spade terminals, plug the jumper wires into the fuse box and connect the test light). There should be voltage present in the circuit. Move the suspected wiring harness from side-to-side while watching the test light. If the bulb goes off, there is a short to ground somewhere in that area, probably where the insulation has rubbed through.

GROUND CHECK

Perform a ground test to check whether a component is properly grounded. Disconnect the battery and connect one lead of a continuity tester or multimeter (set to the ohm scale), to a known good ground. Connect the other lead to the wire or ground connection being tested. If the resistance is low (less than 5 ohms), the ground is good. If the bulb on a self-powered test light does not go on, the ground is not good.

CONTINUITY CHECK

A continuity check is done to determine if there are any breaks in a circuit - if it is passing electricity properly. With the circuit off (no power in the circuit), a self-powered continuity tester or multimeter can be used to check the circuit. Connect the test leads to both ends of the circuit (or to the power end and a good ground), and if the test light comes on the circuit is passing current properly (see illustration). If the resistance is low (less than 5 ohms), there is continuity; if the reading is 10,000 ohms or higher, there is a break somewhere in the circuit. The same procedure can be used to test a switch, by connecting the continuity tester to the switch terminals. With the switch turned On, the test light should come on (or low resistance should be indicated on a meter).

FINDING AN OPEN CIRCUIT

When diagnosing for possible open circuits, it is often difficult to locate them by sight because the connectors hide oxidation or terminal misalignment. Merely wiggling a connector on a sensor or in the wiring harness may correct the open circuit condition. Remember this when an open circuit is indicated when troubleshooting a circuit. Intermittent problems may also be caused by oxidized or loose connections.

Electrical troubleshooting is simple if you keep in mind that all electrical circuits are basically electricity running from the battery, through the wires, switches, relays, fuses and fusible links to each electrical component (light bulb, motor, etc.) and to ground, from which it is passed back to the battery. Any electrical problem is an interruption in the flow of electricity to and from the battery.

CONNECTORS

Most electrical connections on these vehicles are made with multi-wire plastic connectors. The mating halves of many connectors are secured with locking clips molded into the plastic connector shells. The mating halves of large connectors, such as some of those under the instrument panel, are held together by a bolt through the center of the connector.

To separate a connector with locking clips, use a small screwdriver to pry the clips apart carefully, then separate the connector halves. Pull only on the shell, never pull on the wiring harness as you may damage the individual wires and terminals inside the connectors. Look at the connector closely before trying to separate the halves. Often the locking clips are engaged in a way that is not immediately clear. Additionally, many connectors have more than one set of clips.

Each pair of connector terminals has a male half and a female half. When you look at the end view of a connector in a diagram, be sure to understand whether the view shows the harness side or the component side of the connector. Connector halves are mirror images of each other, i.e. a terminal shown on the right side end-view of one half will be on the left side end view of the other half.

3 Fuses and fusible links - general information

FUSES

▶ **Refer to illustrations 3.1, 3.2 and 3.5**

The electrical circuits of the vehicle are protected by a combination of fuses, circuit breakers and fusible links. The fuse and relay box is located inside the vehicle, behind the right kick panel (see illustration). (For help with removing the right kick panel, refer to Chapter 11.) Each of the fuses is designed to protect a specific circuit, and the various circuits are identified on the fuse panel cover. You'll also find a guide to these fuses and relays in your owner's manual.

Miniaturized fuses are employed in the fuse block. These compact fuses, which use blade-type terminals, can be removed and installed without any special tools. If an electrical component fails, always check the fuse first. The best way to check a fuse is with a test light. Check for power at the exposed terminal tips of each fuse. If power is present on one side of the fuse but not the other, the fuse is blown. A blown fuse can also be confirmed by visually inspecting it (see illustration).

Be sure to replace blown fuses with the correct type. Fuses of different ratings are physically interchangeable, but only fuses of the proper rating should be used. Replacing a fuse with one of a higher or lower value than specified is not recommended. Each electrical circuit needs a specific amount of protection. The amperage value of each fuse is molded into the fuse body.

If the replacement fuse immediately fails, don't replace it again until the cause of the problem is isolated and corrected. In most cases, this will be a short circuit in the wiring caused by a broken or deteriorated wire.

FUSIBLE LINKS

The circuit between the battery and the alternator is protected by three fusible links. They're located in the engine compartment near the battery, under a plastic cover (see illustration). They act like a fuse, in that when the electrical load in the circuit they are protecting becomes too great, they melt and break the circuit.

Although the fusible links appear to be a heavier gauge than the wire they are protecting, the appearance is due to the thick insulation. All fusible links are several wire gauges smaller than the wire they are designed to protect.

Conceivably, the fusible links could be replaced individually in the event one or more melts, as long as the replacement link is of the same gauge as the failed one. This would be done by cutting out the old link, splicing in the new one, then soldering and insulating the connections. At the time of writing, however, individual fusible links were not available, which would necessitate the replacement of the entire cable between the battery and the alternator. If you find that a fusible link has melted, first determine the reason why, then consult with an auto parts store or dealer parts department to inquire about parts availability.

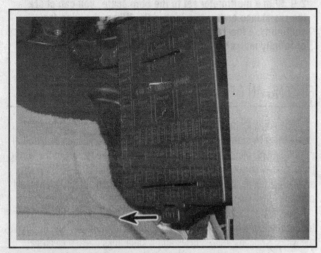

3.1 The fuse and relay box is located inside the vehicle, behind the right kick panel, which has already been removed in this photo. To remove the cover, simply pull it off at the bottom where it says PULL

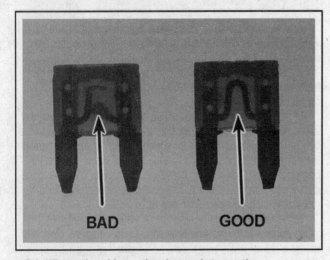

3.2 When a fuse blows, the element between the terminals melts

3.5 The fusible links are located under this plastic cover near the battery, in the harness between the positive battery terminal and the alternator

4   Circuit breakers - general information

Circuit breakers protect certain circuits, such as the power windows or heated seats. Depending on the vehicle's accessories, there might be one or two circuit breakers, and they're usually located inside the vehicle, where they're scattered throughout the area under the instrument panel.

Because circuit breakers reset automatically, an electrical overload in a circuit-breaker-protected system will cause the circuit to fail momentarily, then come back on. If the circuit does not come back on, check it immediately.

For a basic check, pull the circuit breaker up out of its socket on the fuse panel, but just far enough to probe with a voltmeter. The breaker should still contact the sockets.

With the voltmeter negative lead on a good chassis ground, touch each end prong of the circuit breaker with the positive meter probe. There should be battery voltage at each end. If there is battery voltage only at one end, the circuit breaker must be replaced.

Some circuit breakers must be reset manually.

5   Relays - general information and testing

GENERAL INFORMATION

1   Several electrical accessories in the vehicle, such as the fuel injection system, horns, starter, and fog lamps use relays to transmit the electrical signal to the component. Relays use a low-current circuit (the control circuit) to open and close a high-current circuit (the power circuit). If the relay is defective, that component will not operate properly. Most relays are mounted in the fuse and relay box (see illustration 3.1). If you suspect a faulty relay, simply remove it and test it using the procedure below. Or have it tested by a dealer service department. Defective relays cannot be repaired; they must be replaced with a new unit.

TESTING

▶ **Refer to illustrations 5.2a and 5.2b**

2   Most of the relays used in these vehicles are of a type often called ISO relays, which refers to the International Standards Organization. The terminals of ISO relays are numbered to indicate their usual circuit connections and functions. There are two basic layouts of terminals on the relays used in these vehicles (see illustrations).

3   Refer to the wiring diagram for the circuit to determine the proper connections for the relay you're testing. If you can't determine the correct connection from the wiring diagrams, however, you may be able to determine the test connections from the information that follows.

4   Two of the terminals are the relay control circuit and connect to the relay coil. The other relay terminals are the power circuit. When the relay is energized, the coil creates a magnetic field that closes the larger contacts of the power circuit to provide power to the circuit loads.

5   Terminals 85 and 86 are normally the control circuit. If the relay contains a diode, terminal 86 must be connected to battery positive (B+) voltage and terminal 85 to ground. If the relay contains a resistor, terminals 85 and 86 can be connected in either direction with respect to B+ and ground.

6   Terminal 30 is normally connected to the battery voltage (B+) source for the circuit loads. Terminal 87 is connected to the ground side of the circuit, either directly or through a load. If the relay has several alternate terminals for load or ground connections, they usually are numbered 87A, 87B, 87C, and so on.

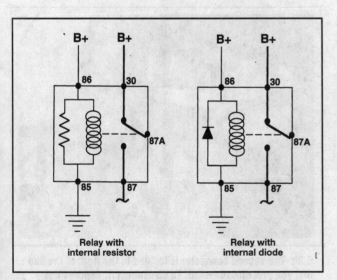

5.2a Typical ISO relay designs, terminal numbering and circuit connections

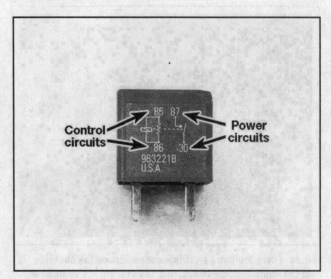

5.2b Most relays are marked on the outside to easily identify the control circuits and the power circuits - four terminal type shown

7   Use an ohmmeter to check continuity through the relay control coil.

  a) *Connect the meter according to the polarity shown in the illustration for one check; then reverse the ohmmeter leads and check continuity in the other direction.*

  b) *If the relay contains a resistor, resistance will be indicated on the meter, and should be the same value with the ohmmeter in either direction.*

  c) *If the relay contains a diode, resistance should be higher with the ohmmeter in the forward polarity direction than with the meter leads reversed.*

  d) *If the ohmmeter shows infinite resistance in both directions, replace the relay.*

8   Remove the relay from the vehicle and use the ohmmeter to check for continuity between the relay power circuit terminals. There should be no continuity between terminal 30 and 87 with the relay de-energized.

9   Connect a fused jumper wire to terminal 86 and the positive battery terminal. Connect another jumper wire between terminal 85 and ground. When the connections are made, the relay should click.

10 With the jumper wires connected, check for continuity between the power circuit terminals. Now, there should be continuity between terminals 30 and 87.

11 If the relay fails any of the above tests, replace it.

6   Multi-function switch - replacement

♦ **Refer to illustrations 6.3a, 6.3b, 6.4a and 6.4b**

✳✳ WARNING:

The models covered by this manual are equipped with Supplemental Restraint Systems (SRS), more commonly known as airbags. Always disable the airbag system before working in the vicinity of any airbag system components to avoid the possibility of accidental deployment of the airbags, which could cause personal injury (see Section 24).

➥ **Note: The multi-function switch is located on the steering column. It includes the turn signal switch, the headlight dimmer switch and the windshield wiper/washer switch.**

1   Disconnect the cable from the negative terminal of the battery (see Chapter 5, Section 1).

2   Remove the upper and lower steering column covers (see Chapter 11).

3   Disconnect the electrical connectors from the multi-function switch (see illustrations).

4   Remove the mounting bolt (see illustration) or two screws (2009 and later models), then remove the switch from the steering column (see illustration).

5   Installation is the reverse of removal.

6.3a There are three electrical connectors on the backside of the multi-function switch, and two of them are somewhat difficult to disconnect. Let's start with the easy one. To disconnect it, depress this release tab and pull off the connector

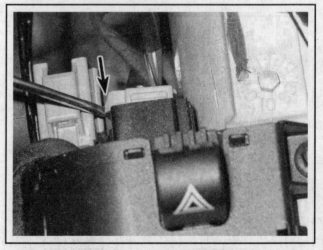

6.3b The second connector is located to the right of the one that you just disconnected. To disconnect it, depress the release tab with a small screwdriver, then pull it off. The third connector (not visible in this photo) is directly below the one shown here

6.4a To detach the multi-function switch from the steering column assembly, remove this bolt (or two screws on later models) . . .

6.4b . . . then depress this release tab (1) and slide the switch straight up to remove it. Note the rail and groove (2) in the switch. When installing the multi-function switch, make sure that the rail and groove on the switch are aligned with their corresponding groove and rail on the backside of the clockspring assembly

7 Key lock cylinder and ignition switch - replacement

✳✳ WARNING:

The models covered by this manual are equipped with Supplemental Restraint Systems (SRS), more commonly known as airbags. Always disable the airbag system before working in the vicinity of any airbag system components to avoid the possibility of accidental deployment of the airbags, which could cause personal injury (see Section 24).

1   Disconnect the cable from the negative terminal of the battery (see Chapter 5, Section 1).

2   Remove the upper and lower steering column covers (see Chapter 11).

IGNITION SWITCH

2004 through 2008 models

▶ **Refer to illustrations 7.4 and 7.5**

3   Remove the multi-function switch (see Section 6).

4   Disconnect the electrical connector from the ignition switch (see illustration).

5   Remove the ignition switch (see illustration).

6   Installation is the reverse of removal.

2009 and 2010 models

7   On models with manual tilt steering wheels, position the steering column in the full-down position.

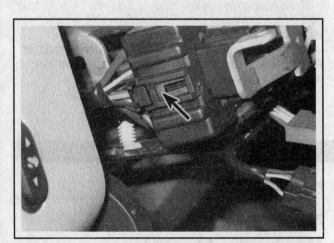

7.4 To disconnect the electrical connector from the ignition switch, depress this release tab and pull out the connector

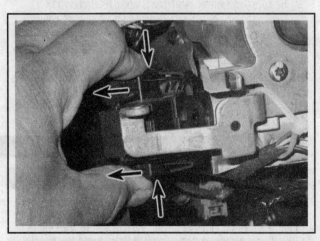

7.5 To detach the ignition switch from the steering column, depress the release tabs on the top and bottom of the switch, then pull the switch out to the left

7.14 Disconnect the electrical connector from the ignition switch

7.19 To detach the PATS transceiver from the steering column assembly, depress the release tab (1) and pull off the electrical connector, then unscrew the bolt (2) and remove the transceiver

12 Remove the ignition switch mounting screw and remove the switch.

13 Installation is the reverse of removal.

2011 and later models

▶ Refer to illustration 7.14

14 Disconnect the electrical connector from the ignition switch (see illustration).

15 To detach the ignition switch from the steering column, depress the release tabs on the top and bottom of the switch, then pull the switch out.

16 Installation is the reverse of removal.

KEY LOCK CYLINDER

▶ Refer to illustrations 7.19 and 7.21

17 Remove the steering wheel (see Chapter 10).

18 Remove the steering column covers (see Chapter 11).

19 Remove the Passive Anti-Theft System (PATS) transceiver (see illustration).

20 Insert the ignition key into the key lock cylinder. On 2004 through 2008 models, turn the key to the ON position. On 2009 and later models, turn the key to the ACC position.

21 Insert an awl or small screwdriver into the hole in the underside of the key lock cylinder, then depress the key lock cylinder retaining tab and remove the key lock cylinder (see illustration).

22 Installation is the reverse of removal.

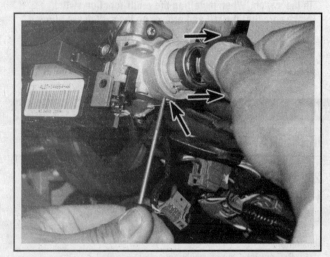

7.21 To remove the key lock cylinder, turn the ignition key to the ON position, then insert an awl or small screwdriver into this hole and depress the locking pin, then pull out the lock cylinder

8 Remove the steering wheel (see Chapter 10, Section 11).

9 Detach the wiring harness retainers from the steering column.

10 Disconnect the electrical connectors from the ignition switch, multifunction switch, clockspring, Passive Anti-Theft System (PATS) and key, and, if equipped, the interlock actuator.

11 On models with manual tilt steering columns, remove the 3 bolts and remove the multifunction switch carrier.

8 Instrument panel switches - replacement

✳ WARNING:

The models covered by this manual are equipped with Supplemental Restraint Systems (SRS), more commonly known as airbags. Always disable the airbag system before working in the vicinity of any airbag system components to avoid the possibility of accidental deployment of the airbag(s), which could cause personal injury (see Section 24).

HEADLIGHT SWITCH AND RHEOSTAT

2004 through 2008 models

▶ Refer to illustrations 8.2, 8.3 and 8.4

1 Disconnect the cable from the negative battery terminal (see Chapter 5, Section 1).

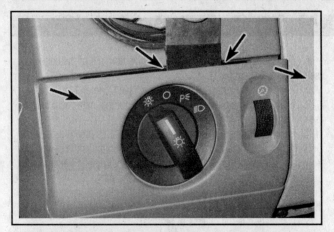

8.2 Carefully pry the headlight switch and rheostat bezel from the instrument panel with a trim panel removal tool or with some other suitable tool with a wide flat blade. Be extremely careful not to scratch or gouge the trim on the instrument panel

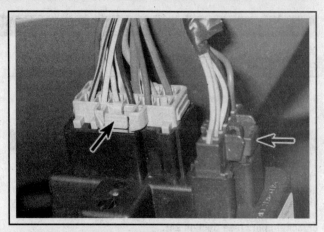

8.3 To disconnect the electrical connectors from the backside of the headlight switch and rheostat, depress these release tabs and pull off the connectors

8.4 To detach the headlight switch and rheostat from the bezel, remove these three screws

8.13 To disconnect the electrical connector from the accelerator and brake pedal height adjustment switch, depress this release tab and pull off the connector

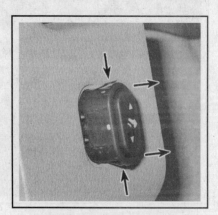

8.14 To disengage and remove the accelerator and brake pedal height adjustment switch from the instrument cluster bezel, squeeze these two retainer springs on the top and bottom of the switch and push the switch out of the finish panel

2   Carefully pry the headlight switch and rheostat bezel from the instrument panel (see illustration).

3   Disconnect the electrical connectors from the headlight switch and rheostat (see illustration).

4   Remove the headlight switch and rheostat mounting screws (see illustration), then remove the headlight switch and rheostat from the bezel.

5   Installation is the reverse of removal.

2009 and later models

6   Disconnect the cable from the negative battery terminal (see Chapter 5, Section 1).

7   Use a dull, flat bladed tool around the front side of the left side finish panel to release it from the clips at the front, then remove the panel.

8   Reach behind the left side of the instrument panel, then release the retaining tabs and partially withdraw the headlight switch assembly.

➡ Note: The retaining tabs are located at the 3, 6 and 11 o'clock positions.

9   Disconnect the electrical connector, then remove the headlight switch assembly.

10 Installation is the reverse of removal.

ACCELERATOR AND BRAKE PEDAL HEIGHT ADJUSTMENT SWITCH

♦ **Refer to illustrations 8.13 and 8.14**

11 Disconnect the cable from the negative battery terminal (see Chapter 5, Section 1).

12 Remove the instrument cluster bezel (see Chapter 11).

13 Disconnect the electrical connector from the accelerator and brake pedal height adjustment switch (see illustration).

14 Remove the accelerator and brake pedal height adjustment switch from the instrument cluster bezel (see illustration).

15 Installation is the reverse of removal.

9   Instrument cluster - removal and installation

2004 THROUGH 2008 MODELS

▶ **Refer to illustrations 9.3a, 9.3b, 9.3c, 9.4a and 9.4b**

✳✳ WARNING:

The models covered by this manual are equipped with Supplemental Restraint Systems (SRS), more commonly known as airbags. Always disable the airbag system before working in the vicinity of any airbag system components to avoid the possibility of accidental deployment of the airbag(s), which could cause personal injury (see Section 24).

1   Disconnect the cable from the negative terminal of the battery (see Chapter 5, Section 1).

2   Remove the instrument cluster bezel (see Chapter 11).

3   Disconnect the electrical connectors from the instrument cluster (see illustrations).

4   Remove the instrument cluster mounting bolts (see illustration). On vehicles with a manual transmission, simply remove the cluster from the instrument panel. On vehicles with an automatic transmission, pull the instrument cluster out of the instrument panel just far enough to disconnect the gear position indicator from the cluster (see illustration), then remove the cluster.

5   Installation is the reverse of removal.

9.3a To disconnect the electrical connectors from the instrument cluster . . .

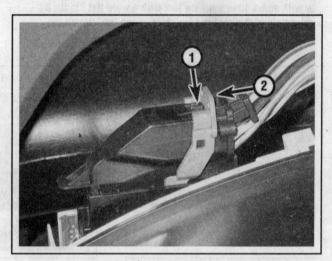

9.3b . . . depress the release tab (1) and push the lock . . .

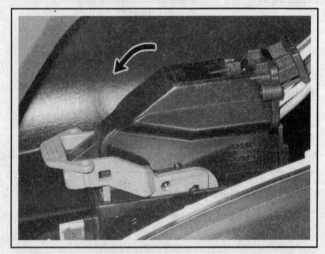

9.3c . . . all the way down, then pull the connector straight up

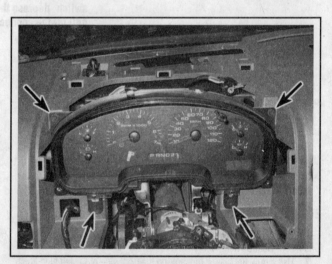

9.4a To detach the instrument cluster from the instrument panel, remove these four mounting bolts

2009 AND LATER MODELS

6 Disconnect the cable from the negative battery terminal (see Chapter 5, Section 1).

7 Lower the steering column to the lowest position.

8 Remove the instrument cluster finish panel two upper screws, then remove it.

9 If equipped, move the column shift lever to the lowest gear position.

10 Remove the four instrument panel mounting bolts.

11 Pull the instrument cluster out of the instrument panel just far enough to disconnect the electrical connector, then disconnect it, and remove the instrument cluster.

12 Installation is the reverse of removal.

9.4b On vehicles with an automatic transmission, pull out the instrument cluster just far enough to access the underside of the cluster, then squeeze these two release tabs together and pull out the gear position indicator

10 Windshield wiper motor - replacement

▶ **Refer to illustrations 10.1, 10.3, 10.4 and 10.5**

1 Mark the positions of the wiper blades on the windshield with a grease pen or pieces of tape. Remove the windshield wiper arms (see illustration).

2 Remove the left and right cowl covers (see Chapter 11).

3 Disconnect the electrical connector from the wiper motor (see illustration).

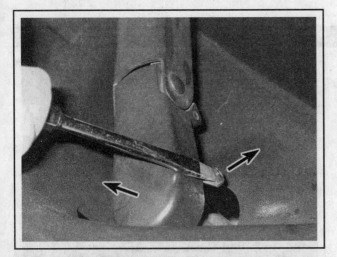

10.1 To remove each windshield wiper arm, pry this lock away from the wiper arm assembly and lift the arm off its shaft

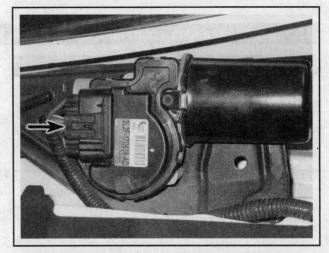

10.3 To disconnect the electrical connector from the windshield wiper motor, depress this release tab and pull off the connector

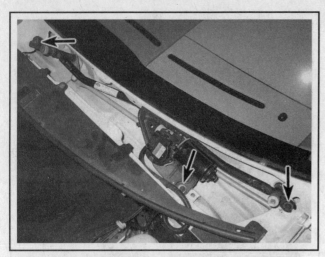

10.4 To detach the windshield wiper motor assembly from the cowl, remove these three bolts and lift the assembly out of the cowl

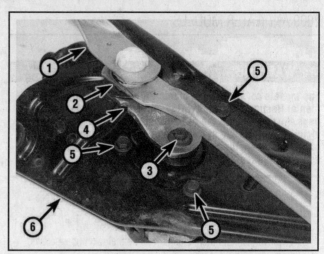

10.5 To detach the wiper motor from the windshield wiper motor assembly:

1   *Pry off this linkage arm from the pin on the end of the crank arm*
2   *Pry off this linkage arm from the pin on the end of the crank arm (these two linkage arms must be reassembled in this same order)*
3   *Remove the crank arm retaining nut*
4   *Remove the crank arm*
5   *Remove the three wiper mounting bolts . . .*
6   *. . . and remove the motor from its mounting bracket*

4   Remove the windshield wiper motor assembly mounting bolts (see illustration) and remove the wiper assembly.

5   Detach the windshield wiper linkage arms from the wiper motor crank arm (see illustration). The linkage arms are pressed onto a pin on the end of the motor crank arm. To detach each linkage arm, simply pry it off with a trim removal tool or a similar suitable tool.

6   Remove the wiper motor crank arm.

7   Remove the wiper motor from its mounting bracket.

8   Installation is the reverse of removal. Be sure to align the wiper blades with the marks made in Step 1 before pushing them onto their shafts.

11 Radio and speakers - removal and installation

✳ WARNING:

The models covered by this manual are equipped with Supplemental Restraint Systems (SRS), more commonly known as airbags. Always disable the airbag system before working in the vicinity of any airbag system components to avoid the possibility of accidental deployment of the airbag(s), which could cause personal injury (see Section 24).

1   Disconnect the cable from the negative terminal of the battery (see Chapter 5, Section 1).

RADIO

▶ **Refer to illustration 11.3 and 11.4**

2   Remove the instrument panel center bezel (see Chapter 11).

3   Remove the radio mounting screws (see illustration), then pull the radio out of the instrument panel just far enough to access the electrical connectors and the antenna cable on the backside of the unit.

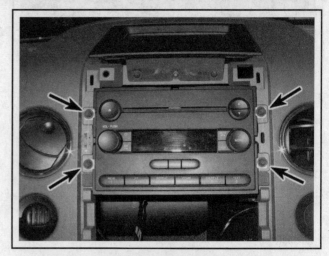

11.3 To detach the radio from the instrument panel, remove these four mounting screws

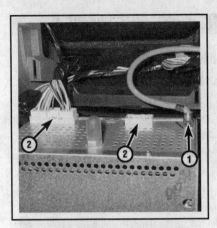

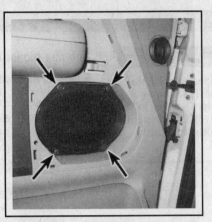

11.4 After pulling the radio out of the instrument panel, disconnect the antenna cable (1) and the electrical connectors (2) (the black electrical connector has already been unplugged in this photo)

11.11 To detach a front door speaker from the door, remove these four screws

11.12 Pull the speaker out of the front door, depress the release tab on the electrical connector and disconnect the connector

4   Disconnect the electrical connectors and the antenna lead from the backside of the radio (see illustration) and remove the radio.

5   Installation is the reverse of removal.

SPEAKERS

Front door speakers

Front door tweeters

6   Remove the front door trim panel (see Chapter 11).

7   Remove the speaker mounting screws.

8   Pull out the speaker, disconnect the electrical connector from the speaker and remove the speaker.

9   Installation is the reverse of removal.

Front door speakers

▸ **Refer to illustrations 11.11 and 11.12**

10 Remove the front door speaker trim panel (see Chapter 11).

11 Remove the speaker mounting screws (see illustration).

12 Pull out the speaker, disconnect the electrical connector from the speaker (see illustration) and remove the speaker.

13 Installation is the reverse of removal.

Rear door speakers

▸ **Refer to illustration 11.15**

14 Remove the rear door trim panel (see Chapter 11).

15 Remove the speaker mounting screws (see illustration).

16 Pull out the speaker, disconnect the electrical connector (see illustration 11.12) and remove the speaker.

17 Installation is the reverse of removal.

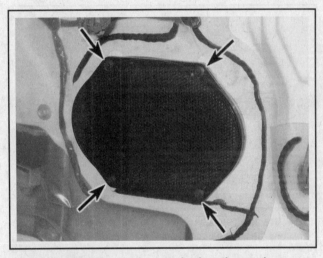

11.15 To detach the rear door speaker from the rear door, remove these four screws

INSTRUMENT PANEL SPEAKER (2009 AND LATER MODELS)

18 Remove the mat from the upper storage compartment.

19 Remove the two screws, then raise the upper storage compartment just far enough to disconnect the speaker electrical connector. Remove the upper storage compartment.

20 If necessary, remove the speaker mounting screws, then remove the speaker.

21 Installation is the reverse of removal.

12 Antenna and cables - replacement

✳✳ WARNING:

The models covered by this manual are equipped with Supplemental Restraint Systems (SRS), more commonly known as airbags. Always disable the airbag system before working in the vicinity of any airbag system components to avoid the possibility of accidental deployment of the airbag(s), which could cause personal injury (see Section 24).

ANTENNA MAST, ANTENNA BASE AND ANTENNA CABLE

Antenna mast

▶ Refer to illustration 12.1

1   Use an open-end wrench to unscrew the antenna mast from the base (see illustration).

2   Installation is the reverse of removal.

12.1 Use an antenna wrench or a small open-end wrench to unscrew the antenna mast from the antenna mounting base

12.5 To detach the antenna mounting base from the fender, remove these three screws

Antenna mounting base and outer antenna cable

▶ Refer to illustrations 12.4, 12.5, 12.7 and 12.11

3   Remove the antenna mast (see illustration 12.1).

4   Remove the antenna mounting base cap (see illustration).

5   Remove the antenna mounting base screws (see illustration).

6   Remove the glove box (see Chapter 11).

7   Disconnect the outer antenna cable from the inner antenna cable (see illustration).

8   Loosen the front right wheel lug nuts. Raise the front of the vehicle and place it securely on jackstands. Remove the right front wheel.

9   Remove the inner fender splash shield from the right front wheel well (see Chapter 11).

10   Trace the outer cable to the rubber grommet where the cable goes through the vehicle body. Note how the outer cable is routed. When you install the new cable, it must be routed exactly the same way, or it won't be long enough to reach the inner cable.

11   Working from inside the wheel well area, pull the grommet out of its mounting hole (see illustration).

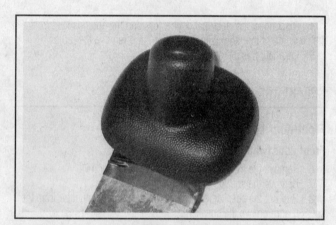

12.4 To remove the antenna mounting base cap, carefully pry it off with a trim panel removal tool or with a similar suitable tool. Put some tape on the tip of your tool to protect the painted surface of the fender from scratches

12.7 To disconnect the outer antenna cable (A) from the inner antenna cable (B), unplug this connector (C)

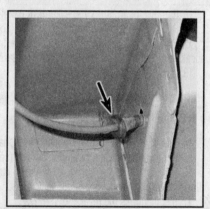

12.11 Working from inside the wheel well, pull the grommet for the outer antenna cable out of its mounting hole, then pull out the cable (the grommet is part of the cable, so you can't remove it from the cable)

12 Pull the outer antenna cable through the grommet hole into the wheel well.

13 Remove the antenna mounting base and outer antenna cable from the wheel well area by pulling the base and the cable straight up through the base mounting hole.

14 Installation is the reverse of removal.

INNER ANTENNA CABLE

▶ **Refer to illustration 12.17**

➡ **Note: The inner antenna cable connects the outer antenna cable to the radio.**

15 Remove the glove box (see Chapter 11).

16 Disconnect the inner antenna cable from the outer antenna cable (see illustration 12.7).

17 Detach the two inner antenna cable locator clips from the trim piece right below the glove box opening (see illustration).

18 Remove the radio (see Section 11) and disconnect the inner antenna cable from the backside of the radio (see illustration 11.4).

19 Installation is the reverse of removal.

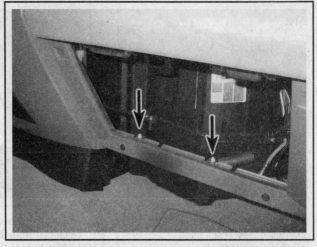

12.17 To detach these two inner antenna cable locator clips from the trim piece right below the glove box opening, carefully pry them loose with a trim removal tool

13 Headlight housing - replacement

▶ **Refer to illustrations 13.1a, 13.1b, 13.1c, 13.2a, 13.2b, 13.2c and 13.2d**

✳✳ WARNING:

These vehicles are equipped with halogen gas-filled headlight bulbs, which are under pressure and may shatter if the surface is damaged or the bulb is dropped. Wear eye protection and handle the bulbs carefully, grasping only the base whenever possible. Do not touch the surface of the bulb with your fingers because the oil from your skin could cause it to overheat and fail prematurely. If you do touch the bulb surface, clean it with rubbing alcohol.

1 Remove the headlight housing retaining bolts (see illustrations).

2 Pull out the headlight housing assembly and disconnect the elec-

13.1a To detach the headlight housing from the vehicle, remove these three bolts (2004 through 2008 models shown)

13.1b Remove the pushpin securing the flap over the side of the headlight housing (2011 and later models)

13.1c Remove the 3 bolts securing the headlight housing and pull it away from the body enough to disconnect the electrical connectors (2011 and later)

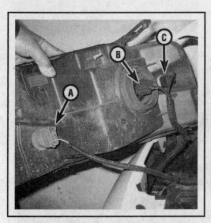

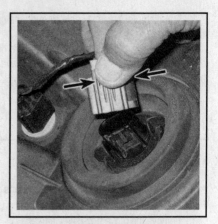

13.2a Pull out the headlight housing and disconnect these three electrical connectors:

A   *Front turn signal/parking light bulb*
B   *Headlight bulb*
C   *Front side marker light bulb*

13.2b To disconnect the electrical connector from the front turn signal/ parking light bulb, depress this release tab and pull off the connector

13.2c To disconnect the electrical connector from the headlight bulb, depress this release tab on top of the connector (release tab not visible) and pull off the connector

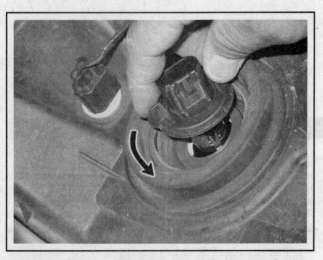

13.2d To disconnect the electrical connector from the front side marker light bulb, depress this release tab and pull off the connector

trical connectors from the front turn signal/parking light, headlight and front side marker light bulbs (see illustrations).

3   If you want to replace the headlight bulb, refer to Section 14. If you want to replace the front side marker or turn signal/parking light bulb, see Section 16.

4   Installation is the reverse of removal. When you're finished, be sure to adjust the headlights (see Section 15).

14 Headlight bulb - replacement

▶ Refer to illustrations 14.2a and 14.2b

❋❋ WARNING:

Halogen gas filled bulbs are under pressure and may shatter if the surface is scratched or the bulb is dropped. Wear eye protection and handle the bulbs carefully, grasping only the base whenever possible. Do not touch the surface of the bulb with

your fingers because the oil from your skin could cause it to overheat and fail prematurely. If you do touch the bulb surface, clean it with rubbing alcohol.

1   Remove the headlight housing (see Section 13).
2   Rotate the headlight bulb retaining ring counterclockwise and pull out the bulb socket (see illustrations).
3   Installation is the reverse of removal.

14.2a To remove the headlight bulb from the headlight housing, turn it counterclockwise and pull it out

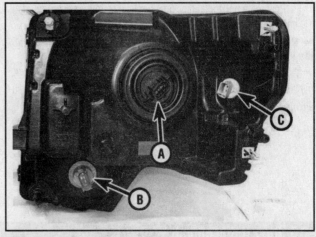

14.2b On 2011 and later models, remove the headlight bulb (A) by twisting it a small amount counterclockwise - remove the park/turn bulb (B) and the side marker light (C) in the same manner

15 Headlights - adjustment

▶ Refer to illustrations 15.1 and 15.4

➡ **Note: The headlights must be aimed correctly. If adjusted incorrectly they could blind the driver of an oncoming vehicle and cause a serious accident or seriously reduce your ability to see the road. The headlights should be checked for proper aim every 12 months and any time a new headlight housing is installed or front-end bodywork is performed. It should be emphasized that the following procedure is only an interim step, which will provide temporary adjustment until a properly equipped shop can adjust the headlights.**

1   These vehicles have a vertical adjustment screw located on the backside of the headlight housing. You can access the adjustment screw through a hole in the radiator crossmember (see illustration). Insert a Phillips screwdriver into the gear-drive mechanism and turn the screw to make adjustments.

2   Adjustment should be made with the vehicle on a level surface, with a full gas tank and a normal load in the vehicle.

3   There are several methods of adjusting the headlights. The simplest method requires masking tape, a blank wall and a level floor.

4   Position masking tape vertically on the wall to indicate the vehicle centerline and the centerline of each headlight bulb (see illustration).

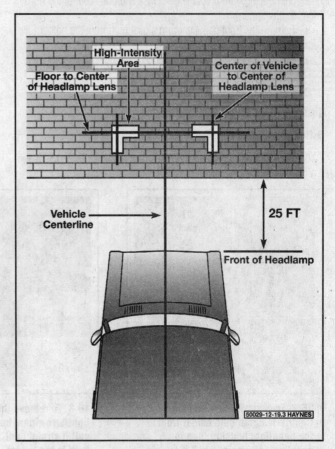

15.4 Headlight adjustment details

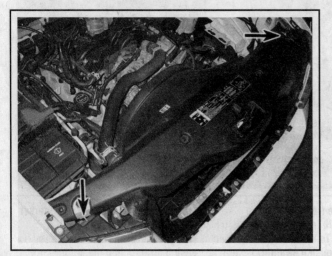

15.1 Headlight vertical adjustment screw locations

5   Position a horizontal tape line in reference to the centerline of all the headlights.

➡ **Note: It may be easier to position the tape on the wall with the vehicle parked only a few inches away.**

6   Adjustment should be made with the vehicle parked 25 feet (7.6 meters) from the wall, sitting level, the gas tank half-full and no unusually heavy load in the vehicle.

7   Position the high intensity zone so it is two inches below the horizontal line and two inches to the side of the headlight vertical line, away from oncoming traffic. Adjustment is made by turning the horizontal adjusting screw to move the beam left or right. The high beams on these aero type headlights are automatically adjusted along with the low beam.

8   Have the headlights adjusted by a dealer service department or service station at the earliest opportunity.

16 Bulb replacement

EXTERIOR LIGHT BULBS

Front parking light/turn signal bulbs

▶ **Refer to illustrations 16.2 and 16.3**

1   Unbolt the headlight housing (see illustration 13.1a or 13.1b and 13.1c), pull it out and disconnect the electrical connectors from the front side marker light, the headlight and the front turn signal/parking light (see illustrations 13.2a, 13.2b, 13.2c and 13.2d).

2   To remove the front parking light/turn signal bulb holder from the headlight housing, turn it counterclockwise and pull it out of the housing (see illustration).

3   Remove the front park light/turn signal bulb from the holder (see illustration).

4   Install the new bulb in the holder by pushing it straight into the holder until it stops.

5   Installation is the reverse of removal.

Front side marker light bulbs

▶ **Refer to illustration 16.8**

6   Unbolt the headlight housing (see illustration 13.1a or 13.1b and

13.1c) pull it out and disconnect the electrical connectors from the front side marker light, the headlight and the front turn signal/parking light (see illustrations 13.2a, 13.2b, 13.2c and 13.2d).

7   To remove the front side marker light bulb holder from the headlight housing, rotate it counterclockwise and pull it out of the housing.

8   Remove the side marker bulb from its holder (see illustration).

9   Install the new bulb in the holder by pushing it straight into the holder until it stops.

10 Installation is the reverse of removal.

Front fog light bulbs

11 The fog lights, if equipped, are located in the lower part of the bumper cover. It's not necessary to raise the front of the vehicle to replace the fog light bulbs. Just use a creeper or throw down an old blanket or towel to lie on, and take a flashlight with you.

12 To remove the fog light bulb socket from the fog light housing, turn it counterclockwise and pull it out of the housing.

13 Disconnect the electrical connector from the fog light bulb.

14 Reconnect the electrical connector to the new fog light bulb.

15 To install the fog light socket in the fog light housing, insert it into its mounting hole and turn it clockwise until it stops.

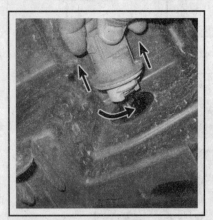

16.2 To remove the front parking light/turn signal bulb holder from the headlight housing, turn it counterclockwise and pull it out of the housing

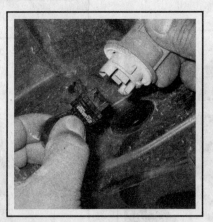

16.3 To remove the front parking light/turn signal bulb from its holder, pull it straight out. To install a new bulb in the holder, push it straight into the holder until it stops

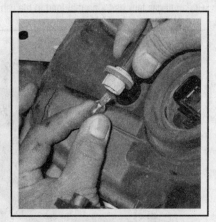

16.8 To remove the front side marker light bulb from its holder, pull it straight out. To install a new bulb, push it straight into the holder until it stops

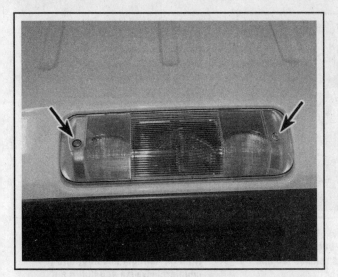

16.16a To detach the high-mount brake light assembly from the roof of the vehicle, remove these two screws . . .

16.16b . . . then carefully pull out the assembly and lay it upside down on the roof

High-mount brake light bulb

▶ Refer to illustrations 16.16a, 16.16b and 16.17

➡ Note: There are three high-mount brake light bulbs. This procedure applies to all three.

16 Remove the two high-mount brake light retaining screws, pull out the center high-mount brake light assembly and lay it upside down on the roof (see illustrations).

17 Remove the socket with the burned out bulb from the center high-mount brake light assembly (see illustration).

18 Remove the old bulb from the socket by pulling it straight out.

19 To install a new bulb in the socket insert it straight into the socket until it stops.

20 Installation is the reverse of removal.

Brake/taillight/turn signal/back-up light bulbs

▶ Refer to illustrations 16.21, 16.22, 16.23a and 16.23b

21 Remove the two taillight housing retaining screws (see illustration).

22 To remove the taillight assembly from the vehicle, pull it out straight to the rear to disengage the two locator pins on the forward edge of the assembly from their corresponding grommets in the fender (see illustration).

16.17 To remove a socket from the high-mount brake light assembly, turn it counterclockwise and pull it out

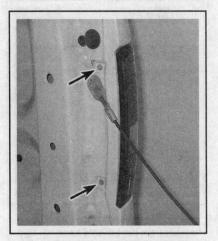

16.21 To detach a taillight assembly from the vehicle body, remove these two screws . . .

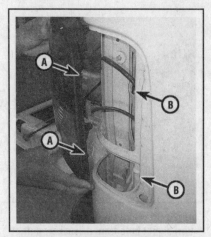

16.22 . . . then pull it out straight to the rear to disengage the two locator pins (A) from their corresponding grommets (B) in the rear fender

16.23a To disconnect the electrical connector from the brake/taillight/turn signal bulb holder, depress this release tab and pull off the connector

16.23b To disconnect the electrical connector from the back-up bulb holder, depress this release tab and pull off the connector

16.25 To remove the brake/taillight/turn signal bulb socket from the taillight housing, turn it counterclockwise and pull it out

23 Disconnect the electrical connectors from the two sockets in the taillight housing (see illustrations) and remove the housing.

24 There are two bulbs in the taillight housing. The upper bulb, a dual-filament unit, is the brake/taillight/turn signal bulb. The lower bulb, a single-filament unit, is the back-up light bulb.

Brake/taillight/turn signal bulb

▶ **Refer to illustrations 16.25 and 16.26**

25 Remove the brake/taillight/turn signal bulb socket from the taillight housing (see illustration).

26 Remove the brake/taillight/turn signal bulb from the socket (see illustration).

27 Installation is otherwise the reverse of removal.

Back-up light bulb

▶ **Refer to illustration 16.28**

28 Remove the back-up light bulb socket from the taillight housing (see illustration).

29 Remove the back-up light bulb from the socket by pulling it straight out.

30 Installation is otherwise the reverse of removal.

License plate light bulbs

▶ **Refer to illustrations 16.31a, 16.31b and 16.32**

31 Remove the license plate light assembly from the bumper and disconnect the electrical connector (see illustrations).

16.26 To remove a brake/taillight/turn signal bulb from its socket, pull it straight out. To install a new bulb, push it straight into the socket until it stops

16.28 To remove the back-up bulb socket from the taillight housing, turn it counterclockwise and pull it out

16.31a Each license plate light assembly is secured to the bumper by this pair of tangs. To remove a license plate light, reach under the bumper and, from the backside of the bumper, squeeze the two tangs together, pull out the light . . .

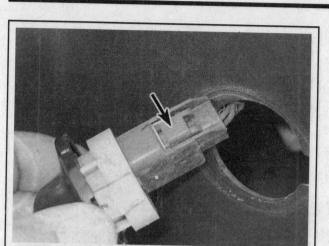

16.31b . . . depress this release tab and disconnect the electrical connector

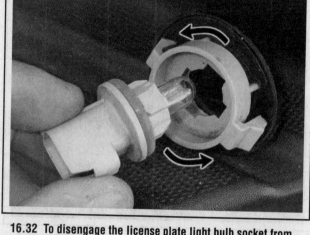

16.32 To disengage the license plate light bulb socket from its mounting base, rotate the socket counterclockwise and pull it out of the base

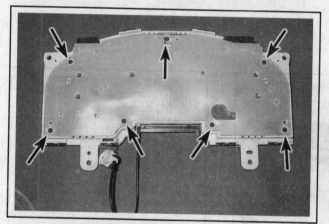

16.37 To remove the protective cover from the backside of the instrument cluster, remove these seven screws and carefully pull off the cover

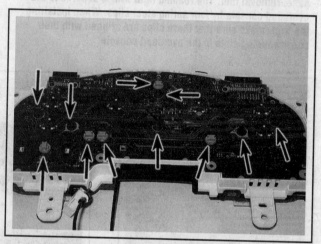

16.38a Instrument cluster light bulb locations

32 Remove the license plate light socket from its mounting base (see illustration).

33 Remove the bulb from the socket by pulling it straight out.

34 Install a new bulb in the socket.

35 The remainder of installation is the reverse of removal.

INTERIOR LIGHT BULBS

Instrument cluster illumination bulbs

◆ Refer to illustrations 16.37, 16.38a and 16.38b

36 Remove the instrument cluster (see Section 9).

37 Remove the protective cover from the backside of the instrument cluster (see illustration).

38 To remove an instrument cluster light bulb socket, turn it counterclockwise and pull it out of the cluster (see illustrations).

➡ **Note: The cluster illumination bulbs are extremely difficult to turn to their released position with your fingers, so use a pair of needle-nose pliers to do so.**

To install an instrument cluster light bulb socket, insert it into the cluster and turn it clockwise until it stops.

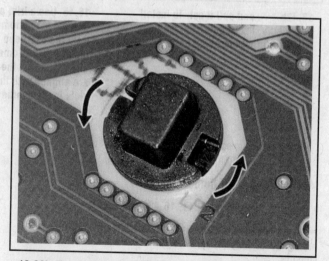

16.38b To remove an illumination bulb from the instrument cluster, turn it counterclockwise and pull it out of the cluster circuit board. These bulbs are difficult to rotate to the released position with your fingers; you'll probably need to use a pair of pliers to do so

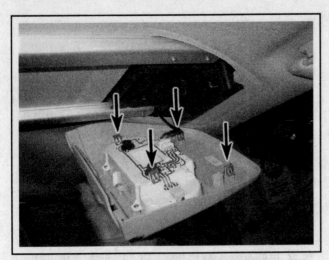

16.41 To remove the map reading light trim piece from the overhead console, carefully pry it loose with a trim panel removal tool. The reading light trim is secured to the overhead console by four spring steel clips. When installing the trim, make sure that these clips are aligned with their corresponding slots in the overhead console

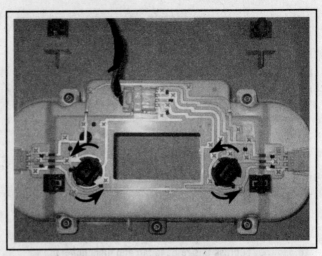

16.42a To remove a map reading light bulb from the reading light assembly, rotate it counterclockwise . . .

16.42b . . . and pull it out. To install a new bulb, insert it into its mounting hole and turn it clockwise until it stops

16.45 Use a trim panel removal tool to remove the dome light assembly from the overhead console. When installing the dome light assembly, make sure that the spring steel clips are aligned with their corresponding slots in the overhead console

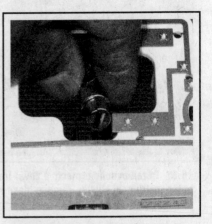

16.46 Remove the dome light bulb from the dome light assembly. When installing the new dome light bulb, make sure that it's fully seated into its two conductor/retainer clips

39 Install the protective cover on the backside of the cluster.

40 Install the instrument cluster (see Section 9).

Map reading light bulbs

▶ Refer to illustrations 16.41, 16.42a and 16.42b

➡ Note: The map reading light bulbs are located in the reading light assembly, which is at the forward end of the overhead console.

41 Using a trim removal tool, remove the map reading light trim piece from the overhead console (see illustration).

42 Remove the bulb from the reading light assembly (see illustrations).

43 Install a new bulb in the reading light assembly.

44 Installation is the reverse of removal.

Dome light

▶ Refer to illustrations 16.45 and 16.46

➡ Note: The dome light is located in the dome light assembly, which is at the rear end of the overhead console.

45 Using a trim panel removal tool or a screwdriver, pry off the dome light lens (see illustration).

46 Remove the bulb from the dome light assembly (see illustration).

47 Installation is the reverse of removal.

17 Horn - replacement

▶ **Refer to illustration 17.1, 17.3 and 17.4**

➡ **Note: The horn is located to the right of the radiator.**

1   To access the horn, remove the upper pin-type retainer (see illustration) and peel back the right radiator side air deflector.

2   Remove the wheel well splash shield (see Chapter 11).

3   Disconnect the electrical connector from the horn (see illustration).

4   Remove the horn mounting bracket bolt (see illustration) and remove the horn assembly.

5   Installation is the reverse of removal.

17.1 To access the horn, remove this pin-type retainer and peel back the right radiator side air deflector

17.3 To disconnect the horn's electrical connector, depress this release tab and pull off the connector

17.4 To detach the horn assembly, remove the mounting bracket bolt

18 Adjustable accelerator and brake pedals - description and component replacement

DESCRIPTION

1   Some models are equipped with optional electrically-adjustable accelerator and brake pedals. Pedal height is adjusted by a switch located to the left of the steering column (see Section 8 for the switch replacement procedure). The switch activates a reversible motor that increases or decreases the height of both pedals simultaneously via a pair of cables. When the motor is activated, the cables drive worm gears inside the pedal assemblies. The worm gears are engaged with teeth on the pedal posts, which allows the pedals to move forward and backward on the posts. If you need more legroom you press the DOWN position on the switch, which moves the pedals away from you (toward the firewall). If you have trouble reaching the pedals, activate the UP position on the switch and the pedals move toward you (away from the firewall).

2   The accelerator pedal is equipped with a small module known as the Electronic Throttle Control (ETC) module, which houses the three Accelerator Pedal Position Sensors (APPS) used by the Powertrain Control Module (PCM) to control the electronic throttle body.

3   The pedals, the pedal posts and the mounting brackets for the posts will probably never wear out, but the motor and/or the drive cables might malfunction someday. So the following replacement procedure applies to the motor and the drive cables. The motor and drive cables are not serviceable separately. They must be replaced as a single assembly.

COMPONENT REPLACEMENT

▶ **Refer to illustrations 18.5, 18.6 and 18.7**

➡ **Note: The motor for the adjustable accelerator and brake pedals is located on the left upper part of the firewall, above the pedal assemblies. The motor isn't easy to get to, but it's easy to remove. You'll need a flashlight for this procedure.**

4   Remove the knee bolster to give yourself some room to work (see Chapter 11). You might also want to detach the speed control deactivation switch from its mounting bracket at the upper end of the brake pedal (see illustration 10.8 in Chapter 9).

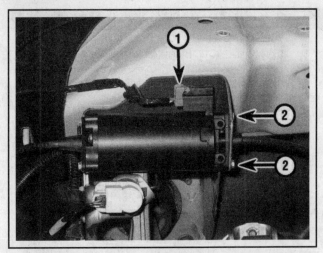

18.5 To disconnect the electrical connector from the motor for the adjustable accelerator and brake pedals, depress this release tab (1) and pull off the connector. To detach the right end of the motor from its mounting bracket, remove these two bolts (2) (instrument panel removed for clarity)

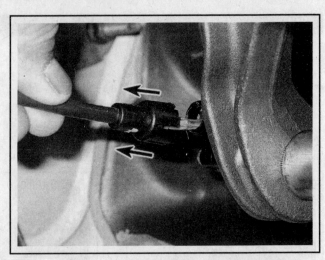

18.6 To disconnect the drive cable from the brake pedal, grasp it firmly and pull it out (detach the cable from the accelerator pedal the same way)

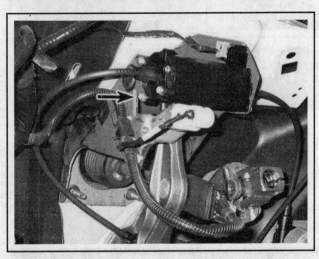

18.7 To detach the left end of the motor from its mounting bracket, remove this bolt (instrument panel removed for clarity)

5   Disconnect the electrical connector from the top of the motor (see illustration).

6   Disconnect the drive cables from the brake and accelerator pedals (see illustration).

7   Remove the left motor mounting bolt (see illustration) and the two right mounting bolts (see illustration 18.5), then remove the motor and drive cable assembly.

8   Installation is the reverse of removal.

19   Electric side view mirrors - general information

1   Most electric side view mirrors use two motors to move the glass; one for up and down adjustments and one for left-right adjustments.

2   The control switch has a selector portion that sends voltage to the left or right side mirror. With the ignition ON but the engine OFF, roll down the windows and operate the mirror control switch through all functions (left-right and up-down) for both the left and right side mirrors.

3   Listen carefully for the sound of the electric motors running in the mirrors.

4   If the motors can be heard but the mirror glass doesn't move, there's a problem with the drive mechanism inside the mirror.

5   If the mirrors do not operate and no sound comes from the mirror

motors, check the fuse (see Section 3).

6   If the fuse is OK, remove the mirror control switch. Have the switch continuity checked by a dealership service department or other qualified automobile repair facility.

7   Test the ground connections.

8   If the mirror still doesn't work, remove the mirror and check the wires at the mirror for voltage.

9   If there's not voltage in each switch position, check the circuit between the mirror and control switch for opens and shorts.

10 If there's voltage, remove the mirror and test it off the vehicle with jumper wires. Replace the mirror if it fails this test.

20 Cruise control system - general information

There are no conventional cruise control system components on these vehicles. The cruise control system is an integral subsystem of the Electronic Throttle Control (ETC) system. If the cruise control system isn't functioning correctly, take the vehicle to a dealer service department or other qualified repair shop for diagnosis.

21 Power window system - description and check

➡ **Note: These models are equipped with a Smart Junction Box (SJB) (manufacturer terminology), otherwise known as a Body Control Module (BCM). Several systems are linked to this centralized control module, which allows simple and accurate troubleshooting, but only with a professional-grade scan tool. The SJB or BCM governs the door locks, the power windows, the ignition lock and security system, the interior lights, the Daytime Running Lights system, the horn, the windshield wipers, the heating/air conditioning system and the power mirrors. In the event of malfunction with this system, have the vehicle diagnosed by a dealership service department or other qualified automotive repair facility.**

1   The power window system operates electric motors, mounted in the doors, which lower and raise the windows. The system consists of the control switches, the motors, regulators, glass mechanisms, the Smart Junction Box (SJB) and associated wiring.

2   The power windows can be lowered and raised from the master control switch by the driver or by remote switches located at the individual windows. Each window has a separate motor that is reversible. The position of the control switch determines the polarity and therefore the direction of operation.

3   The circuit is protected by a fuse and a circuit breaker. Each motor is also equipped with an internal circuit breaker; this prevents one stuck window from disabling the whole system.

4   The power window system will only operate when the ignition switch is ON, and for a period of time after the ignition key has been turned Off (unless one of the doors is opened). In addition, many models have a window lockout switch at the master control switch which, when activated, disables the switches at the rear windows and, sometimes, the switch at the passenger's window also. Always check these items before troubleshooting a window problem.

5   These procedures are general in nature, so if you can't find the problem using them, take the vehicle to a dealer service department or other properly equipped repair facility.

6   If the power windows won't operate, always check the fuse and circuit breaker first.

7   If only the rear windows are inoperative, or if the windows only operate from the master control switch, check the rear window lockout switch for continuity in the unlocked position. Replace it if it doesn't have continuity.

8   Check the wiring between the switches and fuse panel for continuity. Repair the wiring, if necessary.

9   If only one window is inoperative from the master control switch, try the other control switch at the window.

➡ **Note: This doesn't apply to the driver's door window.**

10 If the same window works from one switch, but not the other, check the switch for continuity.

11 If the switch tests OK, check for a short or open in the circuit between the affected switch and the window motor.

12 If one window is inoperative from both switches, remove the switch panel from the affected door. Check for voltage at the switch and at the motor (refer to Chapter 11 for door panel removal) while the switch is operated.

13 If voltage is reaching the motor, disconnect the glass from the regulator (see Chapter 11). Move the window up and down by hand while checking for binding and damage. Also check for binding and damage to the regulator. If the regulator is not damaged and the window moves up and down smoothly, replace the motor. If there's binding or damage, lubricate, repair or replace parts, as necessary.

14 If voltage isn't reaching the motor, check the wiring in the circuit for continuity between the switches and the body control module, and between the body control module and the motors. You'll need to consult the wiring diagram at the end of this Chapter. If the circuit is equipped with a relay, check that the relay is grounded properly and receiving voltage.

15 Test the windows after you are done to confirm proper repairs.

22 Power door lock and keyless entry system - description and check

➡ **Note: These models are equipped with a Smart Junction Box (SJB) (manufacturer terminology), otherwise known as a Body Control Module (BCM). Several systems are linked to this centralized control module, which allows simple and accurate troubleshooting, but only with a professional-grade scan tool. The SJB or BCM governs the door locks, the power windows, the ignition lock and security system, the interior lights, the Daytime Running Lights system, the horn, the windshield wipers, the heating/air conditioning system and the power mirrors. In the event of malfunction with this system, have the vehicle diagnosed by a dealership service department or other qualified automotive repair facility.**

1   The power door lock system operates the door lock actuators mounted in each door. The system consists of the switches, actuators, Smart Junction Box (SJB) and associated wiring. Diagnosis can usually be limited to simple checks of the wiring connections and actuators for minor faults that can be easily repaired.

2   Power door lock systems are operated by bi-directional solenoids located in the doors. The lock switches have two operating positions: Lock and Unlock. These switches send a signal to the SJB, which in turn sends a signal to the door lock solenoids.

3   If you are unable to locate the trouble using the following general steps, consult your dealer service department.

4   Always check the circuit protection first. Some vehicles use a combination of circuit breakers and fuses. Refer to the wiring diagrams at the end of this Chapter.

5   Check for voltage at the switches. If no voltage is present, check the wiring between the fuse panel and the switches for shorts and opens.

6   If voltage is present, test the switch for continuity. Replace it if there's not continuity in both switch positions. To remove the switch, use a flat-bladed trim tool to pry out the door/window switch assembly (see Chapter 11).

7   If the switch has continuity, check the wiring between the switch and door lock solenoid.

8   If all but one lock solenoids operate, remove the trim panel from the affected door (see Chapter 11) and check for voltage at the solenoid while the lock switch is operated. One of the wires should have voltage in the Lock position; the other should have voltage in the Unlock position.

9   If the inoperative solenoid is receiving voltage, replace the solenoid.

10 If the inoperative solenoid isn't receiving voltage, check for an open or short in the wire between the lock solenoid and the relay.

11 On the models covered by this manual, power door lock system communication goes through the Smart Junction Box. If the above tests do not pinpoint a problem, take the vehicle to a dealer or qualified shop with the proper scan tool to retrieve trouble codes from the SJB.

KEYLESS ENTRY SYSTEM

12 The keyless entry system consists of a remote control transmitter that sends a coded infrared signal to a receiver, which then operates the door lock system.

13 Replace the battery when the transmitter doesn't operate the locks at a distance of ten feet. Normal range should be about 30 feet.

KEY REMOTE CONTROL BATTERY REPLACEMENT

14 Use a coin to carefully separate the case halves.
15 Replace the battery.
16 Snap the case halves together.

TRANSMITTER PROGRAMMING

17 Programming replacement transmitters requires the use of a specialized scan tool. Take the vehicle and the transmitter(s) to a dealer service department or other qualified repair shop equipped with the necessary tool to have the transmitter(s) programmed to the vehicle.

23 Daytime Running Lights (DRL) - general information

The Daytime Running Lights (DRL) system, which is required on new Canadian models, illuminates the headlights when the engine is running. The DRL system supplies reduced power to the headlights so they won't be too bright for daytime use, which also prolongs headlight life.

24 Airbag system - general information and precautions

GENERAL INFORMATION

1   All models are equipped with a frontal impact airbag system, which is referred to as the Supplemental Restraint System (SRS). The SRS is designed to protect the driver and the front seat passenger from serious injury in the event of a head-on or frontal collision. The SRS is controlled by the Restraints Control Module (RCM), which is mounted on the center tunnel, between the seats. The SRS uses a pair of airbags to protect the front-seat occupants: the driver's airbag in the steering wheel and the passenger airbag, which is located in the right end of the instrument panel, beneath the instrument panel top pad and above the glove box. Other important components in the SRS include the clockspring, a wind-up coil that delivers battery voltage to the steering wheel airbag, and the airbag readiness light on the instrument cluster.

2   The seatbelts, which are considered a critical part of the SRS, are equipped with pre-tensioners that remove excess slack from the seatbelt webbing. When the RCM detects a frontal or side impact that exceeds the specified threshold, it activates the pre-tensioners right before it deploys the airbags.

Driver airbag

3   The airbag inflator module, which is mounted in the center of the steering wheel, contains a housing incorporating the airbag and the inflator unit. The inflator assembly is mounted on the back of the housing over a hole through which gas is expelled, inflating the bag almost instantaneously when an electrical signal is sent from the system. The clockspring assembly on the steering column under the steering wheel carries this signal to the module. The clockspring assembly can transmit an electrical signal regardless of steering wheel position. The igniter in the airbag converts the electrical signal to heat and ignites the powder, which inflates the bag.

Passenger airbag

4   The airbag is mounted in the right end of the instrument panel, beneath the instrument panel top pad and above the glove box. It uses the same components as the driver's airbag, except that the passenger airbag is larger than the steering wheel-mounted unit. The trim cover is textured and colored to match the instrument panel and has a molded seam that splits when the bag inflates.

Restraints Control Module (RCM)

5   In the event of a collision, the RCM supplies current to the SRS, even if battery power is cut off. Simultaneously, it also activates the seatbelt pre-tensioners to remove all slack from the seat belts.

6   The RCM checks the SRS every time the vehicle is started, and indicates that it is doing so by turning on the airbag readiness light, which is located on the instrument cluster. If the SRS is operating properly, the RCM turns off the airbag readiness light. If it detects a fault in the system, the airbag readiness light will remain on. If this condition occurs, take the vehicle to your dealer immediately for service.

DISARMING THE SYSTEM AND OTHER PRECAUTIONS

⁜ WARNING:

Failure to follow these precautions could result in accidental deployment of the airbag and personal injury.

7   Whenever you are working in the vicinity of the driver airbag in the steering wheel or any of the other airbags on your vehicle, **DISARM THE SYSTEM.** To disarm the system:

a) *Point the wheels straight ahead and turn the ignition key to the LOCK position.*

b) *Disconnect the cable from the negative battery terminal. Isolate the cable terminal so it won't accidentally contact the battery post.*

c) *Wait at least two minutes for the back-up power supply to be depleted. (Back-up power is supplied by a capacitor that takes about two minutes to fully discharge. During this two-minute interval the SRS is still capable of deploying.)*

8   Whenever handling an airbag, always keep the airbag opening (the trim side) pointed away from your body. Never place the airbag on a bench or other surface with the airbag opening facing the surface. Always place the airbag module in a safe location with the airbag opening facing up.

9   Never measure the resistance of any SRS component. An ohmmeter has a built-in battery supply that could accidentally deploy the airbag.

10   Never dispose of a "live" airbag. Return it to a dealer service department or other qualified repair shop for safe deployment and disposal.

COMPONENT REMOVAL AND INSTALLATION

Driver airbag and clockspring

11   Refer to Chapter 10, *Steering wheel - removal and installation*, for the driver's side airbag module and clockspring removal and installation procedures.

Passenger airbag

12   We don't recommend removing the passenger airbag. If you ever have to remove the instrument panel (see Chapter 11), you will have to remove the airbag with it, but it's not necessary to actually detach the airbag from the instrument panel, and we don't recommend doing so. If the passenger airbag must be serviced, take the vehicle to a dealer service department or other qualified repair shop.

Restraints Control Module (RCM)

13   We don't recommend removing the RCM. If the RCM must be serviced, take the vehicle to a dealer service department or other qualified repair shop.

25 Wiring diagrams - general information

Since it isn't possible to include all wiring diagrams for every year covered by this manual, the following diagrams are those that are typical and most commonly needed.

Prior to troubleshooting any circuits, check the fuse and circuit breakers (if equipped) to make sure they're in good condition. Make sure the battery is properly charged and check the cable connections (see Chapters 1 and 5).

When checking a circuit, make sure that all connectors are clean, with no broken or loose terminals. When unplugging a connector, do not pull on the wires. Pull only on the connector housings.

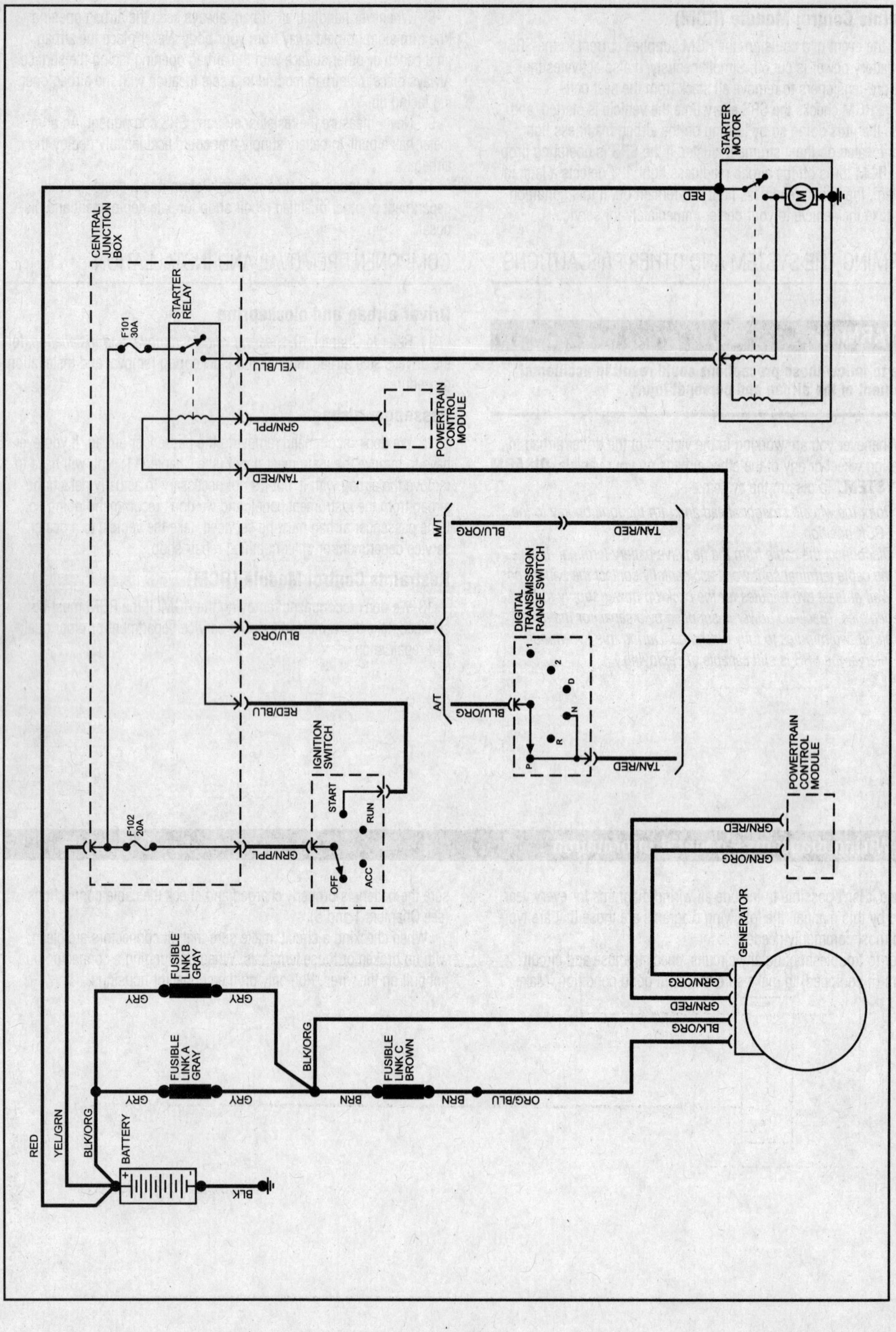

Starting and charging systems

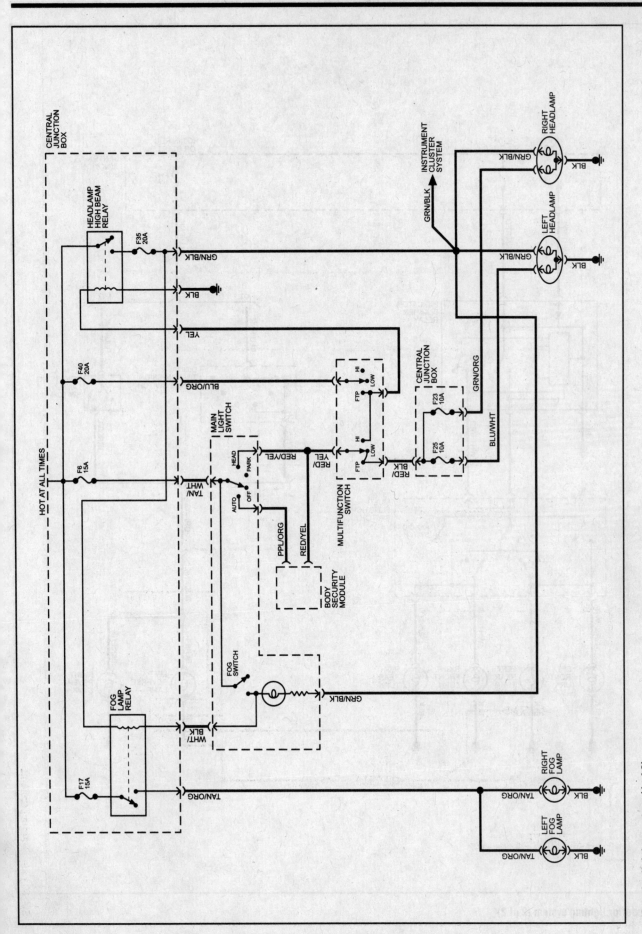

Exterior lighting system (1 of 2)

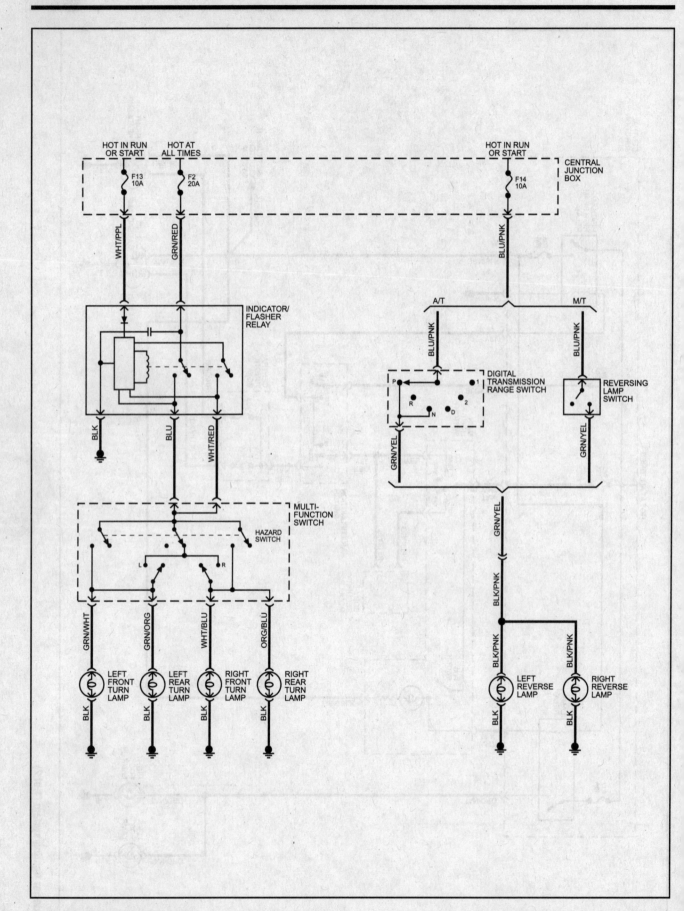

Exterior lighting system (2 of 2)

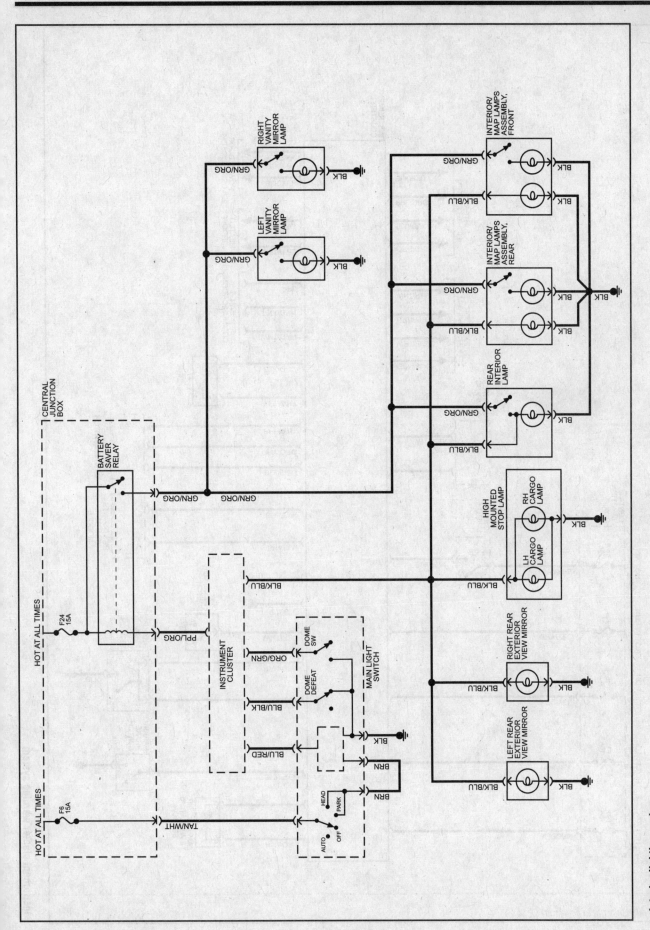

Interior lighting system

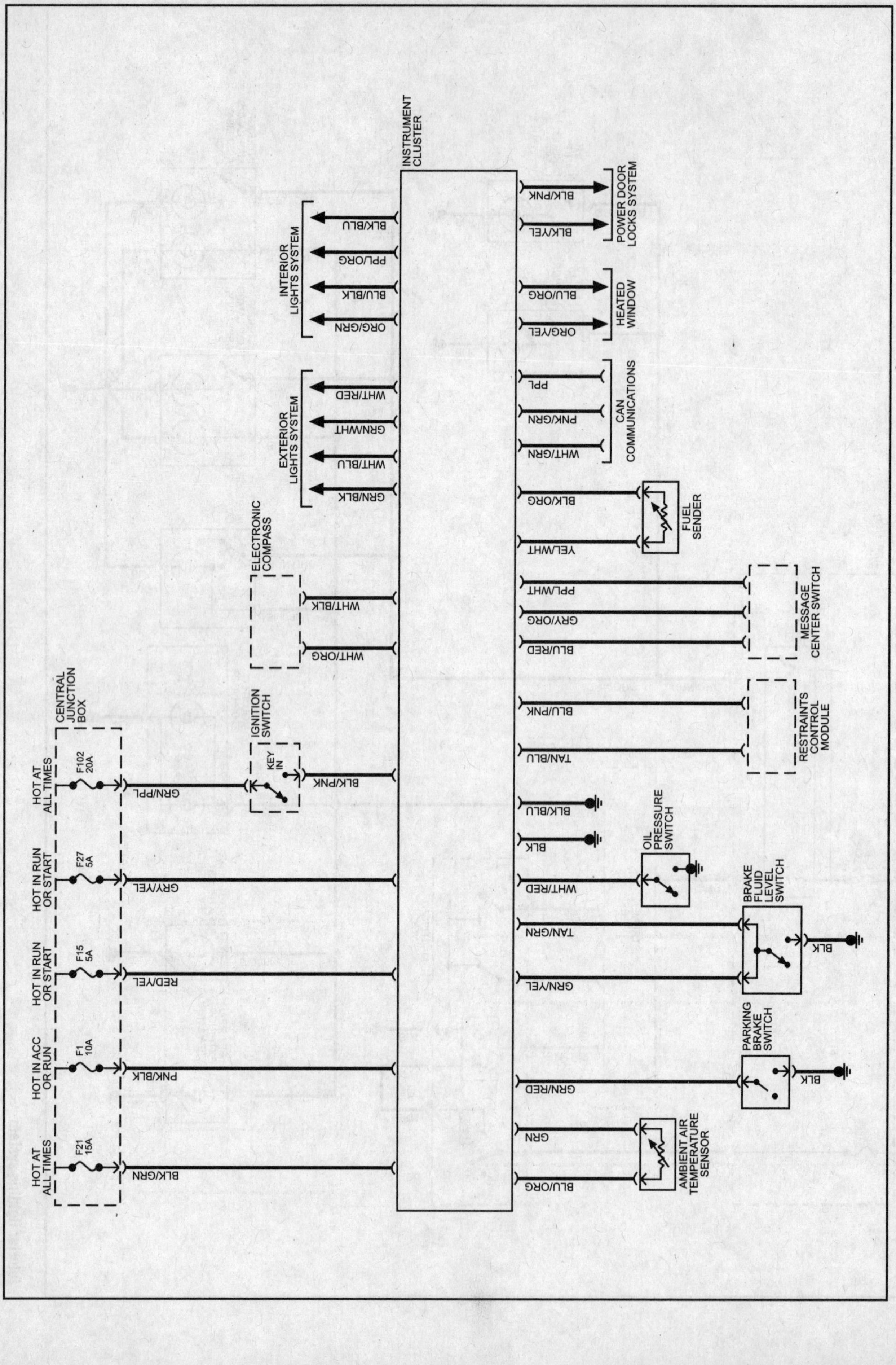

INSTRUMENT CLUSTER

INTERIOR LIGHTS SYSTEM

BLK/BLU
PPL/ORG
BLU/BLK
ORG/GRN

POWER DOOR LOCKS SYSTEM

BLK/PNK
BLK/YEL

HEATED WINDOW

BLU/ORG
ORG/YEL

EXTERIOR LIGHTS SYSTEM

WHT/RED
GRN/WHT
WHT/BLU
GRN/BLK

CAN COMMUNICATIONS

PPL
PNK/GRN
WHT/GRN

FUEL SENDER

BLK/ORG
YEL/WHT

ELECTRONIC COMPASS

WHT/BLK
WHT/ORG

MESSAGE CENTER SWITCH

PPL/WHT
GRY/ORG
BLU/RED

RESTRAINTS CONTROL MODULE

BLU/PNK
TAN/BLU

CENTRAL JUNCTION BOX

HOT AT ALL TIMES

F102 20A

GRN/PPL

IGNITION SWITCH

KEY IN

BLK/PNK

HOT IN RUN OR START

F27 5A

GRY/YEL

HOT IN RUN OR START

F15 5A

RED/YEL

HOT IN ACC OR RUN

F1 10A

PNK/BLK

HOT AT ALL TIMES

F21 15A

BLK/GRN

BLK/BLU
BLK

OIL PRESSURE SWITCH

WHT/RED

BRAKE FLUID LEVEL SWITCH

TAN/GRN
GRN/YEL

BLK

PARKING BRAKE SWITCH

GRN/RED

BLK

AMBIENT AIR TEMPERATURE SENSOR

GRN
BLU/ORG

Instrument cluster warning system

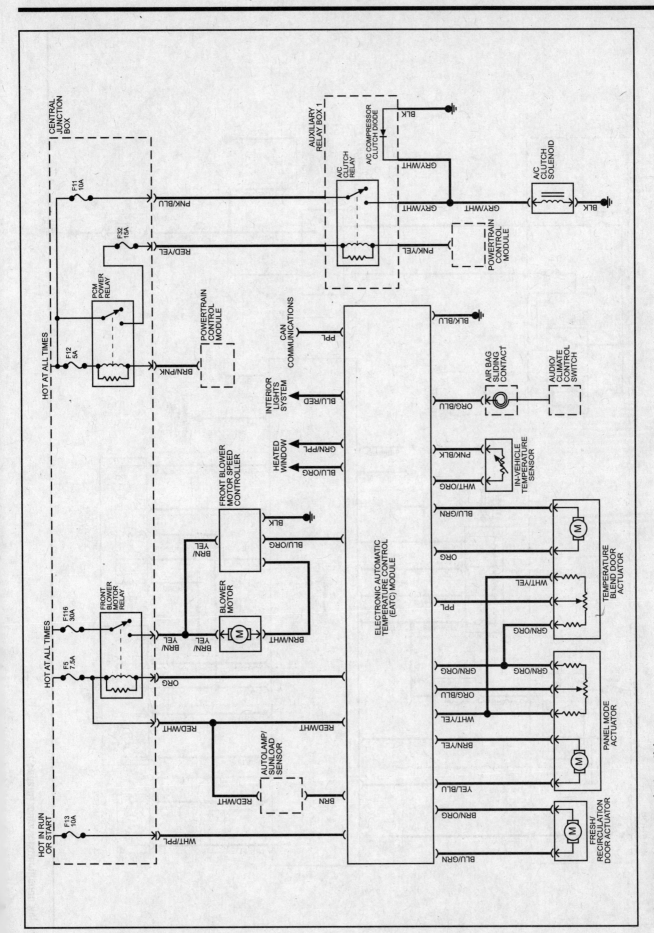

Air conditioning system (automatic)

Air conditioning system (manual)

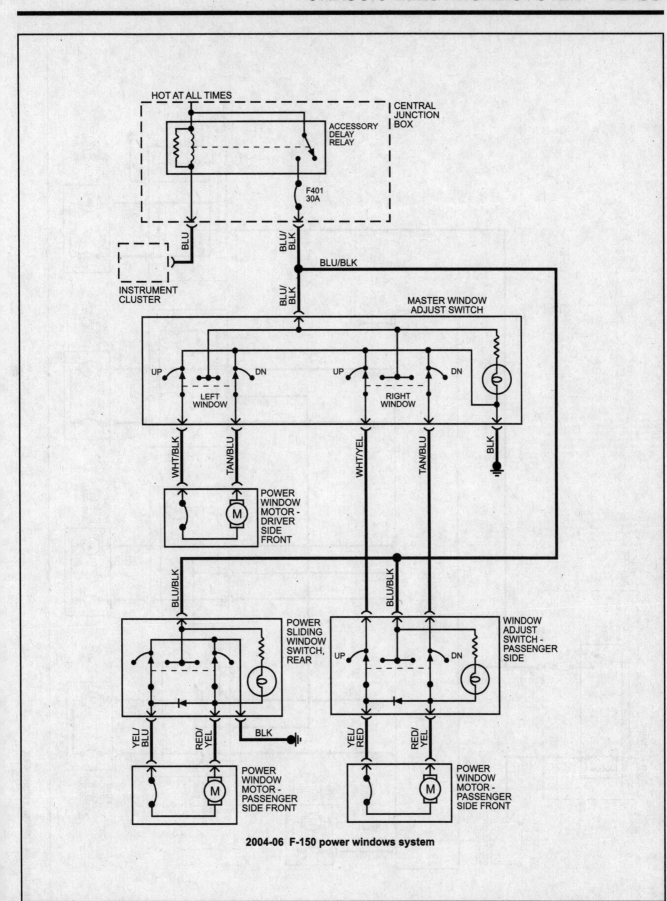

2004-06 F-150 power windows system

Power windows system

Power windows system - super cab

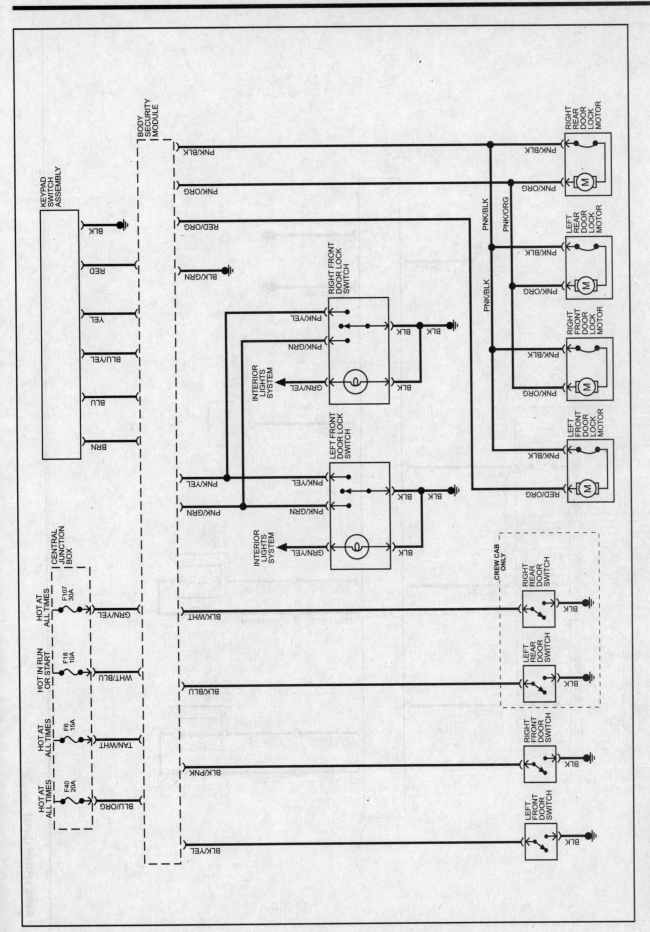

Power door lock system

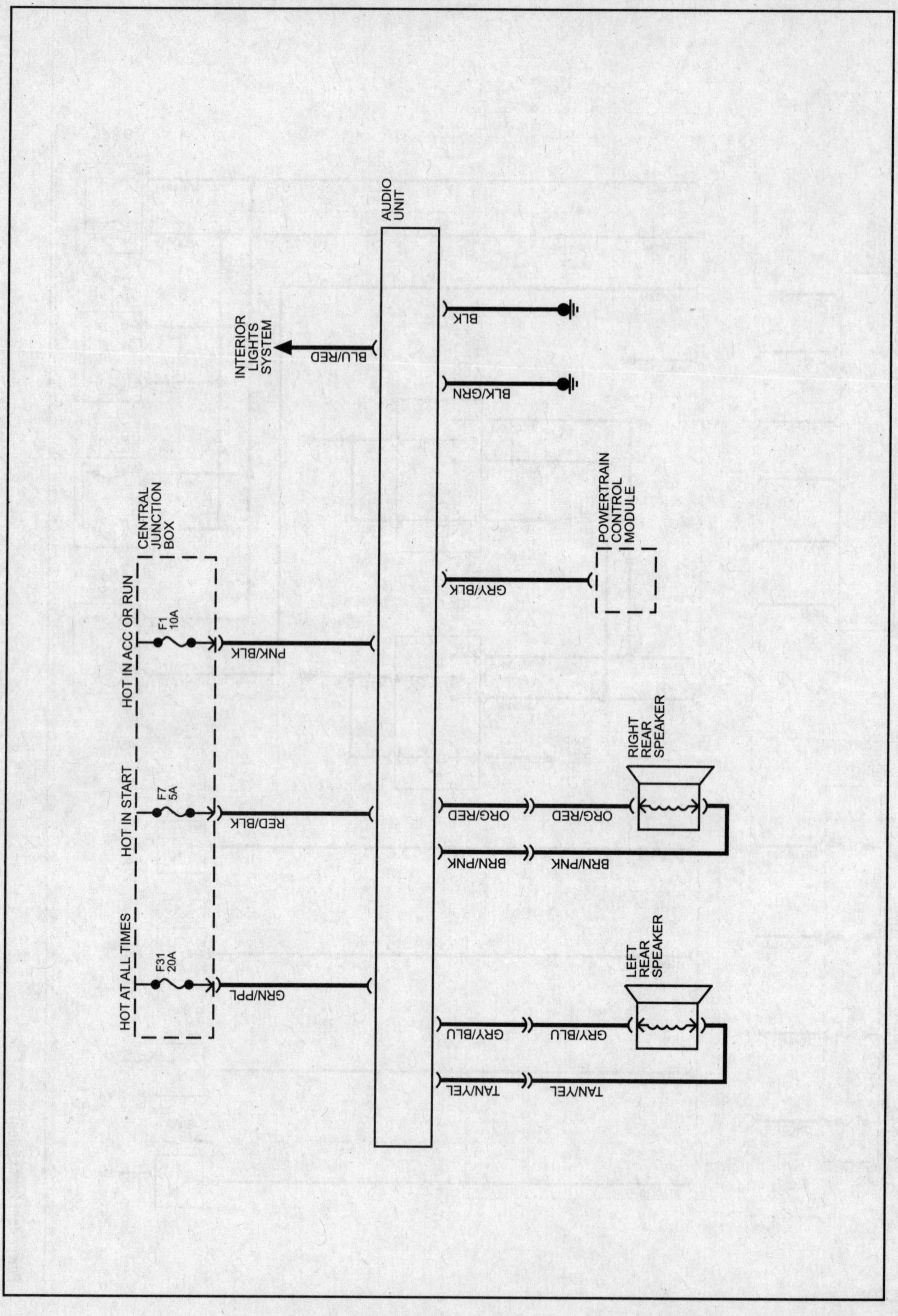

AUDIO UNIT

BLK

BLK/GRN

INTERIOR LIGHTS SYSTEM

BLU/RED

POWERTRAIN CONTROL MODULE

GRY/BLK

CENTRAL JUNCTION BOX

HOT IN ACC OR RUN

F1 10A

PNK/BLK

HOT IN START

F7 5A

RED/BLK

HOT AT ALL TIMES

F31 20A

GRN/PPL

RIGHT REAR SPEAKER

ORG/RED   ORG/RED

BRN/PNK   BRN/PNK

LEFT REAR SPEAKER

GRY/BLU   GRY/BLU

TAN/YEL   TAN/YEL

Audio system⁰ (base)

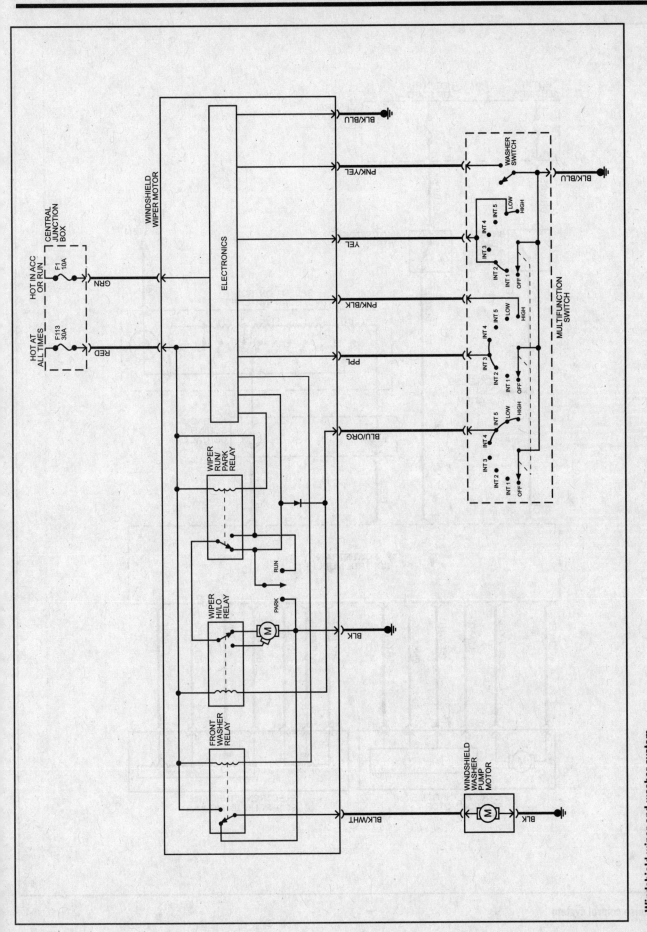

Windshield wiper and washer system

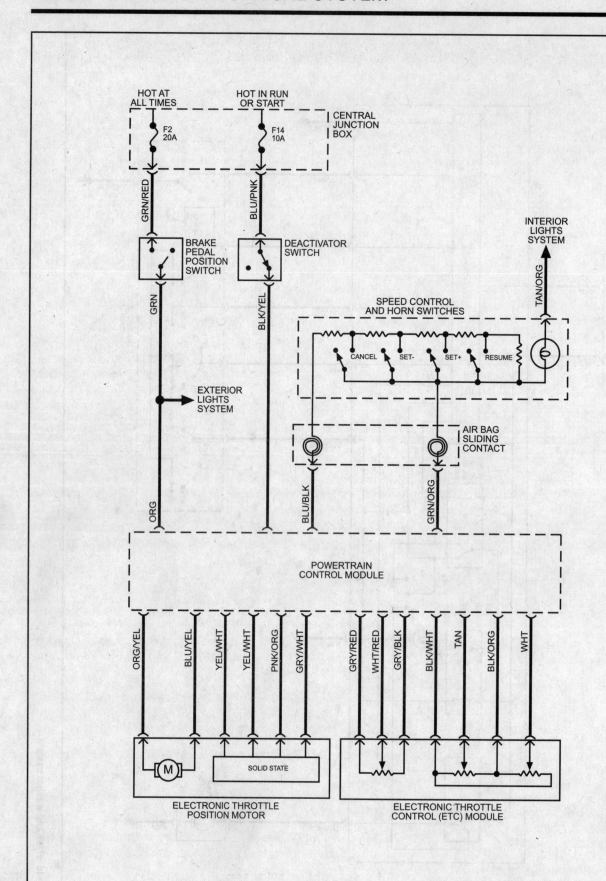

Cruise control system

GLOSSARY

AIR/FUEL RATIO: The ratio of air-to-gasoline by weight in the fuel mixture drawn into the engine.

AIR INJECTION: One method of reducing harmful exhaust emissions by injecting air into each of the exhaust ports of an engine. The fresh air entering the hot exhaust manifold causes any remaining fuel to be burned before it can exit the tailpipe.

ALTERNATOR: A device used for converting mechanical energy into electrical energy.

AMMETER: An instrument, calibrated in amperes, used to measure the flow of an electrical current in a circuit. Ammeters are always connected in series with the circuit being tested.

AMPERE: The rate of flow of electrical current present when one volt of electrical pressure is applied against one ohm of electrical resistance.

ANALOG COMPUTER: Any microprocessor that uses similar (analogous) electrical signals to make its calculations.

ARMATURE: A laminated, soft iron core wrapped by a wire that converts electrical energy to mechanical energy as in a motor or relay. When rotated in a magnetic field, it changes mechanical energy into electrical energy as in a generator.

ATMOSPHERIC PRESSURE: The pressure on the Earth's surface caused by the weight of the air in the atmosphere. At sea level, this pressure is 14.7 psi at 32°F (101 kPa at 0°C).

ATOMIZATION: The breaking down of a liquid into a fine mist that can be suspended in air.

AXIAL PLAY: Movement parallel to a shaft or bearing bore.

BACKFIRE: The sudden combustion of gases in the intake or exhaust system that results in a loud explosion.

BACKLASH: The clearance or play between two parts, such as meshed gears.

BACKPRESSURE: Restrictions in the exhaust system that slow the exit of exhaust gases from the combustion chamber.

BAKELITE: A heat resistant, plastic insulator material commonly used in printed circuit boards and transistorized components.

BALL BEARING: A bearing made up of hardened inner and outer races between which hardened steel balls roll.

BALLAST RESISTOR: A resistor in the primary ignition circuit that lowers voltage after the engine is started to reduce wear on ignition components.

BEARING: A friction reducing, supportive device usually located between a stationary part and a moving part.

BIMETAL TEMPERATURE SENSOR: Any sensor or switch made of two dissimilar types of metal that bend when heated or cooled due to the different expansion rates of the alloys. These types of sensors usually function as an on/off switch.

BLOWBY: Combustion gases, composed of water vapor and unburned fuel, that leak past the piston rings into the crankcase during normal engine operation. These gases are removed by the PCV system to prevent the buildup of harmful acids in the crankcase.

BRAKE PAD: A brake shoe and lining assembly used with disc brakes.

BRAKE SHOE: The backing for the brake lining. The term is, however, usually applied to the assembly of the brake backing and lining.

BUSHING: A liner, usually removable, for a bearing; an anti-friction liner used in place of a bearing.

CALIPER: A hydraulically activated device in a disc brake system, which is mounted straddling the brake rotor (disc). The caliper contains at least one piston and two brake pads. Hydraulic pressure on the piston(s) forces the pads against the rotor.

CAMSHAFT: A shaft in the engine on which are the lobes (cams) which operate the valves. The camshaft is driven by the crankshaft, via a belt, chain or gears, at one half the crankshaft speed.

CAPACITOR: A device which stores an electrical charge.

CARBON MONOXIDE (CO): A colorless, odorless gas given off as a normal byproduct of combustion. It is poisonous and extremely dangerous in confined areas, building up slowly to toxic levels without warning if adequate ventilation is not available.

CARBURETOR: A device, usually mounted on the intake manifold of an engine, which mixes the air and fuel in the proper proportion to allow even combustion.

CATALYTIC CONVERTER: A device installed in the exhaust system, like a muffler, that converts harmful byproducts of combustion into carbon dioxide and water vapor by means of a heat-producing chemical reaction.

CENTRIFUGAL ADVANCE: A mechanical method of advancing the spark timing by using flyweights in the distributor that react to centrifugal force generated by the distributor shaft rotation.

CHECK VALVE: Any one-way valve installed to permit the flow of air, fuel or vacuum in one direction only.

CHOKE: A device, usually a moveable valve, placed in the intake path of a carburetor to restrict the flow of air.

CIRCUIT: Any unbroken path through which an electrical current can flow. Also used to describe fuel flow in some instances.

CIRCUIT BREAKER: A switch which protects an electrical circuit from overload by opening the circuit when the current flow exceeds a predetermined level. Some circuit breakers must be reset manually, while most reset automatically.

COIL (IGNITION): A transformer in the ignition circuit which steps up the voltage provided to the spark plugs.

COMBINATION MANIFOLD: An assembly which includes both the intake and exhaust manifolds in one casting.

COMBINATION VALVE: A device used in some fuel systems that routes fuel vapors to a charcoal storage canister instead of venting them into the atmosphere. The valve relieves fuel tank pressure and allows fresh air into the tank as the fuel level drops to prevent a vapor lock situation.

COMPRESSION RATIO: The comparison of the total volume of the cylinder and combustion chamber with the piston at BDC and the piston at TDC.

CONDENSER: 1. An electrical device which acts to store an electrical charge, preventing voltage surges. 2. A radiator-like device in the air conditioning system in which refrigerant gas condenses into a liquid, giving off heat.

CONDUCTOR: Any material through which an electrical current can be transmitted easily.

CONTINUITY: Continuous or complete circuit. Can be checked with an ohmmeter.

COUNTERSHAFT: An intermediate shaft which is rotated by a mainshaft and transmits, in turn, that rotation to a working part.

CRANKCASE: The lower part of an engine in which the crankshaft and related parts operate.

CRANKSHAFT: The main driving shaft of an engine which receives reciprocating motion from the pistons and converts it to rotary motion.

CYLINDER: In an engine, the round hole in the engine block in which the piston(s) ride.

CYLINDER BLOCK: The main structural member of an engine in which is found the cylinders, crankshaft and other principal parts.

CYLINDER HEAD: The detachable portion of the engine, usually fastened to the top of the cylinder block and containing all or most of the combustion chambers. On overhead valve engines, it contains the valves and their operating parts. On overhead cam engines, it contains the camshaft as well.

DEAD CENTER: The extreme top or bottom of the piston stroke.

DETONATION: An unwanted explosion of the air/fuel mixture in the combustion chamber caused by excess heat and compression, advanced timing, or an overly lean mixture. Also referred to as "ping".

DIAPHRAGM: A thin, flexible wall separating two cavities, such as in a vacuum advance unit.

DIESELING: A condition in which hot spots in the combustion chamber cause the engine to run on after the key is turned off.

DIFFERENTIAL: A geared assembly which allows the transmission of motion between drive axles, giving one axle the ability to turn faster than the other.

DIODE: An electrical device that will allow current to flow in one direction only.

DISC BRAKE: A hydraulic braking assembly consisting of a brake disc, or rotor, mounted on an axle, and a caliper assembly containing, usually two brake pads which are activated by hydraulic pressure. The pads are forced against the sides of the disc, creating friction which slows the vehicle.

DISTRIBUTOR: A mechanically driven device on an engine which is responsible for electrically firing the spark plug at a predetermined point of the piston stroke.

DOWEL PIN: A pin, inserted in mating holes in two different parts allowing those parts to maintain a fixed relationship.

DRUM BRAKE: A braking system which consists of two brake shoes and one or two wheel cylinders, mounted on a fixed backing plate, and a brake drum, mounted on an axle, which revolves around the assembly.

DWELL: The rate, measured in degrees of shaft rotation, at which an electrical circuit cycles on and off.

ELECTRONIC CONTROL UNIT (ECU): Ignition module, module, amplifier or igniter. See Module for definition.

ELECTRONIC IGNITION: A system in which the timing and firing of the spark plugs is controlled by an electronic control unit, usually called a module. These systems have no points or condenser.

END-PLAY: The measured amount of axial movement in a shaft.

ENGINE: A device that converts heat into mechanical energy.

EXHAUST MANIFOLD: A set of cast passages or pipes which conduct exhaust gases from the engine.

FEELER GAUGE: A blade, usually metal, or precisely predetermined thickness, used to measure the clearance between two parts.

FIRING ORDER: The order in which combustion occurs in the cylinders of an engine. Also the order in which spark is distributed to the plugs by the distributor.

FLOODING: The presence of too much fuel in the intake manifold and combustion chamber which prevents the air/fuel mixture from firing, thereby causing a no-start situation.

FLYWHEEL: A disc shaped part bolted to the rear end of the crankshaft. Around the outer perimeter is affixed the ring gear. The starter drive engages the ring gear, turning the flywheel, which rotates the crankshaft, imparting the initial starting motion to the engine.

FOOT POUND (ft. lbs. or sometimes, ft.lb.): The amount of energy or work needed to raise an item weighing one pound, a distance of one foot.

FUSE: A protective device in a circuit which prevents circuit overload by breaking the circuit when a specific amperage is present. The device is constructed around a strip or wire of a lower amperage rating than the circuit it is designed to protect. When an amperage higher than that stamped on the fuse is present in the circuit, the strip or wire melts, opening the circuit.

GEAR RATIO: The ratio between the number of teeth on meshing gears.

GENERATOR: A device which converts mechanical energy into electrical energy.

HEAT RANGE: The measure of a spark plug's ability to dissipate heat from its firing end. The higher the heat range, the hotter the plug fires.

HUB: The center part of a wheel or gear.

HYDROCARBON (HC): Any chemical compound made up of hydrogen and carbon. A major pollutant formed by the engine as a byproduct of combustion.

HYDROMETER: An instrument used to measure the specific gravity of a solution.

INCH POUND (inch lbs.; sometimes in.lb. or in. lbs.): One twelfth of a foot pound.

INDUCTION: A means of transferring electrical energy in the form of a magnetic field. Principle used in the ignition coil to increase voltage.

INJECTOR: A device which receives metered fuel under relatively low pressure and is activated to inject the fuel into the engine under relatively high pressure at a predetermined time.

INPUT SHAFT: The shaft to which torque is applied, usually carrying the driving gear or gears.

INTAKE MANIFOLD: A casting of passages or pipes used to conduct air or a fuel/air mixture to the cylinders.

JOURNAL: The bearing surface within which a shaft operates.

KEY: A small block usually fitted in a notch between a shaft and a hub to prevent slippage of the two parts.

MANIFOLD: A casting of passages or set of pipes which connect the cylinders to an inlet or outlet source.

MANIFOLD VACUUM: Low pressure in an engine intake manifold formed just below the throttle plates. Manifold vacuum is highest at idle and drops under acceleration.

MASTER CYLINDER: The primary fluid pressurizing device in a hydraulic system. In automotive use, it is found in brake and hydraulic clutch systems and is pedal activated, either directly or, in a power brake system, through the power booster.

MODULE: Electronic control unit, amplifier or igniter of solid state or integrated design which controls the current flow in the ignition

primary circuit based on input from the pick-up coil. When the module opens the primary circuit, high secondary voltage is induced in the coil.

NEEDLE BEARING: A bearing which consists of a number (usually a large number) of long, thin rollers.

OHM: (Ω) The unit used to measure the resistance of conductor-to-electrical flow. One ohm is the amount of resistance that limits current flow to one ampere in a circuit with one volt of pressure.

OHMMETER: An instrument used for measuring the resistance, in ohms, in an electrical circuit.

OUTPUT SHAFT: The shaft which transmits torque from a device, such as a transmission.

OVERDRIVE: A gear assembly which produces more shaft revolutions than that transmitted to it.

OVERHEAD CAMSHAFT (OHC): An engine configuration in which the camshaft is mounted on top of the cylinder head and operates the valve either directly or by means of rocker arms.

OVERHEAD VALVE (OHV): An engine configuration in which all of the valves are located in the cylinder head and the camshaft is located in the cylinder block. The camshaft operates the valves via lifters and pushrods.

OXIDES OF NITROGEN (NOx): Chemical compounds of nitrogen produced as a byproduct of combustion. They combine with hydrocarbons to produce smog.

OXYGEN SENSOR: Use with the feedback system to sense the presence of oxygen in the exhaust gas and signal the computer which can reference the voltage signal to an air/fuel ratio.

PINION: The smaller of two meshing gears.

PISTON RING: An open-ended ring with fits into a groove on the outer diameter of the piston. Its chief function is to form a seal between the piston and cylinder wall. Most automotive pistons have three rings: two for compression sealing; one for oil sealing.

PRELOAD: A predetermined load placed on a bearing during assembly or by adjustment.

PRIMARY CIRCUIT: the low voltage side of the ignition system which consists of the ignition switch, ballast resistor or resistance wire, bypass, coil, electronic control unit and pick-up coil as well as the connecting wires and harnesses.

PRESS FIT: The mating of two parts under pressure, due to the inner diameter of one being smaller than the outer diameter of the other, or vice versa; an interference fit.

RACE: The surface on the inner or outer ring of a bearing on which the balls, needles or rollers move.

REGULATOR: A device which maintains the amperage and/or voltage levels of a circuit at predetermined values.

RELAY: A switch which automatically opens and/or closes a circuit.

RESISTANCE: The opposition to the flow of current through a circuit or electrical device, and is measured in ohms. Resistance is equal to the voltage divided by the amperage.

RESISTOR: A device, usually made of wire, which offers a preset amount of resistance in an electrical circuit.

RING GEAR: The name given to a ring-shaped gear attached to a differential case, or affixed to a flywheel or as part of a planetary gear set.

ROLLER BEARING: A bearing made up of hardened inner and outer races between which hardened steel rollers move.

ROTOR: 1. The disc-shaped part of a disc brake assembly, upon which the brake pads bear; also called, brake disc. 2. The device mounted atop the distributor shaft, which passes current to the distributor cap tower contacts.

SECONDARY CIRCUIT: The high voltage side of the ignition system, usually above 20,000 volts. The secondary includes the ignition coil, coil wire, distributor cap and rotor, spark plug wires and spark plugs.

SENDING UNIT: A mechanical, electrical, hydraulic or electromagnetic device which transmits information to a gauge.

SENSOR: Any device designed to measure engine operating conditions or ambient pressures and temperatures. Usually electronic in nature and designed to send a voltage signal to an on-board computer, some sensors may operate as a simple on/off switch or they may provide a variable voltage signal (like a potentiometer) as conditions or measured parameters change.

SHIM: Spacers of precise, predetermined thickness used between parts to establish a proper working relationship.

SLAVE CYLINDER: In automotive use, a device in the hydraulic clutch system which is activated by hydraulic force, disengaging the clutch.

SOLENOID: A coil used to produce a magnetic field, the effect of which is to produce work.

SPARK PLUG: A device screwed into the combustion chamber of a spark ignition engine. The basic construction is a conductive core inside of a ceramic insulator, mounted in an outer conductive base. An electrical charge from the spark plug wire travels along the conductive core and jumps a preset air gap to a grounding point or points at the end of the conductive base. The resultant spark ignites the fuel/air mixture in the combustion chamber.

SPLINES: Ridges machined or cast onto the outer diameter of a shaft or inner diameter of a bore to enable parts to mate without rotation.

TACHOMETER: A device used to measure the rotary speed of an engine, shaft, gear, etc., usually in rotations per minute.

THERMOSTAT: A valve, located in the cooling system of an engine, which is closed when cold and opens gradually in response to engine heating, controlling the temperature of the coolant and rate of coolant flow.

TOP DEAD CENTER (TDC): The point at which the piston reaches the top of its travel on the compression stroke.

TORQUE: The twisting force applied to an object.

TORQUE CONVERTER: A turbine used to transmit power from a driving member to a driven member via hydraulic action, providing changes in drive ratio and torque. In automotive use, it links the driveplate at the rear of the engine to the automatic transmission.

TRANSDUCER: A device used to change a force into an electrical signal.

TRANSISTOR: A semi-conductor component which can be actuated by a small voltage to perform an electrical switching function.

TUNE-UP: A regular maintenance function, usually associated with the replacement and adjustment of parts and components in the electrical and fuel systems of a vehicle for the purpose of attaining optimum performance.

TURBOCHARGER: An exhaust driven pump which compresses intake air and forces it into the combustion chambers at higher than atmospheric pressures. The increased air pressure allows more fuel to be burned and results in increased horsepower being produced.

VACUUM ADVANCE: A device which advances the ignition timing in response to increased engine vacuum.

VACUUM GAUGE: An instrument used to measure the presence of vacuum in a chamber.

VALVE: A device which control the pressure, direction of flow or rate of flow of a liquid or gas.

VALVE CLEARANCE: The measured gap between the end of the valve stem and the rocker arm, cam lobe or follower that activates the valve.

VISCOSITY: The rating of a liquid's internal resistance to flow.

VOLTMETER: An instrument used for measuring electrical force in units called volts. Voltmeters are always connected parallel with the circuit being tested.

WHEEL CYLINDER: Found in the automotive drum brake assembly, it is a device, actuated by hydraulic pressure, which, through internal pistons, pushes the brake shoes outward against the drums.

A

ABOUT THIS MANUAL, 0-5

ACCELERATOR PEDAL POSITION SENSORS (APPS), REPLACEMENT, 6-14

ACCUMULATOR, AIR CONDITIONING, REMOVAL AND INSTALLATION, 3-17

ACKNOWLEDGEMENTS, 0-4

ADJUSTABLE ACCELERATOR AND BRAKE PEDALS, DESCRIPTION AND COMPONENT REPLACEMENT, 12-23

ADJUSTABLE BRAKE PEDAL MOTOR CABLE, REPLACEMENT, 9-19

AIR CONDITIONING

accumulator, removal and installation, 3-17
and heating system, check and maintenance, 3-13
compressor, removal and installation, 3-16
condenser, removal and installation, 3-17
orifice tube, removal and installation, 3-20
pressure cycling switch and high-pressure cutoff switch, replacement, 3-19

AIR FILTER CHECK AND REPLACEMENT, 1-22

AIR INTAKE DUCT AND FILTER HOUSING, REMOVAL AND INSTALLATION, 4-14

AIRBAG SYSTEM, GENERAL INFORMATION AND PRECAUTIONS, 12-26

ALTERNATOR, REMOVAL AND INSTALLATION, 5-9

ANTENNA AND CABLES, REPLACEMENT, 12-14

ANTIFREEZE, GENERAL INFORMATION, 3-2

ANTI-LOCK BRAKE SYSTEM (ABS), GENERAL INFORMATION, 9-2

AUTOMATIC TRANSMISSION, 7B-1

Brake Transmission Shift Interlock (BTSI) system, description, check and replacement, 7B-6
diagnosis, general, 7B-2
fluid
    and filter change, 1-33
    cooler, removal and installation, 7B-8
    level check, 1-10
    type, 1-35
gear position indicator cable adjustment (models with a steering column-mounted shifter), 7B-7
general information, 7B-2
oil seal, replacement, 7A-2
overhaul, general information, 7B-10
removal and installation, 7B-8
shift cable, check, replacement and adjustment, 7B-3
shift lever (center console models), removal and installation, 7B-3

AUTOMOTIVE CHEMICALS AND LUBRICANTS, 0-21

AXLE ASSEMBLY, REMOVAL AND INSTALLATION

front (4WD models), 8-19
rear, 8-15

AXLESHAFT, REAR

bearing, replacement, 8-17
oil seal, replacement, 8-16
removal and installation, 8-16

MASTER INDEX

B

BALLJOINTS, CHECK AND REPLACEMENT, 10-8
BATTERY
cables, check and replacement, 5-5
check, maintenance and charging, 1-16
check and replacement, 5-2
precautions and disconnection, 5-2
**BLOWER MOTOR RESISTOR AND BLOWER MOTOR,
    REPLACEMENT, 3-10**
BODY REPAIR
major damage, 11-5
minor damage, 11-3
BODY, 11-1
BODY, MAINTENANCE, 11-2
BOOSTER BATTERY (JUMP) STARTING, 0-20
BRAKES, 9-1
adjustable brake pedal motor cable, replacement, 9-19
Anti-lock Brake System (ABS), general information, 9-2
caliper, removal and installation, 9-8
disc, inspection, removal and installation, 9-9
fluid
    change, 1-25
    level check, 1-8
    type, 1-35
general information, 9-2
hoses and lines, inspection and replacement, 9-15
hydraulic system, bleeding, 9-16
light switch, replacement, 9-19
master cylinder, removal and installation, 9-14
pads, replacement, 9-4
parking brake shoes, replacement, 9-11
power brake booster, check, removal and installation, 9-17
system check, 1-19
**BRAKE TRANSMISSION SHIFT INTERLOCK (BTSI) SYSTEM,
    DESCRIPTION, CHECK AND REPLACEMENT, 7B-6**
BULB REPLACEMENT, 12-18
BUMPERS, REMOVAL AND INSTALLATION, 11-8
BUYING PARTS, 0-10

C

CABLE REPLACEMENT, BATTERY, 5-5
CALIPER, DISC BRAKE, REMOVAL AND INSTALLATION, 9-8
**CAMSHAFT AND TAPPETS, 3.5L AND 3.7L V6 ENGINES,
    REMOVAL, INSPECTION AND INSTALLATION, 2B-12**
CAMSHAFT POSITION (CMP) SENSOR, REPLACEMENT, 6-14
**CAMSHAFT, BALANCE SHAFT AND BEARINGS, 4.2L V6 ENGINE,
    REMOVAL, INSPECTION AND INSTALLATION, 2A-15**
**CAMSHAFT(S), V8 ENGINES, REMOVAL, INSPECTION AND
    INSTALLATION, 2C-25**
**CATALYTIC CONVERTERS, GENERAL DESCRIPTION, CHECK AND
    REPLACEMENT, 6-32**
CENTER CONSOLE, REMOVAL AND INSTALLATION, 11-23
**CHARGE MOTION CONTROL VALVE (CMCV) (5.4L V8
    MODELS), REMOVAL AND INSTALLATION, 6-30**

CHARGING SYSTEM
alternator, removal and installation, 5-9
check, 5-9
general information and precautions, 5-8
CHASSIS ELECTRICAL SYSTEM, 12-1
CHEMICALS AND LUBRICANTS, 0-21
CIRCUIT BREAKERS, GENERAL INFORMATION, 12-5
CLUTCH
components, removal, inspection and installation, 8-5
description and check, 8-2
fluid
    level check, 1-8
    type, 1-35
hydraulic system, bleeding, 8-4
master cylinder, removal and installation, 8-2
pedal position switch, replacement, 8-8
release
    bearing, removal, inspection and installation, 8-5
    cylinder, removal and installation, 8-4
CLUTCH AND DRIVELINE, 8-1
COIL SPRING (FRONT), REMOVAL AND INSTALLATION, 10-4
COIL(S), IGNITION
check, 1-31
replacement, 5-7
**COMPRESSOR, AIR CONDITIONING, REMOVAL AND
    INSTALLATION, 3-16**
**CONDENSER, AIR CONDITIONING, REMOVAL AND
    INSTALLATION, 3-17**
CONVERSION FACTORS, 0-22
COOLANT
expansion tank, removal and installation, 3-6
general information, 3-2
level check, 1-8
temperature indicator, check, 3-10
type, 1-35
COOLING SYSTEM
check, 1-17
servicing (draining, flushing and refilling), 1-32
**COOLING, HEATING AND AIR CONDITIONING
    SYSTEMS, 3-1**
COWL COVERS, REMOVAL AND INSTALLATION, 11-23
CRANKSHAFT, REMOVAL AND INSTALLATION, 2D-17
CRANKSHAFT OIL SEALS, REPLACEMENT
3.5L and 3.7L V6 engines, 2B-7
4.2L V6 engine, 2A-19
V8 engines, 2C-11
CRANKSHAFT POSITION (CKP) SENSOR, REPLACEMENT, 6-17
CRANKSHAFT PULLEY AND FRONT OIL SEAL(S), REPLACEMENT
3.5L and 3.7L V6 engines, 2B-7
V8 engines, 2C-11
CRUISE CONTROL SYSTEM, GENERAL INFORMATION, 12-25
CYLINDER COMPRESSION CHECK, 2D-4
**CYLINDER HEAD TEMPERATURE (CHT) SENSOR,
    REPLACEMENT, 6-19**
CYLINDER HEADS, REMOVAL AND INSTALLATION
3.5L and 3.7L V6 engines, 2B-8
4.2L V6 engine, 2A-8
V8 engines, 2C-29

D

DASHBOARD TRIM PANELS, REMOVAL AND INSTALLATION
2004 through 2008 models, 11-16
2009 and later models, 11-18
**DAYTIME RUNNING LIGHTS (DRL), GENERAL
    INFORMATION, 12-26**
DIAGNOSIS, 0-25
DIAGNOSTIC TROUBLE CODES (DTCS), 6-7
DIFFERENTIAL
lubricant
    change, 1-31
    level check, 1-11
    type, 1-35
pinion oil seal, replacement, 8-18
**DIGITAL TRANSMISSION RANGE (DTR) SENSOR,
    REPLACEMENT, 6-19**
DISC BRAKE
caliper, removal and installation, 9-8
disc, inspection, removal and installation, 9-9
pads, replacement, 9-4
DOOR
latch, lock cylinder and handle, removal and installation, 11-12
removal, installation and adjustment, 11-11
trim panels, removal and installation, 11-10
window glass regulator, removal and installation, 11-14
window glass, removal and installation, 11-13
DRIVEAXLES, FRONT (4WD MODELS)
boot replacement, 8-11
removal and installation, 8-11
DRIVEBELT
check and replacement, 1-26
tensioner, replacement, 1-27
DRIVEPLATE
3.5L and 3.7L V6 engines, 2B-15
4.2L V6 engine, 2A-21
V8 engines, 2C-32
**DRIVESHAFT SLIP YOKE BOOT AND CENTER BEARING
    (TWO-PIECE DRIVESHAFTS), REPLACEMENT, 8-10**
DRIVESHAFT(S)
general information, 8-8
removal and installation, 8-8
universal joints, replacement, 8-9

E

**ELECTRIC SHIFT MOTOR, TRANSFER CASE (ELECTRIC SHIFT
    MODELS), REPLACEMENT, 7C-2**
ELECTRIC SIDE VIEW MIRRORS, GENERAL INFORMATION, 12-24
ELECTRICAL TROUBLESHOOTING, GENERAL INFORMATION, 12-2
EMISSIONS AND ENGINE CONTROL SYSTEMS, 6-1
ENGINE COOLANT, LEVEL CHECK, 1-8
ENGINE COOLING FAN, CHECK AND REPLACEMENT, 3-4
ENGINE ELECTRICAL SYSTEMS, 5-1
ENGINE FRONT COVER, REMOVAL AND INSTALLATION
3.5L and 3.7L V6 engines, 2B-9
4.2L V6 engine, 2A-10
V8 engines, 2C-12

ENGINE, GENERAL OVERHAUL PROCEDURES, 2D-1
crankshaft, removal and installation, 2D-17
cylinder compression check, 2D-4
engine overhaul
    disassembly sequence, 2D-10
    reassembly sequence, 2D-21
engine rebuilding alternatives, 2D-6
engine removal, methods and precautions, 2D-6
engine, removal and installation, 2D-8
initial start-up and break-in after overhaul, 2D-21
oil pressure check, 2D-3
pistons and connecting rods, removal and installation, 2D-11
vacuum gauge diagnostic checks, 2C-4
ENGINE, IN-VEHICLE REPAIR PROCEDURES
3.5L and 3.7L V6 engines, 2B-1
    camshaft and tappets, removal, inspection and installation, 2B-12
    crankshaft pulley and front oil seal, replacement, 2B-7
    cylinder heads, removal and installation, 2B-8
    driveplate, removal and installation, 2B-15
    engine front cover, removal and installation, 2B-9
    engine mounts, check and replacement, 2B-17
    exhaust manifolds, removal and installation, 2B-7
    intake manifold(s), removal and installation, 2B-5
    oil pan, removal and installation, 2B-14
    oil pump, removal and installation, 2B-15
    rear main oil seal, replacement, 2B-16
    repair operations possible with the engine in the vehicle, 2B-2
    timing chain and sprockets, inspection, removal and installation, 2B-10
    turbocharger(s) (3.5L engine), removal and installation, 2B-16
    valve clearance, check and adjustment, 2B-2
    valve covers, removal and installation, 2B-3
4.2L V6 engine, 2A-1
    camshaft, balance shaft and bearings, removal, inspection and
        installation, 2A-15
    crankshaft oil seals, replacement, 2A-19
    cylinder heads, removal and installation, 2A-8
    engine mounts, check and replacement, 2A-22
    exhaust manifolds, removal and installation, 2A-7
    flywheel/driveplate, removal and installation, 2A-21
    intake manifold, removal and installation, 2A-5
    oil pan, removal and installation, 2A-17
    oil pump, removal and installation, 2A-18
    repair operations possible with the engine in the vehicle, 2A-2
    rocker arms and pushrods, removal, inspection and installation, 2A-4
    timing chain
        and sprockets, inspection, removal and installation, 2A-11
        cover, removal and installation, 2A-10
    Top Dead Center (TDC) for number 1 piston, locating, 2A-2
    valve covers, removal and installation, 2A-3
    valve lifters, removal, inspection and installation, 2A-13
V8 engines, 2C-1
    camshaft(s), removal, inspection and installation, 2C-25
    crankshaft pulley and front oil seal, removal and installation, 2C-11
    cylinder heads, removal and installation, 2C-29
    engine mounts, check and replacement, 2C-33
    exhaust manifolds, removal and installation, 2C-9
    flywheel/driveplate, removal and installation, 2C-32
    intake manifold, removal and installation, 2C-6
    oil pan, removal and installation, 2C-31
    oil pump, removal, inspection and installation, 2C-32
    rear main oil seal, replacement, 2C-33
    repair operations possible with the engine in the vehicle, 2C-2

rocker arms and valve lash adjusters, removal, inspection and installation, 2C-21

timing chain cover, removal and installation, 2C-12

timing chains, tensioners and sprockets, removal, inspection and installation, 2C-14

Top Dead Center (TDC) for number 1 piston, locating, 2C-2

valve covers, removal and installation, 2C-3

Variable Camshaft Timing (VCT) system, general information and component checks, 2C-25

ENGINE MOUNTS, CHECK AND REPLACEMENT

3.5L and 3.7L V6 engines, 2B-17

4.2L V6 engine, 2A-22

V8 engines, 2C-33

ENGINE OIL

and filter change, 1-13

level check, 1-7

type and viscosity, 1-35

ENGINE OIL TEMPERATURE (EOT) SENSOR, REPLACEMENT, 6-21

ENGINE OVERHAUL

disassembly sequence, 2D-10

reassembly sequence, 2D-21

ENGINE REBUILDING ALTERNATIVES, 2D-6

ENGINE REMOVAL, METHODS AND PRECAUTIONS, 2D-6

ENGINE, REMOVAL AND INSTALLATION, 2D-8

EVAPORATIVE EMISSION CONTROL (EVAP) SYSTEM, GENERAL INFORMATION AND COMPONENT REPLACEMENT, 6-33

EXHAUST GAS RECIRCULATION (EGR) SYSTEM, GENERAL DESCRIPTION AND COMPONENT REPLACEMENT, 6-36

EXHAUST MANIFOLDS, REMOVAL AND INSTALLATION

3.5L and 3.7L V6 engines, 2B-7

4.2L V6 engine, 2A-7

V8 engines, 2C-9

EXHAUST SYSTEM

check, 1-24

servicing, general information, 4-24

EXPANSION (ORIFICE) TUBE, AIR CONDITIONING, REPLACEMENT, 3-20

F

FAN, ENGINE COOLING, CHECK AND REPLACEMENT, 3-4

FAULT FINDING, 0-25

FENDER, FRONT, REMOVAL AND INSTALLATION, 11-9

FILTER REPLACEMENT

automatic transmission, 1-33

engine air, 1-22

engine oil, 1-13

fuel, 1-25

FLUID LEVEL CHECKS, 1-7

automatic transmission, 1-10

brake fluid, 1-8

clutch fluid, 1-8

differential, 1-11

engine coolant, 1-8

engine oil, 1-7

manual transmission, 1-10

power steering, 1-9

transfer case, 1-10

windshield washer, 1-9

FLUIDS AND LUBRICANTS

capacities, 1-36

recommended, 1-35

FLYWHEEL/DRIVEPLATE, REMOVAL AND INSTALLATION

4.2L V6 engine, 2A-21

V8 engines, 2C-32

FRACTION/DECIMAL/MILLIMETER EQUIVALENTS, 0-23

FRONT AXLE ASSEMBLY (4WD MODELS), REMOVAL AND INSTALLATION, 8-19

FRONT DRIVEAXLES (4WD MODELS), REMOVAL AND INSTALLATION, 8-11

FUEL

filter replacement, 1-25

high-pressure fuel pump (3.5L V6 engine), removal and installation, 4-23

injection system, check, 4-16

lines and fittings, general information, 4-5

pressure relief procedure, 4-2

pump/fuel level sensor

component replacement, 4-13

removal and installation, 4-11

pump/fuel pressure, check, 4-3

rail and injectors, removal and installation, 4-18

Sequential Multiport Fuel Injection (SFI) system, general information, 4-15

system check, 1-22

tank

cleaning and repair, general information, 4-11

removal and installation, 4-9

FUEL AND EXHAUST SYSTEMS, 4-1

FUEL PUMP DRIVER MODULE (FPDM), REPLACEMENT, 6-30

FUSES AND FUSIBLE LINKS, GENERAL INFORMATION, 12-4

G

GEAR POSITION INDICATOR CABLE ADJUSTMENT, AUTOMATIC TRANSMISSION (STEERING COLUMN TYPE), 7B-7

GENERAL ENGINE OVERHAUL PROCEDURES, 2D-1

crankshaft, removal and installation, 2D-17

cylinder compression check, 2D-4

engine overhaul

disassembly sequence, 2D-10

reassembly sequence, 2D-21

engine rebuilding alternatives, 2D-6

engine removal, methods and precautions, 2D-6

engine, removal and installation, 2D-8

initial start-up and break-in after overhaul, 2C-21

oil pressure check, 2D-3

pistons and connecting rods, removal and installation, 2D-11

vacuum gauge diagnostic checks, 2D-4

GRILLE, RADIATOR, REMOVAL AND INSTALLATION, 11-7

H

HEADLIGHTS
adjustment, 12-17
bulb, replacement, 12-16
housing, replacement, 12-15
HEATER CORE, REPLACEMENT, 3-12
HEATER/AIR CONDITIONER CONTROL ASSEMBLY, REMOVAL AND INSTALLATION, 3-11
HEATING AND AIR CONDITIONING SYSTEM, CHECK AND MAINTENANCE, 3-13
HIGH-PRESSURE FUEL PUMP (3.5L V6 ENGINE), REMOVAL AND INSTALLATION, 4-23
HINGES AND LOCKS, MAINTENANCE, 11-5
HOOD
latch and release cable, removal and installation, 11-7
removal, installation and adjustment, 11-6
support struts, removal and installation, 11-5
HORN, REPLACEMENT, 12-23
HUB AND BEARING ASSEMBLY, REPLACEMENT, 10-7

I

IGNITION SWITCH AND KEY LOCK CYLINDER, REPLACEMENT, 12-7
IGNITION SYSTEM
coil check (3.5L and 3.7L V6, and V8 engines), 1-31
coil(s), replacement, 5-7
general information and precautions, 5-6
system check, 5-6
INITIAL START-UP AND BREAK-IN AFTER OVERHAUL, 2D-21
INJECTION PRESSURE (IPR) SENSOR/FUEL RAIL PRESSURE TEMPERATURE (FRPT) SENSOR, REPLACEMENT, 6-22
INSTRUMENT
cluster, removal and installation, 12-10
panel
switches, replacement, 12-8
removal and installation, 11-18
INTAKE AIR TEMPERATURE (IAT) SENSOR, REPLACEMENT, 6-22
INTAKE MANIFOLD RUNNER CONTROL (IMRC) ACTUATOR, REPLACEMENT, 6-31
INTAKE MANIFOLD TUNING (IMT) VALVE, REPLACEMENT, 6-31
INTAKE MANIFOLD(S), REMOVAL AND INSTALLATION
3.5L and 3.7L V6 engines, 2B-5
4.2L V6 engine, 2A-5
V8 engines, 2C-6

J

JACKING AND TOWING, 0-19
JUMP STARTING, 0-20

K

KEY LOCK CYLINDER AND IGNITION SWITCH, REPLACEMENT, 12-7
KEYLESS ENTRY SYSTEM, DESCRIPTION AND CHECK, 12-25
KNOCK SENSOR(S), REPLACEMENT, 6-22

L

LEAF SPRINGS, REMOVAL AND INSTALLATION, 10-8
LOWER CONTROL ARM, REMOVAL AND INSTALLATION, 10-6
LUBRICANTS AND CHEMICALS, 0-21
LUBRICANTS AND FLUIDS
capacities, 1-36
recommended, 1-35

M

MAINTENANCE SCHEDULE, 1-2
MAINTENANCE TECHNIQUES, TOOLS AND WORKING FACILITIES, 0-11
MAINTENANCE, ROUTINE, 1-1
MANUAL TRANSMISSION, 7A-1
general information, 7A-2
lubricant
change, 1-27
level check, 1-10
type, 1-35
mount, check and replacement, 7A-3
oil seal, replacement, 7A-2
overhaul, general information, 7A-5
removal and installation, 7A-4
shift lever, removal and installation, 7A-2
MASS AIR FLOW (MAF) SENSOR, REPLACEMENT, 6-23
MASTER CYLINDER, REMOVAL AND INSTALLATION
brake, 9-14
clutch, 8-2
MIRRORS, ELECTRIC SIDE VIEW, GENERAL INFORMATION, 12-24
MIRRORS, REMOVAL AND INSTALLATION, 11-14
MULTI-FUNCTION SWITCH, REPLACEMENT, 12-6

O

OIL PAN, REMOVAL AND INSTALLATION
3.5L and 3.7L V6 engines, 2B-14
4.2L V6 engine, 2A-17
V8 engines, 2C-31
OIL PRESSURE CHECK, 2D-3
OIL PUMP, REMOVAL AND INSTALLATION
3.5L and 3.7L V6 engines, 2B-15
4.2L V6 engine, 2A-18
V8 engines, 2C-32

OIL, ENGINE, LEVEL CHECK, 1-7
ON-BOARD DIAGNOSTIC (OBD) SYSTEM AND DIAGNOSTIC
    TROUBLE CODES (DTCS), 6-2
ORIFICE TUBE, AIR CONDITIONING, REPLACEMENT, 3-20
OXYGEN SENSORS, GENERAL INFORMATION AND
    REPLACEMENT, 6-25

P

PADS, DISC BRAKE, REPLACEMENT, 9-4
PARKING BRAKE SHOES, REPLACEMENT, 9-11
PARTS, REPLACEMENT, BUYING, 0-10
PINION OIL SEAL, REPLACEMENT, 8-18
PISTONS AND CONNECTING RODS, REMOVAL AND
    INSTALLATION, 2D-11
POSITIVE CRANKCASE VENTILATION (PCV) VALVE
    REPLACEMENT, 1-27
POWER BRAKE BOOSTER, CHECK, REMOVAL AND
    INSTALLATION, 9-17
POWER DOOR LOCK AND KEYLESS ENTRY SYSTEM,
    DESCRIPTION AND CHECK, 12-25
POWER STEERING
fluid
    cooler, removal and installation, 10-16
    level check, 1-9
    type, 1-35
pump, removal and installation, 10-14
system, bleeding, 10-15
POWER STEERING PRESSURE (PSP) SWITCH,
    REPLACEMENT, 6-26
POWER WINDOW SYSTEM, DESCRIPTION AND CHECK, 12-25
POWERTRAIN CONTROL MODULE (PCM), REMOVAL AND
    INSTALLATION, 6-29

R

RADIATOR GRILLE, REMOVAL AND INSTALLATION, 11-7
RADIATOR, REMOVAL AND INSTALLATION, 3-7
RADIO AND SPEAKERS, REMOVAL AND
    INSTALLATION, 12-12
REAR AXLE
assembly, removal and installation, 8-15
axleshaft bearing, replacement, 8-17
axleshaft oil seal, replacement, 8-16
axleshaft, removal and installation, 8-16
general information, 8-14
REAR MAIN OIL SEAL, REPLACEMENT
3.5L and 3.7L V6 engines, 2B-16
4.2L V6 engine, 2A-19
V8 engines, 2C-33
RECALL INFORMATION, 0-7
RECOMMENDED LUBRICANTS AND FLUIDS, 1-35
RELAYS, GENERAL INFORMATION AND TESTING, 12-5
RELEASE BEARING, CLUTCH, REMOVAL, INSPECTION AND
    INSTALLATION, 8-5

RELEASE CYLINDER, CLUTCH, REMOVAL AND
    INSTALLATION, 8-4
REPAIR OPERATIONS POSSIBLE WITH THE ENGINE IN
    THE VEHICLE
3.5L and 3.7L V6 engines, 2B-2
4.2L V6 engine, 2A-2
V8 engines, 2C-2
REPLACEMENT PARTS, BUYING, 0-10
ROCKER ARMS AND PUSHRODS, 4.2L V6 ENGINE, REMOVAL,
    INSPECTION AND INSTALLATION, 2A-4
ROCKER ARMS AND VALVE LASH ADJUSTERS, V8 ENGINES,
    REMOVAL, INSPECTION AND
    INSTALLATION, 2C-21
ROTOR, BRAKE, INSPECTION, REMOVAL AND
    INSTALLATION, 9-9
ROUTINE MAINTENANCE
operations, 1-1
schedule, 1-2

S

SAFETY FIRST!, 0-24
SAFETY RECALL INFORMATION, 0-7
SCHEDULED MAINTENANCE, 1-1
SEAT BELT CHECK, 1-18
SEATS, REMOVAL AND INSTALLATION, 11-21
SEQUENTIAL MULTIPORT FUEL INJECTION (SFI) SYSTEM,
    GENERAL INFORMATION, 4-15
SHIFT CABLE, CHECK, REPLACEMENT AND
    ADJUSTMENT, 7B-3
SHIFT LEVER, REMOVAL AND INSTALLATION
automatic transmission (center console models), 7B-3
manual transmission, 7A-2
transfer case (manual-shift models), 7C-2
SHIFT RANGE SELECTOR SWITCH, TRANSFER CASE
    (ELECTRICSHIFT MODELS), REPLACEMENT, 7C-2
SHOCK ABSORBER/COIL SPRING (FRONT), REMOVAL AND
    INSTALLATION, 10-4
SHOCK ABSORBERS (REAR), REMOVAL AND
    INSTALLATION, 10-8
SLAVE CYLINDER, CLUTCH, REMOVAL AND INSTALLATION, 8-4
SPARE TIRE, INSTALLING, 0-19
SPARK PLUG
check and replacement, 1-28
torque, 1-38
type and gap, 1-36
wire check and replacement (OHC V6 and 6.2L V8 engines), 1-32
SPEAKERS, REMOVAL AND INSTALLATION, 12-12
STABILIZER BAR AND BUSHINGS, REMOVAL AND
    INSTALLATION, 10-4
STARTER MOTOR
and circuit, in-vehicle check, 5-11
removal and installation, 5-12
STARTING SYSTEM GENERAL INFORMATION AND
    PRECAUTIONS, 5-11
STEERING
and suspension check, 1-21
column covers, removal and installation, 11-20

column, removal and installation, 10-11
gear boots, replacement, 10-13
gear, removal and installation, 10-13
knuckle, removal and installation, 10-5
wheel, removal and installation, 10-9
STOP LIGHT SWITCH, REPLACEMENT, 9-19
**SUPPLEMENTAL RESTRAINT SYSTEM (SRS), GENERAL
    INFORMATION AND PRECAUTIONS, 12-26**
**SUPPORT STRUTS, HOOD, REMOVAL AND
    INSTALLATION, 11-5**
SUSPENSION AND STEERING SYSTEMS, 10-1
SWITCHES, INSTRUMENT PANEL, REPLACEMENT, 12-8

T

TAILGATE
latch and handle, removal and installation, 11-15
removal and installation, 11-15
TENSIONER, DRIVEBELT, REPLACEMENT, 1-27
THERMOSTAT, CHECK AND REPLACEMENT, 3-3
THROTTLE BODY, REMOVAL AND INSTALLATION, 4-17
THROTTLE POSITION (TP) SENSOR, REPLACEMENT, 6-26
TIE-ROD ENDS, REMOVAL AND INSTALLATION, 10-12
**TIMING CHAIN(S) AND SPROCKETS, INSPECTION, REMOVAL
    AND INSTALLATION**
3.5L and 3.7L V6 engines, 2B-10
4.2L V6 engine, 2A-11
V8 engines, 2C-14
TIMING CHAIN COVER, REMOVAL AND INSTALLATION
3.5L and 3.7L V6 engines, 2B-9
4.2L V6 engine, 2A-10
V8 engines, 2C-12
TIRE AND TIRE PRESSURE CHECKS, 1-11
TIRE ROTATION, 1-15
TIRE, SPARE, INSTALLING, 0-19
TOOLS AND WORKING FACILITIES, 0-11
TOP DEAD CENTER (TDC) FOR NUMBER 1 PISTON, LOCATING
4.2L V6 engine, 2A-2
V8 engines, 2C-2
TORQUE SPECIFICATIONS
brake caliper mounting bolts, 9-20
cylinder head bolts
    3.5L and 3.7L V6 engines, 2B-19
    4.2L V6 engine, 2A-23
    V8 engine, 2C-35
sparks plugs, 1-38
thermostat housing cover bolts, 3-21
water pump bolts, 3-21
wheel lug nuts, 1-38
Other torque specifications can be found in the Chapter that deals with the
    component being serviced.
TOWING, 0-19
TRANSFER CASE, 7C-1
electric shift motor, replacement, 7C-3

general information, 7C-2
lubricant
    change, 1-35
    level check, 1-10
    type, 1-35
oil seal, replacement, 7C-3
removal and installation, 7C-3
shift lever, removal and installation (manual-shift models), 7C-2
shift range selector switch, (electric-shift models), replacement, 7C-2
TRANSMISSION, AUTOMATIC, 7B-1
Brake Transmission Shift Interlock (BTSI) system, description, check and
    replacement, 7B-6
diagnosis, general, 7B-2
fluid
    and filter change, 1-33
    cooler, removal and installation, 7B-8
    level check, 1-10
    type, 1-35
gear position indicator cable adjustment (models with a steering column-
    mounted shifter), 7B-7
general information, 7B-2
oil seal, replacement, 7A-2
overhaul, general information, 7B-10
removal and installation, 7B-8
shift cable, check, replacement and adjustment, 7B-3
shift lever (center console models), removal and installation, 7B-3
TRANSMISSION, MANUAL, 7A-1
general information, 7A-2
lubricant
    change, 1-27
    level check, 1-10
    type, 1-35
mount, check and replacement, 7A-3
oil seal, replacement, 7A-2
overhaul, general information, 7A-5
removal and installation, 7A-4
shift lever, removal and installation, 7A-2
TRANSMISSION SPEED SENSORS, REPLACEMENT, 6-28
TRIM PANELS, DOOR, REMOVAL AND INSTALLATION, 11-10
TROUBLE CODES, ACCESSING, 6-7
TROUBLESHOOTING, 0-25
TUNE-UP AND ROUTINE MAINTENANCE, 1-1
TUNE-UP GENERAL INFORMATION, 1-6
**TURBOCHARGER(S) (3.5L V6 ENGINE), REMOVAL AND
    INSTALLATION, 2B-16**
TURN SIGNAL SWITCH, REPLACEMENT, 12-6

U

UNDERHOOD HOSE CHECK AND REPLACEMENT, 1-18
UNIVERSAL JOINTS, REPLACEMENT, 8-9
UPHOLSTERY AND CARPETS, MAINTENANCE, 11-2
**UPPER CONTROL ARM, REMOVAL AND
    INSTALLATION, 10-5**

V

V6 ENGINE, 4.2L, 2A-1
camshaft, balance shaft and bearings, removal, inspection and
    installation, 2A-15
crankshaft oil seals, replacement, 2A-19
cylinder heads, removal and installation, 2A-8
engine mounts, check and replacement, 2A-22
exhaust manifolds, removal and installation, 2A-7
flywheel/driveplate, removal and installation, 2A-21
intake manifold, removal and installation, 2A-5
oil pan, removal and installation, 2A-17
oil pump, removal and installation, 2A-18
repair operations possible with the engine in the vehicle, 2A-2
rocker arms and pushrods, removal, inspection and installation, 2A-4
timing chain
    and sprockets, inspection, removal and installation, 2A-11
    cover, removal and installation, 2A-10
Top Dead Center (TDC) for number 1 piston, locating, 2A-2
valve covers, removal and installation, 2A-3
valve lifters, removal, inspection and installation, 2A-13

V6 ENGINES, 3.5L AND 3.7L, 2B-1
camshaft and tappets, removal, inspection and installation, 2B-12
crankshaft pulley and front oil seal, replacement, 2B-7
cylinder heads, removal and installation, 2B-8
driveplate, removal and installation, 2B-15
engine front cover, removal and installation, 2B-9
engine mounts, check and replacement, 2B-17
exhaust manifolds, removal and installation, 2B-7
intake manifold(s), removal and installation, 2B-5
oil pan, removal and installation, 2B-14
oil pump, removal and installation, 2B-15
rear main oil seal, replacement, 2B-16
repair operations possible with the engine in the vehicle, 2B-2
timing chain and sprockets, inspection, removal and installation, 2B-10
turbocharger(s) (3.5L engine), removal and installation, 2B-16
valve clearance, check and adjustment, 2B-2
valve covers, removal and installation, 2B-3

V8 ENGINES, 2C-1
camshaft(s), removal, inspection and installation, 2C-25
crankshaft pulley and front oil seal, removal and installation, 2C-11
cylinder heads, removal and installation, 2C-29
engine mounts, check and replacement, 2C-33
exhaust manifolds, removal and installation, 2C-9
flywheel/driveplate, removal and installation, 2C-32
intake manifold, removal and installation, 2C-6
oil pan, removal and installation, 2C-31
oil pump, removal, inspection and installation, 2C-32

rear main oil seal, replacement, 2C-33
repair operations possible with the engine in the vehicle, 2C-2
rocker arms and valve lash adjusters, removal, inspection and
    installation, 2C-21
timing chain cover, removal and installation, 2C-12
timing chains, tensioners and sprockets, removal, inspection and
    installation, 2C-14
Top Dead Center (TDC) for number 1 piston, locating, 2C-2
valve covers, removal and installation, 2C-3
Variable Camshaft Timing (VCT) system, general information and
    component checks, 2C-25

VACUUM GAUGE DIAGNOSTIC CHECKS, 2D-4
**VALVE CLEARANCE, CHECK AND ADJUSTMENT, 3.5L AND
    3.7L V6 ENGINES, 2B-2**
VALVE COVERS, REMOVAL AND INSTALLATION
3.5L and 3.7L V6 engines, 2B-3
4.2L V6 engine, 2A-3
V8 engines, 2C-3
**VALVE LIFTERS, 4.2L V6 ENGINE, REMOVAL, INSPECTION AND
    INSTALLATION, 2A-13**
**VARIABLE CAMSHAFT TIMING (VCT) OIL CONTROL SOLENOID,
    REPLACEMENT, 6-31**
VEHICLE IDENTIFICATION NUMBERS, 0-6
VINYL TRIM, MAINTENANCE, 11-2

W

WATER PUMP
check, 3-8
replacement, 3-9
WHEEL ALIGNMENT, GENERAL INFORMATION, 10-17
**WHEEL SPEED SENSOR, ANTI-LOCK BRAKE, REMOVAL AND
    INSTALLATION, 9-2**
WHEELS AND TIRES, GENERAL INFORMATION, 10-16
**WINDOW GLASS REGULATOR, REMOVAL AND
    INSTALLATION, 11-14**
**WINDOW GLASS, DOOR, REMOVAL AND
    INSTALLATION, 11-13**
WINDSHIELD
and fixed glass, replacement, 11-5
washer fluid, level check, 1-9
wiper blade inspection and replacement, 1-15
wiper motor, replacement, 12-11
WIRING DIAGRAMS, GENERAL INFORMATION, 12-27
WORKING FACILITIES, 0-11